Did God Care?

Studies in Platonism, Neoplatonism, and the Platonic Tradition

Edited by

Robert M. Berchman (*Foro di Studi Avanzati Gaetano Massa, Roma*)
John F. Finamore (*University of Iowa*)

Editorial Board

John Dillon (*Trinity College, Dublin*) – Gary Gurtler (*Boston College*)
Jean-Marc Narbonne (*Laval University, Canada*)

VOLUME 25

The titles published in this series are listed at *brill.com/spnp*

Did God Care?

*Providence, Dualism, and Will
in Later Greek and Early Christian Philosophy*

By

Dylan M. Burns

BRILL

LEIDEN | BOSTON

Library of Congress Cataloging-in-Publication Data

Names: Burns, Dylan M., author.
Title: Did god care? : providence, dualism, and will in later Greek and early
    Christian philosophy / by Dylan M. Burns.
Description: Leiden ; Boston : Brill, 2020. | Series: Studies in platonism,
    neoplatonism, and the platonic tradition, 1871-188X ; volume 25 | Includes
    bibliographical references and index.
Identifiers: LCCN 2020020815 (print) | LCCN 2020020816 (ebook) |
    ISBN 9789004432970 (hardback) | ISBN 9789004432994 (ebook)
Subjects: LCSH: Determinism (Philosophy) | Free will and determinism. |
    Providence and government of God.
Classification: LCC B105.D47 B97 2020 (print) | LCC B105.D47 (ebook) |
    DDC 214/.8–dc23
LC record available at https://lccn.loc.gov/2020020815
LC ebook record available at https://lccn.loc.gov/2020020816

Typeface for the Latin, Greek, and Cyrillic scripts: "Brill". See and download: brill.com/brill-typeface.

ISSN 1871-188X
ISBN 978-90-04-43297-0 (hardback)
ISBN 978-90-04-43299-4 (e-book)

Copyright 2020 by Koninklijke Brill NV, Leiden, The Netherlands.
Koninklijke Brill NV incorporates the imprints Brill, Brill Hes & De Graaf, Brill Nijhoff, Brill Rodopi,
Brill Sense, Hotei Publishing, mentis Verlag, Verlag Ferdinand Schöningh and Wilhelm Fink Verlag.
All rights reserved. No part of this publication may be reproduced, translated, stored in a retrieval system,
or transmitted in any form or by any means, electronic, mechanical, photocopying, recording or otherwise,
without prior written permission from the publisher. Requests for re-use and/or translations must be
addressed to Koninklijke Brill NV via brill.com or copyright.com.

This book is printed on acid-free paper and produced in a sustainable manner.

οὐ γάρ εἰσιν αἱ βουλαί μου ὥσπερ αἱ βουλαὶ ὑμῶν
οὐδὲ ὥσπερ αἱ ὁδοὶ ὑμῶν αἱ ὁδοί μου

Isaiah 55:8

Contents

Acknowledgments   XI
Abbreviations   XIII
Author's Note on Translations and References   XX

Introduction   1

PART 1
Providence

1 The *Pronoia* Problem(s)   17
   1   Introduction: Did the Gods Care?   17
   2   The First 'Likely Stories' about Providence: From the Presocratics to Plato   19
   3   Epicurus, Aristotle, and (Pseudo-)Aristotle: "What Difference Is There …?"   26
   4   "Call Him Providence. You Will Still Be Right": The Stoa on God   31
   5   "What Do I Care? For I Have Done My Part": The Stoa on Fate and Determinism   37
   6   Three Providences! Pseudo-Plutarch and the Doctrine of 'Conditional Fate'   45
   7   Conclusions: Aesop and Xanthus in the Weeds   51

2 Which God Cares for You and Me?   54
   1   Introduction: The Personal God of Early Christianity?   54
   2   Philosophers' Personal Gods: Daimonic Intervention in the Stoa and Plutarch   59
   3   Fortune's Favorites: Providence in Early Roman Historians   65
   4   A Different God, Present and Absent in Hellenistic Jewish Literature   71
   5   "So You Do Not Neglect the Nation of the Jews After All!": Philo of Alexandria   76
   6   Flavius Josephus: Providential History is Jewish History   85
   7   Prayer or Care?—Justin Martyr and Trypho the Jew 'Investigate the Deity'   89
   8   Conclusions: A God Personal Enough for a Stoic   96

VIII   CONTENTS

PART 2
Dualism

3 The Other Gods 103
  1   Introduction: Dualism in Doubt 103
  2   Matter, Evil, and Dualism from the Pythagoreans to a
       Neo-Pythagorean 104
  3   'Mitigated Dualism' and Jewish Apocalyptic Literature 112
  4   Athenagoras on "the Archon over Matter and Material Things" 118
  5   Living Idols and Questions That Deserve Punishment according to
       Clement of Alexandria 122
  6   "Nothing Happens without God": Origen on Evil, Demons, and Other
       Absences 128
  7   Marcion asks, "Doth God Clothe the Grass?" 137
  8   Conclusions: 'Religious Dualism' in Roman Philosophy 149

4 Did God Care for Creation? 153
  1   Introduction: Gnostics without 'Gnosticism'? 153
  2   No Idle Hands: The Creation-Theology of Irenaeus of Lyons 155
  3   Archons and Providences at Work in Creation: 'On the Origin of the
       World' and the 'Apocryphon of John' 160
  4   "These Senseless Men Claim That They Ascend above the
       Creator ..." 171
  5   "The Will of the Father" and the 'Tripartite Tractate' 176
  6   Conclusions: The Gnostics on Providence, Creation, and
       'Gnosticism' 184

PART 3
Will

5 Did God Know All Along? 191
  1   Introduction: Origen 'On Fate' (Philocalia 23) 191
  2   Origen's Digression on Divine Omniscience and Future Causes in 'On
       Fate' 194
  3   Chrysippus and Cicero on "Things That Are Simple, Others Complex":
       The Oracle to Laius 196
  4   Upholding the Appearance of Civic Piety: Alexander of Aphrodisias
       and Alcinous Respond to the 'Oracle to Laius' 204
  5   Origen's Oracles to Laius—and David, against Marcion 210
  6   Conclusions: 'The Book of Heaven' 216

CONTENTS   IX

6 What We Choose Now 223
  1   Introduction: Where Does Free Will Emerge in Ancient
        Philosophy? 223
  2   Aristotle on Action and Pseudo-Plutarch on Determinism 227
  3   "All These Things Depend on One's Thinking": Autonomy and
        Fatalism in the 'Book of the Laws of the Countries' 232
  4   "Say Anything Rather Than Call Providence Bad": Clement of
        Alexandria against Basilides the False 240
  5   Origen 'On Free Will' (Princ. 3.1), "Older Causes," and Gnostic
        Determinism 252
  6   Conclusions: Birth, Death, and Eden 262

7 How God Cares 270
  1   Introduction: The One's Providence, Will, and Omniscience 270
  2   "Neither Actuality nor Thought before It": Plotinus (Enn. 6. 7–8 [38–
        39]) and the 'Tripartite Tractate' on the Knowledge and Will of the
        Good 273
  3   Plotinus 'On Providence' (Enn. 3.2–3 [47–48]): Another Engagement
        with the 'Tripartite Tractate'? 281
  4   The "Unspeakable First Thought" according to Porphyry and the
        Anonymous Commentary on Plato's 'Parmenides' 293
  5   'First Thought' and Providence in the 'Platonizing' Sethian Treatises
        of Nag Hammadi 299
  6   Conclusions: A Christianizing Turn in Platonist Conceptions of
        Divine Foreknowledge 306

Conclusions 311

Bibliography 321
Index 366

Acknowledgments

The origins of the present volume are straightforward. When researching my doctoral dissertation in 2009–2011, I found a great deal of language in my sources about something called "providence" (*pronoia*). Dictionary entries and highly specialized articles clarified things enough that I could proceed with the dissertation, but they failed to give me a penetrating sense of the 'big picture' about providence in ancient thought. I asked a theologian I knew to recommend to me a thorough, book-length study of the subject, but he didn't know any. So I thought to myself, "well, that would be a great topic for my *next* book!" Little did I foresee the winding paths down which this well-intentioned resolution would lead me, and I cannot know whether I have walked under the custodianship of *pronoia* or *nemesis*. Yet what I am sure of is that I have been the beneficiary of great care and attention from colleagues, friends, and family, without whom this book would never have come to completion.

Initial research on this book was conducted under the auspices of a postdoctoral position at the University of Copenhagen, as part of the Faculty of Theology's 'Centre for Naturalism and Christian Semantics' (CNCS), headed by Troels Engberg-Pedersen and Niels Henrik Gregersen. I must single Troels out for special thanks: from my first day in Copenhagen he was deeply supportive and encouraging of this project, offering criticisms and corrections of my early stabs and rescuing me from countless errors and *Holzwege*. CNCS roundtables were crucial at this formative phase. I thank all those who participated in them, especially Gitte Buch-Hansen, Stefan Nordgaard, Maria Pantoppidan, and Runar Thorsteinsson. *Det var meget hyggeligt.* Finally, I thank my sister in the *plērōma*, Tilde Bak Halvgaard, who shared her expertise in all things *pronoia-prōtennoia*, and most importantly, her friendship. In late 2012, I accepted an offer from Tonio Sebastian Richter to take up a position as project manager for the project Database and Dictionary of Greek Loanwords in Coptic (DDGLC). This book has been completed with the support of DDGLC, which is funded by the funded by the German Research Council (DFG); I am grateful for their provision.

Drafts of several chapters were presented and discussed at the following conferences and workshops: a draft of chapter two was workshopped at a colloquium at the Max Weber Kolleg in Erfurt (May 2018), where I spent a semester as a junior fellow of the research group 'Religious Individualization'; parts of chapter three were read and discussed at the Faculty of Theology at Aarhus University (April 2018); I gave papers on material from chapter four at the Faculty of Theology at the University of Helsinki (April 2012), as well as Leipzig University's Institute of Egyptology (May and June 2013); I had the pleasure of reading an abridged version of chapter six at the Centre Léon Robin-Centre Jean Pépin-LEM, Paris (May 2019); and what became chapter seven appeared at the annual conference of the International Society of Neoplatonic Studies in Olomouc (June 2017), as well as the Department of Classics, Philosophy, History of Art and Ideas at the University of Oslo (August 2019). I thank all those who participated in these discussions, which were instrumental in refining my work. Certain generous individuals read and critiqued drafts of sections and chapters, at times independently of the aforementioned presentations: Michael Chase, Jean-Daniel Dubois, René Falkenberg, Asuman Lätzer-Lasar, Andreea-Maria Lemnaru Carrez, Colin Marshall, Bernd-Christian Otto, Nils Arne Pedersen, Jörg Rüpke, Einar Thomassen, John D. Turner, Jan Willem van Henten, and Markus Vincent. I am indebted to them all for their invaluable insights and interventions, and have done my best to make good on them. Crucial encouragement and advice were supplied over the years by Crystal Addey, David Brakke, David Butorac, Nicola Denzey Lewis, Anne Eusterschulte, Matthew Goff, Christian Halvgaard, Matyáš Havrda, Danielle Layne, Hugo Lundhaug, Christoph Markschies, Ivan Miroshnikov, Tuomas Rasimus, Luciana Gabriela Soares Santoprete, Alin Suciu, Paivi Vähäkangas, and Kocku von Stuckrad. Finally, I must thank my anonymous reviewer at Brill for his or her incisive discussion of the manuscript, and important recommendations for further secondary literature. The index is by Martin White.

I have been blessed with young gods ('research assistants') who really do operate in the best of possible worlds: Elisabeth Koch, Janik Petersdorff, and Philip Scharfenberger, who played a vital role in the formatting and copyediting of this text. I also thank John Finamore and Robert Berchman for their interest in the volume and for accepting it for publication in SPNP. I met John and Rob at my very first academic conference—New Orleans, in 2003. I had graduated with my bachelor's degree less than a week earlier, but despite my youth, they were more than happy to engage, and to encourage me to study further. I remain grateful to them for their terrific openness, and it is out of that gratefulness and with great pleasure that I contribute to their series.

I met Naida Šehić around the same time I first became interested in *nafaka*, but it was when I married her that I began to really live with it. For a lifetime's worth of inspiration and care, I thank my first teachers of philosophy, Charley Burns and Karin Ryuku Kempe Roshi. I dedicate this book to them.

Dylan Michael Burns
11 February 2020
Berlin-Charlottenburg

Abbreviations

Primary sources referred to only once in this book are not abbreviated. Primary sources referred to more than once are given an abbreviation here. Names of modern series of scholarly publications which are listed three or more times in the bibliography are also given an abbreviation below. Abbreviations here follow those given in the *SBL Handbook of Style* (second ed., 2014, although Nag Hammadi treatises are still given in italics) and, when necessary, the *Oxford Classical Dictionary*.

ACA	Ancient Commentators on Aristotle
ACW	Ancient Christian Writers
Aët.	Aëtius
Plac.	*De placita philosophorum*
Alc.	Alcinous
Epit.	*Epitome doctrinae platonicae* (*Didaskalikos*)
Alex. Aphr.	Alexander of Aphrodisias
Fat.	*De fato*
Prov.	*De providentia*
Ammon. Herm.	Ammonios Hermiou
Comm. interp.	*Commentaria in Aristotelis Libros Peri Hermeneias*
AMP	Ancient and Medieval Philosophy
Anon. *Comm. Parm.*	(Anonymous) *In Platonis Parmenidem commentaria*
ANRW	*Aufstieg und Niedergang der Römischen Welt*
Ap. John	*Apocryphon of John*
Apoc. Adam	*Apocalypse of Adam*
Apollod.	Pseudo-Apollodorus of Athens
[*Bib.*]	*Bibliotheca*
Apul.	Apuleius of Madaura
Apol.	*Apologia* (*pro se de magia*)
Deo Socr.	*De deo Socratis*
Dogm. Plat.	*De dogma Platonis*
Arist.	Aristotle
Eth. eud.	*Ethica eudemia*
Eth. nic.	*Ethica nicomachea*
Metaph.	*Metaphysica*
[*Mund.*]	[*De mundo*]
Phys.	*Physica*
Athenag.	Athenagoras
Leg.	*Legatio pro Christianis*

Att.	Atticus
Aug.	Augustine
Conf.	*Confessionum libri XIII*
Auth. Disc.	*Authoritative Discourse*
BCNH	Bibliothèque Copte de Nag Hammadi
BG	Papyrus Berolinensis 8502
BICSSup	Bulletin of the Institute for Classical Studies Supplement
BLC	*Book of the Laws of the Countries*
Boeth.	Boethius
Cons.	*De consolatione philosophiae*
BzA	Beiträge zur Altertumskunde
Calc.	Calcidius
Comm. Tim.	*Commentarius in Timaeum*
Chald. Or.	*Chaldean Oracles*
Cic.	Cicero
Acad.	*Academicae quaestiones*
Div.	*De divination*
Fat.	*De fato*
Nat. d.	*De natura deorum*
Clem.	Clement of Rome
[*Rec.*]	[*Recognitiones*]
Clem. Al.	Clement of Alexandria
Ecl.	*Eclogae Propheticae*
Exc.	*Excerpta ex Theodoto*
Paed.	*Paedagogus*
Protr.	*Protrepticus*
Strom.	*Stromateis*
Corp. herm.	*Corpus hermeticum*
CQ	*Classical Quarterly*
D. L.	Diogenes Laertius
Diod. Sic.	Diodorus Siculus
Bib. hist.	*Bibliotheca historica*
Disc. Seth	*Second Discourse of the Great Seth*
DK	Diels/Kranz, *Die Fragmente der Vorsokratiker*
1 En.	1 Enoch (Ethiopic Apocalypse)
Ep. Pet. Phil.	*Letter of Peter to Philip*
Epict.	Epictetus
Diatr.	*Diatribai (Dissertationes)*
Epiph.	Epiphanius of Salamis
Pan.	*Panarion*

ABBREVIATIONS

XV

EPRO	Études préliminaires aux religions orientales dans l'Empire Romain
Eur.	Euripides
Herc. fur.	*Hercules furens*
Euseb.	Eusebius of Caesarea
Hist. eccl.	*Historia ecclesiastica*
Praep. ev.	*Praeparatio evangelica*
FC	Fathers of the Church
Gal.	Galen
Usu	*De usu partium corporis humani*
GCS	Die Griechischen Christlichen Schriftsteller der ersten Jahrhunderten
Gell.	Aulus Gellius
Noct. att.	*Noctes Atticae*
Gos. Eg.	*Egyptian Gospel*
Hom.	Homer
Il.	*Ilias*
Od.	*Odyssea*
HTR	*Harvard Theological Review*
Ir.	Irenaeus
Epid.	*Epideixis tou apostolikou kērygmatos*
Haer.	*Adversus haereses*
JAC	*Jahrbuch für Antike und Christentum*
JBL	*Journal of Biblical Literature*
JECS	Journal of Early Christian Studies
Jos.	Josephus
A.J.	*Antiquitates judaicae*
B.J.	*Bellum judaicum*
JSJSup	Journal for the Study of Judaism Supplement Series
JTS	*Journal of Theological Studies*
Jub.	Jubilees
Just. Mart.	Justin Martyr
1 Apol.	*Apologia i*
2 Apol.	*Apologia ii*
Dial.	*Dialogus cum Tryphone*
[*Or. Graec.*]	[*Oratio ad Graecos*]
LCL	Loeb Classical Library
Let. Arist.	*Letter of Aristeas*
LS	Long and Sedley, eds. and trs., *The Hellenistic Philosophers*
LSJ	Liddell, Scott, and Jones, eds., *A Greek English Lexicon*, 9th ed.

Lucr.	Lucretius
Manil.	Manilius
Astron.	*Astronomica*
Marc. Aur.	Marcus Aurelius
Mars.	*Marsanes*
Max. Tyr.	Maximus of Tyre
Or.	*Orationes*
Min. Fel.	Minicius Felix
Oct.	*Octavius*
Nat. Rul.	*Nature of the Rulers*
Nem.	Nemesius of Emesa
Nat. hom.	*De natura hominis*
NHC	Nag Hammadi Codices
NHMS (formerly NHS)	Nag Hammadi and Manichaean Studies (formerly Nag Hammadi Studies)
Num.	Numenius
OECT	Oxford Early Christian Texts
Orig.	Origen
Cels.	*Contra Celsum*
Comm. Jo.	*Commentarii in evangelium Joannis*
Comm. Matt.	*Commentarii in evangelium Matthaei*
Comm. Rom.	*Commentarii in Romanos*
Hom. Jer.	*Homilae in Jeremiam*
Hom. Luc.	*Homiliae in Lucam*
Hom. Num.	*Homiliae in Numeros*
Or.	*De oratione*
Philoc.	*Philocalia*
Princ.	*De principiis (Peri Archōn)*
Orig. World	*On the Origin of the World*
PA	Philosophia Antiqua
Paraph. Shem	*Paraphrase of Shem*
PG	*Patrologia graeca* (Migne)
PGL	Lampe, ed., *Patristic Greek Lexicon*
Philo (of Alexandria)	
Cher.	*De cherubim*
Det.	*Quod deterius potiori insidari soleat*
Deus	*Quod Deus sit immutabilis*
Ebr.	*De ebreitate*
Flacc.	*In Flaccum*
Fug.	*De fuga et inventione*

Her.	*Quis rerum divinarum heresit*
Ios.	*De Iosepho*
Leg.	*Legum allegoriae*
Mos.	*De vita Mosis*
Opif.	*De opificio mundi*
Plant.	*De plantatione*
Praem.	*De praemiis et poenis*
Prov.	*De providentia*
QG	*Quaestiones et solutiones in Genesin*
Sobr.	*De sobrietate*
Somn.	*De somniis*
Spec.	*De specialibus legibus*
Virt.	*De virtutibus*
Plat.	Plato
Leg.	*Leges*
Phaedr.	*Phaedrus*
Pol.	*Politicus*
Resp.	*Respublica*
Symp.	*Symposium*
Tim.	*Timaeus*
Plin.	Pliny the Elder
Nat.	*Naturalis historia*
Plot.	Plotinus
Enn.	*Enneads*
Plut.	Plutarch of Chaeronea
Comm. not.	*De communibus notitiis contra stoicos*
Def. orac.	*De defectu oraculorum*
Fort. Rom.	*De fortuna Romanorum*
Is. Os.	*De Iside et Osiride*
Stoic. rep.	*De Stoicorum repugnantiis*
Polyb.	Polybius
Hist.	*Historiae*
Porph.	Porphyry
Sent.	*Sententiae*
Vit. Plot.	*Vita Plotini*
Procl.	Proclus Diadochus
Comm. Tim.	*In Platonis Timaeum commentarii*
Ref.	*Refutatio omnium haeresiorum*
RGRW	Religions in the Graeco-Roman World
SAMPP	Studies in Ancient Moral and Political Philosophy

SAPERE	Scripta Antiquitatis Posterioris ad Ethicam REligionemque pertinentia
SC	Sources chrétiennes
Sen.	Seneca
Brev. vit.	*De brevitate vitae*
Ep.	*Epistulae*
Nat.	*Naturales quaestiones*
Prov.	*De providentia*
Sent. Sext.	*Sexti philosophi Sententiae a Rufino translatae*
Sext. Emp.	Sextus Empiricus
Adv. math.	*Adversus mathematicos*
Pyr.	*Pyrrhoniae hypotyposes*
Simpl.	Simplicius
Comm. phys.	*In Aristotelis de physica commentaria*
SNAM	Studies in Neoplatonism: Ancient and Modern
STAC	Studien und Texte zu Antike und Christentum
Stob.	Johannes Stobaeus
Ecl.	*Eclogae*
SPNPT	Studies in Platonism, Neoplatonism, and the Platonic Tradition
SVF	von Arnim, ed., *Stoicorum Veterum Fragmenta*
Tac.	Tacitus
Ann.	*Annales*
Tat.	Tatian
Or. Graec.	*Oratio ad Graecos*
Teach. Silv.	*Teachings of Silvanus*
Ter.	Tertullian
An.	*De anima*
Carn. Chr.	*De carne Christi*
[*Haer.*]	[*Adversus haereses*]
Herm.	*Adversus Hermogenes*
Marc.	*Adversus Marcionem*
Praescr.	*De praescriptione haereticorum*
Theoph.	Theophilus of Antioch
Autol.	*Ad Autolycum*
TTH	Translated Texts for Historians
Three Forms	*Three Forms of First Thought*
Tri. Trac.	*Tripartite Tractate*
TUGAL	Texte und Untersuchungen zur Geschichte der altchristlichen Literatur

VC	*Vigiliae Christianae*
VCSup	Vigiliae Christianae Supplement Series
Vit. Aes.	*Vita Aesopi*
WGRWSup	Writings from the Greco-Roman World Supplement Series
WUNT	Wissenschaftliche Untersuchungen zum Neuen Testament
Xen.	Xenophon
Mem.	*Memorabilia*
ZAC	*Zeitschrift für Antike und Christentum*
Zost.	*Zostrianos*

Author's Note on Translations and References

Abbreviations and formatting follow the outlines given in the *SBL Handbook of Style*, second edition (2014). When no standard is given in that manual, I have referred to the Chicago Handbook of Style and abbreviations of primary sources found in the LSJ and PGL. The *Suda On Line* is referred to according to the bibliographic standards given at the resource's website; per the website's custom, the address given following the *Suda* entry in question is not a link to a webpage for the entry, but to the Adler entry under which the lemma in question can be found. Sigla in quotations of ancient texts follow the Leiden Conventions, with the exception that "[…]" indicates a lacuna of unknown length, as well as longer stretches of multiple words or lines where the text is too fragmentary to render in any readable manner. Greek, Coptic, and Aramaic script have been transliterated, so as to facilitate accessibility to a variety of readers across disciplines.

I have endeavored to use existing standard translations where possible, altering them or composing my own translations where I have seen fit, as documented in the footnotes. Biblical translations are NRSV, occasionally modified, as noted. All translations from the Septuagint are from Pietersma and Wright, unless otherwise noted; all translations of Jewish peudepigrapha are those given in Charlesworth, ed., *Old Testament Pseudepigrapha*, as noted. For the early Stoa, I have favored the use of Long and Sedley, *The Hellenistic Philosophers* = LS, noting page numbers of translations and Greek text in the notes ad loc., and keying references to von Arnim = SVF and the original text (according to the citation given in LS and/or SVF). For Greco-Roman literature, I have used the LCL texts and translations as much as possible, altering them when necessary, as noted: for instance, "Cic. *Nat. d.* 3.90, text and tr. Rackham, in LCL 268:376–377, modified" means that I have used Rackham's text and translation on the pages in question, and modified the translation (not the text) as I saw fit. An exception is Plato, where I have used the translations in Cooper and Hutchinson, eds., *Plato: Complete Works*, noting each translator individually. For Patristic literature, I have avoided the translations given in the Ante-Nicene Fathers series, using other translations as noted. Wherever possible, I provided translations with reference to the text as given in Sources Chrétiennes (SC), using a format identical to that employed for the LCL.

Finally, ancient sources are listed in the bibliography by ancient author if known (thus Cicero's works are under "Cicero"), while anonymous works (e.g., *On the Origin of the World*; *Suda*) are listed by modern editor or translator.

AUTHOR'S NOTE ON TRANSLATIONS AND REFERENCES   XXI

This means that a reference in a note to: "Cic. *Nat. d.* 3.90, text and tr. Rackham, in LCL 268:376–377, modified," will be found under "Cicero," and not "Rackham."

However, a reference to: "*Orig. World* NHC II 100.1–101.9, text in Painchaud, "Texte," 152, 154, tr. mine," leads to a critical edition under "Painchaud," not "*Orig. World.*"

"Modified" always refers to translation and not source text, unless noted otherwise. For instance: "*Cels.* 6.55, text Borret in SC 147:316, 318, tr. Chadwick, 371–372, modified," refers to *Against Celsus* 6.55; the text is that of Borret in volume 147 of Sources chrétiennes, while the translation from Chadwick's *Origen Against Celsus*. I have modified the translation of Chadwick with reference to the text as given in Borret. Both Borret and Chadwick are to be found under "Origen" in the bibliography.

Introduction

The title of this book—*Did God Care?*—asks a question which is provocative, but in modernity became acceptable, and in the twentieth century, even pressing.[1] A historian of early philosophy might find this question less than vital, because, with some notable exceptions, ancient philosophers typically argued that the gods do care. Yet ancient philosophers' insistence on affirming divine care does not mean that the question was of no importance to them. More typical of their attitudes is the statement of the early Christian thinker Clement of Alexandria, that someone who asks whether God cares is asking for punishment (*kolasis*)—and this shows us that the question was, in fact, urgent indeed.[2]

The word Clement uses to denote this care is *pronoia*, "providence"—a concept of Greek culture which is virtually absent from the Hebrew Bible and the New Testament.[3] Nevertheless, the notion of providence, or divine care for the world, human beings, and the unfolding of history, became enormously significant in later Greek and early Christian philosophy, to such an extent that Christian theology and Western philosophy are scarcely imaginable without it.[4] Yet, despite the importance of this subject, an Anglophone, scholarly monograph outlining the emergence and transformation of providence in the philosophy of the first centuries CE has, until now, remained to be written.[5] The absence

---

1 As Hans Jonas asked with reference to Auschwitz, "what God could let it happen?" ("Concept of God," 3). To oversimplify his answer: not an omnipotent one.

2 *Strom.* 5.1.6.1–2, discussed below, chapter three.

3 On translating pronoia as care, see Bergjan, *Der fürsorgende Gott*, 31–43; eadem, "Clement," 64.

4 For surveys of the theme in Western theology and philosophy from the approach of contemporary academic theology, see Murphy and Ziegler, eds., *Providence of God*; Ferguson, *Providence of God*. For a study from the perspective of biblical theology, see Schrage, *Vorsehung Gottes?*. Providence was a question of particular importance in Islamic philosophy (*kalām*), particularly for Averroes and Avicenna and their commentators (see for instance Belo, *Chance and Determinism*, or the recent special issue of *Intellectual History of the Islamicate World*, ed. Sebti and De Smet, on *The Reception of Avicenna's Theory of Providence in Post-Avicennism*). Important studies of the problem of evil in contemporary philosophy have to reckon with the problem of providence (e.g., Geach, *Providence and Evil*; Swinburne, *Providence and the Problem of Evil*; van Inwagen, *Problem*). The same is true of the problem of free will (see the discussion in Zagzebski, "Recent Work").

5 As regards studies in ancient philosophy, the monograph of Christian Parma (*Pronoia und Providentia*) is limited in scope and has virtually no discussion of the history of the problem prior to Plotinus—precisely the focus of this book. Magris's *L'idea di destino* is a terrific survey of Classical and Hellenistic texts and includes Christian and Gnostic sources, but sequesters

---

© KONINKLIJKE BRILL NV, LEIDEN, 2020 | DOI:10.1163/9789004432994_002

of a such a monograph owes to an uncomfortable simultaneity of the topic's obviousness and ostensible difficulty, given the various challenges it poses to the prospective author. These challenges are fourfold, and I will outline them here, so as to introduce the aims and strategy of the present study.[6]

The first challenge is that since there is a relative absence of a notion or idiom of providence in everyday and intellectual life today, one might think that providence was never really very important.[7] Yet this present absence of language about a divine 'master-plan' for human beings and history is decidedly young, and in the broader scope of things, it is stunning. To illustrate this point I select three relatively recent (for a book on the first centuries CE), very different examples of the use of the language of providence in public life: American political oratory, a Papal encyclical, and Nazi propaganda. In his Second Inaugural Address (4 March 1865), delivered less than three months before the surrender of the Confederate States of America, President Abraham Lincoln supposed "American slavery (to be) one of those offenses which, in the providence of God, must needs come, but which, having continued through His appointed time, He now wills to remove."[8] Slavery, Lincoln here avers, is an evil which God deemed necessary, but only for a limited time. In 1897, Pope Leo XIII entitled his encyclical on the study of the Bible simply "Providentissimus deus" ("The Most Caring God"). The text of the encyclical only uses the word *providentia* once, in the first sentence: God's providence is His revelation

---

the latter in a final chapter focused on predestination, with little integration with the rest of the study. Robert Sharples's *oeuvre* is excellent and foundational to the present study, but highly specialized, spread across many articles and commentaries, and relatively uninterested in early Christian sources prior to Boethius. George Karamanolis (*Philosophy*) takes up the latter challenge, but his analysis is limited to only part of a book chapter. On the side of theological and religious studies, Bergjan's *oeuvre* is very useful, but her *Der fürsorgende Gott* is chiefly concerned with (proto-orthodox) Christian theology, and so it contents itself with superficial treatment of Greek philosophy on its own terms, and omits Gnostic, Coptic, and Syriac sources entirely. Denzey (Lewis)'s useful book (*Cosmology and Fate*) fills much of the gap as regards Gnosticism, but also presents its own difficulties regarding its treatment of philosophy.

I regret that revised editions of the aforementioned monographs of Magris (2016) and Karamonolis (2020) were not available to me at the time of writing.

6 Cf. Ferguson's account of the problems the topic poses for the theologian at work (*Providence of God*, 2–12).

7 Rightly noted by Bergjan, *Der fürsorgende Gott*, 1. Similarly the theologian G.C. Berkouwer: "one cannot give thought to the Church's confession of faith in Providence without very soon being impressed by the distance between this confession and modern thought" (*Providence*, 7). For similar concerns *im deutschsprachigen Raum*, see Schrage, *Vorsehung Gottes?*, 10–13.

8 Lincoln, "Second Inaugural."

INTRODUCTION 3

as communicated in canonical Scripture.[9] Therefore, questioning the inerrancy of scripture—particularly from the vantage points of historical criticism or the natural sciences—amounts to an attack on divine providence.[10] On 21 July 1944, *Reichskanzler* Adolf Hitler declared the failure of the '20 July plot' on his life to be "a confirmation of the plan of providence."[11] The dictator proceeded to thank "providence and my Creator, not because He has saved me—my life is but care and labor for my people—rather, I thank him simply because He gave me the possibility of being permitted to bear these cares further, and to continue pursuing my work."[12] To me, these examples suffice to show that providence is 'something people in have been talking about,' until fairly recently. Yet I (b. 1981) cannot recall reading much about divine providence until undertaking my study of ancient history and philosophy as a university student. Some secular-minded readers may share this predicament; more religiously-minded ones may bemoan it, but I doubt they will not recognize it.[13]

---

9   Leo XIII, "Providentissimus Deus," 1.

10   Particularly vitriolic is the beginning of chapter ten:

> It must be clearly understood whom we have to oppose and contend against, and what are their tactics and their arms ... Now, we have to meet the Rationalists, true children and inheritors of the older heretics, who, trusting in their turn to their own way of thinking, have rejected even the scraps and remnants of Christian belief which had been handed down to them. They deny that there is any such thing as revelation or inspiration, or Holy Scripture at all ... These detestable errors, whereby they think they destroy the truth of the divine Books, are obtruded on the world as the preemptory pronouncements of a certain newly-invented 'free science' ...

Similarly, chs. 17–19. Despite his reservations about 'modernism,' Leo also fostered biblical scholarship, encouraging the study of ancient languages (ibid., 17; Spiteri, "Specific Contribution," 8) and authorizing in 1892 L'École biblique et archéologique française de Jérusalem. "Providentissimus Deus" would be commemorated fifty years later by Pius XII's "Divino Afflante Spiritu," which does permit the employment of historical-critical approaches to Holy Scripture, earning it the moniker of the "Magna Carta of biblical progress" (Brown and Collins, "Church Pronouncements," 1167; see also Spiteri, op. cit., 6).

11   "Ich selbst bin völlig unversehrt ... Ich fasse dies als eine Bestätigung des Auftrags der Vorsehung auf, mein Lebensziel weiter zu verfolgen" (text in Michalka, ed., *Deutsche Geschichte*, 365, quoted by Feldmeier, "Wenn die Vorsehung," 147–148; tr. mine). Fittingly enough, a British historian in 1952 described Hitler's improbable survival of the 20 July Plot in terms resembling Polybius's notion of *tuchē* (Walbank, *Historical Commentary*, 26).

12   "Ich selber danke der Vorsehung und meinem Schöpfer nicht deshalb, daß er mich erhalten hat. Mein Leben ist nur Sorge und ist nur Arbeit für mein Volk, sondern ich danke ihm nur deshalb, daß er mir die Möglichkeit gab, diese Sorgen weiter tragen zu dürfen, und in meiner Arbeit weiter fortzufahren ..." (text in Michalka, ed., *Deutsche Geschichte*, 367, tr. mine).

13   The question of the disappearance of providence from everyday discourse calls for its own

4   INTRODUCTION

Another challenge one faces when writing about providence is not that there is too little talk about it in the ancient sources; there is too much. The concept is so universal in the ancient sources that language about it begins to take on a nebulous, amorphous character. As the mind's eye glazes over and goes 'snow-blind,' the object of study begins to appear so diffuse and vague that it no longer seems to merit investigation.[14] Yet the universality of language about providence in antiquity does not signify that the concept means nothing; it signifies that it means everything. As the historian Averil Cameron writes, "the idea of Christian providence constituted a totalizing explanation, a kind of theory of everything. It embraced the idea of a divine plan which began with Creation."[15] Such a theory was to be found just about everywhere in ancient philosophy, as is evidenced by the few who attained notoriety by rejecting it, or even questioning it. The ancients themselves recognized that providence was not a single problem as much as a great complex of problems, as we read in Boethius's *Consolation of Philosophy*:

> "Fine," I [Boethius] said, "but it is a part of our business for you to reveal these mysteries and explain those things that are clouded and hidden. I am disturbed by these inconsistencies and beg you to explain a little more fully the apparent randomness of good and bad fortune."
>
> She [Lady Wisdom] hesitated a moment, then smiled, and at last replied, "This is the great question, isn't it? It is a problem that can never be fully solved even by the most exhaustive discourse. When one part of the conundrum is resolved, others pop up, like the heads of the Hydra. What is needed to restrain them is intellectual fire. Otherwise, we are in a morass of difficulties—the singleness of providence, the vicissitudes of fate, the haphazardness of events, God's plan, predestination, free will. All these knotty questions come together and are intertwined."[16]

---

study. For cursory remarks with bibliographies spanning political philosophy and rhetoric of the nineteenth and twentieth centuries, as well as the enormous challenges posed by the World Wars and the Holocaust for theodicy, see Webb, "From Prudentius," 241–243; Ferguson, *Providence of God*, 7–8, 241–242.

14   "It sometimes appears that the idea is so firmly embedded that it often not need be explicated in detail unless perhaps it is central to a particular debate" (Kraabel, "Pronoia at Sardis," 81). Rajak rightly notes how Kraabel's struggle with the "scope and diversity" of the term leads him to, without warrant, diminish its significance in Philo of Alexandria ("Gifts of God," 233–234). Such sentiments have been shared with me by a number of colleagues. One attempted to write a similar study, and failed; another simply told me, "you'll never figure that one out."

15   Cameron, "Divine Providence," 121.

16   Boeth. *Cons.* 4.6, tr. Slavitt, 130–131.

INTRODUCTION 5

Nor is the terminology itself simple. The terms used by the Greeks and Romans to describe the gods' care were already more or less fixed by Plato in various dialogues, and rendered in Latin as early as Cicero: *pronoia/pronoein* (*providentia/providere*; rarely *numen*) stand out as most important by far, but ancient authors use other terms for divine care as well, such as *epimeleia/epemeleisthai* (*carum esse*), *ameleia/amelein* (*neglegare*).[17] Conversely, the terms themselves are not always used in a uniform manner: what one text terms *heimarmenē*, another terms *pronoia* (or worse, 'tertiary *pronoia*').[18] The best one can do, at least within the limitations of a single monograph, is to focus on *pronoia/providentia* and their cognates and address other terminology when it presents itself. Meanwhile, language for the divine mirrors language for the human, and providence is no exception. The verb *pronoein* can refer to forethought or planning on the part of human beings, in entirely mundane environments.[19] Papyrological evidence for the usage of terminology related to *pronoia* begs for a book of its own,[20] but the present study focuses rather on usage in philosophical and theological, and to a lesser extent historical, literature.

The third challenge is that while providence was a central and fascinating problem amongst Roman and especially early Christian philosophers, scholarship on the subject remains balkanized into investigations that proceed along the lines of our modern university faculties, which cloister Greek 'philosophical' sources and Christian 'theological' or 'religious' ones away from one another. The problem is compounded by the fact that crucial sources survive not only in Greek and Latin, but in Coptic and Syriac, languages which historians of philosophy traditionally have not been compelled to learn. Scholarship on providence in later Greek and early Christian philosophy thus tends to focus strictly on (*a*) Greek 'pagan' writers in conversation with one another, and (*b*) Christian, 'theological' writers in conversation with one another, with (*c*) sources in 'oriental Christian' languages relegated to the margins and consulted

---

17 The object(s) of care are usually rendered in terms of wholes and parts: *ta panta/ta tōn holōn/ta kath'hola* (Lat. *magna*), *ta smikra/ta merē/ta kath'hekasta* (Lat. *parva*). As we will see, the vocabulary used by Christian and Gnostic thinkers to discuss divine care is virtually identical to that used by Plato and the Stoics.

18 So Nasrallah, "Lot Oracles," 218–219; on the example of *heimarmenē* versus tertiary *pronoia*, see below, chapter one.

19 See esp. Magris, *L'idea di destino*, 2:612.

20 While the bulk of our documentary papyri postdate the period under discussion this book, it is worth noting that private letters of the third and fourth centuries CE by Christian and non-Christian alike often opened or closed with blessings invoked with respect to *pronoia*. See the discussions of Horsley, *New Documents*, 143–144; Kraabel, "Pronoia at Sardis," 80; further, Preisigke, *Wörterbuch*, 2:379–380.

6 INTRODUCTION

haphazardly, if at all. Most of the attendant secondary literature proceeds along these lines, intersecting only on occasion and adding up to less than the sum of its parts.

I here give three representative examples from philosophy, religious studies, and theology. On the one hand, a flagship philosophical study of Stoic fate and determinism elects at the outset to exclude the themes of political freedom, providence, the concept of the will, and astrological determinism.[21] This works for the project in question, but brackets a huge amount of relevant material, begging for a complimentary project (such as the one attempted here).[22] On the other hand, some recent studies of providence in ancient Jewish and Christian sources appear to dismiss the relevance of these sources' philosophical content qua philosophy.[23] A better approach, as argued below, would be to embrace the philosophical content of Jewish and Christian writers from the standpoint of the history of philosophy. Finally, a recent, learned essay of theology opens with the aforementioned example of Hitler's invocation of providence to illustrate that the notion is "anything but unproblematic," which explains why "biblical tradition itself does not use this notion": it is *out of caution*."[24] Providence, the author attests, presents "divine power without a face. Yet in this manner,

---

21 Bobzien, *Determinism and Freedom*, 13.

22 To her credit, Bobzien does not set these questions aside out of any dismissiveness of 'religious' or 'biblical' evidence, but on grounds that her concern is with Hellenistic rather than Roman Stoicism.

23 Denzey (Lewis) claims that the *De fato* treatises of the fourth and fifth centuries are "tedious," full of "stock arguments ... which no one appears to have embraced with any earnestness" (*Cosmology and Fate*, 8, 184; also eadem, "New Star," 215), a statement refuted by the very fact of the existence of the *De fato* treatises themselves. (What author writes a book s/he does not care about?) Nasrallah waves away an Epictetan taxonomy of school-opinions about providence and fate (*Diatr.* 1.12.1–3) with the claim that "our scholarly attempt to systematize and clarify, whether in relation to Stoic philosophy or ancient Christian theology, runs counter to the diversity of the discussion in antiquity. There were many ancient strategies ... they were contingent and experimental" ("Lot Oracles," 220). While the ancient discussions were diverse, that does not mean that the arguments presented in them were random, unintelligible, or unworthy of scholarly investigation of the merits of their argumentation. Finally, Klawans cuts short his discussion of Stoic fate with the (at best) curt invitation, "readers can follow the subsequent peregrinations [of Stoic compatibilism] in the works of Susanne Bobzien" (*Josephus*, 77). One can—and should, if s/he is serious about understanding Stoic determinism.

24 "Das Beispiel [von Hitler—auth.] zeigt, dass der Begriff der Vorsehung alles andere als unproblematisch ist, dass er zumindest in den Giftschrank der theologischen Wissenschaft gehört" (Feldmeier, "Wenn die Vorsehung," 148). Feldmeier elaboriert that "zum einen finden sich in der biblischen Tradition Elemente, die man dann unter dem Vorsehungsbegriff subsumieren könnte. Zum anderen nötigt die Tatsache, dass die biblische Tradition selbst diesen Begriff nicht verwendet, zur Vorsicht, *denn was nicht entsprechend*

INTRODUCTION 7

it becomes all too easily the mask of inhumanity," which explains why it is virtually absent in the New Testament—the implication being, God's Word knew better than to use the term.[25] These are the approaches of three different fields at work on two different planets, whose fruits must be considered together in this one book.

This brings us to the fourth problem, the question of structure. The nature of the surviving evidence is uneven because some ancient sources have a lot to say about providence, while others preserve only a little, even if they are very important. With this issue compounded by the fact that providence singly tackles several problems that today we treat as distinct from one another, a study which proceeds on a strictly chronological basis—thinker by thinker, school by school—and surveys language about providence in each would make for a choppy, lopsided presentation.[26] Chapters on major thinkers with a great deal of relevant surviving evidence, such as Cicero, Philo, or Origen, would be massive; other bodies of evidence, like those regarding Numenius, Marcion, or Iamblichus, would be quite small, even though they are vital. There would be no chapter on the early Stoa because we can only reconstruct our picture of them from later sources, even if they were arguably the most important Hellenic *pronoia*-theorists of all. Some chapters would treat providence, dualism, and personal accountability together, and others would not. Perhaps most importantly, a sustained discussion that puts the arguments of a thinker in his or her philosophical context would—if it fully engaged the relevant primary and secondary sources—look like one of the thematic chapters offered here in the first place. A strictly chronological presentation could well suit a reference work for the initiated or the forced march of a handbook article, but not a prose

---

  auf den Begriff gebracht ist, von dem kann man nicht ohne weiteres voraussetzen, dass es so begriffen werden will und begriffen werden soll" (ibid., 149, italics author's).

  In any case, Feldmeier's reference to Hitler's appropriation of providence in order to denote *pronoia* as inherently problematic is questionable, given that the following page states that *pronoia* "ist ein philosophiches Theologoumenon, das *über seine Rezeption im hellenistischen Judentum* Eingang in die frühchristliche Theologie gefunden hat" (ibid., italics mine). If one follows the logic of Feldmeier's reading, it is Hellenistic Jewish writers who are ultimately responsible for the incorporation of the notion of providence into early Christian theology—and thus its eventual abuse in the Third Reich.

25 "Damit repräsentiert er ... die göttliche Macht ohne Gesicht. Auf diese Weise aber wird er nur zu leicht zur Maske des Unmenschlichen. Wohl auch deswegen wird der Begriff der Vorsehung im Neuen Testament vermieden" (Feldmeier, "Wenn die Vorsehung," 170; for similar concerns about abuse of the rhetoric of providence, see Ferguson, *Providence of God*, 8). The phrase "göttliche Macht ohne Gesicht" was coined by Jörg Rüpke in a study of divination given at the same conference where Feldmeier delivered his paper.

26 This problem has also been recognized by Denzey (Lewis) ("New Star," 209).

monograph that seeks to cultivate understanding for the advanced student or adventuring scholar. Thus, I have done my best to meet the competing needs of the evidence and the reader alike by organizing the discussion of each chapter along thematic lines that follow the threads of argument pursued in the ancient sources. Within the constraints of this principle, I nonetheless attempt to present the material within each chapter chronologically and with an eye to the structural integrity of individual textual corpora. The study has as its 'bookends' Classical, Hellenistic, and early Roman sources in the first chapter, while the final chapter focuses on sources from the middle to the end of the third century.

There is no way around these difficulties; they are a necessary fact of undertaking the study of the subject in the first place (*anagkē* or a happy coincidence, depending on whether one is a Platonist or Stoic). This book then attempts to communicate the insights of work on providence from 'philosophy,' 'classical philology,' 'religious studies,' and 'theology,' while bridging the gaps between them. Specifically, it hopes to contribute to the history of philosophy by way of treating ancient Jewish and Christian philosophers as ancient philosophers alongside fellow ancient philosophers, rather than 'theologians' only of importance to the history of Judaism or Christianity.[27] As Peter Adamson writes in a recent introduction to Hellenistic and Roman philosophy, "the texts of the Christians represent the last unexplored frontier in ancient philosophy," but some philosophers doubt whether early Christian writers actually made any novel contributions to the history of philosophy as such.[28] Thus for instance theologian George Christopher Stead's remark that "there is no doubt about the contribution which philosophy made to early Christian thought ... But we cannot speak with the same assurance about the contribution which Christian writers made to philosophy."[29] Rather, Stead avers, "what has been called 'Chris-

---

27 This book is thus a humble exercise in the sort of integrative approach to ancient thought pioneered by Pierre Hadot, who revolutionized the histories of later Greek philosophy and Latin Patristics alike through his deeply philological yet multidisciplinary approach to ancient evidence. For a useful discussion and appreciation of Hadot's methods, see Davidson, "Introduction," 2–18, as well as Hadot's own "Philosophy, Exegesis, and Creative Mistakes."

28 Adamson, *Philosophy*, xi; also ibid., 279; Gerson, "General Introduction," 3–4; Karamanolis, *Philosophy*, 3–4, 18; Mitralexis, Steiris, and Lalla, "Introduction," xxi (re: the example of Maximus Confessor). Similarly integrative is the useful survey of Perkams, "Einheit und Vielfalt."

29 Stead, *Philosophy*, 80. Cf. Zachhuber's claim with reference to the first three centuries CE hat "there is practically no evidence until much later that non-Christian philosophers accept the philosophical credentials of Christian thinkers in the way they accept the credentials of philosophers they disagree with" ("Review"). While true, this fact may tell

INTRODUCTION 9

tian philosophy' generally proves to be Christian theology."[30] This latter point is easily dispatched, for it is widely recognized today that the boundary between theology and philosophy is utterly porous in Roman antiquity.[31] Meanwhile, Adamson rightly identifies several examples where such contributions do seem to be evident—causation, personal accountability and 'free will,' and philosophy of language.[32] As will be argued in the conclusion, this book provides a fourth such contribution (closely related to the first two of these): providence. Thus, this is not a study of 'providence in early Christianity' as much as a study on 'providence in Roman philosophy'—but one that takes full consideration of the plentiful and challenging Christian and 'Gnostic' sources, in Greek, Latin, Coptic, and Syriac. These chapters will, the author can only hope, then also be of interest to those scholars of religion and theology who work with these sources.

Part One of the book, 'Providence,' serves as an introduction to the subject in Classical, Hellenistic, and early Roman philosophy, as well as Jewish and the earliest Christian sources of the first and second centuries CE. Chapter one introduces the 'providence problem(s),' i.e., the complex of questions which philosophers discussed with reference to *pronoia* and its cognates. These include God's care for and interaction with the world and its parts, whether directly or via semi-divine intermediaries; evil and theodicy, and their relationship with creation and matter; and human autonomy or responsibility, usually phrased in Greek as 'what is up to us.'[33] The chapter presents crucial proof-texts, problems, and terms of debate for the Roman period by way of reviewing the thought of the Presocratics and Plato, Aristotle, the Epicureans, the pseudo-Aristotelian author of *On the Cosmos*, and the Hellenistic and Roman Stoa on *pronoia* and questions relating to it. It concludes with a close reading of pseudo-Plutarch's treatise *On Fate* and its famous account of the Middle Platonic theory

---

us more about the rhetorical aims—particularly with a view towards construction of a tradition of 'Hellenism,' i.e. paganism—of non-Christian philosophers in late antiquity than it does about whether non-Christian philosophers of the third century were actually engaged in conversation with Christians, and how these conversations may have impacted the history of Greek philosophy.

30   Stead, *Philosophy*, 81; similarly ibid., 89.

31   Karamanolis, *Philosophy*, 17–18, with ample references; similarly, Gerson, "General Introduction," 3–4; cf. the more traditional view (if also more charitable towards Christian philosophy as philosophy) of O'Meara, "Introduction," xvi–xvii.

32   Adamson, *Philosophy*, 280–282. On the distinctive character of early Christian philosophy, see Karamanolis, *Philosophy*, 24–27, 239–240, followed by Janby, et al., "Introduction," 12.

33   Cf. the articulation of Labarriére, who sees providence as posing two kinds of problems: the relationship between God and the world, and human autonomy. These relate, in his account, to two further problems: theodicy and free will ("Providence," 2465).

of 'conditional fate,' which brings these issues together in a remarkable synthesis. Chapter two introduces thought about providence from Hellenistic and Roman Jewish sources, mainly of the first century CE, focusing on the *Letter to Aristeas*, the books of Sirach and Wisdom of Solomon, Philo of Alexandria, and Josephus. While it is a scholarly cliché to denote Jewish and New Testament texts as furnishing a more 'personal' sense of divine care than that found amongst 'pagan' philosophers, the chapter argues otherwise. Some Hellenistic Jewish texts envision God as absent, while some Stoic and especially Hellenistic and early Roman historical authors had an attenuated sense of God's involvement in terrestrial matters and personal attendance to virtuous individuals. Philo and other Jewish writers do present a genuine shift in ancient understandings of providence, but it is not a new thesis regarding God's personal care for individuals: it is a shift in the identity of the divine itself, from the gods of Greek and Roman civic cults to the God of Israel. This context helps us understand a difficult but fascinating discussion of providence and prayer in Justin Martyr's *Dialogue with Trypho*, set against the backdrop of the Bar Kochba Revolt. Meanwhile, the Stoic valence of early Christian philosophers' arguments about the reach of God's care for individuals was highlighted by these same Christian philosophers themselves, who struggled to differentiate their notions of God's immanence from those of the Stoa.

The difficulties presented by the perennial questions of divine transcendence versus immanence, and reconciling a providential character to the creator-god with the experience of evil, are the focus of Part II, 'Dualism.' Chapter three examines philosophers of the second and early third centuries CE who addressed these questions by positing multiple causal principles, some of which are not providential—a position which may reasonably be denoted 'religious dualism.' For Middle Platonists like Plutarch or Numenius, evil was understood in terms of the causality of matter, which possesses an efficacy distinct from that of the caring demiurge or the *daimones* which administer providence. Many early Christian philosophers, meanwhile, dealt with the question of evil's causality with primary reference to Second Temple Jewish apocalypticism, rather than the *Timaeus*. Among thinkers like Athenagoras of Athens, Clement of Alexandria, and Origen of Alexandria, a sort of 'proto-orthodox' stance emerged which identifies human evil as sin, bound up not only with personal responsibility, but with demons and Satan, who were understood to be fearsome cosmic powers who are nonetheless very much subordinate to the awesome and all-pervasive power of the deity. Meanwhile, these Christian philosophers' skepticism about the Middle Platonic model of distributing providence via semi-divine intermediaries reflected their views, influenced by the heritage of Jewish apocalyptic, that the *daimones* of Greek thought were in

INTRODUCTION 11

fact evil beings living off of sacrifices and spreading sin. On the other hand, other thinkers often considered 'heterodox' and identified as 'dualists' today—principally Hermogenes, Marcion, and Apelles—were accused of assigning too much casual agency to principles or beings other than God who were not demons. For Hermogenes and Apelles, the 'dualist' Platonism of Plutarch and Numenius likely served as their chief inspiration, while Marcion appears to have divorced, on scriptural grounds, providential care for human beings from providential care for the world, ruled by a separate, inferior deity—the God of the Old Testament.

Chapter four examines a particular kind of dualism which is of paramount importance to second and third-century philosophical sources, Christian and 'pagan' alike: the dossier of evidence sometimes referred to as 'Gnostic.' Just as chapter three defends the use of the phrase '(religious) dualism' to denote systems with multiple causal (or creative) principles, chapter four defends use of the term 'Gnosticism' to denote the philosophical presuppositions underlying most of the myths associated by ancient writers such as Irenaeus of Lyons and Porphyry of Tyre with individuals called *gnōstikoi* (Grk. "knowers"). Examination of these myths, particularly as preserved in the hoard of Coptic manuscripts discovered near Nag Hammadi (Upper Egypt) in 1945, shows that many of them use the language of providence explicitly and extensively to express the perspective that the world and human bodies are the creation of sub-divine beings, but that a providential God does care for humanity and intervene on its behalf because human beings belong in fact to a divine realm superior to the cosmos and its maker. Such a view contrasts strongly with the theorizations on the relationship between God as providential creator and administrator and humanity developed by Philo or Irenaeus, for whom the providential character of the creator-deity was axiomatic. Other texts dealing with this mythology confirm its tension with competing models of creation and providence when they attempt to mitigate its dualism by emphasizing the universal reach of providence or that everything happens "by the will of the Father." Some term is necessary to denote this complex of evidence in the history of philosophy, and "Gnosticism," the longtime term of choice in modern scholarship for so much of it, presents itself as a strong candidate.

Part III, 'Will,' focuses chronologically on third-century sources, particularly the writings of Origen of Alexandria and Plotinus on divine foreknowledge, individual responsibility and free will, and the question of God's own faculties of knowledge and will. Chapter five offers a close reading of the first of Origen's great works on determinism and free will, an excerpt from his *Commentary on Genesis* preserved in the *Philocalia* under the title *On Fate*. This treatise takes astrological determinism as its subject, but also attacks Marcion, and includes a long digression on the subjects of divine foreknowledge and divination, culminating in its examination of the 'Oracle to Laius,' a stock example among Greek philosophers debating prophecy and determinism. The chapter provides the proper background and context for Origen's arguments on these subjects and the 'Oracle to Laius': Chrysippus's doctrine of co-fated events (preserved in Cicero's dialogue *On Fate*); the Peripatetic Alexander of Aphrodisias's arguments that the practice of divination must be defended even if God does not take an active interest in the world and that Chrysippus's doctrine makes the gods responsible for impious behavior; and Alcinous's exploration of these themes in explaining Middle Platonic doctrine of 'conditional fate' and the role *daimones* play in prophecy. Origen's solution to the problem of the 'Oracle to Laius'—that it is future events which cause divine foreknowledge, not the other way around—is an ingenious response that takes up the logical problems presented by his Hellenic forebears but is primarily directed against Marcionite exegesis of Gen 2–3. His arguments regarding astrological determinism in the remaining chapters of *On Fate*, meanwhile, weave together these themes—the providential and unlimited character of divine foreknowledge, and the removal of the activity of divination from Roman institutions to biblical prophecy— and introduce a new one, the individual responsibility of humans and angels alike.

This is the subject of chapter six, which seeks to shed light on the murky origins of the notion of 'free will' in second and third-century Roman philosophy. The chapter sets the stage by introducing the relevant terminology concerning individual responsibility and autonomy, the bulk of which derives from Aristotle, and its application to the question of a faculty of responsibility in Alexander of Aphrodisias's treatise *On Fate* and the controversial conclusion to pseudo-Plutarch's *On Fate*. The chapter then proceeds to examine the *Book of the Laws of the Countries* from the school of the second-century Christian teacher Bardaiṣan, the Alexandrian Christian philosopher Basilides's discussion of providence and sin (and Clement's response to it), and Origen's mini-treatise *On Free Will* in the third book of *On First Principles*. While most Patrologists would agree that these are the three most important accounts of free will and determinism in Christian literature prior to the fourth century CE, these sources are practically nonexistent in scholarship on the early history of free will conducted from the viewpoint of the history of philosophy. What they tell us is that the emergence of free will in second–third-century Christian philosophical discourse was largely concerned with eschatology, particularly vis-à-vis the existence of the soul as the seat of responsibility even prior to its incarnation in the body. This key instance of influence from Plato's *Republic* on early Christian thought

INTRODUCTION   13

is often neglected in favor of outsize influence accorded to thinkers whose views on the problem more closely resemble those of Augustine, such as Irenaeus or Tertullian.

Finally, chapter seven focuses rather on divine omniscience and providence from the perspective of the first principle itself, particularly as discussed by Plotinus in his great treatises *On the Will of the One* and *On Providence*. While Plotinus typically relegated the acts of willing and knowing to the realm of divine Intellect, not the transcendent One (or 'Good'), in the former work he throws caution to the wind and argues that, in a sense, the first principle does 'will' the production of the universe, an act which one may describe as "prior to intellect (*pro noēseōs*)" or even a divine "first thought (*prōtē noēsis*)." Here, Plotinus assumes a position very closely resembling that taken by the Valentinian text known today as the *Tripartite Tractate*, which also holds significant parallels to his work *On Providence*, perhaps the most thorough and compelling treatise composed on the subject prior to Boethius. The rest of the chapter explores the curious afterlife of this notion of providence qua the 'first thought' of The One in Platonism of the third century CE, which includes Plotinus's student Porphyry of Tyre, the anonymous *Commentary on Plato's 'Parmenides'*, and three 'Platonizing' Sethian texts from Nag Hammadi, *Zostrianos*, *Allogenes*, and *Marsanes*. All of these works explore the notion of divine providence as a faculty of the first principle which may be shared by a human being via contemplative practices such as negative theology, but it is practically impossible to decisively date these works and thus establish a narrative of dependency and development. Nonetheless, it is clear that while Platonists at the beginning of the third century generally eschewed to assign faculties of will or providence to the first principle, by the end of the century it was the standard view for Platonists—just as it had been for most biblically-informed philosophers since Philo. This turn after Plotinus towards views on divine foreknowledge and providence more closely resembling those of the Stoa or the Christians suggests the possibility that third-century Platonists were, owing to their discourses and disputes with Christians and Gnostics, pushed to adapt a more baldly providential notion of the divine.

This book concludes by pursuing the natural implications of its approach to the history of Roman philosophy: while it is commonly recognized that early Christian philosophy drew a great deal from Platonism and especially Stoicism, is it possible that this conversation between 'pagan' and Christian thinkers went in both directions, at least until the end of the third century CE? 'Pagan' Roman philosophy on providence, dualism, and will may not have been, on this reading, only a source for early Christian philosophy; it was developed in conversation with Christian philosophers. Among these Christian philosophers were 'Gnostics,' whose philosophical contributions were invaluable, particularly to the thought of the greatest philosopher of late antiquity, Plotinus. The question of divine care reminds us that it is to our detriment when we tell the story of ancient thought by reading Jewish, Christian, and Gnostic authors solely as sources for ancient religion, rather than sources for the history of philosophy.

PART 1

Providence

CHAPTER 1

The *Pronoia* Problem(s)

1   Introduction: Did the Gods Care?

Sextus Empiricus, a Skeptic of the first century CE, takes as the "usual view (*biōi*)" that "the gods exist, we worship them, and they care (*einai theous kai sebomen theous kai pronoein*)."[1]

For ancient philosophers—and for ancient Roman society—divine providence, or care, was directly tied to the gods' very existence and human interaction with them: 'worship,' or what we might today call something like 'religion.'[2] To deny divine care was tantamount to denying religion. It was no accident that the sole ancient philosophical school to divorce the gods from care for worldly things, the school of Epicurus, did so as part of a greater criticism of civic cult and ritual that was often referred to by its opponents, misleadingly, as 'atheism.'[3]

Seemingly hated by all their contemporaries, Epicurus (ca. 342–271 BCE) and adherents to his philosophy, such as Lucretius, only spoke of providence to reject it.[4] Epicurus believed the gods to be happy—so happy, they had nothing to do with administering the cosmos, a task which would amount to an awful lot of work: "the blessed and the imperishable neither itself engages in affairs nor provides them for another, so that it is affected neither by anger nor by joy; all such things are a kind of weakness. Anger is foreign to the gods; for anger is because of what is against the will, but nothing is against a god's will."[5] Epicu-

---

1   *Pyr.* 3.2, text Bury in LCL 273:326, tr. mine, cit. M. Frede, "Galen's Theology," 111.

2   On the use of the term 'religion' to describe discourses and practices of the ancient Mediterranean world, see the critical treatment of Nongbri, *Before Religion*, which I take as a call for circumspection when using the term 'religion' in an ancient context, rather than an all-out *Verbot*.

3   For accusations of Epicurus's 'atheism,' see Cic. *Nat. d.* 1.85; Plut. *That Epicurus Actually Makes a Pleasant Life Impossible*, 1102c–d, cit. and discussed in Mansfeld, "Theology," 464.

4   For the Epicureans on theology and providence, see e.g. the *testimonia* collected in LS 13F–J, with commentary in Long and Sedley, *Hellenistic Philosophers*, 1:144–149; further, Theiler, "Tacitus," 48–50; Philippson, "Quelle"; Sutcliffe, *Providence and Suffering*, 1; Long, *Hellenistic Philosophy*, 41–49; Mansfeld, "Theology," 462–464; O'Brien, *Demiurge*, 89 (emphasizing that the Stoa were often maligned as badly as were the Epicureans). On dating Epicurus's life and *floruit*, see Dorandi, "Chronology," 43.

5   *Ap.* Nem. *Nat. hom.* 43 [147], tr. Sharples and van der Eijk, *Nemesius*, 211; similarly, Cic. *Nat. d.* 1.52 = LS 13H (quoted below, chapter five); Lucr. 5.146–155 = LS 23L.

© KONINKLIJKE BRILL NV, LEIDEN, 2020 | DOI:10.1163/9789004432994_003

rus and Epicureans thus figure as bogeymen in discussions of providence and evil, attempting to dispatch cherished notions of providential care. In one of the philosophical dialogues of the Roman statesman and philosopher Cicero (first century BCE), the Epicurean 'Lucullus' demands: "I ask why God, when he made everything for our sakes—for that's what you think—made so vast a supply of water-serpents and vipers, why did he dole out so many lethal and pernicious creatures over land and sea?"[6] In a later work, *On the Nature of the Gods* (46 BCE), Cicero's mouthpiece for Epicurean philosophy, Velleius, begins his speech—the first major one of the work—by announcing: "do not listen to pointless and fanciful ideas, like the maker and world-builder deity of Plato's *Timaeus*, or of the old hag of the Stoics, *Pronoia*, which may be rendered in Latin as '*Providentia*' ..."[7] While these figures are never meant to be taken seriously, their persistent appearance in ancient literature about providence and fate indicates that their arguments carried more sway than authors like Cicero would have liked. It indicates that providence mattered.[8]

The present chapter introduces the development of Greek philosophical ideas concerning providence, focusing on the twin problems of care and causality. Beginning with Homer and the Presocratics, it discusses Plato, Aristotle, and the Epicureans' Hellenistic contemporaries the early Stoa, proceeding all the way to the Middle Platonists and Roman Stoa of the second century CE.[9] It seeks to demonstrate that in ancient Greek philosophy, providence was a single issue that dealt with multiple problems. If one surveys the language, arguments, and especially terminology used to discuss providence, it becomes clear that the question of (*a*) *the gods' care* was tightly bound with those relating to (*b*) the *causes of evil and misfortune*, as well as (*c*) *fate and personal accountability*. In other words, even if these multiple questions may be regarded as distinct today, the ancients—and especially the Stoa—considered them all to

---

6 *Acad.* 2.120, tr. Rackham in LCL 268:623, slightly revised. For another attestation of the 'harmful animal' argument, see Lucr. 5.218–220; see further Magris, *L'idea di destino*, 2:677–678; Kalligas, *'Enneads'*, 461; O'Brien, *Demiurge*, 53; below, n. 90. For Lucretius against the argument from design, see Sedley, *Creationism and its Critics*, 148–149.

7 Cic. *Nat. d.* 1.18, tr. Rackham in LCL 268:21, modified. For the date of *Nat. d.*, see Beard, "Cicero and Divination," 34.

8 Cf. Bergjan's argument that, among the philosophers of the second and third centuries CE, "die Frage war nicht, ob Gott Pronoia übt, sondern wie Gott Pronoia übt" (*Der fürsorgende Gott*, 336).

9 This is less material to cover than it may seem. Cf. Bobzien's remark that "the central place providence has in later writings on fate is not documented before the turn of the millennium" to CE (*Determinism and Freedom*, 13; similarly M. Scott, *Journey*, 38). As this chapter makes clear, *pronoia* is of great importance already in Plato, to say nothing of the early Stoa, but our extant textual evidence for *pronoia* before the first centuries CE is relatively meagre.

THE PRONOIA PROBLEM(S)   19

fall under the aegis of providence. This chapter then does not simply provide an introductory survey of the philosophical problem of *pronoia* in Classical and Hellenistic Greek philosophical sources, but attempts to demonstrate the necessity—or at least the usefulness—of the structure of the rest of this book. Nor is our evidence regarding the Platonic, Aristotelian, and Stoic positions on divine care, cosmic causality, and human responsibility dormant in scholarly debate today. While many of the passages discussed here are well-known, their precise meaning and significance, particularly in relationship to passages that are less famous, remain contested amongst historians of philosophy, and these are debates which are worth spelling out in full at the onset of this study.

2   The First 'Likely Stories' about Providence: From the Presocratics to Plato

It is possible to pinpoint a distinctive shift in Classical Greek discourse which marks the appearance of a notion of providential care for humanity. It is not to be found in Greek Epic poetry, which does not treat questions of care, fate and responsibility in a systematic way. Rather, the universe of the Homeric epics is characterized by fatalism about the cosmos and, alternatively, pessimism about human nature. For instance, the *Iliad* states that "no one of men escapes his doom (*moiran*)."[10] "In no way is it possible for another god to escape or nullify the will (*noon*) of aegis-bearing Zeus ..."[11] On the other hand, in the *Odyssey*, human beings are the sole authors of evil, however capricious the gods may appear to be: "look you now, how ready mortals are to blame the gods. It is from us, they say, that evils come, but they even of themselves, through their own blind folly, have sorrows beyond that which is ordained."[12] Conversely, the Archaic poets' gods are not really creators; in Hesiod, they simply appear in a seemingly eternal world that already exists and is already populated. Hesiod knows stories of primordial matters, such as the myth of the four ages of humanity, or of Pandora, but these are not creation-myths.[13] What is absent from all of these passages is the notion that the gods care for human beings and events; if all is fated, it is not to human benefit.

---

10   *Il.* 6.488, text and tr. Murray in LCL 170:296–297, slightly modified. On *moira*, see Russell, *The Devil*, 129–130.
11   Hom. *Od.* 16.137–138 text and tr. Murray in LCL 104:180–181, slightly modified.
12   *Od.* 1.32–34, tr. Murray in LCL 104:5; quoted by Max. Tyr. *Or.* 41.4 (see below, chapter three). Cf. Russell, *The Devil*, 131.
13   Parker, "Origins of Pronoia," 92.

20   CHAPTER 1

Meanwhile, the cosmos of the first philosophers, the 'Presocratics,' is so depersonalized that there is no sense of divine care at all. God's operations and the workings of nature are here completely identified, with no interest in or regard for human life; to Zeus, all things are just.[14] Democritus, Heraclitus, and Empedocles all agreed that "fate exercises the force of necessity (*ut id fatum vim necessitates afferret*)."[15] Anaxagoras, on the other hand, supposedly said that "nothing that comes to be does so in accordance with fate, and that this term is an empty one."[16] All this changes with the flourishing of Greek thought in the fifth century BCE.[17] Diogenes of Apollonia claims that the element *aēr*, operating as something like a universal, divine mind, intelligently organizes everything in the best possible way.[18] God remains accused, on occasion: one of Euripides's characters cries, "you are either a stupid (*amathēs*) god, or there is no justice in your nature."[19] Thus does Herodotus state—using the term *pronoia* for the first time in extant sources to describe divine care for humanity—that "somehow, the forethought of God (*tou theiou hē pronoiē*), in its wisdom—as is fitting—has made all those animals which are submissive and edible fruitful, lest they run out by being eaten up; meanwhile, headstrong and troublesome animals have few offspring."[20]

Although Diogenes Laertius credits Plato with being the first philosopher to discuss *pronoia theou*,[21] the oldest sustained discussion of God's providential care for human beings is to be found in the *Memorabilia* of Socrates's

---

14   Heraclitus, frgs. 102–104 DK, cit. Kalligas, '*Enneads*', 441, n. 1.

15   Cic. *Fat.* 39, tr. Rackham in LCL 349:235.

16   Alex. Aphr. *Fat.* 2, tr. Sharples, 42. Mansfeld ("*Diaphonia*," 191–194) has argued that Alexander's remarks are probably not an unfair reading of Anaxagoras, even if they give a hardly impartial, "hyper-interpretation of a critical interpretation of Anaxagoras" derived mainly from Plato (*Phaedo* 98b) and to a lesser extent Aristotle (*Metaph.* 1.3 984b15–22, 1.4 985a18–21). Sharples appears more skeptical ("Commentary: Alexander," 125–126).

17   Magris, *L'idea di destino*, 2:613; for survey, see ibid., 612–626; Parker, "Origins of Pronoia."

18   Frgs. B3, B5 DK. See Long, *Hellenistic Philosophy*, 150; Magris, *L'idea di destino*, 2:617–619; Kalligas, '*Enneads*', 441.

19   Euripides, *Hercules*, 346, text and tr. Kovacs in LCL 9:340–341, slightly modified. On Euripides's theological critique in his other plays, see Magris, *L'idea di destino*, 2:623–625; Russell, *The Devil*, 133.

20   Herodotus, *Histories*, 3.108, text and tr. Godley in LCL 118:134–135, significantly modified. Kalligas, '*Enneads*', 441 opines that Herodotus is here under the influence of Diogenes, although the evidence is by no means clear (Parker, "Origins of Pronoia," 90–91). "This is not the first text in which the gods are credited with *pronoia*, but previously it had been exercised in particular instances ... Here, for the first time in surviving literature, divine *pronoia* is revealed in the permanent conditions of existence established by the gods" (Parker, op. cit., 87; see also Feldmeier, "Wenn die Vorsehung," 151).

21   D. L. 3.24, followed by Kraabel, "Pronoia at Sardis," 80.

THE PRONOIA PROBLEM(S)   21

most important student after Plato, Xenophon. In the *Memorabilia*, Socrates declares that "the one who created humanity in the beginning (*ho ex archēs poiōn anthrōpous*) had some useful end in view," as is evident in the facility of the sensory organs. "Additionally," he asks, "doesn't it look to you like other things resemble the works of providence (*pronoias ergois eoikenai*)"? The eyeballs have eyelids, eyelashes, and eyebrows to protect them; incisor teeth are sharp, while molars grind food well. The mouth is next to the nose and eyes—so that we can see and smell what we eat—but since our excrement is unpleasant to see and smell, our digestive organs and openings are at the opposite end of the body from our sensory ones. "So, with these matters arranged with care (*tauta ... pronoētikōs pepgragmena*), do you doubt whether they are the works of chance—or of design (*tuchēs ē gnōmēs erga estin*)?"[22]

A very similar passage on the gods' construction of the eye and eyelids is to be found in Plato's great cosmological treatise, the *Timaeus*, which should lead us to suppose that some kind of argument for the existence of God by design (of our bodies) was used by Socrates himself.[23] Here, the care of the "craftsman" (*dēmiourgos*, thus 'demiurge') for creation in general—for the entire universe, in fact—is evident in Plato's argument that God made the universe as good as it could possibly be, and that it is nothing short of amazing, for the cosmos is a thinking, living creature where Being (stability) and Becoming (change) meet:

> Let us, then, state the reason for which the artificer put together Becoming and the All: He is good, and in him no desire for anything else arises, ever; so, not wishing for anything else, he wishes for everything to be as equal to him (in goodness) as possible ... For God wants everything to be good, and for the bad not to exist, to the extent of possibility. Thus, ascertaining that the entirety of what is visible is not in a state of peace, but rather moving about, flailing and confusedly, he leads it from disorder to order, considering that order is manifestly superior to disorder. It is not right for that one who is best to do anything but that which is most noble. Reasoning further, he found that, given that visible things are visible by nature, any creation bereft of intellect will not be more noble than that

---

22   Xenophon, *Socratic Memorabilia*, 1.4.5–6, text and tr. Marchant in LCL 168:56–57, significantly modified. See also ibid., 4.3.2–18, on Socrates's argument that the invisible gods must exist, given the state of visual, natural phenomena. On the latter and its influence, see M. Frede, "Galen's Theology," 100–101.

23   *Tim.* 45b–46a; see Dragona-Monachou, "Divine Providence," 4419–4420, 4429–4430; Feldmeier, "Wenn die Vorsehung," 152; Sedley, *Creationism*, 213; O'Brien, *Demiurge*, 21–22. On the influence of these passages amongst the Stoa, see Long, *Epictetus*, 152.

which possesses intellect, just as with comparing wholes, and it is impossible that intellect could come into being apart from soul. For this reason, then, as he was crafting the all, the artificer put intellect in soul, and soul in the body, so that he might arrange a creation that is by nature most noble and best. Therefore, according to our likely story, it is necessary to say that the world is a living, ensouled, thinking being, and that it truly came into being thanks to divine providence.[24]

Plato here does not only spell out that the world "truly came into being thanks to divine providence," a vital notion for so many of the thinkers discussed in the rest of this book. He also identifies, albeit vaguely, what amounts to a source of evil in the world: the obscure, turbulent 'receptacle' (*chōra*) which is home to the absence of order (*Tim.* 50a–51b), as well as a kind of efficacious, active disorder and confused motion of the visible cosmos (*Tim.* 52d–53b).[25] Such chaotic, disordered motion, he says, is inherent in matter, and so its effects may be referred to as "necessity" (*anagkē*). The demiurge cannot make a world that is completely good, without any faults whatsoever; rather, with recourse to "persuasion"—the means of 'taming' matter—it makes the world as good as it can possibly be.[26]

A second and equally important source of fault in the *Timaeus* is constituted by the demiurge's underlings: the "young gods" of traditional Greek cult, who are fallible beings.[27] To them are entrusted the actual creation of the material cosmos and the human body, to insulate God from responsibility for the necessary evils inherent in material existence: "when he had finished assigning all these tasks, he proceeded to abide at rest in his customary nature. His children immediately began to attend to and obey their father's assignment" and construct the body of the world. Yet, overwhelmed by the chaos of the elements, "the living thing as a whole did indeed move, but it would proceed in a disorderly, random and irrational way ..."[28] As Sarah Broadie notes, the withdrawal of the demiurge at the moment of material creation seems to imply a withdrawal from care for the creation and the temporal realm.[29] We cannot

---

24 *Tim.* 29e–30b, tr. Zeyl, in Cooper and Hutchinson, eds., *Plato: Complete Works*, 1236. See further Magris, *L'idea di destino*, 2:634, 643; Karamanolis, *Philosophy*, 62–63.

25 Rightly emphasized by Reydams-Schils, "Maximus," 135.

26 So Armstrong, "Dualism," 36–37; Magris, *L'idea di destino*, 2:672; Adamson, "Making a Virtue," 9–12; idem, "State of Nature," 89–90, re: *Tim.* 48a; see further ibid., 68e–69a (on divine vs. necessary causes); more generally, Morrow, "Necessity."

27 *Tim.* 40e–42e; see Reydams-Schils, *Demiurge and Providence*, 71.

28 *Tim.* 43a–b, tr. Zeyl, in Cooper and Hutchinson, eds., *Plato: Complete Works*, 1246.

29 Broadie, *Nature and Divinity*, 262; also Reydams-Schils, "Maximus," 130.

THE PRONOIA PROBLEM(S) 23

be certain if this is what Plato intended, but it is clear that, following the creation of the material cosmos and human bodies, care for these creations is in the hands not of the demiurge, but of the 'visible and generated gods'—the planets, as well as *daimones* ('demons'), described in other Platonic dialogues as superhuman intermediaries.[30]

Plato takes up the problem of the cause of imperfection and even evil in different contexts throughout the dialogues. A myth in the *Politicus* describes how in the previous world-age, Cronos attended to the needs of humans and even animals; in the present age ruled by Zeus, there is no such care, as is evident in the strife characterizing our worldly experience.[31] A particularly important discussion is to be found in the *Laws*, where Plato stresses God's care for the 'whole' (*holos*) as well as the 'part' (or 'individual'—*meros*):

> So let us not treat God as less skilled than a mortal craftsman, who applies the same expertise to all the jobs in his own line whether they are big or small, and gets more finished and perfect results the better he is at his work. We must not suppose that God, who is supremely wise, and willing and able to superintend the world, looks to major matters, but—like a faint-hearted lazybones who throws up his hands at hard work—neglects the minor, which we established were in fact easier to look after.[32]

One wonders if the "faint-hearted lazybones" is how a critic pilloried the demiurge of the *Timaeus*, who leaves the 'dirty work' to the young gods. In the *Laws*, Plato is keen to block any such characterization of God, and yet his account of divine care at work in the world is not so different from that of the *Timaeus*: "the supervisor of the universe has arranged everything with an eye to its preservation and excellence ... Creation is not for your benefit; *you* exist for the sake of the universe."[33] The qualification is important: God does not necessarily attend to the welfare of individual lives, and to the extent that God does, it is solely in the interest of the whole. To my knowledge, Plato was the first of the Greeks to frame the question of God's relationship to the world in terms of wholes and parts—the 'big picture' versus the small dramas, however tragic

---

30   *Tim.* 40c–41a.

31   *Pol.* 269c–274e.

32   Plat. *Leg.* x 902e–903a, tr. Saunders in Cooper and Hutchinson, eds., *Plato: Complete Works*, 1559–1560. The greater discussion ranges from 900d–904b. See also Ferguson, *Providence of God*, 14.

33   Plat. *Leg.* x 903b–c, tr. Saunders in Cooper and Hutchinson, eds., *Plato: Complete Works*, 1560, italics his; see also Magris, *L'idea di destino*, 2:645–646.

24   CHAPTER 1

they may be. Whatever position one takes on it, this language remained standard in Hellenistic and Roman antiquity for discussions of providence, fate, and theodicy.[34]

Care attendant to 'the preservation and excellence of the whole' is not tantamount to any kind of divine intervention or involvement in human affairs.[35] How, then, can God be said to attend to human life, aside from the fact that there are lives at all? Effectively, this is still the 'best of possible worlds' of the *Timaeus*, and it is not a very satisfying answer to the experience of human suffering and injustice. Plato must have sensed this. In the *Laws*, the 'Athenian' continues:

> You're grumbling because you don't appreciate that your position is best not only for the universe, but for you, too, thanks to your common origin. And since a soul is allied with different bodies at different times, and perpetually undergoes all sorts of changes, either self-imposed or produced by some other soul, the divine checkers-player has nothing else to do except promote a soul with a promising character to a better situation, and relegate one that is deteriorating to an inferior, as is appropriate in each case, so that they all meet the fate they deserve.[36]

In other dialogues as well, Plato's answer is to look beyond present human lives to the past and future incarnations of souls—to the afterlife described in his eschatological myths, particularly in the *Phaedrus* and the *Republic*.[37] The former dialogue includes a discussion of the lives of exceptional souls who have ascended on their wings after death, following the gods, celestial charioteers whose routes comprise the movement of the circuits of heavenly bodies—the

---

34   This fact can be obscured by the fact that the Greek term *holos* also simply means 'universe' (so LSJ 1218b), and so modern translations often render the term as such. They are not wrong, but where an ancient author has divine care in mind, he or she often refers to care for the 'universe' as care for 'the big picture, not the small stuff,' rather than 'the universe and every single thing in it.' Accordingly, in this study, I translate *holos* and its cognates as 'whole' rather than 'universe,' however wooden that may be, where it may better convey what sort of care the ancient author had in mind—for wholes versus parts, for the big picture versus every little thing.

35   See also Louth, "Pagans and Christians," 280; *pace* Karavites, *Evil*, 118–119.

36   Plat. *Leg.* x 903d, tr. Saunders in Cooper and Hutchinson, eds., *Plato: Complete Works*, 1560.

37   On this point, see Dörrie, "Der Begriff Pronoia," 77–78; Dragona-Monachou, "Divine Providence," 4421; Alt, *Weltflucht*, 123; D. Frede, "Theodicy and Providential Care," 93–95. See further below, in this chapter, on the Middle Platonists.

THE PRONOIA PROBLEM(S)

stars and planets. The most exceptional souls reach the 'plain' where the gods rest their 'horses'—pure reality—and enjoy there a taste of "all things as they are."[38] Nonetheless, they remain subject to the 'law of Nemesis' (*Adrasteia*):

> The law of Nemesis is this: If any soul becomes a companion to a god and catches sight of any true thing, it will be unharmed until the next circuit; and if it is able to do this every time, it will always be safe. If, on the other hand, it does not see anything true because it could not keep up, and by some accident takes on a burden of forgetfulness and wrongdoing, then it is weighed down, sheds its wings and falls to earth.[39]

Reincarnation into nine kinds of lives ensue, better ones granted to those who have led just lives, worse to the unjust.[40]

The *Republic* sets out similar principles with different imagery, in the famous 'Myth of Er' concluding the work. Here, a group of souls in heaven is told by a representative of the Fate Lachesis that they will draw lots so as to determine the order in which they may select their next type of incarnate existence:

> Your daemon or guardian spirit will not be assigned to you by lot; you will choose him. The one who has the first lot will be the first to choose a life to which he will be then bound by necessity. Virtue knows no master; each will possess it to a greater or lesser degree, depending on whether he values or disdains it. The responsibility lies with the one who chooses; God has none (*aitia elomenou, theos anaitios*).[41]

Unlike the accounts in the *Laws* and *Phaedrus*, the language of determinism is present here, for the soul will be "bound by necessity" to the life it chooses. One may read Plato here as indicating that the selection of a life prior to incarnation amounts to a complete determinism of our present situation and behavior, despite Socrates's assertion that responsibility for virtue is nonetheless up to each soul.[42]

---

38   *Phaedr.* 246e–247e.

39   *Phaedr.* 248c, tr. Nehemas and Woodruff in Cooper and Hutchinson, eds., *Plato: Complete Works*, 526.

40   *Phaedr.* 248d–e.

41   *Resp.* x 617d–e, tr. Grube, rev. Reeve, in Cooper and Hutchinson, eds., *Plato: Complete Works*, 1220, slightly modified.

42   Wilberding, "Myth of Er," 88–90. See further Alt, *Weltflucht*, 13; Louth, "Pagans and Christians," 281–282.

26 CHAPTER 1

Yet the all-important statement, for ancient and modern commentators alike, is that "responsibility lies with the one who chooses,"[43] because it highlights in very clear terms the purpose of reincarnation in all three of these accounts: aside from God the benevolent creator, there is a causal principle at work in determining how things are, and this principle is the immortal human soul. Its choices are independent, and, although they are made outside of the present, material world, they can have serious ramifications for the lives we experience during our earthly incarnations. This is the second distinctive contribution of Plato to the emergence of the notion of providence in ancient philosophy. *Pronoia* already denoted God's care for the universe in Herodotus; Xenophon's discussion in the *Memorabilia*, paired with Plato's *Timaeus*, indicates that Socrates taught a version of the 'argument by design' with reference to divine *pronoia*. Plato was the first to designate the human soul as a causal principle independent of God and the present material world created by the 'young gods' of the *Timaeus*, an agent that could be independent of providence. While here, the gods "became creators, and they became kind,"[44] plenty of room was left for people and the semi-divine beings they worshipped to do wrong.

3 Epicurus, Aristotle, and (Pseudo-)Aristotle: "What Difference Is There ...?"

Many writers following Plato, on the other hand, did not find the notion of *pronoia* compelling at all. Epicurus and his followers have already been mentioned; to them, we may add Aristotle. These figures—who differ on so much else—would often be lumped together by later authors, such as Atticus, a Platonist of the second century CE:

> 'What?' someone might say, 'are you aligning Aristotle and Epicurus on the same point?!' Yes, I am, for the following reason: what difference is there for us, if the divine is banished from the world and no connection to it is left to us, or if one confines the gods to the world and removes them from terrestrial affairs? For it is the same with them both—the absence

---

43 See further Bobzien, "Inadvertent Conception,"161, denoting the model of moral responsibility adopted here as one of individual autonomy.

44 Parker, "Origins of Pronoia," 94.

THE PRONOIA PROBLEM(S)   27

of divine care (*to ek theōn ameles*) for humanity, and the absence of fear
of the gods amongst the unjust ...[45]

Atticus tries to conflate the views of Epicurus and Aristotle on the grounds that
they both deny that the gods care for human beings, and that they are to be
feared.[46] It does not matter if Epicurus and Aristotle had two different ends
in mind when making these arguments. What matters to Atticus is that they
made them at all, because for him, providence is the way in which one denotes
divine administration and justice, of God's very presence in the world. Yet Aristotle and a writer pretending to be him, writing in an influential tract *On the
World* (*De mundo*), had views regarding providence that are significantly more
complex, and distinct from those of the Epicureans, than Atticus lets on.

Aristotelian theology is difficult to summarize because our extant corpus of
Aristotle's works is incomplete and contains mutually exclusive views regarding God's relationship to the world.[47] The view usually assigned to Aristotle (as
by Atticus) is that expressed in a classic passage in the *Metaphysics*, which cat-
egorically denies that God, the divine Mind (*nous*), acts at all outside of Its own
self:

> Further, whether its substance is the faculty of thought or the act of think-
> ing, what does it think? ... Evidently, then, it thinks that which is the most
> divine and precious, and it does not change; for change would be change
> for the worse, and this would be already a movement. First, then, if it is not
> the act of thinking but a capacity, it would be reasonable to suppose that
> the continuity of its thinking is wearisome to it. Secondly, there would
> evidently be something else more precious than thought, viz., that which
> is thought. For both thinking and the act of thought will belong even to
> one who has the worst of thoughts. Therefore if this ought to be avoided
> (and it ought, for there are even some things which it is better not to see

---

45 Att. frg. 3.49–63, text des Places, 48, tr. mine. See *inter alia* Opsomer and Steel, "Evil," 233;
    Boys-Stones, "Providence and Religion." Michalewski notes that Atticus is alone amongst
    ancient Platonists in making this argument, which is more typical of Christian authors
    ("Faut-il préférer," esp. 128).

46 As Boys-Stones rightly notes, Atticus's argument does not concern the metaphysical char-
    acter of Aristotle's God, or Its ability to exercise providence—rather, Atticus is concerned
    with the (ostensible) absence of providential care for human beings ("Providence and
    Religion," 320–322). Similarly, see Michalewski, "Faut-il préférer," 128.

47 A brief survey is Sharples, "Aristotelian Theology," 4–12. See further Dragona-Monachou,
    "Divine Providence," 4419–424; Bos, *Providentia Divina*.

than to see), the act of thinking cannot be the best of things. Therefore it must be itself that thought thinks (since it is the most excellent of things), and its thinking is a thinking on thinking.[48]

This passage has enjoyed many interpretations—God is thought thinking thought, God is thinking universals, etc.—but what is clear is that God is not thinking about particulars or individuals.[49] As far as you and I go, this is not a caring God.[50]

And yet: for Aristotle, the whole point of a notion of God is to provide a final cause that explains the observable, eternal motion of the heavens, contrasted with the corruptible state of becoming that characterizes the sublunary realm.[51] Fine enough, but if God is completely separate from even the celestial realm, how can It be a cause of it, much less the sublunary world? There must be some principle of 'like knows like' at work that presumes a relationship of the divine even to the sublunary cosmos, for "it is unclear how these types of becoming can be moved by final causality unless they are somehow envisaged as animate," as John Dudley writes. "Thus," he continues, "we have an indication that matter must be viewed by Aristotle as penetrated by a kind of soul."[52] As much seems to be implied in another passage from the same chapter of the *Metaphysics*, which describes the universe as an army with God as its general.[53] According to Robert Sharples, the point of the analogy "is to argue that the good is present in the universe both in a transcendent and in an immanent way, and that the former is primary."[54] A still third perspective appears to be expressed in a fragment from the third book of Aristotle's lost 'exoteric' work *On Philosophy*, quoted by Cicero: "At one moment he [i.e., Aristotle] assigns divinity exclusively to the intellect, at another he says that the world is itself a god, then again he puts some other being over the world, and assigns to this being the role of regulating and sustaining the world-motion by means of a sort of

---

48 *Metaph.* 12.8 1074b21–35, tr. Ross, in Barnes, ed., *Complete Works*, 1698.

49 So recently Mayhew, with further secondary literature ("Aristotle on Prayer," 295).

50 Louth, "Pagans and Christians," 282.

51 Arist. *On Heaven*, 2.3 286a31; *On Generation and Corruption*, 2.10–11 336a32; *Metaph.* 12.6 1072a10, cit. Sharples, "Alexander of Aphrodisias on Divine Providence," 200 n. 20; see also Magris, *L'idea di destino*, 2:647.

52 Dudley, "Fate of Providence," 65. Cf. Boys-Stones, who contrasts the fashion in which the Prime Mover qua teleological cause of movement affects the universe from the fashion in which the Platonists described "the celestial system ... as a unified *entity* with a single *formal* cause" ("Providence and Religion," 325, italics his).

53 *Metaph.* 12.10 1075a11–15, cit. Sharples, "Aristotelian Theology," 6.

54 Sharples, "Aristotelian Theology," 10.

inverse rotation. Then he says that the celestial heat is god—not realizing that the heavens are a part of that world which elsewhere he has dubbed 'God'."[55] Abraham Bos holds that the Aristotle of *De philosophia* may be reconciled with that known to Atticus and other later writers. The "inverse rotation" is, on this reading, God's cause of motion in the cosmos. Later in life, Bos suggests, Aristotle changed his mind, favoring the more straightforward view we know from the *Metaphysics*.[56]

While Bos is right that one may harmonize the evidence of Atticus with Cicero's testimony, it is the absent God of the *Metaphysics* who became the 'God of Aristotle' in later philosophical discourse—but this god is at least the invisible general leading the army as much as the 'God thinking God,' thanks to the widespread influence of the pseudo-Aristotelian work *On the World*. The work may have been written anywhere from the generation following Aristotle up to the mid-second century CE.[57] To Pseudo-Aristotle, God is "the cause holding the universe (*tōn holōn*) together."[58] The universe is like a continuum stretching forth from this first cause, with somethings being more distant from it than others; nonetheless, "the divine naturally penetrates everything" and so different things receive their proper portion of divinity in inverse proportion to their distance from God.[59] God's influence does not require his immediate presence everywhere, just as the head of a household is not present everywhere in the house at once, or the master of an army or city is not present at every level of his administration.[60] "[What is appropriate] is for example related about the Great King. ⟨For⟩ the pomp of Cambyses, Xerxes, and Darius was ordered in a magnificent manner to the height of dignity and authority. The King himself, they say, was based in Susa or Ecbatana, invisible to everyone ..." Yet he was preceded by bodyguards, soldiers, janitors, stewards, and hunters, and that is

---

55 Cic. *Nat. d.* 1.13.33, tr. Rackham in LCL 268: 35, 37.

56 Bos, *Providentia Divina*, 25–27.

57 For a brief survey of the problem and the attendant secondary literature, see Thom, "Introduction," 3–7; the *Forschungsbericht* is Krayer, "Disputes"; see also Betegh and Gregoric, "Multiple Analogy," 574. While there is no scholarly consensus, the most widely-held position is a later date, i.e., the first or second centuries CE (Thom, op. cit., 7; Krayer, op. cit., 196–197; van Nuffelen, *Rethinking*, 105, 133), acknowledging the text's nods to Stoicism in addition to Plato and of course Aristotle (also Theiler, "Tacitus," 66; Louth, "Pagans and Christians," 283). The thesis of authentic Aristotelian authorship of *De mundo* does have its champions: see e.g. Radice, "Philo's Theology," 135, n. 16. For the arguments made in this book, the date of the text is less important than the clear reception of the theme of the 'Great King' of Persia in more firmly dateable writers such as Philo.

58 Arist. [*Mund.*] 6, 397b9–10, text and tr. Thom in idem, *Cosmic Order*, 42–43.

59 Arist. [*Mund.*] 6, 397b30–398a1, tr. Thom in idem, ed., *Cosmic Order*, 43.

60 On these analogies, see now Betegh and Gregoric, "Multiple Analogy."

only in the palace; in the provinces, he was preceded by generals and satraps. "Now the authority of the Great King compared to that of God who has power over the cosmos must be considered just as much weaker as the authority of the most inferior and weakest creature compared to that of the King."[61] Thus, "it is more dignified and becoming for him to be based in the highest region and for his power, penetrating through the whole cosmos, to move the sun and moon and to cause the whole heaven to revolve and be the cause of preservation for the things on earth."[62]

While the description of the 'Great King' appears to be a riff on Aristotle's *generalissimo* analogy in the *Metaphysics*, it is more vague than it appears. The Great King's interest in affairs of his kingdom is not asserted nor denied, although it appears that he is informed about what is happening in the kingdom, and is not indifferent to it.[63] More importantly, the author of *On the World* himself emphasizes that the analogy has its limits, insofar as while the Great King is dependent on his intermediaries to exert power throughout his kingdom, God projects power throughout the universe with a single, forceful motion, without actually needing subordinates to serve as his proxies.[64] Indeed, while Aristotle's notion of God as too elevated for worldly affairs probably influenced Epicurus,[65] Pseudo-Aristotle actually mocks Epicurus's notion that such affairs would put any kind of strain on the 'Great King.'[66] Interestingly, Platonist authors from Pseudo-Plutarch to Philo and Origen used the same analogy to make a different point, namely that it is precisely through intermediaries that God is present, and that these subordinates are personified with reference to civic metaphors which Plato had eschewed to describe divine care and its agents. For them, the young gods of the *Timaeus* became the "generals and satraps" of the Great King.

---

61   Arist. [*Mund.*] 6 398a10–398b3, tr. Thom in idem, *Cosmic Order*, 45.

62   Arist. [*Mund.*] 6 398b6–9, tr. Thom in idem, *Cosmic Order*, 45; similarly 398b28–30, 400a3–7; Karamanolis, *Philosophy*, 65.

63   Sharples, "Aristotelian Theology," 26, re: [Arist.] *Mund.* 6 398a34–35, 400b13–15.

64   Arist. [*Mund.*] 6 398b10–13; rightly emphasized by Betegh and Gregoric, "Multiple Analogy," 577–578.

65   Dudley, "Fate of Providence," 63 n. 17.

66   "For god is really the preserver of all things and the begetter of everything however it is brought about in this cosmos, without indeed enduring the hardship of a creature hard at work for itself" (Arist. [*Mund.*] 6 397b20–24, tr. Thom in idem, *Cosmic Order*, 43; similarly, 400b6–11).

THE PRONOIA PROBLEM(S)

4 "Call Him Providence. You Will Still Be Right": The Stoa on God

When Cicero's Epicureans 'Lucullus' and 'Velleius' fire on the notion of *pronoia*, they associate it with the Stoics, and for good reason: the Stoa authored the first books devoted exclusively to providence and fate, topics which they set at the center of their philosophy.[67] For the Stoa, in fact, *pronoia* did not simply describe God's care for everything; providence is God, and, in turn, is everything. More specifically: it is omnipresent, omniscient, repetitive, totally focused on creation and particularly focused on the creation and administration of human life. Yet as Susanne Bobzien observes, the Stoa separated providence and fate into distinct topics for distinct works, in contrast to late antique philosophers, who wrote tractates examining providence and fate in the same breath.[68] This fact is striking, given that the Stoa usually identified providence and fate, while Platonist or Christian authors of late antiquity did not. Keimpe Algra notes that it indicates how the Stoa conceived of 'physico-theology' as approachable from two different perspectives, even if the object was the same: "one dealing with gods' goodness, the other dealing primarily with god's causal efficacy and its consequences for individual human autonomy and responsibility"—providence and fate, respectively.[69] In the interests of presentation, the former will take precedence in this section, while the latter will be discussed in the following section.

Stoic philosophy survives largely in fragments, often quoted by hostile witnesses, which makes the task of reconstructing its teachings difficult. Nonetheless, providence assumes such a large place amongst the various Stoa that we may paint some broad strokes of its contours. "They (the Stoics) say," writes Diogenes Laertius, "that god is an animal which is immortal and rational or intelligent, perfect in happiness, not admitting of any evil, provident towards the world and its occupants, but not anthropomorphic (*pronoētikon kosmou te kai tōn en kosmōi, mē einai mentoi anthrōpomorphon*). He is the creator of the whole and, as it were, the father of all, both generally and, in particular, that part of him which pervades all things ..."[70] The founder of the school, Zeno

---

67   *Pace* Elliott, *Providence Perceived*, 8: "If Philo's work [*On Providence*—auth.] was really a polemic against fatalism, rather than a treatment of the theme as a whole, then it could be argued that before Plotinus there was no work dedicated to the topic unless one counts Book x of Plato's Laws. There was much more done on Fate."

68   Bobzien, *Determinism and Freedom*, 5; cf. Bergjan, *Der fürsorgende Gott*, 3 n. 4.

69   Algra, "Plutarch and the Stoic Theory," 119 n. 9.

70   D. L. 7.147 = SVF 2:1021 = LS 54A, text in Long and Sedley, *Hellenistic Philosophers*, 2:321, tr. ibid., 1:323. On the Stoic God as demiurge, see also Cic. *Nat. d.* 2.58; Algra, "Stoic Theology," 165–168; Karamanolis, *Philosophy*, 151.

(d. 262 BCE), seized and accentuated aspects of Plato's thought in novel ways that depart from Plato's—and here, one sees *Tim.* 30b's provident demiurge actually identified with the living world it makes, and so it "pervades all things."[71] In his dialogue *On the Nature of the Gods*, Cicero's exponent of later Academic (Skeptic) philosophy, 'Cotta,' states of the Stoic creator: "the molder and manipulator of this universal substance is divine providence, and therefore providence, wherever it moves, is able to perform whatever it will."[72]

The Stoa often characterized this omnipresent, omnipotent deity with reference to the supreme God of Greek culture, Zeus.[73] Cleanthes, who took over the school from Zeno ca. 262 BCE and remained its scholarch until his death until ca. 230 BCE, wrote an exposition of Stoic theology as a *Hymn to Zeus*.[74] The Roman philosopher Seneca (fl. first century CE) dubs the pantheistic, omnipotent Stoic God Jupiter:

> The (ancient sages) recognized the same Jupiter that we do, the controller and guardian of the universe, the mind and spirit of the world, the lord and artificer of this creation. Any name for him is suitable. You wish to call him fate? You will not be wrong. It is he on whom all things depend, the cause of causes (*causa causarum*). You wish to call him providence? You will still be right. It is by his planning that provision is made for this universe ... You wish to call him nature? You will not be mistaken. It is he from whom all things are naturally born, and we have life from his breath. You wish to call him the universe? You will not be wrong. He himself is all that you see, infused throughout all his parts, sustaining both himself and his own. The Etruscans had the same view ...[75]

The Stoic God is spirit (*pneuma*) and fire, the *Ursubstanz*, and universal active principle underlying and controlling the material, passive principle (*hylē*).[76] A doxographer of the first or second centuries CE, Aëtius, writes that "the Stoics

---

71   Sedley, *Creationism*, 225–230; also O'Brien, *Demiurge*, 90; on the possibility of influence from the Old Academy (esp. Polemo) on Zeno's pantheism, see J.M. Dillon, *Heirs of Plato*, 166–173. On dating Zeno's life and *floruit*, see Dorandi, "Chronology," 39.

72   *Nat. d.* 3.92, tr. Rackham in LCL 268:379.

73   In addition to the following discussion, see J.-P. Martin, *Providentia deorum*, 20; Magris, *L'idea di destino*, 2:654; Bobzien, *Determinism and Freedom*, 45–46; eadem, "Early Stoic," 508–513; Long, *Epictetus*, 143 n. 2; Thorsteinsson, "Justin," 537.

74   On dating Cleanthes's life and service as scholarch of the school of the Stoa, see Dorandi, "Chronology," 38.

75   Sen. *Nat.* 2.45, tr. Corcoran in LCL 450:173, cit. Reydams-Schils, "Seneca's Platonism," 211.

76   D. L. 7.139 = SVF 2:300, emphasized by Bobzien, *Determinism and Freedom*, 17.

THE PRONOIA PROBLEM(S)

defined God as an intelligent, designing fire (*noeron ... pur technikon*) systematically proceeding towards the creation of the world, and encompassing all the seminal principles according to which everything comes about, in accordance with fate, and a breath (*pneuma*) pervading the entire world ..."[77]

The divine spiritual fire, Zeus-Jove, is omniscient, both the principle and object of knowledge on the macro- and microcosmic scales alike. (The similarity to the "its thinking is a thinking on thinking" of Aristotle's God, noted above, is striking.)[78] Thus Cleanthes hymns Zeus:

> This whole universe, spinning around the earth, truly obeys you wherever you lead, and is readily ruled by you; such a servant do you have between your unconquerable hands, the two-edged, fiery, ever-living thunderbolt. For by its stroke all works of nature ⟨are guided⟩ ... Not a single deed takes place on earth without you, God, nor in the divine celestial sphere nor in the sea, except what bad people do in their folly.[79]

It is a perspective very much in line with the Hesiodic perspective on Zeus, but it "persists from the earliest to the latest Stoicism."[80] In Hesiod, the king of the Gods "knows unfailing plots (*aphthita mēdea eidōs*)" of men,[81] while the Stoic Epictetus, writing in the early second century CE, quotes the *Iliad* approvingly concerning men "whose ilk includes both Odysseus and Socrates, who say: 'nor when I move am I concealed from thee ...' "[82] Cicero states that the gods know everything because they are the cause of everything, and his

---

77   Aët. *Plac.* 1.7.33 = SVF 2:1027 = LS 46A, text in Long and Sedley, *Hellenistic Philosophers*, 2:272, tr. ibid., 1:274–275, modified; for further passages and discussion, see ibid., 1:275; Long, *Hellenistic Philosophy*, 147–150; Magris, *L'idea di destino*, 2:515–517; D. Frede, "Theodicy and Providential Care," 104–105; O'Brien, *Demiurge*, 88.

78   Re: Sen. *Ep.* 9.16 = SVF 2:1065 = LS 46O, on Jupiter's self-contemplation during breathers between cosmic world-cycles, discussed by Long, *Hellenistic Philosophy*, 155 n. 2. Any such reminiscence has its limits: as Mansfeld notes, Aristotle's Prime Mover "is definitely not to be identified with providence, whereas Chrysippus's god, being extended and forever remaining united with matter, takes care of it both during total unification at *ekpyrosis* and, in innumerable ways, when it is organized within the created world" ("Providence and the Destruction," 178).

79   Lines 7–17, tr. Thom, in idem, *Cleanthes*, 40.

80   Long, *Hellenistic Philosophy*, 181; see also Magris, *L'idea di destino*, 2:522–523.

81   Hesiod, *Theogony*, 550; for discussion, see Larson, *Understanding*, 95–96. Notably, the only parallels to the Stoic conception of Zeus's omniscience Theiler could find are late Platonist or Christian: Ammonius son of Hermias, and Clement of Alexandria ("Tacitus," 61 n. 70). See further below, chapters five and seven.

82   *Diatr.* 1.12.3, re: Hom. *Il.* 10.279, text and tr. Oldfather in LCL 131:90–91, slightly modified.

Stoic representative in *On the Nature of the Gods*, 'Balbus,' takes this principle to its logical conclusion: divine intelligence and universal causality necessarily entails divine providence.[83]

The omniscience of the Stoic God is inextricable from the Stoa's remarkable notions about cosmic eschatology. According to the Christian bishop Nemesius of Emesa (later fourth century CE), the Stoics believed that the cosmos will be destroyed in a massive explosion of the cosmic, seminal fire (*ekpurōsis*) and then be re-established, setting into motion the universal drama that will repeat itself precisely, forever—the eternal return: "but, they hold, the gods who are not subject to this destruction, having observed one cycle, know from it everything that will come about in the following cycles."[84] Cleanthes's student Chrysippus (ca. 280–205 BCE)—author of the earliest known treatise devoted to the subject of *pronoia*—declares in his treatise *On Fate* that, "when the *ekpurōsis* comes, Zeus, being the only imperishable one among the gods, withdraws into providence, whereupon both, having come together, continue to occupy the single substance of aether."[85] Chrysippus agrees with Zeno that successive world-cycles must be identical because providence can only order things in the best possible way; therefore, providence has created and ordered the best world already, and it will order an equally good—i.e., identical— one again, *ad infinitum*. Providential world-cycles necessarily entail the eternal return of best possible creations.[86]

Stoic teachings concerning providence and creation are thus even more optimistic than those of Plato, who admits the entrance of error into the world

---

83 Cic. *Div.* 2.104; idem, *Nat. d.* 2.75, 2.77. See further Theiler, "Tacitus," 61; Feldmeier, "Wenn die Vorsehung," 152–153; Begemann, "Cicero's Theology," 236. While Cicero may appear to favor the arguments of Balbus (so Begemann, "Cicero's Theology," 227, re: *Nat. d.* 3.95; cf. however Opsomer and Steel, "Evil," 234–235), there is no single 'Ciceronic voice' in *Nat. d.* (Beard, "Cicero and Divination," 35; Schofield, "Cicero For and Against," 59, 63). On the mechanism by which the Stoic gods actually possess foreknowledge, see further below, chapter five.

84 Nem. *Nat. hom.* 38 [111–112], tr. Sharples and van der Eijk, 193 = SVF 2:625 = LS 52C. This passage is discussed more fully with regard to Stoic understandings of divination below, in chapter five. For further references to the Stoic *ekpurōsis*, see LS 46F–P.

85 Plut. *Comm. not.* 1077d–e = LS 28O, tr. Long and Sedley, *Hellenistic Philosophers*, 1:171; for discussion, see Mansfeld, "Providence and the Destruction," 175. The doctrine was also attributed to Chrysippus by Philo of Alexandria, Lactantius, and Alexander of Aphrodisias (LS 52A–B, F, respectively). For Chrysippus as the author of the first known treatise on providence, see Gell. *Noct. att.* 7.2 = SVF 2:1000. On dating Chrysippus's life and *floruit*, see Dorandi, "Chronology," 40.

86 See Cic. *Div.* 1.127 = SVF 2:944 = LS 55O; Mansfeld, "Providence and the Destruction," 163, 179; Long and Sedley, *Hellenistic Philosophers*, 1:311–312; Schallenberg, *Freiheit*, 129.

as a 'necessity' following from the exigencies of material existence and the delegation of material creation to lower deities, while assigning responsibility for vice to human souls alone. This is not to say that the Stoa failed to develop a theodicy. On the contrary, they developed a vigorous one, known to be a response largely to the Epicureans.[87] Their arguments rested on the fundamental understanding of evil as nonexistent, an understanding related in different argumentative contexts in terms of the experience of evil as necessary, occasionally beneficial, or something humans create when they deviate from the natural order of things, i.e. *pronoia*. Stoic thinkers certainly agreed with Plato that some apparent flaws in (the parts of) creation simply follow from the fact of creation (as a whole), but they evaluated these flaws in a different way, with what some historians of philosophy today term 'the concomitance argument' (*to kata parakolouthēsin*): apparent flaws coincide with the fact of a world in the first place, but these flaws are not evil, since the workings of necessity in nature are good.[88] Seneca states that natural evils are not really evils, but things that happen for the sake of the good; earthquakes and natural disasters and the like are normal disturbances, like those that happen in our own bodies—a requirement of existence.[89] Related to this thinking are the arguments which reply that apparent evils are actually divine gifts that make humans stronger in body and mind alike. In a response to the Epicurean complaints that god created harmful animals that are dangerous to human beings, the Stoa reply that such creatures are in fact beneficial for us. Chrysippus claims bedbugs exist to help us get out of bed.[90]

---

87   Plut. *Comm. not.* 1075e = SVF 2:1126 = LS 54K.

88   The classic example is Plato's description of the make of the head and skull (a compromise between the competing needs of sense-perception and safety, made "out of necessity" [*ex anagkēs*]—*Tim.* 75a–c), which was taken up by Chrysippus in his explanation of the 'concomitance argument,' ap. Gell. *Noct. att.* 7.1.1–13 = SVF 2:1169–1170 = LS 54Q. See esp. Reydams-Schils, "Maximus," 135–136; also Mansfeld, "Theology," 467; Adamson, "Making a Virtue," 11; Sedley, *Creationism*, 235; Kalligas, '*Enneads*', 443 n. 12; Reydams-Schils, "Seneca's Platonism," 212–213; Algra, "Plutarch and the Stoic Theory," 124–125; cf. O'Brien, *Demiurge*, 123.

89   Sen. *Prov.* 1.5–6; idem, *Nat.* 6.3; see also *Prov.* 1.3 and Marc. Aur. 2.12, 2.17, 4.14, 4.43, 5.23, 5.33, 6.15, 7.18, 7.23, 7.25, cit. Reydams-Schils, "Seneca's Platonism," 209–210; see also Opsomer and Steel, "Evil," 241.

90   For Chrysippus on bedbugs (and mice), see Plut. *Stoic. rep.* 1044d = SVF 2:1163. On the happy benefits of harmful animals and wild beasts, see also Cic. *Nat. d.* 2.161; Plin. *Nat.* 21.77–78; Philo, *Prov.* 2.56–61; Marc. Aur. 6.36; Orig. *Cels.* 4.75; Plot. *Enn.* 3.2 [47] 9.34–37. Several of these examples are explored below, chapters two, three, and seven; see also Mattila, "Ben Sira," 477–478; Kalligas, '*Enneads*', 461; also Opsomer and Steel, "Evil," 241–242.

As part of the 'concomitance argument,' Chrysippus also argues that goods and evils must co-exist, so the goods that providentially come about are of course accompanied by evils; similarly, virtue can only exist if there is vice.[91] The identification of evil with vice sometimes appears in later sources as part of a separate, influential line of argument amongst the Roman Stoa and some Platonists, which demarcates 'natural evil' (like earthquakes, or bedbugs) from 'moral evil' (a strictly human phenomenon).[92] Seneca even claims that, since the only real evil is moral evil, virtuous people experiencing suffering without losing their virtue are not actually experiencing evil.[93] In fact, according to Seneca, we need not ask why bad things happen to good people; Fortune chooses good people to suffer, for she "seeks out the bravest men to match with her."[94]

While Seneca's *Providentia* sounds somewhat sadistic in her aim to cultivate virtue through suffering, the argument betrays a certain anthropocentrism in Stoic thought which will be explored more below (chapter two), but is usually not articulated in discussions of creation.[95] The exception is Cicero's 'Balbus.' In clear agreement with the *Timaeus*, Balbus declares that providence must exist, on account of the earth's good governance and its beauty: "let someone, therefore, prove that it could have been made better; but no one will ever prove this!"[96] Following upon the Socratic argument from design of the human body—known from Xenophon and Plato, as noted above—he exclaims: "truly, what creator other than Nature, who is more cunning than all, could have achieved such shrewdness in (arranging) the senses? ..."[97] "It will be more easily understood that humanity has been cared for by the immortal gods if we survey the entire structure of the human being (*tota hominis fabricatio*) and

---

91   Gell. *Noct. att.* 7.1.2–6 = SVF 2:1169 = LS 54Q. On this passage, see Sharples, "Introduction: Cicero," 32 n. 1; Bergjan, "Celsus," 198; Opsomer and Steel, "Evil," 242; Reydams-Schils, "Seneca's Platonism," 213; Algra, "Plutarch and the Stoic Theory," 112. Chrysippus was widely followed here: see Sen. *Prov.* 1; Epict. *Diatr.* 1.1.7–13; Marc. Aur. 6.36.

92   Plut. *Comm. not.* 1050f = SVF 2:1181 = LS 61R. On the Stoic conception of evil as a purely human phenomenon, see Long, *Epictetus*, 153–154; Algra, "Stoic Theology," 170–171. The theme is particularly important in Philo, *Prov.* (discussed below, chapter two), and Boeth. *Cons.* 2.4–6, 3.3–8.

93   Sen. *Prov.* 2–3 *passim*. See also Magris, *L'idea di destino*, 2:685.

94   Sen. *Prov.* 3.4; also ibid., 1.6.5–7, and idem, *Ep.* 74.20, both cit. Algra, "Plutarch and the Stoic Theory," 124 n. 22.

95   Rightly Ilievski, "Stoic Influences," 28.

96   Cic. *Nat. d.* 2.86–87, text and tr. Rackham in LCL 268:206–207, modified.

97   Cic. *Nat. d.* 2.142, text and tr. Rackham in LCL 268:258–259, modified.

THE PRONOIA PROBLEM(S)   37

all the shape and perfection of human nature."[98] In fact, "the world itself was
created for the sake of gods and human beings, and everything in it was prepared and contrived for human enjoyment."[99] No 'young gods' were involved
in the making of these human beings or their planet. The Stoa did not need
to postulate them to insulate God from evil, for, Plato's *Laws* notwithstanding,
"Stoic providence is an immanent principle in all of nature," as Dorothea Frede
remarks.[100] God and God alone is responsible for creation.[101]

5   "What Do I Care? For I Have Done My Part": The Stoa on Fate and Determinism

So what, then, are human beings responsible for, if anything at all? According
to the Stoa, people are responsible for that for which they are responsible, and
that amounts at once to nothing and everything—depending on how you look
at it. The keys to unlocking this initially confounding view are two: first, most
(if not all) of the Stoa equated divine providence with fate, the causal web of
all things; second, Stoic epistemology and ethics are largely concerned with
developing a character which reacts in accordance with reason to the circumstances we experience in life. While these circumstances are pre-determined
by providence-fate, it is this character for which we are responsible. Although
the specific issues of fate and responsibility will be treated in detail only in the
concluding chapters of this book ('Part III: Will'), it is nonetheless necessary
to introduce the Stoic perspective on these problems at its onset. Stoic ruminations on these problems comprised a primary foil against which Platonist
and especially Christian philosophers of the first centuries CE developed their
own conceptions of the relationship between providence and fate, as well as
their investigations into the question of whether responsibility for evil could be
extended beyond human beings—whether to angels, demons, or even a malevolent creator-god ('Part II: Dualism').

---

98   Cic. *Nat. d.* 2.133–134, text and tr. Rackham in LCL 268:250–251, modified; similarly, Clem.
      Alex. *Strom.* 4.26.163.1.

99   Cic. *Nat. d.* 2.154, text and tr. Rackham in LCL 268:272–273, modified. The argument comes
      from Chrysippus, *ap.* Porph. *Abs.* 3.20.1 = SVF 2:1152 = LS 54P. See also Epict. *Diatr.* 1.16.17,
      2.23.5, cit. Long, *Epictetus*, 159, n. 11.

100   D. Frede, "Theodicy and Providential Care," 102; also Long, *Epictetus*, 145–152; Reydams-
      Schils, "Maximus," 129.

101   "The Stoics are of the opinion that there is one cause—that which creates (*id, quod facit*)"
      (Sen. *Ep.* 65.4, text Gummere in LCL 76:446, tr. mine); see also Sedley, *Creationism*, 209–
      210.

Practically all of our evidence regarding the relationship between *pronoia* and fate (*heimarmenē*) in the Stoa points towards the equation of these terms. *Heimarmenē* was conceived as the sequence of causes that encompasses everything that was, is, and will be.[102] Although an ancient etymology derived the term from a string of beads—each bead linked to and affecting the next—the concept works more like interlocking chains spreading in all directions.[103] That this sequence of interlocking causes may be traced back to a single, universal cause for everything—God—is a fundamental tenet of Stoic philosophy which follows from the axiom "nothing happens without a cause," dubbed by Bobzien the 'General Causal Principle' (henceforth 'GCP').[104] Cicero articulates this perspective thus: "either everything takes place by fate or something can take place without a cause," and the latter is of course impossible.[105] Thus, we are told Chrysippus believed "no state or process is to the slightest degree other than in accordance with the rationale of Zeus,"[106] and Zeus, as we know, was *pronoia* to him.

Thus Zeno, the founder of the school, "said that (Fate) is the power which moves matter in the same respect and in the same way, and which it makes no difference, whether we call it providence and nature (*pronoian kai physin*)."[107] Chrysippus agreed, and was followed by most other Stoa.[108] In his work *On the World*, he writes: "the essence of *heimarmenē* is spiritual power (*dunamin pneumatikēn*) governing the order of the whole (*taxei tou pantos dioikētikēn*)."[109] In *On Fate*, he is more specific—"Fate (*heimarmenē*) is the rational design

---

102   Cic. *Div.* 1.125–126 = SVF 2:921 = LS 55L, discussed further below, in chapter five; see also Plot. *Enn.* 3.1 [3] 2.30–36; Moore, "Fate," 377; Bobzien, *Determinism and Freedom*, 50. The term was apparently coined by Heraclitus (frgs. A5, 8 and B137 DL, cit. Theiler, "Tacitus," 53 n. 30).

103   The useful metaphor of S. Meyer, "Chain of Causes," validated by a glance at Marc. Aur. 4.40, 7.9, 9.1.4, and 10.5, quoted below. The notion goes back to Chrysippus (Magris, *L'idea di destino*, 2:527; Bobzien, "Early Stoic," 512).

104   *Determinism and Freedom*, 39. This phrasing of the issue of causality is widely followed in the secondary literature on fate and determinism in ancient philosophy; see e.g. Boys-Stones, "'Middle' Platonists on Fate," 431; M. Frede, *Free Will*, 14; Opsomer, "Middle Platonic Doctrine," 142; Reydams-Schils, "Seneca's Platonism," 211.

105   Cic. *Fat.* 26, tr. Rackham in LCL 349:223.

106   Plut. *Stoic rep.* 1056c = SVF 2:997 = LS 55R, tr. in Long and Sedley, *Hellenistic Philosophers*, 1:339; similarly, Calc. *Comm. Tim.* 144 = SVF 2:933 = LS 54U.

107   Aët. *Plac.* 1.27.5, text in SVF 1:176, tr. Mansfeld, "Providence and the Destruction," 163, modified. See also Theiler, "Tacitus," 57 n. 48.

108   Theiler, "Tacitus," 56–57; Mansfeld, "Providence and the Destruction," 178; G. Lloyd, *Providence Lost*, 91. For the equation of *pronoia* and *logos*, see Long, *Epictetus*, 145, 162.

109   Stob. *Ecl.* 1.79.1 = SVF 2:913 = LS 55M; text in Long and Sedley, *Hellenistic Philosophers*, 2:337, tr. mine. For a similar phrasing, see Cic. *Nat. d.* 2.75.

THE PRONOIA PROBLEM(S)   39

(*logos*) of the cosmos," in turn "of the things in the world which are organized by providence (*tōn ... pronoiai diakoumenōn*)."[110] His teacher Cleanthes held that things that are fated happen by providence, but there are also things that are fated in the future that have not yet been produced by providence—amounting to a distinction between providence and fate.[111] No such distinctions present themselves amongst the Roman Stoa. Seneca seems to conflate *fatum* and *providentia*, and Marcus Aurelius appears to refer to providence and fate, as well as providence and chance, interchangeably.[112]

The Stoa recognized that their views on the universal reach of providence-fate led directly to a crisis of moral responsibility,[113] particularly given the withering criticism that their determinist model did away with the entire question of meriting praise or blame for one's actions.[114] One such argument along these lines was the 'lazy argument (*argos logos*)'—whatever happens is already fated to happen, so why bother to try and shift matters one way or another?[115] Notably, 'free will' does not enter the picture here. Greek philosophers did not describe the issue of responsibility with reference to the Greek abstract 'freedom' (*eleutheria*) until the second century CE at the very earliest.[116] Rather, the favored term for denoting moral responsibility was 'what is up to us' (*to*

---

110   Stob. *Ecl.* 1.79.1 = SVF 2:913 = LS 55M; text in Long and Sedley, *Hellenistic Philosophers*, 2:337, tr. mine.

111   Calc. *Comm. Tim.* 144 = SVF 2:933 = LS 54U. This evidence has recently been doubted as second-hand and third-rate (Alessandrelli, "Cleante e Crisippo"). Yet Cicero, presumably following Carneades, admits that there can be some things that happen by elements of chance (*fortuita*), and are not predestined (*Fat.* 5–6). In any case, Algra plausibly hypothesizes that what Cleanthes means is that providence is not responsible for fate insofar as human evil transpires under the scope of fate; thus, fate encompasses human evil, but providence does not ("Plutarch and the Stoic Theory," 122–123; the verity of Calcidius's evidence is assumed by Theiler, "Tacitus," 65; Mansfeld, "*Diaphonia*," 195; Magris, *L'idea di destino*, 2:653; Bobzien, *Determinism and Freedom*, 46–47, 137). Theiler believes Cleanthes to recall Hom. *Od.* 1.32–34 here ("Tacitus," 65–66, 68).

112   Sen. *Nat.* 2.45; idem, *Benef.* 4.7–8; also with Fortune: idem, *Prov.* 1.1, 2.4, 3.4; idem, *Brev. vit.* 5.3, 11.2; Marc. Aur. 2.3, 12.14, 12.24.

113   Theiler, "Tacitus," 51.

114   For criticism of determinism on the grounds of its doing away with human responsibility for praise or blame, see e.g. Alex. Aphr. *Fat.* 16, as well as the sources discussed in the following notes.

115   For the *argos logos*, see Cic. *Fat.* 28–29 = LS 55S (as well as Cic. *Div.* 2.21), and Orig. *Cels.* 2.20. For exhaustive discussion, see Bobzien, *Determinism and Freedom*, 182–217; Schallenberg, *Freiheit*, 196–205; further, Sharples, "Introduction: Cicero," 9–10; Barnes, "Cicero's *de fato*," 501–502; Benjamins, *Eingeordnete Freiheit*, 25–27; Begemann, "Cicero's Theology," 235. Chrysippus's answer is discussed below, in chapter five.

116   Bobzien, "Inadvertent Conception," 135. Cf. e.g. Elliott, *Providence Perceived*, 5: "the [tragic—auth.] playwrights and Cicero maintained free will where the Epicureans gave

40   CHAPTER 1

eph'hēmin), a concept which probably has more to do with moral responsibility than with 'freedom,' and certainly should not be translated as 'free will.'[117] The Greek dative in the expression communicates with what is 'in our power,'[118] and is commonly rendered as 'what is up to us.'

According to Chrysippus, 'what is up to us' is how we react to the predetermined circumstances we experience, whether our impulses (or 'reactions'—Grk. *hormai*) to circumstances are in accordance with reason (*logos*), which is divine. The human soul, or 'ruling-faculty' (*hēgemonikon*), is the seat of this reason.[119] As Diogenes Laertius writes,

> They [the Stoics] say that an animal has self-preservation as the object of its first impulse, since nature from the beginning appropriates it, as Chrysippus says in his *On Ends* book I. The first thing appropriate to every animal, he says, is its own constitution and the consciousness of this ... This is why the animal rejects what is harmful and accepts what is appropriate ... Since animals have the additional faculty of impulse, through the use of which they go in search of what is appropriate to them, what is natural for them is to be administered in accordance with their impulse. And since reason, by way of a more perfect management, has been bestowed on rational beings, to live correctly in accordance with reason comes to be natural for them. For reason supervenes as the craftsman of impulse (*technitēs gar houtos epiginetai tēs hormēs*).[120]

From this, it follows that reasonable action is the same as the impulse or response natural to attendant circumstances, regardless of what pre-determined activity confronts the rational actor in question.[121] This view resembles

---

all to chance and the Stoics to fate." The oldest known attestation of the noun *libera* qua 'free (will)' is Lucr. 2.256 (cit. Theiler, "Tacitus," 67). See further below, chapter six.

117   Magris, *L'idea di destino*, 2:406; Bobzien, "Inadvertent Conception," 139, followed by Popović, "Apocalyptic Determinism," 257; Opsomer, "Middle Platonic Doctrine," 156 n. 78. Such mistranslations still occur in the secondary literature: e.g. Begemann, "Cicero's Theology," 232; Simonetti vacillates here (*A Perfect Medium?*, 167).

118   Opsomer, "Middle Platonic Doctrine," 156 n. 78.

119   Aët. *Plac.* 4.21.1–2 = SVF 2:836 = LS 53H, per M. Frede, *Free Will*, 32; further, Long and Sedley, *Hellenistic Philosophers*, 1:320.

120   D. L. 7.85–86 = SVF 3:178 = LS 57A, tr. Long and Sedley, *Hellenistic Philosophers*, 1:346.

121   The bibliography on impulse and assent to external sense-impressions in Stoicism is enormous; useful cursory discussions include Long, *Hellenistic Philosophy*, 123–131; idem, *Epictetus*, 172–175; Dihle, *Theory of Will*, 61–64; Kahn, "Discovering Will," 246–247; M. Frede, *Free Will*, 35–42; G. Lloyd, *Providence Lost*, 91–95.

THE PRONOIA PROBLEM(S)

what is often called 'compatibilism' in professional philosophy today: the belief that free will is in some way compatible with causal determinism.[122]

The classic presentation of Stoic compatibilism is the metaphor, devised by Chrysippus, of a cylinder. It is the nature (internal cause) of a cylinder to roll down a slope when pushed, but someone has to push it (external cause). "Therefore," writes Chrysippus,

> just as the person who pushed the cylinder gave it its beginning of motion but not its capacity for rolling, likewise, although the impression encountered will print and, as it were, emblazon its appearance on the mind, assent will be in our power (*adsensio nostra erit in potestate*). And assent, just as we said in the case of the cylinder, although prompted from the outside, will thereafter move through its own force and nature. If something were brought about without an antecedent cause, it would be untrue that all things have come about through fate. But if it is plausible that all events have an antecedent cause, what ground can be offered for not conceding that all things come about through fate?[123]

---

122   "For the Stoics a choice is up to us if the decision arises within us and is not determined by external events. The choices are our own if they proceed from our character ..." (Opsomer, "Middle Platonic Doctrine," 153). On Stoic compatibilism, see further Theiler, "Tacitus," 72–78; Bobzien, "Inadvertent Conception," 142–143; Adamson, *Philosophy*, 74–75.

123   Cic. *Fat.* 43 = SVF 2:974 = LS 62C, text in Long and Sedley, *Hellenistic Philosophers*, 2:383–384, tr. in ibid., 1:388, modified; on this passage, see Theiler, "Tacitus," 76–77; Long and Sedley, *Hellenistic Philosophers*, 1:341–343, 392–394; Long, *Hellenistic Philosophy*, 167; Sharples, "Introduction: Cicero," 9; Klawans, *Josephus*, 76; Kocar, "'Humanity'," 196–197; Begemann, "Cicero's Theology," 232. Chrysippus's cylinder is also discussed in Gell. *Noct. Att.* 7.2 = SVF 2:1000 = LS 62D. Epictetus credits to Chrysippus the analogy of a foot delighted to get muddy, should it learn that its muddiness is the rational response to the causal chain (*Diatr.* 2.6.9 = SVF 3:191 = LS 58J). The anonymous, third-century Christian author of the *Refutation of All Heresies* assigns to Zeno and Chrysippus the scenario of a dog tied to a moving cart; it can follow along happily or be dragged along miserably (*Ref.* 1.21 = SVF 2:975 = LS 62A; similarly Max. Tyr. *Or.* 13.8, per O'Brien, *Demiurge*, 133). Bobzien objects that the emphasis on 'freedom to do otherwise' in these examples—not necessarily well-attested in our evidence for the early Stoa—indicate that they are not actually of Chrysippean coinage (*Determinism and Freedom*, 357). This does not seem to bother many readers of the evidence (e.g. Long, *Hellenistic Philosophy*, 182–183; G. Lloyd, *Providence Lost*, 96–97; Kocar, "'Humanity'," 198; Sedley, *Creationism*, 234; Ferguson, *Providence of God*, 44, none of whom mention the problem). In any case, the rest of this book is mainly concerned with the first–third centuries CE, and so even if Bobzien is right, the evidence regarding Stoic compatibilism presently under review merits inclusion in this study.

The 'cylinder' is fated to be pushed, but assents to the manner of its own rolling. The example is useful for emphasizing the physicality of the situation—a sense-impression pushes you—but it is also awkward, insofar as common sense does not regard cylinders as conscious agents. This awkwardness has prompted misinterpretation in the secondary literature,[124] and so it is worth re-phrasing the scenario with reference to an example that actually involves human beings.[125] Take for instance an addict trying to give up a habit. He or she fails, when he or she assents to an offer of the source of addiction: the 'push' was external and the result was fated (given the GCP), but the addict remains a responsible party, since he or she 'assents' and so does goes along with the 'push' in his or her own way. Unless one is physically forced to assent, any such assent is in a sense willing, and so already with Chrysippus we have something of a notion of an act of willing (if not a will).[126]

So, 'what is up to us' is how we react to the options presented to us: even if these are fated, we earn praise or blame for how we respond to them. Centuries after Chrysippus, Epictetus is the most florid exponent of this view.[127] He likens the individual to someone undertaking a voyage:

> What can I do? Select the helmsman, the sailors, the day, the moment. Then a storm descends upon us. Even so, what do I care? For I have done my part ... But even better: the ship goes down. What, then, have I do to? I do the only thing I can. I drown without fear, without screaming or accusing God, but recognizing that what is born must perish. For I am not eternal, but a man—a part amongst the wholes, as an hour is to a day.[128]

---

124   In a seminal (if dated) article on Josephus's explanation of the beliefs of the Second Temple Jewish sects about fate, for instance, Moore (mis)interprets the example as describing whether or not the person who pushes the cylinder was fated to push it. On Moore's reading, the person may or may not assent to the sight of the cylinder, and so may or may not push it; but if the cylinder is pushed, then it will roll the way its shape determines it to roll (Moore, "Fate," 378–379). Yet the example as explained by Moore does not explain Stoic co-determinism, but the theory of 'conditional fate' espoused by the Middle Platonists (see below, in this chapter, and chapter five).

125   Remarkably, such examples are in short supply in the secondary literature. Bobzien, however, phrases the 'cylinder' as expressing what she calls "the Different Person Principle," i.e., that two different people will make two different decisions ('roll' in different directions, if they were cylinders) even when presented with the same situation (*Determinism and Freedom*, 279, 388, 397; also M. Frede, *Free Will*, 8; Adamson, *Philosophy*, 75).

126   Frede, *Free Will*, 42–43.

127   Epict. *Diatr.* 1.12.1–16 is the classic discussion.

128   Epict. *Diatr.* 2.5.10–13, text and tr. Oldfather in LCL 131:238–241, modified, per G. Lloyd,

THE PRONOIA PROBLEM(S)   43

For Epictetus, assent derives from our character (*prohairesis*). Changing one's behavior—one's assent or lack thereof to circumstances—is a matter of changing one's character.[129] The choice of terms is significant: in his *Nicomachaean Ethics*, Aristotle had referred to actions made "by choice" (*ek prohaireseōs*) to denote 'what is up to us,' in contrast to what one wills or desires (which may or may not even be possible).[130] Epictetus's designation of assent as a result of individual *prohairesis* emphasizes not that the wise person assents to what is fated for us—this was argued by Chrysippus already—but that there is some part of us to which this wise assent belongs.[131]

It has been argued that Epictetus "represented a watershed" in "his insistence on a radically undetermined faculty with the capacity to make use of external impressions"—a faculty like that of a 'free will.'[132] Nonetheless, if the GCP holds, then even our developed rational behavior is caused, too; and if this behavior is really the product of the passive experience of external causes, then 'what is up to us' does not amount to much, however vividly a Stoic writer may illustrate it.[133] Seneca seems to have recognized this problem—and not to have cared, favoring what today might be called a 'hard' determinism, abandoning the pretense of carving out a separate causal nexus for human responsibility and so rejecting compatibilism.[134] God "wrote the decrees of Fate, yet follows them;

  Providence Lost, 119. See also *Diatr.* 4.7.20; Kahn, "Discovering Will," 254–255; Frede, *Free Will*, 39.

129 Epict. *Diatr.* 1.12.20, 1.12.34, 1.22.10, 2.14.8–9, per Kahn, "Discovering Will," 252–253; Bobzien, "Inadvertent Conception," 160–161; Frede, *Free Will*, 44–45; G. Lloyd, *Providence Lost*, 112, 119. See also Karamanolis, *Philosophy*, 153, 171–172, re: *Diatr.* 1.4.18–21, 1.17.21–28, 2.2.1–7; Gabor, "When Should a Philosopher," 328–329, re: Epictetus, *Enchiridion*, 32.2.

130 M. Frede, *Free Will*, 24–27, re: Arist. *Eth. nic.* 3 1110b18–1111a21, 1111b20–30; see further Pich, "Προαίρεσις und Freiheit," 105; D. Frede, "Free Will in Aristotle?," esp. 46–51; Wildberg, "Will,"333.

131 Dihle, *Theory of Will*, 60–61; M. Frede, *Free Will*, 46–47, followed by Gibbons, "Human Autonomy," 676–677; most extensively, Pich, "Προαίρεσις und Freiheit." Cf. Wildberg's argument that *prohairesis* denotes for Epictetus less a faculty than a choice ("Will," 344).

132 Harper, *From Shame to Sin*, 120; similarly Long, *Epictetus*, 28–30, 28, followed by Thorsteinsson, "Justin," 551; although see also Wildberg (previous note); Pich is wary of rendering the term with connotations of 'will' or *voluntas*, preferring a sense of the ability of making rational choices ("Προαίρεσις und Freiheit," 123–124).

133 This problem is taken up in more detail below, chapter six.

134 See further the remarks of Marcus Aurelius (both in this chapter and below, chapter two), whose evidence makes it difficult to accept Thorsteinsson's claim that "fate and human autonomy were not on the list of topics specifically dealt with by the Stoics during the second century CE" ("Justin," 569–570).

44   CHAPTER 1

forever he obeys, but once he decreed."[135] At the same time, living in accordance with Fate means that one has a kind of power over it:

> You, praise and imitate that one who does not feel sick at the prospect of dying, even as he enjoys living. For what virtue is there in leaving when one is kicked out? And yet, there is virtue even in this: sure, I am kicked out, but as though I want to go anyways. For this reason, the wise man can never be kicked out, since that would mean removal from a place he were unwilling to leave, and he does nothing unwillingly. He eludes Necessity, because he is willing to do what is forced upon him (*necessitate effugit, qui vult quod coactura est*).[136]

Despite the efforts of Chrysippus and Epictetus, the Stoic cosmos does not really permit any causal force independent of the greater web of causes variously named *pronoia*, *heimarmenē*, Zeus, or Jupiter. Worldly or 'natural' evil is a matter of concomitance, the something that coincides with the fact of the world existing in the first place, as Plato argued in the *Timaeus*—and besides, even most apparent worldly evils are actually benefits. The only evil is human evil, or vice: irrational behavior that disturbs the harmony of the cosmos, even if it does not budge the decrees of providence-fate.

The Stoic universe is like a great, beautiful cosmic symphony. When our solo comes around, it is 'up to us' as to whether we will play a harmonious melody over it—something in tune with reason (*logos*)—or something rebellious and dissonant.[137] Yet here, too, the universality of providence-fate consumes any notion of human action as causally independent. Even defiant music must have been fated to be, and if it is part of the plan, then it cannot be so defiant, really, can it?

---

135   Sen. *Prov.* 5.8; see Theiler, "Tacitus," 58, 72–73; Reydams-Schils, "Seneca's Platonism," 213; Algra, "Plutarch and the Stoic Theory," 126 n. 29.

136   Sen. *Ep.* 54, text and tr. Gummere in LCL 75:362–365, modified; see also idem, *Brev. vit.* 5.3; M. Frede, *Free Will*, 79; G. Lloyd, *Providence Lost*, 104; Thorsteinsson, "Justin," 538.

137   Similarly, Long and Sedley, *Hellenistic Philosophers*, 392; Louth, "Pagans and Christians," 284; Long, *Epictetus*, 154; Ilievski, "Stoic Influences," 30.

THE PRONOIA PROBLEM(S)   45

6 Three Providences! Pseudo-Plutarch and the Doctrine of 'Conditional Fate'

The chief opponents of the Stoa were the Platonists, who were every bit as interested in providence as their contemporaries. Even in the so-called 'Old Academy'—the generations following Plato prior to the Academy's skeptical turn, with the philosophy of Carneades (fl. second century BCE)—providence appears to have been a topic of debate.[138] Following the decline of Academic Skepticism, some Platonists began to believe Plato to have had a consistent philosophy in his dialogues, especially in the *Timaeus* and the *Republic*, and therefore found these works to be absolutely authoritative, even if one resorts to Aristotelian or Stoic ideas to understand them.[139] Scholarship generally denotes these Platonists the 'Middle Platonists,' since they mark a shift from the skepticism of the Academy during the Hellenistic Age, but are prior to the great synthesis of the Egyptian Plotinus in the mid-third century CE (marking the turn to 'Neoplatonism').[140] Amongst the Middle Platonists, there is a more or less consistent teaching concerning providence, fate, and moral responsibility. It is worth closing the present survey with discussion of this '(Middle) Platonist doctrine of conditional fate,' for two reasons. First, this doctrine—and particularly its concomitant gradations of 'levels' of fate, and description of semi-divine intermediaries as cosmic administrators—was of tremendous importance for the development of ancient Jewish and Christian discussions

---

138 If Cicero's 'Varro' in his *Academica* does in fact articulate doctrine from the Old Academy, possibly referring to Polemo (as suggested by Sedley, "Origins of Stoic God," in turn followed by J.M. Dillon, *Heirs of Plato*, 168): "all things in the world are parts of it, held together by a sentient nature (*natura sentiens*), in which inheres perfect reason, and which is also eternal, since nothing stronger exists to cause it to perish; and this force they say is the soul of the world (*animas mundi*), and is also perfect intelligence and wisdom, which they call "god," and is a sort of providence, presiding over all the things that fall under its control, governing especially the heavenly bodies, and then those things on earth that concern mankind (*prudentiam quondam procurantem caelestia maxime, deinde in terries ea quae pertineant ad homines*)" (Cic. *Acad.* 1.28–29, text and tr. Rackham in LCL 268:438–439, slightly modified). On this passage, see further J.M. Dillon, op. cit. 173 (on its deterministic overtones); Sharples, "Threefold Providence," 112–113 (suggesting Aristotelian valency). On dating the life and *floruit* of Carneades, see Dorandi, "Chronology," 33–34.

139 See recently Tarrant, "Platonism," 75–79; Engberg-Pedersen, "Setting the Scene."

140 On 'Middle Platonism,' the categorical, doxographical survey remains J.M. Dillon, *Middle Platonists*. The term is still widely used despite acknowledgement of its weakness; on this, see e.g. the remarks of Tarrant, "Platonism," 66. Boys-Stones has argued for dispensing the term and the focus on doxography in favor of looking more at 'methodology' (i.e., claims to authority—*Post-Hellenistic Philosophy*, esp. viii), which is promising, although the term 'post-Hellenistic philosophy' leaves something to be desired.

of providence and fate. Secondly, the doctrine exemplifies how the three problems of (*a*) divine care, (*b*) the causality of evil, and (*c*) individual accountability are inextricable from one another in the ancient sources, and so often treated as a single problem—that of 'providence' or 'fate.'

Platonizing authors ranging from the second–fourth centuries—such as Alcinous (second–fourth century CE?), and Apuleius (second century CE), Calcidius (fourth century CE), Nemesius of Emesa, and the author of a work *On Fate* erroneously ascribed to Plutarch of Chaeronea (henceforth Pseudo-Plutarch)—all present theories so similar to one another,[141] often using the same precise phrases and terminology, that they must be working from a more or less common doctrine.[142] The doctrine's constituent parts include:

(1) the distinction between providence and fate;
(2) the distinction of fate in essence and in action (*ousia* and *energeia*, respectively);
(3) some kind of human responsibility meriting praise or blame;
(4) necessary consequences for our actions in accordance with fate's law;
(5) a doctrine of three permutations of providence.[143]

Some version of this doctrine appears to be attested as early as Tacitus's *Annals* (early second century CE).[144] The doctrine is interesting because of its novel and coherent integration of Platonic proof-texts, its views on causality and

---

141 For the figures of Calcidius and Nemesius, see respectively Magee, "Introduction," viii–xvii (discussed further below, in chapter five), and Sharples and van der Eijk, "Introduction," 2. The author of the treatise *De fato* transmitted under the name of Plutarch of Chaeronea has long been doubted to have been Plutarch himself; see initially Gercke, "Ein platonische Quelle"; for further bibliography, see Boys-Stones, "'Middle' Platonists on Fate," 433 n. 4.

142 The classic study of the Platonist doctrine of conditional fate remains Theiler, "Tacitus," esp. 79–88; see also J.M. Dillon, *Middle Platonists*, 294–298, 323; idem, "Commentary," 160–161; Sharples, "Alexander of Aphrodisias, *De Fato*"; idem, "Threefold Providence," 109; Hammerstaedt, *Oenomaus*, 274–278; Benjamins, *Eingeordnete Freiheit*, 41–45; Bobzien, "Inadvertent Conception," 146–152; Boys-Stones, "'Middle' Platonists on Fate," 431–436; Opsomer, "Middle Platonic Doctrine"; Bonazzi, "Middle Platonists"; and the discussion in the following notes.

143 Per Chase, "Porphyre sur la providence," 130. For slightly different typologies of the teaching, see Magris, *L'idea di destino*, 2:574–575; Opsomer, "Middle Platonic Doctrine," 140.

144 I.e., Tacitus refers to the idea that fate determines only the results of our freely-made actions according to universal laws, the core of the idea of 'conditional fate' presently under discussion (Tac. *Ann.* 6.22); see Theiler, "Tacitus," esp. 82, 93; also den Boeft, *Calcidius on Fate*, 32–33, 37. This doctrine was once attributed to the elusive 'school of Gaius,'

THE PRONOIA PROBLEM(S)

determinism—whose relationship to Stoic compatibilism remains a topic of debate (see below, chapter six)—and its departure from Stoicism in distinguishing three grades of providence, with an emphasis on the role of *daimones* in the terrestrial realm. Its most detailed expositions are those of Calcidius and Pseudo-Plutarch. Because elements of Calcidius's account may derive from post-Plotinian thought,[145] Pseudo-Plutarch is considered the standard description of the Middle Platonic doctrine of fate, and so will serve as the focus of the present discussion.

As John M. Dillon writes, "Platonists wanted to see the physical world as a series of law-like chains of causation, ineluctable once they were set in train, but needing to be triggered by acts of human free will, and thus 'conditional'."[146] Agreeing with the Stoics in mapping the world into causal networks, the Platonists then sought to defend a coexistence of inescapable (*ex hypotheseōs*) laws of destiny at work next to the free (*kath'hypothesin*) choice of souls. Thus Pseudo-Plutarch: "what is both consequent upon a hypothesis and universal is, then, of the description" given by Plato, namely that actions have consequences in accordance with universal *laws* (*nomoi*)—and these universal laws are fate.[147]

---

see J.M. Dillon, *Middle Platonists*, 266–267 and ensuing discussions; Dihle, *Theory of Will*, 214 n. 18; Benjamins, *Eingeordnete Freiheit*, 41.

145 For instance, Pseudo-Plutarch assigns the third grade (of a fourfold hierarchy) to the 'second providence,' but Calcidius prefers to assign it to *fatum*, the second god or World Soul. Den Boeft proposes that the discrepancy results from Calcidius's substitution of the World Soul for the role of demons in the third grade (*Calcidius on Fate*, 93, re: Calc. *Comm. Tim.* 146–147). Despite his use of the same source as Pseudo-Plutarch and Nemesius, "he wants to harmonize his doctrine with another hierarchy, which greatly resembles Plotinus" (den Boeft, op. cit., 94). As den Boeft points out, if Porphyry, rather than Pseudo-Plutarch, is Calcidius's source for this ostensibly more Plotinian hierarchy, then to whom does Nemesius refer in *Nat. hom.*, a work whose hierarchy of providences certainly follows Pseudo-Plutarch even though he is also certainly dependent on Porphyry? The issue "seems insoluble" (den Boeft, op. cit. 98). On the impossibility of determining the pre- or post-Plotinian character of Calcidius's thought, see Magee, "Introduction," xx–xxii.

146 J.M. Dillon, "Commentary," 163; also Opsomer, "Middle Platonic Doctrine," 145–146; on the Aristotelian elements of this development (i.e., deliberation and contingent possibility), see Bobzien, "Inadvertent Conception," 151–152.

147 Plut. [*Fat.*] 570a, tr. Einarson and de Lacy in LCL 405:325; see also Alc. *Epit.* 26.1, discussed below, chapter five: "Plato's views are roughly as follows. All things, he says, are within the sphere of fate, but not all things are fated. Fate, in fact, has the status of a law" (tr. J.M. Dillon, 34); similarly, Calc. *Comm. Tim.* 143–144, 147. For fate carrying out the decrees of providence, see Apul. *Dogm. Plat.* 1.12; Max. Tyr. *Or.* 5.4 (cf. ibid., 13.4–7). For further citations and discussion of Platonic antecedents, see Theiler, "Tacitus," 88; J.M. Dillon, "Commentary," 162; Boys-Stones, "'Middle' Platonists on Fate," 433–435; Sharples, "Stoic Background," 169; Chase, "Porphyre sur la providence," 128 n. 9; Opsomer, "Middle Platonic Doctrine," 137–148; O'Brien, *Demiurge*, 125–132; Timotin, *Priere*, 87–89.

As Alcinous writes, "fate consists in the fact that if a soul chooses a given type of life and performs such-and-such actions, such-and-such consequences will follow"—note the *double entendre* of 'choosing a life,' alluding to Plato's myth of the souls selecting lives in heaven.[148] Pseudo-Plutarch then takes the 'beads' on the 'chains' of causation to be open-ended, or "contingent" (*endechomenon*). Human responsibility is always a factor: "the contingent is that which is both possible itself and has a possible opposite, whereas what is up to us (*to eph'hēmin*) is one of the two parts of the contingent: namely, what is already happening according to our impulse (*hēmeteran hormēn*)."[149]

Contingents can in turn be split in three: of things that are not just possible but common; of things that are possible and rare; and of things that are equally possible.[150] To explain contingency, the later Platonists used the example of walking.[151] "Walking and not walking and other such things," Pseudo-Plutarch writes, "of which both are equally under the control of human impulse, and what is under its control, is said to be up to us and be a matter of choice (*eph'hēmin kai kata proairesin*). Out of these, what is up to us is the more general, since it has two kinds: namely actions deriving from passion or from reason."[152] While modern commentators are right that "the idea that what is up to us is intermediate in frequency between what is usual and what is infrequent is hardly plausible,"[153] Pseudo-Plutarch's point is probably that choice is best theorized regarding banal cases, rather than situations including extenuating circumstances (like being held at gunpoint). However, "chance" (*tuchē*) is always a factor, according to Pseudo-Plutarch: "chance is an accidental cause,

---

148   Alc. *Epit.* 26.1, tr. J.M. Dillon, 35. The phrasing recalls both *Resp.* x 617e ("the responsibility lies with the one who chooses") and *Phaedr.* 248c ("if a soul ..."—J.M. Dillon, "Commentary," 161–162). Cf. Max. Tyr. *Or.* 41.5; Calc. *Comm. Tim.* 154, adding a reference to Adam and Eve choosing to eat of the Tree of Knowledge.

149   Plut. [*Fat.*] 571d–e, text and tr. de Lacy and Einarson in LCL 405:334–335, slightly modified. Notably, this is actually in agreement with the Stoic notion of responsibility *qua* autonomy (Bobzien, "Inadvertent Conception," 167).

150   Plut. [*Fat.*] 571 c–d.

151   Walking was a favorite scenario of Aristotle. Notably, amongst Roman elites, one's gait was taken to reflect one's moral character and standing (O'Sullivan, *Walking*, esp. 11–33).

152   Plut. [*Fat.*] 571d, text and tr. de Lacy and Einarson in LCL 405:332–333, significantly modified; for parallels, see Nemes. *Nat. hom.* 34 and Calc. *Comm. Tim.* 155–156. The vocabulary regarding possibility (including the walking) is largely determined by Aristotle; see esp. *Eth. nic.* 3.1–3, *Phys.* 2.4–6, *Metaph.* 5.12, (cit. J.M. Dillon, "Commentary," 160–163; see also Opsomer, "Middle Platonic Doctrine," 152). Bobzien notes that this language reflects in fact a systematization of Aristotle, hypothesizing that Pseudo-Plutarch here reworks or repeats an older source, distinct from whoever invented the doctrine of conditional fate ("Inadvertent Conception," 147–148).

153   Sharples and van der Eijk, "Notes," 183 n. 916.

THE PRONOIA PROBLEM(S)   49

found in the class of things directed toward an end which take place in conformity with choice."[154] Therefore, not all particulars are causally determined.[155]

Or are they? Pseudo-Plutarch then describes the doctrine of the 'Great Year,' alluded to in *Tim.* 39d; its presupposition is that "although events are infinite, extending infinitely into the past and future, fate, which encloses them all in a cycle, is nevertheless not infinite, but finite," and so "everything in the heavens and everything on earth whose production is necessary and due to celestial influences, will once again be restored to the same state and once more be produced anew in the same way and manner."[156] In other words, given that there is a finite set of constituent moving parts in an eternal cosmos, these moving parts—particularly the stars and planets—will eventually return to any arrangement they have previously achieved, moving in a cycle.[157] Pseudo-Plutarch appears to flirt with the Stoic notion of the 'eternal return.'[158] Yet he immediately adds that he does not refer to all individual or particular acts (or persons) coming into identical existences *ad infinitum*: "and so even this treatment shows, I dare say, how exactly fate works—but not as regards that fate which deals with particulars or individuals."[159]

While the notion of the Great Year/Eternal Return is belabored, it has a point: to articulate how the "fate that deals with particulars or individuals"—i.e., "what is up to us"—is distinct from fate (the greater web of causes) and so free

---

154   Plut. [*Fat.*] 572b, tr. de Lacy and Einarson in LCL 405:337; again, the definition of chance is Aristotelian, as noted by de Lacy and Einarson, op. cit., re: *Phys.* 2.5 197 a5.

155   Opsomer, "Middle Platonic Doctrine," 147, 153.

156   Plut. [*Fat.*] 569a–b, tr. de Lacy and Einarson in LCL 405:317.

157   See Opsomer, "Middle Platonic Doctrine," 146, re: Calc. *Comm. Tim.* 148.

158   "And so, when the same cause returns again, we shall, once more becoming the same persons, do the same things and in the same way, and so will all men besides ... and everything that is found in a single entire revolution will be repeated in similar fashion in each of the entire revolutions as well" (Plut. [*Fat.*] 569c, tr. de Lacy and Einarson, LCL 405:319). George Boys-Stones has recently taken this to mean that "in identical circumstances, identical events will occur. The stars do not cause particular events, but it is no coincidence that history repeats itself in step with their revolution" ("'Middle' Platonists on Fate," 443), but cf. the following note. Boys-Stones also recalls Orig. *Cels.* 5.21, but Opsomer is right to dismiss Origen's evidence as polemical and offered in bad faith ("Middle Platonic Doctrine," 159–161); it is not obvious that Celsus actually endorsed the Stoic Eternal Return in his *True Doctrine*.

159   Plut. [*Fat.*] 569d, text and tr. de Lacy and Einarson in LCL 405:318–321, significantly modified. Opsomer adds that Pseudo-Plutarch here refers to a *hypothetical* situation of repeated antecedent conditions, which one could take "as meaning that a combination of the same external *and internal* causes ... will produce the same results" ("Middle Platonic Doctrine," 159, italics his). He adds that the text here appears to be corrupt and the original text may have qualified the passage further.

50   CHAPTER 1

individuals from causal determinism. Like other Middle Platonists, Pseudo-Plutarch here distinguished between Fate with a capital 'F'—usually considered synonymous with *pronoia*, providence—and the situations presented to us by fate, a 'second fate.' In fact, Pseudo-Plutarch believes it necessary to break providence-fate down into three grades:

> The highest and primary providence is the thought or will (*noēsis eite kai boulēsis*), beneficent to all things, of the primary God; and in conformity with it each thing belonging to the divine is primordially arranged at its best and most beautiful, throughout the universe. Secondary providence belongs to secondary gods ... The providence and forethought which belongs to the daemons stationed in the terrestrial regions as watchers and overseers of the action of humanity would reasonably be called tertiary.[160]

The rationale for this famous tripartition of providence derives from the *Timaeus*'s distinction between the creation of the Demiurge (29d–30a, 41c) and of the secondary gods (42d), while tertiary providence refers to the arrangement of human affairs (42e). Its goal is clear: to be able to simultaneously maintain divine care, a regular determination of natural phenomena, and some degree of human responsibility for individual actions; providence takes care of the big picture and does it well, while the small stuff is up to fate—an extrapolation of the view of Plato in *Laws* X (see above, in this chapter).[161] The doctrine of conditional fate thus inspired a distinction between providence and fate (or multiple gradations of fate) that is widespread across ancient philosophical and religious in texts—a significant break from Stoic treatments, which usually identified providence and fate.

Its conscription of *daimones* into the divine administration, meanwhile, reflected everyday experience of government and civic religion. Pseudo-Plutarch takes administrative structures as his metaphor of choice for describing the relationship between god and his *daimones*: "God, taking no part in

---

160   [*Fat.*] 572f–573a, text and tr. de Lacy and Einarson in LCL 405:343, significantly modified. On the Middle Platonist doctrine of threefold providence, see J.M. Dillon, *Middle Platonists*, 325; Sharples, "Threefold Providence," esp. 107–110; Boys-Stones, "'Middle' Platonists on Fate," 436 n. 25, 445–447; Sharples and van der Eijk, "Introduction," 27–28; idem, "Notes," 190–191, n. 934; Timotin, *Démonologie platonicienne*, 118–120; Denzey, *Cosmology and Fate*, 32–34; Opsomer, "Middle Platonic Doctrine," 161–164; Kalligas, *'Enneads'*, 444; Chase, "Porphyre sur la providence," 129–130.

161   So articulated, see Chase, "Porphyre sur la providence," 129, re: Plut. [*Fat.*] 573b.

THE PRONOIA PROBLEM(S)

evil,[162] should have no need of laws or fate, but each of them [i.e., the subordinates] carries out its task through the providence of the Begetter, who draws them along in His wake."[163] Divine care is here likened to the attention of a remote monarch who is beyond all access but nonetheless sits before his imperial administration, whose policies are carried out by subordinates—an allusion to the 'Great King' discussed in the pseudo-Aristotelian *On the World* (see above, in this chapter), and one paralleled by other Middle Platonists, such as Maximus of Tyre.[164] The concept of *daimones* enlisted for work in the celestial administration derives in turn from Platonic proof-texts regarding demonology, as systematized by Xenocrates, in the Old Academy: *daimones* are semi-divine beings dwelling in the stratosphere who serve as the intermediaries between human beings and the gods, particularly in cultic activities like divination and sacrifice.[165] Roman philosophers of the first centuries CE lived and worked in close proximity to civic, sacrificial cult.[166] It made sense to enlist the *daimones* they understood to be at work in these cults in the divine administration, of which the earthly administration was a very tangible reflection.

7   Conclusions: Aesop and Xanthus in the Weeds

In the *Life of Aesop* (first century BCE–second century CE?) a farmer offers the witty protagonist and his master, the philosopher Xanthus, free vegetables if he can answer a question: why is it that, despite all the care the farmer lavishes on his crops, do weeds still grow among them?[167] The pompous Xanthus

---

162   There is a nice pun here—*amoiros kakias* can mean both "without a share in evil" and "not fated in evil" (LSJ 85).

163   Plut. [*Fat.*] 573f, text and tr. de Lacy and Einarson in LCL 405:348–349, significantly modified.

164   Max. Tyr. *Or.* 9.12, 11.12; Timotin, *Démonologie platonicienne*, 129–130; generally, see Kalligas, '*Enneads*', 444 n. 21; Opsomer, "Middle Platonic Doctrine," 165–166; cf. Dihle, "Philosophische Lehren," 17. Another reminiscence of the 'Great King' may be Philo, *Prov.* 2.17.

165   Important Platonic demonological proof-texts include *Tim.* 90a–c; *Phaedr.* 246e; *Symp.* 202d–203a; *Resp.* 617e; *Pol.* 271d, 273e; *Phaedo* 107d–108c; [*Epinomis*] 981c–d, 984c–e. Useful, recent surveys include Gasparro, "*Daimôn* and *Tuchê*," 66–82, and esp. Timotin, *Démonologie platonicienne*; see further below, chapters two and three.

166   See recently the discussion of Burns, *Apocalypse*, 16–20; see also below, chapter five.

167   Dating *Vit. Aes.* is a hazardous affair. The text is from the 'G' recension of the *Vit. Aes.* (PM 397), a version of the work to which Perry gives a plausible *terminus post quem* of the first century BCE (given the prominence of Isis in the text) and suggests a milieu of the second century CE (given shared interest with writers like Apuleius or Lucian—Perry, *Studies*,

52   CHAPTER 1

does not know, so he sagely utters a maxim: "everything is directed by divine providence."[168] Aesop laughs heartily, seeing right through the pretense. One modern commentator takes the passage to indicate that the "such exalted language about *pronoia* is a commonplace. That much is evident even to farmers and slaves."[169] Yet the story illustrates the opposite: it is a philosopher—albeit one who is third-rate—who uses the word. The fact that the tale concludes with dear Aesop laughing the pronouncement off does not mean that *pronoia* was a commonplace in speech among farmers.[170] It means that whoever wrote the story found the concomitance argument, and philosophers who walked around pronouncing pseudo-profundities, to be risible. Xanthus even admits to Aesop that his answer to the farmer was insincere: "well, is there any other solution to the question? For whatever is administered by the divine nature is not privy to investigation by philosophers!"[171]

Xanthus's confession to Aesop that he has no idea about how divine administration works is a good joke, because this is precisely what most philosophers of the Roman Empire claimed to know about. As Sextus Empiricus related to us at the beginning of this chapter, they were generally unanimous on the view that the gods exist and that they are good, and almost unanimous that the gods care for the world and human beings. Consequently, a vociferous topic of debate was the reconciliation of the care of these good gods with the apparent existence of worldly evils. Philosophers debated this problem largely in terms of causation: who is involved in the acts of creating the world and human beings, and out of what? To what extent does the divine care for the world and human beings, following creation? And how exactly do human beings have the ability to cause—and thus be responsible for—human actions, independently of

---

      24–26; further, Hägg, "Professor," 180–182). Tomas Hägg has suggested that the 'Xanthus narrative' is of Hellenistic provenance, perhaps with a *terminus post quem* of the fourth century CE (op. cit., 183).

168   *Panta tēi theiai pronoiai dioikeitai* (*Vit. Aes.* 35; text Perry, *Aesopica*, 48, tr. mine; cit. Kraabel, "Pronoia at Sardis," 82).

169   Kraabel, "Pronoia at Sardis," 82.

170   As Hägg notes, the character and lampooning of Xanthus hints at an author with knowledge not only of New Comedy, but of the schools of Hellenistic philosophy themselves ("Professor," 196). "To judge from the *Life of Aesop*, there was little understanding among ordinary people of the more central tenets of the Hellenistic schools of philosophy" (ibid., 192).

171   *Vit. Aes.* 36; text in Perry, *Aesopica*, 48, tr. mine. Unfortunately, recension G does not preserve Aesop's 'solution' to the problem. In recension W, he uses the analogy of a stepmother who favors her natural children over her stepchildren; 'Mother Earth' treats the farmer's crops as stepchildren, since she did not 'plant' them herself. The farmer is satisfied with the answer and gives Aesop the vegetables.

THE PRONOIA PROBLEM(S)   53

divine activity? For Plato and his later readers, the Middle Platonists, the principal cause of fault is matter, which introduced chaos and suffering into a cosmos handled by 'young gods.'[172] These semi-divine beings were transmuted by the Middle Platonists into *daimones*, perhaps inspired in part by the civic cosmos of Pseudo-Aristotle's *On the World*. Human beings, too, bear responsibility, and often what befalls us in this life is a consequence of choices made prior to birth, when the soul exists outside of the body. The Stoa, meanwhile, refused to recognize any evil in the world but human depravity, the consequence of irrational behavior and faulty impulsive reactions to external circumstances.

For both parties, the dictum of Plato's *Laws* that God cares more for greater affairs than the small ones held true, but how this was actually understood differed in accordance with differing notions of causality, particularly regarding matter, demonology, and human responsibility. Meanwhile, divine action was generally restricted to intermediaries in order to safeguard God's transcendence. Many philosophers denied that the gods even have knowledge of human affairs. The Stoa were an exception, defending divine omniscience and omnipresence. In the first and second centuries CE, they would be joined by new, competing groups of philosophers, who identified themselves as belonging not to the schools of Plato and Zeno, but to those of Moses and Christ.

---

172   See further the discussion below, in chapter three.

CHAPTER 2

Which God Cares for You and Me?

1   Introduction: The Personal God of Early Christianity?

How far did *pronoia* go? This question may be interpreted in two ways. Both of them are significant. First, philosophers disagreed about the extent to which the divine gets involved in worldly affairs. Does divine care extend to the whole alone, or to parts as well—and if so, how? Or are the gods entirely removed from human affairs? Secondly, to what degree is the notion of *pronoia* and the terminology of divine care one of specifically Greek philosophical provenance? When a fable portrays a farmer asking a philosopher about divine care, does this mean that discussions of God's *dioikēsis* took place beyond the world of elites—or were such discussions considered so bound to the world of philosophy that lampooning them was an ideal way to mock philosophers?

The previous chapter outlined some 'classic' passages in Classical and Hellenistic Greek philosophy relating to the problem of divine care for the world and individuals and came down decisively on the side of this philosophical literature as the primary locus of talk about providence. However, with Rome's expansion and ascent to military and economic dominance in the Mediterranean basin in the first half of the second century BCE, both of these questions became significantly more complicated. In 63 BCE, the Roman general Pompey absorbed what remained of the Seleucid Empire and conquered Judaea. Known to speakers of Greek as the *Hebraioi* or *Ioudaioi* (terms I translate in this book as "Jews," despite reservations),[1] the inhabitants of this province believed it to be their ancestral homeland. The Jews were restless subjects and their attempts to challenge Roman rule led to unmitigated disasters. The Great Revolt against the Romans (66–73 CE) culminated in the destruction of the Second Temple in Jerusalem, Trajan's crackdown on later revolts (116–117 CE) annihilated Jewry in Egypt and North Africa, and the failure of the Bar Kochba Revolt (ca. 132–135 CE) extinguished ancient Jewish hopes for national independence.[2]

---

1   A useful and (relatively) recent discussion of the attendant problems regarding the word *Ioudaios* and cognate terminology is Mason, "Jews."

2   For the First Jewish War, see Gabba, "Social," 148–166; on the revolts against Trajan and their consequences, see Kerkeslager, "Jews," 59–68; on the Bar Kochba Revolt, see Eshel, "Bar Kochba."

© KONINKLIJKE BRILL NV, LEIDEN, 2020 | DOI:10.1163/9789004432994_004

WHICH GOD CARES FOR YOU AND ME?

Providence 'was there' for all of this. The Stoa and Middle Platonists dedicated close attention to the problem of providential care for particulars. Both *pronoia* and its Latin counterpart *providentia* were appropriated by Greek and Roman sovereigns, respectively, in their propaganda to express and defend their right to rule, and this appropriation is reflected by historians documenting their regimes. Some Hellenophone Jews, meanwhile, struggled to reconcile their own views of God as deeply involved in the history of Israel and its people with their experience of subjugation at the hands of Greeks and Romans, and the philosophically-inclined among them used the language of providence.[3] Finally, the 'new religious movement' that grew up around the figure of a Jew named Jesus of Nazareth and his followers began as early as the second century CE to count among its adherents individuals who practiced philosophy.[4] And as ancient philosophers were wont to do, they, too, discussed providence and the problem of the reach of divine care.

It will be argued at the end of this chapter that, like some of their Jewish predecessors, these first Christian philosophers contributed a new perspective on divine care for particulars and divine intervention. However, this 'new perspective' is not that which many theologians have described as the novel contribution of early Christian theory about providence: an ostensibly more 'personal' God than that known to the Stoa and Middle Platonists, for whom providence was more remote or abstract. The belief that early Christian providence was 'personal' in an innovative and distinctive way usually proceeds in two steps. The first step is to go looking for a personal, providential God in the Bible. He is not difficult to 'find,' even though there is no word for 'providence' in Hebrew,[5] and no New Testament text uses the words *pronoia, epimeleia,* or *dioikēsis* and their cognates with regards to divine care.[6] Nonetheless, New Testament texts are replete with divine interventions and unequivocal statements

---

3   Rajak, "Gifts of God," 233; Aitken, "Divine Will," 284.

4   For early Christianity as a NRM, see Regev, "Early Christianity." For Basilides (*floruit* 130s CE; see Pearson, "Basilides," 1, 27) as the earliest known Christian philosopher—a point often neglected in the secondary literature—see Layton, "Significance," 147. Cf. also the question of philosophical influence on Paul and other first-century members of the Jesus Movement (see e.g., Engberg-Pedersen, "Setting the Scene," 8–10), on which the present study adopts an agnostic stance.

5   Moore, "Fate," 382–383; Scheffczyk, *Schöpfung und Vorsehung*, 11; Braun, *Deus Christianorum*, 128, 135; Sutcliffe, *Providence and Suffering*, 43; L. Martin, "Josephus' Use," 128; Bergjan, *Der fürsorgende Gott*, 108; Feldmeier, "Wenn die Vorsehung," 148–149; Popović, "Apocalyptic Determinism," 257; Ferguson, *Providence of God*, 2, 19; similarly, Attridge, *Interpretation*, 75 n. 1. This 'received wisdom' is demonstrated to be only half-true by Machinist, "Fate, *miqreh*, and Reason," esp. 159–165.

6   For *pronoia* re: human care, see Rom 13:14; Acts 24:3; similarly *pronoein* in Rom 12:17; 2 Cor 8:21. See e.g. Schrage, *Vorsehung Gottes?*, 137; Ferguson, *Providence of God*, 20.

56   CHAPTER 2

of God's care for individual persons.[7] A fine example presents itself in Luke
12:27–30, Jesus's comforting words to the disciples regarding their mission:

> Consider how the wild flowers grow. They neither toil nor spin ... But if
> God so clothes the grass of the field, which is alive today and tomorrow
> is thrown into the oven, how much more will he clothe you—you of little
> faith! And do not keep striving for what you are to eat and what you are
> to drink, and do not keep worrying. For it is the nations of the world that
> strive after all these things, and your Father knows that you need them.
> Instead, strive for his kingdom, and these things will be given to you as
> well.

Similarly, Matt 10:29–30 (= Luke 12:6–7; recalling Ps 84:3): "Are not two sparrows
sold for a penny? Yet not one of them will fall to the ground apart from your
Father. And even the hairs of your head are all counted. So do not be afraid: you
are of more value than many sparrows."[8] Thus, one can read studies of 'implicit'
providence in New Testament literature.[9] The natural result of this approach is
a cottage industry of studies on providence in biblical works that do not explicitly refer to providence.[10] Such an approach is plainly anachronistic (from a

---

7   Jesus works many miracles in the Gospels; some of these recall God's demonstration of
     His worldly omnipotence in earlier Jewish scriptures, such as stilling the waves when the
     disciples are at sea during a storm (Matt 8:26, re: Ps 89:9; Isa 51:9–10; Job 26:11–12; see also
     Matt 14:32). Divine intervention is also the question in Gethsemane, where Jesus asks his
     Father to save him (Mark 14:36; Matt 26:39; cf. John 12:27). The book of Acts is replete with
     such interventions, as when an angel frees Peter from jail, or the Holy Spirit blinds the
     rival magician Elymas (Acts 12:6–11, 13:4–12, respectively). See also Acts 12:23 (an angel
     of the Lord strikes down King Herod); 16:25–34 (a divinely-sent earthquake opens the
     prison); 23:11 (Paul guided by The Lord); 27:22–25.34–35 (Paul assured by an angel of God
     of the success of his journey to Rome). On this point see also Pagels, "Preliminary Sketch,"
     108.
8   On the importance of this passage, see Dihle, "Astrology," 162; idem, "Philosophische
     Lehren," 24; Louth, "Pagans and Christians on Providence," 286; Feldmeier, "Wenn die
     Vorsehung," 157; Scheffczyk, *Schöpfung und Vorsehung*, 22, also recalling Matt 5:45, 6:26.
9   Scheffczyk, *Schöpfung und Vorsehung*, 22; Louth, "Pagans and Christians," 286; Moore,
     "Fate," 380 n. 45. Feldmeier critiques this phrasing as "viel zu unspezifisich" ("Wenn die
     Vorsehung," 149), but his alternative—the use of the same approach to identify "equiva-
     lences" (*Äquivalente*) between the Greek notion of *pronoia* and divine activity in the NT
     (ibid., 157, 169)—is splitting hairs. Cf. Elliott, *Providence Perceived*, 5–6: "the New Testa-
     ment thought that certain things were indeed fixed, the two advents of Christ in particular,
     but little else is predetermined and no plan may be discerned" (following Schrage, *Vorse-
     hung Gottes?*, 157, 170; cf. also Ferguson, *Providence of God*, 21, 41–42).
10   To take a few examples: with regards to Sirach, see Wicke-Reuter: "man kann nun einwen-

WHICH GOD CARES FOR YOU AND ME? 57

diachronic perspective, at least), even if it has the virtue of highlighting proof-texts that were important for Christian philosophers who really did talk about *pronoia* (e.g., Origen on Luke 12:6–7).[11]

The second step is to contrast this construction of 'implicit providence' with the allegedly impersonal gods of the Stoa and Platonists, as does Andrew Louth:

> Providence is to the Christians primarily a religious doctrine—about God's care for his creation ... Their pagan contemporaries, on the contrary, were primarily philosophers; the philosophical debate was presented in terms of fate or destiny and human freedom, providence being either not mentioned at all (despite the prominence of *pronoia* in Plato's doctrine), or introduced as an argument against the determinist consequences of the Stoic doctrine of fate (as its opponents understood it).[12]

---

den, dass bereits im Alten Testament die Vorsehung Gottes eine beachtliche Rolle spielt" ("Ben Sira," 274; similarly ibid., 279); also Mattila: "as firmly as the Stoics, Ben Sira believed in divine providence" ("Ben Sira," 501). For Tobit, see Schellenberg, "Suspense" (for a different reading, see Schmitz, "Gott als Figur," 228–230). For the *megillot*, see Melton, *Where is God*, 136–163. For Paul, see Macaskill, "History" (similarly Feldmeier, "Wenn die Vorsehung," 160–164). In these studies it can be unclear whether the authors write as historians or theologians. For an explicitly synchronic, theologizing account of 'providence in Scripture,' see Ferguson, *Providence of God*, 21–42. Another scholar explains that he uses the term 'providence' in the title of a (historical) study where the work does not otherwise appear at all to express that he wishes to discuss the "technologies" in late ancient Jewish 'magical' and 'mystical' practices (Swartz, *Mechanics*, 22).

11 Orig. *Princ.* 3.2.7; *Hom. Luc.* 32.3; *Cels.* 8.70; discussed below, chapters three and four.
12 Louth, "Pagans and Christians on Providence," 286; similarly Osborn: "Clement replaced the impersonal providence of the Stoics with a saving God" (*Clement*, 49). Schrage, meanwhile, constructs a theology of providence for the New Testament which is based "von dem von Gott gewirkten Heilsereignis in Jesus Christus," in contrast to "die göttliche Weltregierung" theorized by the Stoa (*Vorsehung Gottes?*, 137; followed by Elliott, *Providence Perceived*, 6). Schrage's monograph is strictly concerned with a systematic theology of the New Testament (rather than Greek and Christian philosophers of the first centuries CE), and thus differs not only in methodology but subject matter from the present study. Finally, from a preeminent historian of philosophy (Dörrie, "Der Begriff Pronoia," 63):
   Nur das Christentum konnte die Tatsache, daß Gott seinen Sohn in die Welt entsandt hat, um die Menschen zu erlösen, göttlicher *pronoia* zuschreiben. Das war eine ebenso notwendige wie radikale Umdeutung des bisherigen *pronoia*-Begriffes. Denn dieser ist—das muß mit allem Nachdruck betont werden—bei vorchristlichen Autoren allein auf die Automatik der diesseitigen Abläufe, und das in einem durchaus mechanistischen Sinne, zu beziehen.
   Bergjan responds: "diese ,radikale Umdeutung' fand nicht statt" (*Der fürsorgende Gott*, 339). The present chapter is in agreement with Bergjan on this point, even if its presentation and interpretation of much of the attendant evidence differ.

Reinhard Feldmeier presents a similar perspective, wherein the Hellenic philosophers' concept of *pronoia* amounts to "divine power without a face," which entered early Christian theology via Hellenistic Judaism.[13] Platonists like Philo and Plutarch offered a "a certain *personalization of the concept of providence*, which made it easier for Hellenistic Judaism and thereafter early Christianity to receive it."[14] Thus, "through *this integration of a personally imagined providence in the biblical election- and salvation-history, a theological transformation of the concept of providence takes place*, which will be decisive for the Christian reception."[15]

The present chapter will challenge such views. First, a closer look at the Middle Platonists and especially the Stoa will show that while both schools rejected divine intervention per se, God was hardly 'impersonal' for either of them. Platonists focused on divine intermediaries as administrators of providential care, but these daimonic caretakers were hardly distant, if not 'fully divine.' Stoic theology, meanwhile, was anthropocentric. Its exponents posited that when human beings employ their reason and behave virtuously, they are 'in tune' with providence, and thus under a divine care that is as personal as you and me.[16] This forms an interesting context for historical writers such as Polybius, Diodorus Siculus, and Pliny the Elder. While each had his own view on Roman power, they all found the rhetoric of divine intervention to be useful for advancing their agendas—including, at times, to describe the dominion of Rome as a consequence of its reason and virtue, as a Stoic might. For Hellenized Jewish authors such as Philo and Josephus, too, the Stoic model of providential care for the virtuous proved especially useful—but to describe the God's care in the history of the Jews. Jewish sapiential works such as Sirach and especially Wisdom of Solomon presage this development, but it was hardly a given, as some Hellenistic Jewish writings describe God not as omnipresent, but distant. Finally, the chapter will close with a discussion of the oldest explicit treatment by a Christian philosopher of the problem of the extent of *pronoia*'s reach: Justin Martyr's *Dialogue with Trypho*, set in the aftermath of the Bar Kochba catastrophe. Justin—like Philo and Josephus—does not theorize a *pronoia* which had more of a 'face' than those of the Greeks and Romans, but a *pronoia* exerted by a God with a completely different 'face,' who was nonetheless active in history using much the same machinery as that posited by the Platonists and Stoa.

---

13   Feldmeier, "Wenn die Vorsehung," 170, tr. mine, 149, respectively. See further above, introduction.

14   Feldmeier, "Wenn die Vorsehung," 154, tr. mine, italics author's.

15   Feldmeier, "Wenn die Vorsehung," tr. mine, italics author's.

16   Cf. Kraabel's opposition of the "impersonal Providence of the Stoics" to the 'personal' providence of the Neoplatonists ("Pronoia at Sardis," 92).

WHICH GOD CARES FOR YOU AND ME?   59

2   Philosophers' Personal Gods: Daimonic Intervention in the Stoa
        and Plutarch

The Middle Platonic introduction of *daimones* as the arbiters of fate in the
present cosmos, with some kind of higher providence or fate removed from
the universe, offers a stark contrast to Stoic view of providence as universal and
directly involved in individual human lives—the parts of the whole. As Marcus
Aurelius writes: "whatever befalls you was prepared in advance for you from
eternity, and the complex arrangement of causes wove together (*hē epiplokē
tōn aitiōn suneklōthe*) your very existence and its coincidence with that (which
befalls you)."[17] Nor is it difficult to find criticisms of a Stoic God who cares for
particulars, as in Cicero's *De natura deorum*, where the Epicurean "Veilleius,"
exclaims that

> This (idle) God (of Epicurus) we would call "blessed" in the fullest sense of
> the word; yours is utterly overworked ... And who would not fear a nosy
> busybody of a God, foreseeing and contemplating and paying attention
> to everything, a God who thinks that everything is his business? ... Of
> what value could one possibly reckon a philosophy to be, where every-
> thing appears to happen by fate?—It is an idea for old ladies, and ignorant
> ones at that.[18]

Even if this is an unfair, polemical representation of Stoic theology, its contours must have been representative enough of Epicurean criticism of the
early Stoa that Cicero found it worthwhile to present to his readers in the first
place. The question of how exactly God-providence is involved in human affairs
was therefore a live one, and here there is variety amongst the Stoa—more
than "Veilleius" would have us believe.[19] What is striking is that both Stoics
and Platonists shied away from admitting the possibility of divine intervention in worldly affairs, at least when writing as philosophers. The Platonists
handed involvement in the world over to semi-divine beings, and some evi-

---

17   Marc. Aur. 10.5, text Haines in LCL 58:262, tr. mine. See also Elliott, *Providence Perceived*, 11
      re: Marc. Aur. 5.8.

18   *Nat. d.* 1.52–55: *hunc deum rite beatum dixerimus, vestrum vero laboriosissimum ... Quis enim
      non timeat omnia providentem et cogitantem et animadvertentem et omnia ad se pertinere
      putantem curiosum et plenum negotii deum? ... Quanti autem haec philosophia aestimanda
      est cui tamquam aniculis, et iis quidem indoctis, fato fieri videantur omnis?* (text Rackham
      in LCL 268:52, 54, tr. mine).

19   On this, see esp. Bénatouïl, "How Industrious can Zeus Be?" 36–44. The problem is glossed
      over by M. Frede, *Free Will*, 14.

60   CHAPTER 2

dence suggests that Chrysippus agreed. Yet Stoic writers after him appear to have emphasized a very 'personal' deity at work in an anthropocentric cosmos, eliding divine action (*pronoia*) with human action—provided that the latter is entirely virtuous and reasonable (*logismos*).

Indeed, the Stoa must have been inspired by Plato's *Laws* 903 in arguing that providence extends more to wholes than to parts, although it does extend to both.[20] Thus Chrysippus holds that while providence pervades the whole world, as a soul pervades a body, it is present in some parts more than others.[21] Centuries later, Marcus Aurelius also emphasizes that providence cares for the 'nature of the whole,' and all individual events are to the benefit of the universal, even if it does not look that way: in a swipe at Epicureans, he states flatly that "it's providence, or atoms" (*ētoi pronoia ē atomoi*).[22] Even Cicero's Stoic mouthpiece Balbus concedes that God "leaves the small stuff aside" (*parva neglegunt*).[23] However, the most well-known Stoic rehearsal of the problem was Chrysippus's 'household argument': "[Do misfortunes come about] because some things are neglected, just as in larger houses the odd husk and a little wheat go astray, even though the overall housekeeping is good (*tōn holōn eu oikonomoumenōn*)? Or is it because the sort of matters in which real blameworthy cases of negligence occur have evil spirits in attendance?"[24]

Chrysippus's views on *daimones* are otherwise not known to us, unfortunately,[25] but the simile of the world as a great house that runs well as far as the

---

20   Long, *Hellenistic Philosophy*, 151; Reydams-Schils, *Demiurge and Providence*, 74; D. Frede, "Theodicy and Providential Care," 89; O'Brien, *Demiurge*, 93; idem, "Prayer in Maximus," 61.

21   D. L. 7.138–139 = SVF 2:634 = LS 47O; similarly, D. L. 7.147 = SVF 2:1021 = LS 54A; Cic. *Nat. d.* 2.115. See also O'Brien, *Demiurge*, 91. This likely furnishes the right context for Seneca's remarks on the otherworldly character of the divine spirit, mistakenly taken by Winston to imply a notion of transcendence in Stoicism (Winston, "Philo and the Wisdom," 115, 124, re: Sen. *Ep.* 41).

22   Marc. Aur. 4.3, text Haines in LCL 58:68, tr. mine; see also Magris, *L'idea di destino*, 2:658; van Nuffelen, *Rethinking*, 182. On the issue generally, see ibid., 2.3, 2.10, 2.16, 4.3, 6.10, 6.44, 7.32, 9.39, 5.8, 5.30, 6.43–44, 10.1, 10.6, 10.25, 12.23, 12.32. On some of these passages, Dragona-Monachou, "Divine Providence," 4445, 4450, 4452; Sharples, "Threefold Providence," 114; G. Lloyd, *Providence Lost*, 126–127; Thorsteinsson, "Justin," 555.

23   *Nat. d.* 2.167, text Rackham in LCL 268:282, tr. mine; see also ibid., 3.86; Sharples, "Introduction: Cicero," 32; idem, "Threefold Providence," 110–111; Bénatouïl, "How Industrious can Zeus Be?" 37–39.

24   Plut. *Stoic. rep.* 1051C = SVF 2:1178 = LS 54S, text in Long and Sedley, *Hellenistic Philosophers*, 2:331, tr. ibid., 1:330.

25   We may reasonably assume that if Chrysippus held *daimones* to be responsible for apparent ills, he believed them to be doing providence's work in the service of the whole (Long

WHICH GOD CARES FOR YOU AND ME?

'wholes' go, despite small problems escaping divine care, became popular.[26] Yet the omnipresent, omniscient, omnipotent God of Stoic pantheism is difficult to reconcile with the 'household argument,' already subject to tensions of its own.[27] Thus Cicero's 'Cotta' (giving the arguments of the Academic Skeptic Carneades) points out that an omniscient God could hardly overlook matters in his own 'house.'[28] And with all due respect to Plato's *Laws*, where does one draw the line of an 'individual' versus a 'whole,' or 'small' versus 'great'—a person, a town, or a nation?[29] More generally, if the gods are good, why did they not make people good, too, or keep good men from failure?[30]

The incisiveness of Carneades's attacks on the 'household argument' may have led some of the Roman Stoa to double down on pantheism. Seneca states that the Gods protect humanity "all the while caring for individuals (*interdum curiosi singulorum*)."[31] Despite his reservations about the 'small stuff,' Balbus does claim that "it is indeed not the case that the care and providence of the immortal gods extends only to the human genus in its entirety, but even to individuals (*etiam singulis*)."[32] He even finishes his speech with a list of famous Roman figures and heroes in whose lives the gods have played a role. This passage has led Dorothea Frede to remark, rightly, on the 'anthropocentrism' of

---

and Sedley, *Hellenistic Philosophers*, 2:331; see also Algra, "Plutarch and the Stoic Theory," 134–135; O'Brien, *Demiurge*, 92). Other scholars simply disregard this evidence, given its incommensurability with Chrysippus's more pantheistic moments (Babut, *Plutarque*, 261–262, followed by Sharples, "Threefold Providence," 111).

26 E.g. Philo, *Prov.* 2.54–55; Sen. *Ep.* 110.2; idem, *Nat.* 1.praef.3. See Dragona-Monachou, "Divine Providence," 4438; Sharples, "Threefold Providence," 112 n. 10; Bergjan, "Celsus," 198; Bénatouïl, "How Industrious can Zeus Be?" 37–38.

27 Bénatouïl, "How Industrious can Zeus Be?" 38; see also Sharples, "Aristotelian Theology," 24 n. 112.

28 Cic. *Nat. d.* 3.90, text and tr. Rackham in LCL 268:376–377, modified: "if human rulers knowingly overlook an issue, the blame is great enough; but God cannot even offer the excuse of ignorance." Similarly, ibid., 3.85. 'Cotta' invokes Carneades at ibid., 3.29, 3.44 *passim*. Similarly, Plutarch's own criticisms (*Stoic. rep.* 1051d, discussed in van Nuffelen, *Rethinking*, 173–174).

29 " 'It does not care for individuals.' This is no wonder; no more does it care for cities. Not for these? Not for tribes or nations either. And if it shall appear that it despises even nations, what wonder is it that it has scorned the entire human race?" (Cic. *Nat. d.* 3.93, tr. Rackham in LCL 268:379). Cf. Bergjan, "Celsus," 198.

30 Cic. *Nat. d.* 3.80. This argument would be taken up by Marcion and his followers; see below, chapters three and six.

31 Sen. *Ep.* 95.50, text Grummere in LCL 77:88, tr. mine. The textual evidence in the passage is problematic but salvage-able; see Sharples, "Threefold Providence," 115.

32 Cic. *Nat. d.* 2.164, text and tr. Rackham in LCL 268:280–281, modified.

62   CHAPTER 2

Stoic theology.[33] Yet this all-pervasive divine care is not to be confused with divine intervention or even personal care, as Seneca says in his remarks on lightning and thunder: "Although Jupiter does not do these things now, it is Jupiter who brought it about that they happen. He is not present at every event for every person but he gives the signal, the force, the cause to all."[34] Even a critic of Stoic Pantheism, the Aristotelian Alexander of Aphrodisias (second century CE), mocks the Stoic god as "the demiurge of worms and mosquitos"—creator of everything, not personal administrator of everything.[35]

It is in fact possible to reconcile this Stoic anthropocentrism with Seneca's remarks: as we have seen above and as Balbus himself says, human reason is a gift of providence,[36] and to the extent that humans act reasonably, they participate in the divine. They are divine, in a sense, or at least set apart from other elements of the universe.[37] The obverse of this—that wickedness is 'its own punishment,' insofar as to practice vice is tantamount to punishment from the gods—was argued already by Chrysippus,[38] but we find this notion of providential care for the virtuous explored most widely in Epictetus: "but you, you are a priority; you are an offshoot of God. You have a part of that one inside of yourself. Why then are you ignorant of your lineage? Why do you not know from whence you came?"[39] Like Cicero, Epictetus recounts instances of divine attendance in everyday matters.[40] God is the "caring father of human beings," a fact that mandates the fundamental equality of human beings—slaves and free men are siblings, because of our kinship with God.[41] The substance of this divine kinship is reason, which Epictetus sometimes refers to as a *dai-*

---

33   D. Frede, "Theodicy and Providential Care," 108, 109–115, re: Cic. *Nat. d.* 2.165–167; see also Dragona-Monachou, "Divine Providence," 443o; Mansfeld, "Theology," 466; Bergjan, *Der fürsorgende Gott*, 216 n. 198; Bénatouïl, "How Industrious can Zeus Be?" 40; Karamanolis, *Philosophy*, 155.

34   Sen. *Nat.* 2.46, tr. Corcoran in LCL 450:175; for discussion, see Reydams-Schils, "Seneca's Platonism," 210–211.

35   Alex. Aphr. *De mixtione* 226.24–29 = SVF 2:1048, cit. O'Brien, *Demiurge*, 89. Notably, Alexander in his appropriated the 'household argument' to support the contention that God attends to worldly affairs, but not to particulars: *Prov.* 25.1–18, discussed below, chapter five.

36   Cic. *Nat. d.* 2.147. See also the Stoicizing Manil. *Astron.* 2.105–116, 4.896–897.

37   Reydams-Schils, "Seneca's Platonism," 204.

38   Plut. *Stoic. rep.* 1050e = SVF 2:1176; see van Nuffelen, *Rethinking*, 173.

39   Epict. *Diatr.* 2.8.11. On human kinship with God in Epictetus, see Long, *Epictetus*, 154–162; Thorsteinsson, "Justin," 522.

40   For inventory, see Long, *Epictetus*, 143.

41   Epict. *Diatr.* 1.3.1, 1.13.4; see also Long, *Epictetus*, 144.

mōn (surely with reference to Socrates's 'voice').[42] Yet it is precisely in order to perceive the arrangement of the whole, despite our status as mere individuals, that humans possess reason: "Now, all other animals have been excluded from the capacity to understand the governance of God, but the rational animal, humanity, possesses faculties that enable him to consider all these things, both that he is a part of them, and what kind of part of them he is, and that it is well for the parts to yield to the whole."[43] It is when we behave rationally that *pronoia* attends to us personally.[44]

The elegance of this way by which Stoic writers after Chrysippus irrigated the cosmos with a personal divinity at work in human affairs emerges when one turns to Middle Platonic sources, which also expressed discomfort with divine intervention, but simply displaced the problem by assigning responsibility for worldly care not to the gods, but to *daimones*—beings who are superhuman, but semi-divine.[45] 'Demons' are not exactly gods themselves, but mediators between humans and gods, particularly in a religious cult, inhabiting the sky.[46]

---

42   Epict. *Diatr.* 1.14.11–14, 4.12.11–12; cit. Long, *Epictetus*, 165; see also Thorsteinsson, "Justin," 552.

43   Epict. *Diatr.* 4.7.7, text and tr. Oldfather in LCL 218:362–363, slightly modified, cit. Long, *Epictetus*, 155; see also *Diatr.* 1.12.24–26.

44   I believe we may be in a similar situation with Galen, in a passage where he describes how a god instructed him to give a thorough, mathematically-informed description of why we have double the visual power with two eyes, instead of just seeing double (Gal. *Usu* 10.14). Michael Frede sees the passage as evidence that Galen believed in divine intervention: "surely this god was concerned with what Galen was doing and made him do the right thing, thus showing providence for Galen and those who might read his work ... The providence of Galen's God does extend to individual human beings. Galen's view in this matter seems to be rather along Platonist lines" (M. Frede, "Galen's Theology," 98). The 'god' may have been Asclepius, patron god of Pergamum (ibid., 104–105). A similar reading of Galen has been presented to me by Matyáš Havrda, in conversation. Galen may have, on the other hand, regarded 'Asclepius' as a name for medical science itself and the rational mind's engagement of it, an activity divine and exalted enough to merit a cult. For a reading of Galen as "agnostic" in *Usu* about the source of natural theology, see Adamson, *Philosophy*, 139.

45   *Pace* Opsomer, "Middle Platonic Doctrine," 166 n. 114: "The works of, say, Plutarch, Apuleius or Maximus of Tyre contain plenty examples [sic] of divine and daemonic interventions ... Lesser divinities take care of the destiny of human individuals. They will presumably intervene to change the course of events, whereas primary providence is more likely to be conceived of as a single invariable act by which order is preserved ..." (ibid., 166). But does tertiary providence qualify as 'divine intervention'? Not exactly, since *daimones* are not strictly gods. Moreover, the very purpose of tertiary providence is to establish an area for *daimones* that is on the same grade as 'what is up to us' and chance: actions that are in Fate but not according to Fate (ibid., 163–164).

46   See esp. Plat. *Symp.* 202d–203a; also *Phaedr.* 246e.

Plutarch of Chaeronea, who preserves the bulk of Xenocrates's writing on *daimones*,[47] agrees with his Middle Platonist peers in denoting demons as the distributors of divine providence, a "race" of demigods serving as intermediaries with the gods.[48] "Let us," he writes, "commit these (cultic) matters to those ministers of the gods to whom it is right to commit them, as to servants and clerks, and let us believe that *daimones* are guardians of sacred rites of the gods and prompters in the Mysteries, while others go about as avengers of arrogant and grievous cases of injustice."[49] Plutarch himself distinguishes daimonic and divine activity, when Cleombrotos, the Platonist speaker in his dialogue *On the Decline of Oracles*, attacks both who "make the god responsible for nothing at all and those who make him responsible for all things"—the Epicureans and the Stoa, respectively.[50] Maximus of Tyre, a philosopher of the second century CE, also regards *daimones* as cultic intermediaries made of air—not exactly corporeal, not exactly incorporeal.[51] He even believes them to be formerly human souls freed of the body at death.[52] George Boys-Stones emphasizes in a recent essay that the purpose of the multi-tiered providence of the Middle Platonists was to express that "providence can be passed down the line from the demiurge."[53] He is right—but only if one also keeps in mind that the purpose of designating this means as 'secondary' (and even 'tertiary'), in the hands of *daimones* rather than gods themselves, was to insulate the demiurge from direct involvement in administration of the cosmos.[54]

---

47 Plut. *Is. Os.* 360e, 361b; idem, *Def. orac.* 416c–e; see J.M. Dillon, *Heirs of Plato*, 129–131; Timotin, *Démonologie platonicienne*, 165–166, 173; Gasparro, "*Daimôn* and *Tuchê*," 75–76; O'Brien, *Demiurge*, 97–98. Similarly, Alc. *Epit.* 15; Calc. *Comm. Tim.* 132–136.

48 Plut. *Def. orac.* 414f–415b; also ibid., 416e–417b. See Gasparro, "*Daimôn* and *Tuchê*," 67–68.

49 Plut. *Def. orac.* 417a, text and tr. Babbitt in LCL 306:388–389, slightly modified. See also van Nuffelen, *Rethinking*, 164–167; Boys-Stones, "Providence and Religion," 330; Simonetti, *A Perfect Medium?*, 82–84.

50 Plut. *Def. orac.* 414f, tr. Babbitt in LCL 306:377. See further Opsomer and Steel, "Evil," 239.

51 Max. Tyr. *Or.* 8.8, 9.2–5.

52 Max. Tyr. *Or.* 9.6–7, a belief shared by Philo, *Somn.* 1.137–141; idem, *Plant.* 14; Porph. *Vit. Plot.* 22–23. This point is rightly emphasized by Boys-Stones, "Providence and Religion," 335.

53 Boys-Stones, "Providence and Religion," 331.

54 Thus I cannot agree with Boys-Stones's statement that "the point is rather that the world soul *secondarily exercises* the very same providence, namely the providence of the demiurge" ("Providence and Religion," 332, italics his). For Plutarch's discomfort with equating fortune, fate, and providence (and thus assigning responsibility for evil to God), see *How*

WHICH GOD CARES FOR YOU AND ME?

3 Fortune's Favorites: Providence in Early Roman Historians

The Middle Platonists' tendency to distance providence from worldly affairs by substituting a secondary or tertiary providence (or 'fate') executed by *daimones* is a commonplace in modern scholarship on providence and fate. Yet it is distant indeed from the descriptions of divine care for worldly affairs found in contemporary literature beyond the immediate context of philosophy. When we depart from philosophy in the day of Cicero or Plutarch, literary constructions of providence take upon a deeply immediate and politicized character. The Greek terminology of 'care' in the context of public service—especially the words *epimeleia* and *pronoia*—overlapped with its theological usage since Plato's day.[55] Following the swift political and military ascent of Rome, *pronoia* and *providentia* came to take on a specifically Roman imperial tone in Greek and Latin alike.[56] Even a brief glance at three authors with wildly divergent views of the Romans—Polybius, Diodorus Siculus, and Pliny the Elder—shows that this usage is broadly consistent from the late Republican to the early Imperial period, and consonant with the Stoic notions of divine care for the virtuous outlined above. Whatever one made of the Romans, their rise was dictated by a providence so political as to be deeply personal.

For Polybius, the second-century BCE Greek historian who witnessed and documented the swift rise of Rome to dominant power of the Mediterranean, *pronoia* appears to be entirely involved in terrestrial matters: it takes sides in political machinations, determines which individuals will meet on the battlefield, and the like.[57] Yet his favored term is *tuchē* ('fortune, chance'), which he

---

the Young Should Study Poetry, 23d–24c, cit. van Nuffelen, *Rethinking*, 168–169; further ibid., 172–173.

55 The Attic orator Isocrates referred to running the *polis* as "care for the all (*hē tōn koinōn epimeleia*)" (*Areopagitus* [*Or. 7*] 25). Polybius used a similar formula—*hē tōn koinōn pronoia*—to define democracy (*Hist.* 6.9.3). Both cit. Bergjan, *Der fürsorgende Gott*, 36–37.

56 The definitive survey of this material remains J.-P. Martin, *Providentia deorum*; see also M. Charlesworth, "Providentia et Aeternitas"; Magris, *L'idea di destino*, 2:659; Bergjan, *Der fürsorgende Gott*, 33–35. The question of the relationship between *pronoia*/*providentia* and imperial propaganda is a pressing one and merits a monograph all its own. The present, cursory discussion hopes to lend further context to the philosophical sources discussed in the rest of this chapter.

57 Polyb. *Hist.* 5.48.8, 10.11.8, 10.14.11, cit. J.-P. Martin, *Providentia deorum*, 16 n. 83; cf. Cohen, "Josephus," 377. *Pronoia* is described in similar fashion in Dionysius of Halicarnassus, *Roman Antiquities*, 2.63.3, 3.13.3, 3.14.2, 3.16.2, 3.5.1, and esp. 4.26.2; see also ibid., 1.2–3, on the greatness of the Romans (cit. Sacks, *Diodorus Siculus*, 120).

describes as doing much the same.[58] On the one hand, Polybius specifically denotes *tuchē* as agent behind inexplicable or even irrational events; on the other, he uses the word loosely to label the sudden turnabout of affairs, or the apparent just desserts that visit the wicked.[59] *Tuchē* even played a hand in Polybius's central narrative: the rise of Rome to total dominion in only fifty-three years, a matter the historian tries to render explicable by virtue of the Romans' rationality and discipline.[60] The old question of whether this teleological understanding of fortune may be regarded as a Stoic(izing) theory of history is difficult to entertain, much less solve, given the lack of consistency surrounding Polybius's use of the term in question.[61] What is clear, however, is that Polybius found the rhetoric of cosmic fortune useful for communicating the meaning of great politico-historical events, and, on occasion, for interpreting events as divinely-sanctioned in some sense.

Nearly a century later, another Hellenophone historian, Diodorus Siculus in his *Library of History*, also used the terms *pronoia* and *tuchē* as a kind of shorthand for the way things go.[62] However, at the very beginning of the work, Diodorus reflects on his task and purpose, and here he describes providence somewhat differently. History, Diodorus maintains, is a great boon for humanity, since it allows people to learn lessons of others' misfortune without actually having to experience the misfortune for themselves:

> ... As it were, such people (historians) have become agents of divine providence (*hypourgoi tēs theias pronoias*). For just as Providence, hav-

---

58   The survey of Walbank, *Historical Commentary*, 16–26 remains useful; see also Magris, *L'idea di destino*, 2:485–487; Brouwer, "Polybius," 111–112.

59   Polyb. *Hist.* 36.17, 39.8, 9.81.5, respectively; cit. (with many more examples) Walbank, *Historical Commentary*, 17–21.

60   Key is Polyb. *Hist.* 1.4.5: "I therefore thought it quite necessary not to leave unnoticed or allow to pass into oblivion this the finest and most beneficent of the performances of Fortune. For though she is ever producing something new and ever playing a part in the lives of men, she has not in a single instance ever accomplished such a work, ever achieved such a triumph, as in our own times ..." (tr. Paton, in LCL 128:11). See Walbank, *Historical Commentary*, 22; Sacks, *Diodorus Siculus*, 120. On Polybius's discussions of why the gods favored the Romans, see also Cohen, "Josephus," 379; Brent, *Political History*, 92–94, 101.

61   Rightly Walbank, *Historical Commentary*, 21–25; for a more recent treatment that decides in favor of Polybius's 'Stoicizing' understanding of *tuchē*, see Brouwer, "Polybius." While suggestive, Brouwer's argument relies upon a very tentative reconstruction on what a 'Stoic' teaching on *tuchē* actually would have been, and in any case the reading he suggests is hardly necessary to make sense of the Polybian passages in question.

62   See Diod. Sic. *Bib. hist.* 2.4.1; 16.58.5; further, see Sacks, *Diodorus Siculus*, 36–37; J.-P. Martin, *Providentia deorum*, 100–102; Bergjan, *Der fürsorgende Gott*, 108; Santangelo, "Prediction," 115.

ing brought the orderly arrangement of the visible stars and the natures of men together into a common relationship, continually directs their courses through all eternity, apportioning to each that which falls to it by the direction of fate (*peprōmenēs*), so likewise the (historians), in recording the common affairs of the inhabited world as though they were those of a single state, have made of their treatises a single reckoning of past events and a common oracle (*chrēsmatērion*) concerning them.[63]

Fortune presents history with much chaos, but through the exercise of virtue and reason, one may perhaps find stability in turbulence and earn mercy when all else fails.[64] This attitude, together with the reference to a cosmic *pronoia* at the *Library*'s opening, has led some to hypothesize that Diodorus here relies on the Stoic Posidonius, who was well-known for his belief in the universal administration of the cosmos by the divine *logos*. Yet any such Posidonian influence here is merely hypothetical, and it is if anything more likely that Diodorus was simply tuned in to the same stirrings of cosmopolitanism as was Posidonius himself.[65] Even so, providence is hardly impersonal here, concerned as it is with ordering the "common affairs" experienced by individuals.

Significantly, Diodorus conspicuously avoids tying *pronoia* and *tuchē* to the Romans in particular. As Kenneth Sacks notes, this is a silence that speaks volumes.[66] The *Suda* tells us that Diodorus lived in the Emperor Augustus's times "and earlier," and was at work on the *Library* until at least 30 BCE,[67] so he may have had a taste of Augustus's deliberate strategy of describing his self and rule with terms of abstraction, not least of them being *providentia*.[68] A famous example is an inscription announcing a new calendar for the province of Asia, in 9 BC: "providence (*pronoia*), which has divinely disposed our lives, having employed zeal and ardor, has arranged the most perfect (culmination) for life

---

63   Diod. Sic. *Bib. hist.* 1.1.3–4, text and tr. Oldfather in LCL 279:4–7, slightly modified.

64   So Santangelo, "Prediction," 123–124.

65   Burton, *Diodorus*, 36–38; cf. J.-P. Martin, *Providentia deorum*, 102; Santangelo, "Prediction," 125.

66   Sacks, *Diodorus Siculus*, 120–121.

67   *Suda*, delta 1151, accessed 7 July 2019 at *Suda On Line* ("Diodorus"). On dating Diodorus's life and career, see the discussion of Whitehead (ibid., n. 3) as well as Sacks, *Diodorus Siculus*, 6–7.

68   For Augustus, see Fishwick, *Imperial Cult*, 85–86, 180–183; Charlesworth, "Providentia et Aeternitas," 110–111, 120–121. On the persistence of language about providence on imperial coins, see ibid., 111–121, and esp. J.-P. Martin, *Providentia deorum*, with attention to many other media.

68   CHAPTER 2

by producing Augustus, whom for the benefit of mankind she has filled with
excellence, as if [she had sent him as a savior] for us and our descendants ..."[69]
Diodorus's description of *pronoia* as relatively independent from the infant
Roman Empire of his day is not a sign of the term's distance from political
contexts—it is a sign that such a connotation was one upon which Diodorus
himself frowned.

Nearly a century later, Pliny the Elder discussed providence and divine care
as part of a well-known criticism of contemporary popular religion in the second book of his *Natural History*. He, too, has been diagnosed as an exponent of
a vague, non-systematic Stoicism in these passages.[70] Pliny is skeptical of traditional mythology, and of attempts to placate the gods via cult (such as the 'Temple of Fever' on the Palatine Hill).[71] This is not to say he is critical of the civic
side of Roman cult. On the contrary, he relocates the divine to human political
action: "For mortal to aid mortal—this is god; and this is the road to eternal
glory: by this road went our Roman chieftains, by this road now proceeds with
heavenward step, escorted by his children, the greatest ruler of all time, His
Majesty Vespasian, coming to the succor of an exhausted world."[72] Vespasian is
likened here even to the sun, the center of the universe.[73] Rather, Pliny repeats
the Epicurean complaints that the gods would be sullied by involvement in

---

69   §101 in Sherk, ed., *Rome and the Greek East*, 125. See Charlesworth, "Providentia et Aeter-
        nitas," 109–110; J.-P. Martin, *Providentia deorum*, 90–93. Brent, *Political History*, 170.

70   For instance, a *leitmotiv* of the *Naturalis historia* is that humanity perverts nature's gifts,
        turning the goods furnished by the earth into evil (see esp. Plin. *Nat.* 2.154–159; see also
        34.138). Beagon (*Roman Nature*, 38–39) supposes that Pliny here answers criticism of Stoic
        providence (ap. e.g. Cic. *Nat. d.* 3.78). In substance, Pliny's answer is Stoic: the only evil is
        human evil. On the question of Pliny's relationship with Stoicism, see further Beagon, op.
        cit., 30.

71   First, he states, religious leaders are infestations of eccentricity and hypocrisy (Plin. *Nat.*
        2.5.21; on this passage, see Beagon, *Roman Nature*, 95). Second, fatalism can be danger-
        ous:

             Everywhere in the whole world at every hour by all men's voices Fortune alone is
             invoked and named, alone accused, alone impeached, alone pondered, alone ap-
             plauded, alone rebuked and visited with reproaches; deemed volatile and indeed by
             most men blind as well, wayward, inconstant, uncertain, fickle in her favors and favor-
             ing the unworthy ... And we are so much at the mercy of chance that Chance herself,
             by whom God is proved uncertain, takes the place of God (*Nat.* 2.5.22, tr. Rackham in
             LCL 330:183, 185, slightly modified, cit. Denzey Lewis, "Facing the Beast," 181).

        For his criticism of blind belief in astrology and divination, see *Nat.* 2.23–25.

72   Plin. *Nat.* 2.18, tr. Rackham in LCL 330:181. For the dedication of the work to Vespasian, see
        Nat. praef.1–11. For praise of Livy's service in writing for the Roman nation, see ibid., praef.
        16.

73   Marchetti, *Plinio il Vecchio*, 25; Beagon, *Roman Nature*, 31.

WHICH GOD CARES FOR YOU AND ME? 69

human affairs.[74] Yet Pliny comes down on the side of belief in providence, and the special character of humanity:[75]

> Truly, it agrees with life's experience to believe that in these matters the gods exercise an interest in human affairs; and that punishment for wickedness—though sometimes tardy, since God is occupied with such a heap of things—yet is never in vain; and that humanity was not born His next of kin for the purpose of keeping the company of beasts in baseness. But the chief consolations for nature's imperfection in the case of humanity are that not even for God are all things possible ...[76]

In this discussion, Pliny seeks to have it both ways: he rejects the *accoutrements* of sacrificial cult while affirming the providence of the Emperor, by identifying providential intervention as manifest in nothing other than the (ostensibly) virtuous action of the Roman leader.

Other passages of the *Natural History* are consistent with this view. The preface of the work holds that divine care for individuals can be seen throughout all the natural world, but that such care is not anthropocentric.[77] An introduction to the geography of Italy does not neglect the opportunity to pay homage to "Rome, the capital of the world." "I am well aware," Pliny exclaims,

> that I may with justice be considered ungrateful and lazy if I describe in this casual and cursory manner a land which is at once the nursling and mother of all other lands, chosen by the providence of the gods (*numine deum electa*) to make heaven itself more glorious, to unite scattered empires, to make manners gentle, to draw together in conversation by trade of language the jarring and uncouth tongues of so many nations, to give humanity civilization, and—in short—to become throughout the world the single fatherland of all the peoples. But what am I to do?[78]

Another remarkable passage presents itself in Pliny's account of how the general Marcus Sergius consistently triumphed over his enemies in battle despite literally crippling wounds, thanks in part to his use of a prosthetic hand. "All

---

74 Plin. *Nat.* 2.20.
75 Cf. Marchetti, *Plinio il Vecchio*, 23–25, who focuses only on Pliny's criticism of religion.
76 Plin. *Nat.* 2.26–27, text and tr. Rackham in LCL 330:184–187, modified.
77 Beagon, *Roman Nature*, 38 re: Plin. *Nat.* Praef.14–15.
78 Plin. *Nat.* 3.39–40, text and tr. Rackham in LCL 352:30–33, slightly modified.

other victors truly have conquered men, but Sergius vanquished fortune also."[79] Providence smiles on the virtuous—particularly, virtuous Romans.

Despite their diverse circumstances and literary aims, for Polybius, Diodorus Siculus, and Pliny the Elder alike, language about fortune and providence doubles as describing the parallel involvement of rulers and of the gods in individual lives.[80] Scholarship often reflects on the extent to which these authors' work bears the influence of 'Stoicism,' albeit in such attenuated senses that the word carries little meaning. Rather, it is clear that these historians—writing with some knowledge of philosophy but outside of the immediate rhetorical context of philosophy—found compelling the rhetoric of divine care for particulars, as is manifest in political history, and especially Roman rule. For Diodorus and Pliny, such care is articulated as care for the Romans on account of their *virtus*—a transformation of a more concretely Stoic notion.[81] Remarkably, this ease with which Roman historical writers living under the later Republic and early Empire extended providential care to individuals may explain the curious cases of philosophers who, writing as philosophers, rejected God's care for individuals, but writing in other contexts, affirmed it. As we saw in the previous section, Plutarch assigned providential care for individuals not to gods, but *daimones*.[82] Yet when he wrote as a historian, he made wide use of distinctly un-philosophical understandings of *pronoia*.[83] In *On the Fortune of the*

---

79   Plin. *Nat.* 7.28.106, tr. Rackham in LCL 352:575; see Beagon, *Roman Nature*, 121.

80   Further examples of this could be adduced; see Cassius Dio 43.17.5 (on Caesar); similarly ibid., 66.11.1 (Vespasian). Dio Chrysostom, *On Kingship iii* (*Oratio 3*) 41, 50, 62. On the latter, see Charlesworth, "Providentia et Aeternitas," 117; van Nuffelen, *Rethinking*, 148–153.

81   Although Beagon is strictly correct that Pliny believes "*Fortuna/Natura* distributes her favours in life without any regard for just deserts," this does not mean that virtue for him is simply "its own reward" (*Roman Nature*, 123). As much is made clear in the passages on providence cited above, regarding divine punishment and Rome's primacy (Plin. *Nat.* 2.26–27, 3.39–40, respectively).

82   Another example presents itself in the figure of Apuleius of Madaura. Writing as a philosopher, he argued that divine interference in human affairs is beneath God's dignity, left rather to the *daimones* (*Deo Socr.* 127–137, re: Plat. *Symp.* 203a; see further Harrison, *Apuleius*, 151–152. I thank John F. Finamore for the reference). Yet he gives an entirely different picture in the *Metamorphoses*, where the *fortuna* that leads Lucius from travail to travail is eventually overcome by Isis's *providentia* upon his conversion to the cult of the goddess. A perennial question in the study of the work, then, is whether one can reconcile its presentation of providence and fortune with the views on *daimones* and fate Apuleius relates in his strictly philosophical works. The question and its attendant bibliography are too large to tackle here (see recently Graverini, "*Prudentia* and *Providentia*."; Drews, "Asinus Philosophans"), but the present analysis reminds us that literary convention may have been at least as important for Apuleius as philosophical consistency.

83   Cf. Simonetti, who sees apparently no discrepancy between Plutarch's ideas as expressed

WHICH GOD CARES FOR YOU AND ME? 71

Romans, he personifies *tuchē* as an actor which overturns the status quo, or gives armies to cowards.[84] He even implies that Roman dominion is the work of providence itself.[85] The deeply political and personal connotations of language about providence thus are evident beyond the Stoa, amongst Greek and Roman historians as well as philosophers who formally rejected the notion of divine intervention. Such connotations were without a doubt also understood by—and problematic for—those Hellenophone authors who were also Jews.

4   A Different God, Present and Absent in Hellenistic Jewish Literature

The *Epistle of Aristeas*, a document most likely composed by an Alexandrian Jew in the second century BCE, records the famous legend of the commissioning of the translation of the Hebrew Bible into Greek by the Hellenistic Egyptian monarch Ptolemy II (Philadelpheus, 285–247 BCE).[86] This legend— wherein God intervenes in ensuring the consonance of the seventy Jewish translators of the Bible from Hebrew to Greek—would become a staple of early Christian apologetic.[87] 'Aristeas' begins by imploring Ptolemy to free 100,000 Jewish prisoners of war in Egypt, on grounds that they worship the same God

---

in the contexts of philosophy and historical writing (*A Perfect Medium?*, 166–168) other than that "the precise relation between providence (πρόνοια) and other earthly powers (such as fortune, or human deliberation) remains fundamentally obscure" (ibid., 168).

84   Plut. *Fort. Rom.* 316a–c, 325d–326a; idem, *On the Fortune and Virtue of Alexander the Great*, 336b; *pace* Swain, "Plutarch," 276–279; idem, *Hellenism and Empire*, 160 ("Plutarch's thoughts about providential interference in the world ... owe little or nothing to comparable earlier writers like Polybius, Posidonius, Livy, or Dionysius of Halicarnassus"). However, Plutarch is free with his terminology in the *Moralia*, using, for example, *tuchē* where one might expect *pronoia*, to designate a divine guiding force (Swain, "Plutarch," 273). On *tuchē* in the *Lives*, see Brenk, "Religious Spirit," 305–316; Gasparro, "*Daimôn* and *Tuchê*," 67–68.

85   Even if one discounts *Fort. Rom.* as an early work, see the analysis of Swain, *Hellenism and Empire*, 157–161; idem, "Plutarch," 286–287; more recently, Simonetti, *A Perfect Medium?*, 167–168; van Nuffelen reads Plutarch as more ambivalent here (*Rethinking*, 159), but for ample citations on Plutarch's belief in the general benevolence of Roman rule, see Aalders, *Plutarch's Political Thought*, 54–58. For review of the literature about Plutarch and politics, see de Blois, "Perception," 4573–4578.

86   On the date of the *Let. Arist.*, see e.g. Wright, *Letter*, 21–30, esp. 27–28. Schmitz emphasizes that the (likely Jewish) author of the text need not be identified with the character of Aristeas in the work, even though its narrator is 'Aristeas' himself ("Using Different Names").

87   *Let. Arist.* 407; Philo, *Mos.* 2.37; Ir. ap. Euseb. *Hist. eccl.* 5.8.14; Clem. Al. *Strom.* 1.22.149.2; all cit. Marcovich, "Introduction," 9.

for whom the Greeks have many names, even though one and the same being is the "overseer and creator of all things."[88] As Barbara Schmitz argues, 'Aristeas' employs a loosely Stoic notion of God as a universal monarch (akin to the Zeus of Cleanthes's *Hymn to Zeus*) in his appeal to Ptolemy.[89] Won over, the king invites a team of Jewish translators from Jerusalem to Egypt, and seventy-two of them—six for each of the twelve tribes of Israel—arrive in Alexandria, where they are welcomed with a banquet (*sumposion*) that lasts seven days. During the symposium, Ptolemy poses philosophical questions about politics, ethics, and dialectic to the translators, whose sage responses repeatedly emphasize that God is the creator of the universe and the source of all virtue. At the end of the first day of the party, the king is struck with delight at the wisdom of the translators, "all of them making God the starting point of their reasoning." A philosopher by name of "Menedemus of Eritrea" then turns Ptolemy's words around on him: "indeed, O King. For since all things are governed by providence, and assuming this correctly, that human beings are created by God, it follows that all sovereignty and beautiful speech have a starting point in God."[90] Just as a Hellenistic ruler ought to act providentially towards his or her subjects, so is God the supreme sovereign and the source of all sovereignty—even of that of Ptolemy himself.[91] The author of *Aristeas* here makes a deeply subversive claim: there is indeed a universal, providential God who validates terrestrial rulers, as the Stoa maintain, but it is not Zeus; it is the God of Israel.

The earliest Jewish literature which discusses *pronoia* belongs, like Aristeas, to roughly the same era as the Stoic, Platonic, and historical sources discussed so far in this chapter—the later Roman Republic and earliest Empire (second cent. BCE–first century CE), a deeply transformational period for the Israelites, who reckoned first with Hellenism and then Roman rule. Like the author of *Aristeas*, Jews were forced to negotiate their beliefs about God's involvement in the world with their experiences of military domination from without and the pressure to assimilate from within. Roughly two perspectives on divine care can be discerned in literature from these centuries. On the one hand, sapiential works like Ben Sira (Sirach) and the Wisdom of Solomon affirm that the God of Israel is very much directly involved in worldly matters, particularly the history

---

88   *Let. Arist.* 15–16, tr. Wright, *Letter*, 122.
89   Schmitz, "Using Different Names," 706–709.
90   *Let. Arist.* 200–201, tr. Wright, *Letter*, 336–337.
91   Thus Wright, *Letter*, 348; see also Bergjan, *Der fürsorgende Gott*, 108, n. 9. On Menedemus, see Wright, op. cit. 351–352. The passage is often cited with no interpretation beyond the observation that Menedemus speaks of *pronoia* at all (e.g., Aitken, "Divine Will," 284).

WHICH GOD CARES FOR YOU AND ME? 73

of Israel and its people.[92] According to Sirach, God has created and determined everything from the beginning (Sir 16:26–27). He controls human behavior on the scale of individuals (33:11–12): "the Lord marked them off and made their ways different. Some of them he blessed and exalted ... some of them he cursed and brought low."[93] Earthly governments and history are beholden to God as well: "In the Lord's hand is the governance of the earth, and he will raise up over it the person useful for the time ... Dominion is transferred from nation to nation on account of injustice and insolence and money ..." (10:4.8; also 10:14–17). The work climaxes with a hymn that mixes themes of divine agency in creation, the goodness of creation, and divine direction of worldly events and human history (39:16–34).[94]

Yet on the other hand, Sirach vss 15:11–20 argues that humans are responsible for their own actions; no one is destined to do evil:

> Do not say, "on account of the Lord I fell away," for what he hates, he will not do ... It was he who from the beginning made humankind, and he left him in the hand of his deliberation (*diabouliou autou*) ... Before humans are life and death, and whichever one he desires shall be given to him, because great is the wisdom of the Lord; he is mighty in dominance and one who sees everything (*blepōn ta panta*). And his eyes are on those who fear him, and he will know every human deed. He did not command anyone to be impious, and he did not give anyone leave to sin.[95]

Given its insistence on human autonomy despite God's determination of human affairs high and low alike, one may fairly dub Sirach a compatibilist text.[96] Some have gone further and raised the question of its relationship to Stoicism, particularly given its identification of God's foreknowledge with God's

---

92 Jewish 'Wisdom' literature is generally taken to encompass the textual group of Proverbs, Qoheleth, Job, Ben Sira, and Wisdom of Solomon (Collins, "Wisdom," 1). Although it is a problematic and amorphous category (ibid.; see also Dell, "Wisdom," 413), it is reasonable to group these works given their concern about something they call "Wisdom" (Macaskill, *Revealed Wisdom*, 20). From there, one may provisionally describe the group's formal characteristics as "proverbial sentence or instruction, debate, intellectual reflection" that address "human betterment, groping after life's secrets with regard to innocent suffering, grappling with finitude, and quest for truth concealed in the created order and manifested in Dame Wisdom" (Crenshaw, *Old Testament*, 19).

93 See further Aitken, "Divine Will," 296–297.

94 Wicke-Reuter, "Ben Sira," 275; Aitken, "Divine Will," 286.

95 On this passage, see e.g. Moore, "Fate," 380; Aitken, "Divine Will," 289.

96 So recently Klawans, *Josephus*, 59; without using the term 'compatibilist,' so Mattila, "Ben Sira," 480–481; Aitken, "Divine Will," 285–286.

care.[97] Yet Sirach also disagrees with Stoicism on important points,[98] above all through its opening maxim: "the beginning of wisdom is fearing the Lord" (Sir 1:14a, 16a, 20a). That one must fear the divine is itself a strange enough notion in the Greek philosophical tradition—all the more so when it is in turn identified with obeying the Mosaic Law.[99] The understanding of wisdom as fear of God, and of this fear in turn with keeping the commandments has strong precedent in Deuteronomy and Proverbs.[100] However stirring Sirach's compatibilist musings may be, they clearly identify God as the God of Moses and Israelite cult.

The Wisdom of Solomon, composed somewhere between 30 BCE–50 CE,[101] is no less shy about firmly identifying the God of Israel as the only true deity, even as it goes beyond Sirach in using unmistakably Stoic language—including that of providence—to explain His terrestrial activity. Here, divine Wisdom "pervades and penetrates all things ... and orders all things well (*diēkei de kai chōrei dia pantōn ... dioikei ta panta chrēstōs*)" (Wis 7:24, 8:1).[102] She is an intelligent breath that pervades the world, like the *pneuma* of the Stoics.[103] Like the figure of Wisdom in Proverbs, Wisdom here is a hypostasized co-administrator, "present when You created the universe," and the agent by whom God "formed human beings."[104] Wis 14:3 denotes God's administration of human affairs as providence, probably the earliest known use of the Greek word in this sense by a Jewish author:[105] "it is your providence (*pronoia*), Father, that pilots (the world)." Yet as in Sir, God is not responsible for sin; "God did not make death" (1:13).[106] Rather, "through the envy of the devil, death entered the world, and those who belong to his party experience it" (2:24). Through Wisdom, God

---

97   Most recently Wicke-Reuter, "Ben Sira," 274.

98   Sirach's emphasis on divine retribution (Sir 11:23–28) could be seen as at odds with Stoicism (Mattila, "Ben Sira," 479–480), but one might respond that for the Stoa, the experience of wickedness itself could be read as a divine punishment.

99   Mattila, "Ben Sira," 491, re: 1:26; 2:15–16; 7:31; 10:19; 15:15; 19:20; 21:11; 23:27; 32:16.23–24; 33:2–3; 35:1–2; 41:8.

100   Mattila, "Ben Sira," 491, re: Deut 10:12–13; 30:16; Prov 1:7.29; 2:5; 9:10; 14:16; 15:33.

101   Winston, *Wisdom*, 23–25, 59.

102   See further Wis 6:7, 14:3, 17:2; Sir 24:3–7. See Scheffczyk, *Schöpfung und Vorsehung*, 11 n. 33; Walsh, "Introduction," 12; Winston, *Wisdom*, 189–190, 265; Frick, *Divine Providence*, 12–13; Bergjan, *Der fürsorgende Gott*, 113; Ferguson, *Providence of God*, 19.

103   Winston, "Philo and the Wisdom," 114; Mattila, "Ben Sira," 487. This is not to say there is no sense of divine transcendence in Wis; see the rejection of pantheism at 13:1–2; also Winston, *Wisdom*, 60.

104   Wis 9:9, 2; see also 8:3, 9:4, Prov 8:22, 8:27–31; Schäfer, *Mirror*, 25–26, 34; cf. Winston, *Wisdom*, 193–194, 205.

105   Scheffczyk, *Schöpfung und Vorsehung*, 11 n. 33; Frick, *Divine Providence*, 12–13; Bergjan, *Der fürsorgende Gott*, 113; Klawans, *Josephus*, 47.

106   See further Sutcliffe, *Providence and Suffering*, 124.

always has and always shall punish the sinner and reward the pious: "for grievous is the end of an unrighteous generation" (3:19).[107]

The author of Wis admits that it is difficult to understand God's plan, but is clear that God intervenes on behalf of Israel, as the liberation from Egypt shows: "For great are your judgments and hard to explain; therefore uninstructed souls have gone astray. For when lawless people thought to oppress a holy nation, they themselves lay as captives of darkness and prisoners of long night, shut in under their roofs, fugitives from eternal providence (*phugades tēs aiōniou pronoias*)" (Wis 17:1–2; see also 17:17; cf. Ex 10:21–23).[108] The author alludes to the hardening of Pharaoh's heart, following the departure of the Jews to Sinai, for God "knew in advance what was to happen in respect of them (i.e., the Egyptians), how, having given (the Jews) permission to be away and having eagerly sent them on their way, they would change their minds and pursue them" (19:1–2). Notably, God here does not make the decision for the Egyptians, but knows in advance what they would do, an approach to the story that would be taken up by Christian philosophers as well (see below, chapter five).

Sirach and the Wisdom of Solomon present an omnipotent, omniscient, omnipresent God who actively intervenes in history, and the latter text even uses the term *pronoia* to designate this intervention. For both works, though, it is clear that the God of Israel—and not Zeus, or any other 'foreign' deity, however 'universal' the Stoa may proclaim Him to be—is the "supreme sovereign and the source of all sovereignty" extolled by the author of *Aristeas*. These writers relocated providence from Hellenistic (or Roman) rule to the God of Israel. This was unusual even within the context of biblical literature itself; Jewish legends of the Hellenistic period present a second, more ambivalent picture of divine involvement in the world, even as it maintains God's ultimate sovereignty.[109] The book of Tobit (third–second century BCE),[110] for instance, states that "there is nothing that will escape his hand" (13:2).[111] Thus one modern interpreter clarifies "Tobit's assertion of divine providence" as constituting

---

107 On the juridical aspect of divine (providential) power in Wis 3–6, see Bergjan, *Der fürsorgende Gott*, 112–115.

108 For another catalogue of Wisdom's interventions in history, see Wis 10:1–21; so Winston, "Philo and the Wisdom," 127; cf. also Elliott, *Providence Perceived*, 6.

109 I thank J.W. van Henten for this insight, and for alerting me to the work of Barbara Schmitz on this point.

110 A *terminus ante quem* for the text is furnished by the dating of the scribal hands of the Aramaic fragments of the book discovered at Qumran, but a *terminus post quem* is more difficult to establish. For *Forschungsgeschichte*, see recently Perrin, "Almanac," 113–115.

111 Cit. Schellenberg, "Suspense," 313.

"a world are fully ordered, a world in which every lack has its corresponding fulfillment ... each element is integrated into God's comprehensive plan."[112] Yet no word for 'providence' actually appears in Tobit, and, as Barbara Schmitz has argued, God Himself does not actually appear, or even communicate, in this work. The same is true of later (i.e., second or first century BCE) Hellenophone Jewish works found in the Septuagint, such as Judith, or 1 and 2 Maccabees.[113] Even a recent, maximalist reading of divine activity in Judith and Esther has to admit that divine care is not explicit in the texts but must be read into them.[114] The identification of the divine with the god of Israelite cult did not necessarily connote an active, 'personal' God, much less any notion of 'providence' in Jewish literature where the terminology of providence is absent.

5 "So You Do Not Neglect the Nation of the Jews after All!": Philo of Alexandria

That most prolific of Hellenized Jewish authors, the Philo of Alexandria (25 BCE–50 CE), takes divine providence—and the difficulties it presents—as one of his central operating concepts for philosophical exploration of creation and Jewish history, even as he appears to express some ambivalence as to how and to what extent it actually operates.[115] On the one hand, Philo often portrays God as very personal indeed, exercising providence over individuals and intervening in history—particularly the history of His favored people, the Jews. On the other, he is often wary of assigning too much responsibility to God, preferring to assign responsibility for cosmic faults and evil to intermediary beings or simply humans themselves.[116] Significantly, these two approaches meet in a very Stoic locus: Philo's identification of the rational faculty and concomi-

---

112   Schellenberg, "Suspense," 327.
113   According to Schmitz, Tob, Jdt, and 1–2 Macc "kennen also eine aktive handelnde Figur Gott (praktisch) nicht und füllen das damit entstandene Vakuum der traditionellen und zentralen biblischen Vorstellung des in der Geschichte handelnden Gottes auf höchst unterschiedliche Weise" ("Gott als Figur," 230). Even in LXX Esth, God only intervenes on the margins, and like the four aforementioned deuterocanonical texts, God does not speak directly (ibid., 233–234).
114   Melton, *Where is God*, 149–150.
115   Space does not permit a sustained engagement here of further Hellenophone Jewish texts about providence, such as 3 Macc 4:21, 5:30; 4 Macc 9:24, 13:19, 17:22; *Sib. Or.* 5.227, 5.323; cit. and discussed in Klawans, *Josephus*, 47; Bergjan, *Der fürsorgende Gott*, 108; Ferguson, *Providence of God*, 19.
116   For Philo's wariness of implying that God causes evil, see *On the Preliminary Studies*, 171; *QG* 1.55, 1.89; *Fug.* 69; *Praem.* 32, all cit. Runia, *Philo*, 139.

WHICH GOD CARES FOR YOU AND ME? 77

tant acts of virtue with divine providence, as described in his exegesis of the creation of humanity.

Philo is assured, for instance, of providential care for the cosmos and human beings in *On the Creation of the World*: "God cares for the world (*pronoei tou kosmou ho theos*). For it is necessary, by all laws and ordinances of Nature, that a maker should always care for what he has made (*epimeleisthai gar aei ... anagkaion*), and it is in accordance with them that parents should care for their children."[117] The parental metaphor is not used lightly, for Philo explicitly states that divine care extends to individuals: in *On the Special Laws*, he writes that God "exercises providence over both the whole and the parts."[118] Providence favors the virtuous: "Scripture says that they (i.e., the virtuous) who do 'what is pleasing' to nature and what is 'good' are sons of God. For it says, 'Ye are sons to your Lord God' (Deut 14:1), clearly meaning that He will think fit to protect and provide for you as would a father."[119] In fact, "virtue, without God's care (*aneu theias epiphrosunēs*) is insufficient of itself to do us good."[120]

Philo recounts many examples of divine care for individuals in the history of Israel. God intervenes specifically to demonstrate his special providential care for the Jews, as when he made Sarah barren so that Abraham's children would be born out of providence, not any human activity, so as to demonstrate divine power.[121] Similarly, Joseph wisely concludes that his travails ultimately were wrought not by his brothers' machinations, but by God's providence, as part of his road to good fortune.[122] Above all, providence plays a starring role in the *Life of Moses*, where it is identified with the means by which the prophet and lawgiver to the Jewish people receives special guidance and aid from God.[123] The miracle of the plague of flies (Ex 8:20–24) was intensified by God so that

---

117　Philo, *Opif*. 171–172, text and tr. Colson and Whitaker in LCL 226:136–137, modified. Similarly, idem, *Prov*. 2.4–6.

118　*Pronooumenos kai tou holou kai tōn merōn* (Philo, *Spec*. 3.189, text and tr. Colson in LCL 320:594–595, slightly modified). See also idem, *Her*. 300–301 (God steers all things, like a ship); *Opif*. 46 (God guides everything like a charioteer or farmer—so Radice, "Philo's Theology," 130). For Philo's emphasis on the monarchial, autocratic notion of providential rule, see *De decalogo* 155, as discussed by van Nuffelen, *Rethinking*, 208; Niehoff, *Philo*, 103.

119　Philo, *Spec*. 1.318, tr. Colson in LCL 320:285; similarly, *Sobr*. 18, 63. On these passages, see Frick, *Divine Providence*, 172–173, 178.

120　Philo, *Det*. 61, tr. Colson in LCL 227:245; see Frick, *Divine Providence*, 183.

121　Philo, *QG* 3.18; for discussion, see Frick, *Divine Providence*, 182.

122　Philo, *Ios*. 236; similarly ibid., 99; see Frick, *Divine Providence*, 183–184; Ewing, *Clement*, 46–47.

123　See also Philo, *On the Migration of Abraham*, 171.

its affliction was "due not only to nature but to divine care."[124] Provisions in the wilderness were furnished provided by providence.[125] Upon descending from Mount Sinai with the Ten Commandments, Moses "had become, by divine providence, a living and thinking law."[126] It is *pronoia* that gives Moses the offices of king, lawgiver, priest, and prophet.[127] It also offers Moses special, prophetic insight that transcends what he would be able to uncover by reasoning alone.[128] Such passages recall the invocations of divine care for Greek and Roman heroes uttered by, say, Cicero or Plutarch, as discussed above, in this chapter. Philo knew historical writing and its conventions. Like Polybius and Plutarch, he used the word *tuchē* to denote the rise and fall of empires in world history.[129] A hypothetical first-century, gentile reader of the *Life of Moses* could certainly recall the divine favor enjoyed by virtuous, Roman leaders—this may even have been Philo's point.

At the same time, more is at stake in these moments for Philo than genre clichés. First, Philo seeks not only to explain Jewish piety in the service of Hellenistic apologetics, but to establish, as a Jewish philosopher, that the central story of God's providential activity is Israel's history. This story is not only recounted in Scripture, per the *Life of Moses*, but in contemporary life. An example of the latter presents itself in his work *Flaccus*, a takedown of Aulus Avilius Flaccus, who was appointed prefect of Egypt by Tiberius in 32 CE, serving until his fall from power and execution by Caligula in 39 CE.[130] Philo relates that Flaccus horribly mistreated Egyptian Jews, climaxing in pogroms in Alexandria in 38 CE; yet Flaccus is then deposed, suffers many torments, and finally, "possessed as in a Corybantic frenzy," cries to heaven:

> King of gods and humankind! So you do not neglect the nation of the Jews after all, nor do they falsely speak of your providence; rather, those who say that they do not regard you as champion and defender have

---

124   *Ouketi monon tois phusikois ... alla kai tois ek theias epiphrosunēs* (Philo, *Mos.* 1.132, text and tr. Colson in LCL 289:344–345, slightly modified).

125   Philo, *Mos.* 1.211. For citation and discussion of many of the following passages, see Frick, *Divine Providence*, 184–185.

126   *Autos egineto nomos empsuchos te kai logikos theiai pronoiai* (Philo, *Mos.* 1.162, text and tr. Colson in LCL 289:358–359, modified). This passage is related in Christianized form by Clement of Alexandria (*Strom.* 1.26; see Frick, *Divine Providence*, 184; Ewing, *Clement*, 42 n. 120).

127   Philo, *Mos.* 2.3.

128   Philo, *Mos.* 2.6.

129   Philo, *Deus* 173–176, cit. Winston, "Philo and the Wisdom," 129.

130   On the historical background of *Flaccus*, see van der Horst, "Introduction," 18–38.

WHICH GOD CARES FOR YOU AND ME? 79

completely lost their minds. And I am a clear proof of it, for whatever insanities I have committed against the Jews I have suffered myself![131]

Philo describes in gruesome detail the punishment of the wicked enemies of the Jews, proof of God's care. While Philo, interestingly enough, never seems to tackle the problem of God's hardening of Pharaoh's heart, he does insert an argument against providence into Pharaoh's mouth, without naming him:

> Such was he who said, 'who is He that I should obey Him,' and again, 'I know not the Lord' (Ex 5:2). In the first of these utterances he asserts there is no God; in the second that even if there is a God he is not known to us, which follows in turn from the supposition that there is no providence. For if He cared, He would be known.[132]

Modern commentators on this passage recall the Epicurean denial of providence, but this only applies to Pharaoh's second statement, since the Epicureans never denied the gods' existence; they denied the gods' involvement (*pronoia*).[133] As a paragon of wickedness in the ancient Jewish imagination, Pharaoh's first statement here recalls the wicked of Psalm 73—wicked men behave as if there is no God.

Yet Philo does not explain tales of the miraculous in a philosophically haphazard fashion. Several examples present themselves in the *Life of Moses*. Miracles are copious in this work, but, Philo explains, they are no problem for God, since He "has subject to Him not one portion of the whole universe (*moira tou pantos*), but the whole world and its parts (*ta toutou merē*), to minister as slaves to their master for every service that He wills."[134] The language here is that of Plato's *Laws*, and of the Stoa: providential care and divine control unambiguously extends to particulars. On the other hand, Philo takes care to safeguard the transcendence of the deity in his rendering of the miracle of the burning bush, in whose flame Moses beholds "a form of the fairest beauty ... It might

---

131 Philo, *Flacc.* 170, text and tr. Colson in LCL 363:394–395, significantly modified; see also *Flacc.* 125–126, 191. For commentary, van der Horst, "Introduction," 1–2, 16–17, 45–46 and idem, "Commentary" 144, 201–202 (on providence in *Flacc.* as well as its sequel, *Leg.*), 234–236 (on *Flacc.* 170); more widely, Frick, *Divine Providence*, 185–189.

132 ... *Ei gar prounoei, kan eginōsketo* (Philo, *Ebr.* 19, text and tr. Colson and Whitaker in LCL 247:328–329, significantly modified).

133 Cf. Dragona-Monachou, "Divine Providence," 4457; Frick, *Divine Providence*, 47–48, also re: Philo, *Opif.* 172, vis-à-vis Cic. *Nat. d.* 2.75–77.

134 Philo, *Mos.* 1.202, text and tr. Colson in LCL 289:380–381, modified. On God's absolute control over the universe and His ability to work miracles, see also *Mos.* 1.212–213; 2.261.

be supposed that this was the image of He who Is; but let us rather call it an angel (*aggelos*), since, with a silence that spoke more clearly than speech, it employed as it were the miracle of sight to herald future events," insofar as the flame signified the wicked (i.e., the Egyptians), and the bramble those who suffer torment, but survive and eventually prevail (i.e., the Jews). "The angel was a symbol of God's providence (*pronoias ek theou*), which serenely alleviates great dangers, beyond everyone's expectation."[135] Similarly, in the *Hypothetica*, it is "by daimonic inspiration (*kata daimona*)" that the Jews are inspired to return to their "ancient, native country."[136] Philo assimilates the providential *daimones*, who act as divinely-appointed overseers of the cosmos, to the angels of the nations (Deut 32:8).[137] He also appears to know the analogy of the 'Great King' of Pseudo-Aristotle's *On the World* and to regard the biblical angels as this regent's satraps, serving as His eyes and ears.[138] Angels are protectors of mortals.[139]

In other words, Philo is unequivocal about God's care being personal, but he often takes a step back and adds that this personal care is effected through mediators. That his motivation is philosophical—to safeguard God from direct responsibility, via the insertion of semi-divine mediators—is perhaps most evident in his remarks on demiurgy. To be sure, Philo agrees with Plato and the Stoics that divine providence is manifest in creation,[140] and characterizes God Himself with reference to His creative activity.[141] It is by this creative activity that we know God at all: the patriarch Abraham, he writes, sought "not after God's essence—for that would be impossible—but after His existence and providence."[142] As the Stoa argued, our senses ought to lead us to recognize the existence of a creator and His care for creation.[143] He also uses the 'design argument,' referring to the fortunate location of the intestines between the human's stomach and buttocks.[144] He often employs the metaphor of a caring, provi-

---

135 Philo, *Mos.* 1.66–67, text and tr. Colson in LCL 289:310–311, significantly modified; see also Frick, *Divine Providence*, 53.

136 Philo, *De hypothetica*, 6.1, text Colson in LCL 363:414, tr. mine.

137 Philo, *Somn.* 1.140–141. For this citation and those of the following two notes, I am indebted to Timotin, *Démonologie platonicienne*, 110–111, 129.

138 Philo, *Opif.* 71. See further van Nuffelen, *Rethinking*, 210.

139 Philo, *On Giants*, 16–18. Cf. Ps 91:11; Louth, "Pagans and Christians on Providence," 286.

140 Radice, "Philo's Theology," 133–134; cf. Feldmeier, "Wenn die Vorsehung," 155.

141 Philo, *Cher.* 77; idem, *Leg.* 1.5. See Frick, *Divine Providence*, 42–43; also Runia, *Philo*, 438–444.

142 *Ouchi tēs ousias—touto gar amēchanon—alla tēs huparxeōs autou kai pronoias* (Philo, *Virt.* 215–216; see Frick, *Divine Providence*, 45; Ewing, *Clement*, 46).

143 Philo, *QG* 2.34. See Frick, *Divine Providence*, 99–100; Runia, *Philo*, 101, 241, esp. 458–461.

144 Philo, *QG* 2.7. On the argument from design, see *Opif.* 9; Niehoff, *Philo*, 97–98, 105–106.

WHICH GOD CARES FOR YOU AND ME?

dent father or parent to describe God as creator,[145] as when he remarks in *On the Special Laws* that "God is good—creator, father of the wholes (*tōn holōn*), and caring for (*pronoētikos*) the things he has begotten."[146]

Peter Frick has considered this passage to be the exception which proves the rule that Philo usually emphasizes God's transcendence,[147] although perhaps what is implied is that God is more focused on wholes than individuals. Philo often identifies God's providential activity as a secondary entity, the Word (*logos*). This entity is known by many names in Philo's writing. "The Image of God is the Word (*logos d'estin eikōn theou*) through whom the whole world was built (*edēmiourgeito*)."[148] He often refers to *logos* as a tool or device, as in *On the Cherubim*, where Philo remarks that the world was made by use of the tool *logos*, although God is its architect (*dēmiourgou*).[149] Elsewhere, the *logos* is an angel (likely confirming it to have been the presence in the burning bush).[150] This same being also constitutes one of God's two powers (*dunameis*), which appear to serve as hypostases of divine character: on the right there is the *logos*, which is merciful and creative; on the left is *dunamis*, which is punitive and regal.[151] Philo's *logos* is often associated or even identified with Wisdom (*sophia*).[152]

---

145 Philo, *Opif.* 9–10, 171–172 (the latter quoted above, in this chapter); *Praem.* 42; *Ebr.* 13; cit. Frick, *Divine Providence*, 49–51; Bergjan, *Der fürsorgende Gott*, 39–42; Niehoff, *Philo*, 100–102.

146 Philo, *Spec.* 1.209, text Colson in LCL 320:218, tr. mine.

147 Frick, *Divine Providence*, 51–52.

148 Philo, *Spec.* 1.81, text and tr. Colson in LCL 320:146–147, slightly modified.

149 ... *organon de logon theou di'hou kataskeuasthēi* ... (Philo, *Cher.* 127). See further *Fug.* 66–71 (quoted below); idem, *Conf.* 169, 171–175, 182; esp. *Her.* 133–229; Dragona-Monachou, "Divine Providence," 4458; Radice, "Philo's Theology," 137–138; Litwa, "The God 'Human'," 79–80; most extensively, O'Brien, *Demiurge*, 43–56.

150 Philo, *Cher.* 3, 35; idem, *Mut.* 87; *Fug.* 5; *Deus* 182. For *logos* as an archangel, see *Her.* 205. All cit. Radice, "Philo's Theology," 140; O'Brien, *Demiurge*, 44.

151 Philo, *Cher.* 27–28; idem, *QE* 2.68; see Frick, *Divine Providence*, 72 n. 57, 73, 113. Frick argues that the providential power is to be understood as subordinate, along with the beneficial and punitive, if one recalls *QE* 2.68, where the creative and royal are clearly considered to be the source of the other powers, as well as if one considers the order of the powers listed (*Divine Providence*, 82).

152 For *logos* and *sophia* together at the beginning of creation, see Philo, *Fug.* 101; idem, *Her.* 205; *Det.* 54; *Virt.* 62; *Conf.* 146; cit. and discussion in Denzey (Lewis), "Genesis Traditions," 28; O'Brien, *Demiurge*, 47. Sometimes *sophia* is the source of *logos*, sometimes the other way around: *Somn.* 2.242; *Fug.* 108–109, 146; *Leg.* 1.43; cit. Denzey (Lewis), "Genesis Traditions," 28 n. 39; cf. Winston, "Philo and the Wisdom," 128 (giving priority to *logos*). The two are identified at *Leg.* 1.65 (cit. Radice, "Philo's Theology," 139).

82   CHAPTER 2

Although he never explicitly states that *logos* is the agent of God's *pronoia*, Philo describes divine activity in a way that demands some such inference.[153] Noting Philo's statement that God is *pronoētikos*, Frick suggests that *logos* is the 'immanent' activity of God's providence.[154] Some kind of activity must lie behind his free discussions of divine interventions in history, and his claim in *Allegorical Interpretation* that God directly gives benefits to mortals, "but (gives) the things that concern getting rid of evils through angels and *logoi*."[155] The notion—surely inspired by the *Timaeus*—that God must hold Himself back from dealing with nasty things like material substance, even in creation, is invoked by Philo in *On the Special Laws*:

> For when out of that confused matter God produced all things, it was hands-off (*ouk ephaptomenos autos*), since His nature, happy and blessed as it was, forbade that He should touch the limitless, chaotic matter (*apeirou kai pephurmenēs hulēs*). Instead, He made full use of the incorporeal powers, well denoted by the name "forms" (*ideai*), to enable each species (*genos*) to take its appropriate shape ...[156]

Similarly, in *On Flight*, it is God's helpers (*sunergoi*) who created the irrational part of the soul—the part responsible for evil.[157] God himself grants humanity the Logos, i.e., the human rational soul, by blowing his *pneuma* into Adam's face (Gen 2.7):

---

153   On this problem, see Runia, *Philo*, 242, 482 n. 45; Frick, *Divine Providence*, 125–126; similarly, Feldmeier, "Wenn die Vorsehung," 154; Elliott, *Providence Perceived*, 7. Runia, op. cit. 242 suggests Philo, *On Agriculture*, 51, but Frick, op. cit. 116 n. 90 rightly states that there is no explicit mention of providence here. Radice assumes less consistency on Philo's part regarding God's transcendence, observing a tendency to go one way or another depending on "whether he is dependent on a biblical or a philosophical model at any given point in his exegesis" ("Philo's Theology," 127).

154   Frick, *Divine Providence*, 87; similarly, Radice, "Philo's Theology," 141.

155   Philo, *Leg.* 3.178, tr. Colson and Whitaker in LCL 226:421, modified; on this passage, cf. O'Brien, *Demiurge*, 47.

156   Philo, *Spec.* 1.209, tr. Colson in LCL 320:291, modified. On this passage, see Radice, "Philo's Theology," 143; O'Brien, *Demiurge*, 47. Nonetheless, this sets up a problem (never solved by Philo): "is the Logos the world of Ideas contained within the mind of God, or is the mind of God itself, the cause of the ordering of the world?" (Radice, op. cit.) For *logos*'s creation of the mortal genera, see *Opif.* 62–68; Winston, "Theodicy," 109. Meanwhile, there are other passages where Philo conceives of matter clearly as a source of disorder and problems, out of which only God can produce an ordered creation—a serious concession to Platonism. See Philo, *Spec.* 4.187; idem, *Plant.* 53; QG 1.55; Dragona-Monachou, "Divine Providence," 4460; Runia, *Philo*, 139. Cf. Frick, *Divine Providence*, 169–170.

157   Philo, *Opif.* 72–75; similarly, idem, *Fug.* 68–72 (quoted below); *Mut.* 30–32; *Conf.* 168–

For this reason, then, when (Moses) philosophized about the creation of the world, saying that everything came into being through God, he specified humanity alone as having been formed with other assistants. For he says, "God says, 'let us make humanity according to our image' (Gen 1.26)," showing multiple actors with the phrase "let us make." And so the Father of the wholes is conversing with his powers, those to whom he has given the mortal part of our soul to form by imitating his craft, while he formed the rational part in us, thinking it right that the ruling part in the soul be made by the ruler, and the subjected part of the soul by his subjects. And He also did as he liked with his powers not only for this reason, but because the human soul alone was meant to receive notions of evil and good, and to put into practice one set of them, if both are not possible. So He considered it necessary for the origin of evil to come from other creators, and for the origin of good to come from Him alone.[158]

The identity of these 'helpers' is never clarified throughout Philo's corpus,[159] although one must suppose they are at least like the "angels and *logoi*" who attend to unpleasant matters of administration. Conversely, just as providence is at work in the rational part of the soul, "it was right that the rational (part) of the human soul should be formed as an impression by the divine logos, since the God prior to the *logos* is superior to every rational nature."[160]

Like the authors of *Aristeas*, Sirach, and the Wisdom of Solomon, Philo identified the deity and its active, providential activity exclusively with the personal God of Israel he knew from the Septuagint. Philo believed that insofar as God is a God at all, God is a providential parent, a father, and that His greatest creation, humanity, is capable of rational behavior and thus taking part in the divine drama that is Jewish history. Thus, even when ruminating on divine mediators, Philo identifies the rational faculty with the providential agent—the *logos*—and therefore *pronoia* as most manifest in human life when a person behaves rationally, i.e., virtuously. It is helpful to recall in this context that evil really only enters Philo's world in the sense that it does in Stoicism—which is to say not much at all. His debt to Stoicism is most clear in his dialogue *On Providence*,

---

183; for discussion, see Runia, *Philo*, 242–249; Pearson, "Philo and Gnosticism," 323–330; Winston, "Theodicy," 106–109. The latter observes that only *LA* 1.41 makes clear that Philo probably means that the irrational soul is, in a sense, made by god (*hupo theou*), albeit not through his agency (*dia theou*). See also Frick, *Divine Providence*, 157–158.

158   Philo, *Fug.* 68–70, text and tr. Colson and Whitaker in LCL 275:46–49, modified.

159   On this problem, see e.g. Runia, *Philo*, 248; O'Brien, *Demiurge*, 68–69.

160   Philo, *QG* 2.62, tr. Marcus in LCL 380:150–151, slightly modified; cit. O'Brien, *Demiurge*, 73.

84 CHAPTER 2

where the character of Philo disputes the question of divine involvement in the cosmos with his nephew, Tiberius Alexander. The dialogue is preserved only in part, thanks to two extracts from Eusebius of Caesarea.[161] The first extract is brief, and appears to describe a creation-account familiar to readers of the *Timaeus*, where a good demiurge uses matter in just the right way.[162] The second account is longer: observing that the wicked appear to prosper, young Alexander doubts the existence of providence. His uncle responds that on the contrary, "God cares for human affairs,"[163] and makes his argument not with reference to revealed Scripture—biblical passages and Moses are never mentioned—but Greek philosophical arguments about theodicy, of markedly Stoic provenance.[164] According to Philo, ostensibly evil events, such as natural disasters or the rise and prospering of evil persons, only occur for the betterment of the world in the larger scheme of things.[165] Unpleasant, harmful animals exist to foster human virtue, like courage and fortitude.[166] Consequently, scholars have argued that Philo agrees with the Stoics that the only evils are moral—'the evil that men do.'[167] Where there is vice, there is no providence.

Significantly, Philo's treatise *On Providence* is largely concerned with assuaging doubts about divine care in the face of apparent worldly evil. Yet it says precious little about the life of virtue, save that it is its own reward.[168] Is the life lived under providence simply that of the Stoic sage, regardless of one's fidelity to Moses and the Law? Despite the glaring absence of references to Moses or Scripture in our extant fragments of *On Providence*, the work may

---

161 Useful remains the discussion of Colson in LCL 363:447–450; see also Runia, "Philo and Hellenistic Doxography," 297.

162 See also Runia, "Philo and Hellenistic Doxography," 300.

163 *Ton theon tōn anthrōpinōn epimeleisthai pragmatōn* (*Prov.* 2.72, text and tr. Colson in LCL 363:506–507, slightly modified).

164 For a similar reading of the Stoic background of *Prov.*, see Runia, "Philo and Hellenistic Doxography," 298; Niehoff, *Philo*, 74–76; cf. Ferguson's (unsubstantiated) claim that "here Platonic themes are allied to Jewish theological convictions" (*Providence of God*, 17; similarly Magris, *L'idea di destino*, 2:682).

165 Natural disasters: Philo, *Prov.* 2.53–54; cf. *Praem.* 32–34. See Frick, *Divine Providence*, 146; Dragona-Monachou, "Divine Providence," 4457, 4460. On the apparent prospering of evil men, see *Prov.* 2.3–22; Dragona-Monachou, op. cit. 4459; Magris, *L'idea di destino*, 2:687. on the Stoic background of the argument, see above, chapter 1, n. 89.

166 Philo, *Prov.* 2.56–61; on the Stoic background of the argument, see above, chapter 1, n. 90.

167 Frick, *Divine Providence*, 168, re: Philo, *On the Posterity of Cain*, 133; *Sobr.* 60, 62, 68; similarly, Dragona-Monachou, "Divine Providence," 4458–4459. On the Stoic background of the argument, see above, chapter 1, n. 91, 92, 93.

168 Philo, *Prov.* 2.9–10.

WHICH GOD CARES FOR YOU AND ME?

nonetheless be inextricable from Philo's Jewish context: the nephew Alexander apostatized from Judaism and embarked upon a wildly successful career in Roman politics during Philo's lifetime, serving as regional administrator (*epistratēgos*) of the Egyptian Thebaid, and then as prefect of the province of Judaea from 46–48 CE, a position he took up at the age of thirty-one.[169] Maren Niehoff has recently suggested that Philo's 'philosophical' works were written during the last decade of his life (ca. 40–49 CE) following his embassy to Rome (38 CE), the fruit of his period of immersion in the political and intellectual climate of the empire's capital city.[170] If this is the case, a second possible context for the composition *On Providence* presents itself, for this decade coincides with the beginning of Alexander's political career. The message of the Jewish philosopher may not have been directed to Roman philosophers in the salons,[171] but to his own nephew, embarking or having just embarked upon on a career of collaboration with the Romans. If so, while *On Providence* argues in good Stoic fashion that the wicked do not prosper, its subtext would be more specific: heed Flaccus's last words, "king of gods and humankind! So you do not neglect the nation of the Jews after all, nor do they falsely speak of your providence."

6 Flavius Josephus: Providential History is Jewish History

The histories of Flavius Josephus (37–100 CE)—the *Jewish Antiquities* and the *Jewish War*—are largely concerned with God's diachronic action in history and politics, not with Greek philosophy. As Harold Attridge writes, "the ancient history of the Jewish people is, in the eyes of Josephus, a compendium of the wondrous acts of God in human affairs and of the accurate predictions of future events, both of which reveal the way God relates to man."[172] One might add that Josephus articulates this 'compendium of wonders' using the language of providence, and specifically of God's care for virtuous individuals of Jewish history—an interpretation of divine care for terrestrial events close to that related by Philo.[173]

---

169   For a useful summary of Tiberius Alexander's career, see Mason, "Text and Commentary," 181–182, n. 1378, re: Jos. *B.J.* 2.220 (Alexander's appointment as prefect of Judaea).

170   Cf. Niehoff, *Philo*, 11, 18, 246.

171   *Pace* Niehoff, *Philo*, 76–77.

172   Attridge, *Interpretation*, 104.

173   For a similar reading of Philo and Josephus in a shared Roman, Jewish context, see Niehoff, *Philo*, 106.

86   CHAPTER 2

Josephus speaks so often of God's influence on individual persons and particular actions and situations that it is possible to provide only a handful of
references here.[174] Josephus often uses the term *pronoia* in a banal sense, to
denote the watchful oversight of human leaders.[175] Even more often, however,
the term denotes divine oversight over Jewish history, as when God gives Abraham instructions or frees Israel from exile through His *pronoia*.[176] Unlike Philo,
Josephus is not worried about the implications of God's direct care for worldly
matters: he even uses term *pronoia* as a name for God Himself.[177] He writes
freely of divine interventions and dubs them providential, as in Moses's confrontation of those opposing his selection of Aaron as high priest.[178] Meanwhile, in books 5–10 of the *Antiquities*, prophecy rather than miracles appear
to demonstrate God's providential care, as when Solomon declares the truth of
the prophecies given to King David proves the existence of *pronoia*.[179]

For Josephus, God's providential working in human affairs is hardly limited
to the history of Israel; rather, Jewish history is the most effective lens through
which one may ascertain God's interest in and care for the virtuous, and His
punishment of the wicked. The antepenultimate line of the entire *Jewish War*
states that the madness and eventual death of the ruthless Libyan governor Cat-
ullus, who brought the last of the *sicarii* to Rome for execution, amounted to
"proof of God's providence (*tēs pronoias tou theou tekmērion*), since He visited
punishment upon the wicked."[180] Throughout the *Antiquities* as well, he writes

---

174   For the following citations and discussion, I am chiefly indebted to Attridge, *Interpreta-*
       tion, 71–107; more briefly, see van Unnik, "Attack," 349–350; Bergjan, *Der fürsorgende Gott*,
       141 n. 87.
175   For inventory, see Attridge, *Interpretation*, 71–72, n. 2.
176   Abraham: Jos. *A.J.* 1.225; Israel: ibid., 2.331, 336, 349; see further Attridge, *Interpretation*,
       78–79.
177   Jos. *A.J.* 4.114, in his rendering of Balaam's oracle; see also 4 Macc. 9.24, 13.19, 16.22 (cit.
       Rajak, "Gifts of God," 235).
178   Jos. *A.J.* 4.47–48; further, Attridge, *Interpretation*, 93–99. Cf. Elliott, who sees Josephus as
       more ambivalent as regards God's interventions in human affairs (*Providence Perceived*, 6).
       Elliott's reference is to *A.J.* 18.1–2, which introduces Josephus's discussion of the three Jew-
       ish sects with reference to philosophical schools' teachings on fate (*A.J.* 18.11–22; see also
       ibid., 13.171–173; idem, *B.J.* 2.162, 164). These passages are famous, yet the intention and
       circumstances behind their composition remain stubbornly opaque (see Moore, "Fate,"
       383–384; L. Martin, "Josephus' Use"; Dihle, "Philosophische Lehren," 15; cf. Magris's hypoth-
       esis that Josephus seeks here to describe the problem of predestination—*L'idea di destino*,
       2:711–714). In any case, it is hardly obvious that Josephus himself agrees with the portrait
       he paints of the Sadducees as rejecting fatalism altogether. For reading Josephus instead
       as a kind of compatibilist, see e.g. Klawans, *Theology*, 56, 89; Aitken, "Divine Will," 284.
179   Jos. *A.J.* 8.109–110; so Attridge, *Interpretation*, 99–100; van Unnik, "Attack," 350.
180   Jos. *B.J.* 7.453, text and tr. Thackeray in LCL 210:632–633, modified.

WHICH GOD CARES FOR YOU AND ME? 87

that God rewards the good and punishes the evil.[181] Therefore, when Josephus claims that he himself survived the First Jewish War (66–73 CE) only through divine providence, he implies that he himself is virtuous, and so his account is all the more veritable.[182]

Josephus also uses other terminology to denote God's oversight over and intervention in history. Fate (*heimarmenē*) appears only rarely in the *Antiquities* but is common in the *War*, where it is instrumental in the destruction of the (Second) Temple.[183] It appears to denote the inevitability of unfortunate events.[184] 'Chance' or 'luck' (*tuchē*) is the agent by which many other greater historical events, such as the ascent of Rome, take place, a usage recalling that of Polybius or of Plutarch (see above, in this chapter).[185] In a single passage, he uses both *heimarmenē* and *tuchē* as synonyms of *pronoia*.[186] Even if his language is not philosophically systematic, Josephus's point is clear: everything happens according to God's will (*boulēsis*),[187] but God's will or plan for the world is not coterminous with fate (*heimarmenē*).[188] There are plenty of events that are unplanned, particularly sinful or wicked acts.[189] Indeed, a defining characteristic of wickedness is behaving as if God does not exist (cf. Psalm 73 LXX).[190]

Noting the curious fact that "in the *Antiquities* explicit descriptions of an agreement made between God and man have been deleted," Attridge observes that as far as providence goes, "the language of Josephus is not simply a device for translating the biblical notion of covenant. It seems, rather, to be a replace-

---

181 Jos. *A.J.* 1.14, 1.20, 8.314, 10.278, 10.281, 17.168, 17.170; thus Attridge, *Interpretation*, 83, 86; for further discussion and citations, see ibid., 83–89; Klawans, *Josephus*, 47–48, 84.

182 Jos. *B.J.* 3.391; *Vit.* 425, cit. Frick, *Divine Providence*, 13.

183 Jos. *B.J.* 4.297; Klawans, *Josephus*, 85; cf. L. Martin, "Josephus' Use," 127.

184 So L. Martin, "Josephus' Use," 133; cf. the 'strength of necessity' (*hē tou chreōn ischun*) in Jos. *A.J.* 8.419, a phrase used widely in *B.J.* for divine determinism (Attridge, *Interpretation*, 101, followed by Klawans, *Josephus*, 86).

185 Jos. *B.J.* 3.354, 4.622, 5.367; thus Klawans, *Josephus*, 46, 85. On the parallels between Josephus and Polybius, see Cohen, "Josephus," esp. 368–369. Interestingly, some apostolic-era Christians also regard Rome as divinely-sanctioned (Rom 13:1–7, 1 Tim 2:1–2, Tit 3:1, 1 Pet 2:13–17, 1 Clem. 37); "the Pauline principle differs from Plutarch in being markedly establishmentarian without attention to the benefits of the régime" (Swain, "Plutarch," 298 n. 84).

186 Jos. *B.J.* 4.622, per Moore, "Fate," 375–376; Cohen, "Josephus," 372.

187 Jos. *A.J.* 1.157; for many other citations, see Attridge, *Interpretation*, 74, n. 2.

188 Jos. *A.J.* 19.347, discussed in L. Martin, "Josephus' Use," 130.

189 Klawans, *Josephus*, 88.

190 Antipater "had carried out all his plans as if no divine power existed" (*A.J.* 17.130 in LCL 410:431; cit. Klawans, *Josephus*, 88).

88   CHAPTER 2

ment for it."[191] The Stoic notion that virtuous action is rational action, and therefore attended to by providence, here displaces the articulation of Israel's virtue in terms of a special covenant with God. It is for this reason that breaking God's commandments is tantamount to loss of His care, as David, on his deathbed, tells Solomon:

> I exhort you ... to be just toward your subjects and pious toward God, who has given you the kingship, and to keep His commandments and laws, which He Himself sent down to us by Moses; do not neglect them by yielding either to favor or flattery or lust or any other passion, for you will lose the goodwill of the deity toward you (*tou theiou pros sauton eunoian apoleis*), if you transgress any of His ordinances, and you will turn His benevolent care (*tēn agathēn ... pronoian*) into a hostile attitude.[192]

As Attridge argues, "Josephus substitutes the relationship to more universally applicable and acceptable belief in the governance of the moral order by God. The history of the people is taken to be an example of how that moral governance operates. Whatever special position Israel enjoys is to be understood as a result of its special virtue."[193]

Conversely, should that virtue be abandoned, Israel suffers. As Jonathan Klawans contends, this is precisely what Josephus wishes to express in his descriptions of the fall of both the First and Second Temples: "the fall of Jerusalem was conditionally fated—the inexorable result of the people's free choice to sin."[194] Josephus's notion of God is one where the lord of Israel is omniscient, omnipotent, and omnipresent, intervening as He likes in human affairs to bestow favor upon the righteous and to punish the wicked. He articulates these interventions along Stoic lines, where providential care is synonymous with the exercise of human reason, and the pursuit of vice entails its own punishments. Yet this is no 'impersonal' *pronoia*: on the contrary, the only passage in which Josephus explicitly names a Greek school of thought is a denunciation of the Epicureans, "who toss out providence from human life and do not think that God manages its affairs (*epitropeuein tōn pragmatōn*), or that

---

191   Attridge, *Interpretation*, 80, 79.

192   Jos. *A.J.* 7.384–385, text and tr. Thackeray and Marcus in LCL 281:208–211. With the editors, I read here *tananti'* ("against [you]") instead of MS *hapant'* ("altogether").

193   Attridge, *Interpretation*, 91–92.

194   Klawans, *Josephus*, 87. On determinism and human responsibility, see further below, chapter six.

WHICH GOD CARES FOR YOU AND ME? 89

universe is directed by a blessed and immortal being towards the preservation of the whole (*tōn holōn*)."[195] Nor is it an emptying of Israelite religion: another corollary of Israel's special position resulting from its virtue is that to be truly virtuous, in a Josephan sense, is "to keep His commandments and laws"—to practice Judaism.

7 Prayer or Care?—Justin Martyr and Trypho the Jew 'Investigate the Deity'

The *Dialogue with Trypho* (written 160–165 CE) of the philosopher Justin Martyr is among the most important and difficult specimens of second-century Christian literature:[196] a literary dialogue where Justin himself features as a protagonist engaged in a debate about the exegesis of Scripture with a Jewish philosopher, 'Trypho,' and his companions. Justin's goal in these debates is to demonstrate that Jesus of Nazareth is the Son of God and His Messiah (*christos*), and that the Jews killed him—but they should now believe in his divine identity and status.[197] At the beginning of the *Dialogue*, Justin relates that as he was walking in the gymnasium, he was approached by a stranger. The man says that he had noticed Justin wearing the robes of the philosophers, and so decided to try to begin a conversation with him about philosophy.[198] He introduces himself as Trypho, "a Hebrew of the circumcision, a refugee from the recent war," now residing in Greece.[199] While the specific year of the narrative

---

195 Jos. *A.J.* 10.277–278, text and tr. Marcus in LCL 326:310–313, significantly modified. Notably, the context is the veracity of prophecy (*A.J.* 10.276–277, 280); see further J.-P. Martin, *Providentia Deorum*, 23–24; van Unnik, "Attack," esp. 343, 347. Indeed, the passage echoes the conclusion of the first half of the *Antiquities*—the destruction of the First Temple and a prophecy of the destruction of the second; "the act of divine retribution which has taken place has been made known beforehand by God and that very fact proves that He exercises providential care for His creation and His people" (Attridge, *Interpretation*, 104; see also L. Martin, "Josephus' Use," 134–135; J.-P. Martin, *Providentia deorum*, 205–207). See also *A.J.* 4.47; below, chapter five.

196 A *terminus post quem* is furnished by Justin's *First Apology*, written ca. 153–155 CE, which *Dial.* 120.6 refers to in passing; a *terminus ante quem* by Justin's death in 165 CE. For a more full discussion, see Horner, *Listening*, 7; followed by den Dulk, *Between Jews*, 1.

197 The prominent anti-Judaism of the work is rightly emphasized by Rajak, "Talking," 60, re: e.g. Just. Mart. *Dial.* 16.4.

198 Just. Mart. *Dial.* 1.2. According to Eusebius, the setting is Ephesus (*Hist. eccl.* 4.18), but how much truth there is to this is anyone's guess (see further Rajak, "Talking," 63–64; cf. van Winden, *Early Christian Philosopher*, 28–29).

199 Just. Mart. *Dial.* 1.3, tr. Falls, rev. Halton, 4.

90   CHAPTER 2

is not obvious, it is not important either: the setting is the aftermath of the failed Bar Kokhba revolt (132–135 CE).[200] Trypho asks:

> "Do the philosophers not make just such a discourse about God, and do not their inquiries on such occasions delve into His singular rule and (His) providence? For is this not the task of philosophy, to investigate the deity?"
>
> "Yes," I (Justin) said. "That's what we think, too. But the majority do not pay attention to this matter—namely, whether their gods are single or many, and whether they care for each and every one of us or not—as if this knowledge contributed nothing to our well-being! Rather, they try to persuade us that God cares for the whole, together with its genera and species; yet he does not care for me or you or the class of individuals in general, since we would not need to pray to him through the whole day and night (if, on the contrary, He did care for each and every one of us)."[201]

This passage is the earliest surviving discussion by a Christian philosopher about the extent to which God's providence extends to particulars,[202] and the second-oldest remarks by a Christian philosopher on providence in general.[203] It is also replete with problems, and these are no matter of scholarly arcana. Justin's remarks to Trypho about providence and prayer concern not only the philosophical feasibility of a personal God who cares for individuals, but the question of the identity of this very personal God to whom Justin prays. For Justin, the question of the extent to which God is personal is inextricable from the question of who God is, and this in turn sheds some light on the difficult question of the *Dialogue*'s intended audience.

It is puzzling that Justin states that the "majority" of philosophers do not "pay attention" to the question of one versus many gods or the reach of providence,

---

200 Rightly highlighted by Lieu, *Marcion*, 316–317; Cf. van Winden, for whom Trypho's remarks indicate that the revolt is still underway (*Early Christian Philosopher*, 28).

201 Just. Mart. *Dial.* 1.3–4, text Marcovich, 70, tr. mine. On the translation of this passage ("brevis esse studet auctor, obscurus fit"—so Marcovich, op. cit.), cf. Hyldahl, *Philosophie*, 98–99; van Winden, *Early Christian Philosopher*, 31–35; Joly, *Christianisme*, 16–23.

202 *Pace* Elliott, who claims that Athenagoras of Athens "was possibly the first Christian to distinguish 'general' from 'specific' providence" (*Providence Perceived*, 8). Notably, *Dial.* 1.3–4 is the only passage where Justin weighs in on this specific problem (Bergjan, *Der fürsorgende Gott*, 238).

203 The only older remarks on *pronoia* by a Christian writer trained in philosophy which I have been able to identify are Clement of Alexandria's quotations of Basilides (*Strom.* 4.12.82.2), discussed below, chapter six.

when even a casual reader of Greek philosophy (to say nothing of this book) knows plainly that this is not the case.[204] It is also puzzling that Justin proceeds to disregard his own claim by repeating the argument of some philosophers that God "cares for the whole, together with its genera and species," but not for individuals, since if God did, "we would not need to pray to him ..." A different group of philosophers is meant here, unless Justin simply means that when philosophers do not "pay attention" to a problem, they treat it insufficiently.[205] What is not puzzling, though, is that Justin wishes to frame the discussion he will begin with Trypho by reference to Greek philosophical debates about how God is active in the world; moreover, he wants to bracket these heathen discussions as fundamentally defective. Justin does this by bringing up the question of providential care for wholes versus individuals, with reference to the practice of prayer. That Justin wishes to kick off his discussion with Trypho through bringing up the topic of providence is also no surprise. As Silke-Petra Bergjan notes, it was commonplace in Roman philosophy to distinguish the various philosophical schools with reference to their views on providence, because the question was so closely tied to the practice of philosophy, as Trypho himself states.[206]

---

204 Rightly de Vogel, "Problems," 374; similarly Joly, *Christianisme*, 17; idem, "Notes," 320.

205 See also van Winden, *Early Christian Philosopher*, 32. Hyldahl (*Philosophie*, 35) and Joly (*Christianisme*, 16) suggest emending the text to differentiate those who make the 'care or prayer' argument (see below) from the "majority," an approach rejected by van Winden (op. cit., 35, widely followed; thus Pépin; "Prière et providence," 112; Marcovich, *Iustini Martyris Apologiae*, 70). The question is ultimately immaterial for the present discussion.

206 Rightly Bergjan, *Der fürsorgende Gott*, 245. Examples could include Cic. *Nat. d.* 1.1–5; Sext. Emp. *Pyr.* 3.2–10; Att. frg. 3. For examples from Christian thinkers besides that of Justin (with the comparable rhetorical aim of contrasting the multiplicity of heathen philosophical opinions with the single 'true' philosophy), see Theoph. *Autol.* 3.7 and Ter. *To the Heathen*, 2.2, both discussed below, in this chapter; *Eugnostos* NHC III 70.2–71.13 and par.; *Wisdom of Jesus Christ* NHC III 91.24–93.24 and par.; *Tri. Trac.* NHC I 109.6–35; for recent discussion of these latter sources, see Poirier, "Deux doxographies"; Burns, "Philosophical Contexts." Cf. Nasrallah, who prefers the context of debate about divinatory practices: "one manifestation of the Christian God's caring—and of an answer to this philosophical question of whether God cares for individuals—was the phenomenon of Christian *sortes*" ("Lot Oracles," 225).

Den Dulk also offers a different interpretation: Justin's reference in *Dial.* 1.4 to philosophers who do not "pay attention" to whether God is single or many is a cryptic nod to 'demiurgicalists'—Christians who differentiate between God and the creator (*Between Jews*, 85). Den Dulk rightly notes that Justin follows the argument about care and prayer by accusing the 'philosophers' of licentiousness, in *Dial.* 1.5:

It imparts a certain immunity and freedom of speech to those who hold these opinions, permitting them to do and to say whatever they please, without any fear of punishment or hope of reward from God. How could it be otherwise, when they claim that things

92   CHAPTER 2

In other words, Justin's disregard for theories of providence that extend to
general matters ("genera and species"), but not individuals, is not a matter of
scholarly *minutiae*. It is part of Justin's careful literary construction in the *Dialogue*. The specificity of the argument is revealing. As discussed at the beginning of this chapter, there were many proponents of such arguments about
care for the whole versus parts in Justin's day—Aristotelians, Platonists, and
even some Stoa—and it is by no means obvious that he has any specific one of
them in mind, much less why he brings prayer into the matter, except perhaps
that the relationship of prayer to providence was something second-century
philosophers liked to debate.[207] Robert Joly has argued that Justin seeks to
respond to skepticism regarding the efficacy of prayer.[208] Yet such an interpretation misreads Justin: he writes that "we would not need to pray … (if, on the
contrary, he did care)." The idea is, rather, that there is no reason to ask God for
a favor which God is already providing; therefore, if God cares, prayer is superfluous.[209] The disjunction is then not 'care for prayer' versus 'no care for prayer,'

---

      will always be as they are now, and that you and I shall live in the next life just as we are
      now, neither better or worse. But there are others who think that the soul is immortal
      and incorporeal, and therefore conclude that they will not be punished even if they are
      guilty of sin; for, if the soul if s incorporeal, it cannot suffer; if it is immortal, it needs
      nothing further from God. (*Dial.* 1.5, tr. Falls, rev. Halton, 4)

      Den Dulk is correct that Justin raises the question of providence specifically to set up
      his debate with Trypho over the identity of God as *both* creator and providential being,
      and that Justin's charge of licentiousness amongst those who deny care for particulars
      is related to this debate. Yet Justin can hardly have 'demiurgicalists' (i.e., Marcionites,
      Gnostics) in mind (*pace* den Dulk, op. cit.). The opinions on the soul which Justin here
      assigns to those who act licentiously can only be caricatures of those of the Stoa (the
      eternal return) and the Platonists (the immortality of the soul—rightly van Winden,
      Early Christian Philosopher, 39), the former entirely without parallel in 'demiurgicalist'
      (i.e., Marcionite, Gnostic) sources. Rather, Justin is not exactly slandering the philoso-
      phers as much as drawing the conclusion that many thinkers drew about abandoning the
      notion of even fictive care for particulars: people will do whatever they want (de Vogel,
      "Problems," 379; van Winden, *Early Christian Philosopher*, 39–40, both with ample cita-
      tions).

207   Cf. Hyldahl and van Winden, who take Justin to be targeting Aristotle (*Philosophie*, 100; van
      Winden, *Early Christian Philosopher*, 38, respectively); Pépin suggests rather the Cyrenaic
      philosopher Aristippus ("Prière et providence," 124–125). The importance of the question
      of how prayer relates to providence is emphasized in Timotin, *Priere*, 87–94, 137–142.

208   Joly, *Christianisme*, 19–20; idem, "Notes," 316–317; followed by Bergjan, *Der fürsorgende
      Gott*, 241 n. 99. Of course they are not wrong that some philosophers did express skepticism
      regarding the efficacy of prayer (re: Orig. *Cels.* 2.13; Nem. *Nat. hom.* 42, 44; a useful survey
      of Classical and Hellenistic Greek sources on this point is provided by Dorival, "Modes,"
      27–32).

209   Rightly van Winden, *Early Christian Philosopher*, 33, although his reading of *pronoia* as

WHICH GOD CARES FOR YOU AND ME? 93

but 'care versus prayer'—i.e., 'care or prayer.' As Jean Pépin has observed, such an argument is uncommon, but attested among ancient philosophers, such as Maximus of Tyre:

> If the things for which we pray come to fruition thanks to divine providence, of what use is prayer? For if God exercises providence, He either cares for the whole, without worrying about the parts—just as kings see to the health of the cities of the kingdom by (the rule of) law and justice, without extending care to every detail—⟨or⟩ His providence can be tested amongst particulars as well. So, what should we say? Do you want God to care for the whole (of creation)? Then do not bother Him, for He will not listen, if what you request is not good for the whole ... Now, a doctor, seeing the cause (of a disease), neglects the requests of the parts, and instead serves the whole. For the whole is his concern. But, should one say that God exercises providence on behalf of particulars, then in this sense prayer is also of no use. It is like the case of a sick patient asking his doctor for medicine or food; if that sort of thing would be effective, the doctor would give it unasked; if it would be harmful, he would not give it when asked. To wit: nothing that falls under the care of providence is to be asked for or prayed for.[210]

Justin thus sets up the debate with Trypho about the identity of the providential God to whom Christians pray through the proverbial 'whole day and night.' And pray they do, in the *Dialogue*: Christians pray to Jesus, Justin says, for help

---

  here implying a sense of Stoic *heimarmenē* is unwarranted and lends no sense to the argument (Joly, *Christianisme*, 19; followed by Bergjan, *Der fürsorgende Gott*, 244).

210 Max. Tyr. *Or.* 5.4, text Trapp, 40–41, tr. mine. Cit. and disc. Pépin, "Prière et providence," 121–122, followed by Marcovich, *Iustini Martyris Apologiae*, 70; Burns, "Care or Prayer?," 181–183 (with reservations); see also Timotin, *Prière*, 90. See also *Or.* 13.3, where God's care for parts is rejected (O'Brien, *Demiurge*, 128–129). Notably, Maximus does not reject the practice of prayer per se, but petitionary prayer as presuming care for particulars (Dorival, "Modes," 31, 38–39, re: *Or.* 5.8; also O'Brien, "Prayer in Maximus," 63). As Pépin notes, Maximus's phrasing of the 'care or prayer' argument recalls Aristippus of Cyrene (op. cit., 124–125; see also Dorival, op. cit., 29–30; Timotin, op. cit., 90). Lucian mocks petitionary prayer in *Jupp. conf.* 5 (on which, see L. Martin, "Josephus' Use," 129; Dorival, op. cit., 31; Timotin, op. cit., 92–93). *Pace* Nasrallah, Lucian's point is not that while "doctrine and practice ... are inextricably linked ... there is no clarity to the terms," as she maintains ("Lot Oracles," 219); rather, he brings up a common skeptical argument critiquing sacrifice. The evidence of Maximus and Lucian permits us to disregard Joly's view that the 'care or prayer' argument reflects "un parodoxe énorme" in terms of religious psychology (Joly, "Notes," 317).

when under assault from demons.[211] He recalls the tale of Jonah, who averts the destruction of Nineveh through prayer and donning sackcloth and ashes.[212] Earlier, in his first *Apology*, Justin describes how Christians pray when conducting rituals, such as while fasting before receiving baptism, or prior to the holy kiss or the distribution of the Eucharist.[213] Yet these examples of efficacious prayer could respond to skepticism about prayer in general, rather than the 'care or prayer' argument in particular.

A hint may be glimpsed in the fact that Justin repeatedly invokes prayer for the conversion and salvation for one's persecutors. The 'care or prayer' argument views the object of care in a static manner: to take up the medical metaphor used by Maximus, the patient who is under good care from a doctor does not need to ask the doctor for help. Yet the providential care in which Justin is interested necessarily marks a break with the past, whether of heathen religion or the Old Covenant of the Jews. For instance, Justin defends Christian abstention from Jewish covenantal rituals such as circumcision by invoking the custom of Christian prayer for mercy for one's persecutors as evidence of their secure trust in the New Covenant.[214] Christians also pray for their Jewish persecutors: "we pray for you that you might experience the mercy of Christ; for he instructed us to pray even for our enemies," for God is merciful, but will judge the just and unjust alike.[215] Later, after telling Trypho that some "heretics" "blaspheme the Creator of the universe," "we pray for you and for everyone else who hates us, that you may repent with us, and refrain from blaspheming Jesus Christ ... We pray, also, that you may believe in Jesus Christ."[216] Justin implores Trypho and his friends here to pray to the correct God, not that suggested by "heretics" like the followers of Marcion, Valentinus, or Basilides (on all of whom, see below). Following a long proof from prophecy that the Judgment Day is real and will be administered by Christ, Justin adds:

> We, indeed, have not believed in him in vain, nor have we been led astray by our teachers, but by wondrous divine providence (*thaumastēi pronoiai theou*) it has been brought about that we, through the calling of the new and eternal testament, namely, Christ, should be found more understand-

---

211 Just. Mart. *Dial.* 30.2–3.

212 Just. Mart. *Dial.* 107, re: Jonah 3.

213 Just. Mart. *1 Apol.* 61, 65, 67.

214 Just. Mart. *Dial.* 18.3. Christians are said to pray for the conversion of others at ibid., 133.6, 142 (see below); idem, *1 Apol.* 14.

215 Just. Mart. *Dial.* 96.3, tr. Falls, rev. Halton, 147, re: Luke 6:36; Matt 5:45.

216 Just. Mart. *Dial.* 35.8, tr. Falls, rev. Halton, 55.

WHICH GOD CARES FOR YOU AND ME? 95

ing and religious than you, who are reputed to be, but in reality are not, intelligent men and lovers of God.[217]

The final lines of the *Dialogue* are Justin's prayer for the departing Trypho and his companions to convert.[218] The close association of prayer with the goal of conversion of one's enemies explains Justin's decision to challenge the 'care or prayer' argument, which conceives of providential care as maintenance of a consistent state of affairs which requires no intervention. For Justin, God's personal intervention—and the prayer for it—are themselves works of providence.

Justin's disparagement of those who reject providential care for particulars —and specifically of the 'care or prayer' argument—thus supports a reading of the dialogue as directed towards a readership concerned with the identity of God as portrayed in Jewish Scriptures, and the relationship of this god to the figure of Jesus Christ.[219] The framing device of the world of philosophy need not imply an audience of philosophically-inclined heathens, like that of the *Apologies*; the focus on scriptural exegesis can only presume an audience invested in such debates.[220] Yet the setting of philosophical debate and the opening salvo about providence and prayer are not accidental to Justin's project of theological 'boundary-setting.'[221] Justin's readers were interested in more than circumcision; they wondered how providential the God of Israel could possibly be, given the response of Trajan and Hadrian to the Jewish revolts in 115–117 and 132–135. Justin thus presents a work replete with examples of God's personal intervention—culminating in the arrival of Christ himself as an act of *pronoia*—and of prayers rendered by Christians for the conversion of their enemies. Care and prayer go hand in hand in the *Dialogue*. Like the Wisdom of Solomon, Philo, and Josephus, the *Dialogue with Trypho* relocates providen-

---

217 Just. Mart. *Dial.* 118.3, text Marcovich, 273, tr. Falls, rev. Halton, 176–177. Cf. Scheffczyk, *Schöpfung und Vorsehung*, 39.

218 "And I in turn prayed for them, saying, 'I can wish you no greater blessing than this ... you may one day come to believe entirely as we do that Jesus is the Christ of God'" (Just. Mart. *Dial.* 142, tr. Falls, rev. Halton, 212). The *Second Apology* also closes with a prayer for the conversion of unbelievers (idem, *2 Apol.* 15).

219 See Rajak, "Talking," 78–80 and now den Dulk, *Between Jews*, 38–46, 84–85 *passim*. I do not take Justin to have an 'internal, Christian audience' as opposed to an 'external, Jewish' one; in a mid-second-century context, such a distinction puts the cart before the horse.

220 Rajak, "Talking," 75–77; cf. Perrone, "For the Sake," 256 n. 78; Bergjan, *Der fürsorgende Gott*, 248.

221 For a useful (if ambivalent), recent discussion of the scholarship on Justin's boundary-setting in *Dial.*, see White, "Justin Between," esp. 163–167.

tial care from the world of Roman religion and politics to the history of Israel, complete with an interventionist God, "the Creator of the universe ... and the God of Abraham, and of Isaac, and of Jacob."[222]

8   Conclusions: A God Personal Enough for a Stoic

The term *pronoia* or any developed, philosophical notion of 'providence' are absent from the Tanakh as well as the New Testament. Yet many biblical texts are, of course, deeply concerned with questions of divine care, the problem of evil, and personal accountability, and so present views that resemble some of the presuppositions involved in Greek philosophical debates about providence. Proof-texts such as Jesus's remarks on God's care for even little sparrows (Matt 10:29–30; Luke 12:6–7) have given many theologians the impression that a distinctively 'personal' God is to be found in the Scriptures, one whose care for individuals exceeds that found among the more abstract deities of the Platonists and Stoa. The fact that many Greek-speaking intellectuals—including important writers such as 'Aristeas,' Philo, 'Solomon,' and Josephus—do write about an interventionist providence, and identify it as particularly active in Jewish history, can give further credence to this impression that the God of first-century CE Judaism and earliest Christianity was providential in a new and special way unknown to the heathens.

The present chapter has argued otherwise. There is something distinctive about the treatment of divine care in the biblically-informed literature discussed here, but it is not a 'personalization' of the divine, or even an emphasis on care for parts as well as the wholes. Rather, the very personal providence one reads of in Philo and Josephus 'intervenes' in history on behalf of the virtuous.[223] Such 'personal' attendance to those who use reason and act in a virtuous way is very much in line with Stoic philosophy, particularly that of Epictetus. Even outside of the context of philosophical discourse, one finds historical writers such as Polybius or Pliny the Elder who write of God's providence as active in history and attending above all to the virtuous. What is distinctive about the sort of providence described by Philo and other Jewish authors is that the identity of God Himself changes. What is distinctive about Justin Mar-

---

222   Just. Mart. *Dial.* 35.4–5, text Marcovich, 128, tr. Falls, rev. Halton, 55, modified.

223   *Pace* Kraabel, "Pronoia at Sardis," 86, who claims that "for Josephus, for Philo and other Greek-speaking Jews, the term had not taken on the specificity it appears to carry for Sardis Jews in a later age." Rightly challenged by Rajak, "Gifts of God," 233–234, followed by Aitken, "Divine Will," 284.

WHICH GOD CARES FOR YOU AND ME?

tyr, when he speaks disparagingly of those who view providence and God's response to individual prayers as mutually exclusive, is that the very personal God he takes to be active in prayer is not just the God of Abraham. This god is the Father of Jesus of Nazareth, the Messiah—and Justin wants Trypho, a refugee from the Bar Kochba Revolt, to believe this.

When it came down to care for parts versus care for wholes, Justin was in good company. Many of the first Christian philosophers give the impression that their God was omnipresent, omnipotent and very personal—in other words, a lot like the God of the Stoa. Theologian Leo Scheffczyk has pointed out that such passages reflect the wide influence of the Stoic notion of God's immanence—recall Cleanthes's *Hymn to Zeus*—on Greek Christian literature of the second century.[224] As much appears to be the case when Theophilus of Antioch or Athenagoras of Athens meditate on God's occupation or enveloping of the universe, penetrating space.[225] The second-century Christian Platonist Valentinus expresses the divine penetration of all beings in very Stoic terms in his poem *Harvest*: "everything suspended by spirit (*pneumati*) I see, everything carried by spirit I sense ..."[226]

Yet some of the very same authors were also concerned with the distinctive identity of the active God in question, vis-à-vis the politicized language of providence in elite Roman discourse. Like Justin, Theophilus wishes to emphasize that followers of Jesus are of no threat to Rome and its providence: rather, it is philosophers, like Euhemerus, Epicurus, and Pythagoras, who "deny the existence of religion and destroy providence (*arnoumenois einai theosebeian kai pronoian anairousin*)." Turning to the "majority" of philosophers—who preferred to identify God's care with the ruling state—he emphasizes their disunity: "whatever the others ... said about God and providence, it is easy to see how they contradicted one another; for some absolutely rejected the existence of God and providence, while others gave proof of God and admitted that everything is governed by providence."[227] He responds:

> We too confess a God—only one, the creator and maker and craftsman of this entire universe. We know that everything is ordered by providence—

---

224 Scheffczyk, *Schöpfung und Vorsehung*, 29, 39 n. 28, re: Athenag. *Leg.* 13.3; see additionally, ibid., 5.3; Theoph. *Autol.* 3.26.

225 Theoph. *Autol.* 1.5; Athenag. *Leg.* 8, cit. Spanneut, *Stoicisme*, 325; also Ir. *Haer.* 2.1.1, 2.2.6; Orig. *Cels.* 6.71 (see immediately below).

226 *Ref.* 6.37.7, text and tr. Litwa, 438–441, modified. See recently Dunderberg, *Beyond Gnosticism*, 61–66.

227 Theoph. *Autol.* 3.7 tr. Grant, 109, 111.

98   CHAPTER 2

but by Him alone. We have also learned a holy law—but we have the real
God as legislator, who teaches us to behave righteously and to be pious
and noble.[228]

This legislation is the Ten Commandments. As in Philo and Josephus, God
personally attends to the righteous—perfectly fine Stoicism, on its face—but
righteousness is what God handed over to Moses on Mount Sinai.

Meanwhile, Tertullian, writing in North Africa around the turn of the third
century, goes a step further. He argues that the belief that Christ took on a body
and died for us is what distinguishes Christians from the philosophers—who,
like Epicurus, deny God's care for humans.[229] Rather, he claims, God cares for
and orders all things, even the small things—like the "lilies of the field."[230]
Recalling (and somewhat misreading) the *Letter of Aristeas*, he charges that
even the philosopher Menedemus had to acknowledge the piety of the Jews,
who recognized that God orders all things on earth.[231] The immanent and
active God of the Stoa is elided with the Christ event, as in Justin. Yet in his
apologetic work *To the Gentiles* (*Ad Nationes*), Tertullian struggles to distance
this thinking from Stoicism. Here, he states that once the philosophers figured
out that God existed, "they did not expound Him as they found Him, but rather
disputed about His quality, and His nature, and even about His abode":

> Indeed, the Platonists maintain that He cares about worldly things (*cu-*
> *rantem rerum*) and decides them as a judge; the Epicureans, that He is
> idle and lazing about, and, so to say, a nobody. The Stoics allege Him to
> be outside of the world; the Platonists, within the world. The God whom
> they utterly failed to welcome, they could neither know nor fear—nor,
> therefore, could they be wise, since they have wandered far off from the
> 'beginning of wisdom,' that is, 'the fear of God.'[232]

Tertullian could only have felt a need to differentiate his thought from that
of the Stoa only under compulsion from critics who saw Christian conceptions of providence as precisely the worst kind of Stoicism. It is telling that

---

228   Theoph. *Autol.* 3.9 text and tr. Grant, 110–113, significantly modified.
229   Ter. *Marc.* 2.16. On this passage, see further below, chapter three.
230   Ter. *To His Wife,* 4; see also *On Fasting, Against the Psychics,* 4.
231   Ter. *Apology,* 18.
232   *Platonici quidem curantem rerum et arbitrumet iudicem, Epicurei otiosum et inexercitum,*
       et, ut ita dixerim, neminem; positum uero extra mundum Stoici, intra mundum Platonici ...
       (*Nat.* 2.2, text Dekkers, et al., 42–43, tr. mine).

WHICH GOD CARES FOR YOU AND ME?

some philosophical opponents of Christianity simply applied arguments used by the Epicureans against the Stoics—thus the character "Caecilius," in Minucius Felix's dialogue *Octavius*, of the later second or early third century CE:[233]

> Yet again what monstrous absurdities these Christians devise! This God of theirs—whom they can neither show nor see—carefully looks into everyone's habits, everyone's deeds, even their words and hidden thoughts, no doubt in a hurry and present everywhere; they make him out a troublesome, restless, shameless and interfering being who has a hand in everything that is done, stumbling by at every turn, since he can neither attend to particulars because he is distracted by the whole, nor to the whole because he is occupied with particulars (*cum nec singulis inservire posit per universa distractus nec universis sufficere in singulis occupatus*).[234]

Many Christian philosophers of the latter half of the second century CE were thus very comfortable indeed in asserting divine involvement in the cosmos, and, particularly, care for individuals—so much so that some of them felt they had to distinguish themselves from the Stoa.[235] It is instructive here to contrast their statements with what we saw in Philo. As discussed above, he was committed to a view of God as very much active in the world, and intervening on behalf of the Jews—even within Philo's own lifetime, as evidenced by the demise of Flaccus. Yet he also shares the Greek philosophers' wariness of describing God as a busybody lurking behind even the tiniest of mundane matters, sometimes referring divine actions to one of God's many agents.[236] Philo does not differentiate God from God's tools or helpers because the latter are bad, but because God is transcendent, and the matter out of which the universe is made is problematic stuff—a view very much in keeping with those of Plutarch or Numenius (see below, chapter three). Nor is there any hint in Philo's writings that any beings at work in creating the world or human beings are malevolent (see below, chapters three and four).[237] Rather,

---

233   A precise date for *Oct.* cannot be established. For a brief discussion with bibliography (favoring the later second century), see Price, "Latin Christian," 112.

234   Min. Fel. *Oct.* 10.5, tr. Rendall in LCL 250:341, significantly modified; similarly Cic. *Nat. d.* 1.54–55.

235   See further Clem. Al. *Strom.* 1.11.51.1–52.3 and Orig. *Cels.* 6.71, discussed below, chapter three.

236   The bulk of Philo's comments regarding angelic mediators are confined to his discussion of creation, discussed below, chapter four.

237   Rightly emphasized by Runia, *Philo*, 248–249; O'Brien, *Demiurge*, 38, 69; cf. e.g. Pearson, "Philo and Gnosticism."

he and Josephus focus on the omnipresence of providence not in terms of divine intervention, but in terms of the Stoic optimism that sees rational, righteous behavior without reward as an impossibility. Similarly, Cicero's 'Balbus' and even Seneca stop short of asserting that God runs all affairs. Meanwhile, Christian writers like Theophilus or Tertullian describe divine activity in very Stoic terms—God is present everywhere, especially where human beings exercise *logos* qua reason—but they go beyond Balbus or Seneca in claiming that God really is not just creator, but administrator of everything.

Part of what is striking about the passages from Valentinus, Theophilus, Tertullian, and Minucius Felix discussed presently is the absence of divine mediators as distributors of providence. Philo calls the voice in the burning bush an 'angel,' and refers on many occasions to *daimones* at work in the world, echoing his Middle Platonic contemporaries; yet the Christian philosophers discussed here simply and firmly state the reality of God's unique power and providential care for the whole of creation.[238] Stoic language about divine immanence in God's providential activity was attractive to Christian thinkers, not only because it emphasized God's personal care and omnipotence; it also emphasized the singularity of divine rule, and that mattered to the second-century apologists. Thus Theophilus states, "we know that everything is ordered by providence—but by Him alone."[239] This is not to say that these same writers had nothing to say about other superhuman beings, such as angels and demons. On the contrary, they were reading the Middle Platonists too, and had a great deal to say about God's agents at work in worldly affairs. Yet to a Justin or Athenagoras, the *daimones* of a Plutarch or Apuleius were not dispensers of a tertiary providence—they were the malevolent demons of 'pagan cult.' Conversely, Justin mentions "heretics" who "blaspheme the Creator of the universe,"[240] when they speak of the god who is providential and the god who creates in two different breaths, referring to two different deities of very different characters, intentions, and abilities. It is to these angels and demons, and to these 'other gods,' that we now turn.

---

238 Further passages include Min. Fel. *Oct.* 5, 18; Orig. *Cels.* 4.99; idem, *Prin.* 1.3.1, 2.9.8. Cf. Spanneut, *Stoicisme*, 327. Re: Orig. *Cels.* 4.99, see Koch, *Pronoia*, 30; Bergjan, *Der fürsorgende Gott*, 193–194, 211–216.

239 Theoph. *Autol.* 3.9.

240 Just. Mart. *Dial.* 35.8, tr. Falls, rev. Halton, 55.

PART 2

Dualism

CHAPTER 3

The Other Gods

1 Introduction: Dualism in Doubt

George Karamanolis has recently argued that the first Christian philosophers approached the problem of evil chiefly with recourse to the Stoic belief "that badness enters the world exclusively by man's failure to stick to the good," rejecting Stoic determinism in favor of emergent notions of free will.[1] There is much truth to this, as will be discussed further below in chapter six, but it might be more appropriate to say that there are definitely 'two sides' to the coin. A second, crucial aspect of the problem of evil in early Christian thought is that of dualism, or rather the philosophical notion that the nexus in the causal chain is twofold, rather than singular. This chapter argues that the problem of evil in Jewish and Christian discussions of divine activity and providence was central and articulated through models that can only be described on some level as 'dualistic.' More specifically, it was precisely in dialogue with these more 'dualistic' approaches to evil and demons that early Christian thinkers developed their notion of individual responsibility for evil. This is interesting, because although 'dualism' once constituted a cottage industry in the study of religion, it has of late become an unfashionable term.[2] Yet, it remains in play in the study of ancient philosophy, for good reason. The caricature of Stoicism as a strict 'monism' against the 'dualism' of the Platonists rings true on some level, even if the matter is more complex upon close inspection. Ancient thinkers often did explain and dispute matters of causality in terms of one principle versus two or three, and these positions held important ramifications for questions of ethics, in addition to physics and theology. In other words, the problem of human responsibility was inextricable from the problem of the number of first principles.

---

1 Karamanolis, *Philosophy*, 156; cf. also Russell, *The Devil*, 223–235; Adamson, "State of Nature," 88–89.

2 Recent discussions include e.g. Couliano, *Tree of Gnosis*; Stoyanov, *Other God*; Xeravits, ed., *Dualism at Qumran*; Frey, "Apocalyptic Dualism," 271–272; Gardner, "Dualism"; Jourdan, "Introduction," esp. 7–14. See further the conclusion to this chapter. For a recent discussion of the deadends to which scholarship on the 'dualism' of the Fourth Gospel and Qumran has led, see Aune, "Dualism in the Fourth Gospel."

© KONINKLIJKE BRILL NV, LEIDEN, 2020 | DOI:10.1163/9789004432994_005

Roman philosophers' questions about how many forces in the universe ought to be reckoned as efficacious causes were central to the problem of providence and of how providence functions, whether one looks at care for the universe and for individuals, at divine foreknowledge and omniscience, at responsibility and free will, or even God's own will. If there are other causal forces, are they not other gods, in a sense? And if so, which one cares, and which one does not? The following two chapters investigate this problematic. Chapter four will tackle the problem of 'Gnosticism' and 'Gnostic' literature, evidence of such importance to the development of Roman and especially Christian philosophy about providence to merit its own extended discussion. The present chapter, meanwhile, treats the related but distinct problems of divine creative agency and sources of evil in Roman philosophers of the first to third centuries CE. Following a discussion of the classic examples of Pythagorean-Platonist 'dualism' in Plutarch of Chaeronea and Numenius of Apamea, it takes up some of the most important early Christian treatments of the same themes, notably by Athenagoras of Athens and the great Alexandrian theologians Clement and Origen. Each of these Christian writers closely engaged both Stoic and Platonist approaches to evil, but they did so with recourse to the background of Second Temple Jewish 'apocalyptic' dualism and especially the legend of the fall of the angels, envisioning the creator-God as having a Satanic opponent and demonic minions—the gods of traditional Graeco-Roman religion—who spread sin and death in the world. This seriously complicated early Christian adaptations of the Middle Platonist teaching on providence, with its daimonic administrators, and in fact it may be argued that Athenagoras, Clement, and Origen all understand demons as mechanisms in decidedly Stoic models of human error. Meanwhile, an entirely different approach to the problem of evil was taken up by other Christian philosophers, who appear to have focused rather on the Pythagorean-Platonist speculations about the chaotic character of matter and its ramifications for evil: Hermogenes, Marcion, and Marcion's student, Apelles. For Marcion and Apelles, imperfection in creation could only be the product of the imperfection inherent in the creator—a second, other god inferior to the God of the Christians, a god who doesn't care.

2 Matter, Evil, and Dualism from the Pythagoreans to a Neo-Pythagorean

As we saw in chapter one, Stoicism is essentially a monist philosophy, whose sole causal principle is the divine *pneuma* that permeates everything. Even if

THE OTHER GODS   105

Stoicism identifies matter as a separate principle, it is a passive principle.[3] Evil, for the Stoa, either does not exist, or it is caused in servitude of a greater good that is so great as to render the experience of evil insignificant. Plato, on the other hand, is somewhat less sanguine, offering several explanations for the experience of evil despite the existence of providential care: the assignment of demiurgic tasks to 'young gods,' the chaotic, irrational nature of matter and its unfortunate but necessary effects in creation (re: *Tim.* 40e–42e, 48a, 52d–53b, 68e–69a), and individual choices made prior to and following incarnated existence (re: *Phaedrus* 248c–e; *Resp.* 617d–e). Chapter six will discuss the reception of the latter passages in Roman philosophy of providence, while the reception of the former will be briefly discussed here. While the 'dualist' streak in Platonism is Pythagorean—that is, self-identifying in some way with the figure of Pythagoras and his numeral-based interpretation of reality—in sources both early and late, our Roman 'dualist' Platonists explain their thoughts on matter and evil, significantly, with reference to providence.

Pythagorean thinking was already in Roman antiquity known for its dualism, attesting evil to exist as an opposite of good. In early Pythagoreanism, opposing principles seem independent and eternal, as in the famous 'Table of Opposites' known to Aristotle, a list of antitheses encompassing all walks of human experience.[4] The fusion of Platonism and Pythagoreanism that appears to have transpired in the decades following Plato yielded a metaphysic which postulated at least two causes to the universe: a principle of unity (the Monad), and a principle of number or diversity (the 'indefinite Dyad'), a schema formulated in full for the first time by Eudorus of Alexandria (first century BCE).[5] On the other hand, when later Platonists talk about active and passive principles—i.e., God and matter—they could be working with proof-texts from the dialogues alone. Plato does admit the existence of an opposite of good (Theaetetus 176d) and, some believed, of an evil World Soul (*Laws* x 896e, 898c). Similarly, the *Timaeus* describes a 'receptacle' with which the demiurge operates, and their relationship to matter, chaotic movement, and necessity, albeit in terms that are not at all clear.[6] Yet external witnesses confirm that Plato wrote about two causes.

---

3   D. L. 7.134; Calc. *Comm. Tim.* 297; for discussion, see e.g. Bobzien, *Determinism and Freedom*, 16–28; O'Brien, *Demiurge*, 87 n. 16.

4   Arist. *Metaph.* 1.5 986a. See Dörrie, "Dualismus," col. 337; Armstrong, "Dualism," 34–35.

5   For Eudorus, the *locus classicus* is Simpl. *Comm. phys.* 9:181.7–130, per the recent discussion of Brenk, "Plutarch's Middle-Platonic God," 30–31, 38–40; for Platonists on the two principles in general, see D. L. 8.25; de Vogel, *Pythagoras*, 204; cf. O'Brien, *Demiurge*, 27.

6   On *Thaetetus* 176d, see Magris, *L'idea di destino*, 2:675; Adamson, "Making a Virtue," 18–20. On *Leg.* 896e and 898c, see Dörrie, "Dualismus," col. 338; Russell, *The Devil*, 148; Karamanolis, *Philosophy*, 67; Reydams-Schils, "Maximus,"135. Some doubt that an evil World Soul is what Plato

Aristotle claims that Plato described two principles: one of matter, and one of form (*anagkē* and *nous*, respectively), "cause of the good and bad."[7] Aristotle already identifies the receptacle of the *Timaeus* with matter and evil (*Physics* 1.9 192a15); he is followed first by Moderatus of Gades (first century CE).[8] Consequently, the Middle Platonists generally fall into one of two parties regarding the status of a second creative principle vis-à-vis evil. The first position was that matter might be evil, but the descent of the soul into it, creating the World Soul and the creative activity associated with it, is something that is good—a line of thinking adopted by Alcinous and refined by Plotinus and (as we will see) Origen, eventually becoming standard in Neoplatonism of the later third century onwards.[9] The second party asserted that matter subsists in the malevolent World Soul, which takes on the role of a counter-principle to the First Principle, Mind. Although they differ on important details, this latter view was adopted by Plutarch and Numenius, who consequently are often referred to as 'dualist' Platonists.[10]

Plutarch's classic exposition of his views is his treatise *On Isis and Osiris*, an allegorical reading of the Egyptian theogonic myth featuring the marriage of the regent Osiris to Isis, the former's murder and dismemberment by the evil god Seth, and the ensuing struggle of Seth with the royal heir, Horus.[11] Plutarch sets out from the observation that the universe cannot possibly be

---

       has in mind in *Leg.* (Armstrong, "Dualism," 35; Alt, *Weltflucht*, 11, 23). On the 'receptacle' in *Tim.* 50a–51b and 52d–53b, see above, chapter one.

7   Arist. *Metaph.* 1.6 988a. See Armstrong, "Dualism," 35; Alt, *Weltflucht*, 11; O'Brien, *Demiurge*, 31. If the second principle or dyad is here meant to be the ideas with reference to which the demiurge creates in *Tim.* 29a—which is by no means clear—it cannot be a source of evil in any attenuated sense. For two principles instead of three in the doxographic tradition, see also D. L. 3.69; Theophrastus's remarks, ap. Simpl. *Comm. Phys.* 9:26.7–13; Waszink, "Observations," 130.

8   Simp. *Comm. Phys.* 9:230.5–27; Num. frg. 52. See Armstrong, "Dualism," 37–38; Karamanolis, *Philosophy*, 67; and further below.

9   Alc. *Epit.* 8.6–7; for Plotinus on the soul's (undescending) descent, see *Enn.* 4.8 [6] 5–6; 2.9 [33] 4; 1.8 [51] 14.34–59. The *Chaldean Oracles* sometimes regard matter as positive (frgs. 273, 216), but more often negative (frgs. 88, 100, 105, 129, 134, 172, 180). On the latter, see Denzey (Lewis), *Cosomology and Fate*, 111–112. For more general discussion of the relationship between the World Soul, matter, and evil in Middle Platonism and Gnosticism, see J.M. Dillon, "Descent"; Corrigan, "Positive," esp. 21–23. Plotinus's position—that the soul descends into matter only partially—would be rejected by Iamblichus and the Athenian School (see Wallis, "Soul and Nous"), but their debates need not detain us here.

10   E.g. Dörrie, "Dualismus," 339; Russell, *The Devil*, 160; Armstrong, "Dualism"; Alt, *Weltflucht*; see further the following notes.

11   On Plutarch's treatment of Egyptian mythology, see recently S. Nagel, "Mittelplatonische Konzepte," 82–99.

THE OTHER GODS

the product of atoms (so Democritus and Epicurus), "nor that the creator of undifferentiated matter is one rational principle and one providence—as the Stoics maintain—that prevails and rules over all things."[12] Rather, he continues, "the greatest majority and the wisest" believe that "there are two gods, rivals as it were—one the creator (*dēmiourgon*) of good things, the other of evil," "but power ultimately belongs to the better one (*alla tēs beltionos to kratos estin*)."[13] Perhaps because the Egyptian legend of Osiris has (at least) three main players, Plutarch is interested in three principles, rather than two. Osiris, the demiurge, is the active principle. Isis, his counterpart, is "receptacle and matter (*chōra kai hylē*)," eventually producing reflections of Osiris: "for creation is an image of substance in matter, and what is created an imitation of being."[14] The third party, Seth-Typhon, is the cause and personification of evil, such as harmful plants and animals.[15] "Typhon is that part of the soul which is passible, impulsive, irrational, and capricious ..."[16] On the authority of Plato's *Laws* (896d), Plutarch claims that the evil principle comprises part of the World Soul,[17] and this evil part could only be be Seth-Typhon. It would stand to reason that Isis may be the other, good part of the World Soul, although Plutarch never states this explicitly;[18] as a receptive but good principle, she represents matter divorced from chaos.

Ugo Bianchi regards all this as a 'radical dualism,' but, as Carl O'Brien observes, he misreads the myth on many counts.[19] While Plutarch's point is that good and evil effects must have distinct good and evil causes, he explic-

---

12   *Is. Os.* 369a, text and tr. Babbitt in LCL 306:108–109, modified. Elsewhere, Plutarch attacks the Epicureans who call providence a myth (*Def. orac.* 420b).

13   *Is. Os.* 369d–e, 371a, text and tr. Babbitt in LCL 306:110–111, 120–121, slightly modified; see also ibid., 376f–377a; Alt, *Weltflucht*, 22–23; Opsomer and Steel, "Evil," 235–236.

14   *Is. Os.* 372f, text and tr. Babbitt in LCL 306:310–331, slightly modified.

15   *Is. Os.* 368e–369a, 369c–d, 371d; Alt, *Weltflucht*, 24.

16   *Is. Os.* 371b, text and tr. Babbitt in LCL 306:120–121, slightly modified; see also O'Brien, *Demiurge*, 104; cf. Armstrong, "Dualism," 38.

17   *Is. Os.* 370f. Plutarch argues that evil derives from the irrational movement of the World Soul elsewhere as well (*On the Generation of the Soul in the Timaeus*, 1014–1015; *Def. orac.* 435f). On these passages, relevant remains Thévenaz, *L'ame du monde*. More recently, see Armstrong, "Dualism," 38–39; Dragona-Monachou, "Divine Providence," 4461; Algra, "Plutarch and the Stoic Theory," 130–131; Alt, *Weltflucht*, 23–24; Opsomer and Steel, "Evil," 236; Boys-Stones, "'Middle' Platonists on Fate," 440; Karamanolis, *Philosophy*, 67. Another Platonist of the period, Atticus, identified an evil aspect to the World Soul, the source of irrationality and disorder in the world—see Procl. *Comm. Tim.* 1.381–382, 1.391; Armstrong, "Dualism," 38–39.

18   For Isis as the World Soul, see Alt, *Weltflucht*, 24–25; O'Brien, *Demiurge*, 100–101, re: 372e–f; however, Armstrong identifies her only with matter (Armstrong, "Dualism," 38).

19   O'Brien, *Demiurge*, 105, re: Bianchi, "Plutarch," 354.

itly tempers this view by stating that power in this arrangement ultimately rests with the good principle. Interestingly, although he explains the myth in the first place to counter the Stoic identification of the creator of all with providence, he does not state where providence fits into his reading of Egyptian myth in particular.[20] The reason may lie in his claim that the notion transcends ethno-cultural boundaries: just as the different gods of different nations are actually the same beings worshipped under different names, so is it "for that one rational principle which orders everything and the one providence which watches over them (*henos logou tou tauta kosmountos kai mias pronoias epitropeuousēs*) and the ministering powers that are set over all ..."[21] The phrases "one rational principle ... one providence" echo his initial swipe at Stoic notions of providence, but now it is clear that Plutarch does not deny that providential power is singular, active, or omnipresent. Rather, he disagrees with the Stoa regarding the source of evils, which can only be a second principle. The allusion to "ministering powers" (*dunameōn hupourgōn*) cannot but recall the daimonic administrators of divine providence in the cosmos according to Middle Platonic theory. As we saw above, in chapter two, Plutarch refers to *daimones* as helpful, divine intermediaries, but distinguishes them from the formal cause of goodness. They serve next to providence in ordering the universe, but are not that providence itself.

The second-century Platonist Numenius of Apamea, on the other hand, considered matter to be an evil product of a malevolent World Soul that is redeemed through beautification or ordering (*kosmēsis*) by the divine mind, an act of providence. He famously identifies God as two divine minds (*nooi*), the first a transcendent source of all reality—"good in itself"—the second an active, creating intellect, whose goodness is an "imitation" of the first. The beautiful cosmos is in turn an imitation of the second god.[22] Numenius states that the first God is entirely "simple" and "indivisible," but there are also a second and even a third god. "When it engages matter, which is dual, and is one with it, it is split by it, because it (i.e., matter) has a lustful character and is in flux."[23]

---

20   S. Nagel rightly observes that amongst Isis's epithets in her Roman-era cult was *pronoia* ("Mittelplatonische Konzepte," 94), but even if Plutarch knew of this, he does not refer to it explicitly.

21   *Is. Os.* 378a, text and tr. Babbitt in LCL 306:156–157, slightly modified.

22   Euseb. *Praep. ev.* 11.22.3–5 = Num. frg. 16. For discussion, see Alt, *Weltflucht*, 35; Edwards, "Numenius," 123.

23   Eus. *Praep. ev.* 11.17 = Num. frg. 11.14–16, text des Places, 51, tr. mine, with reference to that of des Places (op. cit., 52) and Edwards ("Numenius" 125). The 'warping' of the creative actor in its approach to chaotic matter may have influenced Hermogenes (ap. Ter. *Herm.* 44.1; see further below, in this chapter).

THE OTHER GODS   109

While scholars are unsure as to what precisely he means by the 'third (god),' the sense appears to be that the second, demiurgic noetic principle is split into two when it confronts matter, yielding a third noetic principle. If this third god is indeed the sundered half of the creative intellect, the doctrine is close indeed to Plutarch's, where the demiurgic World Soul is also split in two over the course of its creative activity.[24]

Calcidius preserves an extensive fragment of Numenius's remarks on the relationship between creation, matter, and providence. Numenius has a habit of describing his view as those of "Pythagoras."[25] He is critical of Moderatus's derivation of the dyad from the monad, preferring two eternal, opposing principles:[26]

> Thus Pythagoras too, Numenius says, thinks that matter is fluid and without quality; unlike the Stoics, however, he does not think that it is of a nature intermediate between good and evil, what they call indifferent (*indifferens*), but that it is noxious in the full sense of the word (*plane noxiam*). For like Plato, he thinks that god is the source and cause of good, and matter of evil, but that the product of form and matter is indifferent, so that the world, not matter, is a blend of the goodness of form and the maliciousness of matter. Finally, he thinks that according to the pronouncements of the ancient theologians the world is held to be the offspring of providence and necessity (*providentia et necessitate*).[27]

Rather than blaming evil on matter, Calcidius continues, the Stoa blame it on "perversity" (*pervesitas*). "Pythagoras," however, "says that since providence

---

24   On the three gods, see also Procl. *Comm. Tim.* 303.27–304.7 = Num. frg. 21. Proclus here identifies the third god as the cosmos (cf. also Num. frg. 16), followed by Brenk, "Plutarch's Middle-Platonic God," 36–37. Yet he was a hostile and perhaps unreliable witness to Numenius's ideas, and so Edwards is probably right to identify the third god as the lesser, cloven part of creative intellect, i.e., the World Soul ("Numenius," 124; for a similar reading of the problem, see M. Frede, "Numenius," 1055–1059). On the similarity to the view of Plutarch, see Opsomer and Steel, "Evil," 243.

25   For instance, in *Comm. Tim.* 299, Calcidius names Numenius explicitly in giving the view that he recounts, concluding with "this is Pythagoras's claim concerning the first beginnings." On Numenius's identification of Platonism—and his own philosophy—with Pythaogreanism, see Alt, *Weltflucht*, 30; M. Frede, "Numenius," esp. 1045–1047.

26   Armstrong, "Dualism," 39, re: Calc. *Comm. Tim.* 295 = Num. frg. 52.15–24. On this fragment, see also M. Frede, "Numenius," 1053.

27   Calc. *Comm. Tim.* 296, tr. Magee, 589 = Num. frg. 52.33–44.

110   CHAPTER 3

exists it was necessary for evil to have come to be as well, given that Matter exists and is endowed with the same principle of evil ..."[28]

All this is very much in the spirit of the *Timaeus*. Calcidius seems to say as much when (speaking for himself) he adds that the 'confused and turbulent' state of matter described at *Tim.* 30b "was due to ill-fated chance rather than to the salutary plans of providence (*improspera sorte habebatur nec ex providentiae consultis salubribus*)." He continues, switching back to the doctrine of 'Pythagoras' (i.e., Numenius):

> According to Pythagoras, then, soul as it pertains to Matter is not the absence of any being, as many suppose, and it resists providence, struggling through the force of its own malice to impugn its plans. Providence however, is the work and function of God, whereas blind and capricious rashness (*caeca ... fortuitaque temeritas*) is the inheritance of matter, so that according to Pythagoras it is clear that the mass of the universe was constructed through the convergence of God, Matter, providence, and fortune, but that upon receiving order matter itself (*postquam silvae ornatus*) became the mother of corporeal and generated gods while the fortune it confers is for the most part prosperous but not entirely so, since the natural defect could not be eliminated altogether.[29]

In short, God orders chaotic matter and so renders it beautiful (*ornatus*)—an act of providence—but the world is of necessity not perfect, a fact Numenius here expresses in terms of human experience of *fortuna*, which is "capricious" (*fortuita*).[30] Thus, "everywhere a lower nature is expiating its sin, as it were, by intermingling with providence."[31] This final remark (which closes the fragment) has been misinterpreted as indicating that Numenius saw providence as malevolent.[32] Rather, it is precisely thanks to the activity of providence that we witness any order or beauty in the natural world at all—and this beauty is abundant, and good.

---

28   Calc. *Comm. Tim.* 297, tr. Magee, 591 = Num. frg. 52.53–58.

29   Calc. *Comm. Tim.* 298, text and tr. Magee, 592–593, slightly modified = Num. frg. 52.89–104.

30   Cf. Pseudo-Plutarch's emphasis on the role that "chance" (*tuchē*) plays in contingent events ([*Fat.*] 572b); see above, chapter one.

31   *Ubique miscente se providentiae deterioris naturae uasi quodam piaculo*—Calc. *Comm. Tim.* 299 = frg. Num. 52.119–121, tr. Magee, *On Plato's 'Timaeus'*, 595.

32   *Pace* Denzey (Lewis): "in his [Numenius's] view, pronoia did not act beneficially toward humankind. It had been compromised by the *pathemata* ..." (*Cosomology and Fate*, 111). See rather O'Brien, *Demiurge*, 161–163.

THE OTHER GODS   111

The distinctively 'dualist' character of the views of Plutarch and Numenius may be brought into relief by way of a brief comparison with remarks made about the origins of evil by a contemporary of Numenius, the rhetor Maximus of Tyre, in his oration *If God Makes Good, Whence Comes Evil?*[33] Maximus begins by quoting Homer's *Odyssey*:

> Look you now, how ready mortals are to blame the gods. It is from us, they say, that evils come, but they even of themselves, through their own blind folly, have sorrows beyond that which is ordained.[34]

Therefore, declares Maximus, worldly imperfections owe to physical matter and human freedom.[35] "What we call evil and ruin, the things we lament over, the craftsman calls the preservation of the whole."[36] Such instances of lamentable acts of preservation are familiar: earthquakes and plagues. Maximus's distinction between natural evil—which he determines to be no evil at all, but a necessary byproduct of God's care for a creation formed from a chaotic substance—and human evil, which is entirely up to us, of course recalls the Stoa. Plutarch and Numenius would agree that the present cosmos is good, yet touched by chaos due to the nature of matter.[37] However, they went beyond Maximus and the Stoa in formalizing the cause of that chaos; it is not an aspect of God that we happen to not like, but something that is genuinely bad, that comes from somewhere bad, and it should be recognized as such.

At the same time, Plutarch and Numenius hardly agreed on what the source of evil actually is, even assuming they both evinced a split in the World Soul. For Plutarch, the source of evil is the negative part of the World Soul, represented in Egyptian myth by Seth-Typhon, that comprises the source of evil and chaos; matter, represented by Isis, appears at once neutral and passive, and yet is also responsive to goodness and ultimately productive. For Numenius, the

---

33 Tr. mine of the title given in the manuscript, *Tou theou ta agatha poiountos pothen ta kaka* (see Trapp, 321). The titles of Maximus's orations may not be original to him, but the product of later editors (Trapp, xv). In this case, the manuscript title accords well with the work's content. For a useful overview of Maximus's engagement with Greek philosophical traditions about *pronoia*, see Reydams-Schils, "Maximus."

34 Hom. *Od.* 1.32–34, tr. Murray in LCL 104:5.

35 Max. Tyr. *Or.* 41.4.

36 Max. Tyr. *Or.* 41.4, tr. Trapp, 328. See also O'Brien, *Demiurge*, 121–124. Maximus's use of a craftsman metaphor (worldly evil is like sparks from a blacksmith's anvil) here parallels that of Origen (*Cels.* 6.55, quoted below, in this chapter).

37 Rightly O'Brien, *Demiurge*, 121. As Reydams-Schils puts it, Maximus here "oscillates between more Platonist and more Stoic leanings" ("Maximus," 136).

112   CHAPTER 3

question of evil's source is more complicated: matter is inherently "noxious," and so leads a part of the World Soul to become noxious too. Their respective positions were highly innovative and influential in their own times, and, as O'Brien has observed, help mark two significant developments in the ancient philosophy of creation: first, the emergence of the conception of the creator-god an actual, literal figure—a big maker in the sky—at times even without reference to the *Timaeus*; and second, the emergence of the notion of matter as a principle which is not entirely passive, but resistant to the ordering of the active principle.[38] The contested identities of the demiurge and daimonic intermediaries, of source(s) of evil, and of material substance were at the heart of discussions about providence and creation in this period for Roman philosophers of all stripes. Yet many of those who considered themselves followers of Jesus Christ brought to these same discussions a different set of beliefs and proof-texts regarding the sources of evil in the world, generally known today as 'apocalyptic.'

3   'Mitigated Dualism' and Jewish Apocalyptic Literature

In a classic treatment of dualism in the history of Greek philosophy, Arthur Hilary Armstrong, identifies one of the most important sources of evil in early Christian thought as "the fall of angels and of men." These two falls refer, of course, to the descent of the "sons of God" (*bnai ha-Elohim*) to mate with human women (Gen 6:1–4 MT) and Adam and Eve's poor choices in the Garden of Eden (Gen 2–3).[39] Both of these stories are about the introduction of sin, and its connotations for death, into the world.[40] Loren Stuckenbruck reminds us that this plurality of explanations—angels, devils, sin, etc.—emerged from a culture where these forces were thought to be working independently of one another, and not as part of a greater 'system' waiting to be reconstructed by us today.[41] Nonetheless, we may speak of these explanations for evil foundational to a worldview underlying so much Jewish and Christian literature of the first centuries CE, in which the cosmos is beset by a universal, personified evil force, as well as demons, who inculcate sin—but over whom God and

---

38   O'Brien, *Demiurge*, 27–28, 88, respectively.

39   Armstrong, "Dualism," 49.

40   Cf. the list of Collins, *Seers*, 292–298, discussed in turn by Reed, *Fallen Angels*, 101–102. Collins (op. cit.) offers two additional explanations: the equation of evil with primordial chaos and God's determination of evil in the Two Spirits doctrine. The former will be discussed below; on the latter—the "wicked inclination" which became prevalent in Rabbinic literature—see Rosen-Zvi, *Demonic Desires*.

41   "Satan and Demons," 174.

THE OTHER GODS   113

his followers are assured of eventual triumph. Because such a view is prevalent in many biblical and parabiblical texts which are written or transmitted in the genre 'apocalypse,' it is often called 'apocalyptic.'[42] Armstrong recognized that such themes are pivotal to the question of evil in early Christian philosophy, and so the present section elucidates them more fully by way of surveying the emergence of this apocalyptic heritage in Second Temple Jewish literature, ranging from the Septuagint to the Dead Sea Scrolls, Enochic literature, and the Gospels and Paul. The 'apocalyptic' perspectives of these Second Temple Jewish sources furnished some of the central issues and proof-texts which the earliest Christian philosophers had in mind when they talked about providence: the identification of the gods of Graeco-Roman cult with evil demons, the leadership of these demons by a greater personification of evil, the notion that these beings are fallen angels, and the connotation of evil itself in terms of the sin these beings introduce to the world.

The Aramaic-Hebrew 'Dead Sea Scrolls,' the first of which turned up at Qumran (Israel-Palestine), in 1947, contain a bonanza of Jewish literature from the last two or three centuries BCE where 'apocalyptic' language about the agents of darkness is prolific and profound.[43] Scholarship has divined at least five chief demons responsible for evil in the Scrolls: Melki-Resa, the Angel of Darkness, Satan, Mastema, and Beliar.[44] The most prominent of these is Beliar. According to Stuckenbruck, Beliar is distinctive in two aspects: first, while many apocalyptic texts refer to groups of demonic beings (packs of fallen angels, etc.), the work known as the *Community Rule* singles out Beliar and his followers for denunciation, giving a clear, explicit identity to evil beings.[45] Second, the *Community Rule* describes Beliar as possessing dominion over the cosmos and the evil in it, firmly locating evil's power in the world.[46] Qumran also pre-

---

42   So Russell, *The Devil*, 176. On 'apocalyptic vs. apocalypticism,' see Collins, "Introduction"; more recently, idem, "What is." A problem with the term 'apocalypticism' and its cognate adjective is that not all apocalypses (i.e., revelatory texts) are particularly 'apocalyptic' (i.e., eschatologically-oriented—so Collins, "Introduction," 2–4; Reed, *Fallen Angels*, 61–64). On use of the term 'parabiblical' to denote extracononical biblical sources, see recently e.g. Shoemaker, "Early Christian."

43   For survey of the themes of apocalyptic, dualism, and evil at Qumran, see respectively Collins, *Apocalypticism*; Frey, "Apocalyptic Dualism," 276–288; Leonhardt-Balzer, "Evil."

44   A useful survey is Stuckenbruck, "Satan and Demons," 176–180.

45   1QS II 4–10 par.; 4Q256 II 12–III 4.

46   1QS I 23–24, II 19; 1QM XIV 9–10/4QMa = 4Q491 8–10 I 6–7. For these passages, see Stuckenbruck, "Satan and Demons," 180; Frey, "Apocalyptic Dualism," 286–287. On this point more generally, see Collins, "Mythology"; Pagels, "Preliminary Sketch," 124–127. The expansion of Beliar's domain is also visible in the *Testaments of the Twelve Patriarchs*; for inventory, see Collins, op. cit., 612 n. 64.

serves an early and memorable personification of such a counter-principle as an external impulse to evil in the *Community Rule*, which describes the two spirits implanted in human beings: spirits of truth, and spirits of deceit, ruled by the "Prince of Lights" and "Angel of Darkness," respectively.[47] Such personifications of evil as a causal entity independent from God and with his own distinct person are a radical departure from earlier biblical texts. To be sure, in Deuteronomistic and Prophetic literature, Satan makes people sin, tests humans on God's command, and accuses the anointed (1 Chron 21:1; Job 1–2; Zech 3:1–2, respectively).[48] He is not a particular individual, but "*the* Satan" (*ha-šāṭān*)—"the prosecutor," always translated *diabolos* in the Septuagint.[49] The autonomy of this 'prosecutor' is not clear; rather, he appears to work for God.[50] The Dead Sea Scrolls thus preserve traditions where Beliar and other causes of evil become figures that are both more independent and universal than the demons and this 'prosecutor' working for God in earlier Jewish literature.[51] This is an important step in the direction of the notion of a 'counter-God,' such as Satan in the four canonical Gospels, who serves as God's archenemy.[52]

The identification of angels as agents of cosmic evil first appears in the tradition we know best from the *Book of the Watchers*, whose origins remain murky but which appears to have begun circulating in the third century BCE, eventually being incorporated into the anthology we today call *1 Enoch*.[53] Expanding on the myth of the descent of the "sons of god" into the world to mate with human women and the subsequent spawning of the Nephilim (Gen 6:1–4),[54] the *Book of the Watchers* interprets these "sons" to have been angels, and transmits what appears to be two separate traditions regarding the effects the

---

47   1QS III 18–25. On this section of the *Community Rule*—known today as the *Treatise on the Two Spirits*—see recently Frey, "Apocalyptic Dualism," 279–283; Leonhardt-Balzer, "Evil," 18–22. Cf. D. Martin's remark that none of the demonic or evil beings at Qumran are equated with angels ("When Did Angels," 669).

48   For detailed discussion with many more passages, see Russell, *The Devil*, 197–203.

49   Russell, *The Devil*, 198–199; Stuckenbruck, "Satan and Demons," 173.

50   Recently, re: Job and Zech, see Rollston, "Ur-History." See also Dörrie, "Dualismus," cols. 345–346; Russell, *The Devil*, 204–206; Stoyanov, *Other God*, 58–59; cf. Pagels, "Preliminary Sketch," 116–117.

51   Collins, "Mythology," 612.

52   Stuckenbruck, "Satan and Demons," 181.

53   Generally, see Reed, *Fallen Angels*, 16–22; see also Frey, "Apocalyptic Dualism," 275. On the date of the *Book of the Watchers*, see Reed, op. cit., 3.

54   On the exegetical problem of "angels of god" versus "sons of God" in Gen 6:1, see e.g. Stroumsa, *Another Seed*, 29; Reed, *Fallen Angels*, 116; Grypeou and Spurling, *Book of Genesis*, 166–167.

THE OTHER GODS   115

angels' transgression had for the appearance of evil amongst humanity. The two traditions are named for the chief rebel angels in their respective parts of the text. In the 'Asa'el strain of the text (1 En. 8:1–3; see also 7:1b, 9:8, 10:7), the evil angels illicitly teach human beings about various "reprehensible forms of knowledge," such as the production of weapons, cosmetics, and magic and astrology.[55] In the Shemiḥazah strain, on the other hand, the sexual union of the angels and human women leads to giant, monstrous beings (1 En. 6:1–4, 7:1–2; 9:7–8; 10:9–11; 14:3–7.12). The reason such union is monstrous is that the spiritual and fleshly realms must be kept separate (14:4.9–10).[56] As in Genesis 6, God sends a flood to kill the Nephilim, who die and become "evil spirits" (15:8–9); these spirits 'survive' the Flood in bodiless form and exist on earth even today, explaining the presence of evil demons in the world.[57] The Shemiḥazah narrative of the *Book of the Watchers* thus provides a bridge from Genesis 6's angels to the existence of demons, while the 'Asa'el legend denotes evil human crafts as angelic in origin.

Another human evil that takes on superhuman origins in *1Enoch* is idolatry. In the *Book of the Watchers*, the demonic spawn of the angels and human women trick humans into offering them sacrifices, pretending to be the gods (1 En. 19:1; cf. Ps 95:5 [LXX]; Deut 32:17).[58] Another Enochic text incorporated into 1 En., the *Astronomical Book* (*terminus ante quem* third century BCE), takes up the origins of evil and idolatry in terms of the operations of celestial nature and their terrestrial effects.[59] After establishing the order and harmony of the created world in the sky (1 En. 72–79), the *Astronomical Book* describes the irruption of disorder (80–82), first among the planets above and then above humans below. In biblical and parabiblical literature, the natural world serves not only as evidence of God's authority as creator and ruler of the cosmos, but also as a model or template for human righteousness.[60] The natural cosmos has a will or personality, and is depicted as capable of choosing whether to run the course decreed for it by God—yielding a harmonious world—or to do otherwise, as in the *Book of the Watchers* (1 En. 5:3): "look at the seas.

---

55   Russell, *The Devil*, 192; Stuckenbruck, "Origins of Evil," 99; Reed, *Fallen Angels*, 6, 29–44.

56   Russell, *The Devil*, 186–188; Stuckenbruck, "Origins of Evil," 101.

57   Cf. Jubilees 10:5; generally, see Russell, *The Devil*, 193–194; Stuckenbruck, "Origins of Evil," 103, 112; D. Martin, "When Did Angels," 667–668; Frey, "Apocalyptic Dualism," 275; Wasserman, "Beyond," 193–194.

58   See Russell, *Satan*, 70; Timotin, *Démonologie platonicienne*, 213.

59   On the date of the *Astronomical Book*, see Reed, *Fallen Angels*, 3.

60   On the former point, see above, chapter two; on the latter, see e.g. Sir 43:1–13; Testament of Naphtali 2–3; 1 En. 2–3; Wyse Rhodes, "Natural World."

116   CHAPTER 3

They do not part; they fulfill all their duties."[61] Not so with the planets of the *Astronomical Book* (1 En. 80:6–8):

> Many of the chiefs of the stars shall make errors in respect to the orders given to them; they shall change their courses and functions ... All the orders of the stars shall harden (in disposition) against the sinners and the conscience of those that dwell upon the earth ... Then they (the sinners) shall err and take them (the stars) to be gods. And evil things shall be multiplied upon them; and plagues shall come upon them, so as to destroy all.[62]

Many passages in the Septuagint refer to 'demons' (*daimones*) as the imposters pretending to be gods in heathen, sacrificial cults.[63] The *Astronomical Book* elides these demonic beings with celestial powers in the context of idolatry.

These two strands of explanations for evil and its coexistence with God's rule—the presence of demons and even an arch-demon, and the human ills that demons or evil angels introduced to society—come together in various ways in New Testament texts. Thus in the canonical Gospels, we already see Satan as a proper name, denoting "the Devil."[64] "Demons" operate under his authority.[65] He is able to offer Jesus "all the kingdoms of the world" (Matt 4:8/Luke 4:5–7), and so, it is implied, a sort of ruler of the cosmos. Matthew and Luke speak of Satan as an angel.[66] Paul refers relatively often to evil angels,[67] and in 1 Cor 10:19–22, demons are associated with sacrificial cult and idols—

---

61   Tr. Isaac in Charlesworth, ed., *Old Testament Pseudepigrapha*, 15. See also *Pss. Sol.* 18:11–12.

62   Tr. Isaac in Charlesworth, ed., *Old Testament Pseudepigrapha*, 59; see further Wasserman, "Beyond," 191.

63   D. Martin, "When Did Angels," 657–663, esp. 662: "Ancient Jews thus used *daimonion* to translate five or six different Hebrew words. In the original Near Eastern context, those words referred to different kinds of beings: goat-man gods; superhuman beings that either are or cause diseases; abstract qualities or goods that may also be seen as gods, such as Fortune or Fate. What they have in common, nonetheless, is that they all were thought of as gods—in fact, as gods other people falsely worship: the gods of the nations" (ibid., 662).

64   Matt 4:1–10; John 13:2, 27; cf. Mark 4:14/Luke 8:12/Matt 13:39; see Stuckenbruck, "Satan and Demons," 174, 181.

65   Mark 3:22–26/Matt 12:24–28/Luke 11:14–20; Luke 10:17–18; see Russell, *The Devil*, 236–239; D. Martin, "When Did Angels," 673; Stuckenbruck, "Satan and Demons," 174.

66   Satan falls from heaven in Luke 10:18; Satan and his angels will eventually go into the fire in 25:41. See D. Martin, "When Did Angels," 673; also Russell, *The Devil*, 228–229.

67   D. Martin, "When Did Angels," 674 refers to 1 Cor 6:3, 2 Cor 12:7; more ambiguous cases are 1 Cor 11:10, Gal 3:19 (re: Acts 7:53), and 1 Cor 2:6.8 (cf. Rom 8:38).

exactly the usage we know from the Septuagint and 1 Enoch.[68] On the other hand, while the fall of Adam and Eve from Paradise due to their primordial sin is entirely absent in the Gospels,[69] Paul regards "all creation" to be captive to sin because of Adam, through whom sin entered the world (Rom 8:22, 5:12, respectively; similarly 5:18–19, 1 Cor 15:20–22).[70] While the canonical Gospels depict Jesus as teaching that sin is breaking the Ten Commandments, sin for Paul is a totalizing, universal force that plagues all humanity.[71]

What stands out from this very brief survey of biblical and parabiblical literature on the sources of evil in the Second Temple period is that throughout all these works, there is something wrong in the present cosmos. It is sin, which connotes death: demons are responsible for introducing sin into the world, and with time these agents are universalized from more specific, particular into universal, cosmic forces—Beliar or Satan. Consequently, it was once common to denote the 'apocalyptic' perspective underlying these sources as "pessimistic."[72] The term 'dualism,' curiously enough, has been used more often in the context of apocalypticism to describe eschatology rather than theodicy, and perhaps for good reason.[73] Even in the literature surveyed here, the independence from God of all of these explanations for evil is ambivalent at best. Some biblical proof-texts state that it is God who is responsible for evil (e.g. 1 Sam 2; Is 45:7; Job 1–2; Micah 1:12–13; cf. Qur'ān 6:112).[74] Throughout sapiential and apocalyptic literature, there is a strong sense that all of history, even the bad parts, has been predetermined by God in some way.[75] Beliar's cosmic dominion at Qumran appears to be temporary and fixed by God.[76] As Emma Wasserman has observed, whatever 'dualism' one finds in Jewish apocalyptic literature is of a mitigated variety, because it depicts even demonic beings "as nonthreatening to the supreme deity, and must construe them as lesser powers relating to disfavored peoples ... The framework of heav-

---

68   D. Martin, "When Did Angels," 674; also Fredriksen, *Sin*, 25–26.

69   Russell, *The Devil*, 232; Stuckenbruck, "Satan and Demons," 182.

70   Russell, *The Devil*, 232; further, Sutcliffe, *Providence and Suffering*, 42–47.

71   Fredriksen, *Sin*, 16–19, 32–36.

72   Hanson, *Dawn*, 11–12, 28; for further examples and discussion, see Burns, "Apocalypses," 358.

73   Vielhauer and Strecker, "Apocalypses," 549; Hanson, *Dawn*, 436–442; Gammie, "Spatial and Ethical Dualism," 357.

74   So Couliano, *Tree of Gnosis*, 24; further, Russell, *The Devil*, 174–184; Ferguson, *Providence of God*, 22.

75   A recent, useful discussion with extensive survey of secondary literature is Klawans, *Josephus*, 50–52, 62.

76   Rightly emphasized by Cohen, "Josephus," 373; Russell, *The Devil*, 213–214; Stoyanov, *Other God*, 62.

enly hierarchy allows for a relativizing explanation that displaces conflict onto lower-level beings while also affirming the ongoing just and providential rule of the supreme powers in heaven."[77] Like Wasserman, Christian philosophers of the second and early third centuries CE found the language of providence to be ideal for articulating this mitigated character of their apocalyptic world-view. Less ideal to these writers, steeped in Enochic lore as they were, was the Middle Platonists' identification of *daimones* as the mediators of God's providence.

4   Athenagoras on "the Archon over Matter and Material Things"

As discussed in chapter two, two philosophers deeply engaged with Judaism, Philo and Justin Martyr, were interested in the notion of divine providence and committed to a worldview in which divine activity was visible across the minutiae of everyday life—care for individuals—as well as greater salvation-history, a perspective deeply indebted to Stoicism. The problem of evil then presented difficulties for their ideas about providence, much as they did for the Platonists and Stoa. Philo, for instance, inclined more towards Stoic views of evil as well as providence, and showed relatively little interest in Enochic lore, even as he theorized the fallible character of matter and divine intermediaries and the imperfect byproducts of their activity largely in terms of contemporary Platonism. For Christian philosophers of the second and third centuries, on the other hand, the existence of demons—fallen angels who exalted themselves as deities while they fed from sacrificial entrails—and the Devil himself were a reality that could not be ignored or explained as benign. Making sense of their role in the providential scheme of things rendered it impossible for these thinkers to easily adapt Middle Platonic ideas of multiple gradations of providence to their own ends. Superhuman intermediaries could not simply be imperfect transmitters of goodness; some of them had to be evil.

The authors of what would become New Testament texts did not take up the Greeks' notion of *daimones* as benevolent overseers; rather, they operated from the more popular view that demons "like just about all gods, were unpredictable persons, sometimes blessing, sometimes harming ... The very reason for sacrifices was to feed, mollify, and influence *daimones* to be beneficient."[78] By the mid-second century CE, Justin Martyr, in both of his works

---

77   Wasserman, "Beyond," 197–198; similarly the 'permissive dualism' of Gammie, "Spatial and Ethical Dualism," 357.

78   D. Martin, "When Did Angels," 663.

THE OTHER GODS 119

entitled *Apology*, had identified the Greek gods made famous by "poets and mythologers" as sinning angels who set themselves up as gods and are responsible for spreading sin.[79] His student Tatian the Assyrian made similar claims, and alluded to a Satanic figure who perversely drew the worship of human and angel alike on account of being "first-born" (*prōtogonon*), who subsequently became a demon, and whose followers become demons as well.[80] In North Africa, where reception of *1 Enoch* appears to have been particularly warm, Tertullian defended the authenticity of the work and referred to its myth of the descent of the Watchers to explain the existence of evils.[81] It was distinctive to understand the relationship between demons and sin in terms of fallen angels and sacrificial cult: Valentinus, for instance, described the inner struggle with sin in terms of a demonic infestation of the heart, entirely without reference to the Enochic myth or demons feeding on sacrifices.[82]

Yet some of the most important early Christian philosophizing about matter, evil and providence took these matters to be inextricable from the mitigated apocalypticism of Enochic literature, understood with reference to the sinful practice of blood sacrifice and the demons who participate in it. Foremost of

---

79 "Poets and mythologers": *2 Apol.* 5; responsible for evil, receiving sacrifices as gods: *1 Apol.* 5.2–6.1, 14; *2 Apol.* 5. See further *Dial.* 79, where Justin's Jewish interlocutor is disturbed by the notion of sinning angels. On these passages, see Russell, *Satan*, 64–65, 70–71; Pagels, "Preliminary Sketch," 106; Rankin, *Athenagoras*, 66; Grypeou and Spurling, *Book of Genesis*, 168; Thorsteinsson, "Justin," 564–565.

80 *Or. Graec.* 7–8; see Russell, *Satan*, 73–76; Dihle, "Astrology," 164–165; Petersen, "Tatian," 147; D. Martin, "When Did Angels," 676. On the role of personal responsibility (*autexousia*) in this passage, see below, chapter six. On matter and creation in Tatian (relatively distant from the issue of theodicy), see Karamanolis, *Philosophy*, 75–76.

81 For Tertullian's remarks on the authenticity of 1 En., see *On the Apparel of Women*, 1.3.1; on the Watchers as the gods of idolatry, see *Idol.* 4.2–3, 15.6; on the descent of angels, see *On the Veiling of Virgins*, 7; for cit. and discussion, see Russell, *Satan*, 96–97; vanderKam, "1 Enoch," 47–54, 67–70; Reed, *Fallen Angels*, 195–197. On the predominance of North Africa in early Patristic reception of 1 En., see VanderKam, "1 Enoch," 59–60. For Tertullian also emphasizes the Devil and human sin as sources of evil: see Russell, *Satan*, 90–101; Aland (Ehlers), "Sünde und Erlösung," 148; Norelli, "Marcion," 125; D. Martin, "When Did Angels," 676. For Tertullian's treatment of human free will and original sin, see further below, chapter six.

82 Clem. Al. *Strom.* 2.20.114 = frg. H Layton (*Gnostic Scriptures*, 245). Ancient parallels indicate that the metaphor refers to demons inhabiting the embodied soul (Whittaker, "Valentinus"). See further Markschies, *Valentinus*, 54–82; Thomassen, *Spiritual Seed*, 455–457; Brakke, "Valentinians," 15 (recalling Luke 10:34). The metaphor of brigands in a hostel for demons in the heart is extrapolated on (without reference to *pronoia*) in *Interp. Know.* NHC XI 6.30–37; see further Brakke, op. cit., 18.

120   CHAPTER 3

these are the remarks of Athenagoras of Athens, in his apologetic work *Embassy for the Christians* (ca. 176–180).[83] Athenagoras agrees with his Platonist contemporaries "that which always is, the intelligible, is uncreated, whereas that which is not, the perceptible, is created"—i.e., the active, providential principle is Mind.[84] It is a single maker—"God, the creator of the world, is from the beginning one and alone"—and only a creator can administer providence.[85] Yet, in an extensive discussion of the fall of the angels and the origin of evil, he argues that angelic intermediaries do play a role in caring for the cosmos.[86] "Suppose," he asks,

> that the poets and philosophers did not recognize that God was one and did not have critical opinions about the other gods, some regarding them as demons, others regarding them as matter, others regarding them as men who once lived, would it make sense to have us banished because we have a doctrine which distinguishes God and matter and their respective substances?[87]

This doctrine begins with the Trinity: God, Son (Word), and Holy Spirit, "united in power yet distinguished in rank." Yet there are "other powers," he says,

> ... which are concerned with matter and operate through it. One of them is opposed to God, not because there is a counterpart to God (*mian men tēn antitheon, ouch hoti antidoxoun ti esti tōi theōi*) ... but because the spirit which is concerned with matter is opposed to God's goodness (*enantion esti to peri tēn hulēn echon pneuma*) ... The spirit opposed to him was in fact created by God just as the rest of the angels were also created by him, and he was entrusted with the administration of matter and material things.[88]

---

83   For the dating of *Leg.*, see Schoedel, "Introduction," xi–xii.
84   Athenag. *Leg.* 19.2, tr. Schoedel, 41.
85   Athenag. *Leg.* 8.7–8, tr. Schoedel, 19. As Schoedel notes (op. cit. 17 n. 3), this statement follows a convoluted argument regarding what space God may (not) occupy that reminds one of Hermogenes, although his reference to "Gnostics" here is misleading.
86   On these chapters of *Leg.*, see VanderKam, "1 Enoch," 40–42, 65; Reed, *Fallen Angels*, 175 n. 32; Rankin, *Athenagoras*, 61, 65; Barnard, *Athenagoras*, 114; Bergjan, *Der fürsorgende Gott*, 316–324.
87   Athenag. *Leg.* 24.1, tr. Schoedel, 59.
88   Athenag. *Leg.* 24.2, tr. Schoedel, 59. See also *Leg.* 10.5.

THE OTHER GODS

"These angels were called into being by God to exercise providence over the things set in order by him, so that God would have universal and general providence over all things whereas the angels would be set over particular things."[89] When Athenagoras refers earlier to the providence that only a sole creator can administer, he must mean this general providence over the wholes; the administration of particulars is assigned to intermediaries, per the model of Middle Platonists like Pseudo-Plutarch or Apuleius.[90]

God created these angels with the power of free choice (*authaireton*).[91] Some angels carried out their duties, yet:

> Others violated both their own nature and their office. These include the archon over matter and material things (*ho tēs hylēs … archōn*) and others who are of those stationed at the first firmament … The latter are the angels who fell to lusting after maidens and let themselves be conquered by the flesh, the former became uncaring and wicked (*amelēsas kai ponēros … genomenos*) in his administration of what had been entrusted to him.[92]

The fallen angels now dwell in the air, while their offspring with the human women, the giants, roam the earth.[93] Quoting Euripides on how lawless and chaotic the world appears to be, Athenagoras concludes that it is no surprise that Aristotle came to believe that "things are not guided by providence"; rather, rather, it is "the demonic impulses and activities of the hostile spirit (*hai apo tounantiou pneumatos daimonikai kinēseis kai energeiai*)" which move people to behave in irrational and evil ways.[94] These external, irrational movements recall Stoic philosophy,[95] but their agent is literally a spiritual one—the fallen angels and their leader, an archon, i.e., the demons and Satan of the Gospels. As observed above, Athenagoras goes out of his way to emphasize that there is only one causal principle, and it is God, so these evil agents are ultimately not

---

89   *… tēn men pantelikēn kai genikēn ho theos ⟨echōn⟩ tōn holōn pronoian, tēn de epi merous hoi ep' autois tachthentes aggeloi*—Athenag. *Leg.* 24.3, text and tr. Schoedel, 58–59.

90   See further Pouderon, *Athénagore*, 142–148.

91   Athenag. *Leg.* 24.4–5. See further below, chapter six.

92   Athenag. *Leg.* 24.5, text and tr. Schoedel, 60–61, significantly modified.

93   The details of the impurity of mixing spiritual and fleshly bodies, as well as the giant offspring of the angels and women roaming the world in what appears to be an innocuous way, belong to the *Book of the Watchers* and point to Athenagoras's knowledge of the text.

94   Athenag. *Leg.* 25.2–3, text and tr. Schoedel, 62–63.

95   Giulea, "The Watchers' Whispers."

agents at all. Yet they began as divine administrators, who must have had some kind of causal efficacy of their own, albeit restricted to particulars (and this is indeed how humans experience the impulses caused by demons). Athenagoras thus adopts the Middle Platonic model of daimonic administration of providence wholesale, even though it sours somewhat when asked to process the apocalyptic demonology of Enoch and the Gospels. The philosophical difference with the Platonists is one more of emphasis and color than substance: the demigods of the *Timaeus* are fallible, too, but Plato and his Middle Platonic exegetes do not dwell on this fact; nor do they describe this fallibility in terms of sin, understood in turn as participation in civic sacrifice.

5 Living Idols and Questions That Deserve Punishment according to Clement of Alexandria

Clement of Alexandria (ca. 150–215 CE) also struggled with Middle Platonic notions of evil and daimonic administration of worldly providence, in passages largely found in books one and seven of his *Stromateis* (*Miscellanies*), probably written in the last decade of the second century.[96] The fact that these discussions to some extent provide bookends for this massive, sprawling work is appropriate, since they present complementary portraits of divine intermediaries of opposing characters and traits. While *Stromateis* book one condemns demons and their relationship to 'pagan' philosophy, book seven contrasts their teaching with the providential tutelage of the most advanced Christian teacher—whom Clement calls the 'Gnostic,' a nigh-superhuman, philosophical pastor. Like Athenagoras, Clement adopts the Middle Platonic structure of a hierarchy of angelic administrators of providence, but he trades out the problematic figures of *daimones* in exchange for authoritative, Christian teachers.

In book one of the *Stromateis*, Clement's discussion of divine care is largely focused on the universal divine dispensation or administration (*oikonomia*), its identification with the Word Christ, and its extension to particulars.[97] Like some Classical Greek authors, he uses the term *pronoia* occasionally to refer to banal human foresight or care for everyday matters, but in his corpus the word

---

96   We possess very little information regarding Clement's life. For the date given here, see recently Ashwin-Siejkowski, "Clement," 85.

97   On Clement's notion of divine economy, see esp. Osborn, *Clement*, 31–37. Irenaeus also used the term 'economy' to describe the Spirit's descent at Pentecost (*Haer.* 3.17.2–4). Clement even authored a lost work *On Providence*; for *status quaestionis*, see Bergjan, "Clement," 63, 90–92.

THE OTHER GODS 123

chiefly denotes divine activity.[98] According to Clement, God intervenes in biblical salvation-history: as Philo argued, the barren Sarah became pregnant thanks to providence, and in like fashion was Noah rescued from the Flood.[99] Good angels serve as His agents, watching over individuals: "for regiments of angels occupy nations and cities—and perhaps some of them are established over individual persons as well."[100] Like Tertullian or Minucius Felix, Clement is at pains to distinguish his view of a God actively caring for particulars from Stoicism (see above, chapter two):

> Nor do the Stoics speak nobly, when they say that God, being a body, inhabits even the vilest matter (*tēs atimotatēs hylēs pephoitēkenai*) ... For the teaching, which is in accordance with Christ, deifies the Creator, attributes providential care even to particulars, shows that the nature of the elements is both subject to change and generation, and teaches us to devote our conduct to that power which brings similitude to God, and to welcome the divine plan as the directing agent of all education.[101]

Characteristic of Clement are his closing words here, which identify God's care with a Christian educational program. Clement's rhetoric of providence thus serves as part of his greater project of adapting Greek philosophy to a Christian context, and so, when he states that all good things are attributable to providence, this must of course include Greek literature.[102] Just as providence is able to turn evils to goods, so did angelic theft result in the gift of philosophy, a teaching that prepares one for Christianity and whose appearance is no accident or chance event in human history:[103]

> Philosophy was not sent out by the Lord, but came, says Scripture, either as an object of theft or a robber's gift. Some power, some angel learned a

---

98   On the former point, see Bergjan, "Clement," 63–64.

99   Clem. Al. *Strom.* 1.5.30.4, 2.19.99.1, respectively.

100   Clem. Al. *Strom.* 6.17.157.5, discussed by Spanneut, *Stoicisme*, 329 n. 32, recalling Cic. *Nat. d.* 2.164–167. See further *Strom.* 6.16.148.6 (on secondary causes mediating universal providence).

101   Clem. Al. *Strom.* 1.11.51.1–52.3, text Stählin in GCS 52:33–34, tr. mine.

102   Clem. Al. *Strom.* 1.5.28.1.

103   For God's ability to turn the evil to good, see the discussion of Osborn, *Clement*, 49. On the preparatory nature of Greek philosophy, see (in addition to the passages cited in the following notes), see e.g. Clem. Al. *Strom.* 1.19.94.1–3, 6.17.153.1–4. For Clement's thoughts on the origins and usefulness of philosophy, the classic treatment remains Lilla, *Clement*, 9–59.

124   CHAPTER 3

portion of the truth, but did not remain within the truth, and stole these things and taught them to human beings by way of inspiration. The Lord has known the outcome of the future from before the foundation of the world and of individual beings; he knew all about this but did not stop it. For the transmission of the theft to human beings did bring some advantage at the time ... but providence straightened out the result of the crime and turned it to our advantage.[104]

Clement refers to the angels' illicit instruction of humankind—especially human women—on many other occasions, where he makes clear that their sin was sexual in nature.[105] While Clement never explicitly identifies the fallen angels with demons, he seems to imply as much when he refers to the traditional gods of Greek and Roman cult as either angels or demons, and so it is probable that he has something in mind like the belief of Justin or Athenagoras that the fallen angels became instigators of idolatry.[106] As Athenagoras argued, demons here act as external impulses for humans to sin.[107] The Devil is "the lord of demons" (*ton tōn daimonōn archonta*), and, in another parallel to Justin and Athenagoras, responsible for his own evil character.[108]

Clement devises a kind of inversion of the daimonic transmission of divine knowledge in book seven of the *Stromateis*, which describes the life and practice of the 'true knower (*gnōstikos*).' Here, too, he emphasizes the omnipres-

---

104   Clem. Al. *Strom.* 1.17.81.4–5, tr. Ferguson, 85. See also *Strom.* 1.17.86.1–87.2, where he surmises these events to lie behind the myth of Prometheus, and 7.2.6.4. See further Lilla, *Clement*, 10–11 n. 3, 29; Karavites, *Evil*, 127–128. Russell's account of this passage is misleading (*Satan*, 115–116).

105   Clem. Al. *Strom.* 3.7.59.2; 5.1.10.2; idem, *Paed.* 3.2.14.2. For cit. and discussion, see VanderKam, "1 Enoch," 44–47, 66–67; Karavites, *Evil*, 42, 100; Osborn, *Clement*, 51; Reed, *Fallen Angels*, 178, 181–184; eadem, "Beyond," 161. For Clement's defense of the authenticity of the Enochic writings, see *Ecl.* 2.1, 53.4, cit. Reed, *Fallen Angels*, 148, 152.

106   For the pagan gods of idolatry as evil demons (among other things), see Clem. Al. *Protr.* 2.40–41, 3.43.1–44.1, 4.51.6–4.52.1, 4.55.4–5, a work in which the only angels mentioned are good ones. For "demons and angels" as the causes of natural evils, see idem, *Strom.* 6.3.31.1. On this question in general (deciding in favor of the identification), see Karavites, *Evil*, 42–43; also Russell, *Satan*, 113 n. 16; Timotin, *Démonologie platonicienne*, 213.

107   E.g., Clem. Al. *Strom.* 6.12.98.1; 7.11.66.1–2; Karavites, *Evil*, 46. For many more citations, see Russell, *Satan*, 115. For Clement on the soul's assent to external impulses (*sugkatathesis*) as identified with spiritual powers, see e.g. *Strom.* 2.20.110–111, on which see Löhr, "Gnostic Determinism," 384; Brakke, "Valentinians," 17.

108   Clem. Al. *Strom.* 5.14.92.5, text Stählin in GCS 52:387, tr. mine, and 1.17.83.2, respectively. The Devil envies the forgiveness God has extended to humans, and works to make them sin further (ibid., 2.13.56.2).

THE OTHER GODS   125

ence of divine care, turning on its head the 'household argument' that some
Stoa used to clear God of responsibility for neglecting individuals:

> At any rate it always belongs to him who is naturally superior to direct the
> inferior, and to him who is able to manage anything well, that he should
> have received the government of it as his due. But the true ruler and direc-
> tor is the Word of God and his providence, superintending all things and
> neglecting the charge of none of her household.[109]

Silke-Petra Bergjan has argued that Clement ultimately conceives of *pronoia*
as a hierarchically organized movement, beginning with God's action through
the Son and culminating in pastoral activity on the part of Christian philosophers—'true Gnostics'—in the Church. Indeed, he writes that the one who
takes care of others "actually preserves a faint image of the true providence
(*eikona ... oligēn tēs tēi alētheiai pronoias*)."[110] The movement begins with the
Word God, but manifests in the everyday activity of the Christian philosopher
who instructs those around him or her. Jesus

> ... is the teacher who educates the Gnostic by means of mysteries ... he
> is the source of providence both for the individual and the community
> and for the universe at large. And that there is a Son of God, and that this
> Son is the Savior and Lord that we assert him to be, is directly declared
> by the divine prophecies ... This is he who bestows on the Greeks also
> their philosophy through the inferior angels. For by an ancient and divine
> ordinance angels are assigned to the different nations; but to the Lord's
> portion (Deut 32:8–9) is the glory of the believers.[111]

Bergjan and others have compared Clement's model to that of the 'Persian
King' of Pseudo-Aristotle's *On the World*, a remote, ultimately transcendent
God whose influence nonetheless emanates, with waning force, into the cos-
mos (see above, chapter one); the difference is that, through the Son's power,

---

109 Clem. Al. *Strom.* 7.2.8.3–4, text Stählin in GCS 17:7–8, tr. Mayor, rev. Chadwick and Oulton
     in idem, *Alexandrian Christianity*, 98; see also 1.11.52.3, 1.17.85.5. Puzzlingly, Bergjan refers
     to this argument as an "aesthetic explanation" of evil (*Der fürsorgende Gott*, 217).

110 Bergjan, "Clement," 85–87, re: Clem. Al. *Strom.* 7.12.70.7, quoted here, text Stählin in
     GCS 17:51, tr. mine; 6.16.148.6; 7.2.8; although the latter rather speaks to God's direct involve-
     ment, the other citations are apposite. See further 7.9.52.1; Bergjan, *Der fürsorgende Gott*,
     327–329.

111 Clem. Al. *Strom.* 7.2.6, tr. Mayor, rev. Chadwick and Oulton in idem, *Alexandrian Christian-
     ity*, 96.

126 CHAPTER 3

God's reach remains undiminished everywhere in it.[112] There is truth to this. However, Clement also contrasts this mediation with the foolish practices of idolatry—the false 'divine' administration governed, as we have seen, by the fallen angels:

> But the dignity of the Gnostic is carried to an even further pitch by the one who has undertaken the direction of the teaching of others, assuming the management (*tēn oikonomian*) in word and deed of that which is the greatest blessing on earth, by virtue of which he becomes a mediator to bring about a close union and fellowship with God. And as those who worship earthly things pray to the idols (*hoi ta epigeia thrēskeuontes tois agalmasi ... proseuchontai*) as though they (i.e., the idols) actually understand them—reinforcing the firmness of their pacts with them—so is the true majesty of the Word received from the trustworthy teacher in ·the presence of human beings, the living idols (*tōn empsuchōn agalmatōn*). And the charity done for them is credited to the Lord himself, after whose likeness the true human creates and molds (*ho tōi onti anthrōpos dēmiourgei kai metarruthmizei*) the character of the person under instruction, renewing that person to salvation.[113]

In other words, "it is the Gnostic who is 'in the image and likeness' (Gen 1:26), who imitates God so far as possible."[114] Clement here empties the divine administration of Pseudo-Aristotle's satraps—and the Middle Platonic *daimones* operative in traditional Greek and Roman religion—and fills it instead with angels, and more importantly, human teachers.[115] He conceives the 'Gnostic' teacher's distribution of providence in Christian instruction to be a kind of anti-idolatry. Christ the Word inverts the perverse activity of the fallen angels in the Enochic narrative by turning mere philosophers into enlightened Chris-

---

112   Bergjan, "Clement," 88 and Timotin, *Démonologie platonicienne*, 130, re: *Strom.* 7.2.9. 7.2.6, respectively.

113   Clem. Al. *Strom.* 7.9.52.1–2, text Stählin in GCS 17:38–39, tr. Mayor, rev. Chadwick and Oulton in idem, *Alexandrian Christianity*, 126, significantly modified; see also *Strom.* 6.13.107.2, as well as Bergjan, "Clement," 65–67 (re: *Strom.* 1.34.1, 7.3.1).

114   Clem. Al. *Strom.* 2.19.97.1, text Stählin in GCS 52:166, tr. Ferguson, 221, slightly modified; see also *Strom.* 1.11.52.3.

115   Thus, although it is strictly true that Clement "übernimmt die platonischen Einsichten seiner [mittelplatonischen] Zeitgenossen über die Pronoia nicht" (Bergjan, *Der fürsorgende Gott*, 330), he appears to respond to these Platonist contemporaries, subverting their models of multi-tiered providential administration.

THE OTHER GODS

127

tian teachers, engaged in the demiurgic activity of shaping people's behavior.[116] Educators are the true administrators of providence, human beings who come to act as 'living images,' as opposed to lifeless, material objects whom demons trick humans into worshipping.

It is worth noting, however, that Clement's idealized educators are not modern, free-wheeling humanities professors, or even ecumenical harmonizers of the Greek and nascent Christian traditions. The 'Gnostic' vehicle of pedagogical providence sets and enforces boundaries, including those of enquiry. This point may be obscured by some apologetic passages in *Stromateis* book six, which emphasize the universal accessibility of Christianity and attempt to subsume the Greek philosophical tradition to it: since the workings of providence and the economy of salvation are evident in creation, Clement here avers, Jesus's teaching is universal and may be grasped by everyone.[117] Even Plato was able to predict the providential crucifixion, based upon his observance of the workings of nature.[118] The philosophy of the Greeks is a kind of gospel, but incomplete:

> But whatever contributes to the discovery of the truth is not to be rejected out of hand. In fact, Greek philosophy (*philosophia*), which proclaims the gospel of providence (*pronoian kataggellousa*)—namely the reward of a happy life, as well as the punishment of a life of misery—teaches theology comprehensively, but it does not preserve matters of accuracy or detail. For it discusses neither the Son of God nor the dispensation that is in accordance with providence (*oute peri tēs kata tēn pronoian oikonomias ... dialambanei*) as we do, and it did not know the worship of God.[119]

Yet Clement argues in *Stromateis* book five that philosophical enquiry must be subordinated to the authority of the Christian instructor:

> Who, then, is so impious (*atheos*) ⟨as⟩ to fail to believe in God, and to demand proofs (*apodeixeis*) from God as from people? Conversely,

---

116   The imagery also recalls the fake demiurges of Gnostic myth (discussed below, in chapter four). I hope to pursue Clement's possible allusions to such myths in a future study.

117   Clem. Al. *Strom.* 6.6.47.1; also ibid., 1.4.3, 7.26.

118   Clem. Al. *Strom.* 5.14.108.2. Cf. also the remarks of pseudo-Justin Martyr ([*Or. Graec.*] 14.2, 36.4), to the effect that learning, wherever it is to be found—as in many Greek writers— was imparted by *pronoia*. As Marcovich notes ("Introduction," 9–10), the author here essentially substitutes *pronoia* for the *logos spermatikos* of Justin Martyr in 2 *Apol.* 10.2–3, 13.5.

119   Clem. Al. *Strom.* 6.15.123.1–2, text Stählin in GCS 52:493–494, tr. mine.

while some questions merit the evidence of sense-perception—like when someone asks if a fire is warm, or snow is white—, others merit scolding and criticism, as Aristotle says, like the question of whether one ought to honor one's parents. And there are those (questions) that deserve punishment (*kolaseōs*), like the demand for proofs if providence (*pronoia*) exists. Now, given the existence of providence, it would be impious to maintain that the entirety of prophecy and the dispensation (*oikonomian*) regarding the Savior did not take place in accordance with providence. It is probably not even necessary to try to demonstrate such things, with divine providence being evident from the sight of all the adept and wise creations (*technikōn kai sophōn poiēmatōn*) which are seen, and of the things that transpire in an orderly fashion (*taxei*) and things that have appeared in an orderly fashion.[120]

Clement's subtext is clear: the program of Christian education that Clement denotes God's providential administration to be is not one that entertains free enquiry into the Scriptures, nor into human experience, nor even into Greek philosophy.[121] It is one where the pastor, garbed in the self-legitimizing rhetoric of *pronoia* and *oikonomia*, shapes and leads the flock along as he sees best.

6 "Nothing Happens without God": Origen on Evil, Demons, and Other Absences

A generation after Clement, Origen of Alexandria offered a particularly ingenious set of approaches to the questions surrounding providence and its relationship with the experience of evil. Like Clement, Justin, Theophilus, and Tertullian (see above in this chapter, and chapter two), Origen states over and over again, firmly, that God cares for individuals, a belief which he consistently maintained from his early theological tour de force *On First Principles*, written in Alexandria (ca. 219–230 CE),[122] through his final works. In the third book of *On First Principles*, Origen takes Matthew 10:29—"… not one of (the

---

120 Clem. Al. *Strom.* 5.1.6.1–2, text Stählin in GCS 52:329, tr. mine.

121 I thank Markus Vinzent for highlighting the authoritarian valence of this passage for me, in conversation. The interpretation of the passage's implications is my own.

122 On dating *Princ.* and Origen's early career in Alexandria, useful remains Butterworth, "Introduction," xxxix–xliii; cf. e.g. Trigg, *Origen*, 18 and Behr, "Introduction," xvii (preferring 229 and 229–230 CE, respectively), both following Nautin, *Origène*, 370–371.

THE OTHER GODS   129

sparrows) will fall to the ground apart from your Father ..."—to teach that even evil occurs "neither by God nor yet without Him," for "nothing happens without God."[123] One can unpack this vague statement with reference to Origen's more sustained discussions of evil in several ways. On some occasions, Origen makes use of familiar Stoic and Platonist arguments to explain the experience of something we could mistake for evil as consonant with the reality of divine care. However, he was also familiar with the Enochic tale of the Watchers' introduction of sin into the world, and so, like Athenagoras, rejects the Platonists' reading of traditional Graeco-Roman deities as benevolent but faulty *daimones*, Yet, rather than simply replacing the actors in this hierarchy (as does Clement) with God's servants to oppose the forces of evil, Origen flattens the ontological basis of this hierarchy altogether, rendering the opposition of 'good' and 'evil' in terms of the presence and absence of God's "power."

Origen understands providence to care for individuals in very strong terms. In book one of *On First Principles*, Origen writes that the "power (*virtus*)" of God is "that by which He is strong, that by which he establishes, preserves, and governs all things visible and invisible, and that by which he is sufficient for all things, for whom he exercises His providence and with whom he is present, as if united with them (*qua ad omnia sufficiens est, quorum providentiam gerit, quibus velut unita omnibus adest*)."[124] Origen also highlights God's care for worldly particulars in his *Homilies on Luke*, written after his move to Caesarea (ca. 231).[125] The young Jesus's visit to the Temple and 'chance' reading of a passage from Isaiah about the Messiah (i.e., himself—Luke 4:16–18), was, we are told, no accident, but a work of divine providence (*non fortuitu ... sed et hoc providentiae Dei fuit*): "for Scripture says, 'a sparrow does not fall into a net without the Father's willing it,' and 'the hairs of the head' of the apostles 'have all been counted'" (Matt 10:29; Luke 12:6–7).[126] The sparrows and the hairs are favorite proof-texts of Origen's on the question of God's care for individu-

---

123   Orig. *Princ.* 3.2.7, tr. Behr, 399.

124   Orig. *Princ.* 1.2.9, text and tr. Behr, 54–55. For Origen's designation of this "power" that cares for individuals as "Wisdom," see ibid., 1.2.12, discussed below, in chapter four.

125   For Origen's move to Caesarea in the winter of 231–232 CE, see Nautin, *Origène*, 68–70. *Hom. Luc.* could have been written anywhere between 231 (the earliest dating of the move to Caesarea—see Behr, "Introduction," xx) and 244 (the year of his completion of the *Commentary on Matthew*, which mentions *Hom. Luc.*, furnishing a *terminus ante quem*); for discussion and *Forschungsbericht*, see Leinhard, "Introduction," xxiv, agreeing with Nautin, *Origène*, 376.

126   Orig. *Hom. Luc.* 32.3, text Crouzel, Fournier, and Périchon in SC 87:388, tr. Lienhard, 131, modified.

130   CHAPTER 3

als.[127] Finally, care for individuals is also maintained in his polemical apologetic work *Against Celsus*, composed still later in Caesarea (ca. 248–249).[128] Here, Origen emphasizes the interventionist quality of the Christian God.[129] "A religious person," he argues,

> will not suppose that even a physician concerned with bodies, who restores many to health, comes to live among cities and nations without divine involvement (*atheei*); for no benefit comes to humanity without divine involvement ... How much more must that be true of him who cured, converted, and improved the souls of many, and attached them to the supreme God?[130]

This great 'physician' can only be Jesus Christ. Like Tertullian, Minucius Felix, and Clement, Origen was also wary to ward off any implication that this omnipresent, omniprovident God was simply the immanent deity of the Stoa:

> Celsus claims that we, in "saying that 'God is Spirit (*pneuma*—John 4:24),' in no way differ from the Stoa among the Hellenes, who assert that God is a Spirit permeating everything and containing everything in Himself."
> Now, the oversight and providence (*episkopē kai pronoia*) of God does indeed extend to all things, but not as does that Spirit of the Stoics. While providence does contain everything—all things being foreknown

---

127 See e.g. Orig. *Princ.* 3.2.7 and idem, *Cels.* 8.70, both discussed in this section; further, idem, *Comm. Rom.* 3.1.15; idem, *Hom. Luc.* frg. 192 (whose authenticity may be questioned, but is translated by Leinhard anyways; see Leinhard, "Introduction," xxxix).

128 So Nautin, *Origène*, 375–376, followed by Trigg, *Origen*, 52.

129 Warding off charges that divine intervention warrants a change in God's character (and thus perfection, since only what is imperfect is susceptible to change), Origen states that God, "while remaining unchanged in essence, He sweeps down to the rescue, in His providence and administration of human affairs (*sugkatabainei tēi pronoiai kai tēi oikonomiai tois anthrōpinois pragmasin*)" (Orig. *Cels.* 4.14, re: Ps 101:28 LXX; Mal 3:6; text Borret in SC 136:216, tr. Chadwick, 193, modified).

130 Orig. *Cels.* 1.9, text Borret in SC 132:100, tr. Chadwick, 13, slightly modified. Note the implication that such must be believed by anyone who is "religious": Celsus serves not only as Origen's target throughout the treatise, but his foil, accused throughout the first books of the work as deliberately denying or misunderstanding providence in the manner of an Epicurean (Orig. *Cels.* 1.8, 10, 3.35, 4.74–75, *passim*). On Celsus's putative 'Epicureanism,' see e.g. Bergjan, "Celsus," esp. 185–189, 204–205; eadem, Bergjan, *Der fürsorgende Gott*, 213–215; Cook, *Interpretation of the Old Testament*, 55–56, 85–86; Trigg, *Origen*, 53. That Origen's arguments are in somewhat bad faith is evidenced by his citations of Celsus's remarks which presume the existence of providence, e.g. *Cels.* 7.68 (discussed below, in this chapter); see further Bergjan, "Celsus," 193–198.

THE OTHER GODS   131

by God—and apprehend everything, it is not like a body that contains its own parts (the contents of the body is itself the body), but like a power (*dunamis*), divine and apprehending the things that it contains.[131]

Such strong statements of God's care for individuals naturally raised the question of the relationship of this care with the experience of evil. In *Against Celsus*, Origen employs some well-known Stoic and Platonist arguments to explain evil. Noting that some critics are concerned by biblical passages where God is said to be the author of all, even evils (Job 2:10; Is 45:7; Micah 1:12–13), he responds that "God did not make evils, metaphysical evil and the deeds which result from it … But evils which are few in comparison to the orderly arrangement of the wholes (*tēn tōn holōn diataxin*) are concomitant with (*epēkolouthēsen*) the works which were His primary intention, just as spiral shavings and sawdust are concomitant with the primary works of a carpenter …"[132] Origen here thus levies a form of 'concomitance argument' (see above, chapter one), that any creation out of matter at all will, of necessity, produce something like evils; nonetheless, the 'big picture' is good.[133] Elsewhere in *Against Celsus*, he also writes that wild beasts are not harmful, but exist to make humans more courageous.[134]

Origen also explains evil with reference to the activity of demons. In *Princ.*, written early in his career, Origen cited Enoch as an authority, but became less sure with time.[135] Yet his ideas about demons as fallen angels in some sense are in keeping with those of his fellow apologists, who saw a connection between the myth of fallen angels and the demonic beings exalting themselves in idolatrous practice. As much is reflected in the *Homilies on Luke* and *Against Celsus*. Here, Origen describes opposing angels set over each nation or region,

---

131   Orig. *Cels.* 6.71, text Borret in SC 147:356, 358, tr. Chadwick, 375, significantly modified; see also Koch, *Pronoia*, 29; O'Brien, *Demiurge*, 287. For God's containing all things, see also Orig. *Princ.* 1.2.9, quoted above, in this chapter; idem, *Comm. Jo.* 13.123–130. For God containing all things in second-century Christian sources, see the discussion above, chapter two.

132   Orig. *Cels.* 6.55, text Borret in SC 147:316, 318, tr. Chadwick, 371–372, modified; on this passage, see Chadwick, "Origen, Celsus," 38, recalling Marc. Aur. 8.50; one might add Max. Tyr. *Or.* 41.4. See also Russell, *Satan*, 129; A. Scott, *Origen*, 134 n. 109; M. Scott, *Journey*, 25–26.

133   So Chadwick, "Origen, Celsus," 38–39. On the created, temporal nature of matter, see *Princ.* 1.3.3, 2.2, cit. Russell, *Satan*, 126 n. 51.

134   Orig. *Cels.* 4.75; the Stoic valence is noted by Chadwick, "Origen, Celsus," 38. See also Philo, *Prov.* 2.56–61, discussed above, chapter two, and other sources given in chapter one, n. 90.

135   Orig. *Princ.* 1.3.3, 4.4.8, but cf. idem, *Comm. Jo.* 6.25; *Hom. Num.* 28.2; *Cels.* 5.52–55. See Russell, *Satan*, 132; VanderKam, "1 Enoch," 54–59; Reed, *Fallen Angels*, 197–198; Grypeou and Spurling, *Book of Genesis*, 168.

132   CHAPTER 3

responsible for their diverse customs. The evil angel is responsible for injustice committed on a mass scale, the good for national benefits—and the gentile nations made the error of worshipping the evil ones.[136] Christ put an end to their evil power,[137] but some wicked demons continue to work unpleasantries, operating like "like public executioners."[138] Angels continue to watch over individual human beings (amounting to care for particulars), and to run the natural planet.[139] All this is according to divine plan, in *Against Celsus*:

> As for us Christians, when God turns to the Devil and gives him authority to persecute us, we are persecuted; when he does not wish for us to suffer such things, we enjoy peace, even though we are in a world that hates us ... For "two sparrows sold for a penny," as it is written, "do not fall on the ground except as by the will of our Father in heaven." In just this way does divine providence apprehend all things (*panta hē theia perieilēphe pronoia*), so that "not even the hairs on our heads escape being counted by Him" (Matt 10:29–31).[140]

All this sounds like good, orthodox Middle Platonism—the 'Great King' and his angelic satraps again, even if some of them have been installed as "executioners," nasty beings who nonetheless have their own role to play in the divine administration. Celsus recognized as much, and so asked why it is wrong to worship lesser, local deities, if they are actually servants of that great "providence" which is ultimately derived from God; Origen's answer is revealing:

> Notice here also how he jumps to conclusions on problems which need considerable study and also knowledge of very profound and mysterious doctrines about the administration of the universe. For with regard to the assertion that all things are administered according to God's will, we have to examine what is meant, and whether the administration extends even to the sins which are committed or not. If the administration extends even

---

136   Orig. *Hom. Luc.* 12.4, 35.6; see also idem, *Princ.* 1.5.2, 1.8.2, 3.3–4; *Cels.* 4.32, 5.27, 5.30, 8.33–42; *Mart.* 18; cit. and discussion in Russell, *Satan*, 124, 141.

137   Orig. *Hom. Luc.* 35.7; *Cels.* 1.31, 3.36.

138   Orig. *Cels.* 8.31. See also ibid., 1.31, 5.30–31, 7.70; Russell, *Satan*, 133–134.

139   Angels appointed over humans: *Hom. Luc.* 12.4, 23.6–8, 35.3; *Or.* 6.4, 11.5, 31.5; *Princ.* 1.8.1, 3.2.1–4; angels appointed over nature: *Hom. Jer.* 10.6; *Cels.* 4.92–93. Cit. and discussion in Russell, *Satan*, 133–135.

140   Orig. *Cels.* 8.70, text Borret in SC 150:336, 338, tr. Chadwick, 506, modified; see also ibid., 4.74; Chadwick, *Early Christian Thought*, 106, 109; Walsh and Walsh, *Divine Providence*, 46. See also *Princ.* 3.1.14, 3.3.5.

THE OTHER GODS   133

to the sins which are committed not only among men but also among *daimones* and any other being without a body which is capable of sinning, let the person who says this notice the difficulty in holding that all things are administered according to God's will ... We also have to make a similar distinction concerning providence, and say that there is an element of truth in the statement that "all providence is derived from him," when providence is the cause of what is good. But if we are saying without qualification that everything which takes place is according to the will of providence, even if anything evil occurs, then it will be untrue to say that all providence is derived from him—unless perhaps one were to say that even the accidental results of the works of God's providence were caused by the providence of God![141]

Origen begins here innocuously enough, stating that the providential scheme of things is ultimately mysterious; but even if it were not, God cannot be responsible for evil, and therefore is not actually responsible for everything—particularly the sins of humans and demons alike.[142] Yet the way in which Origen absolves the divine of responsibility for evil is distinctive: the divine administration is staffed by intermediaries who are not merely imperfect but sinners themselves in the same way that people are sinners, and so the very basis for the administration—the putatively superhuman character of the divine intermediaries—fades into the background. Origen leaves intact the cosmic administration populated by the 'satraps' of the 'Great King,' but drains it of any sense of ontological hierarchy. We are left with the divine monarch's omnipresence—but not extended through the intermediaries of angels and demons. Rather, the intermediary is the "power" (*dunamis*, *virtus*), who is everywhere—except where there is sin, in which case there is nothing at all. Sinners themselves, angels, demons, and the Devil are here less agents of providence than fellow seekers of it.

This passage is interesting because, in *Against Celsus*, Origen usually attempts to respond to the heathen critic using his own tools—mastery of the Greek philosophical tradition—against him. Yet here, Origen's argument is unintelligible without reference to his idiosyncratic teaching that angels, demons, and humans are all fallen intellects responsible for their own movement back to God. In *On First Principles*, he famously theorizes that all sentient

---

141   *Cels.* 7.68, text Borret in SC 150:172, tr. Chadwick, 450–451, modified. On Celsus's views regarding traditional religion, see e.g. Trigg, *Origen*, 89–90.

142   On the mysterious nature of God's workings, see also Orig. *Princ.* 1.4.4, 3.5.8; see further M. Scott, *Journey*, 66–69. Cf. van Nuffelen, *Rethinking*, 227.

134 CHAPTER 3

beings began as pre-existent minds contemplating God, who eventually and of their own free will became distracted, allowing their thinking to fall away from divinity, a 'fall from heaven' eventually leading to embodiment.[143] This embodiment takes place at the opposite end from God on the spectrum of reality, the material world, which is evil, non-being—as later Platonists would agree, in sharp distinction to Plutarch and Numenius (see above, in this chapter).[144] Not only humans, but angels, demons, and even the Devil are amongst these fallen minds. Christ is the one mind that remained and has descended to pull the rest back in;[145] it is this same Christ, the Word, God's Wisdom, who is the "power" that exercises providence on behalf of the Father.[146] Thus, Origen is not sure as to whether angels and demons are really distinct types of beings, rather than fallen intellects of different moral grades.[147] Even so, he puts everything on this 'fall' to explain the causality of evil: demons and the Devil are present inso-

---

143 Orig. *Princ.* 1.3.8, 1.4.1, 2.9.2, 3.3.5; for Origen's application of this teaching to Scripture, see recently Martens, "Origen's Doctrine"; on its philosophical antecedents (particularly in Plato, *Resp.* x), see idem, "Embodiment," and Karamanolis, *Philosophy*, 171.

144 On the privative character of evil in Origen, see M. Scott, *Journey*, 24–25, re: *Comm. Jo.* 2.92–99. For a useful, recent survey of later Platonic notions of evil as privative, see Opsomer and Steel, "Evil."

145 Orig. *Princ.* 1.8.3.

146 In Wisdom, Origen writes,

> every capacity and form of the creation that would come to be—both of those things which exist in a primal way and of those accidents which occur in consequence (*vel eorum quae principaliter exsistunt vel eorum quae accidunt consequenter*), having been formed beforehand and arranged by the power of foreknowledge regarding these very created things (*virtute praescientiae praeformata atque disposita pro his ipsis*), which had been as it were outlined and prefigured in Wisdom herself. (*Princ.* 1.2.2 text and tr. Behr, 42–43, slightly modified)

Origen dubs providential activity a "power," explaining that

> Wisdom is also called "the flawless mirror of the *energeia* (that is, the 'working') of God" (Wis 7:26). It must first be understood, then, what the "working" of the power of God is. It is a kind of strength (*vigor*), if I may so speak, by which the Father works—whether when He creates or when He exercises providence (*vel cum creat vel cum providet*) or judges, or when He arranges and orders individual things, each at the right time (*vel cum singula quaeque in tempore suo disponit atque dispensat*). (*Princ.* 1.2.12, text and tr. Behr, 62–63, slightly modified)

See also *Princ.* 1.2.10, 1.4.3, 1.6.2, 2.1.1.

147 Orig. *Princ.* 1.5.2, 1.8.4, 3.1.23 (a case where Rufinus preserves a passage omitted by the *Philocalia*—Rist, "Greek and Latin Texts," 109); Jackson, "Sources," 14; D. Martin, "When Did Angels," 676; Martens, "Embodiment," 610–611. Harl ("Préexistence") and Edwards (*Origen Against Plato*, 91–93, 100–101) have argued that Origen actually did not teach the preexistence of souls/intellects (cf. M. Frede, *Free Will*, 121; M. Scott, *Journey*, 60–61; Gibbons, "Human Autonomy," 674 n. 6), but see the convincing response of Martens, op. cit., 614 n. 73.

THE OTHER GODS   135

far as they try to make humans sin, but they do not constitute a 'second' or
'third' oppositional principle independent of God and human beings.[148] Rather,
angels, demons, and humans alike together progress up (or down) along the
scale of moral excellence and depravity, each soul guided to its best instruction in accordance with God's plan.[149]

The radical and distinctive character of Origen's views on evil and demons
is most easily brought into relief by way of a brief recapitulation of this chapter
thus far. Christian philosophers of the second and third centuries CE certainly
made use of contemporary Platonic models of divine activity featuring ranks
of heavenly intermediaries, albeit with inchoate results. A major factor here
was their treatment of the Enochic tradition of the Fall of the Watchers, and
the more widespread belief that the *daimones* of the Greek philosophers were
identical with evil spirits, imposters posing as divinities in idolatrous cult.[150]
Thus, Athenagoras argued that the divine administration had been broken
up into good and evil parties, of angels and demons; the latter are the gods
of traditional Greek and Roman religion, led by the Devil. Clement, rather
than splitting the divine administration in two, simply switched out the actors
designated for it by the Middle Platonists for angels and especially human
mediators—the 'true Gnostics'—who execute providence on God's behalf. As
"living images" of divinity, these human authorities serve as sort of counter-
idols to the demons attempting to lure humans into worshipping them. Origen,
meanwhile, employed some traditional explanations for evil and described
both angels and demons as at work in the divine administration. Yet he flat-
tened the ontological basis of the hierarchy of angels, demons, and humans,
regarding all as fallen intellects equally capable of repentance, fellow travel-
ers at different stages of progress in their journeys back to God. Athenagoras

---

148   For the Devil and demons as causing sin, see Orig. *Princ.* 3.2.2; idem, *Hom. Luc.* 35.5. The
       Devil is at the center of the problem of evil (*Cels.* 4.65) and is present wherever there is
       sin (*Comm. Jo.* 20.103–105). He was elected leader of the angels when they all fell (Russell,
       Satan, 124, 132; M. Scott, *Journey*, 50–52), and is lord of this world (*Philoc.* 14.2, re: 1John
       5:19; similarly, *Comm. Matt.* 13.20; both cit. A. Scott, *Origen*, 130; further, *Hom. Num.* 12.4.3).
       For Origen, matter is not evil, since it was created by God (*Princ.* 2.1.4; see further O'Brien,
       Demiurge, 271).
149   Orig. *Princ.* 1.5.3, 1.6.2, 1.8.4; Russell, *Satan*, 127; also D. Martin, "When Did Angels," 676. For
       individual responsibility for sin, see also *Hom. Jer.* 17.4.3; Koch, *Pronoia*, 111–112; Jackson,
       "Sources," 14; A. Scott, *Origen*, 134 n. 109.
150   Cf. Magris, who rightly discusses Enochic and Qumran literature (*L'idea di destino*, 2:728–
       750), but does not relate it to the early Christian texts dealing with providence and
       demonology discussed here. I thank Carlos Steel for encouraging me, early in this project,
       to pursue the problems posed by demons for early Christian thought about evil vis-à-vis
       providence.

and Clement viewed demons and the Devil as causal forces which are genuine, but also subordinate to God, much like (and certainly inspired by) the 'attenuated dualism' of Jewish apocalyptic teaching.[151] Origen, remarkably, took this demonological framework for explaining evil, but removed any sense of distinctive 'being' from the evil character that defines matter, demons, and the Devil. In this way, when Origen says that evil occurs "neither by God nor yet without Him," he has this privative understanding of evil in mind, rather than the 'concomitance argument.'

In terms of the distinction made early in this chapter between the two approaches to evil in Roman Platonism, Origen, like Plotinus, understands evil to occupy the position of absence in the continuum of being. Athenagoras and Clement, on the other hand, appear at first glance to agree with Plutarch and Numenius in taking evil to be something, albeit something subordinated to the good, just as the power of demons and the Devil are subordinate to that of God. Yet they articulate the manifestation of evil not in terms of the chaotic matter or fallible 'young gods' of the *Timaeus*, but of demonic activity bringing sin into the world. In fact, Athenagoras, Clement, and Origen all agree in explaining evil in terms of sin and the external demonic impulse to it (recall the 'two spirits' of Qumran's *Community Rule*), all the while reinterpreting this demonology in the Stoic terms of external impulses leading one to error. This is ultimately a Stoic framework of how human evil occurs, even if it is explained in terms of the Jewish apocalyptic demonology: sin is the result of poor choices, but the external 'push' to those choices is called 'demon.' An interesting, complicating factor here is that Athenagoras, Clement, and Origen all view humans, angels, and demons alike as responsible for their decisions. This theme will be pursued further in chapter six, but presently it suffices to observe that demonology was a principal venue for early Christian development of a concept of personal autonomy, insofar as the evil angels and demons in question began precisely as divine mediators of *pronoia* before they chose to be otherwise. There is no fully-developed explanation of the matter prior to Origen, but both Athenagoras and Justin, already in the second century CE, describe angels as possessing an autonomous faculty of decision-making.

Finally, it is a truism that the angelic interpretation of Gen 6:1–4 is "the greatest contribution of the Enochic apocalyptic tradition to early Christian thought," an interpretation that waned and eventually disappeared amongst Byzantine authors, who favoured the belief that the bnai ha-Elohim were not

---

151   Emphasized by Russell, *Satan*, 72, 76, 92, on Justin, Tatian, and Tertullian, respectively.

THE OTHER GODS   137

angels at all, but the sons of the patriarch Seth.[152] The reading of the evidence offered here identifies a further ripple of this apocalyptic tradition: even as the angelic reading of Gen 6 went out of fashion, the philosophy of providence which excluded demons and fallen angels from roles in divine administration and identified them with external impulses to sin remained. The effects of the Enochic tradition on ancient Christian philosophers' understanding of divine mediators outlived the widespread popularity of the tradition itself.

7   Marcion asks, "Doth God Clothe the Grass?"

The legend of the fall of the angels furnished only one of several avenues by which early Christian philosophers explained the origin and effects of evil with respect to divine providence. Some thinkers of the second century CE were aware of the new theories on the relationship between chaotic matter and evil as developed by Platonists such as Plutarch and Numenius, and adopted them in formulating their own ideas. Some remarks of Hermogenes—a shadowy figure who taught the eternal co-existence of matter with God, known only from Tertullian's polemic against him—appear to recall Numenius's teaching in particular.[153] Others, such as Marcion of Sinope and his student Apelles, went so far as to propose a distinction between the providential God and the inferior god of creation working with matter. These models are known only from polemical texts written against them, and so our knowledge of them is slim and provisional. Nonetheless, even a cursory reading of this evidence shows that a central criticism of Marcion and Apelles was that each, in their own way, assigned too much causal efficacy to non-divine powers, thus infringing on the unity and sovereign character of God. Specifically, a brief look at Mar-

---

152   VanderKam, "1 Enoch," 100; see also Stroumsa, *Another Seed*, 29 *passim*; Reed, *Fallen Angels*, 190–206.

153   On Hermogenes's adaptation of Platonic dualistic models, see Greschat, *Apelles und Hermogenes*, 173–191; Pleše, "Evil," 102 n. 2; Karamanolis, *Philosophy*, 87; still relevant is Waszink, "Observations," 129–135. For the parallel to Numenius, see Ter. *Herm.* 44.1 and Num. frgs. 11, 16 (the latter discussed in Edwards, "Numenius," 123 and above, in this chapter). Greschat, *Apelles und Hermogenes*, 198 n. 12 recalls Num. frg. 12.17–19 on God's creative activity as an emanation, but not frg. 16 on beauty. Tertullian does not discuss *providentia*, *prudentia*, or *praescientia* in *Against Hermogenes* or his related work *On the Soul*, and so I omit detailed discussion of Hermogenes's thought in this book. In the interests of space, I also omit the doctrine of the Valentinian character Droserius in Methodius of Olympus's *On Self-Determination* (*De autexousio*), whose broad outlines resemble those of Hermogenes, although Methodius (as "Droserius") says it goes back to Valentinus himself, an attribution recently defended by Dunderberg (*Beyond Gnosticism*, 67–72).

cion's earliest critics—Justin Martyr, Irenaeus of Lyons, and Tertullian—shows that Marcion used philosophical arguments about providence in his scriptural exegesis and text-criticism to try to demonstrate that the 'good' God who sent Jesus is providential, even though Tertullian attempts to portray Marcion as a denier of providence.[154] Apelles, meanwhile, appears to have married this schema to the notion—so important for Athenagoras, Clement, and Origen—that evil angels could be responsible for the human inclination to sin, but by identifying the second god as a malignant angel of fire, responsible for making the human body.

In his work today known as the *First Apology*, Justin Martyr refers to "a certain Marcion of Pontus, who even now teaches his followers to think that there is another God greater than the demiurge (*allon tina ... meizona tou dēmiourgou theon*)."[155] Justin adds that the 'other, greater' God has "done greater works." In a passage alluded to above (chapter two) in the *Dialogue with Trypho*, he is more specific:

> Dear friends, there were—and still are—many men who come and teach others godless and blasphemous doctrines and practices, in the name of Jesus; we call them by the name of the originator of each false doctrine. For others teach, each in his own peculiar method, how to blaspheme the Creator of the universe (*ton poitēn tōn holōn*), and the God of Abraham, and of Isaac, and of Jacob, and Christ, whose advent was prophesied by Him ... These men call themselves Christians in much the same way as some heathens engrave the name of God upon their statues, and then indulge in every kind of wicked and godless rite. Some of these heretics are called Marcionites, some Valentinians, some Basilidians, and others by still other names ...[156]

---

154   The Valentinian teacher Ptolemy's remarks on what has often been taken by scholars to be Marcionite teaching will be discussed below, in chapter four. For Origen on Marcion, see below, chapters four and six. The evidence about Marcion in the third-century *Refutatio omnium haeresiorum* (7.30–31, 10.19) is generally considered wildly inaccurate (see e.g., Roth, "Evil," 351; Lieu, *Marcion*, 91, 96). Ephraem Syrus does not discuss providence or fate with regards to Marcion and so is somewhat less relevant to the scope of this study, but referred to in some of the following notes.

155   Just. Mart. *1 Apol.* 26.5, text Marcovich, 70, tr. mine. Dieter Roth considers this passage to be the most reliable *Kern* of Marcion's teaching on the two gods: the distinction is between a 'high' and 'low' one, and 'low' here has both metaphysical and ethical connotations ("Evil," 345, 354).

156   Just. Mart. *Dial.* 35.4–6, text Marcovich, 128–129, tr. Falls, rev. Halton, 54–55, modified.

THE OTHER GODS   139

Justin here disputes Marcion's divorce of the demiurge, the God of the Jews, from the God who sent Jesus Christ and who foretold his coming in the Jewish Scriptures. What is important about this passage for the present discussion is that Justin's argument against Marcion is not that the high God is not active; it is that the high God is not the same as the creator. This means our earliest testimony about Marcion does not know him to have argued that God is not provident.

The heresiographer Irenaeus of Lyons, in his work *Against Heresies* (ca. 180 CE),[157] agrees with Justin in seeing Marcion's error as the introduction of a second god, rather than simply denigration of the creator.[158] However, Irenaeus goes beyond Justin in claiming that Marcion believed the lower god to be the creator of evil, and judgmental or 'just' rather than 'good.'[159] Irenaeus relates this dichotomy between the 'good' and 'just' gods with reference to how even the "heathen" philosophers recognize the demiurge to be provident:

> God, however, does hold providence (*pronoian ... echei*) over all things. Consequently, He also gives counsel, and by giving counsel, He assists those who have a care (*pronoian*) for morals. It is necessary, therefore, that those who are provided for and governed (*ta pronooumena kai kubernōmena*) should recognize their director, since they are not irrational or purposeless, but have received perception of divine providence (*aisthēsin ... peri tēs pronoias theou*). Consequently, certain ones of the heathens, who were less addicted to allurements and pleasures and were not led away to so great a superstition in idols—having been moved by His providence, even if slightly—nevertheless were converted to say that the creator of everything is the Father who provides for all and arranges the world for us (*Patera pantōn pronoounta kai dioikounta ton kath'hēmas kosmon*). Yet in order that they might take away from the Father the power of reproving and judging, thinking that it is unworthy of God, and believing that

---

157   The Greek *Vorlage* of *Haer.* is now lost, known only through quotations by later writers; when possible, I refer to it as given in the SC edition, otherwise referring to the later Latin translation that survives completely. Chiapparini has recently argued for dating the "conception of the work and the retrieval of the sources" of *Haer.* earlier (to ca. 160–165—"Irenaeus," esp. 97–101), but the question of a mid- or late-second century dating are unimportant for the purposes of this book.

158   Lieu, *Marcion*, 37, re: Ir. *Haer.* 2.30.9, 4.2.2 ("Marcionites," not Marcion); Just. 1 *Apol.* 26.5.

159   Ir. *Haer.* 1.27.2, 3.25.3 respectively (see Löhr, "Did Marcion Distinguish," 136; Roth, "Evil," 348). For the belief of the followers of Marcion in a good versus an evil god, see *Haer.* 3.12.12; Löhr, "Did Marcion Distinguish," 136; Roth, "Evil," 348 n. 45; cf. Moll, *Arch-Heretic*, 50.

they have found a god that is good and free from anger, they asserted that one god judges and the other saves. But they are unaware that thus they deprive [God] both of intelligence and justice.[160]

The polytheistic philosophers may be right that the demiurge is provident, but they believe that the characteristics of anger and wrath are "unworthy of God" (*anaxion*) and so divorced them from divinity, assigning the role of punisher—of executor of justice—to another being.[161]

When he argues that Marcion's distinction between the rebuking and saving deities originated amongst heathen philosophers who believe in providence but were troubled by the notion of the providential God as a god who punishes, Irenaeus paints Marcion as a heathen philosopher—even though Marcion's views have no parallel in ancient Greek philosophy. And sure enough, Irenaeus immediately introduces Marcion as differentiating the 'good' and 'just' deities:

> Consequently, Marcion, by dividing God in two, asserting the one to be good and the other to have judicial power, destroys God on both counts. For the one who has judicial power, if he is not also good, is not God, because he who lacks goodness is not God. On the other hand, the one who is good, if he is not also just, suffers the same fate as the former, namely, he is deprived of something without which he is not God.[162]

To Irenaeus's mind, Marcion ignores the willingness to punish as essential to the just and wise character of a divine sovereign.[163] Thus, Marcion's 'blasphemy' is "not denial of the existence of the creator, but of his supremacy and hence of his meriting worship,"[164] and denial of the fully divine character of the God of Israel, giver of the Law and recognized by the Prophets.[165]

---

160   Ir. *Haer.* 3.25.1. Here I translate the Greek text of Doutreleau and Rousseau in SC 211:479, 481, with reference to Unger, rev. Steenberg, 111–112.

161   It is unclear what philosophers Irenaeus has in mind; no known Greek school fits the bill (also Adamson, *Philosophy*, 286). At the end of the chapter, he even contrasts Marcion's views with those of the Greek schools: Plato unites the good and juridical characters of the demiurge, a differentiation between a punishing and forgiving God would not fit the Stoa at all, and the Epicurean deity would neither punish nor forgive, being entirely disassociated from human affairs (Ir. *Haer.* 3.25.5).

162   Ir. *Haer.* 3.25.3, tr. Unger, rev. Steenberg, 112.

163   The eschatological valence of divine vengeance (on which see below, chapter six) is thus highlighted here by Irenaeus; see Karamanolis, *Philosophy*, 79; cf. Lieu, *Marcion*, 48.

164   Lieu, *Marcion*, 35.

165   Ir. *Haer.* 4.9.3; see also Lieu, *Marcion*, 23.

THE OTHER GODS   141

Marcion's Jesus "has his origin in the Father who is above the God who made the world … He abolished the prophets and the law and all the works of the God who made the world, whom he also styled the World-Ruler (*kosmokrator*)."[166] Notably, Irenaeus never claims that Marcion denies providence, like the Epicureans or Aristotelians. Rather, he claims that Marcion was inspired by the philosophical notion that the providential God is one who does not experience passions like wrath, and so went beyond the philosophers in distinguishing this providential God from the wrathful god of the Old Testament. In other words, Irenaeus relates that Marcion reasoned that a good god exerts providence (*pronoia*), and therefore does not punish. Such a reading would clear up an old problem in research on Marcion, namely his debt to philosophy: it seems evident that Marcion was concerned in some sense with what contemporary intellectuals deemed 'behavior proper to a deity' (*theoprepēs*), but any particular philosophical valence to his thought proves elusive.[167] The answer would then be that Marcion used arguments about providence in his scriptural exegesis, but to make a novel argument about God (providential) and creation (not cared for, but punished) without parallel in Greek philosophy.

Tertullian confirms this, which is all the more remarkable given the fact that he attempts to tar Marcion with the brush of Epicureanism. His early writings against heretics allude to Marcion, but evince little knowledge of his thought.[168] His later work *Against Marcion*, on the other hand, dwarfs our other evidence about Marcion in both girth and detail. Tertullian claims that all heretics brood over the question *unde malum*, none moreso than Marcion.[169] As with Justin and Irenaeus, Tertullian's central point of contention with Marcion is the identity of the creator,[170] particularly whether Scripture shows the

---

166 Ir. *Haer.* 1.27.2, tr. Unger, 91; so Aland (Ehlers), "Marcion: Versuch," 308, with other citations.

167 A representative passage is Ter. *Marc.* 1.25; so Aland (Ehlers), "Marcion: Versuch," 94; more recently, Löhr, "Did Marcion Distinguish," 145–146; Norelli, "Marcion," 113. On the issue in general, see Gager, "Marcion and Philosophy"; Norelli, op. cit.; Moreschini, "Tertullian's *Adversus Marcionem*." Norelli emphasizes Marcion's possible debts to the Middle Platonism which designated matter as evil (discussed above, in this chapter), but diagnoses the theologian's thought as consciously anti-philosophical (op. cit. 122, 128; similarly Aland (Ehlers), "Sünde und Erlösung," 155–156).

168 Rightly Moreschini, "Tertullian's *Adversus Marcionem*," 151 n. 67, re: e.g., Ter. *Praescr.* 7.2–3, which refers to Marcion as a Stoic—a claim which at first sight appears baffling, but perhaps should be read in terms of *Marc.* 5.19.7 (discussed below; cf. also Meijering, *Tertullian*, 76).

169 Ter. *Marc.* 2.2, 1.2.2, respectively, on which see Pleše, "Evil," 102–103; M. Scott, *Journey*, 35.

170 763 of the 800 usages of the word "creator" in Tertullian are in *Against Marcion* (Lieu, *Marcion*, 66 n. 51).

qualities of supremacy and vengeful judgment to be coincident or mutually exclusive.[171] Again, we are told that Marcion explicitly distinguished between a 'good' and a 'just' god.[172] It is the latter who stated that "it is I who create evil things" (Is 45:7), who hardened Pharaoh's heart, and who had ferocious bears maul the little children who mocked the prophet Elijah (2 Kgs 2:23).[173] It is this same punishing god who, Tertullian maintains, created the present cosmos out of pre-existing matter, perhaps indicating Marcion's acquaintance with the sort of Middle Platonic exegesis of the *Timaeus* we know from Plutarch or Numenius (see above, in this chapter).[174] The punishing god also created humanity, which is fundamentally as alien to the good God as is the world itself; thus, by sending Christ to redeem humanity, the good God invades our planet and steals the just god's property away, a scenario Tertullian likens to a brigand breaking into a nobleperson's house and robbing them of their slaves.[175] According to Marcion, sin is disbelief in the salvation offered by Christ; the just demiurge offers a stumbling-block in the Law, albeit a necessary one in the overall salvific plan.[176] Tertullian has none of this: he responds that the essence of divinity is to create, not to be alien from creation, that God's providence is responsible for punishment as well as love, and that the Law was designed to keep humanity focused on God even when performing the smallest tasks.[177] All this speaks for an argument not over whether the lower god is 'evil,' but 'just';[178] the demiurge here is not evil, exactly, but creates using matter, and then punishes its creation for matter's attendant failures. Tertullian's reply is like that of Justin or Irenaeus: this willingness to punish is not, he avers, mutually incompatible with a divine,

---

171   Lieu, *Marcion*, 67, re: Ter. *Marc.* 2.29.2.

172   Roth, "Evil," 340–342, re: Ter. *Marc.* 2.12.1, 5.13.2; cf. Moll, *Arch-Heretic*, 47–52; Pleše, "Evil," 103 n. 3.

173   Ter. *Marc.* 2.14, cit. Lieu, *Marcion*, 68. On the hardening of Pharaoh's heart, see also below, chapter six.

174   Ter. *Marc.* 1.15.4. See Karamanolis, *Philosophy*, 82; Aland (Ehlers), "Marcion: Versuch," 298–299, underlining the parallel with Hermogenes. That Marcion held such views regarding matter is also supported by Ephraem Syrus; for a recent, critical discussion of this evidence, see Lieu, *Marcion*, 162–163, 176. Cf. Clem. *Strom.* 3.3.12–13; Löhr, "Did Marcion Distinguish," 141.

175   Ter. *Marc.* 1.23.1, 6–8; Norelli, "Marcion," 116–117, 122; Lieu, *Marcion*, 83.

176   Aland (Ehlers), "Sünde und Erlösung," esp. 152–153, 156–157, re: Ter. *Marc.* 1.11, rightly noting a parallel to Irenaeus's theology; see further Meijering, *Tertullian*, 38.

177   Ter. *Marc.* 1.11, 2.15, 2.19, respectively.

178   The question of whether Marcion taught the creator to be 'evil' or 'just' is of course Harnack's enquiry, on which the dossier is enormous; recent contributions include Löhr, "Did Marcion Distinguish"; Moll, *Arch-Heretic*; Lieu, *Marcion*, 328, 343–349; Norelli, "Marcion," 117–119; Roth, "Evil."

THE OTHER GODS   143

providential quality. On the contrary, it is integral to it. In order to be a caring
deity, these thinkers believe, God must punish.

Irenaeus associates Marcion with the philosophers in order to make him
look like a polytheist, but Tertullian goes further, accusing Marcion of teaching that even the good God is not active in the world. According to Tertullian,
Marcion claimed that knowledge of God comes from the prophets, not from
"the philosophers and Epicurus."[179] He continues:

> At least let Marcion admit that the principal term of his faith is from the
> school of Epicurus, for to avoid making him an object of fear he introduces
> a dull sort of god, and puts on loan even with God the Creator matter from
> the porch of the Stoics when he denies the resurrection of the flesh, which
> in fact no philosophy admits.[180]

As John Gager has pointed out, Jerome argues that Marcion and other heretics
who criticize the Old Testament are even worse than Epicurus, "for although
they accept providence, they reproach the creator and claim that he failed in
most of his works."[181] And indeed, Tertullian tells us that Marcion argued the
following, about Adam's disobedience of the command not to eat of the Tree
of Knowledge (Gen 3):

> If God is good, you ask, and has knowledge of the future (*praescius futuri*),
> and also has power to avert evil, why did he suffer the man, deceived by
> the Devil, to fall away from obedience to the law, and so to die? For the
> man was the image and likeness of God, or even God's substance, since
> from it the man's soul took its origin. So if, being good, he had wished
> a thing not to happen, and if, having foreknowledge (*praescius*), he had
> been aware that it would happen, and if he had had power and strength to
> prevent it from happening, that thing never would have happened which
> under these three conditions of divine majesty it was impossible should
> happen.[182]

---

179   Ter. *Marc.* 2.16; see also Meijering, *Tertullian*, 130.
180   Ter. *Marc.* 5.19.7, tr. Evans, 633.
181   Jerome, *Commentariorum in Isaiam libri XVIII*, 7 (re: Is 18:1–3), tr. Gager, "Marcion and Phi-
      losophy," 55.
182   Ter. *Marc.* 2.5.1–2, text and tr. Evans, 97, 99. On Tertullian's use of the term *providentia*
      (as well as *praescientia*, *praescire*, etc.) to render Greek *prognōsis*, see Braun, *Deus Chris-
      tianorum*, 135–137. Braun's suggestion (ibid., 138) that *praescientia* was first coined by the
      Marcionites to denote God's foreknowing in distinction to his *providentia* is speculative at
      best.

... Therefore, the god who created Adam was not really God. As Gager argues, the same argument—that if God wills for some x not to happen, knows beforehand that x will happen, and has the power to prevent x from happening, it is impossible for x to occur—was a stock line of reasoning used by Epicureans to deny the existence of providential care.[183] Thus, Gager alleges that "Marcion was familiar with Epicurean philosophy and borrowed from it a key element in his argument for the existence of his higher god."[184] One can add that Tertullian claims Marcion's followers "put to scorn those tiny animals," such as bed-bugs, ants, and mosquitos. Epicureans took the existence of pests to indicate the absence of providence; conversely, Tertullian's arguments in defense of these irritating little beasts recall the Stoa.[185]

Yet this evidence does not show that Marcion 'was an Epicurean.'[186] Marcion's good God did act, since He sent Jesus to save humanity.[187] As Tertullian himself remarks, a truly Epicurean deity would never have been stirred to care for humans.[188] Meanwhile, practically *all* philosophically-educated commentators on Scripture of the first centuries CE struggled with God's statement "let *us* make" (implying a need for fellow creators—Gen 1:26) or His apparent lack of knowledge that Adam will sin, or where Adam is after he sins (Gen 2:8–13).[189] Altogether, it appears that Marcion used an Epicurean argument to show that the just god of the Old Testament is not providential, and that there is no providence for the world—but this does not mean that he denied the providence of the good God who sent Christ.

It is instructive here to look at how Tertullian reacts in book four of *Against Marcion* to the heretic's treatment of passages from the Gospel of Luke that appear to refer to personal, divine care for even minute affairs in the present creation. For example, Tertullian tells us the following about Luke 12:27–30 ("consider how the wild flowers grow ... how much more will He clothe you ... Your Father knows you need them [i.e., clothes and food]"):

---

183   Lactantius, *On the Wrath of God*, 13.20–21 and Sext. Emp. *Pyr.* 3.9–11.

184   Gager, "Marcion and Philosophy," 55.

185   Ter. *Marc.* 1.14.1–2, tr. Evans, *Adversus Marcionem*, 37; so also Meijering, *Tertullian*, 44–45 (whose reference to Ir. *Haer.* 2.30.8 on this point is misleading).

186   So Pedersen, *Demonstrative Proof*, 220 n. 91. As Opsomer and Steel note, the argument was popular, "fashionable amongst sceptic and Academic philosophers" ("Evil," 229).

187   Rightly Löhr, "Did Marcion Distinguish," 144; Norelli, "Marcion," 119, 129–130; the point is understated by Gager, "Marcion and Philosophy," 57.

188   Ter. *Marc.* 1.25.3–5; see Meijering, *Tertullian*, 75; Norelli, "Marcion," 126; Lieu, *Marcion*, 330; Moreschini, "Tertullian's *Adversus Marcionem*," 147.

189   Lieu, *Marcion*, 341–343, 363. See further below, chapter five.

THE OTHER GODS 145

But the Father knows that you have need of these things, I must first inquire whom Christ wishes them to understand by the Father. If he means their own Creator, he thereby affirms the goodness of the one who knows what his sons have need of: but if he means that other god, how does this one know that food and clothing are what man has need of, when he has provided none of these? For if he had known, he would have made provision ...[190]

Marcion does not remove Jesus's statement that (the good) God knows that His followers have worldly needs. This indicates that Marcion believed God to care for Christians; otherwise, he would have excised the passage. The import of Marcion's retention of the verse is obscured by Tertullian's criticism, which disingenuously asks which God is meant here: the 'just' demiurge of humans (in which case Marcion is betraying himself by paying the lower god a compliment), or the good God (in which case it is silly that a 'good' deity would not have taken care of human needs in the first place).

Luke 22:22 ("woe to that one by whom the Son of Man is betrayed") presents us with a similar case. This verse presupposes that God the Father knew in advance who would betray Jesus—and therefore that the 'good' God is *praesciens*, providential in the sense of 'foreknowing.' This fact leaves Tertullian somewhat flustered, since he had tried to pigeonhole Marcion as an Epicurean. He tells Marcion that, because he includes Luke 22:22 in the Gospel,

... You can no longer bring under discussion concerning the Creator, in the matter of Adam, objections which recoil back on your own god as well—that he either did not know, seeing he did not by providence prevent the sinner: that he was unable to prevent him, if he did not know: or was unwilling to do so, if he both knew and was able: and therefore must be judged of evil intent, as having permitted his own man to perish for his sin. I advise you therefore to recognize the Creator in this ⟨Christ⟩, rather than make your supremely good god like him, contrary to your own doctrine![191]

---

190   Ter. *Marc.* 4.29.3–4, tr. Evans, *Adversus Marcionem*, 427.

191   Ter. *Marc.* 4.41.1–2, tr. Evans, *Adversus Marcionem*, 497. For a similar sentiment, see *Marc.* 1.22.8–10, tr. Evans, *Adversus Marcionem*, 59, 61:

The whole indictment they bring against the Creator has to be transferred to the account of that one who, by this check on his own goodness, has become a party to the other's savageries ... The same judgement will have to be pronounced upon Marcion's god, for permitting evil, favoring wrong, currying favor, offending against that kindness which he did not immediately exercise when cause arose. Evidently he would

146   CHAPTER 3

Tertullian here seizes and turns around the Epicurean argument he said earlier, in book two, Marcion had used: if the 'good' God cared for humanity and foresaw that Adam would sin, why did He fail to prevent him from it? Evidently, in Marcion's Gospel, only the 'good' God cares for humans—their creator, the demiurge, does not. As much is also clear in one of Epiphanius of Salamis's remarks on Marcion's Gospel: it "does not have, 'God doth clothe the grass'!"[192] If both he and Tertullian give accurate testimony, this means that Marcion's Gospel simply states that (the good) God attends to the clothing of humans, but not to grass, i.e., the world. Epiphanius also writes: "he did not have, 'are not five sparrows sold for two farthings, and not one of them is forgotten before God'."[193] Here too, the absence from Marcion's Gospel of one of the most important proof-texts for ancient Christian explanations of providential care for individuals does not mean that Marcion denied care for human beings; he denied care for the cosmos. It is a position that has no parallel among the traditional, Greek philosophical schools—even if an argument used to support this position could be filched from the Epicureans, or if the conception of the demiurge's relationship to matter is in line with those of some contemporary Middle Platonists (so Tertullian).

While the tradition of the descent of the Watchers and the concomitant appearance of evil and the Devil is markedly absent from our evidence about Marcion,[194] one of his students, Apelles, attempted to wed his teacher's doctrine to traditions about evil angels. Eusebius of Caesarea, writing in the first quarter of the fourth century, claimed that

> Others, such as the captain himself (Marcion), introduced two Principles. To them belong Potitus and Basilicus. These followed the wolf of Pontus [i.e. Marcion], not perceiving the division of things any more than he, and, turning to a simple solution, announced two principles, baldly and without proof. Others again, passing into worse error, supposed that there are not only two but even three natures ...[195]

---

       have exercised it if kind by nature and not by afterthought, if good by character and not by rule and regulation, if god since eternity and not since Tiberius, or rather—to speak more truly—since Cerdo and Marcion.

192   Epiph. *Pan.* 42.11.17, tr. Williams, 306, re: Luke 12:28. See also Roth, *Text*, 156–157, 423.

193   Epiph. *Pan. Schol.* 29, tr. Williams, 325, re: Luke 12:6; see BeDuhn, *First New Testament*, 163; Lieu, *Marcion*, 225; Roth, *Text*, 313, 422.

194   Marcion apparently did argue that the angels who appeared to Abraham and Lot, agents of the demiurge, could not have taken on flesh; Tertullian replies that of course they could have, if God had wanted them to (*Marc.* 3.9).

195   Euseb. *Hist. eccl.* 5.13.4, tr. Lake in LCL 153:467, 469.

THE OTHER GODS   147

One of those exponents of 'worse error' was Marcion's student Apelles. Eusebius, who claims as his source the late second-century teacher Rhodon, relates that Apelles "confesses that there is one principle, but says that the sayings of prophecy derive from a counterfeit (*ex antikeimenou*) spirit."[196] "He kept on saying that there is only one Principle," Eusebius continues, "just as our doctrine states ... but as to how there is one principle, he said that he did not know; rather, that he merely leaned towards this view."[197]

If Rhodon is to be trusted, Apelles's insistence on the ultimate superiority of monism is vital for understanding his comments on second and third principles. Again, Tertullian is our chief source. According to Tertullian, Apelles followed Marcion in rejecting the identity of the god of Moses, creator of the world, with the first, good God.[198] However, he claimed that the creator of the body was a different figure, an angel of fire:

> Even if this fragile, pointless, little body, which they [i.e., heretics] are not afraid to call an evil thing, had been the handiwork of angels, as Menander and Marcus maintain—even if it had been fabricated by some fiery being, this one an angel too, as Apelles teaches—the patronage of a second deity (*secundae divinitatis patrocinium*) would have sufficed for the value of the flesh. We do acknowledge angels—after God![199]

Souls apparently were pre-existent and 'lured into flesh' by this fiery angel; Tertullian considers this to be the influence of Plato's teachings on metempsychosis.[200] While Katharina Greschat maintains that the extant evidence does not make it clear if Apelles simply identified the human soul as 'divine' in origin,[201] Meike Willing rightly replies that some sort of identification appears to

---

196   Euseb. *Hist. eccl.* 5.13.2, text Lake in LCL 153:466, tr. mine.

197   Euseb. *Hist. eccl.* 5.13.5–7, text Lake in LCL 153:469, tr. mine. See further Aland (Ehlers), "Marcion: Versuch," 313; Greschat, *Apelles und Hermogenes*, 74.

198   Ter. *Carn. Chr.* 6.

199   Ter. *Res.* 5, text and tr. Evans, 14–15, significantly modified. See further Greschat, *Apelles und Hermogenes*, 90–91.

200   Ter. *An.* 23.3, text Waszink, 31, tr. mine: "Apelles claims that souls were seduced from (their) superheavenly abodes with earthly foods by a fiery angel, the God of Israel—and of ours, who then set them in sinful flesh." Greschat accordingly reads this dualism between flesh and soul and their origins as of Platonic character (*Apelles und Hermogenes*, 83, 95), but it also reminds one of Gnosticism (so also Willing, "Neue Frage," 228–229, albeit only with reference to Irenaeus's Valentinians, noting further that any scheme of emanations is missing from our evidence about Apelles; cf. Greschat, op. cit. 126–127, 132).

201   *Apelles und Hermogenes*, 127: "Doch bereits an dieser Stelle hört die Strukturähnlichkeit auf, denn die Quellen lassen offen, ob das Gott nicht Entsprechende und von seinem

148 CHAPTER 3

be presupposed, and this would supply a motive for the Son's incarnation (in an astral body made from stellar matter, nonetheless) and ministry—a question on which Marcion was notoriously silent.[202] Tertullian goes on to argue that it was the Word, not angelic intermediaries, who created the human body with God: again, exegetical concerns force one to ask about the character and fallibility of secondary actors in the creation of humanity (cf. Gen 1:26 and *Tim.* 42d–e).[203] Notably, Tertullian concedes the existence and potency of angels— just not that they are bad, although he had accorded credence to the story of the fall of the Watchers and their role in the spread of human evil and idolatry, like Athenagoras, Clement, or Origen (see above, in this chapter).

If Apelles was then a student of Marcion, as his critics say, he was an original one. We have no evidence that he regarded the world itself as evil—rather, the problem lies in fleshly embodiment—and this is a substantial departure from Marcion.[204] A second difference with Marcion is his sense that human souls belong to the heavenly realm, not the world. Christ's incarnation, ministry, and death has a different meaning here: rather than alerting humans to the existence of an alien God in an alien realm who wants to adopt them, Jesus reminds humans of their true home—for humans belong to heaven, not to earth. Our knowledge of even the outlines of Apelles's thought is very limited and does not permit assessment of his theological vocabulary, so we cannot know if he used the language of providence. Yet he seems to have held a view distinct from all the other authors treated in this chapter, namely that the creation of the world and of human beings transpired beyond God's care, but that nonetheless the divine intervened when it came to the salvation of humans, because humans belong to the divine realm. Finally, and perhaps most importantly, Apelles departs from Marcion and, say, Numenius alike in envisioning some kind of break of divine powers in the appearance of the fiery angel,[205] designated as having played a (*the*) central role in the construction of the human body.[206]

   Wesen her von Gott Unterschiedene durch eine Art von Fall aus der ursprünglichen Einheit Wirklichkeit geworden ist."

202 Willing, "Neue Frage," 227; see also Aland (Ehlers), "Marcion: Versuch," 313; cf. Drijvers, "Bardaisan's Doctrine," 25. For the Son's incarnation in a body of star-stuff, see Ter. *Car.* 6, 8; see also [Ter.] *Haer.* 6.5; Greschat, *Apelles und Hermogenes*, 129–130.

203 A similar answer is given by Justin (*Dial.* 62.3); on angels as co-constructors of the body, see below, chapter four. On this point in general, see Greschat, *Apelles und Hermogenes*, 87, 92; Willing, "Neue Frage," 226 n. 26.

204 Greschat, *Apelles und Hermogenes*, 127; Willing, "Neue Frage," 225–226.

205 Greschat, *Apelles und Hermogenes*, 85–87, 125.

206 Here I follow Greschat in reading Tertullian's identification of the fiery angel with the demiurge as confused (*Apelles und Hermogenes*, 90 n. 51, re: *Carn. Chr.* 8.2; *Praescr.* 34.4),

THE OTHER GODS   149

Ambrose of Milan tells us that this creator of human beings was, according to Apelles, itself created by God.[207] Putting this evidence together, it is reasonable to hypothesize that Apelles was as inspired by myths regarding evil angels (probably the Fall of the Watchers) as were most of his contemporaries. He turned to this myth to explain the exegetical problem of who was responsible for the creation of the human body and its attendant complications: an angel gone awry, despite having been made by God.[208] The 'mitigated dualism' of Enochic tradition would be in keeping with Rhodon's account of Apelles's beliefs about first principles: there is a second god, and there is an angel who created the body of flesh—nonetheless, "there is only one Principle."

8   Conclusions: 'Religious Dualism' in Roman Philosophy

In all of the sources discussed in this chapter, the problem at hand is whether there is one causal principle, or two—or even three. Tertullian articulates the 'proto-orthodox' position of the second- and third-century Christian philosophers well: God is absolutely great (*summum magnum*), and *summum* really does mean 'to the exclusion of all else.'[209] Such statements coexisted with a decided binitarianism of Father and a subordinated Son that turns up in so many sources of the second and third centuries.[210] As we have observed in this chapter, they also coexisted with a serious reckoning with evil as possessing some degree of causal efficacy, of reality, even as part of God's providential plan for the world and human beings. One historian of the concept of evil in

---

despite Willing, who affords Tertullian more plausibility ("Neue Frage," 224 n. 14). Pseudo-Tertullian denotes the demiurge as a good angel ([*Haer.*] 6.4; so Geschat, op. cit. 83) who is unable to create a world as good as the celestial paradigms upon which he bases his work (Greschat, op. cit. 84; Willing, op. cit. 224; re: Ter. *Carn. Chr.* 8.2; Ter. [*Haer.*] 6.4).

207   Ambrose, *On Paradise*, 8.40, cit. Greschat, *Apelles und Hermogenes*, 90 n. 52.

208   Greschat refers only in passing to the possibility that Apelles's teaching about the firey angel presupposes legends about fallen angels in Judaism (*Apelles und Hermogenes*, 92–93 n. 71).

209   Rightly Moreschini, "Tertullian's *Adversus Marcionem*," 151, re: Ter. *Marc.* 1.3.2–5; similarly, Lieu, *Marcion*, 64.

210   Tertullian again serves as a good example: "all the things you [Marcion] repudiate as unworthy, are to be accounted to the Son, who was both seen and heard, and held converse, the Father's agent and minister, who commingles in himself man and God, in the miracles God, in the pettinesses man …" (Ter. *Marc.* 2.27.6–7, tr. Evans, *Adversus Marcionem*, 163, per Moreschini, "Tertullian's *Adversus Marcionem*," 152–153). Other examples of subordinationism include Just. Mart. *1 Apol.* 13; Athenag. *Leg.* 10.5; Ir. *Haer.* 4.20.1–4.

Christianity, Jeffrey Burton Russell, has thus stated that "Christianity is a moderate dualist religion."[211] I have expressly tried to leave this question open in the present chapter, hitherto avoiding use of the term 'dualism' until the concluding discussion of Apelles to designate these sources' discussions of providence and evil. At this point, however, I think it safe to say that they prove Russell right, in some sense.

More specifically, second- and third-century philosophical debates about providence were to a large extent occupied with the question of the number of causal principles, given a belief in divine care and acknowledgment of cosmic evil. Even for thinkers attuned to Stoic lines of thinking about divine activity, like Clement or Origen, the reality of a personal confrontation with evil was not negotiable given the 'apocalyptic heritage' of the canonical Gospels and of Enochic literature. Philosophers who took this apocalyptic framework to be authoritative presupposed a world populated by demons and the devil, by evils resulting from the fall of the angels, or both. It is useful, from the viewpoint of the history of philosophy, to denote this emergent philosophical view 'dualism,' if we acknowledge that what is in question in arguments about 'dualism' is a matter of degree rather than a strict demarcation with monism,[212] and if we focus on the question of creation, acknowledging the ethical element implicit therein.[213] Indeed, the conception of a second power that causes evil in the universe is so basic as to be nigh-transcultural,[214] and it is a principal

---

211 Russell, *Satan*, 32; also ibid., 159–160; idem, *The Devil*, 228.

212 Indeed, the purest monism would be a unity that admits no change or movement whatsoever, a scenario envisioned by nobody discussed in this book, even the Stoa. Conversely, there is no conception of dualism which is not beholden to monism, since there is no two without two ones, so to speak—see Dörrie, "Dualismus," col. 340; similarly Edwards, "Numenius," 124.

213 Scholars have explored many iterations of 'dualism.' The most general level is described aptly by Bianchi: "dualism means the doctrine of the two principles" ("Category of Dualism," 15). For a detailed 'taxonomy of dualism' see Bianchi, "Category of Dualism," 16, critically discussed in Couliano, *Tree of Gnosis*, 45 n. 17; for other broad discussions, see Gammie, "Spatial and Ethical Dualism," 357–360; Armstrong, "Dualism," 34; *Weltflucht*, 10; Gardner, "Dualism." The term 'dualism' was first coined by Thomas Hyde in 1700, to refer to the co-eternal principles of Zoroastrianism, one good and one evil (Dörrie, "Dualismus," col. 334; Couliano, *Tree of Gnosis*, 23; Stoyanov, *Other God*, 2; Gardner, "Dualism"). The importance assumed by dualism in Persian thought—recognized as early as Plutarch, as we have seen in this chapter—has misled some scholars into dubbing it 'oriental,' as if it were alien to the Greeks (e.g. van Winden, *Calcidius on Matter*, 117, 246; J.M. Dillon, *Middle Platonists*, 379; the 'oriental' character to Numenius's dualism is today rightly rejected, as by Alt, *Weltflucht*, 42).

214 Couliano, *Tree of Gnosis*, 24.

THE OTHER GODS   151

tangle in the skein of any ethical dimension of monotheism: if there is one
cause, and it is good, *unde malum*?[215]

The Epicureans claimed that the gods did not cause anything we experience; the Stoa, that only we are responsible for anything like evil, namely moral
evil. The Platonists offered multiple responses to the problem, pointing towards
poor choices made prior to incarnation (see chapters one and six), recalcitrant
matter in creation, and fallible, semi-divine beings who introduce imperfection
and chaos into the world. The Christian thinkers examined in this chapter wrestled with all of these options as they addressed the problem of evil in a context
that presupposed some form of the apocalyptic heritage of the gospels, and,
occasionally, the Enochic tradition. The latter led to a sort of 'despoiling' of the
heavenly intermediaries of the Platonists: as discussed above (chapters one and
two), Pseudo-Plutarch, Apuleius, and their like regarded *daimones* as imperfect, but not as malevolent. In developing such a rich demonology which took
into account the personality of *daimones* themselves, philosophers from Justin
to Origen offered a new way of thinking about the specific kind of causality daimonic administrators played in introducing evil into the world: rather than taking these beings to be imperfect 'young gods,' demons became sinners who, like
humans, make bad choices and in so doing spread sin. Other thinkers, such as
Hermogenes—and Marcion and Apelles, although our evidence here is much
more scanty—appear to have tried to adapt Pythagorean-Platonic notions of
matter as a source of chaos and disruption in creation. For Marcion and Apelles,
the question was addressed in the context of a scriptural hermeneutic which
read biblical texts as documenting the creation and rule of the material world
by a lesser God; all three were pilloried by their contemporaries for assigning
too much of an external, causal role to cosmic evil beyond the sin proffered by
demons and the Devil, over which God will triumph. In the terms of the present
chapter, their 'dualism' was not 'attenuated' enough.

So, given the emphasis on the reality of evil across this wide spectrum of
early Christian thought, were all these thinkers—from Athenagoras to Apelles—equally dualist, because they were partisans of Christianity, a "moderate dualist religion," in Russell's words? It is useful here to recall what Yuri
Stoyanov calls 'religious dualism': cases where both good and evil principles
are at work in cosmogony and anthropogony.[216] The previous chapter con-

---

215   Stroumsa, *Making*, 16.
216   Stoyanov, *Other God*, 3; see also idem, "Religious Dualism," 410; Heger, "Another look at
       Dualism," 48. Karamanolis makes the interesting observation that both Monists and Dual-
       ists assume that "the world must be similar in character to its creator" (Karamanolis,
       Philosophy, 65).

cluded by highlighting the deeply Stoic valence of early Christian philosophizing about the omnipresence and personal character of divine providence. The present account has tried to show that, even for thinkers employing a Middle Platonic framework of superhuman intermediaries, the human experience of these intermediaries—especially the ones who have gone bad—amounts to what is essentially a Stoic model, where humans are responsible for embracing rational, providential activity or resisting it, and falling into irrational sin. For Athenagoras, Clement, and even Origen, it is not the creation of human beings that explains the origins of evil; it is the phenomenon of demons, however philosophically they interpreted this phenomenon. This is not the case with Marcion or Apelles, who postulated a secondary, evil principle not just occupying administration, but creation—of the world or of human beings, or of both. Here, a secondary causal force is at work and demands some kind of recognition. This is a step beyond the *Timaeus*, where fallible young gods are responsible for making the human body, but Plato nonetheless stresses the providence of the demiurge as extending to everything. It is even a step beyond the Middle Platonists who are usually called 'dualists'—Plutarch and Numenius—for whom the 'World Soul' must split in its engagement with matter while making the body of the cosmos, but who are silent as to how this may affect our understanding of the creation of the souls and bodies of human beings. Out of the thinkers discussed in this chapter, only Marcion and Apelles qualify as 'religious dualists' *sensu* Stoyanov: Marcion thought both the world and humans were created by the lower God, and a higher God providentially sent his Son to redeem humanity. Apelles agreed about the world, but seems to have thought humans were from a separate, divine realm, which would explain why this higher God would reach out to them. Other Christian thinkers of the first centuries CE had a similarly dualistic belief that divine care extended to human beings, but not the cosmos. They were called Gnostics.

CHAPTER 4

Did God Care for Creation?

1   Introduction: Gnostics without 'Gnosticism'?

Even beyond Marcion, the most famous case of 'dualism' in ancient Roman religion is 'Gnosticism,' together with the related but distinct phenomenon of Manichaeism. Scholars have severely criticized the term 'Gnosticism,' but they generally agree on the body of sources to which the term refers: the 'biblical demiurgical' myths largely (but not strictly) preserved in the Nag Hammadi Codices, discovered in Upper Egypt (ca. December 1945).[1] As Bentley Layton has argued, these myths recall the story that Irenaeus of Lyons claims was taught by individuals who belonged to a 'school of thought' comprised of self-described 'Gnostics' (*gnōstikoi*, "knowers"). The third-century CE philosopher Porphyry of Tyre also writes that works circulating amongst certain Christian "heretics" were known to the seminar of Plotinus around 263 CE. They were criticized by Plotinus in a tractate which Porphyry titled *Against the Gnostics* and *Against Those who say the World and its Maker are Evil*.[2] Thus, for much of the twentieth century, scholarship referred to the thought of these Gnostics as 'Gnosticism.' Following Michael Allen Williams's seminal critique of the term's vagueness and association with "clichés" that have little or no correspondence to the sources in question, Anglophone scholarship now tends to investigate sources formerly known as 'Gnostic' without recourse to the modern notion of 'Gnosticism,' but to other aspects of their ancient social and intellectual environments. Some scholars simply call these sources 'Christian.'[3] Meanwhile, David Brakke has recently defended Layton's identification of the 'Gnostic school of thought' with the myths from the Nag Hammadi corpus, while

---

1   On the discovery, editing, and publication of the Nag Hammadi Codices, see recently Robinson, *Nag Hammadi Discovery*. On the viability of M.A. Williams's phrase 'biblical demiurgical' as a replacement for the term 'Gnostic,' see the conclusion to this chapter. The present chapter revises and expands my article "Providence, Creation, and Gnosticism," and, to a lesser extent, "First Thoughts."

2   Layton, "Prolegomena," re: Ir. *Haer.* 1.29–30 and Porph. *Vit. Plot.* 16. For the interpretation of the latter passage provided here, see Burns, *Apocalypse*, 45–46, 161–163. On *Enn.* 2.9, see recently Spanu, *Plotinus*; Burns, op. cit., 32–47; Gertz, *Plotinus*.

3   King, *What is Gnosticism?*, 231. Recent examples of such an approach include King, *Secret Revelation*, viii–x; Dunderberg, *Beyond Gnosticism*, 1–2, 5–6; Dunning, "What Sort," 60; G. Smith, *Guilt*, 166–171.

© KONINKLIJKE BRILL NV, LEIDEN, 2020 | DOI:10.1163/9789004432994_006

eschewing the term 'Gnosticism,' given Williams's incisive criticism of the term.[4] Did the Gnostics, then, teach no Gnosticism?

To be sure, much has been learned by studying the Gnostic dossier without recourse to the category of 'Gnosticism.' Above all, it is increasingly clear that the materials sometimes dubbed 'Gnostic' were embedded in and alongside early Christian communities; from a socio-historical perspective, they are difficult—perhaps impossible—to extricate from the phenomenon of early Christianity. Nonetheless, this chapter will argue that some connotation of the term 'Gnosticism' remains useful and even necessary for historians of philosophy and theology to denote the philosophical presuppositions regarding creation and salvation that underlie the body of myths that Layton and Brakke rightfully associate with the *gnōstikoi*. It can be difficult to understand these presuppositions because these stories do not express themselves in reasoned propositions designed to be read by historians of philosophy, but in the language of revealed mythology.[5] Yet the authors of some of these myths were knowledgeable about Greek thought and sometimes used the jargon of the Greeks in making their point. Amongst this jargon is that of "providence" (*pronoia*), which is remarkably commonplace throughout our evidence regarding Gnosticism.[6]

More specifically, Gnostic anthropogonies like those found in the Nag Hammadi tractates the *Apocryphon of John* and *On the Origin of the World* use language about divine care to highlight an idea expressed in their myths: the world and material bodies were created by entities who are not providential, yet God cares for human beings, who belong to the heavenly realm and so are divine in some sense. From the perspective of Roman philosophy, this is a highly distinctive view on providence and creation. This chapter will thus begin by briefly surveying passages on providence and creation from second- and early

---

4   Brakke, *Gnostics*, 27, 36–51, following Bentley Layton, "Prolegomena." These myths Brakke considers to have belonged to the Gnostic school of thought are more or less identical to those from the 'Sethian' group identified by Schenke, "Phenomenon" (on 'Sethian Gnosticism,' see further Turner, *Sethian Gnosticism*, and Burns, *Apocalypse*), and what Layton called 'Classic Gnosticism' (Layton, *Gnostic Scriptures*, 5–22, and Rasimus, *Paradise Reconsidered*, esp. 55). While I find the terms 'Classic,' 'Ophite,' and "Sethian" useful to denote particular Gnostic literary traditions—in agreement with Rasimus, op. cit.—the question is peripheral to the argument made in this chapter, and so I eschew them here.

5   Most Gnostic works are apocalypses, works which seek to persuade via claims to possess celestial authority; see Burns, "Apocalypses."

6   Cf. Magris, who, despite devoting many pages to analysis of evidence about Gnosticism, relates almost nothing of what this evidence specifically says about *pronoia* (*L'idea di destino*, 2:774–817).

third-century Christian writers, above all Irenaeus himself, who wrestled with a similar set of biblical and Greek philosophical perspectives in developing their ideas about the origin of the world and humanity, but posed no such divorce between providential care for the world and for human beings. It will be argued that the use of language about providence in the myths associated with the Gnostics known to Irenaeus and Porphyry shows that these Gnostics did, in fact, espouse ideas distinct from their Christian and heathen brethren alike, ideas which are most conveniently referred to as 'Gnostic.'

2   No Idle Hands: The Creation-Theology of Irenaeus of Lyons

As argued in chapter one, all Platonic and Stoic philosophers, despite many differences of emphasis and detail, defended the notion of divine care for the world and for human beings, and articulated this notion in terms of God's care for creation. The demiurge of the *Timaeus* makes the world as good as a creation can possibly be, given the complications presented by matter and necessity (*anagkē*), while leaving the construction of human bodies to the young gods, later identified by the Middle Platonists as *daimones*. The God of the Stoa is itself both creator and present in creation, caring for the universe insofar as it permeates and rationally orders it. Chapter two observed that for some Stoa, this omniprovidence amounted, in a sense, to personal care for individuals. Some ancient Jewish and Christian thinkers of the first two centuries CE conceived the God of Israel to be at least as involved in the world as the deity of Stoic philosophy, starting with the act of creation itself, as witnessed for instance in the *oeuvre* of Philo of Alexandria.[7] Finally, the previous chapter highlighted the notable exception of Marcion and his student Apelles, whose God was said by their opponents not to create, but only to save. As chapter three also showed, the adaptations of Middle Platonic models of multi-tiered providence to a Christian worldview proved complex and difficult, given widespread belief in the myth of the Fall of the Watchers and the identification of *daimones* with the false deities of heathen cults. Each of these issues—divine care for wholes versus parts, the problem of care for the world, and the problem of the status of demons and other superhuman beings in the universe—was also at work in speculation among Roman philosophers about the providence's role in the creation not just of the world, but the creation of human beings themselves.

---

7   On this point see also Armstrong, "Dualism," 44.

The earliest Christian philosophers generally presented a similar approach to providence's role in creation as we found in Philo, where the Word (*logos*)—also known as Wisdom (*sophia*)—serves as a kind of secondary entity, who is at once God's tool in fashioning things and the rational faculty acquired by human beings when God blew *pneuma* into Adam's face (Gen 2:7).[8] Furnished with ample proof-texts from the authors of 2 Peter and Colossians (2 Pet 3:5; Col 1:16), Justin Martyr, Theophilus, Athenagoras, and Tertullian all assign responsibility for creation to Christ the *logos*, often in the same breath as Wisdom.[9] Clement of Alexandria also insists on God's identity as creator of the world, and the identity of the *logos*, His Son, as His agent.[10] Like Philo and the Stoa, he employs the argument from design, trotting forth the claim that human beings were created erect so better as to gaze on the heavens.[11] Origen holds that belief in providence is tantamount to belief that the world is the creation of God and God alone: "everyone who perceives that providence exists (*providentiam esse sentiunt*)—in whatever way—confess that God, who created and arranged all things (*universa creavit atque disposuit*), is unbegotten and confess Him as the Father of the universe (*parentem universitatis*)."[12] Origen's *On First Principles* identifies *logos*, *sophia*, and *pronoia* all at once as God's divine activity; even if God the Father is the architect, it is Wisdom who does the building, and "forming beforehand and containing within herself the species of and calculations behind the entire creation (*species scilicet in se et rationes totius praeformans et continens creaturae*)."[13] In *Against Celsus* as well, *pronoia* is a consummately demiurgic power whose work is evident in the florid diversity of creation, such as the manifold kinds of birds one can observe.[14] Providence has made all things for the sake of cultivating the human rational faculty: in a riff on the Stoic defense of pests as part of the divine plan, Origen argues that even animals that appear to behave rationally—like bees and ants build-

---

8   On these points see Philo, *Spec.* 1.81, *Fug.* 68–70, 101, all discussed above, chapter two, with many more references.

9   Just. Mart. *Dial.* 61.3, 129.3; Athenag. *Leg.* 10.2; Theoph. *Autol.* 1.3 (cit. Scheffczyk, *Schöpfung und Vorsehung*, 16–17, 36 n. 14). For Tertullian, see *Herm.* 33 (re: Prov 8:22; so Karamanolis, *Philosophy*, 86); *Marc.* 1–2; *Res.* 6; *An.* 17.

10   God alone is the creator (Clem. Alex. *Strom.* 5.14.92.3), albeit through the Word (ibid., 5.1.6.3; idem, *Protr.* 63.3); cit. Karamanolis, *Philosophy*, 88–89.

11   Clem. Alex. *Strom.* 4.26.163.1, cit. Scott, *Origen and the Life*, 106 n. 19, re: Sen. *Ep.* 92.30.

12   Orig. *Princ.* 1.3.1, text and tr. Behr, 66–67, slightly modified.

13   Orig. *Princ.* 1.2.3, text and tr. Behr, 42–43, discussed in O'Brien, *Demiurge*, 253–256. This creative activity extends to matter: *Princ.* 1.2.6, 2.9.1, 4.4.8; cit. and discussed by Karamanolis, *Philosophy*, 92; O'Brien, *Demiurge*, 256. See also *Princ.* 1.2.2, 1.2.12, discussed above, chapter three, n. 146.

14   Orig. *Cels.* 4.98.

DID GOD CARE FOR CREATION? 157

ing colonies—are nonetheless irrational creatures which behave in this way so as to remind rational creatures to pursue greater industry.[15]

Besides Philo, however, no Jewish or Christian writer of the first three centuries explores God's role as benevolent, providential creator of the universe and human beings with as much vigor as does Irenaeus of Lyons.[16] Amongst his goals is dispatching the threat of dualism: As noted in chapter three, Irenaeus, in the final discussion of book three of *Against Heresies*, accuses Marcion of wrongly introducing a second deity, divorcing God's loving and punitive aspects as found in Scripture. While Tertullian attempts to paint Marcion as an Epicurean, Irenaeus does not, probably because Marcion himself had argued that the high God was providential. Yet immediately before he turns to Marcion, he charges a different party, the followers of the second-century Christian Platonist Valentinus, with introducing a deity who recalls the lazy, inactive gods of Epicurus, who exercise no providence at all:

> So they dream up a god who in actuality does not exist, as being above Him, so that they maintain that they have found a great god whom no one will be able to know, because he does not have fellowship with the human race and does not administer earthly affairs (*ou ... ta epigeia dioikounta*), having obviously 'found' the god of Epicurus, a god who does not help him nor any others—that is, a god who cares for no one at all (*oudenos pronoian echonta*).[17]

Rather, Irenaeus argues, Plato was right to teach that God is active in the world (*Leg.* 715e) and good (*Tim.* 29e).[18] Indeed, goodness is implied in creation: "for

---

15   Orig. *Cels.* 4.81.

16   Origen's remarks on the creation of Adam and Eve are, to the extent we know them at all, rather minimal. For a recent discussion, see Martens, "Origen's Doctrine."

17   Ir. *Haer.* 3.24.2. Here I translate the Greek text of Doutreleau and Rousseau in SC 211:477, 479, with reference to Unger, rev. Steenberg, 111. Cf. van Unnik, "Attack," 344; Bergjan, *Der fürsorgende Gott*, 122 n. 76.

18   Ir. *Haer.* 3.25.5: "Plato is shown to be more religious than these men, since he acknowledged that the one and the same God is both just and good and has power over all things, and even exercises judicial power ..." (tr. Unger, rev. Steenberg, 113). Lashier rightly notes that Irenaeus's reference to Plato in positive terms in this passage does not indicate the theologian's positive evaluation of Greek philosophy, but his extreme exasperation with Marcion (*Irenaeus on the Trinity*, 39 n. 85). See also *Haer.* 3.25.1–3 (quoted above, chapter three); Osborn, *Irenaeus*, 85. As Karamanolis observes, Irenaeus's attacks on Gnosticism as 'mythical, non-rational' ("they *dream up* a god ..."—*Haer.* 3.24.2, quoted previous note) imply that "Irenaeus sees Christianity as a continuation of the rational enterprise of Hellenistic philosophy" (Karamanolis, *Philosophy*, 82, re: *Haer.* 1.12.1, 2.13.3).

the act of creating (*facere*) is a property of God's goodness."[19] It is creation that allows the transcendent God to be known, even to those who do not know Christ, like the pagan philosophers.[20] In book two of *Against Heresies*, he vigorously defends the goodness of the material creation, even if it is a mere echo of the Platonic forms upon which it is modeled. If the celestial models are arranged via providence, Irenaeus claims, then the creation executed with reference to those models must be honored as providential; to not honor the creation as such is tantamount to denying providence.[21]

As with Philo, the question is how exactly God creates. Irenaeus does not speak of any kind of pre-existent, chaotic matter God uses to shape creation, but simply states that God is at once identical with the tool He uses to create; His Word:

> God has no need of anything that exists since he created all things and made them by his Word. He did not need angels as helpers to make the things that are made, nor did he need any power much inferior to himself and ignorant of the Father; neither any degeneracy nor ignorance in order that he who would become man might know him. On the contrary, he predetermined in himself all things in advance according to His nature—which is ineffable and inscrutable to us—and he made them as He willed, bestowing on all things their form and order, and the principle of creation ... It is proper to God's preeminence not to be in need of other instruments for creating things to be made. His own Word is sufficient for the formation of all things. Thus John, the Lord's disciple, says of him: All things were made by him and without him was made nothing (John 1:3).[22]

Irenaeus here does not want to imply that God is a *deus otiosus* who sits back while a second being is at work making and administrating the cosmos. He even

---

19   Ir. *Haer*. 4.39.2, tr. mine, text Rousseau and Doutreleau in SC 100:966, 968, per Steenberg, *Irenaeus on Creation*, 33; Karamanolis, *Philosophy*, 79–80. Karamanolis (op. cit., 66), notes that Irenaeus is inspired by *Tim*. 29e throughout.

20   Ir. *Haer*. 2.6.2; for discussion, see Perkins, "Logos Christologies," 386; eadem, "Ordering the Cosmos," 235; Steenberg, *Irenaeus on Creation*, 146. Steenberg (ibid., 37) also recalls Theoph. *Autol*. 2.10.

21   Ir. *Haer*. 2.15.3; cf. Perkins, who reads Irenaeus as claiming that providential care for material creation implies that the creation itself is of equal status to the heavenly forms upon which it was modeled ("Ordering the Cosmos," 214).

22   Ir. *Haer*. 2.2.4–5, tr. Unger, rev. J.J. Dillon, 20–21; cf. Perkins, "Ordering the Cosmos," 235. See also *Haer*. 3.11.8, 5.18.3; also 3.11.8, cit. Steenberg, *Irenaeus on Creation*, 69.

DID GOD CARE FOR CREATION?

adds that to posit such an entity would be tantamount to limiting God's freedom, rendering Him subject to a principle of Necessity.[23] Irenaeus's reticence to distinguish God from the creating Word is surely informed by his wariness of the doctrine he believes professed by the Marcosians, Valentinians, and Marcionites: that there is another maker than the Father.[24] Thus, when presented with the passage where God says "let *us* make" (Gen 1:26) humanity, he says that God is talking to "his hands," i.e. the Son and the Spirit, who are with him always.[25] This 'hand' belongs to none other than the God of Abraham Himself:

> He alone is omnipotent and alone the Father who, by the Word of his power, created and made all things ... He ordered all things by his Wisdom. He comprehended all things, but himself alone cannot by comprehended by anyone. He is the Builder, he is the Creator, he is the Originator, he is the Maker, he is the Lord of all things. Neither is there anyone beside him nor above him; neither a mother, as they falsely assert, nor another God, whom Marcion imagines ... No, there is only one God the Builder ... He who is Father, God, Creator, Maker, Builder, made them by himself, that is, by his Word and Wisdom, namely the heavens and the earth and the sea, and all things that are in them. He it is who is just and good. He it is who fashioned man, planted paradise, made the world, and brought on the flood that saved Noah. He is the God of Abraham, the God of Isaac, the God of Jacob, the God ... of the Living ...[26]

Imperfection and error do not appear to present much of an issue in Irenaeus's theology of creation. Evil is the result of sin, responsibility for which belongs to humanity alone. Irenaeus writes that God created humanity as an immature, imperfect creature, which needs to grow into maturity; he even speculates

---

23   Ir. *Haer.* 2.5.3–4. Plotinus addresses such questions as well, in *Enn.* 6.8 (see below, chapter seven).

24   Ir. *Haer.* 1.20.3, 4.18.4, 4.27.4, respectively, cit. Steenberg, *Irenaeus on Creation*, 67; see also *Haer.* 2.1.1; idem, *Epid.* 4, 99; Karamanolis, *Philosophy*, 78–79.

25   Ir. *Haer.* 4.20.1, cit. Steenberg, *Irenaeus on Creation*, 75. Similarly Ir. *Epid.* 11.

26   Ir. *Haer.* 2.30.9, tr. Unger, rev. J.J. Dillon, 100, cit. Steenberg, *Irenaeus on Creation*, 68, 79, 147, re: also *Haer.* 4.7.4, 4.18.4 (with a liturgical valence); see also idem, *Epid.* 5. Schefczyk's citations on this point are misleading (*Schöpfung und Vorsehung*, 45, re: *Haer.* 3.9.3, 3.16–18). Bingham also recalls *Haer.* 2.6.1, 4.6.1–7 (*Irenaeus' Use of Matthew's Gospel*, 47). Finally, see *Haer.* 2.26.3, which attacks heretical ways of counting the various parts of creation (only God—providentially!—can do that, per Matt 10:29–31 = Luke 12:6–7).

160   CHAPTER 4

that Adam and Eve were created as children, not adults.[27] He valuates the creation so highly that assigning the creative portion of God's activity—even with respect to the creation and maintenance of humanity—to a being so tied to the Father (the Son, "hand") does not, to him, imply divine responsibility for evil. Creation, for Irenaeus, is not a problem.

3   Archons and Providences at Work in Creation: 'On the Origin of the World' and the 'Apocryphon of John'

Irenaeus is at such pains to clarify the singularity and identity of the creator and His "hands" because, he tells us, creation was a serious problem for some of his contemporaries. In the first book of *Against Heresies*, he seeks to link various groups he opposes—particularly the followers of Valentinus—to the teaching of "Gnostics" (*gnōstikoi*).[28] He describes the teaching of these individuals in chapter twenty-nine of the book, which is mostly concerned with the procession of various heavenly beings, including a primordial human being (*anthrōpos*), as well as a corrupt demiurge, the son of Wisdom (*Sophia*), who creates the subordinate angels, heavens, and the earth. In chapter thirty, he turns to "other (Gnostics)," and relates a similar story, with more detail regarding this bad demiurge and his minions. His name is Yaldabaoth:

> On this account, Yaldabaoth, rejoicing over all those below him, swelled up with pride and exclaimed, "I am father, and God, and above me there is no one." But his mother, upon hearing this, cried out against him, "Do not lie, Yaldabaoth: for above you is the Father of everything, the First Man; and so is Man the Son of Man." Then, with all of them being upset at this new voice due to the unexpected declaration, and as they were asking where they sound had come from, Yaldabaoth, in order to lead them back to himself—so they say—exclaimed, "Come, let us make humanity after our image" (Gen 1:27). The six powers, upon hearing this as their mother gave them the idea of a human being (in order that by means of him she might empty them of their original power), together formed a man of immense size, both in regard to breadth and length. However, as he could merely writhe along the ground, they carried him to their

27   Ir. *Haer.* 3.22.4; idem, *Epid.* 12. For further passages and discussion, see Aland (Ehlers), "Sünde und Erlösung," 156; Russell, *Satan*, 83; esp. Steenberg, "Children in Paradise."

28   Ir. *Haer.* 1.praef, 1.11.1, 1.29.1. Recent scholarship on Irenaeus's construction of heretical teachings in these passages includes Brakke, *Gnostics*, 29–35; cf. G. Smith, *Guilt*, 131–171.

DID GOD CARE FOR CREATION?

father. Wisdom was doing all this so that she might empty him of the sprinkling of light in him and so that he would no longer stand against those who were above him, having been deprived of his power. So, when that one breathed the spirit of life into the man—so they say—he was secretly emptied of his power, while humanity came to possess thenceforth intellect and thought, and—they say—these are the faculties which enjoy salvation.[29]

It is striking that, according to this myth, God cares for human "intellect and thought" alone—these are the only things "which enjoy salvation." A corollary of this view is that God does not care for material bodies and the present world. Such a reading is validated by the fact that several versions of this same anthropogony, preserved in Coptic—*On the Origin of the World* and the *Apocryphon of John*—mark this divorce between care for humanity and care for the cosmos in terms of divine providence. At the same time, they express a certain suspicion or rejection of worldly authority, by using terms typically associated with divine and terrestrial administrations—*archon*, *exousia*, and even *pronoia* itself—to refer to antagonists.

Orig. World (NHC II,5, henceforth *Orig. World*) relates how providence intervened when terrible superhuman beings named archons, seeking to create slaves for themselves, went about creating humanity. Thanks to providence, the archons mistakenly pattern their creation on an image of God, the "Adam of Light," a being they cannot possibly hope to subdue. The text distinguishes between two Wisdom-figures: the celestial Pistis Sophia ("Faith-Wisdom") and the terrestrial Sophia Zoē ("Wisdom-Life").[30] Pistis Sophia gives birth to Yaldabaoth, an *archon* (Grk. "leader, administrator"; see further below) who "possesses authority over matter" (*euᵉntaf ᵉmmau ᵉntexousia ᵉnthulē*), out of which he creates both heaven and earth.[31] Androgynous, he possesses both a male and a female name; the latter is *"pronoia sambathas*, which means, 'the week (*thebdomas*)'."[32] Blindly thinking himself to be the sole existing being, he wishes to be glorified, and so creates seven androgynous sons who "appear from the Chaos," the greatest of whom is named Sabaoth, as well as a host of angels. Basking in their worship, "his heart was filled with joy, and he began to boast

---

29 Ir. *Haer.* 1.30.6, text Rousseau and Doutreleau in SC 264:370, 372, tr. mine.

30 The distinction between the two wisdoms is a marked feature of Valentinian literature; see Perkins, *"On the Origin,"* 40.

31 *Orig. World* NHC II 100.1–101.9, text in Painchaud, "Texte," 152, 154, tr. mine.

32 *Orig. World* NHC II 101.26–27, text in Painchaud, "Texte," 156, tr. mine; see further idem, "Commentaire," 276; Good, *Reconstructing*, 46–47.

162   CHAPTER 4

constantly, saying to them, 'I do not need anything!' and saying, 'I am God, and
there is no one beside me!' But when he said these things, he sinned against
all the immortal beings who are responsible ..."[33] Pistis Sophia rebukes him,
and Sabaoth, recognizing the truth of her words, repents for his previous ignorance of the higher realm beyond Yaldabaoth; in return, he is raptured and
given authority over all of Chaos.[34]

Pronoia is not an unambiguous figure in *Orig. World*; rather, the two Wisdoms appear to have as counterparts a higher and lower "Providence."[35] The
work tells us that, following Sabaoth's rapture, this lower *Pronoia(-Sambathas)*
was involved in the introduction of sexuality to the world:[36]

> When this light manifested, a human image appeared within it, being very
> splendorous, and nobody saw it, except for the Prime Begetter alone and
> Providence, who was with him. But its light appeared to all the powers of
> heaven; for this reason, they were all troubled by it. Then, once Providence
> saw this emissary (*aggelos*), she fell in love with him; but he despised her,
> because she was on darkness. Now, she wanted to embrace him, but she
> was not able to.[37]

The divine human image is also seen by the "powers of heaven," who are also
known in this text as "authorities" (*exousia*) or especially "archons." Both the
beings and the names used for them are common in myths like that of *Orig.
World*. Although they fulfill many of the roles of demons,[38] they are only occasionally referred to as such. The word *archon* was commonly used in Greek and
Coptic alike, not just for sovereigns, but for local administrators and authority-
figures.[39] The connotation of the word as used in this story is then distinc-

---

33   *Orig. World* NHC II 103.8–14, text in Painchaud, "Texte," 158, 160, tr. mine.

34   *Orig. World* NHC II 103.32–106.18.

35   That two characters rather than one is meant is admittedly implicit, but there is no ques-
      tion that the two 'providences' play very different roles in *Orig. World*.

36   *Orig. World* NHC II 111.15–20, 111.31–33; see further Williams, "Higher Providence," 498, fol-
      lowed by Denzey (Lewis), *Cosmology and Fate*, 42; cf. Perkins, "On the Origin," 39.

37   *Orig. World* NHC II 108.7–18, text in Painchaud, "Texte," 170, 172, tr. mine; cf. Painchaud,
      "Commentaire," 344–345. The scene recalls the famous 'seduction of the archons,' an
      important tale in Manichaean mythology; see recently Burns, "Gnosis Undomesticated,"
      140–144.

38   Despite their importance in Gnostic myths, there are remarkably few studies of the
      archons themselves. For a recent discussion of how the *Book of the Watchers* may have
      influenced descriptions of the archons, see Losekam, *Sünde der Engel*.

39   For Greek usage, see LSJ 254a; Preisigke, *Wörterbuch*, 1:222. For Coptic usage, see Förster,
      Wörterbuch, 112–113.

DID GOD CARE FOR CREATION? 163

tively anti-authoritarian: do not trust the administrators![40] The use of the term *pronoia*—a term that typically designates favorable, caring authorities in Hellenistic and Roman sources—to designate a malevolent entity speaks for this reading.[41]

The archons are disturbed, because the appearance of the divine image proves that Yaldabaoth was wrong or even lying when he had claimed "It is I who am God. No one exists besides me":

> When they approached him, saying, "is this the god who has destroyed our work?" he answered, "Aye. If you wish that he should not be able to ruin our work, let us go, then, and create a human being from the earth, according to the image of our body and according to the likeness of that one (i.e., the luminous Adam—*kata thikōn ᵉmpensōma auō kata pine ᵉmpē*), so that he might serve us; moreover, so that he, when he sees his likeness (*eine*), might fall in love with it. No longer shall he ruin our work; rather, as for those who shall be begotten from the light, we shall turn them into our slaves for the entire duration of this age." But: all this came to pass through the providence of Pistis (*kata tpronoia ᵉnpistis*), so that humanity might appear in his likeness, and come to condemn them through their modeled form ... Then, the authorities received the knowledge so that they might create humanity. Sophia-Zoē—she who was with Sabaoth—had anticipated them, and she mocked their decision. For they are blind; they created in a state of ignorance, against their own interests, and they do not know what they are going to do. For this reason, she anticipated them, creating her own human being first, so that it might instruct their modeled form, how to despise them and thus be saved from them.[42]

---

40   A fundamental insight of Kippenberg, "Versuch"; more briefly, also Magris, *L'idea di destino*, 2:790–791. Kippenberg (op. cit.) extrapolated further that the authors of such texts were politically disempowered intellectuals making calls for rebellion; for a similar reading taking archons to be ecclesiastical rather than administrative authorities, see Pagels, "'The Demiurge'." Subsequent scholarship (surveyed in Dunderberg, *Beyond Gnosticism*, 163–165) has been wary of inferring too specific a social context for this pejorative language about authority-figures. Nonetheless, such usage strikes me as both marked and distinct, particularly in the context of Coptic literature, where the terms *archon* and *exousia* only very rarely appear with a pejorative sense outside of 'Gnosticizing' literature.

41   On the connotation of *pronoia* as specifically just, see Bergjan, *Der fürsorgende Gott*, esp. 107–122.

42   *Orig. World* NHC II 112.29–113.20, text in Painchaud, "Texte," 180, 182, tr. mine.

164   CHAPTER 4

When we are told that "all this came to pass through the Providence of Pistis,"
it must be the higher, good Providence is meant, for two reasons. First, the story
relates that the nefarious scheme of the archons was actually all part of the plan
of a benevolent God.[43] Moreover, *pronoia* here belongs to *pistis* ("faith"), a figure who in this text is also identified on some level with *sophia* ("wisdom").[44]
As discussed above (in this chapter, and in chapter two), *pronoia* and *sophia*
were often associated in Hellenistic Jewish and Christian literature, and so *Orig.
World*'s further absorption of these beings into a benevolent 'providence' is only
natural.

Meanwhile, the diabolical Prime Begetter and his archons appear to parody the creator-deities of Plato's *Timaeus*, where the good Demiurge sows the
immortal part of human souls and then assigns the construction of the body
to the "young gods."[45] Thus, *Orig. World* proceeds to tell us that "from that very
day on, the seven archons have molded humanity; while its bodily form resembles their body, its true likeness resembles the human being that had appeared
to them."[46] However, *Orig. World* and Irenaeus's "others" also go considerably
beyond Plato's account insofar as they explicitly assign the implantation of a
divine, immortal element (God's "likeness," Copt. *eine*, as manifest in the celestial Adam who appears) to divine intervention—here, executed by the figure of
the good *Pronoia*. This divine intervention is entirely distinct from the creative
activity of the archons, who make, in *Orig. World*'s parlance, "the image (*hikōn*)
of our body": the material Adam.[47] They operate under the jurisdiction of Yaldabaoth, who is identified in turn with a sort of lower *pronoia*. Scholars have
noted that this latter feature is probably inspired in part by Middle Platonic
models of divine administration,[48] but in light of our analysis in chapter three,
we can be more precise. Yaldabaoth's identification with a malevolent *pronoia*

---

43   Perkins, "*On the Origin*," 40, followed by Onuki, "Die dreifache Pronoia," 252; see also Burns,
      "First Thoughts," 41–42.

44   On the figure of Pistis Sophia, see Good, *Reconstructing*, 46–47; additionally, MacRae, "Jew-
      ish Background," 91; Turner, *Sethian Gnosticism*, 223; Rasimus, *Paradise Reconsidered*, 136;
      Bak Halvgaard, *Linguistic Manifestations*, 79, 118. Fittingly, Wisdom-Life (*sophia-zoē*) in
      Orig. World prepares a 'beast' to instruct humanity: the Serpent who bears salvific knowl-
      edge (NHC II 113.10–120.6).

45   See above, chapter one; further, in the context of Gnosticism, Pleše, "Fate, Providence, and
      Astrology."

46   *Epefsōma men eine ᵉmpousōma, pefeine de efeine ᵉmprōme ntahouōnh ebol nau*—*Orig.
      World* NHC II 114.29–32, text in Painchaud, "Texte," 184, tr. mine.

47   On *Orig. World*'s interpretation of the terminology of "image" and "likeness" (re: Gen 1:26–
      27), and its description of the created Adam as material, see Dunning, "What Sort," 66–74,
      77–78.

48   Perkins, "*On the Origin*," 40–43, followed by Painchaud, "Commentaire," 384.

DID GOD CARE FOR CREATION? 165

is in line with early Christian philosophers who struggled with the Middle Platonists' identification of demons as providential administrators. In *Orig. World*, the providential 'powers' at work in the creation of the human body are agents of the 'demonic,' cosmic *pronoia*, which may be overcome thanks to the salvific plan steered by the *pronoia* of Pistis Sophia.

A similar intervention of a higher providence in the creation of human beings, overcoming a lower, cosmic providence, is also central to one of the most famous Gnostic texts, the *Apocryphon of John* (BG 8502,2; NHC II,1; III,1; IV,1, henceforth *Ap. John*). This tractate is preserved in four manuscripts and two recensions, long and short (NHC II,1 and IV,1; NHC III,1 and BG 8502,2, respectively).[49] These recensions are differentiated in part by their use of language about *pronoia*, which, as Bernard Barc and Louis Painchaud have demonstrated, appears much more frequently in the long version.[50] *Ap. John* is a long work that appears to be a compilation of several pre-existing sources.[51] The diverse literary provenances of these sources is indicated in part by use of their language about *pronoia*, which is very distinctive.[52] In the text's theogony, *pronoia* is repeatedly identified with the generative maternal-deity named Barbelo or "Mother."[53] (In one passage of the theogony, she is rather denoted with a Coptic nominal phrase for "first thought": *šorᵉp ᵉmmeue*, or *houeite ᵉnnennoia*, "first-/fore-thought" < Grk. *prōtennoia*, viz., *protennoia*, on which see further below, and in chapter seven.)[54] Barbelo gives birth to the aeonic beings of the pre-existent, celestial realm, and one of these aeons, Wisdom, does something unwise: she chooses to give birth alone, without her male consort:

---

49 On the manuscripts and recensions of *Ap. John*, see esp. Waldstein and Wisse, "Introduction." As is customary, I refer here to the long recension as LR and the short recension as SR. The best manuscript of the text is NHC II and so I base the present analysis upon it, referring to significant parallels (and differences) in SR ad loc.

50 Barc and Painchaud, "Réécriture." On *pronoia* in *Ap. John*, see also Onuki, *Gnosis und Stoa*, and esp. idem, "Die dreifache Pronoia," discussed in the following.

51 Waldstein and Wisse, "Introduction," 1; King, *Secret Revelation*, 17; Burns, "First Thoughts," 29–30.

52 Burns, "First Thoughts."

53 For Barbelo as *pronoia* in *Ap. John*, see NHC II 4.32 = BG 27.10–11; BG 28.4; NHC II 5.16 = BG 28.10; NHC II 6.5; [NHC II 6.22] = BG 30.14; NHC II 6.30 = BG 31.4; NHC II 14.20. For brief discussion, see Burns, "First Thoughts," 35; also Rasimus, *Paradise Reconsidered*, 151–152; cf. Pleše, "Fate, Providence, and Astrology," 262 n. 52; King, *Secret Revelation*, 125. This usage is paralleled in a number of other Nag Hammadi treatises that, in Rasimus's parlance, have 'Barbeloite' features: *Gos. Eg.*, *Three Forms*, *Zost.*, *Allogenes*, and *Mars*, as discussed below, in chapter seven. On the feminine incarnation of *pronoia*-Barbelo, see below, in this chapter.

54 *Ap. John* NHC II 5.4 (*šorᵉp ᵉmmeue*) = BG 27 18 (*houeite ᵉnnennoia*).

166   CHAPTER 4

> She (i.e., Wisdom) desired to manifest a likeness out of herself, without [the will] of the Spirit—He did not consent—and [without] her consort, and without his consideration. So, despite the person of her maleness not having consented, and without her having found her partner, she fell deep into thought—without the will of the Spirit, and the knowledge of her partner—and she brought something forth.[55]

This being is Yaldabaoth, the same figure known to Irenaeus's 'Others' and *Orig. World*. As in these former sources, this malevolent demiurge creates demonic angels and archons to help him rule the cosmos, and exalts in their glorification of him. Then,

> ... And a voice came forth from the exalted aeonic heaven: "Man exists, and the Son of Man." And the first archon, Yaldabaoth, heard it, thinking that the voice had come from his mother. And he did not know from where it had come. And He, the holy and perfect Mother-Father—He, the perfect providence, He, the image (*hikōn*) of the Invisible One, (the image of) the Father of the universe, in whom the universe came into being—He, the First Man, taught them; for he revealed his likeness (*eine*) in masculine form (*tupos ⁿnandreas*) ... And when all the authorities and the first archon looked, they saw the lower part (of the abyss) illuminated; and thanks to the light, they beheld in the water the form of the image. And he (Yaldabaoth) said to (the) authorities before him, "come; let us make man after the image of God (*kata thikōn ⁿmpnoute*), and after our own likeness (*kata peneine*), so that his image might become a light for us ..."[56]

---

55   *Ap. John* NHC II 9.28–35 and par., italics mine; text in Waldstein and Wisse, "Synopsis," 59, 61, tr. mine. See also Ir. *Haer*. 1.29.4, and *Ep. Pet. Phil*. NHC VIII [135].8–17, where Jesus says: "Yes, about [the deficiency] of the aeons—this [is] the deficiency, which is the disobedience and foolishness of the mother which appeared without the command of the greatness of the Father. She desired to set up aeons. And when she spoke, the Arrogant One ⟨appeared⟩ ..." (text and emendation Wisse, 238, 240, tr. mine; the reading of *de* as *te* [dental interchange, not uncommon in Coptic manuscripts] in line 10 is the helpful suggestion of John D. Turner, communicated via Lance Jennot, November 2016).

56   *Ap. John* NHC II 14.13–15.5, text in Waldstein and Wisse, "Synopsis," 85, 87, tr. mine. The appearance of the heavenly being is in response to the prayer for redemption of Wisdom, a response that is glossed as providential in SR (BG 47.6–7 = NHC III 21.10–11; Onuki, *Gnosis und Stoa*, 114).

DID GOD CARE FOR CREATION? 167

As in *Orig. World*, the theophany of an image of the First Man inspires Yald-abaoth and his archons to create the primal human being. In the theogony of both recensions of *Ap. John*, this First Man is identified with the Barbelo, the "image" of the first principle, the "Great Invisible Spirit."[57] Now, the long recension of the text also refers to Barbelo repeatedly as *pronoia*.[58] Therefore, the long recension holds that it is providence that inspired the creation of humanity, in contrast to the cosmos. In fact, humanity is a "likeness" of providence herself![59]

Yaldabaoth and his archons proceed to build the human body out of limbs and organs made of an "animate" (*psuchikos*) substance over which they have power, yet they cannot bring it to life—i.e., 'animate'—it. It is a 'soul-body,' but one that fails to do what souls are supposed to do, namely move, or be animated.[60] As in *Orig. World*, we also see here a 'lower providence': *pronoia* is one of the seven powers belonging to Yaldabaoth's archons, and assists in the creation of Adam's 'soul-body.'[61] Wisdom prays for help, which she receives: angels trick Yaldabaoth into blowing into Adam's face. Receiving *pneuma*, Adam becomes capable of movement and so truly alive. Recognizing Adam to be a superior being, the chief archon and his underlings grow jealous of him and cast him into matter (*hylē*). Heaven responds by sending another emissary, Consciousness (*epinoia*, i.e. the rational faculty), to enter Adam and become externally available on the Tree of Knowledge.[62] Both recensions of *Ap. John* describe Adam's acquisition of *epinoia* to be an act of providence, but in different ways. In the long recension, it is the Barbelo who sends Consciousness,

---

57 On the First Man as Barbelo, see NHC II 6.2–8 = BG 29.8–14; Litwa, "The God 'Human,'" 73–74; cf. King, *Secret Revelation*, 120. As King and Litwa have noted, *Ap. John* uses the term "image" rather than "likeness" to denote the divine similitude; it prefers "likeness" for the similitude of the archons. Such usage reverses the terminology of *Orig. World* (see above), as well as Philo, both re: Gen 1:26 LXX (King, "Distinctive Intertextuality," 13–14; Litwa, "The God 'Human,'" 61–62).

58 See above, n. 53, in this chapter.

59 See also King, "Distinctive Intertextuality," 11.

60 *Ap. John* NHC II 15.5–19.14 = BG 48.14–50.16. The former account includes a catalog of the angels involved in the creation of individual body parts.

61 *Ap. John* NHC II 12.17 = BG 43.12 (*pronoia* as a power of the authorities). *Ap. John* and *Orig. World* work from a common list of planetary powers also known to Celsus, in his account of the 'Ophite Diagram' (see Good, *Reconstructing*, 40–45; Onuki, "Dreifache Pronoia," 244; and esp. Rasimus, *Paradise Reconsidered*, 103–128). In the two recensions, this malevolent *pronoia* assists is the creation of different body parts: in LR, it helps make the "animate sinew" (NHC II 15.16). In SR, it helps make the "animate marrow" (BG 49.16, NHC III 23.1). See further Burns, "First Thoughts," 33 n. 16.

62 *Ap. John* NHC II 20.5–28, 21.14–16, 22.3–5 = BG 52.11–54.4, 55.15–18, 57.8–12. See also Pleše, "Evil," 123.

168   CHAPTER 4

while in the short recension, Wisdom's restoration to the true heaven is said to have happened thanks to divine providence.[63]

The complex of the mythological figures of *sophia* (Wisdom), *epinoia* (Consciousness), and *pronoia* (Providence)—complicated further by the latter's occasional identification with the Barbelo and the First Man—has occasioned many conflicting hypotheses about how exactly these various hypostases may be related to one another in different stages of the transmission of *Ap. John*.[64] For the present purposes, it suffices to observe that Hellenistic Jewish and early Christian literature often described divine wisdom and providence not as distinct, but as occupying the same spectrum of divine thoughtfulness for the cosmos and human beings.[65] This thoughtful care (*pronoia*) manifested in divine interventions in Jewish or Christian salvation-history, and this is also the case in *Ap. John*, where Wisdom, Consciousness, and Providence (especially in the long recension) aid Adam and Eve, watch over their progeny, and warn Noah about the Flood.[66] Jewish and Christian writers also followed the Stoa in holding that God's care manifested further in the indwelling of divine reason in humanity, and this, too, is expressed in *Ap. John* via *epinoia*'s providential visit to Adam. However, the long recension of *Ap. John* goes even further, appending to the end of the treatise a beautiful poem where *pronoia* herself describes her multiple interventions on behalf of humanity. In her first two descents into Chaos (or "Hell"), she delivers a message of salvation, is persecuted, and driven away. Then,

> Still for a third time, I went—it is I, the light that exists in the light; it is I, the remembrance of the Providence (*pronoia*)!—so that I might descend

---

63   For Barbelo's agency, as the "Mother-Father," see NHC II 20.10. This is the rectification of Wisdom's "deficiency"; SR had referred to this rectification as taking place thanks to providence (BG 47.6–7 = NHC III 21.10–11).

64   The most recent discussions are M. Meyer, "Thought," and Bak Halvgaard, "Life, Knowledge, and Language" (focusing rather on *Nat. Rul.* NHC II,4 and *Thunder* NHC VI,2). For a brief *Forschungsbericht*, see Burns, "First Thoughts," 33 n. 14. That such a line of enquiry is likely a red herring is recognized by Pleše, *Poetics*, 3–4 n. 4.

65   See above, chapter three and in this chapter. On this point see also Burns, "First Thoughts," 43–44.

66   *Ap. John* NHC II 23.23–29 (Eve's naming: in the SR, *epinoia* intervenes), 24.13–15 (Life escapes from Eve: scene not in SR), 28.1–5 (*pronoia* intervenes on behalf of the 'seed of Seth': in the SR, *epinoia* intervenes), 29.1–3 (Noah: in the SR, *epinoia* intervenes and is also identified with *pronoia*). On these episodes and their relationship to the '*pronoia* hymn,' see Waldstein, "Providence Monologue," 388–393; Barc and Painchaud, "Réécriture," 330–331; King, *Secret Revelation*, 134–135, 253; Rasimus, *Paradise Reconsidered*, 153; Turner, "Johannine Legacy," 113–120.

DID GOD CARE FOR CREATION? 169

into the middle of darkness, and the lower depth of Hell. I filled my face
with the light of the completion of their aeon, and I descended into the
center of their prison: the prison ⟨of⟩ the body. And I said, "he who hears,
awaken from the deep sleep." And he wept, and shed tears. Bitter tears he
wiped from himself, and he said, "who is it who calls my name, and from
where has this hope come to me? For it is in the bonds of the prison that I
dwell." And I said, It is I, the Providence (*pronoia*) of the pure light. It is I,
the recollection of the Virgin Spirit, the one who shall take you up to the
honored place. Wake up, and remember! For it is you who have hearkened;
and follow your root, which is me, the merciful one. And guard yourself
from the clutches of the angels of poverty, and the demons of Chaos, and
all of those who ensnare you …[67]

Providence then 'seals' the human supplicant and so delivers him unto salvation.[68] Louis Painchaud and Bernard Barc have observed that the redactor(s) of
the long recension of *Ap. John* added language about providence to the text, to
accompany their insertion of this 'Pronoia Hymn' into its conclusion.[69] However, they do not say why someone would have wanted to do this—a problem
we will attempt to answer in the following section.

Meanwhile, the dualism of light and darkness, forgetfulness and recognition,
of salvific descents met with rejection by those who ought to be saved, and,
finally, the liturgical seals—a reference to baptism?—led scholars to compare
this 'Pronoia Hymn' to the prologue of the Fourth Gospel.[70] The hymn appears
to undergird the structure of another Nag Hammadi work which is probably based off of the long recension of *Ap. John*, *Three Forms of First Thought*
(Grk. *protennoia trimorphos*, NHC XIII,1ʹ, henceforth *Three Forms*), a revelation-
discourse narrated in the first-person feminine by a figure who appears to be
identical to Barbelo-Providence of the 'Pronoia Hymn,' but here is named "First
Thought."[71] Here too, the cosmos is the result of an error committed by a heav-

---

67   *Ap. John* NHC II 30.32–31.19, text in Waldstein and Wisse, "Synopsis," 171, 173, tr. mine.
68   On this passage, see now Rasimus, "Three Descents."
69   "Réécriture," esp. 322–333, followed by Onuki, "Die dreifache Pronoia," 247.
70   For an overview, see Waldstein, "Providence Monologue," esp. 398–402.
71   The dependence of *Three Forms* on *Ap. John* LR was initially suggested by Yvonne Janssens
      and established by Paul-Hubert Poirier as all but certain, on thematic and linguistic
      grounds in several studies; see most recently Poirier "*Three Forms*," esp. 28–32, cautiously
      followed by Bak Halvgaard, *Linguistic Manifestations*, 43, 53–54 (highlighting that *Three
      Forms*'s linguistic terminology is absent from *Ap. John*). In the titular subscript to the work,
      the full title is given first in Coptic, then Greek: "*plogos ᵉntepiphania 3, prōtennoia trimor-
      phos*." On the term *prōtennoia* (viz., *protennoia*), see further below, chapter seven.

enly being, while the material world is created by "the Great Demon" (*pnoq
^{e}ndaimonion*) and his "archons," into which First Thought must descend to save
human beings.[72] *Three Forms* is replete with allusions to Johannine literature,
and so responds to some kind of Johannine theological context:[73] indeed, the
(re-)incarnating *Prōtennoia* is content with nothing less than taking upon and
exceeding the role of the Logos-Christ in John's Gospel:

> [The archons] thought [that I] was their "Christ," while [I was] actually
> [in everyone], actually, in fact, inside of those who [...] archons. It is I,
> their beloved; for [in] that place I clothed myself [as] the child of the
> Prime Begetter, and I [came to resemble him] up until the end of his
> judgment, that is, the ignorance belonging to Chaos. And amongst the
> angels I revealed myself, using their appearance, and amongst the pow-
> ers (I revealed myself), as if I were one of them. But amongst humanity,
> (I revealed myself) as if I were a human being, even though I am father to
> all. I have hidden amongst all those who are mine, until I reveal myself in
> my members, who are mine.[74]

As Elaine Pagels and Marvin Meyer have suggested, the universal presence of
Pronoia-Prōtennoia, the divine rational faculty, in human beings is something
of an affront to the Fourth Gospel's Jesus Christ, who unequivocally states that
"I am the Way and the Truth and the Life. Nobody comes to the Father, but
through me" (John 14:6).[75] In *Ap. John* and *Three Forms*, providence's interven-

---

72   The process of creation begins when the aeon Eleleth (not Sophia!) commits the sin
      of arrogance and thus produces the Great Demon, Yaldabaoth (*Three Forms* NHC XIII
      39.13–32). On this passage, see Turner, *Sethian Gnosticism*, 99, 169–170, 228–230; Bak Halv-
      gaard, *Linguistic Manifestations*, 76–80; Burns, "Magical, Coptic, Christian," 146–148. For
      the Great Demon's creation of the world and the creation of the human being inspired by
      the appearance of *Prōtennoia*, see *Three Forms* NHC XIII 40.4–29; for the parallel of this
      scene to Barbelo-First Man's manifestation to Yaldabaoth and the archons in *Ap. John*, see
      Poirier, "*Three Forms*," 33.
73   See e.g. Turner, *Sethian Gnosticism*, 151–155; idem, "Johannine Legacy," 123–139; Bak Halv-
      gaard, *Linguistic Manifestations*, 50–53.
74   See e.g. *Three Forms* NHC XIII 49.8–22, text in Poirier, *La pensée première*, 166, tr. mine.
      The relationship between Christ and *Pronoia-Prōtennoia* in *Ap. John* and *Three Forms* is
      complex; the two are superimposed over one another in the latter, while the issue is
      more ambiguous in the former (see King, *Secret Revelation*, 134–135, 136; Rasimus, *Paradise
      Reconsidered*, 153, 259; idem, "Three Descents," 246–247; Burns, "First Thoughts," 38).
75   Pagels, *Beyond Belief*, 64, followed by Meyer, "Thought," 221; cf. King, *Secret Revelation*, 237–
      238; Rasimus, *Paradise Reconsidered*, 262–270. See also Bak Halvgaard, *Linguistic Man-
      ifestations*, 66: "Protennoia reveals how as the real, hearable Sound she functions as a

DID GOD CARE FOR CREATION?   171

tion in the creation of humanity is capped by the indwelling of the divine—providence herself—in all human beings who exercise reason.

4   **"These Senseless Men Claim That They Ascend above the Creator ..."**

What all four of the witnesses reviewed in the previous section—Irenaeus's 'others,' *Orig. World*, *Ap. John*, and *Three Forms*—share is a myth wherein the world and the physical (and in the case of *Ap. John*, animate) human body were created outside of the sphere of divine influence, but where God intervenes in some way to rescue the human being, who is ultimately identified with the divine by virtue of some mental faculty. As Irenaeus states: "when that one breathed the spirit of life into the man—so they say—he was secretly emptied of his power, while humanity came to possess thenceforth intellect and thought, and—they say—these are the faculties which enjoy salvation." The myths from Nag Hammadi discussed above gloss this story with the language of providence, which was not active in the creation of the world nor of the human body—these activities are left to Yaldabaoth and his minions—and yet served as the inspiration and even template for the making of the human essence. Providential care for human beings and their creation is divorced from providential care for the creation of the cosmos and of material bodies, a position regarding *pronoia* which the investigations of the previous chapters did not encounter, except perhaps in the thought of Apelles.

The usage of the language of providence to underscore divine activity for the creation and care for human beings but not the world may first appear difficult to isolate in sources beyond the Nag Hammadi documents. Yet Irenaeus relates that according to the followers of the second-century teacher Valentinus,

> ... as for the offspring of the mother, Achamoth, which she brought forth in accordance with her contemplation of the angels surrounding the Savior, being of a similar, spiritual substance, subject to the mother—they say that the demiurge himself was ignorant of it, and that it was secretly deposited in him, without his knowing, so that it might be, through him, sown into the soul that comes from him, and into this material body, and so that, having been carried by them as in a womb and grown, it might

promoter of Gnosis. Thus, through herself and her message, hearers may gain access to the place from which she comes: the ineffable and the unknowable. Hence, she also claims to be Perception and Knowledge."

come to be for the reception of the perfect ⟨Word⟩. And so, as they say, the spiritual Human Being, thanks to ineffable ⟨power and⟩ providence (*arrētōi ⟨dunamei kai⟩ pronoiai*), escaped the attention of the demiurge, having been sown into his breath by Wisdom. For just as the demiurge failed to recognize his mother, so it was with her seed, which—they say—constitutes the church, being a reflection of the celestial Church.[76]

Just as in *Orig. World* and *Ap. John*, this demiurge was produced has created the cosmos outside of the scope of providence, but has been manipulated by divine agency so that humanity can be said to possess a divine (i.e., rational) element thanks to God's care.[77] In fact, as Pheme Perkins and Pierre Létourneau have recognized, a corollary of these myths is the elevation of humanity above the creator-god.[78] As much is stated explicitly in *Ap. John*: once the animate body of Adam receives the divine *pneuma*, "the body moved, became powerful, and radiated light. At that moment, the rest of the powers became jealous; for it had come into being through all of them, and they had given their power to the human being—and his intelligence was stronger than those who had made him, and than the First Archon."[79]

The novelty and transgressive character of such a position was recognized and disparaged in antiquity. Irenaeus writes, "these senseless men claim that they ascend above the Creator. They proclaim themselves superior to the God who made and adorned the heavens, the earth, the seas, and all things in them."[80] The third-century philosopher Plotinus exclaims in *Against the Gnostics* that his opponents claim that human souls are immortal and divine, unlike the souls of stars—i.e., that the human elect is superior to the world.[81] Other Nag Hammadi treatises feature Jesus explaining to the Apostles how his revelation will permit them to overcome the servants of an evil creator-god. The *Letter of Peter to Philip* (NHC VIII,2; Codex Tchacos, 1) tells yet another variant of the myth discussed in the previous section: the "Arrogant One" is worshipped by his "powers of the world" who do not know the true God, "and he ordained the powers under his authority to form dead bodies."[82] It is the humans in these bodies whom Jesus was sent to redeem, he tells his disciples:

---

76   Ir. *Haer.* 1.5.6, text Rousseau and Doutreleau in SC 264:88–89, tr. mine.

77   On this point see also Thomassen, "Saved by Nature?" 131.

78   Perkins, *Gnostic Dialogue*, 173; Létourneau, "Creation," 432.

79   *Ap. John* NHC II 19.32–20.5 = BG 51.20–52.11; similarly, NHC II 20.30–33 = BG 54.7–11.

80   *Haer.* 2.30.1, tr. Unger, 95.

81   Plot. *Enn.* 2.9 [33] 5.8–12; see further ibid., 8.32–38, 16.10–15.

82   *Ep. Pet. Phil.* NHC VIII [135].17–1[36].3, 1[36].11–13, respectively, text in Wisse, "*Letter*," 240, tr. mine.

DID GOD CARE FOR CREATION? 173

"When you divest yourselves of what is corrupt, then shall you become luminaries in the midst of mortals. [And] this: it is you who shall struggle with the powers, for [they] have no reprieve [like] you, since they do not wish for you to be saved." Then, the apostles worshipped once more, saying: "Lord, teach us: in what way shall we combat the archons? For [the] archons are above us."[83] Then [a] voice called unto them [from] that one (i.e., Christ) who had appeared, saying: "Now, you shall combat them in this way. You see, the archons fight with the inner man; [but] you shall combat them in this way.[84] Come together and teach, in the world, salvation with a promise. And you, guard yourselves with the power of my Father, and show your prayer, and He—the Father—shall help you, just as He has helped you when he sent me."[85]

As in *Orig. World* and *Ap. John*, the message is that the Messiah's followers are exempt from their physical bodies' subjugation to astral forces: the archons "above" who serve the "Arrogant One." As Nicola Denzey (Lewis) has shown, such rhetoric of liberation from cosmic enslavement to fate was common in early Christianity.[86] Yet the emphasis on the superiority of the human being not only to demonic forces, but even to the creators of the world and human bodies, is distinctive and without parallel in Christian philosophers like Clement or Origen, to say nothing of their Platonist and Stoic contemporaries. Similarly, in the polemical homily entitled the *Second Treatise of the Great Seth* (NHC VII,2), Jesus declares,

But, thanks to my Father, I am the one whom the world did not know. And for this reason, it rose up against me and my brethren. But we are innocent as regards it; we did not sin. For the Archon was a joke, since he said, "I am God, and there is none greater than me," "I alone am the Father, the Lord, and there is none other besides me," "I am a jealous God, bringing the sins of the fathers upon the(ir) children for three and four generations"—as though he had become stronger than me and my brethren! But we, we are innocent regarding him, for we did not sin.[87]

---

83   Similarly *Dial. Sav.* NHC III [138].11–20; text in Emmel, "Text," 76, tr. mine: "Judas said, 'Look! The archons are above us; therefore, it is they who shall rule over us!' The Lord replied, 'it is *you* who shall rule over *them*. Rather, once you divest yourselves of jealousy, then shall you clothe yourselves in light and enter the bridal chamber.' "

84   Perhaps a dittography.

85   *Ep. Pet. Phil.* NHC VIII [137].6–30, text in Wisse, *"Letter,"* 242, 244, tr. mine.

86   Denzey (Lewis), *Cosmology and Fate,* 8.

87   *Disc. Seth* NHC VII 64.12–29, text in Riley, *"Second Treatise,"* 184, 186, tr. mine.

174   CHAPTER 4

Theologians, philosophers, and historians of religion have all recognized the relationship between this distinctive view regarding humanity, God, and the world, and contemporary religious and philosophical thought about providence, but struggle to formulate it precisely. Leo Scheffczyk writes that Gnosticism proposes a "divorce between the activity of creation and salvation" that is ultimately without basis canonical Christian Scripture.[88] Jaap Mansfeld notes that it was completely novel in the ancient philosophical context to conclude that the demiurge is evil on the premise that the world is evil.[89] Ioan Couliano describes Gnosticism as a rejection of the principle that the human and cosmic are of fundamentally similar character: for the Gnostics, while humans are good, the world is bad.[90] All of these observations ring true, but do not communicate the whole picture, and the reader who has fought through these long excerpts from Coptic myths given in this chapter will understand why: Gnostic literature is opaque, esoteric stuff. It is for this reason that the glossing of these myths with ancient philosophical jargon—the jargon of providential care (*pronoia*)—is important: the ancient authors' usage of terminology recognizable to us from the philosophical context serves as a trustworthy guide as to the intended meaning of the narratives in question.

Chapters one and two highlighted the anthropocentrism of Stoic and early Christian conceptions of providence, since so many Stoic and biblically-informed sources accept the notions of God's direct involvement in the creation of human beings and interventionist care for them. The myths under review here may then be taken as the apex of early Christian anthropocentrism: according to *Orig. World* and *Ap. John*, providence was at work in the creation of the first human being and its rational, divine character, elevating the primal human above the demiurge himself. This sort of 'extreme Stoicism' is accompanied by a close, if very critical, engagement with Platonism: the arrogant, foolish Yaldabaoth and his bumbling archons parody the "young gods" of the *Timaeus* or Philo's creative "powers" even as it explores the same philosophical territory, namely the question of who is responsible for creating the irrational soul. In the *Timaeus*, Plato delegates the creation and administration of human beings to fallible intermediaries. Yet such intermediaries are only partially responsible for the creation of humanity for Irenaeus's "others" and the myths related to it. In fact, the appearance of two kinds of providence in *Ap. John* and *Orig. World*—that exerted by God in his genuine interventions on

---

88   "... Eine Abtrennung der Schöpfungs- von der Erlösungswirklichkeit" (Scheffczyk, *Schöpfung und Vorsehung*, 19).

89   Mansfeld, "Bad World," 313.

90   Couliano, *Tree of Gnosis*, 108–111.

behalf of humanity, and that exerted by the demonic rulers in their control of the "psychic" body, in addition to evil Fate (*heimarmenē*), which governs the body of matter (*hulē*)—may recall the Middle Platonic tripartitions of providential administration which came into vogue in the second century CE.[91] At this point, Irenaeus's "others," *Orig. World, Ap. John*, and *Three Forms* abandon Stoicism and Platonism alike, by divorcing the creation of the world and of human bodies (on both the 'animate' and 'material' levels) from providence. In fact, the primal human on whose behalf providence intervenes in these anthropogonies is not identified with its *psychē* or material self at all, but a being entirely comprised of *pneuma*. Such a view is very much at odds with Stoicism, where the universal spirit is not identified with matter, but always embodied; positive language about 'bodies' is conspicuously absent in the aeons of *Ap. John* and related texts (see below).

Early Christian philosophers commonly accounted for the existence of evil by recourse to a variety of arguments—the work of Satan and demons, personal freedom, the concomitance argument, and more, as discussed in chapter three—and the myths under discussion here take up some of these views as well, particularly in their descriptions of the demiurge and his archons as external causes of worldly evil and human irrationality. Their optimism about the ability of God to intervene on humanity's behalf is in keeping with the 'attenuated dualism' of Jewish and Christian apocalyptic literature.[92] Yet *Ap. John, Orig. World*, and their like go further in distinguishing between providential care for humans (maximal) from that for the worldly creation humans experience, including their physical bodies (minimal).[93] These Nag Hammadi anthropogonies then appear to employ philosophical terminology to highlight an idea already implicit in our earliest evidence about Gnostic myths, such as the

---

91   On the 'secondary providence' of the archons, see above. For Fate as the enslaver of human bodies in *Ap. John*, see NHC II 28.11–32 = BG 72.2–12; generally, see Pleše, "Fate, Providence, and Astrology," 253, n. 34. On Middle Platonic tripartitions of providence, see above, chapter one. The classic discussion of the relationship between these Nag Hammadi texts' gradations of providence and Middle Platonic models remains Williams, "Higher Providence"; see also Perkins, "*On the Origin*"; Denzey (Lewis), *Cosmology and Fate*, 35 (recalling Athenagoras's remarks on divine administration—see above, chapter three), and Pleše, "Evil," 125–126 n. 30.

92   Rightly Williams, "'Wisdom, Our Innocent Sister,'" 280 (re: *Three Forms*); on 'attenuated dualism,' see above, chapter three.

93   As much appears to be sensed by Williams in his remark that in *Ap. John*, Wisdom's repentance and ensuing work as an agent of providence are "with her focus not on the material cosmos in general but rather on, essentially, perfecting the creation of humanity in Adam, Eve, and Seth and his progeny" ("'Wisdom, Our Innocent Sister,'" 289).

176   CHAPTER 4

teaching of Menander in the early second century:[94] if God cares for and intervenes on behalf of human beings but the present world and our present bodies do not appear to benefit from any such care, then the latter must be the creation of powers who are not providential at all.[95] These powers are, in fact, inferior to the beings that God does care for—humanity, which is divine, unlike the world and its maker.

5   "The Will of the Father" and the 'Tripartite Tractate'

Two objections may be levied here, related but distinct. First, M.A. Williams has recently argued that many of the myths discussed presently emphasize that Wisdom was ultimately 'innocent,' and therefore that the birth of Yaldabaoth and his subsequent creation is not, in the "big picture," to be regarded as an "accident or mistake." There is some truth to this: at different points in *Ap. John*, *Three Forms*, and *Disc. Seth*, Wisdom is redeemed and/or regarded as a benevolent force.[96] However, these statements of Wisdom's innocence and goodwill do not mean that Wisdom's creation of Yaldabaoth without the Father's consent was not an error.[97] Nor does the absence in these treatises of an Epicurean-esque disparagement of nature indicate that their view of the natural cosmos is a sunny one.[98] The focus of these works on celestial, primordial matters precludes much discussion of present reality,[99] except as regards its physical foundations, which are described in negative terms: *Ap. John* disparages 'matter' and the archons who employ it,[100] and while little is said there

---

94   *Haer.* 1.23.5–24.1, on which see recently Drecoll, "Martin Hengel," 152–161.

95   As Rudolph recognized, "the world is not (the Gnostic God's) work, but that of a subordinate being. But nevertheless he (God) exercises influence in varying ways for the well-being of men ... it is "providence" (*pronoia*) which here comes to expression" (*Gnosis*, 62).

96   Williams, "'Wisdom, Our Innocent Sister,'" 274 *passim* re: Ir. *Haer.* 1.29.4; *Ap. John* NHC II 23.20–24 (LR); BG 51.1–6 = NHC III 23.19–22 (SR); *Three Forms* NHC XIII 39.13–34, 40.11–19, 47.28–34; *Disc. Seth* NHC VII 50.22–51.3.

97   *Pace* Williams, "'Wisdom, Our Innocent Sister,'" 256.

98   *Pace* Williams, "'Wisdom, Our Innocent Sister,'" 273.

99   Cf. Layton's observation that the topics of interest in Gnostic myths offer virtually no context for use of the social self-designation 'Gnostic' ("Prolegomena," 344; similarly Brakke, *Gnostics*, 47–48).

100   The material substance (*hulē*) into which the archons cast Adam (after he has received *pneuma*) is "the shadow of death ... the ignorance of darkness and desire" (NHC II 21.3–8 = BG 55.2–8). According to the *Book of Zoroaster* (LR only), matter is the "mother of demons" (NHC II 18.3–6; also ibid., 18.6–13).

DID GOD CARE FOR CREATION? 177

of the monstrous demiurge's making of the world, there is no doubt that he is its author.[101] Similarly, *Orig. World* begins with a "proof" (*apodeixis*) that matter (*hulē*) originated in "Chaos," a "shadow" (*haibes*) outside of the celestial realm of the aeons.[102] It "came into being from shadow" as a result of the appearance of "envy," which was like an "abortion, without any *pneuma* in it"— perhaps an anti-Stoic polemic.[103] Finally, the intervention of the divine in the creation of human beings does not amount to the involvement of the divine in the creation of everything, including the material cosmos and the demiurge himself—creative acts where the language of providence is conspicuously lacking in *Ap. John* and *Orig. World*.

The second objection is that many of the myths discussed in this chapter also emphasize that everything transpired according to the divine will or plan.[104] For instance, a work closely related to *Orig. World*, the *Nature of the Rulers* (Copt. tthupostasis *ᵉnᵉnarchōn*, NHC II,4) also relates the intervention of the divine in the creation of humanity: divine "Immortality" (*tmᵉntattako*) appeared in the terrestrial waters and inspired the creation of Adam, "so that, by the will of the father (*hᵉm pouōš ᵉmpeiōt*), it should join the universe with the light."[105] As noted above, *Orig. World* says that "all this came to pass by the providence of Pistis."[106] The "First Thought" (*prōtennoia*) of *Three Forms* claims to be everywhere, even "amongst the archons and the powers, and amongst all the angels, and in every movement that exists, in all matter (*hulē*)!"[107] The *Paraphrase of Shem* (NHC VII,1) intones repeatedly that cosmological movements all transpire "by the will of the Majesty," despite describing the cosmos itself (*phu-*

---

101   Once Yaldabaoth has finished creating the heavenly firmaments and the archontic angels who attend him, he glances around at his work: in SR, it is "the creation (*sōnt*) which is beneath him"; in LR, "the creation (*ktisis*) which surrounds him" (BG 44.10 = NHC II 13.5–6, text in Waldstein and Wisse, "Synopsis," 78–79, tr. mine).

102   *Orig. World* NHC II 97.24–99.1.

103   *Orig. World* NHC II 99.6–13; further ibid., 99.20–100.10. For the anti-Stoic context, see Perkins, "*On the Origin*," 37–38; Painchaud, "Commentaire," 245–246.

104   In addition to the following passages, see Jenott, "Emissaries of Truth", re: the salvation-historical narratives of *Ap. John*, *Apoc. Adam*, and *Gos. Eg.*; Lundhaug and Jenott, *Monastic Origins*, 88.

105   *Nat. Rul.* NHC II 87.22–23, text Layton, "*Hypostasis of the Archons*," 236, tr. mine (similarly, 88.10–11, 88.34–39.1, 96.11–12).

106   *Orig. World* NHC II 113.5–9. Perkins and Denzey (Lewis) have suggested that the text here could rearticulate, using the philosophical term "providence," the text from *Nat. Rul.* on which (they surmise) *Orig. World* is dependent ("Gnostic Physics," 41, and *Cosmology and Fate*, 40, respectively).

107   *Three Forms* NHC XIII 47.19–22; see further Lundhaug and Jenott, *Monastic Origins*, 88; Williams, "'Wisdom, Our Innocent Sister'," 279–280.

178 CHAPTER 4

sis, "nature") as ruled (*dioikein*) by "winds and demons."[108] A Nag Hammadi treatise which regards matter (but not the demiurge) in very negative terms, the *Authoritative Teaching* (NHC VI,3), emphasizes that "nothing has transpired without his (i.e., the Father's) will."[109]

Such asides that everything transpires according to God's will—even as the text relates a story of how God was not the creator—may perhaps indicate that the authors of these texts recognized that the myths in question were in a serious tension with the views of contemporary Christian and Greco-Roman thinkers, and that they sought to resolve this tension. Thus, these works acknowledge this fundamental difference of perspective with their contemporaries insofar as they attempt to hedge and mollify it. Another useful illustration of this dynamic presents itself as some of our evidence regarding the school of Valentinus, which was much more hesitant to demonize the demiurge. The disciple Ptolemy, for instance, deigns to identify the demiurge with "the devil," or as a being who exercises no providential care.[110] Ptolemy acknowledges the world to be imperfect, but also emphasizes:

> The apostle says that the creation of the world is ⟨the Savior's⟩, and that everything came into being through him, and that without him nothing came into being—thus pulling out the rug from under the baseless wisdom of the liars—not of some destructive God, but of a righteous God who hates iniquity. Rather, ⟨this⟩ is the view of idiots who do not ascribe providence to the creator (*tēs pronoias tou dēmiourgou mē atian lambanomenōn*), and who have been deprived not only the eyes of the soul, but of the body as well.[111]

Irenaeus reports that the Valentinians claimed that the demiurge, having created the world in ignorance, came to repent and "will accomplish the adminis-

---

108   "Will of the Majesty": *Paraph. Shem* NHC VII 2.29, 4.15, 6.30–31, 8.15–16, 9.4, 10.16, 11.7, 12.15–16, 13.33–34, 18.2, 21.21, 25.4–6, 29.20–21. "Winds and demons": ibid., 44.13–21. For the text, see Wisse, "*Paraphrase of Shem*"; tr. mine.

109   *Auth. Disc.* NHC VI [26].6–7, text in MacRae, "*Authoritative Teaching*," 268, tr. mine.

110   Epiph. *Pan.* 33.3.1–2; see further Markschies, "New Research," 239–246. As O'Brien notes, Ptolemy's language about whether the Devil is the "father and maker of the universe" recalls Plat. *Tim.* 28e (*Demiurge*, 236).

111   Epiph. *Pan.* 33.3.6. Scholars have often believed Ptolemy to be targeting Marcion in this passage (most recently Moll, *Arch-Heretic*, 48–49; see the criticism of Roth, "Evil," 347), although others have doubted this (Layton, *Gnostic Scriptures*, 307; Löhr, "Die Auslegung," 80 n. 11; cit. Roth, op. cit. 346). The inference is reasonable but hardly secure (Markschies, "Valentianische Gnosis," 166–167).

DID GOD CARE FOR CREATION? 179

tration of the world (*tēn kata ton kosmon oikonomian*) until the given time."[112] Some Nag Hammadi myths also feature repenting demiurges, perhaps a response to discomfort with a disparaged creator-god.[113]

The only complete Valentinian theological treatise to survive from antiquity, the *Tripartite Tractate* (NHC I,5), offers perhaps the most sophisticated rehearsal of the view that the present cosmos resulted of some kind of precosmic catastrophe, but that this was all nonetheless God's providential plan.[114] Significant parallels of the text with the thought of Origen and Plotinus indicates that the work is a translation of a Greek text composed in the first half of the third century CE.[115] *Tri. Trac.* famously identifies the catalyst for the break within the aeonic realm as a *logos*—a 'Word' informed by *sophia* but not identified with her. The text emphasizes that this being acted on its own free will

---

112 Iren. *Haer.* 1.7.4, text Rousseau and Doutreleau in SC 264:109–110, tr. mine; see also Tertullian, *Against the Valentinians*, 28. On the demiurge in Irenaeus's *grande notice*, see Dunderberg, *Beyond Gnosticism*, 121–123. The "Archon" also comes to realize his lesser nature in a fragment of Basilides preserved by Clem. Al. *Strom.* 2.36.1 = frg. 4 Löhr (*Basilides*). This evidence is glossed in the anonymous *Refutatio* with the detail that the "Great Archon" administers providence up to but not beyond the sublunary realm, like Aristotle's God, and upon learning this fact becomes first afraid and then wise (*Ref.* 7.24.3; Bergjan, *Der fürsorgende Gott*, 140 n. 85; Bos, "Basilides," 53). Both *testimonia* describe the episode with reference to Prov 1:7; see further Pearson, "Basilides," 16–17. Finally, the demiurge of Apelles also 'repents' for creation (Ter. *Carn. Chr.* 8.3; Ter. [*Haer.*] 6.4; cf. Willing, "Neue Frage," 225).

113 *Nat. Rul.* NHC II 95.13–96.2; *Orig. World* NHC II 103.32–106.18.

114 Cf. Williams, "'Wisdom, Our Innocent Sister'," 275, n. 65. It is typical of Valentinian sources to describe aeonic production as beginning with a singular act of the Father's will—see recently G. Smith, "Irenaeus," esp. 96–109. The process of celestial generation eventually leading to the demiurge, all as part of God's plan for creation (*pronoia, oikonomia*), is described in another Nag Hammadi Valentinian tractate, *A Valentinian Exposition* NHC XI [36].10–[37].36 (noted by Onuki, "Dreifache Pronoia," 257), but the MS is too poorly preserved to be of much use here. Irenaeus ascribes such a view to his Valentinian foes in *Haer.* 2.15.3: "if they will claim that it was according to the Father's providence (*providentiam Patris*) that the Fullness was so emitted for the sake of creation, in order that this be arranged well (*uti bene rhythmizata ipsa esset*) ..." (text Doutreleau and Rousseau in SC 294:150, tr. Unger, rev. J.J. Dillon, 53, slightly modified).

115 On dating *Tri. Trac.*, see Attridge and Pagels, "*Tripartite Tractate*: Introduction," 178; Thomassen, "Introduction," 11–13, 18. Most scholars date the work to the third century CE; the main debate is over whether the text was known to Origen (Dubois, "*Traité Tripartite*"), or in fact responds to Origen (Thomassen, "Introduction," 18–20). For the argument made in the present chapter, it suffices to adopt the parsimonious view of Attridge and Pagels, op. cit., favoring the first half of the third century, without excluding the possibility of a date after the *floruit* of Origen and even Plotinus. However, the discussion below in chapter seven will argue that the closely shared themes of two of Plotinus's treatises (*Enn.* 6.7–8 [38–39] and 3.2–3 [47–48]) with *Tri. Trac.* may indicate his knowledge of a Greek version of the latter treatise, engaged multiple times in his career.

180   CHAPTER 4

(*piouōše ^ennautexousios*),[116] but that it was also by the will of the first principle
("Father") that this Word desire to create, and so accidently beget trouble:

> Therefore, the Father and the wholes pulled themselves back from it, so
> that the limit which the Father had set could be established, for it does
> not result from accessing the inaccessible, but by the will of the Father;
> and moreover, in order that these things that happened, happen for the
> future dispensation (*auoikonomia esnašōpe*). If it (i.e., the future dispen-
> sation) were to come about, it would not happen [by] the appearance of
> the Fullness (alone).[117]

That is, God's salvific plan requires a production that is imperfect, unlike that
of the heavenly realm, the "Fullness" (*plērōma*). "For this reason," the text continues,

> It is not right to blame the movement—namely, the Word—[118] but it is
> fitting for us to say concerning [the] movement of the Word that it was a
> cause [of] a dispensation ordained to be. For, on the one hand, the Word
> begat itself, perfect, single, alone, for (the) glory of the Father, who willed
> it and was pleased with it; on the other hand, these things which it wished
> to receive [by] establishing (them) did it beget in shadows [and] reflec-
> tions and semblances, for it was not able to bear the sight of [the] light,
> but it looked into [the] abyss, and doubted.[119] For this reason, it is divi-
> sion [which] it suffered … For its act of self-elevation, and its expectation

---

116   *Tri. Trac.* NHC I 75.22–76.4:
        [Although] it is a Word of the unity, [and although] it is one, it does not come from
        the harmony of the wholes, nor from He who brought them forth—He who brought
        forth the universe, the Father. For the aeon came forth from those to whom had been
        given the wisdom that pre-existed each one of them, as His thought … For this rea-
        son did it receive a wise nature, so that it may enquire after the secret form, since it is
        a fruit of wisdom (*karpos ^ensophia*). This free will (*piouōše ^ennautexousios*) which was
        begotten with the wholes was a cause for this one, so to speak, so that it would do what-
        ever it wanted without anything holding it back. Therefore, the decision of the Word
        (*tproairesis … ^emplogos*)—which is this one—was something good (text Thomassen in
        Thomassen and Painchaud, "Texte," 111, 113, tr. mine, with reference to that of P. Nagel,
        Tractatus, 39).

117   *Tri. Trac.* NHC I 76.30–77.5, text Thomassen in Thomassen and Painchaud, "Texte," 113, 115,
        tr. mine, with reference to that of P. Nagel, *Tractatus*, 40.

118   So Thomassen. Cf. P. Nagel's suggested emendation, "movement of the Logos," but I do not
        see this as necessary to make sense of the passage, despite *Tri. Trac.* NHC I 77.9.

119   Cf. Plot. *Enn.* 2.9 [33] 10–12; *Zost.* NHC VIII 8–10.

DID GOD CARE FOR CREATION? 181

to comprehend the incomprehensible became firm in it; it remained in it. Yet the weaknesses which followed it after it had gone beyond itself, it is from doubt that they came into being—i.e., ⟨from its own inability to comprehend⟩ the glories of the Father, whose grandeur is infinite![120]

Unable to beget with reference to the Father's light (for the Father is unknowable), the Word begets instead with reference to "shadows [and] reflections and semblances" (*henhaibes m*[*ⁿ*] *heneidōlon mⁿ hⁿtantⁿ*), terms that indicate faulty, inferior representations of reality, especially in Platonic contexts.[121] Generation of an aeonic realm of negative mental states proceeds apace and begins to run amok (see further below, chapter seven), until the intervention of the Father's agent, the Son, among whose many titles includes "the illumination of the ones He illuminates, the will of the ones He wills, the providential care for the ones for whom He providentially cares (*tpronoia ⁿnetⁿfⁿr pronoia ⁿmmau*), the intelligence of the ones who he has made intelligent, the power of the ones to whom he gives power ..."[122] The Word, redeemed, sets about ordering the three different orders of pre-existent beings, subsuming to the "spiritual" (*pneumatikon*) order the "animate" (*psychikon*) and the "material" (*hylikon*).[123] To the latter—who are called "archons," "angels," and "archangels"—are assigned fiefdoms over various terrestrial activities, ranging from administering "punishment" and "judgment" (*kolasis, hap*) to healing, teaching, and guarding.[124] Finally, "he appointed over all the archons an(other) archon, with no one to command him. He is Lord of them all"—a being with many names, such as "'father,' and 'god,' and 'craftsman' (*refⁿr hōb*) and 'king' and 'judge' and 'place' and 'dwelling' and 'law'." While these epithets recall the second god of Marcion, this great archon's activities are those of Yald-

---

120   *Tri. Trac.* NHC I 77.6–35, text Thomassen in Thomassen and Painchaud, "Texte," 115, 117, tr. mine, with reference to P. Nagel, *Tractatus*, 40. The importance of this passage is rightly highlighted by Pleše, "Evil," 113; similarly Armstrong, "Dualism," 45; Dunderberg, *Beyond Gnosticism*, 166; Kocar, "'Humanity'," 202.

121   On the terminology of 'image' (*eikōn*) versus 'reflection' (*eidōlon*, etc.) from Plato through Plotinus and some 'Platonizing' Nag Hammadi treatises, see Burns, *Apocalypse*, 64–70.

122   *Tri. Trac.* NHC I [66].19–24, text Thomassen in Thomassen and Painchaud, "Texte," 89, tr. mine, with reference to that of P. Nagel, *Tractatus*, 33. See further NHC I 6[1].1–[62].38, a lengthy description of the Father's providential generation of the Son; on the relationship between Son, Word, and demiurge in this text, see Perkins, "Logos Christologies," 388. Notably, the *Gospel of Truth*, many of whose themes are echoed in *Tri. Trac.*, also emphasizes "nothing happens apart from the Will of the Father" (NHC I 37.22–24, text in Attridge and MacRae, "The *Gospel of Truth*," 110, tr. mine), but does not use the language of *pronoia*.

123   *Tri. Trac.* NHC I 95.17–98.11.

124   *Tri. Trac.* NHC I 99.19–100.18.

182   CHAPTER 4

abaoth: he is glorified by his underlings and mistakenly exalts himself. Yet he is entirely under God's control, for the Word uses him as a "hand."[125] The Word moves the demiurge to create a human being, who is led astray by a Serpent:

> This is the expulsion that was [made] for him, when he was cast out from the delights of the things that belong to semblance and those which belong to [likeness]. Truly was it a work of providence (*pronoia*), so that it would be found out (that) it is a short period of time until humanity will receive the enjoyment of the eternal, good things in which lies the place of rest, which has been fixed; for the Spirit had thought it out in advance (*eaf^{e}r šar^{e}p {p}mmoukmoukf*) ...[126]

The general scheme of *Tri. Trac.*—that the production of a material universe requires that God permit some kind of error or fault in creation—is close to that of third-century Platonism, in particular Plotinus (see further below, chapter seven), but differs in its fixation on the moribund character of the cosmos and the negative character of the superhuman beings who administrate it.[127]

Tri. Trac. and other works discussed in this section then agreed with Marcion in postulating the existence of a God above and beyond the demiurge, but they took great care to stress that God permitted the world to be created out of evil; in *Tri. Trac.*'s case, precisely so that human beings be created out of good—a view that strongly echoes not only Plato but, as we have seen in this chapter, the thought of Irenaeus himself! Ptolemy, the author of *Tri. Trac.*, and others must have recognized that the insistence of some myths, like *Ap. John*, that the demiurge and its cosmos came into being without God's consent opened one up to the charge of denying providence.[128] Not only did such insistence invite

---

125 On the demiurge in *Tri. Trac.*, see esp. NHC I 100.18–103.12. For the titles of the demiurge, see 100.28–30. For the demiurge as the 'hand' of the Word, see 100.31–32 (discussed below, chapter five), 103.4; cf. Irenaeus's own descriptions of the Son as the Father's hand (above, in this chapter).

126 NHC I 107.19–28, text Thomassen in Thomassen and Painchaud, "Texte," 187, tr. mine, with reference to that of P. Nagel, *Tractatus*, 65.

127 Armstrong, "Dualism," 45; Pleše, "Evil," 120; Kocar, "'Humanity'," 202–203; cf. Lundhaug and Jenott, who read this view of the creator as "positive" (*Monastic Origins*, 88); cf. also Magris, recalling the "Catholic" *felix culpa* (*L'idea di destino*, 2:799).

128 *Ap. John* NHC II 9.28–35 and par., quoted above. Cf. Pleše, seeing the causal break a result of God's transcendence and thus unknowability, rather than a lower principle's impulse to create without God's assent ("Evil and its Sources," 108–112). This is true for *Tri. Trac.*, but is not so clear in the case of *Ap. John*.

DID GOD CARE FOR CREATION?

tarring with the brush of Epicureanism or of Aristotelianism, but it also opened one up to the charge of inconsistency, should one then affirm providential care for the elect. Such inconsistency was noted by Plotinus, in his treatise *Against the Gnostics*: "Moreover, how is it pious for providence to fail to extend to anything here—indeed, to anything at all? And how are they at all consistent in holding this view? For they say that God does care for them, and them alone (*legousi gar autōn pronoein au monōn*)."[129]

Finally, the present reading of the evidence permits us to say why the redactor(s) of *Ap. John* added language about providence to the long recension of the text. For some of their interlocutors, this Gnostic anthropocentrism must have implied denial of providential care for the "present evil age" (Gal 1:4)—and these redactors wished to show otherwise, insofar as *pronoia* herself has descended into Hades three times, on the behalf of humanity.[130] Some writers of Gnostic literature therefore chose to emphasize the universal power and extension of *pronoia* to the world and human beings, even though such a perspective is at odds with the myth the same literature relates.[131] The problem of providence thus furnishes a rare glimpse into how the authors of Gnostic texts grappled with the implications of Gnostic myth for negotiating their greater identity and worldview amongst Christian and Greek philosophers. There was a clear tension between 'Gnostic' and 'proto-orthodox' sources regarding care for humanity versus care for the world and its creation, a tension most evident in works like *Nat. Rul.*, *Orig. World*, or *Paraph. Shem*, whose myths express Gnostic anthropocentrism but add that nothing happens except by divine will. If there is no such tension in these myths, then asides about the 'will of the Father' are mere banalities. Their significance hinges upon the degree to which it was a problem, in a second or third-century philosophical context, to assert that the present creation was the product of a God who did or could not exercise providence.

---

129   Plot. *Enn.* 2.9 [33] 16.15–17, text and tr. Armstrong in LCL 441:286–287, modified.

130   *Ap. John* NHC II 30.11–31.28.

131   As the examples given in this and the previous two sections hopefully illustrate, this emphasis was not limited to Valentinian writers; therefore, we need not postulate that the language of providence in *Orig. World* was the work of a Valentinian redactor (*pace* Painchaud, "Commentaire," 389).

6 Conclusions: The Gnostics on Providence, Creation, and 'Gnosticism'

These tensions regarding myths where God cares for human beings, but not the creation of the world, demand some sort of name or second-order term of description.[132] It is hard to imagine the authors discussed in the previous three sections agreeing with an early Christian sapiential work, the *Sentences of Sextus*, that "just as the ruler (*to archon*) welcomes the ruled, God welcomes the wise man. Just as the ruler is inseparable from the ruled, so God cares for and attends to (*pronoei kai kēdetai*) the wise."[133] Here, *to archon* is provident. Even the author of *Nature of the Rulers*, insisting that everything transpires "by the will of the father," had a very different idea of what an archon's oversight meant: the problem, not the solution. Nor does one imagine that this author had a similar view of creation and God's care for it as Epictetus, who remarked that God "has no need of a fussy spectator" who has been granted to witness the festival that is the present life.[134] The term 'Gnosticism,' which has traditionally been used to denote the thought of so many of the works discussed in this chapter, may perhaps be rehabilitated to describe the view that responsibility for the creation of the world falls not to God but an inferior being, to whom and to whose creation human beings are superior, because humanity is divine. It has been argued above that such a view was promulgated, defended, and hedged—in diverse permutations, often using the language of providence—in the various extant works associated with ancient individuals known to Irenaeus and Porphyry as "Gnostics," such as *Ap. John* and *Orig. World*.[135]

---

132   Indeed, scholars who study early Christian discourse about superhuman beings and ritual life in the ancient Mediterranean world do this already, when we heuristically employ terms like 'early Christianity,' or ancient 'religion.' On the problem of defining religion in an ancient Mediterranean context, see recently Nongbri, *Before Religion*, 153.

133   *Sentences of Sextus*, 422–423, text in Chadwick, *Sentences*, 60, tr. mine.

134   Epict. *Diatr.* 4.1.108, text and tr. Oldfather in LCL 218:280–281; see also Long, *Epictetus*, 168–172.

135   For a similar typology of 'Gnosticism,' see Marjanen, "Gnosticism," 210–211. Brakke criticizes this typology for setting the origin of the cosmos and the divine quality of the soul at the center of the teaching of ancient Gnostics, who probably identified themselves rather as proponents of the message of salvation offered by Jesus Christ (*Gnostics*, 26–27). One might reply that the ancient Gnostics described their message of salvation precisely in terms of this typology. Other typologies in which the tension highlighted here figures strongly include those of Pleše, "Gnostic Literature," 177–182, 189–196; Markschies, *Gnosis*, 15–17.

DID GOD CARE FOR CREATION?

Why 'Gnosticism'? Let us briefly examine two alternatives currently in use that ring true in some way, but also leave something to be desired, since they lead us far afield from the 'Gnostics' known to Irenaeus and Porphyry and the extant works which resemble their thought. One is Williams's term 'biblical demiurgical(ism),' generally favored in North American scholarship.[136] Its advantage is highlighting the significance of the works in question as having to do with their portrayal of the biblical demiurge, without the baggage of outdated 'clichés' associated with 'Gnosticism.'[137] The present analysis highlights two issues with the term.[138] For instance, one of these clichés—that Gnosticism is tantamount to a sort of 'anticosmic dualism'—may hold more water than Williams allows.[139] To be sure, Williams is correct that Gnostic and 'proto-orthodox' sources sought "different strategies for explaining evil," rather than describing two qualitatively different "experiences" of evil; nor is it always clear that Gnostic sources "viewed their world with more antagonism than, for example, contemporaries who believed that the world had been created by one good God but had subsequently come under the strong influence or control or evil angels."[140] Both Gnostic and non-Gnostic sources are, as far as their outlook on salvation-history goes, party to the 'mitigated dualism' that permeated early Christianity: 'pessimism' is hardly the right designation these works, because they describe the mechanism for salvation of humanity, not the absence of such.[141] Yet these same Gnostic sources remain ambivalent regarding the goodness and salvation of the cosmos and, often, of the material bodies of human beings—a distinction these sources attempt to illustrate by employing the language of providence.[142] The 'powers' of Philo are not the archons of *Orig. World*,

---

136   On 'biblical demiurgical' myths, see Williams, *Rethinking "Gnosticism"*, 265.

137   Williams, *Rethinking "Gnosticism"*, 265; cf. also Pleše, "Evil and its Sources," 101, 107–108.

138   Setting aside its unwieldiness.

139   Perhaps the classic description of Gnosticism as an 'anticosmic, dualistic' perspective is that of Kurt Rudolph: "the gnostic dualism is distinguished from these (Platonic, Buddhist, etc.) above all in the one essential point, that it is 'anti-cosmic'; that is, its conception includes an unequivocally negative evaluation of the visible world together with its creator; it ranks as a kingdom of evil and of darkness …" (Rudolph, *Gnosis*, 60).

140   Williams, *Rethinking "Gnosticism"*, 100.

141   Cf. Dunderberg, *Beyond Gnosticism*, 133. Conversely, "a dualistic and pessimistic anthropology alone does not yet constitute a 'Gnostic' phenomenon. Gnostic anthropology is unthinkable without a very definite and pessimistic view of the universe and its creator" (Mansfeld, "Bad World," 293, re: Orphism).

142   So Pépin, recalling biblical passages which are critical of the present cosmos, but clearly less so than Gnostic texts: Deut 4:19; Wisd. 13:2–3; Luke 9:25; Rom 1:25; Gal 4:8–11; Col 2:20 ("Cosmic Piety," 408–409).

and Irenaeus's Son (the 'hand' of the Father) is a far more knowledgeable and benevolent being than even the ignorant but ultimately benign demiurge of *Tri. Trac.* (the 'hand' of the *logos*), much less the malevolent Yaldabaoth. These disparities are significant.

A second issue with 'biblical demiurgicalism' is that its strict focus on the dualism of God and creator could also describe Marcion.[143] In other words, 'biblical demiurgicalism' does not only describe the Gnostic myths of Nag Hammadi; it describes dualism in general (see the conclusion to chapter three). This can, for instance, lead one to conflate Marcionism and Gnosticism, when in fact Marcionites and Gnostics appear to have been two distinct social groups.[144] Even so, a comparison of Marcion's dualism with that of the Gnostic sources surveyed here is instructive.[145] While Karamanolis has argued that Marcion's belief that there are two gods is a "variation of this Gnostic view," this is not quite right.[146] Rather, as Barbara Aland writes—echoing Scheffzyck, noted above—the Gnostic myths identify the essential, save-able human portion from heaven in contrast to the created cosmos, while Marcion unambiguously identifies the human being as a creation of the lower deity alone.[147] This same distinction may be articulated in terms of Tertullian's response to the 'heretical' question of *unde malum?*, which is *unde bonum?*—i.e., if the

---

143   Thus also Williams, *Rethinking "Gnosticism"*, 25–28; Räisänen, "Marcion," 107; Marjanen, "Gnosticism," 211.

144   Cf. e.g. Karamanolis: "Gnostics and also Marcion and his followers in one way or another advocated the view that the world as a whole or in large part is essentially bad ... Marcion and the Gnostics distinguished sharply between God-the creator-of-this-world, the God of Genesis and the Old Testament, whom they considered ignorant, bad, irascible and envious, and a higher God, the Christian God of the New Testament, whom they considered wise and essentially good" (*Philosophy*, 64, re: Ter. *Marc.* 1.6; similarly, Karamanolis, op. cit. 78). Den Dulk embraces 'biblical demiurgicalism' as a term for understanding Justin's polemic against Marcion and Valentinus, et al. in *Dial.* (*Between Jews*), thus using the phrase to replace 'dualism' rather than 'Gnosticism' (cf. also above, chapter two, n. 206).

145   For *Forschungsbericht* on the question of Marcion's relationship to Gnosticism, see Roth, "Evil," 343 n. 21, and esp. Aland (Ehlers), "Marcion: Versuch"; 157; see also Markschies, "Valentinianische Gnosis," 173–175.

146   Karamanolis, *Philosophy*, 78, re: Ir. *Haer.* 2.1.14, 3.25.3. For contrasting readings of these passages, see above, chapter three. Cf. also Lieu, *Marcion*, 337, 366.

147   Aland (Ehlers), "Marcion: Versuch," 304. See also ibid., 301; Brakke, *Gnostics*, 96; Lieu, *Marcion*, 381; Norelli, "Marcion: ein christlicher Philosoph," 122, 124–125. Aland (Ehlers) supposes that Marcion knew Gnostic myths but consciously avoided Gnostic terminology ('aeons' and the like—op. cit. 302). As Lieu points out, Irenaeus never accuses Marcion of stipulating kinship between the human soul and the divine, while he does exactly this regarding the Valentinians (Ir. *Haer.* 1.5.5–6, 1.7.3, 1.7.5; cit. Lieu, *Marcion*, 44).

world is made by a false god, how can there be any good in it?[148] Marcion does not have an answer, since the world and humans really are alien to god. Yet the Gnostic myths surveyed here do have an answer to *unde bonum?*: "human beings!"

Another alternative to the typology of 'Gnosticism' offered here is 'Gnosis' (with a capital 'G'), a wider category, favored on the Continent. 'Gnosis' is most often defined as a religion concerned with salvation through knowledge of one's divine origins.[149] It is a current that ostensibly encompasses not only ancient Gnosticism, but Manichaeism, the Hermetic literature, and the *Gospel of Thomas*.[150] The difficulty of this term is that it appears to be used more or less synonymously with 'mysticism,'[151] and this can take us far indeed from the circles of individuals who, according to Irenaeus and Porphyry, claimed to be *gnōstikoi*. To take up the counterexample of Epictetus once more, his query, "you are an offshoot of God … Why do you not know from whence you came?" (quoted above, chapter two) would ostensibly qualify as emblematic indeed of 'Gnosis.' Yet Stoicism can hardly qualify as a kind of 'Gnosis' in any useful sense of the word. What is distinctive about the use of language about divine care in the ancient sources associated with the *gnōstikoi*, particularly so many Nag Hammadi texts, is that they postulate a dualism of God and creator, simultaneously with some sort of kinship between human and divine.

Regardless, even if one chooses to eschew the term 'Gnosticism,' the myths belonging to the Gnostic dossier—above all, the Nag Hammadi Codices—present us with a general perspective on divine providence distinct from Christian and Greek philosophical discourses alike. From the standpoint of the history of philosophy, we are obliged to speak of the Gnostic myths as distinct, compelling, and controversial in their ancient context, because they describe how the world came to be and is currently administrated absent God's care, while the divine was nonetheless involved in the creation of human beings.

---

148 Ter. *Marc.* 5.13, cit. Russell, *Satan*, 89 n. 27. Tertullian's question assumes it is self-evident that there is some good in the world.

149 Most recently and forcefully, see van den Broek, *Gnostic Religion*, 2–3. See Hanegraaff, "Gnosticism," 790–793; similarly, DeConick, "Crafting Gnosis", 300–301. Interestingly, there is no critique of the category 'Gnosis' in Williams, *Rethinking "Gnosticism"*, except to the extent that the term is often used as a synonym for 'Gnosticism.'

150 Van den Broek, *Gnostic Religion*, 4–5, 11; DeConick, "Crafting Gnosis," 293. On the relationship between Manichaeism and Gnosticism, see P. Nagel, "Über das Verhältnis." In any case, it is deeply misleading to denote the Manichaean demiurge "evil" (*pace* Crouzel, "Theological Construction," 248).

151 Cf. von Stuckrad, "Entangled Discourses."

Language about *pronoia* is plentiful in Gnostic myths because it makes clear what is at stake in these stories. Even if the historian of religion regards the persons who authored such works as sociohistorically inextricable from early Christianity, the historian of philosophy or theology is in need of another name for their distinctive and transgressive notions about providence.

PART 3

Will

∴

CHAPTER 5

Did God Know All Along?

1 Introduction: Origen 'On Fate' (Philocalia 23)

The third body of philosophical problems that late ancient philosophers described in terms of providence was that involving fate, determinism, and responsibility, a complex out of which emerges the first notions of free will in Western thought. Our evidence for this complex is relatively thin prior to the third century CE, where we find two near-contemporaries of towering importance in ancient philosophy: Origen of Alexandria and Plotinus. Origen's discussions of fate, determinism, and responsibility are by far the most erudite and influential of any Christian writer prior to the *floruit* of Boethius, while Plotinus, widely regarded as the greatest philosopher of late antiquity, authored a treatise *On Providence* (*Enneads* 3,2–3) that is unrivaled in both its intellectual sophistication and state of preservation. Consequently, the present and final section of this book will focus on the treatments of providence by Origen and Plotinus with respect to questions of determinism, divine foreknowledge, and individual accountability.

There are two great 'treatises' on providence and free will in Origen's extant corpus: the twenty-third book of the *Philocalia*, and the long, first chapter of book three of *On First Principles*. The latter is concerned with individual accountability and free will, and will be taken up in the next chapter; the former focuses on the issue of divine foreknowledge, or prophecy, and will be discussed here. These two treatises serve as a fine point of departure for both topics, not least thanks to Origen's preservation of and engagement with the thoughts of his predecessors. Finally, chapter seven moves into the second half of the third century CE by seguing to the corpus of Plotinus, whose writings on providence encompass all the themes treated in this book, and so furnish an appropriate point of closure for it. An exciting new venue of research on Plotinus brings his works into conversation with Coptic treatises discovered near Nag Hammadi, whose language and interests bear hallmarks of third-century Platonism, and so shed new light on the engagement between Christian and Hellenic philosophers in the third century—particularly where *pronoia* and *protennoia* ('first thought') are concerned. What these three chapters attempt to show is the original and innovative character of Christian thought already in the third century CE, regarding divine foreknowledge, individual accountability, and the intersection of divine forethought with language about providence.

© KONINKLIJKE BRILL NV, LEIDEN, 2020 | DOI:10.1163/9789004432994_007

The ancients themselves assembled a guide to Origen's thought: the *Philocalia*, a 'greatest hits' collection compiled by Basil of Caesarea and Gregory Nazianzus, well into the second half of the fourth century CE.[1] The final third (books twenty-one to twenty-seven) of this compilation is devoted to Origen's views on free will. The longest and most poignant of these books is number twenty-three, whose title (the invention of Basil and Gregory), nicely summarizes Origen's thoughts:

> On Fate, and how human responsibility is preserved, even admitting God's foreknowledge of what is done by each person; and in what way the stars are not the makers of human affairs, but merely indicate them; and that humans are not able to possess sure knowledge about these things, but the signs are published by divine powers; and who is the cause of these things.[2]

Most of *Philocalia* book twenty-three (henceforth referred to as *On Fate*) is an extract drawn from the third book of Origen's *Commentary on Genesis*, an early work composed around 229 in Alexandria (shortly before *On First Principles*).[3] However, the compilers of *On Fate* have inserted two other sources into the discussion: chapters twelve and thirteen, right in the middle, are an extract from one of Origen's last works, *Against Celsus*; and at the end, one finds a long extract from the Pseudo-Clementine *Recognitions*. The structure of the book is thus as follows:

> *On Fate* 1–2 = Origen, *Commentary on Genesis*, book 3: against astrology; against Marcion
> *On Fate* 3–11 = Origen, *Commentary on Genesis*, book 3: the causality of divine foreknowledge
> *On Fate* 12–13 = Origen, *Against Celsus*, 2.20: the causality of divine foreknowledge
> *On Fate* 14–21 = Origen, *Commentary on Genesis*, book 3: against astrology
> *On Fate* 22 = Pseudo-Clement, *Recognitions*, 10.7–13.1: against astrology

---

1 On the date (between 364–378 CE), compilation, and reception of the *Philocalia*, see Junod in SC 226:11–13, 62–65 (re: *Philoc*. 23), followed by Benjamins, *Eingeordnete Freiheit*, 55. M. Frede takes these chapters as "fairly representative of the Christian position in the East in the third and fourth centuries A.D." regarding freedom and human responsibility (*Free Will*, 106).

2 Orig. *Philoc*. 23.1, text Junod in SC 226:130, tr. mine.

3 On dating the *Commentary on Genesis*, see Nautin, *Origène*, 370–371, followed by Trigg, *Origen*, 86.

DID GOD KNOW ALL ALONG? 193

This chapter walks with Origen through *On Fate*. However, as we will see, the logic of his presentation is not immediately clear. What is the connection between Marcionite thought and astrology? And why the massive digression—ten chapters' worth, including the passage from *Against Celsus*—on divine foreknowledge?

The key, it will be argued, is to be found precisely in the excursus from *Against Celsus*, which engages a favorite literary *topos* of earlier Greek thinkers considering the relationship between causal determinism and personal responsibility ("what is up to us"—*to eph'hēmin*), in the context of ancient divination: Apollo's oracle to the legendary Theban Laius regarding his death at the hands of his own son, Oedipus. Origen's account of this *topos* is well-trod ground for historians of philosophy, who have taken it as crucial evidence in the reconstruction of the Stoic Chrysippus's response to the 'lazy argument' (*argos logos*). As we will see, most of Origen's modern exegetes lose the forest for the trees, neglecting the rhetorical and theological contexts of these passages in the attempt to mine them for the modern doxography of Stoicism and Middle Platonism. Rather, a close examination of the theme of the 'Oracle to Laius' in Hellenistic and early Roman philosophical literature—particularly Chrysippus, Cicero, Alexander of Aphrodisias, and Alcinous—reveals that some thinkers asked if prophecies indicate that the gods who utter them are not necessarily providential. Keeping this in mind when we come back to Origen's discussion in the *Commentary on Genesis*, it becomes clear that while he wished to refute the deterministic implications of astrology, he also wished to preserve biblical prophecy and the providential, benevolent character of the God operative within it—precisely what Marcionite exegesis of Genesis 2–3 challenges.[4] In doing so, Origen presented a view of divine omniscience that extended to God's knowledge of future conditionals—a view characteristic of later Platonism, not the Platonism of the early third century—and located prophecy as operative not in civic divination, but in the Bible.

---

4 *Pace* Bergjan's claim that "die Vereinbarkeit von Vorherwissen und Entscheidungsfreiheit fand in der Antike nicht dadurch eine Forsetzung im Begriff der göttlichen Pronoia, daß man sich auch in diesem Zusammenhang mit der Frage der Notwendigkeit auseinandersetzte" (*Der fürsorgende Gott*, 188–189 n. 69). On the general importance of divination and prophecy for understanding the development of Christian notions of providence, see Cameron, "Divine Providence," 121, 130–131. Here I set aside the discussion of Calc. *Comm. Tim.* 153–154, since its sources may be of later provenance than most of the sources discussed in this book, and it is sufficiently complex to warrant a study of its own.

2 Origen's Digression on Divine Omniscience and Future Causes in 'On Fate'

Book three of the *Commentary on Genesis* takes as its point of departure Gen 1:14 LXX, that the stars were established "for signs," *eis sēmeia*. Origen sets up several problems at the outset, and they concern all humanity:

> The many nations who are strangers to the faith of Christ are not the only ones who lose their footing concerning the topic of destiny (*heimarmenēs*). They reckon that everything that occurs on the earth, as well as to each individual person, and indeed even to irrational animals, is due to the combination of the stars called planets with those of the zodiac.[5]

If this is so, Origen asks, how do praise or blame serve any purpose? And what indeed is the purpose of the arrival of Christ and

> the entire divine plan (*oikonomia*) of the law and the prophets and the efforts of the apostles to establish God's Church through Christ. Even Christ himself, according to some who dare to say so, has been subjected to the constraint (*anagkēn*) of the movement of the stars on account of his birth (*genesin*) ... From such godless and impious doctrines it also follows that believers must believe in God because they have been induced to do so by the stars! Let us inquire of them, what was God's will (*ti ho theos boulomenos*) when he made such a world? ...[6]

The answer, Origen says, is not to postulate "another good God who is the source of none of these things"—surely a swipe at Marcion or some of his followers.[7] Such people are either under the power of the second, 'just' god who is the source of evils and the stars (in which case their access to the 'good' god is mitigated), or they are not under the influence of the stars of the just god at all (a scenario which, he says, they cannot explain).[8] Finally, he exclaims, what would be the use of prayer, since "if events must necessarily occur ... it is irrational to ask of God that he give us such things?"[9]

---

5 Orig. *Philoc.* 23.1, text Junod in SC 226:130, 132, tr. Trigg, *Origen*, 87.
6 Orig. *Philoc.* 23.1, text Junod in SC 226:134, 136, tr. Trigg, *Origen*, 87–88, modified.
7 Orig. *Philoc.* 23.2, tr. Trigg, *Origen*, 88; see further Trigg, *Origen*, 257.
8 Orig. *Philoc.* 23.2, tr. Trigg, *Origen*, 88.
9 Orig. *Philoc.* 23.2, text Junod in SC 226:138, 140, tr. Trigg, *Origen*, 87, 88. Notably, Origen's invocation of prayer here is a use of the 'lazy argument' for rhetorical purposes, rather than a

DID GOD KNOW ALL ALONG? 195

The line and targets of Origen's argumentation here are not clear. The most obvious question is: what has Marcion to do with astrology? The rhetoric of liberation from enslavement to cosmic fate is common across early Christian sources (see above, chapter four, and below, chapter six), so the presence of Marcionite thinking in a discussion of astrology and determinism—to say nothing of the ostensible implication of the former in the latter—is puzzling. In fact, in the discussion above (chapter three) of early evidence about Marcion and Marcionite exegesis, astrology did not come up at all. Origen does not tell us why he takes dualist exegesis to be a necessary byproduct of belief in astrology, but this is the position he argues against. Thus, some scholars hypothesize that Origen has some vaguely 'gnostic' adherents to astrology in mind, even though his rhetoric of a 'just' versus a 'good' god can only recall Marcionites.[10]

Origen then introduces a second hermeneutical problem, moving on to eleven chapters' worth of discussion of how divine foreknowledge works. He begins by claiming that the stars and planets do not determine all human action, but merely serve as signs. Yet he proceeds by simply dropping the question of astrological determinism to take up that of divine foreknowledge: specifically, biblical prophecies of Judas's betrayal of Jesus. While God inspired Scripture by a kind of 'imprinting' (*entupoun*) of knowledge of future events, he says, God is not the cause of Judas's betrayal. "The one who foreknows is not at all the cause of the things foreknown (*oute ho prognous pantōs aitios tōn proegnōsmenōn*), any more than are the texts that receive the imprints of the words of foreknowledge from the one who foreknows."[11] Origen then gives examples from Scripture illustrating God's faculty of foreknowledge, such as Sus 42–43 LXX: "dear God eternal who knows secrets, who knows everything before it comes to be (*ho eidōs ta panta prin geneseōs autōn*), you know that these men have borne false testimony against me."[12] Noting that Greek

---

defense against the 'care or prayer' argument known to Justin Martyr (on which see above, chapter two).

10   Junod and Benjamins, for instance, take Origen's target to be "einige (gnostischen) Anhänger der astrologischen Lehre" (Benjamins, *Eingeordnete Freiheit*, 79, following Junod's remarks in SC 226:138 n. 2), re: Clem. Al. *Exc.* 69. Yet *Exc.* 69 refers responsibility for evils to the stars, not to God, and in any case does not oppose the 'good' and 'just' gods. Magris suggests "gnostici (probabilmente i valentiniani)" (*L'idea di destino*, 2:838).

11   Orig. *Philoc.* 23.3, text Junod in SC 226:142, tr. Trigg, *Origen*, 89.

12   Orig. *Philoc.* 23.4–5, text Junod in SC 226:142, 144, tr. Trigg, *Origen*, 89. It is a favorite passage of Origen's, also quoted in *Princ.* 3.1.12, 3.1.16 (discussed below, chapter six). All the other examples Origen gives are *ex eventu* prophecies: 1Kgs 12:42, 13:1–3; Is 45:1–4; Dan 8:5–9.

philosophers have enquired as to the compatibility of human responsibility and divine foreknowledge,[13] he counters that foreknowledge of another's action is not tantamount to causation of it:

> And, if it is necessary to say that foreknowledge is not the cause of what happens, it follows that when someone does sin, God is not implicated in the action of the person whose future sinning He has foreknown. But, paradoxical as it may seem, we shall state the truth, namely that the future event is itself the cause of such foreknowledge about it. For it does not happen because it was known; rather, it was known because it is going to happen.[14]

This is not to say that divine foreknowledge extends only to definite events. Rather, Origen asserts, God knows that Judas will betray Christ, but that it will also be possible for Judas to do otherwise. Thus, "God's knowledge could say, 'It is possible for him to do this, but the opposite is also possible; both being possible, I know that he will do this'."[15] In fact, he adds, if human decisions were planned in advance by virtue of God's foreknowledge of them, the many prophetic injunctions to repent would be meaningless.[16] At this point, chapters twelve and thirteen of *On Fate* take up the extract from *Against Celsus* concerned with the 'Oracle to Laius,' a *topos* to which we now turn.

3   Chrysippus and Cicero on "Things That Are Simple, Others Complex": The Oracle to Laius

The language of providence is pronounced in divinatory contexts even beyond philosophical literature, and points to an understanding of the revelatory forethought of the gods as a personified deity. "Honor *Pronoia*," intones a Delphic oracle of the third century BCE.[17] An avatar of Athena named "Athene Pronoia"

---

13   "They say that from God's foreknowledge of the future it follows that what is up to us cannot be preserved" (Orig. *Philoc.* 23.7, text Junod in SC 226:152, tr. Trigg, *Origen*, 93, slightly modified).

14   Orig. *Philoc.* 23.8, text Junod in SC 226:158, tr. Trigg, *Origen*, 93, slightly modified.

15   Orig. *Philoc.* 23.9, tr. Trigg, *Origen*, 94. On the importance of 'freedom to do otherwise' in the development of notions of free will, see below, chapter six.

16   Orig. *Philoc.* 23.10.

17   See J.-P. Martin, *Providentia deorum*, 15–16. To my best knowledge, there is no study of the language of *pronoia* in oracular inscriptions.

even dwelt at a temple opposite Delphi, as reported by a Greek poet of the first century BCE, Parthenius:

> The tyrant Phayllos fell in love with the wife of Ariston, chief of the Oitaian ... Now she had a great longing for a necklace that was at that time hanging in the temple of Athene of Providence (*en tōi tēs Pronoias Athēnas*): it was said formerly to have belonged to Eriphyle; and this was the present for which she asked. Phayllos took a great booty of the offerings at Delphoi, the necklace among the rest.[18]

The tenth-century, Byzantine lexicon *Suda* explains the location of this temple of Athena vis-à-vis Delphi in its entry on *pronoia*: "*Pronoia*: A particular temple of Athena at Delphoi was named Pronoia, because of its being situated *pro tou naou* ('in front of the temple'). Herodotos names her Proneie in his book eight."[19] The entry on *Pronoia Athena*, however, reveals that the name *pronoia* was not taken by all as a toponym, empty of theological content: "some say that her statue was so-called because it stood before (*pro*) the temple (*naos*) at Delphoi (so *pronaia*); others because she foresaw (*prounoēsen*) that Leto would give birth."[20] The goddess's knowledge of the future was her *pronoia*.

By the time Plutarch of Chaeronaea assumed the role of one of the two high priests at Delphi, probably in the last decade of the first century CE, the great oracular shrines had declined enough in popularity and importance that would feel compelled to write a treatise explaining the unfortunate phenomenon.[21] However, philosophers continued to debate about how exactly divination worked and what its relationship to divine providence might be. One prophetic episode of Greek myth in particular took on great vigor in the doxographic record of Roman philosophy: Apollo's oracle to Laius, Oedipus's father, that if he sleeps with a woman, he will be killed by his own child. Ancient sources preserve the story in several versions, but pseudo-Apollodorus relates

---

18   Parthenius, *Love Romances* 25.1–2, text and tr. Gaselee in LCL 69:326–327, slightly modified.

19   *Suda*, pi 2534, tr. Whitehead, accessed 29 July 2019 at *Suda On Line* ("Pronoia"). For further citations, see J.-P. Martin, *Providentia deorum*, 14–15.

20   *Suda*, pi 2535, tr. Roth, accessed 29 July 2019 at *Suda On Line* ("Pronoia Athena").

21   The date of Plutarch's ascension to high priest at Delphi is uncertain; the present guess follows Ziegler, "Plutarchos," 660; similarly Brenk, "Imperial Heritage," 254–255. For recent discussion and bibliography of the general matter, see Casanova, "Plutarch." By the end of the second century CE, Clement of Alexandria was able to crow that the great oracular sites of old had faded into obscurity (Clem. Alex. *Protr.* 2.11.1–3; see Eidinow, *Oracles*, 63). See further Athanassiadi, "Fate of Oracles."

an apposite version which contains all the details at issue, in his *Bibliotheca*: the Theban noble Laius was sent into exile, and found refuge with Pelops. He also took a fancy to his host's son, who happened to have the name Chrysippus (!), and absconded with the boy.[22] Later becoming king of Thebes, Laius married, but "the oracle had warned him not to beget, for the son that should be begotten would kill his father; nevertheless, flushed with wine, he had intercourse with his wife. And when the babe was born he ... gave it to a herdsman to expose ..."[23] The child of course survived and was named Oedipus.

We might casually remark that 'the rest is fate' as regards the Oedipus story, but it is precisely this point which was fiercely debated in antiquity, beginning (so far as we know) with the Stoic Chrysippus himself. Chrysippus takes up Apollo's 'Oracle to Laius' as a case study in his explanation of 'co-determined fate,' a notion meant to preserve the compatibility of causal determinism and human responsibility, and explored with reference to the usefulness of divination.[24] Three of Chrysippus's Roman interpreters—Cicero, Alexander of Aphrodisias, and Alcinous—all examine the 'Oracle to Laius' as well. For them, the story's logic and presuppositions about the divine are not only of scholastic import, but have significant implications for conceptions of Roman civic cult.

---

22   Apollod. [*Bib.*] 3.3.5.

23   Apollod. [*Bib.*] 3.3.7, tr. Frazer in LCL 121:343, 345.

24   Bobzien has argued forcefully that the Laius oracle was not included in Chrysippus's reply to the lazy argument, because the example is not 'compatible' (no pun intended) with the lazy argument; i.e., it is not concerned with action, but abstention. Rather, she proposes, Chrysippus's views on divination and compatibilism were laid out in distinct contexts, and only brought together—erroneously—in the later, doxographic record (*Determinism and Freedom*, 215–216). Sharples has offered the plausible reply that Chrysippus may have conceived of the matter as follows: the 'lazy argument' would have held that if it is fated for Laius to have a child, he might as well sleep with a woman because the child is coming whether he abstains from sex or not, and this situation merits a response ("Stoic Background," 180). Secondly, Bobzien prefers the evidence of Diogenianus, for whom there is only a 'vague hint' linking Chrysippus's name to the Laius oracle, which seems to Sharples to be a misreading (Sharples, op. cit. 181, *pace* Bobzien, op. cit. 208, re: Euseb. *Praep. Ev.* 6.8.25–38 = SVF 2:998 = LS 62F). (Diogenianus's account of 'the woman example' makes the necessary condition for the co-fated event "not the action itself but the wanting and making an effort" [Bobzien, op. cit. 212]—a more substantial reply to the 'lazy argument' than explained by Cicero.) I here side with Sharples in taking Cicero's evidence referring the oracle to Chrysippus to be more or less accurate (similarly Whittaker, "Notes," 134, with reference to the witness of Alcinous—see below—and Barnes, "Cicero's *de fato*"). As far as this chapter is concerned, the matter is only relevant as regards its presentation of the evidence, not its conclusions, which are concerned with the development of notions of divine foreknowledge.

DID GOD KNOW ALL ALONG? 199

The teachings of Chrysippus and other Stoa on divination are mainly known through their engagement by Cicero in his 'theological treatises' *On Divination* (45–44 BCE) and *On Fate* (44 BCE).[25] Cicero tells us that Chrysippus regarded divination not as superstition or magic, but as a kind of science, a technique (*technē*).[26] According to Cicero, Chrysippus argued that the gods do not extend their attention to every little piece of sacrificial flesh consulted by a priest; rather, the state of the entrails is indicative of general, universal laws about what is happening.[27] Stoic divination is a science of signs, describing correlation rather than causation.[28] For Chrysippus and other Stoa, belief in the efficacy of traditional divinatory practices thus serves as a presupposition in demonstrating the existence of the great network of causes that is God, the 'General Causal Principle (GCP).'[29] Critics of the Stoa responded that such an understanding of divination and the GCP is incompatible with Stoic modal logic, which sought to retain the notion of contingency, i.e., non-necessary future possibilities: how can something be fated, foreseen via divination, and yet *not* be necessary?[30] In *On Fate*, Cicero reports Chrysippus's reply that prognosticators ought to formulate their prophecies as negated conjunctions, rather

---

25 Cicero himself states that these works, together with *Nat. d.*, comprise a consistent set of theological investigations: *Div.* 1.7, 2.1–4; idem, *Fat.* 1. See Schofield, "Cicero For and Against," 48–49; Sharples, "Introduction: Cicero," 3–4; Begemann, "Cicero's Theology," 226. For the date of *Div.*, see Beard, "Cicero and Divination," 34; for the date of *Fat.*, see Sharples, op. cit. 5–6.

26 So Chrysippus, ap. Sext. Emp. *Math.* 9.132; also Cic. *Div.* 2.130. See Theiler, "Tacitus," 60; Algra, "Stoic Theology," 173–174, n. 56; similarly, Bobzien, *Determinism and Freedom*, 87; followed by Gabor, "When Should a Philosopher," 326.

27 Cic. *Div.* 1.118, widely quoted, e.g. Algra, "Stoic Theology," 173–174; Larson, *Understanding*, 74.

28 Rightly Barnes "Cicero's *de fato*," 506, n. 26, and Bobzien, *Determinism and Freedom*, 159–175, esp. 166.

29 On the GCP, see above, chapter one. On the Stoic strategy of referring to divination as evidence of the existence of the GCP, see Bobzien, *Determinism and Freedom*, 87–96 (re: Cic. *Fat.* 11; Euseb. *Praep. Ev.* 4.3.1–2, *inter alii*), followed by Schallenberg, *Freiheit*, 113–114; Gabor, "When Should a Philosopher," 326–327; Burkert, "Signs," 36; see also Boyd, "Two Ancient," 49; Begemann, "Cicero's Theology," 233. For Chrysippus's definition in his *On Providence* of God qua fate as the universal causal network, see Gell. *Noct. att.* 7.2.3, discussed in Bobzien, op. cit., 47–48.

30 Here, the Stoa responded to the (in)famous 'Master Argument' of Diodorus Cronus (third century BCE), on which see esp. Gaskin, *Sea Battle*; Schallenberg, *Freiheit*, 17–22. For thorough discussion of the Stoic response and criticism of it, see Bobzien, *Determinism and Freedom*, 97–143; see also Benjamins, *Eingeordnete Freiheit*, 24–27; Schallenberg, op. cit., 127–139. The crux of the Stoic view as understood by Bobzien is that even if it is fated that Dio will go for a walk on such-and-such a day in the future, this fact is compatible with the possibility of his not being externally, physically hindered from walking at certain times

200 CHAPTER 5

than conditionals. For example, instead of stating that 'if someone is born with a horoscope where the star Sirius is rising, he or she will not die at sea,' it should rather be said that 'it is not the case that someone has been born with Sirius rising and will die at sea.'[31] Cicero mocks this suggestion, but Chrysippus's point is that if divination deals with correlation rather than causation, then the logic of prophecy is not mutually exclusive with future contingency, and the words of soothsayers and oracles could perhaps better reflect that.[32]

Thus, according to the Stoa, humans do not possess knowledge of the future, but can gain foreknowledge of some events via the technique of divination.[33] The gods possess advance knowledge of what is to be, and so grasp the causes behind all events, including future ones—what the Stoic Posidonius termed 'sympathy' (*sumpatheia*).[34] Our sole witness to how the Stoa understood the mechanism by which the gods possess this foreknowledge is late: Nemesius of Edessa (fourth century CE). The famous Stoic doctrine of the 'eternal return' dictates that history proceeds in a cycle which the gods re-live over and over again. Nemesius identifies this doctrine as the basis of divine foreknowledge among the Stoa—the gods know everything will happen because they have experienced it already:

> The reconstitution of the universe occurs not once but many times, or, rather, to infinity, and the same things will be re-established without end. But—they hold—the gods, who are not subject to this destruction, having observed one cycle, know from it all the future events that will happen (*panta ta mellonta esesthai*) in the following cycles. For there will be nothing foreign beyond what happened before, but everything will be the same without change even in the last detail.[35]

   (*Determinism and Freedom*, 142). This aspect of Chrysippus's teaching is omitted by Boyd at a key point in his presentation of the issue ("Two Ancient," 45–48).

31   Cic. *Fat.* 15. There is extensive bibliography on this passage: see Sharples, "Commentary: Cicero," 169–171; Schallenberg, *Freiheit*, 141–155; additionally, see Long and Sedley, *Hellenistic Philosophers*, 1:236, 393.

32   ... And thus there is (ostensibly) no contradiction between Stoic modal logic and Stoic physics after all (Bobzien, *Determinism and Freedom*, 156–175; Schallenberg, *Freiheit*, 154–155). We are still waiting for the prognosticators to comply with Chrysippus's request.

33   Cicero agrees with them. See *Div.* 1.127 = SVF 2:944 = LS 55O; see further *Div.* 2.18; Sharples, "Commentary: Alexander," 164; idem, "Introduction: Cicero," 8, 25–26; Schallenberg, *Freiheit*, 208.

34   For Posidonius's doctrine of *sumpatheia*, see e.g. Cic. *Fat.* 7; idem, *Div.* 2.34 = SVF 2:1211. Further, Sharples, "Introduction: Cicero," 8–9; Burkert, "Signs," 33; Schallenberg, *Freiheit*, 100–104; Begemann, "Cicero's Theology," 235.

35   Nem. *Nat. hom.* 38 [112] = SVF 2:625 = LS 52C, text in Long and Sedley, *Hellenistic Philoso-*

DID GOD KNOW ALL ALONG? 201

Divine foreknowledge is therefore incumbent upon a chain of events which is inalterably determined, since any deviance in the repetition of the chain would amount to an event that the gods cannot know. It is no coincidence that Nemesius emphasizes the gods' omniscience, the totality of divine knowledge.

The 'lazy argument' responds that if the chain of events is already completely determined, why bother to make an effort to change anything—including to consult divination regarding pressing matters? In *On Fate*, Cicero introduces the case of Laius as illustrative of Chrysippus's response to the 'lazy argument': the doctrine of co-fated events (or "co-determination"): if *a* is fated, it may still be incumbent on condition *b* being fulfilled.[36] As Robert Sharples has argued, Chrysippus's aim must have been to show that "prophecy has some point because it can serve as a warning and we can take action to avoid the outcome, which we can do because some events are co-fated with others."[37] Thus Chrysippus, Cicero tells us, claims that

> There are some cases in things that are simple, others complex ... If it is fated that 'Oedipus will be born to Laius,' one will not be able to say 'whether Laius has slept with a woman or not'; the matter is complex and 'co-fated'—for that is what he [Chrysippus] calls it, because it is fated, both that Laius will sleep with his wife and that he will beget Oedipus by her.[38]

That is, the fated event that 'Oedipus will be born to Laius' is also fated (or 'co-fated') with Laius sleeping with a woman, since it is impossible (in the ancient context, at least) for Laius to sire a child without intercourse.[39] Thus, even though it is fated for 'Oedipus to be born to Laius,' this is incumbent upon Laius's co-fated decision to have intercourse with a woman. Chrysip-

---

phers, 2:306, tr. Sharples and van der Eijk, 193–194, slightly modified, quoted above, chapter one. On the importance of this passage for Stoic concepts of divination, see Sharples, "Commentary: Cicero," 182. Otherwise, it is strangely neglected in this sector of the secondary literature.

36   Cic. *Fat.* 31.

37   Sharples, "Stoic Background," 178–179; also Adamson, *Philosophy*, 158; cf. Boyd, "Two Ancient," 59 n. 37.

38   Cic. *Fat.* 30, text and tr. Sharples, 76–79, slightly modified.

39   Cicero makes this clear in *Fat.* 30 by glossing the example with a second example from sports: if it were prophesied that 'Milo will wrestle at the Olympics,' this event would be co-fated with Milo having an opponent, since there is no such thing as a solo wrestling match. The Milo example illustrates the example of Laius, not the Lazy Argument (Bobzien, *Determinism and Freedom*, 202 n. 57; see also Schallenberg, *Freiheit*, 202–203; cf. Benjamins, *Eingeordnete Freiheit*, 26).

pus here offers a compatibilist view of how the foreknowledge of determined events operates: while it is fated that Laius be killed by his son, it is Laius's own choice to sleep with Jocasta and get rid of the offspring. (Down the road, Oedipus chooses to leave those whom he believes to be his parents, which is how he winds up meeting his real parents and unwittingly fulfilling the terrible prophecy.) On Chrysippus's reading, the story illustrates both the inescapability of fate and the way in which human choices play a role in destiny's consummation. This destiny includes, of course, the utterance of the prophecy itself.[40]

The Academic Skeptic Carneades—Chrysippus's arch-critic, and one of Cicero's chief sources for Hellenistic thought—recognizes this explanation of future foreknowledge (epistemic determinism) to be distinct from the question of future truth (logical determinism): something that will happen but is contingent on preceding events outside of the causal chain will not be foreknown by the gods, even if it is true.[41] "It makes a great difference," Cicero writes,

> whether a natural cause makes future things true from eternity, or whether even those things which are going to be in the future without a natural eternity of preceding cause can be understood to be true. And so Carneades used to say that not even Apollo could say what was going to be in the future, except for those things whose causes were contained in nature in such a way that it was necessary for them to come to be.[42]

The gods, Cicero believes (following Carneades), then do not have knowledge of future contingents, but only of things that are determined to be. If it was not naturally determined for Oedipus to kill his father—if the choices of Laius and Oedipus really had belonged to them alone—then Apollo could not have foretold the event.[43] No Stoic answer to this argument is preserved for the

---

40 As Bobzien recognizes, divinatory signs offered by the gods themselves are different than those discovered by human seers insofar as "the condition prediction itself is understood as part of the causal network of fate ... however, it does not indicate unconditionally what is going to happen" (Bobzien, *Determinism and Freedom*, 178–179; see also Sharples, "Commentary: Cicero," 180–181).

41 Long and Sedley, *Hellenistic Philosophers*, 1:466; cf. Begemann, "Cicero's Theology," 230–231.

42 Cic. *Fat.* 32, tr. Sharples, 79; cf. Begemann, "Cicero's Theology," 239.

43 Cic. *Fat.* 33, tr. Sharples, 79: "It was, in short, by knowing the causes that brought each thing about that it was possible to know what was going to be in the future. Therefore Apollo could not have made a prediction about Oedipus, since there were no causes laid down beforehand in the nature of things making it necessary for his father to be killed by him; nor could he make any other prediction of that sort." See Cic. *Div.* 2.15–18 for a catalog of arguments that there can be no foreknowledge of things that happen by chance. For dis-

record, but one could imagine Chrysippus agreeing that while the gods only know determined events, there are no undetermined events, including human choices; therefore, the gods foreknow all events, even if some of them happen to be co-fated.[44]

Notably, Cicero in *On Fate* does not deny divine foreknowledge nor the efficacy of divination in general. Rather, the gods foreknow everything that must be, and the technique of divination may succeed in unveiling some of that. *On Fate* is a scholastic treatise, and Cicero surely wrote it at least in part to burnish his academic credentials and further the development of Greek philosophy written in Latin, an enterprise that was still very new in his day.[45] Yet *On Fate* is also as animated by civic values as much as its companion 'theological' treatises, *On Divination* and *On the Nature of the Gods*. As Mary Beard has observed, all of the interlocutors in these dialogues are elites of roughly equal status, and their main speakers (Cotta and Marcus, respectively) are priests.[46] Cicero's fellow elites shared with him the responsibilities of serving in the Roman priesthood, such as the performance of augury, and it is likely that these readers had very tactile questions about what exactly they were doing when they read a liver.[47] This political context may help explain why Cicero esteems civic religion in the theological treatises even as he pens characters who deliver scathing critiques of divination, while appearing himself to favor a skeptical or at least open-minded approach to cultic practice.[48] As Cicero himself argues (in his own voice) at the beginning of *On the Nature of the Gods*, religious observance and piety themselves inculcate virtue; if these practices are abolished on the

---

cussion of all these passages, see also Schallenberg, *Freiheit*, 208–209; also Magris, *L'idea di destino*, 2:569–570. The Epicurean Oenomaus also claims that Apollo could have no way of knowing how Laius would act, against both Stoic and Middle Platonic interpretations of the story (Euseb. *Praep. ev.* 6.7.22–26 = SVF 2:978; see further Hammerstaedt, *Orakelkritik*, 273–276).

44 Sharples, "Commentary: Cicero," 182. On the extension of the gods' knowledge to individuals, see Cic. *Div.* 2.104; idem, *Nat. d.* 2.75, 2.77; Epict. *Diatr.* 1.12.3 (discussed above, chapter one).

45 See Barnes, "Cicero's *de fato*," 497–500; Beard, "Cicero and Divination," 36–39, 45; Schofield, "Cicero For and Against," 50–61.

46 Beard, "Cicero and Divination," 44.

47 Rightly emphasized by Beard, "Cicero and Divination," 45–46; see also Schofield, "Cicero For and Against," 49; Magris, *L'idea di destino*, 2:571; Begemann, "Cicero's Theology," 241.

48 For criticism of traditional divinatory practices, see *Div.* 2.148–149, discussed in Schofield, "Cicero For and Against," 60, 62. On *fatum* as a superstitious, socially corrosive concept in the theological treatises, see Begemann, "Cicero's Theology," 229–230. The final lines of *Div.* (2.150) invite the reader to make up his or her own mind (Beard, "Cicero and Divination," 35).

204 CHAPTER 5

presumption that the gods do not exist or pay no notice of the human realm, "in all probability the disappearance of piety towards the gods will entail the disappearance of loyalty and social union among men as well, and of justice itself, the queen of all the virtues."[49]

4 Upholding the Appearance of Civic Piety: Alexander of Aphrodisias and Alcinous Respond to the 'Oracle to Laius'

A Peripatetic philosopher of the later second century, Alexander of Aphrodisias, took up the Laius oracle with different aims in his treatise *On Fate* (*Peri Heimarmenēs*), a digest of arguments against determinism. The work is dedicated to the emperor Septimius Severus (193–211 CE) and his son and co-ruler, Caracalla (198–217 CE), and so was probably written during the period of their shared reign (198–209 CE).[50] He begins the work by declaring it to be a token of thanks for their support of his public teaching of the philosophy of Aristotle (likely his installation in one of the chairs of philosophy in Athens, established by Marcus Aurelius), "together with a testimonial (*meta marturias*) that I was worthy (*dikaios*) of receiving such things upon asking."[51] Alexander never takes up this line anew, but the subtext is clear: his various supplications to his patrons over the years were those of a just man, he maintains, and the ensuing arguments against determinism ought to remind us that we bear responsibility for the quality of the supplications we make, and the response they elicit. (One wonders if his tenure was in question.)[52]

Twice in *On Fate*, Alexander breaks off his discussion to take up the problems of foreknowledge and divination. In the first case, he poses a version of the 'lazy argument': if the acts which ultimately led to the Trojan War were all

---

49   Cic. *Nat. d.* 1.3–4, tr. Rackham in LCL 268:7; see also *Nat. d.* 1.121 1.124, 3.5; idem, *Div.* 2.28, 2.70–71, 2.75; see Beard, "Cicero and Divination," 43; Schofield, "Cicero For and Against," 59–60; Begemann, "Cicero's Theology," 244.

50   Sharples, "Introduction: Alexander," 15.

51   Alex. Aphr. *Fat.* 1, text Sharples, 179, tr. Sharples, 41, slightly modified.

52   Alexander uses the occasion to proclaim himself the foremost interpreter of Aristotle of his day and to distinguish himself from rivals who adhere to Skepticism (Mansfeld, "*Diaphonia*," 204–205). Unfortunately, we possess no other evidence regarding the circumstances of this dedication. Alexander states further (*Fat.* 1) that his work is presented as a votive offering from afar, just as sacrifices are made to Rome from those all over the Empire. Caracalla was not sympathetic to the teaching of Aristotle (Sharples, "Commentary: Alexander," 125); perhaps Alexander found his distance from Rome preferable, even as he sought to justify the existence of his academic post.

DID GOD KNOW ALL ALONG? 205

determined and possible to divine, how did any of the actors involved merit praise or blame?[53] This leads directly to concern about the compatibility of divinatory practices and human responsibility:

> And how, saying such things, could [the determinists] preserve the providential concern exercised by the gods on behalf of mortals (*tēn hypo tōn theōn ginomenēn tōn thnētōn pronoian*)? For if the manifestations of the gods, which they say happen to certain people, come about in accordance with some cause laid down beforehand ... how would it still be right for anyone to call this providence, when it comes about not in accordance with merit, but in accordance with some necessity laid down beforehand?[54]

Alexander then asks further what would be the point of prophecy if its fruits are determined in the first place.[55] He drops the issue, only to raise it again, later in the treatise:

> Well, if someone says these things, does one preserve prophecy, or teach pious conceptions concerning the gods, or show that prophecy has any usefulness? For prophecy is thought to be a prediction of the things that are going to happen, but they make Apollo the author of the things he predicts ... According to what [the determinists] say, at least, the Pythian Oracle does not contribute anything good for Laius, but strives and does everything for the end that his house escapes nothing of what is most unholy and impious! Having heard these things, who would not call the

---

53   Alex. Aphr. *Fat.* 16.

54   Alex. Aphr. *Fat.* 17, text Bruns, 188.1–6 in Sharples, 195, and tr. Sharples, 66, slightly modified.

55   "And how would they not do away with prophecy as well, when the usefulness of prophecy is done away with? For what would anyone either [take pains to] learn [from the prophets] or guard against as a result of having learned from the prophets, if we are only able to learn, and they to reveal, those things which it was necessitated even before our birth we should learn and do or not do in each case ...?" (Alex. Aphr. *Fat.* 17, tr. Sharples, 67) Sharples has suggested that the passage is an allusion to the incompatibility of determinism with prayer ("Commentary: Alexander," 151, re: Plut. [*Fat.*] 574d; Nem. *Nat. hom.* 38). More likely, Alexander simply raises the issue which Chrysippus had attempted to address via the doctrine of co-fated events, namely the point of engaging in prophecy in the first place if future events are already determined. Rather, philosophical reflection on the practice of supplication lies behind the work's opening dedication. On philosophical criticism of prayer and supplication, see also above, chapter two.

absence of providence (*apronoēsian*) asserted by the followers of Epicurus more pious than *this* sort of providence (*toiautēs pronoias*)?[56]

As Sharples notes, Alexander's criticism "questions the motive of Apollo in giving the oracle when he knew what the outcome would be. There is nothing here that is incompatible with determinism as such, as opposed to providential determinism."[57] Alexander rejects not only Chrysippus's notion that Laius is responsible for his actions, but also his belief that the causal nexus, if it exists, is a benign one!

Alexander's presentation of Chrysippus's view is unsympathetic,[58] but revealing: divine foreknowledge of human affairs and the practice of divination are rejected as incompatible with praise or blame, yet Alexander stops short of condemning either. In fact, he presents the Stoic view as fundamentally impious: the idea that a superhuman being may deliver an oracle as part of a causal chain that leads to terrible ruin is so offensive that the mere implication of its possibility disqualifies the entire argument. Alexander does not elaborate here on his precise beliefs regarding what the gods do foreknow,[59] but we may gather that even if he follows the 'classic' Aristotelian view that God is not involved in the sublunary realm, he believes piety regarding the gods' benevolence and providence to be good, and worth defending. As much is confirmed by his treatise *On Providence* (preserved only in Arabic), where Alexander vehe-

---

56   Alex. Aphr. *Fat.* 31, text Bruns, 202.25–203.12 in Sharples, 205, tr. Sharples, 82–83, modified.

57   Sharples, "Commentary: Alexander," 166; similarly Magris, *L'idea di destino*, 2:603–604; Michalewski, "Faut-il préférer," 134–135; cf. D. Frede, who charges Sharples with having neglected this question ("Could Paris," 291–292). Other ancient commentators also observed that Apollo utters the oracle to Laius, knowing perfectly well that that the mortal will not heed the warning (Epict. *Diatr.* 3.1.16; Max. Tyr. *Or.* 13.5; cf. also Oenomaeus, *apud* Euseb. *Praep. ev.* 6.7.36; generally, see Sharples, op. cit.; idem, "Stoic Background," 184–185; Benjamins, *Eingeordnete Freiheit*, 49; and Bobzien, *Determinism and Freedom*, 178; cf. O'Brien, *Demiurge*, 132; idem, "Prayer in Maximus," 68). The problem bothers Magris so much that he wonders whether Chrysippus—otherwise an optimist regarding the gods' activity—actually believed his own interpretation of the Oracle to Laius (op. cit., 2:531).

58   Sharples, "Stoic Background," 186; D. Frede, "Could Paris," 290.

59   A vexing problem; the *crux interpretationis* is *Fat.* 30. Some argue that Alexander here indicates that he thinks the gods to have knowledge of conditionals as such (i.e., neither true nor false)—thus Sharples, "Commentary: Alexander," 165, followed by Benjamins, *Eingeordnete Freiheit*, 37. Schallenberg seems to indicate as much by virtue of referring to this passage alongside Cic. *Div.* 2.15–18 (*Freiheit*, 208 n. 385). See further Alex. Aphr. *Prov.* 65.9–67.13, discussed in Sharples, "Aristotelian Theology," 30. Mignucci suggests rather that Alexander means that the gods have knowledge of propositions about individuals which do not change their truth values, but not knowledge of propositions whose truth values change ("Logic and Omniscience," 232–234).

DID GOD KNOW ALL ALONG? 207

mently rejects the notion that the gods do not exercise providential care over worldly affairs and turns to the 'household argument'—but a version of the 'household argument' where the gods strictly attend to greater matters (i.e., universals), not particulars, for it would be beneath the dignity of the master of the house to attend to the mice and ants that live in it.[60] Alexander does not deviate here from Aristotle's insulation of the divine from the sublunary realm, but appropriates the 'household argument' in an attempt to formulate a Peripatetic view that is in keeping with at least the rhetoric of public piety. While Alexander and Cicero have distinctive views on divine foreknowledge and the efficacy of divination, they agree on the importance of at least the appearance of civic devotion. Alexander's opening dedication to the emperors in *On Fate* reminds us that the context for such arguments about piety could be very immediate: on the one hand, he takes the providential beneficence of his patrons to be beyond question; on the other, he reminds them that he merits this beneficence.

A different problematic emerges in a third witness to the 'Oracle to Laius,' the *Handbook of Platonism* (*Didaskalikos tōn Platōnos Dogmatōn*), whose author is given in its manuscripts as one 'Alcinous,' otherwise entirely unknown. It is a systematizing introduction to the philosophy of Plato, but one that presupposes such a high degree of familiarity with Greek philosophy on the part of its reader(s) that it is probably meant as a manual for teachers or learned amateurs, rather than beginners;[61] an audience of Roman elites, in any case. While nothing of the date or location of the composition of the *Handbook* is known, its content fits comfortably with what is commonly termed the Middle Platonism of the second and third centuries CE, prior to the *floruit* of Plotinus.[62] The *Handbook* presents philosophy as comprised, in a popular paradigm, of three parts: logic, physics, and ethics. In a chapter bridging physics and ethics, Alcinous presents an abbreviated account of the Middle Platonist doctrine of 'conditional fate' elaborated with much more detail by Pseudo-Plutarch in his *On Fate* (see above, chapter one). After stating that according to Plato, all things are encompassed by fate but not all things are fated, and that fate is a law which sets consequences for the choices made by souls, Alcinous illustrates this model by way of two examples: (*a*) it was fated that if Paris steals Helen, the Greeks will

---

60 The household argument: Alex. Aphr. *Prov.* 5.6–7.13 (text Ruland); God does not attend to small matters: ibid., 25.1–18, per the discussion of Adamson, "State of Nature," 85–88; similarly Magris, *L'idea di destino*, 2:668; Sharples, "Threefold Providence," 121–122; idem, "Aristotelian Theology," 36.

61 J.M. Dillon, "Introduction," xiv–xv.

62 J.M. Dillon, "Introduction," ix–xiii. One still occasionally sees the work attributed to Albinus in the secondary literature (e.g. Benjamins, *Eingeordnete Freiheit*, 41; G. Smith, "Irenaeus," 110–111).

208   CHAPTER 5

go to war over her;[63] (b) Apollo told Laius, "if you beget a son, that offspring will kill you."[64] "Here, in the oracle," Alcinous writes, "Laius and his begetting a son are taken as premises, and the consequence is fated (*katheimartai*)."[65] The following discussion elaborates the problem of the truth-value of future events in terms resembling those of Pseudo-Plutarch.

Most scholarly commentary on this passage has focused on exegesis on Alcinous's use of the 'Oracle to Laius' to explain the doctrine of conditional fate,[66] yet as Sharples astutely notes, the oracle does not actually fit this doctrine very well. The doctrine illustrates general conditions and consequences that follow from a soul's choices made prior to incarnation, as described by Plato in the Myth of Er ("the responsibility lies with the one who chooses; God has none"):[67] "fate consists," writes Alcinous, "rather in the fact that if a soul chooses a given type of life and performs such-and-such actions, such-and-such consequences will follow."[68] "What general rule, exactly," Sharples asks, "is the conditional oracle meant to express? Under what circumstances does having a child, generally speaking, inevitably lead to the child killing its father? The destiny that Apollo laid upon Laius was not indeed an arbitrary whim; it was a punishment for Laius's rape of—interestingly enough—a boy who in the myth was named *Chrysippus*."[69] The Laius oracle assumes a god whose interest in human matters is so specific that it must exercise providence over particulars, not only universal laws—a god like the God of the Stoic philosopher Chrysippus.

---

63   For the example of Paris, see also Alex. Aphr. *Fat.* 17; Whittaker, "Notes," 134. Cf. Calc. *Comm. Tim.* 154, on Achilles.

64   This line is a quote of Euripides's *Phoenician Women*. Use of the quote in testimony about the 'Oracle to Laius' is found only in Origen and Middle Platonic writers (Sharples, "Commentary: Cicero," 180); Barnes stretches in taking Origen's use of the quote as proof that his source was not just any Stoic, but Chrysippus himself ("Cicero's *de fato*," 506).

65   Alc. *Epit.* 26.2, text Whittaker, 52, tr. J.M. Dillon, 35.

66   Koch, *Pronoia*, 286–287; Theiler, "Tacitus," 63; Chadwick, "Origen, Celsus," 46 n. 2; Barnes, "Cicero's *de fato*," 505 n. 24; Magris, *L'idea di destino*, 2:577–578; Alt, *Weltflucht*, 152–153; Whittaker, "Notes," 134; J.M. Dillon, "Commentary," 162; Blank, "Commentary," 123–124 n. 39; Benjamins, *Eingeordnete Freiheit*, 42–43, 91 n. 74; Bobzien, *Determinism and Freedom*, 179 n. 84; Boys-Stones, "'Middle' Platonists on Fate," 431–432; Sharples, "Stoic Background," 173–174; Opsomer, "Middle Platonic Doctrine," 148 n. 48; Bonazzi, "Middle Platonists," 285–286. Other discussions of the 'Oracle to Laius' in the context of conditional fate include Calc. *Comm. Tim.* 153; Lucian, *Iuppiter confutatus*, 13; Euseb. *Praep. ev.* 4.3.12; Max. Tyr. *Or.* 13.5.

67   Plat. *Resp.* x 617d–e, tr. Grube, rev. Reeve, in Cooper, ed., *Plato: Complete Works*, 1220, slightly modified.

68   Alc. *Epit.* 26.1, tr. J.M. Dillon, 35. See also Plut. [*Fat.*] 570a; Calc. *Comm. Tim.* 143–144, 147; further above, chapter one.

69   Sharples, "Stoic Background," 174, italics his.

DID GOD KNOW ALL ALONG? 209

Sharples wonders if Alcinous's recourse to the 'Oracle to Laius' and its (ostensibly) determinist God indicates that the Middle Platonists were compatibilists after all,[70] but Alcinous's use of Platonic proof-texts referring to the soul's choices prior to embodiment may indicate otherwise (see further below, chapter six). In fact, Alcinous explicitly excludes God (the "Father") from direct involvement in anything, for the first principle is transcendent and ineffable, only possible to conceive by way of analogies and abstractions; it is intellect (*nous*) that, "set in order by the Father, itself imposes order on all of nature in this world."[71] A later chapter of the *Handbook* describes the *daimones* as operative in prophecy: "the whole sublunary and terrestrial sphere has been assigned to their administration (*hupotetaktai*) ... From them derive portents, ominous sounds, dreams, oracles, and all divinatory practice conducted by mortals."[72] To use Pseudo-Plutarch's terminology, it is 'secondary and tertiary providence'—the provenance of necessity and *daimones*, respectively—that are at work here, in the realm of human affairs.[73] Public cult and the human art of divination are not discussed on their own in the *Handbook*, but they are presupposed—as is the providential administration in which its *daimones* play a crucial role. In the *Handbook*, Alcinous invokes the 'Oracle to Laius' not only to illustrate the general laws administered by conditional fate, but that individual human affairs are under the administration of *daimones* like Apollo, who will present human beings with praise or blame, in accordance with their actions.

Despite the diversity of positions on divine foreknowledge and the truth-value of future conditionals taken by Cicero, Alexander, and Alcinous, their arguments about these positions revolve around and even derive their importance from the presupposition of the providential character of the divine and worldly administrations and the cultic life which serves as an integral part of them, not least in civic institutions of divination. This bond between the 'Oracle to Laius' and the ethical character of the divine order was nothing new in the first centuries CE: already in Sophocles's *Oedipus Rex* (fifth century BCE), the Chorus laments the possibility that the oracle's prophecy could be avoided and therefore false; thus their final line, "the divine is dis-

---

70   Sharples, "Stoic Background," 179, 187.

71   Alc. *Epit.* 10.3, tr. J.M. Dillon, 18. For Alcinous's *via negativa*, see *Epit.* 10.3–6; discussions include e.g. J.M. Dillon, "Commentary," 107–111; Burns, "Apophatic Strategies," 168–169, with bibliography.

72   ... *hōn klēdones kai otteiai kai oneirata kai chrēsmoi kai hosa kata manteian hupo thnētōn techniteuetai* (Alc. *Epit.* 15.1–2, text Whittaker, 35, tr. J.M. Dillon, 25, modified).

73   For Middle Platonic notions of *daimones* operative in divination, see above, chapter two (re: Plutarch); further, Apul. *Deo Socr.* 133–137; Alc. *Epit.* 15.2; Max. Tyr. *Or.* 8.8; Calc. *Comm. Tim.* 255; all cit. Timotin, *Démonologie platonicienne*, 282.

210   CHAPTER 5

appearing!" The play is resolved with the 'good news' that, on the contrary, "this"—Oedipus's entire ordeal—"was Apollo!"[74] When Alexander wrote *On Fate* roughly six hundred years later, the oracle at Delphi had faded, but *pronoia* still lived opposite Apollo's temple—not only as Athena *pro naou*, but as the *providentia* of Rome's civic institutions, which these philosophers sought to defend.

5   Origen's Oracles to Laius—and David, against Marcion

Finally, we may return to chapters twelve and thirteen of *On Fate*, a passage drawn from Origen's late work *Against Celsus*, where he, too, discusses the 'Oracle to Laius.' While the *Commentary on Genesis* and *Against Celsus* comprise bookends to Origen's literary career, the principle invoked in his arguments about the causality of divine foreknowledge is the same in each work: it is the future event that causes God to foreknow it, rather than God's foreknowledge which causes the future event. This unity of argumentation helps explain why the relevant excerpt from the latter was brought in to supplement the excerpt from the former in *On Fate*. However, modern scholars looking at these arguments have reached variant conclusions as to what they mean and against whom they were directed, which has led to a fundamental misunderstanding of what was at stake for Origen in these passages. The present discussion will first outline the argument given in *Against Celsus* (and excerpted in *On Fate*), before turning to its rhetorical context, as well as that of the *Commentary on Genesis*. While determinism is at issue in the *Commentary*, it is not the only issue; rather, it shares with *Celsus* a different concern: the providential character of prophecy, a question over which the spectre of Marcion loomed, explaining why the *Commentary* brought up Marcionite exegesis in the first place.

According to Origen, Celsus charged that God, having foreknowledge of Judas's betrayal of Christ, is Himself responsible for this betrayal: "being a god he foretold these events, so it was altogether necessary (*pantōs echrēn*) that what he foretold come to pass. A god, therefore, led his own disciples and prophets with whom he used to eat and drink so far astray that they became impious and wicked ..."[75] The upshot of Celsus's argument is that a god whose prophecies lead people to do bad things can only be wicked, and therefore

---

74   Lines 898–910, 1329, respectively—so Burkert, "Signs," 36.
75   Orig. *Cels.* 2.20, text Borret in SC 132:336, tr. Chadwick, 84, modified.

DID GOD KNOW ALL ALONG? 211

Christian myth is impious. Origen responds to Celsus by repeating the same principle he had outlined on this subject years before, in the *Commentary on Genesis*, namely that "the one who prophesies is not the cause of the future event because he foretold that it would happen; rather, the future event— which is going to happen even if it has not been prophesied—constitutes the cause of the foreknowing of the person who foretells it."[76] Celsus, he avers, is trying to use the 'lazy argument,' an argument which may be refuted with reference to this principle of the causal efficacy of the future event's truth.

Origen then adds two examples of the principle at work, one with reference to "divine scriptures," the other to "Greek stories." Christ the *logos*, singing through David the Psalmist (Ps 108), "foreknew that Judas would betray the Savior, so also he [David] implies that he [Judas] was responsible for the betrayal and deserved the curses uttered in the prophecy on account of his wickedness."[77] "And addressing Greeks," he continues,

> we will use the utterance to Laius which goes as follows, whether these are the actual words of the oracle, or words to the same effect composed by the tragedian. This is what was said to him by the one who had foreknowledge of the future:
>
> *Sow no furrow of offspring against the will of the gods,*
> *For if thou dost produce a child, thy offspring shall slay thee,*
> *And thy house entire shall come to bloodshed.*
>
> Here too, then, it is clearly shown that it was possible for Laius not to sow "a furrow of offspring," for the oracle would not give him an impossible command; yet it was also possible for him to have children. Neither of these alternatives was determined (*oudeteron autōn katēnagkasto*).[78]

Finally, Origen explains the structure of the 'lazy argument' in terms very close to those of Cicero in *On Fate*.[79] Celsus is wrong, he maintains, that it "was altogether necessary (*pantōs echrēn*) that what [the *logos* in Psalm 108] foretold come to pass" if 'altogether (*pantōs*)' means 'deterministically (*katēnagkasmenōs*)':

---

76   Orig. *Cels.* 2.20, text Borret in SC 132:336, tr. Chadwick, 85, modified.

77   Orig. *Cels.* 2.20, tr. Chadwick, 85, gloss mine.

78   Orig. *Cels.* 2.20, text Borret in SC 132:340, tr. Chadwick, 85–86, modified.

79   Jonathan Barnes has argued that the language is so similar that Origen must here preserve for us Chrysippus's own Greek *ipsissima verba*, which Cicero had rendered into Latin in *Fat.* 28–29 ("Cicero's *de fato*," esp. 502–507). Bobzien is skeptical, for good reason (*Determinism and Freedom*, 207–208).

For it was also possible for it not to happen. But if by 'altogether' he means simply that 'it will come to pass' (and nothing prevents that from being true, even if it is possible for it not to happen), then it doesn't affect my argument. For it does not follow from the fact that Jesus correctly predicted the actions of the traitor and the one who denied him, that he was the cause of their impiety and wicked conduct. For he saw his wicked state of mind, knowing—according to our Scriptures—"what was in each person" (John 2:25), and seeing whatever one will venture to do ...[80]

As noted above, the principle Origen outlines in response to critiques of divine foreknowledge in the *Commentary on Genesis* and *Against Celsus* is clear: it is not God's foreknowledge of future misbehavior which causes said misbehavior; rather, the future misbehavior—for which the misbehaving one alone is responsible—causes God's foreknowledge of it. However, there is less scholarly agreement about whom Origen wrote against, and why. Interpreters focusing on the *Commentary* have understood Origen to here challenge Academic Skeptics or Middle Platonists, who would have deemed divine foreknowledge of future events and human responsibility to be incompatible.[81] Meanwhile, historians of philosophy have focused on the 'Oracle to Laius' in *Celsus* in hopes of better reconstructing Chrysippus's response to the 'lazy argument,' coming to impressively divergent conclusions about Origen's sources.[82] Significantly, none of these interpreters of Origen's presentation of the 'Oracle to Laius' take up the parallel argument in the *Commentary* nor the example of Judas, which provides the occasion in *On Fate* for the discussion of the Laius legend in the first place.

A closer look at the rhetorical contexts of both the discussion of Judas in the *Commentary on Genesis* and the 'Oracle to Laius' in *Against Celsus* shows that in

---

80   Orig. *Cels.* 2.20, text Borret in SC 132:342, 344, tr. Chadwick, 87, modified.

81   See Junod in SC 226:152 n. 1 and Benjamins, *Eingeordnete Freiheit*, 82 n. 63, respectively; see also Boys-Stones, "Human Autonomy," 490–491.

82   (*a*) Origen quotes Chrysippus, in agreement with him: Jackson, "Sources," 20; Barnes, "Cicero's *de fato*"; (*b*) the argument is Stoic, but not necessarily Chrysippus: thus von Arnim's inclusion of *Cels.* 2.20 without attribution to any particular Stoic (SVF 2:957; notably, the passage is not included in LS); (*c*) Origen draws on Carneades: Chadwick, "Origen, Celsus," 35; (*d*) Origen "invokes the Platonic hypothetical-fate argument": Gibbons, "Human Autonomy," 688; Bobzien regards Origen as having (*e*) no distinct position at all, rather being "entirely neutral as regards the—notable—differences between Stoic and Middle Platonic fate doctrine" (*Determinism and Freedom*, 208). Craig does not address the question of Origen's sources, nor the rhetorical context of the passage beyond the confrontation with Celsus himself (*Problem*, 59, 80–81).

DID GOD KNOW ALL ALONG? 213

both, Origen is concerned not just with determinism, but the providential character of prophecy.[83] As noted earlier in this chapter, Origen in the *Commentary* addresses unnamed individuals whose belief in the power of the stars leads them to claim that astral fate is ruled a lower, "just" god, opposed to "another good God who is the source of no (evils)" who is "good."[84] This opposition of the 'good' and 'just' gods recalls Marcion's followers. Yet the problem is not any 'deterministic' character to Marcionite dualism, but the implications of a philosophical exegesis of stories of divine prophecy of evil deeds. As we saw in the previous section, this problem was flagged by Alexander of Aphrodisias, for whom the Stoic reading of the 'Oracle to Laius' is impious because it implies Apollo's malevolence. Origen does not accuse Marcionites of being determinists; rather, he seeks to counter their reading of Scripture wherein some prophecies act in causal chains that lead to evil, and so may imply that the prophesying deity is not benevolent.

God's foreknowledge as portrayed in Jewish Scripture was a primary target of Marcionite and Gnostic exegesis alike. As Judith Lieu writes, Marcion's concern was that "if humanity was created in the image of the Creator, then the Creator models human behaviour"—and given how poorly humans behave, we are presented with a poor Creator indeed in Gen 1:26–27 and 2:7.[85] According to Tertullian, Marcion asked why God, if He has "foreknowledge of the future (*praescius futuri*)," would allow Adam to fall?—therefore, the deity of Genesis is neither fore-knowing nor good.[86] As Nils Arne Pedersen has argued, Marcion's later followers continued to make such arguments, according to fourth-century witnesses such as Titus of Bostra, Ephraem Syrus, or St. Jerome.[87] Marcion's disciple Apelles also appears to have used some version of this proof, in fragments quoted by Ambrose.[88] The 'Gnostic' Justin known to the early third-century

---

83   Cf. D. Frede's remark ("Could Paris," 292), in a review of Sharples's edition of Alex. Aphr. *Fat.*, that "as a child I always felt sorry for Judas. After all, he had to do it, hadn't he?"

84   Orig. *Philoc.* 23.2, tr. Trigg, *Origen*, 88.

85   Lieu, *Marcion*, 343.

86   Ter. *Marc.* 2.5.1, text and tr. Evans, 96–97; see Lieu, *Marcion*, 341.

87   Pedersen, *Demonstrative Proof*, 199–200.

88   Ambrose, *On Paradise*, 8.38, tr. Savage, 315–316, cit. Pedersen, *Demonstrative Proof*, 221–223: Another problem. Did God know that Adam would violate His commands? Or was He unaware of it? If He did not know, we are faced with a limitation of His divine power. If He knew, yet gave a command which He was aware would be ignored, it is not God's providence to give an unnecessary order. It was in the nature of a superfluous act to give to Adam, the first created being, a command which He knew would not at all be observed. But God does nothing superfluous. Therefore, the words of Scripture do not come from God. This is the objection of those who do not, by interposing these questions, admit the authenticity of the Old Testament ... The following example should

214   CHAPTER 5

author of the *Refutation of All Heresies* states that the first principle is "fore-knowing of the wholes" (*prognōstos tōn holōn*), while the male and female creator-deities "are bereft of foreknowledge (*aprognōstos*)."[89]

Finally, God's ignorance of the whereabouts of Adam in the Garden of Eden (Gen 3:9) is highlighted in several Gnostic treatises from Nag Hammadi, such as the *Testimony of Truth*:

> Of what sort is he, this God? [Now], first of all, [he was] jealous (*af*ᶜ*rphtho-nei*) of Adam, insofar as he ate from the Tree of Knowledge; and second, he said, "Adam, where are you?" For God did not have foreknowledge (*pro⟨g⟩nōsis*), that is to say, he did not know from the start (what would happen) ... And if he has showed himself to be an envious malefactor, and he is a god, of what sort is he? Indeed, great is the blindness of those who read (this story) and did not understand it![90]

While Pedersen has argued that the Coptic Gnostic works which highlight the ignorance of the creator are "not connected with the theodicy problem in the same way as the Marcionite arguments above," this is misleading. As Chrysippus, Cicero, Alexander, and Alcinous recognized, the gods' foreknowledge was intimately bound to their dispensation; that is part of what makes their administration providential.[91] In the Gnostic myths, the lack of fore-

---

convince them that a command to one who will disobey is not something superfluous or unjust. The Lord Himself chose Judas, one who, He knew, would betray Him. If these men think that he was chosen unwisely, they restrict the power of God. But they cannot hold this opinion, since Scripture declares: *'For Jesus knew who it was who should betray him.'* [John 6:65] These defamers of the Old Testament should therefore hold their peace.

Amusingly, Epiphanius turns the argument around on Apelles: the Marcionite's first God would not be worthy of the name, because He evidently did not have had foreknowledge that the demiurge's creation would be faulty, or that the fiery angel would trap divine souls in flesh (*Pan.* 44.1.7–9, 44.5.6).

89   *Ref.* 10.15, text in Litwa, 722, tr. mine; see also Williams, *Rethinking "Gnosticism"*, 18–19.

90   *Testimony of Truth* NHC IX 47.14–48,4, text in Mahé, *Le Témoignage Véritable*, 112, tr. mine. On this passage, see also Pedersen, *Demonstrative Proof*, 212–214. For the Chief Archon as ignorant of Adam and Eve's whereabouts, see also *Nat. Rul.* NHC II 90.19–31. For subordinate archons as ignorant of Adam and Eve's whereabouts, see *Orig. World* NHC II 119.23–120.5. Cf. also the inability of the demiurge or his archons to recognize the voice from heaven responding to their boasts of sovereignty: Ir. *Haer.* 1.30.6; *Ap. John* NHC II 14.13–15.14; *Orig. World* NHC II 112.29–113.20, discussed above, chapter four.

91   *Pace* Pedersen's claim that "in the Marcionite (and in general the Christian) context(-s) the concept of 'Providence' acquired other meanings than at any rate in philosophical systems such as Stoicism and Platonism: the problem had to do with a personal God's

DID GOD KNOW ALL ALONG? 215

knowledge exhibited by the demiurge and his archons in their creation of the
world pose a striking contrast to the *pronoia* that intervenes in the creation of
human beings, as discussed in chapter four.[92]

At last, we are in a position to say why Origen brings up Marcionite exegesis in the third book of the *Commentary on Genesis*, purportedly dedicated to
combatting astrological determinism, and why he devotes ten chapters to it.
The reason is that, as Alexander of Aphrodisias, Marcion, and the *Testimony of
Truth* all stress, the benevolent care (*pronoia*) of the gods was always at stake
in discussions of the gods' foreknowledge (*prognōsis*) of human affairs. Origen
wishes to refute astrological determinism but not biblical prophecy, and the
importance of prophecy in Scripture raised exegetical questions about how
prophecy worked and its implications for God's character. Origen does not
want cede any ground to the Marcionites, and so attempts to defend God's
foreknowing quality by explaining how foreknowledge could be benevolent
and providential. Keeping the anti-Marcionite aims of Origen's argument from
the *Commentary* in mind, we may then in turn better understand his use
of the same argument decades later against a heathen critic. Celsus did not
only argue that scenes of biblical prophecy fall victim to the 'lazy argument';
he impugned the providential character the God of the Prophets, hoping to
paint the god of the Christians as wicked and therefore unworthy of the title
'god.' While the aims of Origen's opponents were thus very distinct, in both
cases, Origen employs the same innovative maneuver—the argument that
foreknowledge of something is not tantamount to responsibility for it, and this
is the case with God's foreknowledge of Judas's betrayal—for the same end:

---

foreknowledge, while the systems mentioned did not envisage a personal God, and therefore understood *pronoia* as a mechanism and not as God's caring, saving power in the life
of the individual" (*Demonstrative Proof*, 220–221 n. 91).

92   Another Nag Hammadi text, the Valentinian *Tripartite Tractate* (NHC I,5), struck a more
conciliatory pose regarding the demiurge's character, and this is also the case in its reading
of the demiurge's foreknowledge:

Thus, the Word used this one (i.e., the demiurge) like a hand to fashion and craft
what was below; and he used him like a mouth to say what would be prophesied.
As for the things which he said and did, when he saw that they are great and good
and wondrous, he celebrated himself and became [joyous, as] if it were he, from his
own thoughts, who had said and done them, ignorant (*efoei ᵉnatsaune*) that the movement in him derived from the Spirit who moved him through a predetermination of
what he wants (*hᵉnn outōše anetᵉfouašou*). (*Tri. Trac.* 100.30–101.5, text in Thomassen
and Painchaud, "Texte," 111, 113, tr. mine, with reference to that of P. Nagel, *Tractatus*,
39)

Cf. Also *Tri. Trac.* NHC I 113.5–35, on the Prophets' garbling of the Word's communication
of future events, including the time and manner of the Savior's advent.

216   CHAPTER 5

to preserve the providential, benevolent character of the foreknowing God as portrayed in Scripture.[93]

6   Conclusions: 'The Book of Heaven'

In his discussion of the 'Oracle of Laius' in *Against Celsus*, Origen explicitly claims that God has knowledge of future conditionals: the course of events is unalterable and God has foreknowledge of it, but the 'lazy argument' does not apply because what will happen is not the only thing that could happen.[94] Carneades, meanwhile, rejects the notion of divine foreknowledge of undetermined events.[95] We have no knowledge of what Chrysippus or other Stoic philosophers would have made of Origen's position, but it is worth considering the possibility that they would have agreed with it, since both Chrysippus and Origen agree that prophesied future events may be true without being necessary, and that what is fated is unalterable.[96]

Yet while Origen illustrates the argument by recourse to the 'Oracle to Laius' for a superficially similar reason as did Chrysippus—to refute the *argos logos*— he does not exactly adopt a 'Stoic' position either. Firstly, the mechanics by which divine foreknowledge operates are quite different. If Nemesius's testimony is accurate, the Stoa held that the gods knew what would happen because they had experienced it all already, in the infinite, unalterable loop of recurring universes. Origen, on the other hand, argued that God knows what would happen because he agreed with Christian writers as diverse as Justin Martyr, Irenaeus, Clement of Alexandria, and the author of the *Teachings of Silvanus* in taking it as given from Scripture that God is omniscient.[97] Such a position

---

93   Chadwick seems to have grasped this, as indicated by his note to *Cels.* 2.20 referring to Jerome's attack on Marcionite criticism of prophecy (*Contra Celsus*, 84, n. 3).

94   Origen elaborates the same point in *Comm. Rom.* 1.3 (for the Greek, see *Philoc.* 25.2); for discussion, see Junod in SC 226:72–93, esp. 74; Benjamins, *Eingeordnete Freiheit*, 91 n. 77, 95 n. 85.

95   Thus Sharples, "Commentary: Cicero," 196.

96   Recognized by Bobzien, *Determinism and Freedom*, 207; without caution, Magris, *L'idea di destino*, 2:837.

97   Justin: *1 Apol.* 28, (on God's foreknowledge of who will convert to Christianity), 44 (foreknowledge of each person's deeds and their just desserts); *Dial.* 141 (on foreknowledge of the angels' sins). Irenaeus: *Haer.* 3.16.7, on passages in the Gospel where Jesus appears to foreknow the future. See also Min. Fel. *Oct.* 36.2; Clem. Al. *Strom.* 1.17.81.4–5 (re: Prov 9:3–5), 2.12.54, 2.13.56.2, 6.17.158.4. Cf. also Acts 2:23, where Peter, addressing the crowd of Jews on Pentecost, declares that Jesus was "handed over" through the "foreknowledge of god (*prognōsei tou theou*)" to be crucified (Braun, *Deus Christianorum*, 133). A particularly

DID GOD KNOW ALL ALONG? 217

was argued already in the first century CE, explicitly, on multiple occasions, by Philo of Alexandria, who claimed that God is "beholding distant events, and seeing the future no less than the present."[98] In a striking passage from *On the Unchangeableness of God*, he boldly states God's absolute knowledge of all events, including what appear to be contingents (human decisions and future events), on grounds on His eternal nature:

> For one cannot foresee the course of future events, or the judgments of others, but to God all things are manifest, as in pure sunlight. For already He has penetrated the recesses of our souls, and what is invisible to others

strong example presents itself in the *Teachings of Silvanus*, a (non-Gnostic) Nag Hammadi text:

> For God does not need to test any person. He knows all things before they happen, and He knows what is hidden, belonging to the heart. Rather, they are all revealed and found wanting in his presence. Let no one ever say [that] God is ignorant, for it is not right to throw the craftsman of all creation into ignorance. Furthermore, things that are in darkness are before him, in the manner of light; for no thing is hidden, except God alone. (*Teachings of Silvanus*, NHC VII 1[1]5.36–116.13, text Peel, 362, tr. mine)

The date of the Greek *Vorlage* to this work remains contested; van den Broek has stressed the possibility of the compilation of the Coptic version we possess in the 320s or 330s CE ("Theology"). Notably, Augustine would defend the notion of God's foreknowledge against Cicero's rejection of it in *Fat*. (*City of God* 5.9, per Schallenberg, *Freiheit*, 208 n. 385).

Boys-Stones is somewhat misleading in highlighting Origen's statement at *Princ*. 3.5.2 that God's knowledge is finite ("Human Autonomy," 494), since the same passage also affirms God's knowledge of everything, i.e., omniscience—i.e., the finitude of divine knowledge is incumbent on the finite nature of things to know, rather than God's powers, which are without limit (even more clearly stated at *Philoc*. 23.20, quoted below, in this chapter). Thence Gibbons's mistaken claim that God's instructive punishments of mortals could "fail" because God ostensibly would not know in advance if His punishments would work, as Gibbons takes Boys-Stones to imply (Gibbons, "Human Autonomy," 688), even though Origen explicitly states the contrary (*Philoc*. 23.4–5, 23.8, 23.20; *Princ*. 3.5.2; see also Koch, *Pronoia*, 113–114, 288).

The present framing of the issue differs from that of Benjamins, for whom Origen adopts a position "zwischen dem 'stoisch-peripatetischen' und dem 'neuplatonischen' Paradigma," since he locates the truth of the fore-known event in question in its future occurrence rather than as caused in the past. Thus, according to Benjamins, Origen arrives at a similar conclusion as the Neoplatonists while framing the question in Stoic-Peripatetic terms, namely the status of the object, not subject, of knowledge (*Eingeordnete Freiheit*, 93–96, followed by Jacobsen, "Freedom," 74–75). For discussion of the issues at work from the approach of modern philosophy of religion, see Boyd, "Two Ancient"; also Craig, *Problem*, 59–60, 80–82.

98   Philo, *Ios*. 236, tr. Colson in LCL 289:255.

is clear as daylight to His eyes, for he employs forethought and foreknowledge (*promētheiai kai pronoiai chrōmenos*)—qualities unique to Him—and permits nothing to run wild or happen outside His comprehension. For not even about the future can uncertainty be found with Him, since nothing is uncertain or future to God ... Future events lie shrouded in the darkness of time that is yet to be at different distances, some near, some far. But God is the maker of time also ...[99]

This deity exceeds even the determinist God of the Stoa insofar as He experiences both past and future as the present—a position explaining divine foreknowledge which would only be taken up again five hundred years later, by Augustine and Boethius.[100] Meanwhile, the belief that the gods have foreknowledge even of future conditionals is a position that would be assumed in later 'pagan' philosophy again by the Neoplatonists; the only exponent of this view in ancient philosophy prior to the end of the third century (Iamblichus and perhaps Porphyry) besides Philo is Origen. This point will be belabored in greater detail below (chapter seven), but the grounds for this shift may not simply be a question of innovation in Neoplatonism after Plotinus.

Secondly, the entire framework for the divinatory practices in which divine foreknowledge functions is radically different for Origen than it was for the thinkers surveyed in the previous sections, because Origen theorizes a Christian cult which operates independently of Roman civic cult and its own divinatory practices. Chrysippus, Cicero, Alexander, and Alcinous address the problem of divine foreknowledge from a variety of perspectives, but always with the question of the legitimacy of civic divinatory practices in mind. Origen is concerned with legitimacy, too—but with respect to the correct interpretation of Scripture, as his engagement with Marcionites in the *Commentary on Genesis* makes clear. In a Roman cultic context, Origen's move amounts to a trading out of civic, sacrificial divinatory practices for belief in the inerrancy of biblical prophecy (as interpreted 'correctly' by the philosophically sophisticated exegete, of course).[101] Origen's adaptation of the 'Oracle to Laius' to explore

---

99 Philo, *Deus* 29–31, text and tr. Colson and Whitaker in LCL 247:24–25, significantly modified.

100 Aug. *Conf.* 11.31; Boeth. *Cons.* 5.6.15–43; see further Craig, *Problem*, 73–80, 96–97; Sharples, "Introduction: Cicero," 27, n. 4; idem, Sharples, "Commentary: Cicero," 227–230. As Boys-Stones notes, the principle animating divine foreknowledge here—God's transcendence of time—is distinct from that discussed by Origen ("Human Autonomy," 494, n. 19).

101 Perrone, "Ἴχνος ἐνθουσιασμοῦ," 326, re: *Hom. Jer.* 15.1, and Bammel, "Origen's Definitions," 493; more generally, Boys-Stones "Human Autonomy," 496–498.

DID GOD KNOW ALL ALONG? 219

exegetical questions regarding biblical prophecy thus foreshadows the rise of 'Bible-centered' divinatory practices in later fourth century CE, such as bibliomancy.[102]

All three of these points—the defense of divine foreknowledge as providential and benevolent, the reach of such foreknowledge as unlimited and thus beyond what we know to have been stated by Stoic and Platonist contemporaries, and the 'relocation' of the nexus of divination from Roman civic institutions to biblical prophecy—are woven together by Origen in the remainder of *On Fate*. Following the insertion of the discussion of the 'Oracle to Laius' in chapters 12–13, *On Fate* picks up once more the *Commentary on Genesis*. These chapters (fourteen through twenty-one) also deal with divine foreknowledge, but as related to the practice of astrology, featuring Origen's famous argument that the stars are not agents, but signs that indicate future events without necessarily causing them. This view was articulated in similar terms by Plotinus and the passage was taken up by Eusebius, and so these chapters from the *Commentary on Genesis* are usually discussed with regards to the contexts of the possibility of Origen's relationship with Plotinus, and the doxography of ancient arguments against astrology.[103] Yet Origen hardly abandons the arguments he has pursued thus far in the *Commentary on Genesis* regarding the character and medium of divine foreknowledge.[104]

Origen marshals three arguments for his belief that the stars are signs (not causes), and against astrological practice as he understood it. First, targeting the notion that a horoscope can relate information regarding the circum-

---

102   The earliest testimony of bibliomancy known to me is Aug. *Conf.* 8.12; idem, *Epistle* 55.20, discussed by Graf, "Rolling the Dice," 52 n. 8; Karanika, "Homer the Prophet," 265; Wiśniewski, "Pagans, Jews, Christians," 556, 565. On the complex relationship of bibliomancy to antecedent divinatory practices involving use of sacred texts, see Karanika, op. cit., 264–273; Wiśniewski, op. cit., esp. 567–568.

103   See Plotinus's treatise *On Fate* (*Enn.* 3.1 [3] 6), which some (Junod in SC 226:57–58, followed by Trigg, *Origen*, 86) take as evidence that the Christian Origen learned this doctrine, with Plotinus, from Ammonius Saccas. However, the notion that the stars indicate the future but do not determine it is a very common perspective in late ancient thought, hardly limited to Ammonius's circle (for index, see Junod in SC 226:58–62; Hegedus, *Early Christianity*, 330). In any case, a real difference between Origen and Plotinus on this point is that, according to the former, only superhuman beings can read the stars (*Philoc.* 23.6, 23.20–21), while the latter allows for mortals to be able to do so (Junod in SC 226:56; Trigg, *Origen*, 87; Hegedus, *Early Christianity*, 128, 331–332). For the passage in Eusebius, see *Praep. ev.* 6.11.69–70. On the stars as signs, cf. Clem. Al. *Ecl.* 55; idem, *Exc.* 70.2; cit. A. Scott, *Origen*, 105 n. 7.

104   Cf. Benjamins, who omits discussion of Orig. *Philoc.* 23.14–21 in *Eingeordnete Freiheit*, 57, n. 30.

stances of one's parents, he asks how one's past could be determined at birth; rather, he maintains, "it is as if someone should comprehend the past and future, not from the stars, but from the mind of God through a particular prophetic word"—i.e., the best guide to the past and future is not heaven, but Scripture.[105] This is not to say the stars play no role in God's revelation of what is to come: Scripture itself refers to the stars as "signs" (Gen 1:14, which is the occasion for this entire book of the *Commentary*; Jer 10:2), and the sky is like a book to be read that "shews" what is to be.[106] His second argument is that people are born into hugely diverse circumstances, but this is not, as the astrologers claim, due to the influence of the stars.[107] On the one hand, each individual's fate is tied up with the fate of countless other individuals, every one of whom has their own horoscope—an infinite regression of horoscopes. On the other hand, while astrologers associate certain characteristics with astral signs, these characteristics are derivative of cultural mores, not the stars—the so-called *nomima barbarika* argument. Most famously known from the *Book of the Laws of the Countries* (on which see below, chapter six), the *nomima barbarika* argument examines the 'barbarian (i.e., not Hellenized) customs' of nations as established by ancient ethnography. The terrific variety of customs pertaining to basic theatres of human life (food, sex, death, etc.) show that it is people and their cultures which are responsible for what transpires in these theatres, not the stars.[108] Significantly, though, Origen concludes his recitation of the *nomima barbarika* with a swipe at Roman divination: "with so many purported means of foreknowledge, I do not know how men have been so inconsistent as to admit that auguries from birds and sacrifices, even auguries from shooting stars, do not contain the efficient cause but are indications only, while making horoscopes a special case."[109] Finally, he offers arguments concerned with the technical difficulty inherent to astrology, and the concomitant inability of people to master the art.[110]

---

105 Orig. *Philoc.* 23.15, tr. Trigg, 97.

106 Orig. *Philoc.* 23.15, 20; see also A. Scott, *Origen*, 145–146, Karamanolis, *Philosophy*, 173. Cf. also his discussion of the story of the Magi (Matt 2:1–12), where God uses an astral phenomenon to signal the birth of Jesus (*Cels.* 1.58–59; Hegedus, *Early Christianity*, 330; Denzey (Lewis), "New Star," 216–217).

107 Orig. *Philoc.* 23.16. See also idem, *Princ.* 2.9.4; *Cels.* 5.27; A. Scott, *Origen*, 136.

108 Besides the BLC, the argument is extant in early Christian sources in Eus. *Praep. Ev.* 6.10.48; Clem. [*Rec.*] 9.19–29 (which is appended to the end of *Philoc.* 23). For further literature on the *nomima barbarika*, see the notes to the discussion of the BLC below, chapter six.

109 Orig. *Philoc.* 23.16, tr. Trigg, 99.

110 "I think that, if one were to pay attention to such issues, one would despair of obtaining

DID GOD KNOW ALL ALONG?

So why are the stars "for signs" at all? Origen's answer is telling:

> Believing in the greatness of the whole knowledge of the mind of God—which embraces every existing thing, so that nothing, no matter how ordinary and trivial it may be considered, escapes the notice of his divinity—includes the opinion that God's mind embraces in itself, for all practical purposes, an infinite number of things. This is not, indeed, something capable of proof, but is a corollary to our belief that God's mind is ingenerate and surpasses all of nature.[111]

"So then this book of heaven," he continues, "is understood experientially by those with superhuman abilities and by holy souls freed from the present bondage"—i.e., the Prophets.[112] Knowing everything that will happen, God wishes to demonstrate his power for propaedeutic reasons: "since Scripture says to Pharaoh: 'For this cause I have raised you up, so as to demonstrate my power to you and so that my name might be proclaimed in all the earth' (Rom 9:17)."[113] Like the figure of Pharaoh in Scripture, the stars serve as signs testifying to God's majesty.

There is a second reason, Origen maintains, that God in His omniscience set the stars as signs in heaven: so that the celestial powers working in the divine administration might use this celestial 'book' in carrying out their duties relating to His *oikonomia*. Origen opens the final chapter of the excerpt from his *Commentary* by stating that even angelic beings fail to heed these signs—and God is not the cause of that, either:

> If bad powers different from men do certain things that have been foreknown and signified in heaven, this does not necessarily mean they have done these things because they were recommended by the letters of God ... The hostile powers, granted that God knows in advance the evil of men and adverse powers who have depraved intentions, accomplish what they do out of their own most shameful choice (*tēi idiai aischistēi ... proairesi*).[114]

---

the sort of information astrologers claim because it is entirely inaccessible to men, and, even at best, does no more than provide signs" (Orig. *Philoc.* 23.19, tr. Trigg, 100).

111   Orig. *Philoc.* 23.20, tr. Trigg, 101.

112   Orig. *Philoc.* 23.20.

113   Orig. *Philoc.* 23.20.

114   Orig. *Philoc.* 23.21, text Junod in SC 223:202, tr. Trigg, 102; see also Hegedus, *Early Christianity*, 127–129; A. Scott, *Origen*, 146. On evil angels in Origen and other early Christian writers, see above, chapter three.

Throughout the entirety of the third book of the *Commentary on Genesis* as excerpted in *On Fate*, then, Origen is concerned not only to refute astrology, but to maintain notions of divine foreknowledge and benevolence in the face of dualism. In the first chapters, Marcion and his followers remain in view; at the end of the excerpt, quoted immediately above, he is concerned with the question of what kind of causal efficacy is at work in demons. Here, the compilers of the *Philocalia* felt it best to leave Origen, and finish this book *On Fate* with a set of anti-astrological arguments taken from the Pseudo-Clementine *Recognitions*.[115] At least in this slight, extant section of the *Commentary on Genesis*, Origen is not at occasion to relate the details of his beliefs regarding individual responsibility, and how it is that angels and humans alike may make shameful choices (*proaireseis*). In later works, some of whose Greek is preserved in following books of the *Philocalia*—*On First Principles*—Origen tackled just these questions and even some of these same biblical examples.

---

115 See Junod in SC 223:25–33, particularly with regard to the question of whether Origen himself or Basil and Gregory introduced the citation of Clem. [*Rec.*] 10.7–13.1 to this discussion; Junod argues persuasively for Basil.

CHAPTER 6

What We Choose Now

1 Introduction: Where Does Free Will Emerge in Ancient Philosophy?

The notion of 'free will' is not a given in the history of philosophy. Historians generally agree that philosophical discussions of a full-fledged seat of responsibility denoted 'the will' is something that emerged in the later first or second centuries CE, and which achieved particular fruition among early Christian theologians in conflict with Gnosticism, such as Justin Martyr and especially Origen.[1] Specifically, scholarly consensus is that the insistence of ancient Christian theologians on the existence of human free will had a biblical rather than a philosophical basis, but was explained in deeply Stoic terms: while there are only hints of something like a faculty of human responsibility in biblical sources,[2] these sources basically agree with the Stoa that responsibility is to be taken as compatible or at least co-existent with God's providential administration of even minute worldly affairs.[3] Early Christian philosophers such as Justin and Origen even adopted a coinage of Epictetus to denote a faculty of moral accountability: *to autexousion* (best translated as "personal responsibility" or, under certain circumstances, "free will").[4]

---

1 See variously Kahn, "Discovering Will"; Benjamins, *Eingeordnete Freiheit*, 9; Magris, *L'idea di destino*, 2:818–825; Bobzien, "Inadvertent Conception"; Müller and Pich, "Auf dem Weg"; M. Frede, *Free Will*, 1–18; and the following notes.

2 See M. Frede, *Free Will*, 103; Karamanolis, *Philosophy*, 144–145, re: Matt 26:41; Mark 14:38; Rom 7:19–24, 8:6.

3 Spanneut, *Stoicisme*, 236; further Dihle, "Philosophische Lehren"; Attridge, "Divine Sovereignty," 198. Emphasizing Stoicism are Karavites, *Evil*, 115; M. Frede, *Free Will*, esp. 89, 103; Adamson, *Philosophy*, 281.

4 On the Stoic background of *to autexousion*, see Kahn, "Discovering Will," 250–251; M. Frede, *Free Will*, 68–75. For use of the term in Justin, Tatian, and Origen, see below, in this chapter. The term achieved a Judaeo-Christian valency by Plotinus's day (Corrigan and Turner, "Commentary," 170–171). It is usually translated as 'self-determination,' which is precise but unwieldy in modern English. 'Personal responsibility' is a loose translation, but treats what is basically the same notion—a seat of praise and blame accorded to each person for their actions, which is independent of external causal forces—while remaining much closer to modern idiom. When the term is used to denote MR2 (on which, see below)—as it is by Origen—then the translation "free will" is justified.

© KONINKLIJKE BRILL NV, LEIDEN, 2020 | DOI:10.1163/9789004432994_008

224 CHAPTER 6

Yet scholarly literature on this question is rather meagre,[5] and to the extent that it has developed, any kind of consensus regarding the details of the appearance of 'free will' in ancient philosophical sources dissipates into a handful of competing theses. Primary is that of philosopher and theologian Albrecht Dihle, who in his celebrated Sather lectures contrasts the allegedly 'nominalistic' notion of human responsibility in Greek philosophical sources with the 'voluntaristic' notion of freedom in the Bible.[6] Christian philosophers of the second to fourth centuries, Dihle alleges, filled the empty wineskins of Greek 'intellective' epistemology with biblical 'voluntarism' over the course of their conflict with Gnosticism, a process culminating in the thought of Augustine.[7] Despite many criticisms,[8] worthy challenges to Dihle's thesis have emerged only recently. Philosopher Susanne Bobzien, meanwhile, focuses on what sort of freedom language about choice and 'will' actually entails. What scholars means when they talk about 'free will,' she argues, is a philosophical notion of a part of the self which governs behavior and can choose between alternatives. This she calls "freedom to do otherwise" ('Moral Responsibility 2' = 'MR2')—i.e., to choose between one thing and its opposite—as opposed to freedom qua physical and mental agency, wherein "it was the agent, and not something else, that was causally responsible" for the action in question ('MR1').[9] The notion of 'freedom to do otherwise' is something that first begins to emerge in the second century CE—specifically, in Alexander of Aphrodisias's response to later Stoicism.[10] Third, in his own Sather lectures, philosopher Michael Frede also underscores the importance of Stoicism in later Greek and early Christian reflection on human responsibility. Frede too highlights the central role played by the conflict with Gnosticism and astral determinism in developing the basic sense among early Christian philosophers "that the world does not put such constraints on us from the outside"—like stars

---

5   Rightly noted by Denzey (Lewis), "New Star," 211 n. 11; Wildberg, "Will," 331.

6   Dihle, *Theory of Will*, 13–17, 105.

7   Dihle, *Theory of Will*, 112–113; followed by Benjamins, *Eingeordnete Freiheit*, 148–149.

8   The notion of the 'Bible' as 'voluntaristic' is problematic, as is the assumption that Augustine's *oeuvre* is the decisive turning-point in the trajectory; both of these issues contribute to the greater weakness of Dihle's anachronistic projection of modern Christian notions of the will on ancient sources. See e.g. Kahn, "Discovering Will" 236–237; Müller and Pich, "Auf dem Weg," 1–6; Rapp, "Tackling," 69–70.

9   Bobzien, "Inadvertent Conception," 135, 139–141. This distinction is surprisingly absent in Patristic scholarship (e.g., Karavites, *Evil*, 115).

10   Bobzien, "Inadvertent Conception," 139–141, 145; eadem, *Determinism and Freedom*, 276–280.

WHAT WE CHOOSE NOW

or archons—"as to make it impossible for us to live a good life."[11] Finally and most recently, Roman historian Kyle Harper walks something of a Foucauldian path between Dihle and Frede, declaring that the emergence of a seat of human responsibility is a specifically Christian development which was from the start tied up in discussions of the body, sexuality, and the regulation thereof.[12]

Each of these studies is deeply penetrating, and each has its blind spots: Dihle and Harper anachronistically focus on Augustine as the *telos* to whom leads all other, earlier developments in the history of will, while Bobzien sets aside the difficulties presented by Gnosticism and astral determinism.[13] A more specific loose thread in these scholarly debates is the recognition—made widely, yet only in passing—that when early Christian philosophers adopted Stoic language to describe a seat of human responsibility, they located this seat beyond the body, in agreement with contemporary Platonic reflection on the Myth of Er.[14] Describing the soul's selection in heaven of its next embodied life and personal *daimōn*, Plato states that "the responsibility lies with the one who chooses; God has none (*aitia elomenou, theos anaitios*)."[15] As discussed above (chapters one and five), this passage was a central proof-text for the Middle Platonic theory of conditional fate, wherein fate serves as a kind of law (*nomos*) that decrees the consequences that follow from the free choice(s) the pre-natal soul makes.

Other scholars, meanwhile, have noted that some notion of a faculty of human responsibility was needed by Christian philosophers to make sense of biblical proof-texts regarding final judgment at the eschaton.[16] Bobzien shrewdly observes that the location of a faculty of choosing in the pre-natal soul implicates the problem of human responsibility in the problem of providence, rather than the (decidedly physical) causal determinism of the Stoa, and that

---

11   M. Frede, *Free Will*, 11; similarly ibid., 10–11, 17, 120.

12   Harper, *From Shame to Sin*, 82–83.

13   For Dihle, see above, n. 8; for Bobzien, see *Determinism and Freedom*, 13 (despite eadem, "Inadvertent Conception," 162 n. 52). On 'Gnostic determinism,' see further below, in this chapter. Harper states that he wishes to liberate the discussion of early Christian freedom from "the ghetto of gnostic-orthodox controversy" (Harper, *From Shame to Sin*, 118), but whether he actually does so is another question.

14   Dörrie, "Der Begriff Pronoia," 70; Dihle, "Philosophische Lehren," 23; Bobzien, "Inadvertent Conception," 172; M. Frede, *Free Will*, 16; cf. also Kahn, "Discovering Will," 245.

15   *Resp.* x 617d–e, tr. Grube, rev. Reeve, in Cooper and Hutchinson, eds., *Plato: Complete Works*, 1220, slightly modified. See further above, chapter one.

16   Already Jackson, "Sources," 13. See also Harper, *From Shame to Sin*, 122; Wildberg, "Will," 333–334.

this development in philosophical discourse is somehow related to the emergence of the notion of free will in early Christian philosophy.[17] This assimilation of the seat of human accountability to an immaterial soul, Bobzien suggests, rendered the physical causal determinism of the Stoa no longer "attractive or plausible, let alone a threat" from the third century CE onward.[18]

The present chapter will confirm and complicate this picture. If we examine our three most sustained discussions of the problem by Christian writers from the second and third centuries CE, we find that it is indeed the case that the emergence of language about a seat of human accountability and 'freedom to do otherwise' (MR2) was inextricable from speculation about the soul's existence prior to birth, and about providence. These discussions are to be found in the Syriac anti-fatalist tract the *Book of the Laws of the Countries*; Clement of Alexandria's refutation of the teaching about the providential punishment of martyrs by the second-century Alexandrian teacher Basilides; and Origen's famous treatise *On Free Will* in Book Three of *On First Principles* (excerpted as book 21 of the *Philocalia*) and his remarks about 'Gnostic determinism.' While each of these sources has been recognized as pivotal to the issue at hand, an integrated, protracted discussion of them together is still lacking—in fact, the first two are usually absent from the key studies of the early history of free will discussed above.[19] However, in order to clarify some of the issues and terminology at hand as well as the background of these debates, this chapter will begin with a brief detour back to the debates about accountability, determinism, and providence in the second century we find in Alexander of Aphrodisas and the Middle Platonist doctrine of 'conditional fate.' The chapter concludes by highlighting the distinctive character of the sources discussed here against the backdrop of the more limited discussions of the problem of free will in second-century apologists, principally Justin Martyr.

---

17   Bobzien, "Inadvertent Conception," 172–173.

18   Bobzien, "Inadvertent Conception," 174.

19   The only historian of philosophy discussed in the introduction to this chapter who analyzes the *Book of the Laws of the Countries* in detail is Dihle; Harper's treatment is superficial, and the source is omitted by the others. Basilides is omitted from all four authors. Denzey (Lewis)'s discussion of Basilides ("New Star," 210) in an article on early Christian discourse about astrology is spurious.

WHAT WE CHOOSE NOW

2   Aristotle on Action and Pseudo-Plutarch on Determinism

If Plato set the terms for discussion of providence and cosmic administration in the Greek philosophical tradition, it was Aristotle who set the terms for debating responsibility and volition.[20] Strikingly, this is the case even though there is no discussion of a faculty of 'willing' in Aristotle's corpus. The *locus classicus* is in book three of the *Nicomachaean Ethics*, where Aristotle uses four key terms to describe his theory of action: 'what is up to us' (*to eph'hēmin*), 'what is voluntary' (*to hekousion*), 'what is chosen' (*to ek prohaireseōs*), and 'desire' (*boulēsis*), i.e., the object of choice.[21] There is no notion of 'will' or *voluntas* to weave all this together;[22] rather, there is a notion of choice (*to ek prohaireseōs*)—namely of things for which we are accountable or not accountable, things done voluntarily or involuntarily (*hekontes* or *akontes*, respectively).[23] Key to this discussion is that something is voluntary only if it is (*a*) committed without external force and (*b*) without ignorance of consequences.[24] To wit, for an action to be voluntary, the person doing it must (*a*) be physically autonomous and (*b*) fully intend the action. Of course, intention is not result: we can will things we cannot achieve (e.g., 'walking to the moon'), but we can only choose 'what is up to us' (definitely not 'walking to the moon'). All of these terms are key for early Christian discussions of individual accountability and its relationship with providence.

Aristotle's articulation of choice is also pivotal for subsequent philosophical developments regarding the complex of character/behavior, autonomy, and determinism. As Michael Frede emphasizes, Aristotle does not make the distinction between choosing x or the consequence being that x does not happen, such that 'I will walk to the store, or I will not walk to the store.' Rather, he distinguishes between choosing x or failing to choose x, such that 'if it is up to me to walk to the store—if I am physically unhindered from doing it and know what it means to do it—then I can choose to walk to the store or fail to

---

20   For a recent *Forschungsbericht* on Aristotle and will, see Rapp, "Tackling." On the various cognitive and volitional terminology one finds in classical Greek literature, see Dihle, *Theory of Will*, 20–31; D. Frede, "Free Will in Aristotle?," 39.

21   Thus Kahn, "Discovering Will," 239–240; similarly Magris, *L'idea di destino*, 2:413–415.

22   Magris, *L'idea di destino*, 2:413; Kahn, "Discovering Will," 240; D. Frede, "Free Will in Aristotle?," 39–41; Rapp, "Tackling," 71–72.

23   *Eth. nic.* 3 1110b18–1111a21, 1139b4 per the discussion of Kahn, "Discovering Will," 240–241; M. Frede, *Free Will*, 24–27.

24   *Eth. nic.* 3 1109b35–1111b3; thus Magris, *L'idea di destino*, 2:415; D. Frede, "Free Will in Aristotle?," 40; also Dihle, *Theory of Will*, 56.

choose to walk to the store.' This is no mere semantic difference, Frede avers.[25] This distinction is important, because Aristotle understands the problems of action, choice, and responsibility in the context of virtue and character (*prohairesis*).[26] Arguably, all classical Greek discussions of agency are concerned with the development of a personality imbued with education (or 'training'— *paideia*).[27] For Aristotle, choosing is a form of desiring, and one's choices reveal the degree to s/he has been educated to have the knowledge that allows one to desire what is good,[28] rather than to fail to desire what is good. 'Freedom to do otherwise' (MR2) would be the ability to choose what is *worse*, rather than the ability to choose consistently what is better.[29]

Our earliest attestation of 'freedom to do otherwise' (MR2) in an ancient source appears in the context of this debate, as noted by Bobzien. In his treatise *On Fate*, Alexander of Aphrodisias attacks the view of an anonymous Stoic philosopher that "if all the antecedent circumstances are the same, only one result can ensue," but, nonetheless, 'what is up to us' is preserved.[30] The problem this anonymous Stoic philosopher attempts to address is that from the perspective of Stoic physics, there is a tremendous physical force—the General

---

25 "To fail to choose to do it, given Aristotle's notion of choice, is not the same as choosing not to do it" (M. Frede, *Free Will*, 29).

26 Dihle, *Theory of Will*, 57.

27 Wildberg, "Will," 332; similarly Magris, *L'idea di destino*, 2:407–408.

28 *Eth. nic.* 3 1111b20–30; cit. M. Frede, *Free Will*, 27; see also D. Frede, "Free Will in Aristotle?," 52–53.

29 M. Frede, *Free Will*, 29.

30 Alex. Aphr. *Fat.* 13. Nemesius of Emesa also preserves a version of this argument, attributing it to Chrysippus and more recently to Philopator, teacher of the famous second-century CE physician Galen (*Nat. hom.* 35 [105]):

> Some say that both our freedom and fate are preserved. From fate [they say] contributes something to each thing that happens, such as to water its chilling, to each plant its bearing a certain fruit, to stone its downward motion and to fire its upward motion, and in the same way to a living thing its assenting and having impulse; so when nothing external and fated obstructs this impulse, then it is entirely up to us to walk and we shall by all means walk. Those who say this, of the Stoics Chrysippus and Philopator and many other famous men, prove nothing other than that everything happens by fate: for if they say that our impulses are given to us by fate and those are sometimes hindered by fate, sometimes not, it is clear that everything happens by fate, including what seems to be up to us. (tr. Sharples and van der Eijk, 184–185)

> Bobzien therefore suggests that the teaching may be that of the historical Philopator ("Inadvertent Conception," 143; eadem, *Determinism and Freedom*, 358–396; Theiler had already noted the similarity of the accounts and assigned them to Philopator—"Tacitus," 79; see also Sharples and van der Eijk, "Introduction," 29; idem, "Notes," 185 n. 921). On the argument in general, see D. Frede, "Dramatization," 279–280, 288–292.

WHAT WE CHOOSE NOW

Causal Principle (GCP; see above, chapter one)—running the entire universe, and so 'what is up to us' is severely limited to how we assent or co-determine it.[31] One's character (*prohairesis*) is here is elided with 'what is up to us'—a notion of autonomy (MR1)—but this begs the question of whether these terms are even of any significance when the universe is a single, divine causal mechanism.[32] As Susan Sauvé Meyer puts it, "even when we exercise our causality as agents, we are subject to the influence of other causes."[33] While Chrysippus argues that autonomy could be envisioned within the context of the GCP insofar as individuals 'co-determine' particular actions, it may be objected that even if this is so, the 'co-determining' human agents would be subject to external causes as well.[34] Alexander disagrees:

> For we assume that we have this power in actions, that we can choose the opposite, and not that everything which we choose has causes laid down beforehand, on account of which it is not possible for us to choose it; this is sufficiently shown also by the regret that often occurs in relation to what has been chosen ... It is clear even in itself that 'what depends on us' is applied to those things over which we have the power of also choosing the opposite things.[35]

Two aspects of Alexander's view are pivotal to the emergence of a faculty of free will in philosophical writing: first, the element of choosing (*elesthai*) between opposites as the decisive element of the character of an action (MR2), and second, the notion of a power or ability (*exousia*) of choosing which belongs to each individual.[36] Yet the term *exousia* does not alone constitute free will for Alexander, since he believes, like Aristotle, that the soul is part of the body and so is susceptible to causation resulting from its corporeality. Nor does he believe in universal providence; thus, all that he needs to guarantee responsibility for actions is to deny the predetermination of these same actions.[37] On this read-

---

31   M. Frede, *Free Will*, 68. On the GCP and the theory of assent, see above, chapter one.

32   Bobzien, "Inadvertent Conception," 136.

33   S. Meyer, "Chain of Causes," 88.

34   S. Meyer, "Chain of Causes," 88–89. Similarly, Sharples, "Commentary: Cicero," 189; Benjamins, *Eingeordnete Freiheit*, 21–22; Bonazzi, "Middle Platonists," 288; cf. Klawans, *Josephus*, 77–78. On Chrysippus's theory of co-determined fate, see above, chapter five.

35   Alex. Aphr. *Fat.* 12, tr. Sharples, 58. On the Aristotelian valence of the passage, see Sharples, "Commentary: Alexander," 142, re: Arist. *Eth. nic.* 3.3 1113a10; see further Alex. Aphr. *Fat.* 20; Bobzien, "Inadvertent Conception," 144; M. Frede, *Free Will*, 96–98.

36   Bobzien, "Inadvertent Conception," 159, 164–167.

37   Bobzien, "Inadvertent Conception," 166, 172.

230 CHAPTER 6

ing, for Alexander as well as for Aristotle, the opportunity to develop a virtuous character becomes, to an extent, a matter of chance.[38]

This question of the relationship between character, the external circumstances which shape it but are determined by chance, and providence feature strongly in a recent scholarly debate regarding the curious conclusion of Pseudo-Plutarch's treatise *On Fate*. Following the exposition of the theory of 'conditional fate' whereby a set of predetermined laws 'determine' the consequences for actions freely made, the Platonist wraps up the discussion by presenting a digest of the Stoic theory of fate.[39] As George Boys-Stones notes, Pseudo-Plutarch cites these Stoic views approvingly, so as to say that his own approach allows for them and additionally, solves problems neglected by the Stoa.[40] This raises the question of how much the Middle Platonic teaching on conditional fate actually departs from Stoic compatibilism in the first place. Platonists like Plutarch or Nemesius regarded the Stoic GCP to be fundamentally incompatible with the possibility of human accountability,[41] but Boys-Stones believes ancient Platonists made this argument in bad faith, because they were themselves compatibilists.[42] Rather, he avers, Platonists departed from the Stoa in allowing for the possibility of events to happen outside of the great web of causes, in two ways: by chance (*tuchē*),[43] and by the absence of governance of variable particulars in the cosmos by necessity (*anagkē*), which maintains only general patterns of cosmic events.[44]

---

38 As Dorothea Frede observes, "though he [Aristotle—DMB] repeatedly affirms that it is 'up to us' to become the persons we turn out to be, he seems to be aware of the fact that this is true only to a limited degree. For the chances for good practice are not divided evenly among humankind. One person may have good cards in that respect ... The next person has bad cards ... It is these circumstances that justify speaking of 'moral luck'" (D. Frede, "Free Will in Aristotle?," 50; similarly eadem, "Could Paris," 277; more hesitatingly, eadem, "Dramatization," 289; cf. Magris, *L'idea di destino*, 2:421–422).

39 Many scholars believe this to represent the views of Chrysippus (Sharples, "Stoic Background," 172 n. 15).

40 Boys-Stones, "'Middle' Platonists on Fate," 444–445, followed by Opsomer, "Middle Platonic Doctrine," 144.

41 Plut. *Stoic rep.* 1056c–d; Nem. *Nat. hom.* 35 [105].

42 Boys-Stones, "'Middle' Platonists on Fate," 439. Cf. Theiler: "hier ist deutlich, wie die Lehre [des Ps.-Plutarchs] chrysippische Sätze voraussetzt; der Einbruch stoischer Gedanken in den Vorneuplatonismus ist ebenso bekannt wie der von aristotelichen" ("Tacitus," 86).

43 "While events *within* the cosmos follow one another with predictable regularity, Platonists (unlike Stoics) insist that *the cosmos itself need not have been this way*," (Boys-Stones, "'Middle' Platonists on Fate," 432, italics his; see also ibid., 441).

44 Boys-Stones, "'Middle' Platonists on Fate," 440–442; similarly, idem, "Human Autonomy," 492–493; Dihle, *Theory of Will*, 103–104.

WHAT WE CHOOSE NOW 231

These arguments are ingenious, but present difficulties of their own.[45] The primary issue, as Jan Opsomer recognizes, is that, if one elevates chance to a cause of human choices in Ps.-Plutarch's account, our choices "are random," and "responsibility goes out the window."[46] Rather, human choices belong to human souls, which possess their own causal web. The Platonists are "causal dualists, or in any case causal pluralists," because they take souls to "have their own causal history—a history that is not determined primarily by antecedent physical causes, although physical events may to some extent interfere with it. Hence, the choice that souls make on their own are free, but not uncaused ..."[47] This animate (i.e., *psychikos*, as opposed to 'material') 'causal history' pre-exists and will post-date bodily incarnation, and therefore renders pre-natal and post-mortem existence key to Platonic notions of fate and determinism.[48]

---

45 Chase rejects the argument, but deigns to elaborate ("Porphyre sur la providence," 128 n. 13).

46 Opsomer, "Middle Platonic Doctrine," 157. An additional, if less pressing, issue is that 'chance' does not appear to play as major a role in Ps.-Plutarch's argument as it does in Boys-Stones's articulation of it. Moreover, the factor of chance is entirely absent from the parallel discussion of possibility in Alcinous, which is otherwise close, although it belongs to a different tradition of transmission (for Alcinous on possibility, see *Epit.* 26.3: Bobzien, "Inadvertent Conception," 154; J.M. Dillon, "Commentary," 164; cf. Dihle, who, maintaining that the chaotic nature of matter accounted for disorderly events in the Middle Platonic cosmos, claims that there is no need for chance in [*Fat.*]—"Astrology," 163).

47 Opsomer, "Middle Platonic Doctrine," 155; similarly Bonazzi, "Middle Platonists," 288. Sure enough, Ps.-Plutarch does not say anything about a soul's character being determined by external causes, and his focus on "what is up to us" occupying the domain of the 'possible' suggests that he is an incompatibilist (ibid. 155–156).

48 Recognized as early as Theiler, "Tacitus," 90. Boys-Stones anticipated this, arguing that Ps.-Plutarch's choice of scenarios of 'what is up to us'—e.g., walking—"makes it clear that Platonists sought the cohabitation of fate and autonomy in the choices of one's sublunary existence—not, or not only, in the pre-incarnation choice of one's life" ("'Middle' Platonists on Fate," 436 n. 24). This appears to me to be an overreading. Rather, the case of 'walking' was selected by Ps.-Plutarch simply because it was a standard example used by his contemporaries; cf. Opsomer, "Middle Platonic Doctrine," 155, who adds that in any case the example can be read as indicating the existence of autonomy in the present life regardless of whether the soul is a separate causal agent for Ps.-Plutarch. Historians of Greek philosophy often refer to the causal agency of incarnated souls in the present life as a 'secularization' of Plato's eschatological myths (Theiler, "Tacitus," 80; Dörrie, "Der Begriff Pronoia," 77–78; Jackson, "Sources," 18; Benjamins, *Eingeordnete Freiheit*, 140–141; Bobzien, "Inadvertent Conception," 161–162; Opsomer, "Middle Platonic Doctrine," 141 n. 15; cf. also Alt, *Weltflucht*, 153; Bergjan, *Der fürsorgende Gott*, 199). To the extent that the pre-existence of the soul was invoked in part to explain its terrestrial character, this is true, but it must be remembered that virtually all ancient Platonists did believe in reincarnation (on Platonist doctrines of metempsychosis, see Stettner, *Seelenwanderung*, esp. 72–77; more recently, Dörrie and Baltes, *Platonismus in der Antike*, 6:2.348–351).

232   CHAPTER 6

The Middle Platonic doctrine of conditional fate, then, is not best understood as compatibilist. Although they differed from one another in the details of this picture, the Middle Platonists articulated human agency in terms of Plato's eschatological myths, and so followed Plato in designating the soul as derivative of a causal web independent of the material world it comes to inhabit upon incarnation in a body. Embracing 'causal dualism,' as it were, the Platonists cleared room for a faculty of human autonomy independent of providence-fate.

3   "All These Things Depend on One's Thinking": Autonomy and
       Fatalism in the 'Book of the Laws of the Countries'

The earliest Christian treatise on something like free will may be the Syriac (West Aramaic) *Book of the Laws of the Countries* (henceforth *BLC*), a product of the circle around the second-century Syrian philosopher Bardaiṣan, if not written by him himself.[49] Scholarly consensus takes the *BLC* as at least indicative of Bardaiṣan's views on the subject, with a *terminus ante quem* of the late third century, since the catalogue of customs which crowns the dialogue appears to have been paraphrased in part by later writers.[50] It is for this catalogue (of the 'laws of the countries') that the treatise is named, but work's central aims

---

49   Scholars who read the *BLC* as a more or less faithful transmission of the thought of Bardaiṣan himself include Drijvers, "Bardaisan's Doctrine"; Dihle, "Zur Schicksalslehre," 123; B. Wilson, "Bardaisan," 168–169; Hegedus, "Necessity," 333; idem, *Early Christianity*, 260; Denzey (Lewis), "New Star," 209; Ramelli, *Bardaiṣan*, 65–68. Yet the attribution is by no means sure: see Aland (Ehlers), "Bardesanes von Edessa," 359; Possekel, "Bardaisan and Origen," 521–522. Alberto Camplani has argued that the *BLC* is a work of a later disciple responding to Catholic or Marcionite criticisms of Bardaisan's views on the soul and the co-eternity of matter, which would explain the focus on free will—not at all the central theme of his philosophy as known from other witnesses ("Bardesane et les bardesanites," 46).
       While Eusebius of Caesarea (*Hist. eccl.* 4.30; *Praep. ev.* 6.9) and other late ancient authors mention a dialogue *Peri heimarmenē* authored by Bardaiṣan. This dialogue could have been a translation of the *BLC* into Greek, or, if the work was originally authored in Greek, the *Vorlage* of the Syriac version we possess, but no such identifications are sure. See Drijvers, *Bardaiṣan*, 60–75; Drijvers, "Bardaisan's Doctrine," 13–14; Denzey (Lewis), "Bardaisan," 159 n. 1; Ramelli, *Bardaiṣan*, 55 ff.; Possekel, "Bardaisan's Influence," 90 n. 29.
       All translations given of the *BLC* here are my own, with reference to the page and line numbers of the text given in Drijvers, *Book of the Laws*, unless noted otherwise.
50   Euseb. *Praep. ev.* 6.10.48; Ps.-Clem. *Rec.* 9.19–29; see Drijvers, *Bardaiṣan*, 62–72; Camplani, "Bardesane et les bardesanites," 46; Hegedus, *Early Christianity*, 94. Aland (Ehlers), expresses skepticism that these authors know the *BLC* ("Bardesanes von Edessa," 359).

WHAT WE CHOOSE NOW

are to exonerate God from responsibility for evil and to reconcile individual accountability with the natural and astral causal forces whose activity is evident in creation. Thus, while the term 'providence' does not appear in the BLC, the text does deal with the same set of problems as contemporary discussions of providence, dualism, and determinism.[51] It is remarkable for both the felicity of its prose and for the distinctive character of its argument, which is heavy on Peripatetic argumentation even as it accords a significant degree of causal efficacy to the stars over human bodies and even souls.

Like Socrates in Plato's dialogues, the character of Bardaiṣan features as a didactic figure clearing up the misconceptions of his pupils, whose enquiries propel the discussion. Chief among the pupils is a certain Awida, whose first question does not concern free will, but evil: "If God is one, as you say He is, and He has created humanity, and wanted you to do what you are charged to, why did He not create humanity such that they would not be able to transgress, but always did what is right?"[52] Bardaiṣan answers:

> If humanity were created thus [as Awida supposes—DMB], he would be nothing in his own self (*nafšeh*),[53] but merely an instrument of whoever set him in motion. Is it clear that whoever set him in motion set him in motion intentionally for good or for evil?[54] In what respect then would humanity then be different from a cither with which another plays, or from a vehicle which another drives? Both praise and blame depend on the creator (*awmānā*) ... But God, in His kindness, did not so want to create humanity; rather, with respect to autonomy (*ḥi'rutā'*) did He raise him above many creatures and make him equal to the angels.[55]

---

51 There are many possible reasons for the absence of the Greek loanword *purnāsā'* (cf. also *prnw'* < *pronoia*—Sokoloff, *Syriac Lexicon*, 1171a, 1243a, respectively) in the BLC. The work owes much to Peripateticism, where providence was not the favored notion for discussing the problems of determinism and human responsibility; like Alexander of Aphrodisias, the BLC prefers to talk about 'fate.' The chronology of West Aramaic as a vehicle for philosophical literature is also a relevant factor which remains understudied, but for background, see Healey, "Edessan Milieu."

52 BLC 4.9–13, tr. Drijvers, *Book of the Laws*, 5, modified. A version of this question was also posed to the Stoa by Carneades (Cic. *Nat. d.* 3.80; see above, chapter one).

53 Significantly, this word also means 'soul.'

54 The line of argument—that human beings are not instruments or marionettes entirely manipulated by external forces—seems to demand a leading question here, but cf. Drijvers, who rather translates a statement: "It is clear, that he who gave an impulse to man would do so for good or for ill" (*Book of the Laws*, 11).

55 BLC 10.2–14, tr. mine.

234   CHAPTER 6

From the start of the dialogue, then, the BLC maintains that dualism (likely Marcionite)[56] is the problem and *ḥiʾrutāʾ* the solution.[57] God's bestowal of individual accountability is what makes God good (i.e. benevolent), a point Bardaiṣan elaborates by comparing the agency possessed by humans and angels with the endless toil to which the natural world is compelled. Creation is there to serve not just God, but humanity, too:

> Those things which are destined to serve, are put in the power of humanity, because he is created after the image of God ... And it is also given to him to lead his life voluntarily (*bṣebyān nafše*),[58] and to do all he is able to, if he will—or not to do it, if he will not—justifying himself, or being found guilty. For if he were so created that he could not do evil—so that he could not incur guilt—then in that way the good he did would not be his own either, and he could not justify himself by it. For the justification and guilt of someone who does not do good or evil voluntarily (*men ṣebyāneh*) depends on (*bged*)[59] the one who made him ... God's goodness towards humanity is great, insofar as he grants humanity more autonomy (*ḥiʾrutāʾ*) than all the elements we have spoken of. Through this autonomy he justifies himself, leads his life divinely, and is associated with the angels, who also possess an autonomy of their own.[60]

In both of these passages, Bardaiṣan identifies *ḥiʾrutāʾ* as a distinctive faculty which is the seat of individual accountability, i.e., receiving praise or blame for one's actions. This faculty is associated with freedom. Moreover, some kind of potestative notion of 'what is up to us' as freedom to do otherwise (MR2) appears to be implied in the statement that a person must "do all he is able to, if he will—or not to do it, if he will not ..." It is thus no surprise that *ḥiʾrutāʾ* as well as *ṣebyānāʾ* are nigh-universally rendered as 'free will' in trans-

---

56   Emphasized by Drijvers, *Bardaiṣan*, 76; Ramelli, *Bardaiṣan*, 62; Possekel, "Bardaisan and Origen," 523; eadem, "Bardaisan's Influence," 104, 107. Later, he simply says "he who has power over everything is One" (BLC 28.24–25, tr. Drijvers, *Book of the Laws*, 29).

57   Drijvers, "Bardaisan's Doctrine," 16; Dihle, *Theory of Will*, 109; Ramelli, *Bardaiṣan*, 62.

58   For the rendering of the phrase *bṣebyān nafše*, see Payne Smith, *Compendious*, 472b; cf. Sokoloff, *Syriac Lexicon*, 1271b.

59   I.e., "is up to" (Grk. *epi*); see Sokoloff, *Syriac Lexicon*, 204a.

60   BLC 12.9–14.1, tr. mine. Cf. also Just. Mart. *1 Apol.* 43, tr. Falls, 80: "God did not create man like the other beings, trees and quadrupeds, for example, which can do nothing by free choice. For, neither would he deserve reward or praise if he did not choose good of his own accord ..."

WHAT WE CHOOSE NOW

lations of the *BLC*.[61] Yet on further inspection, it is not obvious that it must be translated as such,[62] and in fact one troublesome passage may demand that we interpret it as translated here, more in the sense of moral autonomy (MR1).

Bardaiṣan explains individual accountability with recourse to the tale of the Fall of the Watchers (on which see above, chapter three). Some angels, he says, chose to descend and mate with human maidens, while others chose to carry out their duties and have been rewarded.[63] Even the stars and planets will be judged on the basis of their (severely limited) *ḥiʾrutā*.[64] Another pupil, Philip, asks how these natural forces can be judged if their freedom to choose is limited, and Bardaiṣan answers that the powers are judged only for that which they are themselves responsible. Awida then bursts in, complaining that it is impossible to comply with God's commandments.[65] Despite initial appearances, Awida does not change the subject: Bardaiṣan replies that God's commandments may be boiled down to two injunctions: to avoid committing evil, and to do good. "All these things," he avers, "depend on one's thinking (*reʿyānā*);[66] not on one's bodily strength, but on the will of the soul (*nafšā*)."[67] It is his elaboration of this point that introduces the question of whether *ḥiʾrutā* is better regarded as 'autonomy' than 'free will/choice':

> ... Humanity's strength lies in these commandments. They are easy, and there is nothing that can confuse them. For we are not charged to carry

---

61   Thus Drijvers, *Book of the Laws*; Magris, *L'idea di destino*, 2:829; Hegedus, *Early Christianity*, 260–263; Ramelli, *Bardaisan*, 80–90 *passim*; Possekel, "Bardaisan of Edessa: Philosopher," 455. Other translations include: "freedom of choice" (Dihle, "Zur Schicksalslehre," 123 *passim*; B. Wilson, "Bardaisan," 171) and simply "freedom" (Possekel, "Bardaisan and Origen," 525 *passim*).

62   Cf. Sokoloff, *Syriac Lexicon*, 403a. A detailed study of the term in as used in Ephaem Syrus's *First Discourse to Hypatius* would shed light on the matter.

63   *BLC* 14.1–6; see Possekel, "Bardaisan and Origen," 527.

64   *BLC* 14.8–11; see also Drijvers, *Bardaiṣan*, 77–78; Drijvers, "Bardaisan's Doctrine," 16–17.

65   *BLC* 14.12–21 (Philip to Awida).

66   Sokoloff, *Syriac Lexicon*, 1480b also has "thinking, will, deliberation." Grk. *gnomē* seems a likely equivalent.

67   *BLC* 16.6–8, tr. Drijvers, *Book of the Laws*, 17, slightly modified. See further Possekel, "Bardaisan of Edessa: Philosopher," 453, n. 66, 458–459. Ramelli, *Bardaisan*, 88–89 terms this an 'intellectual' ethic instead of 'voluntaristic' ethic, noting that Bardaisan, like Plato and most of the Fathers, agrees that the will depends on intellect and knowledge (*pace* Dihle, *Theory of Will*, 109, who argues just the opposite: "here we find, for the first time, that biblical voluntarism has been formulated, however imperfectly, in terms of philosophical anthropology").

236   CHAPTER 6

heavy loads of stone or wood or anything else, which can only be done by
persons with a strong body. Neither to build fortresses and found cities,
which only kings can do ... Nor to exercise one of those crafts which some
people have mastered and the rest have not. Rather, as by God's goodness, the commandments were given to us without malice. Every human
being with a soul (*nafšā'*) can keep them with joy. For there is no man
who does not feel joy when he acts rightly, nor anyone who is not glad at
heart when he avoids wrong, apart from those persons who are not made
(*'etbriw*) for this good and who are called 'weeds' (*zizāne'*—cf. Matt 13:24–
30, 13:36–43). For were that judge not unjust, who would blame someone
on account of something he is not able to do?[68]

The determinism implicit in the notion that some persons are simply made as
'weeds' has led some scholars to suggest that the passage is an interpolation,[69]
or a dualistic tendency in the thinking of the historical Bardaiṣan which the
authors of the BLC failed to purge.[70] A third possibility is that what the BLC
means by *ḥi'rutā'* is not an 'ability to do otherwise' (MR2), but autonomy (MR1).
A more strictly Aristotelian notion of responsibility is implied by Bardaiṣan's
examples: like 'what is up to us' in the *Nicomachean Ethics*, God's commandments are physically and mentally possible to achieve; no external force prevents people from practicing them. Yet not everyone does.

For Aristotle, the failure of some people to practice virtue is in part a matter
of luck, since not everyone is born into circumstances where they can become
sufficiently educated to consistently choose virtue. The BLC explores the same
problem by recourse to the 'parable of the weeds.' The source of evil, Bardaiṣan
continues, is not the soul, "for good belongs to humanity; for this reason, he
is glad when he does good. Evil, on the contrary," he states, "is the influence of
The Enemy," i.e., the Devil.[71] Like Plato and Aristotle, Bardaiṣan assumes that an
individual with no external force forcing him or her to evil will do good. Sinning
is not part of human nature, contrary to Awida's view.[72] Sinning is the result
of the wrong reaction to external stimuli—caused, it seems, by a malevolent

---

68   BLC 16.17–18.10, tr. Drijvers, *Book of the Laws*, 17, 19, significantly modified.
69   "The present bit, if it suggested predestinationism, would be absurd and completely at
      odds with the rest of the dialogue" (Ramelli, *Bardaiṣan*, 76). Her solution is to emend the
      passage, but Camplani has shown that the emendation is both unwarranted and ungram-
      matical ("Bardaisan's Psychology," 266 n. 25).
70   Camplani, "Bardaisan's Psychology," 266. This 'dualistic tendancy' is presumably the
      notion that the 'enemy' who sowed the weeds (Matt 13:28.38–39) created evil people.
71   BLC 18.21–23, tr. mine.
72   BLC 20.22–23.

WHAT WE CHOOSE NOW

force. This Stoicizing reading of early Christian demonology recalls Athenagoras (discussed above, chapter three),[73] but only to an extent: the BLC describes the soul as endowed with a faculty that is not prevented from choosing good (MRI) when under assault from the Devil.

Why then do some people sin and fall prey to "the enemy"? The BLC famously explains this by introducing two causal forces at work in human life beyond autonomy: nature and fate. "As for us, we are led, equally but distinctly, by nature, by fate, and by our autonomy, each according to their wont."[74] Nature (*kinyā'*) has power over immutable, elemental functions.[75] Insofar as we are embodied, we suffer the limitations of embodiment, such as death. While this 'naturalistic determinism' does not extend to the soul,[76] a second external cause does: fate. After offering a brief taxonomy of different contemporary notions of fate,[77] Bardaiṣan states that "there exists 'fate' (*ḥalkā'*), as it is called by the Chaldaeans. And not everything happens voluntarily (*bṣebyān*)."[78] Rather, fate has power over external circumstances of life (e.g., poverty or riches) and even death (e.g., early or late):

> That principle which is called fate is that order of the course of stars which has been granted by God to the rulers and the elements. According to this course and order do intellects (*mād'e'*) undergo change while entering the soul, and do souls (*nafše'*) undergo change while descending to bodies (*pagre'*). And that agent of change is called "fate" and "natal horoscope" (*beit yaldā'*), belonging to that grouping (of qualities) which was mixed and is being purified for the benefit of what, by the grace and goodness of God, was and will be cared for until the consummation of the universe.[79]

In other words, part of what accounts for the diversity of human behavior is the change worked by the "course and order" of astral fate on the pre-existent intellects descending into souls, souls into bodies, and bodies birthed into lives

---

73   Thus Possekel, "Bardaisan of Edessa: Philosopher," 457.

74   *BLC* 32.8–10, tr. mine.

75   *BLC* 22.5–24.2.

76   B. Wilson, "Bardaisan," 175.

77   *BLC* 26.16–28.13. On this taxonomy, see most recently Poirier, "Deux doxographies"; additionally, Dihle, "Zur Schicksalslehre," 125; B. Wilson, "Bardaisan," 175; Hegedus, "Necessity," 336–337; idem, *Early Christianity*, 263.

78   *BLC* 30.3–4, tr. mine.

79   *BLC* 32.11–19, tr. mine. See also Drijvers, "Bardaisan's Doctrine," 20–21.

238 CHAPTER 6

of diverse circumstances and concomitant effects on behavior.[80] Souls are not themselves made evil, but some of them are affected by fate such that they are hindered from following God's commandments.

Thus, according to the BLC, fate has power over the soul as well as the body, insofar as it affects how the soul's life on earth begins.[81] Thus, the BLC offers a distinctive tripartition of causal forces—nature, fate, and autonomy—as a "modification of the Peripatetic system" of Alexander of Aphrodisias,[82] in which responsibility is conceived of in terms of the soul's autonomy, which is nonetheless not entirely sovereign. The three causes are interwoven with one another throughout life, often affecting and even competing with one another, but at a certain point each has its own sovereignty.[83] The dominion of fate therefore extends to all external circumstances of both life and death as well as an integral part of the human being, without annulling human autonomy—a genuinely distinctive view on determinism in early Christian literature.[84]

Awida is convinced by these arguments that human beings are not compelled by their nature (*kinyā'*) to sin, but still desires to be shown "that it is not due to fate and destiny (*ḥalkā' w pusqānā'*) that sinners sin. Then," he says, "it will be necessary to believe that humanity has its own autonomy (*ḥi'rutā' dnafšeh*) and is by nature inclined to what is noble and averse to what is hateful—and for this reason too, it is just that he be judged on the Last Day."[85]

---

80 To the extent that this is so, I then agree with Dihle's suggestion that the stars in the BLC play the role which fortune (*tuchē*) plays for Alexander of Aphrodisias, i.e., of determining randomly allotted but causally efficacious events (Dihle, "Zur Schicksalslehre," 130; idem, "Astrology," 166). As he notes, for Alexander, the stars rather fall under the domain of *physis*. On the tripartite anthropology (intellect, soul, body) of the BLC, see Dihle, "Zur Schicksalslehre," 124; B. Wilson, "Bardaisan," 173; Camplani, "Bardaisan's Psychology," 267–268, 274.

81 Camplani has explained further parallels to Bardaiṣan's psychology as reconstructed from later Syriac sources ("Bardaisan's Psychology," 268–272).

82 Dihle, "Zur Schicksalslehre," 134 *passim*, re: Alex. Aphr. *Fat.* 2–6, on which see Sharples, "Commentary: Alexander," 125–131; D. Frede, "Dramatization," 277–279; see also Dihle, *Theory of Will*, 109. On the BLC's distinctive tripartition of individual responsibility, nature, and fate, see also Drijvers, *Bardaiṣan*, 71, 85–89; Dihle, "Astrology," 166–167; Hegedus, "Necessity," 334; idem, *Early Christianity*, 260–263; Ramelli, *Bardaisan*, 79; Harper, *From Shame to Sin*, 127; Burns, "Astrological Determinism," 213–214.

83 BLC 36.17–25.

84 On the distinctiveness of the BLC, see Drijvers, "Bardaisan's Doctrine," 20–21; B. Wilson, "Bardaisan," 176; Hegedus, "Necessity," 337–338; idem, *Early Christianity*, 264; Denzey (Lewis), "Bardaisan," 179–180; Possekel, "Bardaisan and Origen," 530; Harper, *From Shame to Sin*, 128.

85 BLC 38.10–15, tr. mine; see also Drijvers, "Bardaisan's Doctrine," 21–22.

WHAT WE CHOOSE NOW

Bardaiṣan's answer—the famous *nomima barbarika* argument—encompasses the rest of the dialogue: the famous catalogue of the customs of far-flung lands, whose diversity is mutually exclusive with astral determinism: people born under the same stars behave in different ways, and so "the laws of human beings are stronger than Fate."[86] The dialogue concludes by briefly (but significantly) reminding the reader that the present world of mixture will be annulled by God, in favor of a more peaceful age.[87] The *nomima barbarika* enjoyed a lively reception beyond the BLC in ancient Christian polemics against astrology, as we saw with Origen's use of it in the *Commentary on Genesis* (see above, chapter five).[88] However, it does not appear that the *nomima barbarika* demonstrates what Awida asks of it, which is the complete autonomy of the soul ("that it is not due to fate and destiny that sinners sin"). Rather, it demonstrates the soul's *partial* autonomy, which co-exists with the causal forces of nature and fate. Bardaiṣan has argued that humans, like astral bodies and angels, shall be judged on the basis of how they have (ab)used their autonomy; the decision to follow the commandments, he has added, depends "on one's thinking (*reʿyānāʾ*); not on one's bodily strength but on the will of the soul (*nafšāʾ*)."[89] And yet the way the soul enters the world is not free of intervention from fate. Strangely enough, the argument for which the BLC is named is an awkward fit to the modified Peripateticism which most of the dialogue explores.

---

86 "In all places, every day and each hour, people are born with different horoscopes, but the laws of human beings are stronger than destiny, and they lead their lives according to their own customs" (BLC 52.8–11, tr. Drijvers, *Book of the Laws*, 53, slightly modified; see also ibid., 38.16–22). The arguments in this lengthy section of the BLC are diverse, but this is the principle animating all of them (B. Wilson, "Bardaisan," 176–178; Hegedus, "Necessity," 341; idem, *Early Christianity*, 91–94, esp. 94). Harper cherrypicks the various customs at hand when he characterizes the *nomima barbarika* as showing that "the inability of the stars to predict sexual phenomena was proof positive of the limits of astrology" (Harper, *From Shame to Sin*, 128).

87 While the passage does recall some sense of *apokatastasis*, it is hardly evidence that Bardaiṣan held the same beliefs regarding the end as Origen allegedly did (Camplani, "Bardaiṣan's Psychology," 264–265, *pace* Ramelli, *Bardaiṣan*, 10; cf. also Hegedus, "Necessity," 342–343).

88 Orig. *Philoc.* 23.16; see further Hegedus, *Early Christianity*, 94; Possekel, "Bardaisan and Origen," 537; Burns, "Astrological Determinism," 215. For the *nomima barbarika* in the fourth century CE and beyond, see Euseb. *Praep. ev.* 6.10.48; Clem. [*Rec.*] 9.19–29; Hegedus, op. cit., 95–100. All these sources probably go back to the BLC, and from there ultimately to Carneades, ap. Cic. *Div.* 2.96–97, as argued first by Boll ("Studien über Ptolemaeus," 181–188), widely followed, e.g. by Amand, *Fatalisme et liberté*, 55–60; Drijvers, *Bardaiṣan*, 76; Dihle, "Zur Schicksalslehre," 125; Hegedus, *Early Christianity*, 94; Possekel, "Bardaisan's Influence," 92.

89 Text Drijvers, *Book of the Laws*, 16.6–8; tr. Drijvers, ibid., 17, slightly modified.

240 CHAPTER 6

Probably the earliest—and most influential—early Christian refutation of astral determinism, the BLC denotes the pre-existent soul as the seat of human accountability, and in rendering the ultimate reward or punishment for one's actions in eschatological terms.[90] It presupposes the existence of both 'intellect' and 'soul,' but does not describe their causal efficacy prior to birth. Yet the pre-existent soul does appear to possess some kind of autonomous power of decision-making (*ḥiʾrutā*'), and this is precisely what fate limits at birth when it furnishes the diverse circumstances into which every human being is born. While the claim that fate exerts control over the body contributed to Bardaiṣan's later notoriety,[91] the BLC shows fate as also affecting the soul, when it determines—in part—who will be able to show themselves to be grass or weeds when confronted by the Devil. While some passages appear to describe the decisive faculty of individual accountability at work choosing between two options, Bardaiṣan's description of the Ten Commandments indicates that even though it is the soul's faculty of choosing, *ḥiʾrutā*' appears to function more in terms of Aristotelian autonomy (MR1) than a potestative 'free will' (MR2). A co-existence of both senses of accountability in even third-century sources is neither surprising nor unique.[92] Rather, the BLC's account of human accountability is particularly striking for tackling the problem of dualism by employing a deeply Aristotelian conception of action alongside Platonizing psychology and Christian demonology, while carving out significant compatibility between human autonomy and natural and astral determinism—a compatibility which sat uneasily with many of its later Christian readers.

4   "Say Anything Rather Than Call Providence Bad": Clement of Alexandria against Basilides the False

Meanwhile, one recent study goes so far as to denote Clement of Alexandria the first Christian philosopher of 'free will.'[93] Yet Clement does not really refer to *to autexousion* or some other, recent coinage for 'free will'—rather, in pas-

---

90   Cf. Ramelli, *Bardaiṣan*, 83: "Justin's, Clement's and Origen's defenses of human free will find a close correspondence in Bardaiṣan's contemporary theory, and at least Clement and Origen supported free will in polemic against Gnosticism, just as Bardaiṣan did."

91   Thus Diodore of Tarsus, who understood Bardaisan as liberating the soul, but not the body, from the sphere of fate's influence (Possekel, "Bardaisan's Influence," 91–92).

92   Bobzien, "Inadvertent Conception," 167–168, taking the examples of Plot. *Enn.* 3.1 [3] 9–10; 6.8 [39] 7; 3.2 [47] 10.

93   Karavites, *Evil*, 117.

WHAT WE CHOOSE NOW

sages scattered throughout the second book of the *Stromateis*, his phrasing for the notion is diverse, and owes much to the Stoa and Aristotle alike.[94] While he often uses the word *prohairesis* to denote 'choice' or 'free choice' (as might Epictetus),[95] he describes 'what is up to us' as the willingness to be persuaded by the *logos*—i.e., to have a refined desire (*boulēsis*).[96] As Matyáš Havrda has demonstrated, in the fifth book of the same work, Clement emphasizes that while rational response to our sense-impressions is necessary for virtuous action, it is not sufficient; it requires God's grace, too.[97] For Clement, the ultimate goal for the Christian 'gnostic' is to lead such a refined, pure life as to be divine.[98] Yet Clement's most penetrating exposition of freedom and accountability to be found in book four of the *Stromateis*, a disputation about martyrdom with the early second-century Christian philosopher Basilides 'the False,' who taught in Alexandria in the 130s CE, during the reigns of Hadrian and Antoninus Pius.[99] These passages are strangely muted in the secondary literature on early Christian notions of autonomy and determinism,[100] and it is not difficult to see why: Clement here argues in a digressive, obscure fashion with an opponent about whom we have little reliable knowledge beyond

---

94 On the diversity of Clement's terms, see Karavites, *Evil*, 115; on their Hellenistic valence, see M. Frede, *Free Will*, 104.

95 Clark, *Clement's Use*, 57; Karavites, *Evil*, 120; Havrda, "Grace and Free Will," 29–30, 32–33.

96 Havrda, "Grace and Free Will," 33, re: *Strom.* 2.6.26.3. Similarly, *Strom.* 2.15.62 describes "what is up to us" as our choice to obey or disobey God's commandments and the educational program of the *logos*. See also *Paed.* 1.6.30.3–31.1, where the convert enjoys the tutelage of the *logos* and the life of free choice it offers, rather than the blind obedience to the law (cit. Havrda, "Grace and Free Will," 28). The Jews in fact offer a life based on *anagkē* rather than *prohairesis* (ibid., 1.9.87.1–2, cit. Havrda, "Grace and Free Will," 28), an amusing play on the early Christian cliché that Christian teaching liberates the convert from cosmic fate.

97 Havrda, "Grace and Free Will," 139–142, re: Clem. Al. *Strom.* 5.1.7.1–2; see also Karavites, *Evil*, 121–122; Karamanolis, *Philosophy*, 168. In book three's refutation of the 'libertine' Gnostics, meanwhile, Clement emphasizes that grace extinguishes desire, even as it preserves marriage (see Harper, *From Shame to Sin*, 112).

98 For an extensive discussion, see Havrda, "Grace and Free Will," 35–42; see also Bergjan, "Clement," 71–72 re: *Strom.* 7.11.65.1, 7.11.65.5.

99 For a recent, thorough *Forschungsbericht* on this figure, see Pearson, "Basilides." For Basilides's tenure in 130s-Alexandria, see ibid., 1, 27. For a critical edition and commentary of the few quoted fragments of his works, see Löhr, *Basilides*; English translations (but different ordering) of the same fragments are given in Layton, *Gnostic Scriptures*. I refer to both these latter works in my treatment of the fragments. I bracket here the question of Basilides's alleged 'Gnosticism,' as it is immaterial to the present discussion (but cf. above, chapter four).

100 Cf. however the treatment of Bergjan, discussed in the following.

Clement's highly selective quotations. Yet these same quotations of Basilides preserve what appears to be the oldest known remarks on providence and personal accountability made by a Christian philosopher.[101]

At the outset of *Stromateis* book four, Clement elucidates each of the central themes he will contest with Basilides in chapter twelve and later chapters: the correction of the heterodox; the problem of right conduct in times of persecution; and the character and meaning of a martyr's suffering and death.[102] Clement declares the book to be a discourse on ethics (*ēthikon logon*) in which he is concerned to introduce and put an end to "the claims of the heterodox" (*ta tōn heterodoxōn*).[103] Facing the threat of death at the instigation of the Devil, he claims, the 'true Gnostic' will give up his body easily, "not maltreating the tempter, but rather, I think, educating and convincing him."[104] Clement denotes martyrdom the most honorable death, an act of perfection and love.[105] Christian martyrs are more worthy of veneration than the fallen war heroes of whose worship Heraclitus and Plato· write—that "golden race" which dwells with the gods in heaven, and "who above all wield command over the providence which extends to humanity (*tēn hēgemonian ... tēs kat'anthrōpous pronoias*)"— probably a reference to a Middle Platonic reading of the idolatrous worship of *daimones* as administrators of lower providence.[106] Some Christian heretics, he adds, either reject martyrdom or are too quick to embrace it;[107] rather,

---

101 Rightly Bergjan, *Der fürsorgende Gott*, 141.

102 On martyrdom in Clement's corpus, see van den Hoek, "Clement."

103 Clem. Al. *Strom.* 4.1.3.3, text Stählin in GCS 52:249, tr. mine.

104 Clem. Al. *Strom.* 4.4.13.1, text Stählin in GCS 52:254, tr. mine. Both these themes—education, and the Devil as the instigator of persecution—will figure largely in the polemic against Basilides.

105 Clem. Al. *Strom.* 4.4.14.3. See van den Hoek, "Clement," 328; Bergjan, *Der fürsorgende Gott*, 134.

106 Clem. Al. *Strom.* 4.4.16.1–2, text Stählin in GCS 52:255–256, tr. mine; cf. Bergjan, *Der fürsorgende Gott*, 135 n. 58, as well as *Strom.* 5.13.90–91, a discussion of the Myth of Er where the *daimones* of Lachesis are taken to be angels, who help people choose and pursue the right life (see Karamanolis, *Philosophy*, 168; Bergjan, "Clement," 88). Havrda argues convincingly that the latter passage is not concerned with election, but God's foreknowledge of what choices humans will make ("Grace and Free Will," 46, adducing *Strom.* 7.7.107.5.). On Clement's understanding of demons as the objects of civic cult, see above, chapter three; on God's foreknowledge of human actions in early Patristic sources, see above, chapter five.

107 Clem. Al. *Strom.* 4.4.16.3, 4.4.17. The latter is a *locus classicus* for the question of whether 'Gnostics' practiced martyrdom; see van den Hoek, "Clement," 329–330; Tite, "Martyrdom and Gnosticism," 28–29, 42, noting the parallel of Clement's language with that of *Test. Truth*. NHC IX 31.22–32.5, 32.19–21.

WHAT WE CHOOSE NOW

Plato himself exhorts his readers to care for the body, even as one is ready to give it up.[108]

Clement elaborates the goods of correct martyrdom further in the ensuing chapters, eventually arriving at the problem of reconciling God's providence with the persecution of his followers, a commonplace in early Christian apologetics.[109] Clements presents the issue in the fashion of a diatribe,[110] delivered to (likely fictional) heathen critics: when asked "if God cares for you (*kēdetai humōn*), why are you persecuted and put to death?", Clement answers that God does not wish for his followers to be persecuted, but is "training us to endurance" (*eis karterian gumnasas*).[111] When the heathen claims that martyrs really are being punished righteously, Clement insists that the judges who condemn martyrs are not righteous, and they are responsible for their unjust conduct:

> Thus do they involuntarily bear witness to our righteousness, when we are unrighteously punished for our righteousness! Yet the unrighteousness of the judge does not affect providence (*oude to adikon tou dikastou tēs pronoias haptetai*). For the judge must be master of his own judgment, not pulled by strings, like marionettes, set in motion only by external causes. In any case, he is tested with respect to his judgment—just as we are, too, with respect to both our selection of options, and our endurance.[112]

In order to reconcile providential care with the experience of persecution, Clement reframes the issue in terms of determinism versus human accountability—for the martyrs and persecutors alike.[113] He also reframes it in terms of eschatology: when the fictional interlocutor asks why Christians are not rescued from persecution, the answer is that there is nothing wrong with "being

---

108 Clem. Al. *Strom.* 4.4.18.

109 Ter. *Apol.* 5.5–6; Min. Fel. *Oct.* 12.4 (cf. also 27.8); Clem. Al. *Strom.* 4.11.78; Orig. *Cels.* 8.39, 41, 69. For citations and discussion, see Cook, *Interpretation of the Old Testament*, 147; Löhr, *Basilides*, 125; Bergjan, *Der fürsorgende Gott*, 123 n. 1. There is no study of language about *pronoia* in early Christian martyr-acts; a sampling of relevant passages can be found in Musurillo, *Acts*, 3, 29, 61, 93, 357.

110 Notably, the quotation from book 23 of Basilides's *Exegetica* given immediately following is also written in diatribe form. On Basilides's literary style in the fragment, see Löhr, *Basilides*, 126.

111 Clem. Al. *Strom.* 4.11.78.1–2, text Stählin in GCS 52:283, tr. mine.

112 Clem. Al. *Strom.* 4.11.79.1–2, text Stählin in GCS 52:283, tr. mine. Schüngel rightfully notes this passage as furnishing the context for the ensuing discussion of Basilides ("Gnostische Gotteslehren," 363 n. 9).

113 Osborn, *Clement*, 50.

244   CHAPTER 6

released by death to the Lord—just like a change in age, and thus, undergoing an adjustment of one's way of life."[114]

Finally, Clement turns to his decidedly non-fictional opponent, Basilides:

> Basilides, in the twenty-third book of the *Exegetica*, concerning those who are punished in martyrdom, says with these words:
>
> "For I tell you: whatever persons fall under the so-called 'afflictions' are brought to this good end since they have sinned with respect to other lapses, but forgotten. By the kindness of the Guide,[115] rather, they stand accused on other grounds—lest they suffer as people condemned for admitted bad deeds, or be reproached like adulterers or a murderer, but (so that they suffer) because they are Christians—a fact which will console them, so that they do not appear to suffer. Even if one who has not sinned at all should come into suffering—which is rare—that one, however, will not suffer due to the machinations of authority. Rather, he will suffer as does the child who appears not to have sinned."[116]

Basilides compares a person with the capacity to sin to someone who will benefit from punishment, just as a child needs training.[117] He continues:

> (Basilides): "For just as whoever wants (*thelōn*) to commit adultery is an adulterer even if he does not happen to commit adultery, and whoever wants to commit murder is a murderer even if he is not able to kill, so also, should I see that blameless person of whom I speak suffering—even if he has not done anything bad, I dub him bad, by virtue of his wanting to sin. For I will say anything rather than call providence (*to pronooun*) bad!"[118]

Finally, Clement adds, Basilides "explicitly speaks about the Lord as if about a human," apparently claiming that the suffering Jesus was like a suffering

---

114 Clem. Al. *Strom.* 4.11.80.1, text Stählin in GCS 52:283, tr. mine. Cf. also Plot. *Enn.* 3.2 [47] 15.25–29.

115 God, in His capacity as leader of souls—a loose rendering of *tou periagontos*. On the Platonic resonances of this rare word, see Löhr, *Basilides*, 128–129.

116 Clem. Al. *Strom.* 4.12.81.1–3 = frg. 7 Löhr = frg. G Layton, text Stählin in GCS 52:284, tr. mine.

117 Clem. Al. *Strom.* 4.12.82.1, tr. mine.

118 Clem. Al. *Strom.* 4.12.82.2 = frg. 7 Löhr = frg. G Layton, text Stählin in GCS 52:284, tr. mine. The final clause makes clear that Basilides's thinking about providence was distant from that of the Nag Hammadi texts which refer to providence as a malevolent power (see above, chapter four).

WHAT WE CHOOSE NOW

child—someone who did not sin except by virtue of being human. Basilides quotes Job 14:4 LXX: "for no one is free from pollution."[119]

Basilides's concern here is theodicy, and specifically the goodness of providence, which he is at pains to defend.[120] At least in these fragments, he holds a monistic view of the cosmos which does not assign responsibility for evil to malevolent external actors, like demons.[121] While it is possible that Basilides anticipated the sort of Hellenic critics who asked why martyrs suffer,[122] his occasion for reflection on martyrdom may not be apologetic, as much as a paraenetic exegesis of 1 Pet 4:12–19 (if it is bad to be punished as a wrongdoer, it is good to be punished for being a Christian).[123] Basilides's theory appears to have been that the persecuted suffer, because they are sinners, for all people are sinners (thus Job 14:4 LXX), and even small children suffer for sin; martyrs just get to suffer in the best way possible.[124] He pushes back against the Peripatetics, insofar as Aristotle, and the *BLC*, as we have seen, argue that one must be physically unhindered from doing something in order to be voluntary and thus 'up to' him or her.[125] Basilides disagrees: he says that the desire (*boulēsis*) suffices to assign accountability (cf. Matt 5:27). According to Basilides, praise or blame may be accorded even for sins which are intended but not possible to accomplish.

To be sure, this fragment says nothing about where these bad desires come from, nor how the punishment of sinners actually works, which indicates that these were not the questions Basilides was trying to answer here.[126] Yet Clement explains how he thinks Basilides saw the matter:

> But the hypothesis of Basilides says that the soul, having sinned earlier in another life, endures punishment here (*proamartesasan ... ten psuchen en*

---

119 Clem. Al. *Strom.* 4.12.83.1, text Stählin in GCS 52:284–285, tr. mine.

120 Nautin, "Les fragments," 206; van den Hoek, "Clement," 332; *pace* Schüngel, "Gnostische Gotteslehren," 362 n. 3.

121 Löhr, *Basilides*, 133, 136–137; Schüngel, "Gnostische Gotteslehren," 363.

122 Löhr, *Basilides*, 137; Tite, "Martyrdom and Gnosticism," 49–50. As is widely recognized, only later witnesses claim that Basilides discouraged martyrdom altogether (Nautin, "Les fragments," 399 n. 4; Layton, *Gnostic Scriptures*, 441; Tite, op. cit. 50).

123 Layton, *Gnostic Scriptures*, 440; Procter, *Christian Controversy*, 57 n. 11. Löhr is skeptical (*Basilides*, 129). Cf. Bergjan, who prefers 2 Macc 7:18 as Basilides's object of exegesis (*Der fürsorgende Gott*, 130, 144).

124 Bergjan, *Der fürsorgende Gott*, 140, 144; eadem, "Clement," 73–74; cf. also Havrda, "Grace and Free Will," 31 n. 45.

125 *Eth. eud.* 2.7 1223a–b; *Eth. nic.* 5.8–9 1135a–1136b; *Rhetorics* 1.13 1374b. Clement knows these terms (*Strom.* 2.15.62). Cf. further M. Frede, *Free Will*, 95, re: Alex. Aphr. *Fat.* 14.

126 Rightly Bergjan, *Der fürsorgende Gott*, 129–130.

heterōi biōi tēn kolasin hupomenein entautha)—the elect soul honorably, by martyrdom, and the other cleansed by the appropriate punishment. How is this truly up to us, when the act of confessing and suffering punishment or not is already established? For in the case of the person who shall deny (Christianity), Basilides's notion of providence is done away with.[127]

Clement here alleges that Basilides taught reincarnation: the sufferings we endure in the present life are punishments for sins from previous lives. Scholars are split as to the veracity of Clement's claim. There is no fragment of Basilides's writings which refers explicitly to the transmigration of souls,[128] but as Birger Pearson has argued, it would not be at all strange for a Platonist like Basilides to have taught reincarnation.[129] In the second and third centuries, there were a variety of Christians who believed in metempsychosis of some kind.[130] In support of this view, Clement's arguments in the remainder of *Stromateis* book four presuppose that Basilides believed that even prior to this life, the soul makes decisions for which it must be held accountable. While we cannot know for sure what Basilides really taught, it is clear that Clement combats the view he ascribes to Basilides—shared with Plato, the *BLC*, and (as we will see) Origen—that the soul's faculty of accountability was an active cause prior to its incarnation on the material plane.

Clement certainly understands as much when he charges Basilides's psychology as mutually exclusive with the decision to confess or deny Christianity being 'is up to us,' and with providence, drawing upon arguments commonly levied against the Stoa. If providence is responsible even for persecutions, then it is also responsible for the lapsed Christian who denies the faith and is unjustly rewarded, while the confessor is unjustly punished for affirming the faith.[131] Rather, it must be the Devil who instigates persecution.[132] It must be possible, Clement believes, to accord persecuted and persecutor alike praise or

---

127   Clem. Al. *Strom.* 4.12.83.2 = frg. G Layton, text Stählin in GCS 52:285, tr. mine.

128   Nautin, "Les fragments," esp. 397; Löhr, *Basilides*, 216–218; Schüngel, "Gnostische Gotteslehren," 366 n. 14; Bergjan, *Der fürsorgende Gott*, 126–128, n. 25. Scholars who have taken Clement and Origen (*Comm. Rom.* 5.1.27 = frg. 18 Löhr = frg. F Layton) at their word on the matter include Layton, *Gnostic Scriptures*, 439; idem, "Significance," 139–140; van den Hoek, "Clement," 332; Procter, *Christian Controversy*, 36–37, 57–58 n. 12.

129   Pearson, "Basilides," 18, 26.

130   Useful remains the survey of Hoheisel, "Seelenwanderung"; additionally, Burns, *Apocalypse*, 227–228 n. 112.

131   Clem. Al. *Strom.* 4.12.84.1–3.

132   Clem. Al. *Strom.* 4.12.85.1; similarly, 4.12.86.2; on these passages, see also Löhr, *Basilides*, 145–150; Bergjan, *Der fürsorgende Gott*, 146–154.

WHAT WE CHOOSE NOW

blame, but if one's actions in a previous existence determine if one will punish or be punished, then praise and blame are superfluous—the old 'lazy argument.'[133] Clement then backtracks once more to the question of whether God is responsible for persecution:

> But if, as Basilides himself says: "we presuppose one part of the aforementioned will of God to be the act of loving everything,[134] because everything makes sense as regards the whole (*logon aposōzousi pros to pan apanta*)";[135] and another: "desire nothing"; and thirdly: "hate nothing"—by the will of God there will be punishments, too, which is impious to think![136]

Basilides's words here—that the universe is ordered for the best, and so it is best to love how it is ordered—make good Stoicism, and so Clement again argues, as one might against a Stoic, that Basilides imputes even evil to God.[137] Clement agrees that "nothing at all happens apart from the will of the Lord of the universe (*thelēmatos tou kuroiou tōn holōn*). It remains to state in brief, that such things happen, without God preventing them; for this alone preserves both the providence and the goodness of God."[138]

---

133 Clem. Al. *Strom.* 4.12.85.3; so also van den Hoek, "Clement," 332; Löhr, *Basilides*, 148 n. 10; cf. Clark, *Clement's Use*, 54.

134 With Layton in regarding this clause to be the words of Basilides (*Gnostic Scriptures*, 435); cf. Löhr, opting for Clement's words (*Basilides*, 152).

135 With Löhr in regarding this clause to be the words of Basilides, and to their meaning (*Basilides*, 152 n. 2); cf. Layton, opting for Clement's words, with a different rendering (*Gnostic Scriptures*, 435: "and they reserve the word 'all' to refer to the entirety").

136 Clem. Al. *Strom.* 4.12.86.1 = frg. 8 Löhr = frg. D Layton, text Stählin in GCS 52:286, tr. mine. Clement writes much the same—almost verbatim—at *Strom.* 7.81.1–2 (Chadwick and Oulton, *Alexandrian Christianity*, 145 n. 68; Löhr, *Basilides*, 153–154).

137 On the Stoic flavor of the passage, see Layton, *Gnostic Scriptures*, 434; van den Hoek, "Clement," 332; Löhr, *Basilides*, 154; Pearson, "Basilides," 25. Löhr also notes Rom 7:7; Ex 20:17/Dt 5:21 (*Basilides*, 155). Thus Layton (op. cit.): "the 'will of god' is providence (fate), which according to Stoic ethics controls all events in the universe. A virtuous person assents to all ('loves all') that is and that comes to pass ..." For the anti-Stoic nuance of Clement's reply, see Pearson, op. cit. Löhr has argued that this fragment exculpates Basilides of accusations of 'world-hating dualism' in favor of a 'cosmic piety' (*Basilides*, 154–155), but as we have seen (above, chapter four), Gnostics spoke warmly of God's *pronoia* even as they rejected its extension to the present cosmos; the question is whether "the whole" here refers to the created cosmos or not. Surely Löhr is right (op. cit. 155) that the context is theodicy (also Procter, *Christian Controversy*, 37).

138 Clem. Al. *Strom.* 4.12.86.3, text Stählin in GCS 52:286, tr. mine; see also Bergjan, *Der fürsorgende Gott*, 148; Löhr, *Basilides*, 149–150.

248 CHAPTER 6

In book one of the *Stromateis*, Clement had argued that God permits but appropriates evil, providentially turning it to the good of education or discipline (*paideia*)—a poignant example being the introduction of forbidden arts by the Watchers to human beings, which God has led to the spread of Greek learning.[139] Conversely, the punishments that are at work in *paideia* are a form of *pronoia*, rather than the work of an overly wrathful deity (a knock against Marcion).[140] Clement argues much the same here, highlighting that punishment is providential only if it is disciplinary, i.e., educational.[141] "'I shall destroy,' He (God) therefore says, 'the wall, and it shall be for treading upon,' because providence is such that it is a disciplinary art (*paideutikēs technēs tēs toiautēs ousēs pronoias*) ..."[142] Continuing his diatribe with a (likely fictive) interlocutor, he returns to the scenario of the martyr as punished for sins from a previous existence: if the punishment is instituted by providence, then either the persecutors are just, or providence wreaks injustice.[143] One cannot render the

---

139 Clem. Al. *Strom.* 1.82.1–2; Bergjan, "Clement," 74; see also above, chapter three.

140 Clem. Al. *Strom.* 1.27.173.5; Bergjan, "Clement," 68 (in his debt to Philo); Havrda, "Grace and Free Will," 22 n. 3, 26–27 (on the Marcionite context).

141 Clem. Al. *Strom.* 4.12.87.1; Bergjan, *Der fürsorgende Gott*, 158 *passim*. In addition to the ensuing discussion, see *Strom.* 6.6.46.3, per Solmsen, "Providence and the Souls," 366 n. 55; Bergjan, "Clement," 70–71. See also Bergjan, *Der fürsorgende Gott*, 125, re: *Strom.* 7.16.102.3–5 (when God punishes, He does not take revenge; He educates). On the theme of discipline via punishment in ancient philosophy and Clement's engagement with it, see Löhr, *Basilides*, 129–130; Bergjan, *Der fürsorgende Gott*, 125–126, 129, 156–168.

142 Clem. Al. *Strom.* 4.12.87.2, text Stählin in GCS 52:286, tr. mine.

143 "If, then, one of them were to say in defense that 'the martyr is punished for sins committed prior to this embodiment, and that he will hereafter reap the fruit of his conduct in this life—for such has the administration been arranged'—we shall ask if retribution is caused by providence. For if it were not caused by divine administration, then the element of divine planning of purifications disappears, and their hypothesis falls; but if purifications are caused by providence, punishments are also caused by providence" (*Strom.* 4.12.88.1–2, text Stählin in GCS 52:286–287, tr. mine).

The following passage presents a puzzle: "but if providence begins to be moved by the Archon—as they say—it has rather been sown in substances at the time of their creation by the God of the universe" (ibid., 4.12.88.3, text Stählin in GCS 52:287, tr. mine). The exact meaning of this passage remains unclear (unconvincing are the interpretations proposed by Löhr, *Basilides*, 150; Schüngel, "Gnostische Gotteslehren," 367, 369), but it is difficult not to recall the *Refutatio*'s account of Basilides's 'pseudo-Aristotelian' teaching that providence extends only to the supralunary realm (*Ref.* 7.24.3; Procter, *Christian Controversy*, 8; Bos, "Basilides," 53). With Bergjan (*Der fürsorgende Gott*, 140 n. 85) I bracket the question, which merits a study of its own. In any case, Clement's argument remains the same: "with things being so, it is necessary for them to agree either that punishment is unjust—and the condemners and persecutors of the martyrs practice righteousness—or that even persecutions are wrought by the will of God" (*Strom.* 4.12.88.4, text Stählin in GCS 52:287, tr. mine).

WHAT WE CHOOSE NOW

pain and fear which result from persecution as "incidental to affairs, like rust is to iron"—the 'concomitance argument'—"rather, by one's own intention (*ek bouleseos idias*) do they come upon the soul."[144] Following lengthy digressions, he explains their purpose with reference to the story of the fall of Adam—but also the Myth of Er. The ability to choose, he writes, is a divine gift which belongs to humans alone.[145] For Adam, who was created complete and had no reason to sin, "the responsibility lies with the one who chooses, and particularly in his choosing what was forbidden; God has none."[146] Clement glosses *Resp.* x 617d–e with the clarification that it was "choosing what was forbidden" for which Adam was to blame.

Clement's appropriation of the classic Platonist proof-text for the soul's pre-existence and concomitant pre-natal accountability is no accident. He proceeds to elaborate a view of two-sided, potestative responsibility delimited to voluntary, completed actions:

> To take the example of what is up to us, we are equally in control both over the one thing and its opposite—like whether to philosophize or not, and whether to believe or disbelieve. So, on account of us being in control equally over each of the opposites, what is up to us is found to be possible. Indeed, the commandments, too, are such that they may or may not be observed by us, to whom follows praise and blame, as is reasonable. Moreover, whoever is punished on account of the sins which befell them is punished for them alone.[147] For whatever happened, happened; and what has happened is never going to be something that didn't happen.[148]

The final sentence is no empty truism: Clement agrees with Aristotle that something is only up to us if it is 'possible' for us to do (and this holds for the Ten Com-

---

144 *Strom.* 4.12.88.5 = frg. 9 Löhr, text Stählin in GCS 52:287, tr. mine. Löhr recognizes parallels to this metaphor (*Basilides*, 157–159, re: Plat. *Resp.* 609a and esp. *Corp. Herm.* 14.7); Schüngel rightly notices that the argument (for Plato and Basilides alike) is a concomitance argument ("Gnostische Gotteslehren," 365).

145 Clem. Al. *Strom.* 4.19.124.2–3, per Karamanolis, *Philosophy*, 166.

146 Clem. Al. *Strom.* 4.23.150.4, text Stählin in GCS 52:315, tr. mine (*aitia de elomenou, kai eti mallon to koluthen elomenou, ho theos anaitios*).

147 Löhr rightly dispels Nautin's suggestion that the passage means Basilides took martyrs to be suffering on behalf of others; Clement simply means that punishments are in accordance with that for which people are responsible (*Basilides*, 161).

148 Clem. Al. *Strom.* 4.24.153.1–2, text Stählin in GCS 52:316, tr. mine. Cf. Karamanolis, *Philosophy*, 167. Later, Clement alludes to the 'two spirits' doctrine (*Strom.* 4.26.165.1; on the 'two spirits,' see above, chapter three).

250   CHAPTER 6

mandments, as argued in the *BLC*), thus rejecting Basilides's contention that all human beings are sinners, and even responsible for sins intended but not acted upon. He elaborates with recourse to the example of pre- and post-baptismal sin: "so, forgiven by the Lord are the ⟨sins committed⟩ prior to faith—not so that they are things that didn't happen, but as if they had not happened. 'But not all,' says Basilides, 'but only (sins) involuntary and in ignorance (*akousious kai kata agnoian*), are forgiven'—as would be the case were it a human, and not God, who conferred such a boon!"[149] In other words, Basilides maintains that only involuntary sins are forgiven to converts; voluntary sins committed prior to baptism—including those intended but not committed—are to be punished.[150]

Clement's counterargument presupposes that these pre-baptismal voluntary sins must include those made prior to birth. The point of punishment, Clement writes, is not to undo sin (an impossibility), but to help people stop sinning, or at least sin less: a punished sinner may come to recognize his or her sinful habit and abandon it, while those who witness the punishment may be deterred from the sin in question, and accept the person who has sinned back into the fold.[151] For Clement, suffering must be disciplinary for it to be providential, but Basilides's notion of punishment educates no one. If the sins for which one is being disciplined occurred in a previous existence, there is no sin on display for the instruction of the spectator, nor in the memory of the one being punished; rather, both punished and spectator are left with the gruesome spectacle of the punishment alone. In other words, if Basilides held the sins punished in martyrdom to be only those made in this life, there is no reason that this punishment could not be educational (and thus providential) as well. Yet this is precisely what Clement is as pains to contest.

The closing passages of *Stromateis* book four show Clement concerned with clarifying exactly how the soul is granted accountability for its actions, with

---

149   Clem. Al. *Strom.* 4.24.153.3–4 = frg. 10 Löhr = frg. H Layton, text Stählin in GCS 52:316, tr. mine.

150   Rightly Pearson, "Basilides," 27; similarly, Procter, *Christian Controversy*, 57 n. 11. Löhr has argued that Basilides's view here is virtually the same as Clement's (that voluntary sins prior to baptism are punished while involuntary sins altogether are forgiven—*Basilides*, 163), but Clement says explicitly otherwise. Moreover, if Clement and Basilides had the same view, why would the former bring it up for debate at all (thus Clem. Al. *Strom.* 4.24.154.2–3)? On *Strom.* 5.1.3.2–3, see below, in this chapter.

151   Clem. Al. *Strom.* 4.24.135.5–4.24.154.1. Cf. also Clark's discussion of how Clement regards even sins made out of ignorance to be punishable offenses—unlike Aristotle and Basilides (*Clement's Use*, 58–63).

WHAT WE CHOOSE NOW

respect to the fact of its embodiment and eschatological fate. The 'true Gnostic' sojourns in the body, which he treats respectfully, although he knows he will abandon it:

> "I am a stranger in the earth, and a sojourner with you" (Gen 23:4 LXX) it is said. And hence Basilides says that "he apprehends that the elect is a stranger to the world, being supramundane by nature (*huperkosmion phusei*)." But this is not so. For everything is of one God, and no one could be a stranger to the world by nature, for their essence is one, and God is one. Rather, the elect individual conducts oneself like a stranger (*hōs xenos*), knowing everything to be given and taken away.[152]

The 'resident alien' motif—the notion that the elect Christian is a stranger to the present world—was itself not uncommon in early Christian literature.[153] What is at issue for Clement here is what the motif means: does the soul really belong to another plane, or is it at one with the rest of creation in the present life? He appears to have taken Basilides's teaching to be misleading regarding not only the meaning of suffering or of accountability in this life, but the import of these questions for soul's fate after life as well.

Clement thus developed his notions about responsibility and freedom in *Stromateis* book four against the backdrop of a conflict with Basilides over the involvement of providence in persecution and suffering, and of the soul's relationship to the beyond. Basilides appears to have been something of an eclectic,[154] favoring a highly monistic view of God's providential involvement in the cosmos but where all humans are sinners, facts reconciled by God's punishment of sinners, even martyrs. Clement used anti-Stoic arguments to paint this view as incompatible with any coherent notion of accountability, and his claims that punishment can be providential only if it is disciplinary—and that Basilides's claims about punishment are mutually exclusive with any such disciplinary function—indicate that Basilides probably taught that souls are punished for voluntary sins committed even prior to birth. Albeit in a different manner, the soul possesses its own causal efficacy in its pre-exis-

---

152   Clem. Al. *Strom.* 4.26.165.3–4 = frg. 12 Löhr = frg. E Layton, text Stählin in GCS 52:321, tr. mine. Clement says much the same at *Strom.* 7.12.78. Layton reads the passage as referring to reincarnation (*Gnostic Scriptures*, 436).

153   For survey of the motif, see Dunning, *Aliens*; on its wide use in Sethian Gnostic literature, see Burns, *Apocalypse*, 102–105.

154   On Basilides's eclecticism, see Layton, *Gnostic Scriptures*, 418; Löhr, "Gnostic Determinism," 388 n. 16; idem, *Basilides*, 136.

252   CHAPTER 6

tence, as in the BLC. For Clement, Plato's statement that "responsibility lies with the one who chooses" can only refer to the soul's potestative, two-sided judgment (MR2) employed in this life—even if it answers for it to God, after death.[155]

5   Origen 'On Free Will' (Princ. 3.1), "Older Causes," and Gnostic Determinism

As discussed in the introduction to this chapter, a red thread in modern scholarship on the emergence of 'free will' in early Christian philosophy is the conflict with 'Gnostic determinism': Christian philosophers developed their notions of free will, the story goes, in order to overcome the threat of 'Gnostic determinism.'[156] Sure enough, even in passages beyond those treated in the previous section, Clement charges Basilides with having taught a determinist soteriology mutually exclusive with personal accountability, grouping him with Marcion and Valentinus as adherents to the belief that salvation is 'by nature' rather than incumbent upon one's actions.[157] Given the paucity and highly polemicized character of our extant evidence to the matter, all that can be readily said is that Basilides and Valentinus probably did employ the phrase 'saved by nature' or something like it, although what they meant by it is largely unknown to us.[158] Some Valentinian primary sources demarcate between humanity based upon their soteriological capacity, largely owing to

---

155   Clement says nothing here about what happens to the soul after death, but in other books of the *Stromateis*, he refers to the soul's postmortem purgation by fire (5.1.9.3–6, 6.14.109, 7.6.34.4), different abodes for the virtuous in heaven (6.14.114; cf. 7.10.57.5, a sort of entrance to the Ogdoad), and (vaguely) the Final Judgment (7.2.12). Cit. May, "Eschatologie v. Alte Kirche," 301–302.

156   Representative is the articulation of Dihle, "Astrology," 162: "To the Gnostics, the conception of Fate and Necessity as underlying the theory and practice of astrology simply indicated the worthlessness of the world as we experience it by our senses. The Gnostic, by his intellectual effort, left far behind this miserable world of matter which was ruled by Fate or Necessity. He had been freed from the bounds [sic?—DMB] of matter ..." Similarly, see idem, "Philosophische Lehren," 19; idem, *Theory of Will*, 150; Jacobsen, "Freedom," 71–74; Ramelli, *Bardaisan*, 64–65; Martens, "Origen's Doctrine," 546–547 n. 96; Karamanolis, *Philosophy*, 144; Adamson, *Philosophy*, 292–294; M. Scott, *Journey*, 38.

157   Clem. Al. *Strom.* 2.3.10.1–3; 5.1.3.2–3 = frg. 13 Löhr = frg. C Layton.

158   See Löhr, *Basilides*, 186–190; similarly, Pearson, "Basilides," 19–21, 24. For criticism of the modern reconstruction of 'Gnostic determinism' more generally, see Schottroff, "*Animae naturiliter salvandae*," and the scholarship discussed in the following notes.

WHAT WE CHOOSE NOW

exegesis of Gen 2:7 by way of 1 Cor 2:14–15.[159] The rhetorical context for these demarcations appear not to be philosophical ruminations on accountability, but exegesis of Pauline and Johannine theologies of election,[160] and in any case it should not surprise us if some early Christian writers expressed views about accountability more in line with Stoic compatibilism than a modern notion of 'free will.'[161]

Clement pillories the notion of 'salvation by nature' with the 'lazy argument' as he might attack a Stoic,[162] but his engagement is brief and relates precious little regarding his opponents' ideas about personal accountability. The case is different, however, with Origen of Alexandria, who was deeply concerned with the same problem. 'Determinism' of some kind is the primary question of the first sub-treatise in the third book of *On First Principles*, entitled *Peri Autexousiou*, which as we will see, may here fairly be translated as *On Free Will*—a discussion of freedom and determinism which is widely recognized as the first truly great treatment of these questions by a Christian philosopher.[163] The compilers of the *Philocalia* even excerpted this discussion to open its anthology of Origen's discussions of freedom and human responsibility, and so this is one of the sections of *On First Principles* where we possess the Greek text.[164] The stakes are high: both at the start of *On Free Will* and of *On First Principles* itself, Origen states that a crucial doctrine of the Church is that the soul merits praise or blame—specifically, reward or punishment in the afterlife—for its actions, and this is why a philosophically tenable notion of personal accountability matters.[165] Although Origen's discussion of free will here is well-known,

---

159 Theodotus, ap. Clem. Al. *Exc.* 54–56, 61–65; Heracleon, ap. Orig. *Comm. Jo.* 13.16, 20.20, 20.24 *passim*; *Tri. Trac.* NHC I 105.29–106.25, 118.28–120.22; cf. also Ir. *Haer.* 1.6–1.7; *Ref.* 6.34.3–8. For discussion, see recently Dunderberg, "Valentinian Theories"; Thomassen, "Saved by Nature?"; Kocar, "Humanity"; Dubois, "Once Again." On the scriptural proof-texts behind this speculation, see van Kooten, "Anthropological Trichotomy." Elliott's remarks on the subject exceed the primary sources themselves in obscurity (*Providence Perceived*, 10).

160 So Pagels, *Johannine Gospel*, 100, followed by Clark, *Clement's Use*, 46.

161 Burns, "There Is No Soul"; a new study on this question is Linjamaa, *Ethics*.

162 Clem. Al. *Strom.* 2.3.11.1–2; see Löhr, "Gnostic Determinism," 384; see further Havrda, "Grace and Free Will," 22 n. 4; Bergjan, "Clement," 76. Irenaeus also used the 'lazy argument' in this context (Löhr, op. cit., 382–383, re: *Haer.* 2.29.1, 4.37.2, followed by Kocar, "'Humanity'," 201; further, Karamanolis, *Philosophy*, 147 re: *Haer.* 5.6.1).

163 Karamanolis, *Philosophy*, 90; similarly, M. Frede, *Free Will*, 105.

164 While Basil and Gregory appear to have removed some references to the pre-existence of souls in the texts, the Greek of *Philoc.* 21 appears to be a more reliable text of *Princ.* 3.1 than is Rufinus's Latin (Crouzel, "Theological Construction," 239). On the Greek text in general, see Junod in SC 226:18–20.

165 Jackson, "Sources," 13; Crouzel, "Theological Construction," 239–240; see more recently

254   CHAPTER 6

detailed scholarly treatment of it is more rare than one might expect.[166] Nor is there much agreement about the identity of his exegetical opponents, or the philosophical valence of his response to them. In light of the preceding discussion, it is worth closely examining Origen's remarks in this little but significant treatise 'on free will'—a notion he explains via scriptural exegesis as the two-sided ability 'to choose otherwise,' bound up with the soul's education through punishment and its existence and capacity to choose for itself even prior to embodiment.[167]

As is widely recognized, *On Free Will*'s opening pages present us with an essentially Stoic explanation of how personal accountability works: we can choose to react one way or another to the sense impressions with which we are presented, despite our initial disposition to them.[168] Origen even uses an example drawn straight from Epictetus—the visage of a beautiful woman, whose appearance may instigate lust in the heart of the beholder.[169] (Significantly, he does not here denote this stimulus as demonic in origin.)[170] However, Origen then pivots to apply this theory to exegesis, selecting problematic passages from both the Old and New Testaments that could mislead someone into thinking "that it is not within our power either to keep the commandments and to be saved or to transgress them and be lost."[171] While Origen entertains many examples from scripture in his disputation with his 'deterministic' opponents, the

---

      Jacobsen, "Freedom," 66–67, and esp. M. Frede, *Free Will*, 107–108, re: *Princ.* Praef.4–5, 3.1.1; cf. ibid., 2.8.3.

166   Noted by Boys-Stones, "Human Autonomy," 493 n. 32; for a more detailed bibliography re: Origen and Greek notions of free will, see Benjamins, *Eingeordnete Freiheit*, 3–6.

167   As is clear in the following, I agree with Dihle's assessment that *Princ.* 3.1 offers three lines of argument in response to soteriological determinism: Stoic co-determination, providential pedagogy, and metempsychosis ("Philosophische Lehren," 22; idem, *Theory of Will*, 110–111; cf. Jacobsen, "Freedom," 70–71; Ferguson, *Providence of God*, 52).

168   Orig. *Princ.* 3.1.1–5. See Crouzel, "Theological Construction," 241–244; Dihle, "Philosophische Lehren," 21–23; Jacobsen, "Freedom," 67–68; Perkams, "Ethischer Intellektualismus," 242–247; M. Frede, *Free Will*, 111–113, 120; Karamanolis, *Philosophy*, 173–175; Gibbons, "Human Autonomy," 678.

169   Orig. *Princ.* 3.1.4. Epictetus's example includes a comely young man, as well as a woman (*Diatr.* 2.18.15–18). It is an important passage for Harper's argument that early Christian discourse about free will was tied up in thinking about sexuality (*From Shame to Sin*, 128). The passage may rather be read as indicative simply of Origen's debt to Stoicism (M. Frede, *Free Will*, 118; Jackson, "Sources," 20).

170   Unlike Orig. *Princ.* 3.2.1–2, which explicitly denotes external stimuli to desire as demonic (Benjamins, *Eingeordnete Freiheit*, 132–136).

171   Orig. *Princ.* 3.1.7, tr. Behr, 301, 303. This is not to agree with Elliott that "for Origen moral praxis rather than philosophical theory mattered" (*Providence Perceived*, 20).

WHAT WE CHOOSE NOW 255

primary body of proof-texts up for debate is that relating to God's hardening of Pharaoh's heart in the book of Exodus.[172]

> Since some of the heterodox use these passages, practically also destroying self-determination themselves by introducing natures which are lost, incapable of being saved, and other natures which are saved, unable to be lost—they say that Pharaoh, being of a lost nature, is on this account hardened by God, who has mercy upon the spiritual but hardens the earthy—come, let us now see what they mean.[173]

His answer is that if Pharaoh was earthy and therefore disobedient, why did God need to harden his heart to get him to disobey, more than once? Rather, "it was possible for him to obey ... but God needs him to be more disobedient in order to demonstrate his mighty deeds for the salvation of the many."[174]

Pharaoh thus played a key role as part of God's pedagogy, which is entirely benevolent—but he was no mere 'instrument' or 'marionette' bereft of autonomy (as feared by Bardaiṣan and Clement, respectively).[175] Rather, there are two kinds of land which receive rain: some bloom, and some not (Heb 6:7.8), and in the same way, different people react differently to God's works.[176] Yet God is not responsible for their reaction; instead, having knowledge of everything, God foresees providentially what people will do, and instrumentalizes their actions accordingly in service of the divine plan.[177] In the case of Pharaoh,

---

172 The passages in question are: Ex 4:21, 7:3 (Pharaoh); Ez 11:19.20 (stony hearts vs. hearts of flesh); Matt 13:10 and Mark 4:12 (Jesus's description of esoteric parables); Rom 9:16 (nobody resists God's will), 9:20–21 (the vessels and the lump); Phil 2:13 (only God wills).

   Origen treated the problem of Pharaoh in largely similar fashion in a number of his writings: *Or.* 29.16; *Homilies on Exodus*, 3.3, 4.1–7, 6.3–4, 6.9; *Comm. Rom.* 7.16; above all, *Philoc.* 27; cit. Koch, *Pronoia*, 131 n. 1; Crouzel, "Theological Construction," 246 n. 23; Junod in SC 226:118 n. 1. For discussion, see Junod, op. cit. 118–119.

173 Orig. *Princ.* 3.1.8, tr. Behr, 307.

174 Orig. *Princ.* 3.1.8, tr. Behr, 307.

175 Orig. *Princ.* 3.1.9–10. The Greek from *Philoc.* 21 focuses on the evil present in Pharaoh's heart already, but Rufinus's Latin translation emphasizes the instructive aspect more. Origen adds that Pharaoh's wavering shows that it was also up to him (*Princ.* 3.1.11). See also Magris, *L'idea di destino*, 2:843.

176 "In this way, then, the wonders done by God are, as it were, the rain, while the differing human wills are, as it were, the cultivated and neglected earth, both being, as earth, of one nature" (tr. Behr, 315). On this passage, see Crouzel, "Theological Construction," 248–249.

177 Koch, *Pronoia*, 129; Crouzel, "Theological Construction," 247; Dihle, *Theory of Will*, 110. Cf. *Cels.* 5.1.

256 CHAPTER 6

his heart was hard already, so God hardened it some more—Stoic co-determinism.[178] Amusingly, Origen adds that God even knows in advance who will "find fault with his providence" (*tōn aitiōmenōn autou tēn pronoian*) and "blame his administration" (*dioikēsin autou*) and so punishes them accordingly—implying that his exegetical opponents have in store some nasty punishments indeed.[179]

The sort of omniscience presumed on God's part here recalls Origen's discussion of the foreknowledge of Judas's sin in the *Commentary on Genesis* and *Against Celsus* (see above, chapter five).[180] Yet his second line of argumentation—God providentially appropriates sinful activity for pedagogical purposes, with a view to eschatology—is distinctive, if familiar from Clement (see above, in this chapter).[181] Silke-Petra Bergjan has argued that Origen here has a more juridical than pedagogical notion of punishment, but the Greek text of *On First Principles* certainly has the goal of instruction in mind.[182] The worst thing God can do, he claims, would be not to punish us, since it is through punishment that we become better:

---

178   God is "not intending to harden, but [acting] with a good purpose, upon which the hardening follows on account of the underlying element of evil (*dia to tēs kakias upokeimenon*), the evil present in such people, so that he is said to harden the one who is hardened" (Orig. *Princ.* 3.1.10, text and tr. Behr, 312, 313). Notably, this detail is removed by Rufinus. See also *Princ.* 3.1.12–13.

179   Orig. *Princ.* 3.1.17, text and tr. Behr, 348–349.

180   Strangely enough, Stead seems to think that this is the main argument of the work (*Philosophy*, 89), a notion which would fit better to *Comm. Gen.* (*Philoc.* 23, discussed above, chapter five).

181   The element of *paideia* was first highlighted by Koch, *Pronoia* (esp. 137–138); see further Crouzel, "Theological Construction," 251–252; Elliott, *Providence Perceived*, 20–22; Gibbons, "Human Autonomy."

182   Bergjan claims that Koch (see prev. note) overemphasizes the element of *paideia* in Origen's *oeuvre* (*Der fürsorgende Gott*, 172–174, esp. 172 n. 5, 176), but at times overstates her case. She uses Clement as a foil, arguing that because Origen does not discuss *paideia* in the same way that Clement does, then *paideia* is of little importance to Origen altogether (Bergjan, *Der fürsorgende Gott*, 174–179, 219)—a straw man. More significantly, Bergjan prefers Rufinus's Latin in reading *Princ.*, because the relevant texts are ostensibly not preserved in Greek (*Der fürsorgende Gott*, 179 n. 25). Yet her choice of passages is selective and misleading: she does not at all discuss *Princ.* 3.1 (where the Greek is preserved, ap. *Philoc.* 21, as discussed presently), and elsewhere reads the Latin where the Greek is available (op. cit. 187 n. 20, re: *Princ.* 1.6.3). Moreover, Rist has observed that Rufinus gives a juridical cast to Origen's ideas about punishment, both as regards his translation (*condemnatio* < *kolasis*, etc.) and his expansions regarding the just character of God qua judge ("Greek and Latin Texts," 99, re: *Princ.* 3.1.9). Bergjan's thesis may then speak more to Rufinus's Latin translation than Origen's original Greek (Bergjan cites Rist but does not appear to see the problem—Bergjan, *Der fürsorgende Gott*, 179 n. 25).

WHAT WE CHOOSE NOW

257

He abandons most people by not punishing them, in order that, from the things within our power, the character of each may be tested and the better ones may become manifest from the trial applied, while the others ... may later come upon the way of healing, for they would not have known the benefit if they had not condemned themselves; and this is beneficial to each, that he perceive his own particularity and the grace of God.[183]

God instructs souls in this way "because, with regard to the immortality of the soul and the limitless age, it will be for their advantage that they may not be too quickly assisted to salvation, but be slowly led to it after experiencing many evils."[184] In fact, God was educating Pharaoh himself, too: "even Pharaoh by means of great events and by drowning in the sea, at which his dispensation for Pharaoh (*oikonomia tou Pharaō*) does not end, for he was not destroyed when drowned ..."[185]

Origen specifies that the souls being trained by God through punishment do not merely possess a faculty of autonomy (MR1), but are educated so as to be able to make good choices between opposite options (MR2). In his reading of Phil 2:13, he writes that we "received the ability to will (*to thelein*) from the Creator (*dēmiourgou*), while we employ the facility of willing either for the noblest purposes or the opposite (*tois kallistois ē tois enantiois*), and likewise the facility of doing."[186] As we saw above in this chapter, Clement described MR2 in a similar way, with reference to choices made in the present life. Origen's discussion, however, seems to presuppose that the soul was already choosing between opposites prior to embodiment. While some scholars have argued that Origen

---

183 Orig. *Princ.* 3.1.12, tr. Behr, 323; see Koch, *Pronoia*, 32, 39–40, 129–130, 135; Dihle, *Theory of Will*, 111; A. Scott, *Origen*, 140; Gibbons, "Human Autonomy," 680–681. Much the same is argued at *Princ.* 3.1.5, 3.5.4; idem, *Comm. Jo.* 19.20.132; *Cels.* 3.38, 6.44; and especially *Comm. Rom.* 8.13.4.

184 Orig. *Princ.* 3.1.13, tr. Behr, 327; see further ibid., 3.1.15; Koch, *Pronoia*, 93; Bergjan, *Der fürsorgende Gott*, 194–196. Significantly, Origen ties this as a notion of providence into his *Homilies on Jeremiah*: "whenever then everything arises for us from Providence so that we may be *brought to completion* and made mature, yet we do not *receive* what belongs to the Providence which draws us to maturity, then it would be said to God by one who understands: *Lord, you have brought them to completion and they did not want to receive instruction*" (*Hom. Jer.*, 6.2.5, tr. J. Smith, 65; see Koch, *Pronoia*, 31).

185 Orig. *Princ.* 3.1.14.

186 Orig. *Princ.* 3.1.20; text and tr. Behr, 360–361. The passage is useful insofar as it shows that the term 'will' was used already by Origen in Greek, and so Rufinus's *voluntas* is no anachronism (Perkams, "Ethischer Intellektualismus," 249).

258   CHAPTER 6

did not teach the pre-existence of the soul,[187] Origen's discussion of human freedom in *On First Principles* does appear to presume it.[188]

This third avenue of Origen's response to determinism begins to reveal itself when he takes up the passage of Rom 9:18–21 (God the potter makes some vessels unto honor, others unto dishonor).[189] To his opponents, the passage implies some kind of salvation by nature; Origen responds that such a reading is mutually exclusive with the many occasions where Paul's writing seems to presume some kind of faculty of autonomy, and in any case God in His foreknowledge knows which vessels will and will not purify themselves, and so makes them unto honor and dishonor accordingly (co-determinism again).[190] But he adds in conclusion, "it is from causes older (*ek presbuterōn aitiōn*) than the fashioning *of vessels unto honor* and *unto dishonor* that one came to be *unto honor* and another *unto dishonor*."[191] The designation of the seat of the ability to choose wrongly as an older "cause" (*aitia*) marks the statement as distinct from the argument of co-determination, where Origen claimed (like Chrysippus) that divine foreknowledge of an event is not a cause of the event.[192] Rather, the "older causes" (or in Rufinus's Latin, 'preceding causes' [*praecedentibus causis*]) refer to the choices made by the soul prior to embodiment, as Origen makes clear in the immediately following discussion by invoking Jacob and Esau— one was favored even before birth (Gen 25:21–26; Rom 9:10–13).[193] At least at

---

187   E.g. Harl, "Préexistence"; Edwards, *Origen Against Plato*, 91–93, 100–101. Cf. also the discussion above, chapter three.

188   Rightly Dihle, *Theory of Will*, 111.

189   Origen also discusses Rom 9:18–21 at *Comm. Rom.* 8.11, where he offers a somewhat different take on the problem. His opponents are explicitly denoted "those who come forth from the school of Valentinus or Basilides" (8.11.2., tr. Scheck, 175–176). Origen's answer is that there is one nature for all beings, but multiple species—in this case, the good and bad species of people (8.11.3–4). "But if something external approaches the freedom of will, either to incite it to evil or to exhort it to good through certain ineffable superintending activities of divine providence, in no respect does this now offend against the consequence of the proposed finish. For the rational nature possesses within itself a freedom of will alive for even these things" (8.11.5., tr. Scheck, 177), i.e., the will remains responsible, regardless of the external impressions given or their source—very Stoic (cf. *Princ.* 3.1.5). "So, then, each one becomes either a good or a wild olive tree by the power of choice" (8.11.7, tr. Scheck, 178; similarly 8.11.11).

190   Orig. *Princ.* 3.1.21.

191   Orig. *Princ.* 3.1.21, text and tr. Behr, 366–367, italics his.

192   See above, chapter five.

193   Orig. *Princ.* 3.1.22 per Jackson, "Sources," 15; Crouzel, "Theological Construction," 260; both also re: *Princ.* 2.9.7. Cf. Jerome's remarks on the passage (*Epistulae* 124.8.1), discussed in Behr's note to *Princ.* 3.1.22, re: 2.8.3 (ad loc., 367; also Crouzel, "Theological Construction," 262–263).

WHAT WE CHOOSE NOW

this early stage of his career, in Alexandria, Origen appears to have conceived of human freedom as a free choice between opposites, already active prior to embodiment and for which we are answerable and punishable throughout life, in hopes of our being providentially trained to become nobler before the Final Judgment.[194]

To whom does Origen speak in these passages? Michael Frede and others have argued that Origen attempts to refute the astral determinism of "Gnostics."[195] There is no such trace of astral determinism in this discussion, but Frede is on firmer ground when he observes that Origen says his opponents went to Scripture to support their views, which is why so much of the discussion (*Princ.* 3.1.6–17) is occupied with scriptural exegesis.[196] Specifically, Origen tries to refute the view that "that it is not within our power either to keep the commandments and to be saved or to transgress them and be lost,"[197] which means that someone must have been arguing precisely this view—the same view brought forth by the Marcionizing Awida and which the BLC and Clement were both at pains to disprove. He begins the discussion by noting that "many have been troubled" by the story of Pharaoh—evidence that criticism of the story was an exegetical commonplace, probably not limited to any

---

194   No other conclusion is permitted from another treatise in *Princ.* 3, preserved only in Rufi-nus's Latin (*On the Opposing Powers*):

>   To all these instances, those who maintain that everything in the world is governed by the providence of God, as also our faith holds, as it seems to me, can give no other answer, so as to show divine providence exempt from any reproach of justice, than say there were certain antecedent grounds by which souls, before they were born in the body, contracted a certain amount of guilt in their thoughts and movements (*quibus antequam in corpore nascerentur animae aliquid culpae contraxerint in sensibus uel motibus suis*), in respect of which they have been deemed worthy by divine providence to suffer these things (*pro quibus haec merito pati a diuina prouidentia iudicatae sint*). For the soul is always in possession of free will (*liberi namque arbitrii semper est anima*), when in the body and when out of the body; and freedom of will always moves either towards good or evil ... It is probable that these movements furnish grounds for merit even before they do anything in this world, so that in accordance with these grounds or merits they are arranged by divine providence immediately upon their birth, indeed even before birth, so to speak, to endure either good or evil. (*Princ.* 3.3.5, text and tr. Behr, 408–409)

195   M. Frede, *Free Will*, 113–114; similarly, Benjamins, *Eingeordnete Freiheit*, 2–3, 147–149; Wild-berg, "Will," 334. However, Frede disavows any knowledge of what the actual Gnostic position was (op. cit. 117).

196   M. Frede, *Free Will*, 115. This fact alone suffices as evidence to dismiss Elliott's claim that *Princ.* 3.1.10–11 "is directed against Alexander of Aphrodisias, for whom any divine entities were completely blind" (*Providence Perceived*, 15).

197   Orig. *Princ.* 3.1.7, tr. Behr, 301, 303; rightly emphasized by M. Frede, *Free Will*, 115.

group.[198] Yet his focus throughout on demonstrating that God is both "just and good" and that someone might "stand, denouncing with uncovered head that the Creator is inclined towards evil" could refer to Marcionite or Gnostic exegesis.[199] Similarly, in countering those who say the creator is wicked and not good, Origen attempts to demonstrate that their scriptural hermeneutic would show the God of the New Testament to be just as bad as that of the Old—again, Marcion's followers come to mind.[200]

Certainly Origen wanted us to think as much, as is reflected in his famous diatribe against "Marcion, Valentinus, and Basilides" towards the end of book two of *On First Principles*. Here, he argues that they claimed the world was not made by god or administered by his providence because humans are born into diverse kinds of life, and diverse cultures (some of which are evil, and without access to Hebrew wisdom).[201] His response is substantially the same to what we have discussed above, from book three: all souls were created equal, but their diversity owes to their "free will" (*voluntas*):

> On this account, the Creator will neither appear unjust, when, according to the antecedent causes, he distributes to each one according to his merit; nor will the happiness or unhappiness of each one's birth, or whatever be the condition that falls to him, be deemed accidental; nor will it be believed that there are different creators and diverse natures of souls.[202]

Some scholars have argued that Origen formulated the pre-existence of souls as articulated here so as to respond to "Gnostic determinism,"[203] but the relative paucity of arguments regarding 'salvation by nature' in our Gnostic primary sources renders such a reading tentative.[204] However, it is clear that Origen here envisions causality as multiple, insofar as the soul is said to possess an autonomy separate from both God and world.[205] Perhaps Origen was here inspired—

---

198   Orig. *Princ.* 3.1.7.

199   Orig. *Princ.* 3.1.9, tr. Behr, 311.

200   Orig. *Princ.* 3.1.16; see also Crouzel, "Theological Construction," 254; Magris, *L'idea di destino*, 2:842–843.

201   Orig. *Princ.* 2.9.5–6.

202   Orig. *Princ.* 2.9.6, tr. Behr, 247.

203   Crouzel, "Theological Construction," 261 *passim*; Martens, "Origen's Doctrine," 543; idem, "Embodiment," 607–615 (also recalling Orig. *Princ.* 1.6.2, 1.8.1, 2.1.1); similarly, Jacobsen, "Freedom," 73–74; M. Scott, *Journey*, 37–38.

204   Re: Marcion, see Lieu, *Marcion*, 136.

205   A. Scott, *Origen*, 137, M. Frede, *Free Will*, 116–118, Possekel, "Bardaisan and Origen," 536; Martens, "Origen's Doctrine," 542; cf. Löhr, "Gnostic Determinism," 389 n. 27.

WHAT WE CHOOSE NOW

like the *BLC* or Basilides—by Plato's remark that "the responsibility lies with the one who chooses; God has none."[206] In fact, the argument bears a passing resemblance with the Middle Platonist doctrine of conditional fate: the soul made a decision prior to embodiment, and some aspects of its lot in life are thereafter determined.[207]

Despite the impression given by opening chapters of *On Free Will*, Origen's treatment of the problem is not simply an adaptation of Roman Stoic theory.[208] It is well-known, for instance, that for Origen, humans retain their faculty of free will even when they make bad decisions; for the Stoa, using one's freedom poorly is coterminous with not using it at all, since one is only free when one behaves virtuously.[209] However, what makes the faculty of choosing autonomous in the first place is that it is causally independent both of God and of worldly (i.e., physical) forces. Like the *BLC* and, it seems, Basilides, Origen appears to have articulated this in terms of the soul's pre-existence. The soul's active exercise of free choice prior to embodiment is what he refers to as "preceding causes" which affects our present existence—an explicit jump beyond the Chrysippean theory of co-determination.[210] In *On Free Will*, Origen explains this notion of the soul's faculty of accountability in order to oppose a viewpoint which strongly resembles the determinism of the Marcionite opponents of the *BLC*, and (however vaguely) the doctrine of 'salvation by nature.'

---

206   Louth, "Pagans and Christians," 286–288; Jackson, "Sources," 16; Bergjan, *Der fürsorgende Gott*, 175, 196–197; Karamanolis, *Philosophy*, 171.

207   The main difference is that Origen does not distinguish between providence and fate (as first noted by Theiler; see Benjamins, *Eingeordnete Freiheit*, 144–147; also Bergjan, *Der fürsorgende Gott*, 196, 206, 220). Further differences with the teaching of 'Ammonius' are noted by Benjamins, op. cit. 143–144: for Origen, God knows in advance what choices the soul makes in advance (the 'Platonizing' gods do not); secondly, Origen's pre-natal souls choose to descend, and then are provided with the education they need to return to heaven, whereas in Plato, the souls first see the Spindle of Necessity and only then make their choice.

208   Misleading is Crouzel's claim that beyond *Princ.* 3.1's opening discussion of Stoic theory of sense-impressions, "we do not find in these expositions important philosophical theories" ("Theological Construction," 264).

209   M. Frede, *Free Will*, 120–122; Karamanolis, *Philosophy*, 176; Gibbons, "Human Autonomy," 679.

210   Jackson, "Sources," 19; cf. Perkams, "Ethischer Intellektualismus," 244. I hesitate to join Boys-Stones in reading Origen's notion of responsibility in a volitional sense: "there is literally no explanation that can be given of the fall based on the prior condition of the intellects, either internal or external. It was a genuinely *spontaneous* act ... His claim that psychological characters themselves are determined by no pre-existing cause (strictly, no rationally comprehensible cause at all) is a striking innovation" ("Human Autonomy," 495, italics his; followed by Gibbons, "Human Autonomy," 677–678).

262   CHAPTER 6

For Origen, the human faculty of free choice lies and was already active in the
soul prior to embodiment, and experiences suffering in the present life as part
of its providential education on the road to an eventual return to God.

6   Conclusions: Birth, Death, and Eden

Pace Harper, the emergence of early Christian language about free will was not
all about sex; it was about death—and what happened to the soul prior to birth.
The *BLC*, Clement, and Origen each developed their ideas about autonomy
and personal accountability in order to counter the notion that it is impossible to comply with God's Commandments, given the causal forces at work in
the present cosmos. Thus, these Christian philosophers derived the causal force
of the seat of decision-making from outside of the cosmos and invested it with
eschatological importance, much as Pseudo-Plutarch and other Middle Platonists did when responding to Stoic determinism.

Significantly, the *BLC*, Basilides, and Origen describe this seat of volition not
with respect to the post-mortem fate of the soul, but the pre-natal status of the
soul—and the implications of this status for the character of God's activity, as
manifest in providence. For each of these thinkers, human beings are responsible for what they do in the present life because they were already making
decisions before they were born, as Plato teaches. Why, then, is this 'pre-natal'
notion of human responsibility so obscured in the attendant scholarly literature on the earliest notions of free will and autonomy in Christian philosophy?
It is worth closing the present chapter with an answer to this question: because
other, second-century Christian intellectuals better known today rejected the
pre-existence of the soul as expressed in the all-important Platonic proof-text
from the Myth of Er. Some, like Clement, used the same proof-text to describe
the soul as the seat of decision-making in the present life and answerable in the
next. Others, meanwhile, preferred an altogether different story about human
autonomy, one which is much more familiar to us today: God's test of Adam's
obedience, and Adam's subsequent failure. As much can be seen even in a cursory examination of the (admittedly) brief extant remarks on this question as
found in Justin Martyr, Tatian the Assyrian, and Theophilus of Antioch.[211]

---

211   Athenagoras seems to allude to the doctrine of 'conditional fate' when he remarks on
       how each person's rational disposition does not "transgress the law appointed for it"
       (Athenag. *Leg.* 25; cf. Barnard, who notes that the passage begins with an attack on Epi-
       curean atomism—*Athenagoras*, 119).

WHAT WE CHOOSE NOW

While Harper overstates things in writing that Justin was "the first philosopher on record to make unambiguous use of the term 'free will,'"[212] Justin certainly does employ the term preferred by the Stoa to designate the seat of accountability: *to autexousion* ('personal responsibility').[213] Yet his most concrete description of this faculty, in the *First Apology*, explicitly ties this faculty to an immaterial soul and the rewards or punishments it will face after life. Like Philo, Irenaeus, or Origen, Justin takes Scripture to show that God foreknows the deeds of human beings, and this foreknowledge was shared by the biblical Prophets.[214] "Now," he continues,

> lest some persons conclude from what we have just stated that whatever takes place must necessarily do so by force of destiny (*kath' heimarmenēs anagkēn*), because of the prediction of things foreknown, we make answer to this, too. Through the Prophets we have learned, and we profess as true, that punishments, and torments, and wonderful rewards are distributed according to the merit of each man's actions. If such were not the case, but everything were to happen by fate, no choice would be in our power at all. For, if fate decrees that this man is to be good and this other man evil, neither the former is praiseworthy, nor the latter blameworthy. Furthermore, if man does not have the free faculty to shun evil and to choose good, then, whatever his actions may be, he is not responsible for them. But we will now prove that only by free will does man act rightly and wrongfully. We observe a man in pursuit of opposite things; if, however, he were destined to be either evil or good, he would not be able to attain both opposites nor would he change his mind so often. Nor would some men be good and others evil ... This, however, we say is inevitable fate—that they who choose good have merited rewards, just as those who prepare the contrary have appropriate punishments.[215]

In presenting fate as simply the summary external determination of human choices, Justin caricatures Stoicism much as did Plutarch or Alexander of Aphrodisias.[216] Justin describes here a sort of Middle Platonist theory of con-

---

212 Harper, *From Shame to Sin*, 117; cf. Spanneut, *Stoicisme*, 236. A better candidate would be Lucr. 2.251–262 (*libera ... voluntas*; see Kahn, "Discovering Will," 250).

213 On Justin and *to autoexousion*, see Karavites, *Evil*, 115–116; M. Frede, *Free Will*, 102.

214 Just. Mart. *1 Apol.* 28; see further above, chapter five. The discussion of prophecy continues in *1 Apol.* 31–53.

215 Just. Mart. *1 Apol.* 43, tr. Falls, 79–80.

216 Karamanolis *Philosophy*, 159–160; Opsomer, "Middle Platonic Doctrine," 156–157. Further

ditional fate, i.e. that appropriate rewards and punishments are fated to be reckoned for individual actions, which are up to us.[217] The framing of choice as the selection of opposite options reminds one of Alexander of Aphrodisias (MR2), as does the argument that such choices must be possible given that people change their minds (Alexander noted the phenomenon of regret). Most instructive, however, are the proof-texts Justin goes on to introduce: God tells Adam that he can choose either good or evil (1 Deut 30:15.19); humanity is presented with the choice to do good deeds, such as caring for orphans and widows, or face the Lord's punishment (Isa 1:16–20); "Plato, too, when he stated: 'the responsibility lies with the one who chooses; God has none' (*Resp.* 617e) borrowed the thought from the Prophet Moses."[218] While personal responsibility (*to autoexousion*) is a term of markedly Stoic provenance, Justin regards it as a natural endowment (for humans and angels alike!) rather than an achieved state.[219] At the same time, Justin locates this natural faculty of decision-making where Plato located it—in the soul that derives from the non-material world. Yet unlike Plato, Justin does not regard the soul as actually having made a choice prior to birth. Rather, its ability to employ its rational faculty (*logos*) is incumbent on its liberation from cosmic necessity (*anagkē*) via baptism: birth into the body takes place under necessity, but via baptism, "we do not continue as children of necessity and ignorance, but of deliberate choice (*prohairesis*) and knowledge."[220]

Justin was not the only second-century Greek apologist to address the soul's faculty of choosing between good and its opposite, its freedom via liberation from cosmic fate, and its earning of praise or blame in the form of its postmortem reward or punishment. Perhaps wary of Justin's invocation of *Resp.* 617e, Tatian the Assyrian rejects the notion of the existence of a pre-natal self, even as the resurrected self will be judged by God the creator:

> Before I was born, I did not exist; I did not know who I was and was only present in the substance of fleshly matter (*sarkikēs hylēs*); it was through

---

anti-Stoic passages include *2 Apol.* 7; see Denzey (Lewis), "Facing the Beast," 176–179, and esp. Thorsteinsson, "Justin, 563."

217   Similarly Rankin, *Athenagoras*, 62; Possekel, "Bardaisan of Edessa: Philosopher," 457; Thorsteinsson, "Justin," 563.

218   Just. Mart. *1 Apol.* 44, tr. Falls, 81, slightly modified; rightly noted by Magris, *L'idea di destino*, 2:836; Ferguson, *Providence of God*, 45.

219   Harper, *From Shame to Sin*, 121 (similarly M. Frede, *Free Will*, 121, on Origen). For the angels' ability to make choices, see *2 Apol.* 7; *Dial.* 88.5, 141; Russell, *Satan*, 64; Rankin, *Athenagoras*, 63.

220   Just. Mart. *1 Apol.* 61, tr. Falls, 100; see further Denzey (Lewis), *Cosmology and Fate*, 149–152.

WHAT WE CHOOSE NOW

my birth that I, previously non-existent, came to believe that I did exist. And in the same way, when I who was born, cease to exist through death and am no more seen, I shall once more be as in my previous state of non-existence which was followed by birth ... God the ruler, when he wishes, will restore to its original state the substance that is visible only to him.[221]

Yet Tatian does not do away entirely with the notion of the immaterial soul, either. "We have knowledge of two kinds of spirit (*pneumatōn*)," he states: a material one—the soul (*psychē*)—and "an image and likeness of God."[222] The Creator, he believes, will resurrect the soul along with the fleshly body as it was on earth to be rewarded or punished.[223] Significantly, Tatian's discussion here segues directly to the topic of personal responsibility (*to autexousion*), with which humans and angels alike are endowed,[224] and the problem of determinism. Evil is integral to the ability to choose: "free will has destroyed us," when Adam wrongly rejected the "image and likeness of God."[225] Angels who have turned to evil, the *daimones*, adopted the guise of the deities of classical Greek mythology and introduced divinatory practices such as astrology and lot oracles to humanity in order to bring it into sin.[226] Determinism, then, is a problem for Tatian too, but he draws on another one of Justin's ideas in explaining the way out of it: baptism. Through baptism "we are above fate," Tatian declares, "and instead of planetary demons we have come to know one Lord who does not err; we are not led by Fate and have rejected its lawgivers."[227] It is those

---

221   Tat. *Or. Graec.* 6.2, text and tr. Whittaker, 12–13, slightly modified.

222   Tat. *Or. Graec.* 12.1, tr. Whittaker, 23; cf. also Basilides's son Isidore, ap. Clem. Al. *Strom.* 2.20.114.2 (cf. also ibid., 6.16.136, for Clement's own thoughts); Theodotus ap. Clem. Al. *Exc.* 50.1; Ter. *An.* 10–11; cit. Martens, "Embodiment," 601 n. 34; Petersen, "Tatian," 147, 151.

223   Tat. *Or. Graec.* 13.

224   Tat. *Or. Graec.* 7.1.

225   Tat. *Or. Graec.* 11.2, tr. Whittaker, 23. See further Petersen, "Tatian," 151.

226   Tat. *Or. Graec.* 7–11; discussed by Hegedus, *Early Christianity*, 125–126; Nasrallah, "Lot Oracles," 227–228. See also above, chapter three.

227   Tat. *Or. Graec.* 9.2, tr. Whittaker, 19. See further Denzey (Lewis), "New Star," 210; eadem, *Cosmology and Fate*, 159; Nasrallah, "Lot Oracles," 228. Cf. Karamanolis ("Tatian rejects astral determinism as an aspect of Hellenic atheism without offering an explicit argument"—*Philosophy*, 161); cf. also Russell, *Satan*, 75–76; Petersen, "Tatian," 150 (whose charges of Tatian's 'predeterminism' are unconvincing). As Nasrallah shrewdly notes, Tatian's rhetoric (*Or. Graec.* 11.1–2) amounts to an inversion of lot-oracle queries (op. cit. 228–229; eadem, "'I Do Not'," 299–302. Denzey [Lewis], *Cosmology and Fate*, 158–159 sees Tatian rather as inverting an astrological schema resembling that of *Corp. Herm.* 1.25; cf. also Hegedus, *Early Christianity*, 126).

266 CHAPTER 6

who chose correctly at baptism (rather than in a past life) whose souls will be rewarded, as part of the fleshly body, at the Resurrection and Final Judgment.

In *To Autolycus*, Theophilus also describes individual accountability as at the center of human evil, explicitly tying it to the notion of freedom, when he argued that Adam was free and responsible for himself (*eleutheron kai autexousion*).[228] Rather than focusing on liberation from cosmic fate, he states that the Prophets and Greek poets alike understood divine providence, as is evidenced by their descriptions of the decidedly physical punishments of the wicked in the afterlife:

> Therefore the Sibyl and the other prophets, as well as the poets and philosophers themselves, also spoke about justice and judgment (cf. John 16:8) and punishment, and furthermore about providence; God cares not only for us who are living but also for the dead. All of them said these things, for they were convinced by the truth (cf. John 16:13). Among the prophets, Solomon said concerning the dead: "There will be healing for the flesh and treatment for the bones" (Prov 3:8). Similarly David: "The humiliated bones will rejoice" (Ps 50:10). In harmony with them, Timocles too spoke these words: "For the dead, Pity is a gentle god." So even though the writers spoke of a multitude of gods, they ended with monotheism; though they denied providence they also spoke of providence; though they said there was no judgment they admitted that there will be a judgment; those who denied the existence of sensation after death also admitted it.[229]

Like Tatian, Theophilus here envisions the seat of accountability and free choice as the soul, yet nonetheless tied to the resurrected, fleshly body at the moment of its final reward or punishment. Yet Theophilus tells a different story than the Assyrian and Justin in relating the character of choosing. The primordial Adam, he attests, was like a child; when God commanded him and Eve not to eat of the Tree of Good and Evil, he wished to test their obedience.[230] By disobeying instead, Adam (and thus humanity) acquired suffering and death, and was expelled from Paradise. Nonetheless, Theophilus maintains that expulsion

---

228 Theoph. *Autol.* 2.27. "The fact that Theophilus puts together freedom (*eleutheron*) and power to choose (*autexousion*) means that the latter now comes close to meaning 'the ability to choose freely'" (Karamanolis, *Philosophy*, 161).

229 Theoph. *Autol.* 2.38, tr. Grant, 97, 99, rightly noted by Ferguson, *Providence of God*, 45.

230 Theoph. *Autol.* 2.25.

WHAT WE CHOOSE NOW

was a favor (*euergesian*), a punishment that enables humanity to expiate its sin and, "having been properly educated" (*paideutheis*) eventually return to Paradise.[231]

Nicola Denzey (Lewis) has argued that the rhetoric of Justin, Tatian, and their contemporaries regarding baptismal liberation from cosmic fate is evidence that "certain Christians conceptualized two fundamentally different ontological strata. Society operated within the constraints of a lower level of creation—flawed and contingent—while those who were baptized and thus initiated participated in a new order, the laws of which were entirely alien."[232] This is an important insight, and the discussions of chapters two, three, and five support it: many early Christian articulations of providence were distinctive insofar as they envisioned a different God operating through providence as did their Roman contemporaries, who argued that the care of the gods was consonant with the established political order and the civic cult that was part of it. Yet the example of Theophilus reminds us that the way in which Christian philosophers conceived of freedom in this 'new order' was hardly uniform. Rather, two notions of how free choice relates to determinism vis-à-vis the soul emerge in Christian sources of the second and early third centuries. In *Against Heresies*, Irenaeus, who was deeply influenced by Theophilus, relates a very similar story regarding God's test of Adam's obedience.[233] As we saw above in this chapter, Clement does much the same; Ephraem Syrus avers as much concerning Bardaiṣan as well.[234] In *Against Marcion*, Tertullian also absolves God from responsibility for people's misuse of their freedom; rather, in order to be able to choose good at all, humans have to be able to choose evil, and so God endowed them with the gift of choosing between these opposites.[235] In *On the Soul*, he refers to this gift as the 'personal responsibility' (*to autexousion*)

---

231   Theoph. *Autol.* 2.25–26.

232   Denzey (Lewis), *Cosmology and Fate*, 162.

233   See Ir. *Haer.* 4.9.1 and esp. 4.37–39 (on God's creation of Adam as free), 5.26.2, and 5.27.2 (on the importance of obedience to God); Dihle, *Theory of Will*, 112. For Theophilus's influence on Irenaeus here, see Schoedel, "Theophilus," 293.

234   Ephraem refers allusively to Bardaiṣan's ostensible belief that Adam, in his disobedience, is responsible for humanity's state of sinfulness (*Prose Refutations of Mani, Marcion, and Bardaisan*, 2:lxxvii, noted by Drijvers, *Bardaiṣan*, 155). If one takes Ephraem at his word, it is possible that Bardaiṣan took the story of Adam's fall to explain the reason for which souls descend into bodies in the first place, much as Clement did.

235   Ter. *Marc.* 2.9.9, 2.6.5, respectively; cit. and discussed in Karamanolis, *Philosophy*, 164–165. Cf. further *Marc.* 2.6.6, 2.7.2 (basically a doctrine of conditional fate; see Meijering, *Tertullian*, 106–107; Moreschini, "Tertullian's *Adversus Marcionem*," 159–160). The former argument is still used in modern Catholic theology (Sutcliffe, *Providence and Suffering*, 43).

268 CHAPTER 6

which is possessed by every human being.[236] Their discussions of responsibility and its relationship to Final Judgment do not touch on the Platonic proof-texts of Pseudo-Plutarch or Justin, or even the otherworldly character of the soul. Rather, both Irenaeus and Tertullian employ the story of Adam to describe the human soul as a seat of accountability immune from cosmic determinism and subject to reward or punishment at the resurrection of the flesh, without having to denote the soul as existing prior to embodiment.[237] This story—not "the responsibility lies with the one who chooses"—is the one more familiar to us today.[238]

To be sure, Irenaeus and Tertullian were addressing fellow Christians in these works (mitigating the value of an appeal to Plato), while Justin, Tatian, and Theophilus all wrote as apologists in the passages discussed here. Yet when we turn from these fleeting reflections on 'free will' to the protracted discussions of the question in the BLC, Basilides, and Origen—none of which have an apologetic context—we find that is precisely the character of the seat of human accountability with respect to both its pre-natal and post-mortem existence, and to divine providence, that were at issue. Recognizing this fact may help us clarify a problem one last problem regarding providence, causation, and determinism in early Christian philosophy: Bergjan argues that Christian thinkers established a notion of divine care which was conceived not in terms of God's causation of human action, but God's interaction with humanity.[239] As chapter two argues, a shift indeed took place in Roman philosophy regarding the character of human response to God's providence, but it is not a shift from an 'impersonal' Stoic God to a 'personal' Christian one; rather, the identity of God Himself changed (see above, chapter two). We can now add that the notion of what human accountability in one's response to God's care could be began to change as well, from autonomy (MR1) to freedom (MR2). The stakes of this change were high, for they were concerned with one's fate after death, and our understanding of the soul's existence prior to birth.[240] Finally, a related

---

236 Ter. *An.* 21.

237 Ir. *Haer.* 2.34.2–3; Ter. *An.* 3–4, 23–24, 27–28; see the recent survey of Givens, *When Souls,* 86, 88–90. Cf. Tertullian's attack on Apelles's ostensible belief in the pre-existence of the soul, lured into human bodies by "a fiery angel" (*An.* 23.3, quoted above, chapter three, n. 200).

238 Cf. Magris, for whom the 'Adam in the Garden'-model of Theophilus et al. predominates (*L'idea di destino,* 2:847).

239 Bergjan, *Der fürsorgende Gott,* 334, followed by Elliott, *Providence Perceived,* 13; similarly Magris, *L'idea di destino,* 2:826.

240 Bergjan rightly notes the eschatological overtones in how Clement and Origen discuss providence (*Der fürsorgende Gott,* 334–336), but does not discuss the shifting notions of

WHAT WE CHOOSE NOW

third marked change in notions of providence and causation took place over the course of the third century CE, amongst the philosophers who mark the beginnings of Neoplatonism, this time regarding the question of whether a transcendent first principle can know, will, or care for anything at all.

───────────

personal accountability, nor of the two different narratives among the Patres regarding the soul's pre-existence.

CHAPTER 7

How God Cares

1 Introduction: The One's Providence, Will, and Omniscience

As discussed in the previous chapter, it is a scholarly cliché that ancient Christian philosophers put a much greater stress on the scope and operation of God's faculty of will than their Platonizing counterparts.[1] Yet in the third century CE, Platonists, nonetheless, began to describe God's forethought as synonymous with divine thought and will.[2] Moreover, they explored anew how the thought and will of the human agent could assimilate itself to those of God, by attaining a supra-cognitive state called 'first thought' (*prōtē noēsis*) that is 'prior to Intellect' (*pro tēs noēseōs*). So writes the greatest philosopher of late antiq-

---

1 Armstrong, "Dualism," 49.
2 Cf. G. Smith, who claims that already in the second century, Middle Platonists, ostensibly under the influence of Philo of Alexandria, began to describe God's creative activity in terms of divine will ("Irenaeus," 115). The present chapter, too, argues for the influence of biblically-informed philosophers on the Platonic tradition, but identifies the bulk of evidence for this shift in the third, rather than the second century CE. G. Smith's sole reference is Plut. [*Fat.*] 573b, where God's *noēsis* is mentioned in passing as equivalent to his *boulēsis*. This is so, but the context of the passage is to exculpate God from all but the most general activity governing the "wholes" (his 'first' *pronoia*) while leaving the administrative structure of the universe as a divine law (his 'second' *pronoia*, or fate) administered on the level of particulars by *daimones* (tertiary *pronoia*)—see above, chapter one. Now, other Middle Platonic sources describe God's will, as adduced by Thomassen, "Commentaire," 278: Alc. *Epit.* 10.4; Att. frg. 4; *Corp. Herm.* 4.1; Calc. *Comm. Tim.* 144. Of these sources, only Atticus may be firmly located in the second century (J.M. Dillon, *Middle Platonists*, 247–249); a third-century date for Alcinous is certainly plausible (J.M. Dillon, "Introduction," xiii), the same is true for Pseudo-Plutarch (Boys-Stones, "'Middle' Platonists on Fate," 433 n. 4), our evidence regarding Calcidius locates him rather in the fourth century CE (Magee, "Introduction," viii–xvii), and the *terminus ante quem* for *Corp. Herm.* 4 is its citation by Johannes Stobaeus (Copenhaver, *Hermetica*, xlii, dating Stobaeus's *floruit* to ca. 500 CE, although one may date his work a century earlier if one wishes, since the latest authors he excerpts are from the later fourth century). Thus, evidence for Middle Platonist speculation on God's 'will' in the second century CE is very thin. In any case, there is no hint that Pseudo-Plutarch (or any of the Middle Platonists mentioned above) shares the view of Philo and the Apostle Paul that "God's will does not follow cosmic rules; it determines them" (G. Smith, op. cit., 114 n. 60). Meanwhile, all of our evidence regarding the reception of the Philonic corpus is Christian (Runia, "Philo and the Early Christian"); any suggestion of his direct influence on the Hellenic Platonist doxography is speculative. For Philo's tendency to emphasize God's omnipotence and ability to do as He wills, unlike Plato's demiurge (rightly noted by G. Smith), see Runia, *Philo*, 139–140, with ample references.

© KONINKLIJKE BRILL NV, LEIDEN, 2020 | DOI:10.1163/9789004432994_009

HOW GOD CARES

uity, Plotinus, in several treatises on the One: *Enneads* 6.7–6.8 (treatises 38 and 39, in the chronological numeration of his editor, Porphyry of Tyre). This 'first thought' appears to be related to Plotinus's famous meditations on mystical contemplation of the One, which rank amongst the most powerful and lasting contributions of Greek thought to the history of philosophy. Its etymology as well as its usage are inextricable, as we will see, from the problem of providence. His descriptions of the first stirrings of the process of emanation of the universe in God's causative first thought, where all reality was willed into existence, he takes to be intimately linked to the question of divine knowledge of and providential care for this reality—a question discussed at length in our sole work of systematic Valentinian theology to survive from antiquity, the *Tripartite Tractate* (NHC I,5). In this Coptic Gnostic work as well as *Enneads* 6.7–6.8, to talk about how God wills and knows the world to be requires one to talk about how God cares.

Plotinus's language in these treatises about God's 'first thought' and will reflects a stark departure not only from the other second and early third-century thinkers we have examined in previous chapter; it reflects a departure from his own thought, in the rest of the Plotinian corpus. As discussed in Chapter one, Platonists of the first and second centuries CE argued that that *pronoia* exists, but only administers the greater things in life, the universals, as Plato argued in the *Laws*. Fate governs contingent, particular circumstances, while God does not determine or even know particular, contingent choices, which are literally "up to us." Plotinus gives a fairly standard rendering of this Middle Platonist view in Treatise 3, *On Fate*.[3] Later, in his polemic *Against the Gnostics* (*Enn.* 2.9 [33]), he is at pains to defend the notion of divine providence against the Gnostic view that the present cosmos did not come into being nor is administered by providence.[4] Yet he agrees with Plato that God does not know or care for everything, either. Already in Treatise 27, the first part of *On Difficulties About the Soul*, Plotinus denies God's omniscience by way of rejecting the notion that God could have a memory.[5] God exists beyond time and the par-

---

3 On Plot. *Enn.* 3.1 [3], see Louth, "Pagans and Christians," 292; Kalligas, *'Enneads'*, 413–439; Eliasson, "Plotinus on Fate," 202–210. For a similar Middle Platonic view, see *Enn.* 4.8 [6] 2.27–38; Kalligas, op. cit., 449, 478.

4 See above, chapter four; additionally, Burns, *Apocalypse*, 88–89; Kalligas, *'Enneads'*, 369, 401–402, 404, 406, 408; Spanu, *Plotinus, 'Ennead II 9 [33]'*, 190, 196–197.

5 "We must certainly not attribute memory to God, or real being or Intellect; for nothing [external] comes to them and there is no time, but eternity in which real being is, and there is neither before nor after, but it is always as it is, in the same state not admitting of change" (4.3 [27] 25.13–17, tr. Armstrong in LCL 443:113). For discussion, see Mignucci, "Logic and Omniscience," 235–236.

ticulars embedded in time, and so God has no memory, because memory deals with temporality; therefore, God does not know (nor remember) everything. Similarly, in an early treatise, *On the Good, or the One*, he states that "He does not wish for anything (*oude boulēsis toinun oudenos*), but He transcends good, and is good not for Himself but for the others if anything is able to participate in Him. And He does not think, because there is no otherness; and He does not move: for He is prior to movement and prior to thought (*pro noēseōs*)."[6]

While there are allusive and fleeting references to some sort of providential quality to the Good in Plotinus's works prior to Treatises 38 and 39, there are no such references in subsequent works. Indeed, his later, grand treatise *On Providence (Enn.* 3.2–3 [47–48])—generally recognized as the most sophisticated disquisition on providence produced in late antiquity—retreats from language about God's will and 'first thought.'[7] This is not, it will be argued, because he has ceased to engage biblically-informed sources altogether; sections of *On Providence* are strongly paralleled, again, by the *Tripartite Tractate*. Yet Plotinus was hardly alone in treating God's forethought not only as an issue of theodicy and free will, but of contemplative practice. The same complex of language relating to a supra-cognitive faculty 'prior to' intellect is found in other Platonist sources of the third century CE, such as Plotinus's student Porphyry, as well as the anonymous *Commentary on Plato's 'Parmenides.'* It is also found in a number of Coptic treatises discovered at Nag Hammadi in 1945. Some, *Zostrianos* and *Allogenes*, are Coptic versions of works that circulated in Plotinus's circle. They refer to a 'first thought' or 'forethought' out of which all intelligible reality is generated—the same terminology as that of the feminine incarnation of providence, *prōtennoia*, we met in chapter four's discussion of the Gnostic text *First Thought in Three Forms*. This chapter will demonstrate that Porphyry, the anonymous *Commentary*, and the aforementioned Coptic Gnostic works all incline towards the belief in God's omnipresence and omniscience of particular beings and events, marking a curious shift in thought about these subjects after Plotinus, wherein Greek philosophers begin to adopt views more closely resembling those of their Christian contemporaries than their 'Pagan' predecessors.

---

6 Plot. *Enn.* 6.9 [9] 6.40–44, text and tr. Armstrong in LCL 468:326–328, slightly modified.

7 *On Providence* "represents the most ambitious attempt related to us by late antiquity to provide a comprehensive theoretical vision of the world as the realization of a divine plan" (Kalligas, *'Enneads'*, 445; similarly Magris, *L'idea di destino*, 2:708; Ilievski, "Stoic Influences," 29).

HOW GOD CARES

2 "Neither Actuality nor Thought before It": Plotinus (Enn. 6. 7–8 [38–39]) and the 'Tripartite Tractate' on the Knowledge and Will of the Good

Enn. 6.7 [38], entitled by Porphyry *How the Multitude of Forms Came into Being, and on the Good*, is an extended meditation on creation and causality. Significantly, Plotinus begins with the familiar Socratic proof for the existence of providence, observing that "when God or one of the gods was sending the souls to birth," he gave them the right organs for their senses in worldly life, "foreseeing that safety would be ensured in this way (*prooromenos hos houtos an sozoito*)." "But really," he asks, "where did this foreseeing (*proïdon*) come from?"[8] The problem, then, is how a divine Intellect (*nous*) could providentially emanate and administer an entire universe without engaging in the sort of mundane, plodding planning we associate with craftsmen and bad demiurges.[9] He alludes to his answer immediately: *nous* exists beyond time and therefore does not have knowledge and care of the temporal realm, and yet the universe exists as if it did: "Eternal existence must be there, too. So the future must also already be present there ... And if the future is already present, it is necessary for it to be present as if it had been thought out beforehand with a view to what comes afterwards (*anagke houto pareinai, hos pronenoemenon eis to hysteron*)."[10] Even though Intellect cannot have a sense of future and past (and thus of forethought), the universe is designed in such a way that it appears to enjoy the fruits of some such forethought.

Plotinus returns to this problem of reconciling a providential causality with the transcendence of first principles at the very end of the treatise, this time with reference not to Intellect, but the transcendent One, which he refers to here simply as the 'Good.' In other words, he begins to ask about the foreknowledge and care not of the Intellect, but the Good itself:

> Will He not know other things, nor Himself? The other things are posterior to Him, and He was what He was prior to them, and the thought of them would be something picked up, and not always the same ... But it is enough for providence that He exists from whom all things come.[11]

---

8   Plot. *Enn.* 6.7 [38] 1.1–6, text and tr. Armstrong in LCL 468:82–83; on the proof 'from nature' for providence's existence, see further above, chapter one.

9   For discussion of Plotinus's ideas about demiurgic causality in 6.7 [38], see Gurtler, "Providence," 108–113; Noble and Powers, "Creation and Divine Providence," 57–61; and esp. Chiaradonna, "Plotinus' Account."

10   Plot. *Enn.* 6.7 [38] 1.48–52, text and tr. Armstrong in LCL 468:86–87, slightly modified.

11   Plot. *Enn.* 6.7 [38] 39.20–27, text and tr. Armstrong in LCL 468:208–209, slightly modified.

274   CHAPTER 7

Like Intellect, the Good exists beyond time and the particulars ensconced in time, so He does not have knowledge of everything; yet we can speak of providence all the same, since He is the cause of everything. In a way, this forethought that is not thought out can be described as simply prior to thought: "if the thought of the Good is different from the Good, the Good is there already prior to the thought of Him (*pro tēs noēseōs autou*)."[12] Once it becomes causal, it is the 'first thought' of the Good:

> And this is the first active actuality, which has generated an existent which came to be substance, and, being the image of another, is the image of one so great that substance came to be. But if it belonged to that and did not derive from it, it would be nothing other than something belonging to that and would not be an existent of its own. Certainly, as this is the first active actuality and the first thought (*prōtē dē ousa hautē energeia kai prōtē noēsis*), it would have neither actuality nor thought before it.[13]

As argued by Pierre Hadot, this 'first thought' (*prōtē noēsis*) likely derives from the Stoic notion that there is a natural human "preconception" of universals.[14] In late ancient religious literature, the language of foreknowing is occasionally alluded to in order to describe divine knowledge.[15] Can this 'first thought' of God be regarded as God's 'fore-thought' (*pronoia*), His providence?

Plotinus does not systematically reflect on the term; rather, he alludes to it and moves on. However, he takes the discussion in an unexpected direction in the following treatise, *On the Will of the One*, *Enn.* 6.8 [39]. Here, and only here, does Plotinus seem to throw caution to the wind, and ascribe character and activity—and providence—to the One. While in earlier treatises he had emphasized the desire of all things to revert to the One—which amounts to an omnipresence of the One in creation—the One itself has no such desire for

---

12   Plot. *Enn.* 6.7 [38] 38.21–23, text and tr. Armstrong in LCL 468:208–209, slightly modified.

13   Plot. *Enn.* 6.7 [38] 40.19–25, text and tr. Armstrong in LCL 468:210–211, slightly modified.

14   Hadot, *Porphyre et Victorinus*, 1:117–118 n. 6. According to Chrysippus, "preconception is the natural conception of universals" (*esti d'hē prolepsis ennoia physikē tōn katholou*— D. L. 7.54.5–9 = SVF 2.105 = LS 42A; tr. mine). See further Algra, "Stoic Theology," 157 n. 11.

15   Hadot, *Porphyre et Victorinus*, 1:117–118 re: *Corp. herm.* frg. 12 in Nock and Festugière, *Corpus Hermeticum*, 4:111; Plot. *Enn.* 5.3 [49] 10.42–44 (the One is *pronooousa*); Marius Victorinus, *Adversus Arium*, 1:49.26–29, 50.1–3 (God has *praeintellentia*). For Porph. *Sent.* 26 see below. Generally, see further Turner, "Commentary: Zostrianos," 588; idem, *Sethian Gnosticism*, 493.

HOW GOD CARES 275

its particulars.[16] In *Enn.* 6.8, he reverses himself to answer "some reckless statement" (*tis tolmēros logos*):

> Unless some reckless statement starting from a different way of thinking says that since [the nature of the Good] happens to be so, and that He has no control over what He is, and is what He is not through Himself, He would not have freedom ... This statement is indeed contrary and absurd and would altogether do away with the nature of the voluntary and self-determination and the notion of what is up to us, as if this was empty talk and names for non-existent things. For not only must the one who says (the reckless statement) say that nothing is up to anybody, but he must say that he does not think or understand this term.[17]

The argument presented here—that if the Good is so transcendent that free will cannot be ascribed to it, then it is (*a*) not free, and (*b*) human free will is not derivable from it, since the Good is the source of everything—regards, as Kevin Corrigan states, "a Will that goes beyond anything in the earlier tradition" of Greek philosophical enquiry.[18]

A long and difficult, Valentinian treatise from Nag Hammadi—the *Tripartite Tractate* (NHC I,5, henceforth *Tri. Trac.*)—is an important comparandum for the "different way of thinking" Plotinus is at pains to combat in *Enn.* 6.8. Scholarship established long ago that *Tri. Trac.* work employs a distinctively Neoplatonic, rather than Middle Platonic, model of ontogenesis, wherein the transcendent Father overflows with Being, first exteriorizing a hitherto latent unity-in-multiplicity (the 'Son') who then proceeds to emit the aeons (the 'Church'), identified as individual "intellects."[19] Yet even as it maintains the absolute transcendence of the "Father," *Tri. Trac.* also assigns this first principle faculties of willing, knowing, and providential care. Immediately following a detailed negative theology, the treatise then turns from apophasis to kataphasis in describing the Father's will:

---

16   E.g. Plot. *Enn.* 5.5 [32] 12, per the discussion of J.M. Dillon, "Signs and Tokens," 228–229.

17   Plot. *Enn.* 6.8 [39] 7.19–25, text and tr. Armstrong in LCL 468:246–249, modified.

18   Corrigan, "Divine and Human Freedom," 146.

19   Early and largely descriptive studies of the Neoplatonism of *Tri. Trac.* include Zandee, *Terminology*; Thomassen, "Structure"; Kenney, "Platonism." For recent discussions with updated bibliography, see Berno, "Rethinking Valentinianism"; Turner, "Plotinus and the Gnostics," esp. 387–402 (on the point made here).

Whatever He thinks, whatever He sees, whatever He says, whatever He has as a thought supersedes any wisdom, and is superior to any intellect, and is superior to any glory, and is superior to any beauty and any sweetness, any greatness, and any depth and any height! So, as for this one—who is unknowable in His nature, to whom all these great things which I have just mentioned pertain—should He, out of the abundance of His sweetness, will (*ouōše*) to grant knowledge in order that He be known, He is able.[20]

A (if not the) central theme of *Tri. Trac.* is that while the present cosmos resulted from an error of one of these intellects in the celestial realm—the Word (*logos*)—this error transpired in fact "by the will of the Father," for the sake of the great salvific plan (*oikonomia*).[21] Only through some such error could the cosmos be produced in the first place, with the purpose being the ultimate good: that the world's inhabitants come to know God insofar as they are able. This is the "knowledge" that the Father is "able" to grant, "should He, out of the abundance of His sweetness, will" to do so.[22] A similar perspective is expressed several pages later, in a description of the growth of the aeonic realm from which the error will eventually proceed: "it was for this reason [too][23] that the Father exercised forethought for them (*ᶜr šarᶜp ᶜmmeue araou*)—not only so that they would come into being for Him, but that they would come into being for themselves, too …"[24] Towards the end of the work, speaking of the incarnated Jesus, *Tri. Trac.* states that "the Father had foreknowledge of him, when he was, in his thought before anything came into being," thus assigning the faculty of foreknowledge to the First Principle.[25]

---

20   *Tri. Trac.* NHC I 55.17–34, text Thomassen in Thomassen and Painchaud, "Texte," 60, 62, tr. mine.

21   *Tri. Trac.* NHC I 76.30–77.35, discussed above, chapter four. See also Corrigan and Turner, "Commentary," 171–172.

22   On the Father's 'will' in Valentinian as well as Hermetic literature, see Attridge and Pagels, "*Tripartite Tractate*: Notes," 234; Thomassen, "Commentaire," 277–279; Corrigan and Turner, "Commentary," 298–301.

23   Rightly Thomasson and Painchaud, "Texte," 75; *pace* Attridge and Pagels, "*Tripartite Tractate*: Notes," 251; P. Nagel, *Tractatus*, 29.

24   *Tri. Trac.* NHC I 6[1].1–5, text Thomassen in Thomassen and Painchaud, "Texte," 74, tr. mine, with reference to those of Thomassen and Painchaud, "Texte," 75, and P. Nagel, *Tractatus*, 29.

25   *Tri. Trac.* NHC I 125.24–27, text Thomassen in Thomassen and Painchaud, "Texte," 230, tr. mine. See also NHC I 126.9–37; Attridge and Pagels, "*Tripartite Tractate*: Notes," 471; Thomassen, "Commentaire," 440 (recalling the 'book of the living' in *Gos. Truth* NHC I 19.35–20.3, 21.3–5).

The date of the Greek *Vorlage* of this treatise is disputed,[26] but one need not presume pre-Plotinian authorship of it in order to recognize its significance for Plotinus. Some scholars have identified the "different way of thinking" to which Plotinus avers in *Enn.* 6.8 [39] with positions held by known Epicurean or Aristotelian thinkers, or a thought-experiment of Plotinus's own invention.[27] (The first chapter of Treatise 39, for instance, includes a criticism of Aristotle's notion of the voluntary, with reference to the 'Oracle to Laius.')[28] *Tri. Trac.* and its insistence on the transcendent, unknowable Father's providential activity and his faculties of will and foreknowledge directly address the themes Plotinus tackles in *Enn.* 6.8.[29] This in turn speaks for identifying the "reckless statement" as one belonging to a Christian interlocutor, 'Gnostic' or not.[30] Indeed, Gnostic sources' use of the term "One" to denote God may explain Plotinus's preference in *Enn.* 6.8 for the distinctively Platonic nomenclature of "Good."[31]

As regards human will, Plotinus responds to the "different way of thinking" with a more or less Platonizing adaption of Stoic notions of the coincidence of divine and human wills, insofar as he ties human free will to the soul's ascent to Intellect. The further the soul dives into *nous*—away from the body and the soul's own irrational impulses—the more free it is:

---

26   See above, chapter four, n. 115.

27   For useful surveys, see Narbonne, *Plotinus in Dialogue*, 135–140; Corrigan and Turner, "Commentary," 217–218. M. Frede appears to believe that Plotinus here simply recognized and addressed a structural problem in his own thought, without an external catalyst (*Free Will*, 144–146).

28   Plot. *Enn.* 6.8 [39] 1.30–45. See Corrigan and Turner, "Commentary," 145–147, a reading of Plotinus as conciliatory with Aristotle in this case.

29   Rightly emphasized already by Zandee, *Terminology*, 30.

30   For Christians, see Armstrong, "Two Views of Freedom," 401; cf. Karamanolis, *Philosophy*, 146. J.M. Dillon and Corrigan are right to suggest that any adherent to an Abrahamic religion could levy such a complaint ("Signs and Tokens," 331, and "Divine and Human Freedom," 140–141, respectively; see also Corrigan and Turner, "Commentary," 219–220). Narbonne presents many examples of Gnostic sources describing the causative will of the First Principle (*Plotinus in Dialogue*, 129–134). M. Frede remains skeptical (*Free Will*, 150–151, with reference only to Armstrong, op. cit.). Alternatively, *Chald. Or.* frg. 1 describes the productive will of the First Intellect. As Corrigan and Turner point out, "the problem here is that the position Plotinus argues *for* looks very like a Gnostic position itself, and so how can he be arguing against the Gnostics?" ("Commentary," 217, italics theirs).

31   Corrigan and Turner, "Introduction," 18. To select examples of Gnostic works referring to 'the One' solely from the Nag Hammadi treatises discussed in this chapter, see e.g. *Tri. Trac.* NHC I 51.8–10, 51.16, 51.21–23; *Zost.* NHC VIII [64].13–22, [66].6–14, [74].3–14, 7[9].16–25, 1[1]8.13–17; *Allogenes* NHC XI [48].19–21, [48].32–38, [54].26–37, [67].24–32.

278 CHAPTER 7

> We shall grant personal responsibility (*to autexousion*) to one whose actions depend on the activities of Intellect and who is independent of sensual experience. We trace what is up to us back to the noblest principle—the activity of Intellect—and shall grant that the premises of action derived from this are truly free, and that the desires roused by thinking are not involuntary, and we shall say that the gods who live in this way have freedom of choice.[32]

Indeed, thinking and willing are synonymous, and the activity of the contemplative, first Intellect (*theōrētikos nous kai prōtos*) is independent: "for its will is its thought, but it is called will, because it is 'according to Intellect'."[33] "The soul, then, becomes free when it presses on to the Good, unimpeded, by means of Intellect."[34] Conversely, the Good is free of fortune or chance (*tuchē*), which characterizes so much of our experience in worldly life.[35] Our freedom may then be viewed as a continuum between fortune and embodiment, on the one hand, and reason and the Good, on the other. "Insofar as it [i.e., the soul] advances towards reason, it leaves chance behind; for whatever is in accordance with reason is not by chance."[36]

However, Plotinus here jettisons Middle Platonic models in arguing that the Good certainly has will, but "He does not will and act as it is His nature to, any more than His substance is as he wills and acts"—for the Good is not constrained by Nature—"so He is absolute master of Himself, for even His being is up to Him."[37] What does the Good will, then? It wills the Good: "for the nature of the Good is truly the will of Himself."[38] All the while, Plotinus repeats that he speaks here of that which may not be properly spoken of under the constraints of language, but in order to correct serious misconceptions about God,[39] and in this context, he may say that God cares.

---

32 Plot. *Enn.* 6.8 [39] 3.20–26, text and tr. Armstrong in LCL 468:234–237, modified. As Corrigan and Turner note, Plotinus's very use of the term *autexousion* here signals his engagement with Christian or Gnostic thought ("Commentary," 173).

33 Plot. *Enn.* 6.8 [39] 6.36–37, text and tr. Armstrong in LCL 468:244–245, slightly modified. Armstrong notes ad loc. that *kata noun* is a Greek idiom for "as one likes it," i.e., as one wills.

34 Plot. *Enn.* 6.8 [39] 7.1–2, text and tr. Armstrong in LCL 468:244–245, slightly modified.

35 Plot. *Enn.* 6.8 [39] 14.37–41, 15.17–24. See Corrigan and Turner, "Commentary," 308–310.

36 Plot. *Enn.* 6.8 [39] 15.30–32, text and tr. Armstrong in LCL 468:278–279, slightly modified.

37 Plot. *Enn.* 6.8 [39] 13.9–12, text and tr. Armstrong in LCL 468:268–279, slightly modified.

38 Plot. *Enn.* 6.8 [39] 13.38, text and tr. Armstrong in LCL 468:270–271, slightly modified. See Corrigan and Turner, "Commentary," 295–296.

39 Plot. *Enn.* 6.8 [39] 13.47–50.

HOW GOD CARES 279

Plotinus emphasizes here the omnipresence of the Good: "But He, since He has the highest rank—or rather does not have it, but Himself is the highest, has all things as slaves—He is not an accident of them, but they of Him, or rather they are accidents around Him ..."[40] This inevitably leads us into contradiction: "this one is everywhere and again is nowhere."[41] To summarize, then, "so He was complete will, and there is nothing in Him which is not that which wills—nothing, then, prior to willing. So He himself is His will, first."[42]

Therefore, the Good does not care, exactly, but it would be wrong to simply leave the matter at that, for "we affirm that each and every thing is in the All, and this All here itself is as it would have been if the free choice (*proairesis*) of its maker had willed it, and its state is as if this maker, proceeding and looking ahead in his calculations, had made it according to providence (*hōs an proïemenos kai proïdōn en logismois kata pronoian houtos eirgasato*)."[43] Yet this statement, like everything in this treatise, is qualified—here by "as if it would have been ...", echoing the beginning of previous treatise, *Enn.* 6.7. It is more precise to say that, as far as the world of Intellect goes, "things there transcend providence ... and transcend free choice (*epekeina pronoias ... kai epekeina proaireseōs*)."[44] Nonetheless, we ought to affirm divine providence: "so if someone calls this dispensation of things providence, he must understand it in this way: that Intellect is the standing still before this All (*hoti esti pro toude nous*), and this All here is from and according to Intellect."[45]

As is well-known, Plotinus locates providential activity in diverse reaches of the intelligible realm throughout the *Enneads*, which are a collection of texts responding to a variety of philosophical problems and rhetorical situations: in earlier treatises, it is the World Soul that exercises *pronoia*; in *Enn.* 3.2–3 [47–48], as we will discover, it is the *logos*; in 6.7 [38], universal intellect is

---

40 Plot. *Enn.* 6.8 [39] 16.8–13, text and tr. Armstrong in LCL 468:280–281, slightly modified.

41 Plot. *Enn.* 6.8 [39] 16.1–2, tr. Armstrong in LCL 468:281; cf. Porph. *Sent.* 31. Thus, as Corrigan writes, existence is "providentially present to all individual beings, against the Peripatetic view that providence does not extend to sublunary individuals. Consequently, the Divine will is supremely causal" ("Divine and Human Freedom," 145).

42 Plot. *Enn.* 6.8 [39] 21.14–16, text and tr. Armstrong in LCL 468:296–297, slightly modified. See Corrigan and Turner, "Commentary," 385–387.

43 Plot. *Enn.* 6.8 [39] 17.1–5, text and tr. Armstrong in LCL 468:282–283. See Corrigan and Turner, "Commentary," 343–344.

44 Plot. *Enn.* 6.8 [39] 17.7–9, text and tr. Armstrong in LCL 468:282–283.

45 Plot. *Enn.* 6.8 [39] 17.10–12, text and tr. Armstrong in LCL 468:282–285.

the providential agent.[46] Yet Plotinus's language about God's 'first thought' and the Good's will as 'prior to intellect' introduces a different sense of providence, a sort of 'hyper-noetic' or supra-intellectual divine cognitive faculty. In other words, insofar as the Soul and the universe it governs are derivative of Intellect, they can be said to be *pro-noia*. In *Enn*. 6.8 [39], however, since Intellect can be said to be prior to the universe which is derived from the Good through Intellect, one may call "this dispensation of things providence," and this a radical step beyond Middle Platonism, in two ways. On the one hand, Plotinus here describes a near-total removal of providence from everyday human experience.[47] On the other hand, Treatise 39 concludes with an account of the soul's ascent to the Good via absorption in the universal intellect—i.e., thinking one's way to unity through contemplation of the universals. Plotinus never states it formally, much less theorizes it, but it follows that achievement of God's 'first thought' is the final step in the self's disrobing of body, soul, and intellect before absolute unity.[48]

Thus, *Enn*. 6.8 denotes providence as something one does; it is the ultimate goal of mystical contemplation.[49] A recent article by Erik Eliasson may provide some context for Plotinus's motivation for exploring the question of God's providence not only with respect to abstract arguments about fate, but with respect to the human soul's ability to ascend to the Good and think its 'first thought' for oneself. In a treatise prior to 6.8, *On Difficulties About the Soul* (*Enn*. 4.3–4 [27–28]), Plotinus discusses the descent of souls into bodies and their concomitant adherence to the laws of fate that govern the material cosmos— a standard Middle Platonic view (see above, chapters one and five). However, Eliasson notes, Plotinus goes further here, insofar as he describes how the 'good soul,' living a life of contemplation and thus of immersion the intelligible world, is not subject to the laws of fate:

---

46   See further Magris, *L'idea di destino*, 2:663; M. Frede, *Free Will*, 138; Chiaradonna, "Plotinus' Account," 32; Corrigan and Turner, "Commentary," 343–345.

47   Thus Kalligas, *'Enneads'*, 447; J.M. Dillon, "Signs and Tokens," 330; Noble and Powers, "Creation and Divine Providence," 61, who denote it a "radically austere" position. Cf. Schroeder, "Aseity and Connectedness," 306–307, n. 3; Chiaradonna, "Plotinus' Account," suggesting that Plotinus is here under Aristotelian influence insofar as he removes providential activity from the mundane (sublunary) realm.

48   See Mazur, "Platonizing Background," 251–253; also Turner, *Sethian Gnosticism*, 484–485, 689. I have emphasized elsewhere that Plotinus uses various terminology throughout his treatises for how contemplation of the Good operates and does not theorize it, unlike later Platonists (Burns, "Apophatic Strategies," 172–173 n. 57).

49   See further Corrigan, "Divine and Human Freedom," 148; cf. Michalewski, "Faut-il préférer," 137–138, who seeks rather to harmonize the idea of providence as 'prior to intellect' in *Enn*. 6.8 with that given in *Enn*. 3.2–3.

HOW GOD CARES

And some of them have altogether become subject to the destiny of the present cosmos (*heimarmenēi tēi entautha*), but others are sometimes subject to it and sometimes independent; others again accept what is necessary to endure (*hosa ... anagkaia hypomeinai*), but are able to be independent with respect to their own deeds, living according to another code of laws which governs the universal reality (*tōn sumpatōn tōn ontōn*), and submitting themselves to [this] other ordinance.[50]

Plotinus proceeds to describe how this separate code of laws to which good souls adhere is in harmony with the world of Intellect.[51] He (and Eliasson) then take the discussion in a different direction, to the question of the post-mortem punishments of souls. The question of what the good soul's life looks like is left open, except that it is embodied yet independent of fate insofar as it participates in the intelligible, "universal reality." Plotinus answers this question in *Enn.* 6.8. The soul ascending to Intellect and beyond, insofar as it comes to participate in the Good's will and 'first thought,' participates in providence—not as a recipient of divine care, but from the perspective of the very source of this care, the Good.

3 Plotinus 'On Providence' (Enn. 3.2–3 [47–48]): Another Engagement with the 'Tripartite Tractate'?

In his later, great treatise *On Providence* (*Enn.* 3.2–3 [47–48]), Plotinus achieves a remarkable synthesis of all of his ideas about the titular subject while responding to the entirety of Greek philosophical speculation on providence, fate, and will explored thus far. Interestingly, he abandons in this treatise any 'mystical' sense of *pronoia*, returning to a conception of providence as a kind of non-deliberative activity of Intellect binding together the intelligible and material worlds.[52] Moreover, unlike in Treatise 39, he insists on the exclusion of providence from the Good, and of the Good's knowledge of particulars—although, recalling Treatise 38, he maintains that we should speak as if prov-

---

50   Plot. *Enn.* 4.3 [27] 15.11–15, text and tr. Armstrong in LCL 443:84–85, modified; cit. and discussion in Eliasson, "Plotinus on Fate," 214, 218. A very similar perspective is found in Boeth. *Cons.* 5.2.8–9.

51   Plot. *Enn.* 4.3 [27] 15.15–24.

52   Mazur plausibly suggests that Plotinus dropped the association of pre-intellection with providence in *Enn.* 3.2–3 because of its ostensibly "Gnostic origin" ("Platonizing Background," 269).

idence extended to everything and as if it were caused by the Good. Finally, while most of his arguments in the treatise will be familiar to a reader who has read the previous chapters of this book and many of them ring of Stoicism,[53] his focus at a crucial point in the argument on the divine *logos* as a binding force between the intelligible and terrestrial worlds has its strongest parallels in Jewish and Christian philosophers. The work also opens by issuing a challenge to Gnostic perspectives (among others) on demiurgy, and articulating a view of strife in creation that is closely paralleled, again, in *Tri. Trac.* Plotinus's engagement with biblically-informed thinkers on the subject of providence may not have ceased following Treatise 39 after all, to say nothing of his treatise *Against the Gnostics.*

On Providence begins by targeting those who deny providential care for the world: first, the Epicureans ("to attribute the being and structure of this All to accident and chance is unreasonable"), then the Gnostics ("it has occurred to some people to say that it [i.e., providence] does not exist at all, and to others that the world has been made by an evil maker [*hōs hypo kakou dēmiourgou esti gegenēmenos*]").[54] His strategy is twofold: to defend the creation of the cosmos via emanation rather than deliberation in much the same terms as he did in *Enn.* 6.7 and elsewhere,[55] and to make wide use of traditional Platonic and Stoic arguments regarding theodicy. The latter set of arguments occupy the bulk of *Enn.* 3.2. One should not blame the whole for the parts, as Plato argues in the *Laws*, and many Stoa affirm after him.[56] Indeed, "if, then, it is possible for souls to be doing well in this universe, and if some are not doing well, we must not blame the place but their own incapacity."[57] Worldly evils are no evils at all, for poverty, sickness, and other troubles are useful for the whole and have come into being in accordance with *logos*.[58] The happy service of bedbugs and other pests in the greater scheme of creation, as espoused by their champion, Chrysippus, even puts in an appearance.[59] Plotinus also discusses the

---

53 So also Armstrong, "Dualism," 40; Adamson, *Philosophy*, 225; Ferguson, *Providence of God*, 17.

54 Plot. *Enn.* 3.2 [47] 1.1–2, 7–9, text and tr. Armstrong in LCL 442:42–43; Kalligas, '*Enneads*', 446.

55 Plot. *Enn.* 3.2 [47] 2.8–9, 3.4–5; see Schroeder, "Aseity and Connectedness," 309; Kalligas, '*Enneads*', 447; Michalewski, "Faut-il préférer," 136–137.

56 Plot. *Enn.* 3.2 [47] 3.9–13.

57 Plot. *Enn.* 3.2 [47] 5.1–4, tr. Armstrong in LCL 442:59.

58 Plot. *Enn.* 3.2 [47] 5.5–23; on the Stoic resonances here, see Kalligas, '*Enneads*', 456; above, chapter one, n. 89.

59 Plot. *Enn.* 3.2 [47] 9.34–37. As Ilievski points out, this argument is not to be found in Plato; Plotinus must know it either from the Stoa or one of their Middle Platonic readers, such as

HOW GOD CARES

classic Platonic proof-texts (*Resp.* 617e; *Phaedrus* 248) regarding the immaterial, pre-natal soul as the seat of volition, whose choices are then administered by providence: "the blame lies with the chooser," not the creator of the world, for our experiences.[60]

Yet Plotinus goes beyond Plato's *Laws* in stating that providence extends to everything—even to parts. The primary aim of the treatise is to establish the universal reach of Intellect, and thus of the sovereignty whereby it exercises care for the world. Indeed, even before he launches into the traditional arguments regarding theodicy mentioned in the previous paragraph, he is sure to state that the defense of the emanationist scheme of creation is his ultimate goal: "the nature of Intellect and Being is the true and first universe, which does not stand apart from itself and is not weakened by division and is not incomplete even in its parts, since each part is not cut off from the whole; but its whole life and the whole intellect lives and thinks all together in one …"[61] Plotinus concedes that one might think otherwise, in a remarkable description of how apparent evils and strife are a necessary byproduct of Intellect's creative activity:

> For from that true world which is one does this world, which is not truly one, come into existence; for it is many and divided into a multiplicity, and one part stands away from another and is alien to it, and there is not only friendship but also enmity because of the separation, and through their deficiency one part is of necessity (*ex anagkēs*) at war with another. For the part is not self-sufficient, but in being preserved is at war with the other by which it is preserved. This universe has come into existence, not as the result of a process of reasoning that it ought to exist but because it was necessary (*anagkē*) that there should be a second nature … So Intellect, by giving something of itself to matter, made all things in unperturbed quietness; this something of itself is the rational formative principle (*logos*) flowing from Intellect.[62]

      Philo ("Stoic Influences," 32); on the Platonic background of the notion of the 'necessity' of such creatures, see Adamson, "Making a Virtue," 25. On the general usefulness of pests and other harmful animals in the cosmic plan, see above, chapter one, n. 90.

60   Plot. *Enn.* 3.2 [47] 7.20, 9.4–10, 13.2–18; Kalligas, '*Enneads*', 460; Adamson, *Philosophy*, 225. On the relationship between the soul's pre-natal choices and 'what is up to us,' see above, chapter six.

61   Plot. *Enn.* 3.2 [47] 1.27–32, tr. Armstrong in LCL 442:45.

62   Plot. *Enn.* 3.2 [47] 2.1–17, text and tr. Armstrong in LCL 442:46–49, slightly modified.

284   CHAPTER 7

Three things stand out in this passage: first, the hasty retreat from the position regarding the will of the Good in Treatise 39, for here, the universe appears because "it was necessary";[63] second, both the content and the instrument of Intellect's creative activity is the *logos*; third, the acknowledgment that the multiplicity which emerges from unity must be characterized not only by fellowship, but strife as well. Thus, Plotinus continues, "so from Intellect which is one, and the formative principle which proceeds from it, this All has arisen and separated into parts, and of necessity some became friendly and gentle, others hostile and at war," yet eventually "they began a single melody, each of them uttering their own sounds, and the forming principle over them producing the melody and the single ordering of all together to the whole."[64]

The argument amounts to a sort of 'Plotinization' of Plato's explanation of disorder as resulting from causes necessary for creation (cf. *Tim.* 68e–69a): it was necessary for the world to exist, and strife is part of that existence.[65] Yet remarkably enough, *Tri. Trac.* presents itself once more as a close parallel. As discussed above in chapter four, in this Valentinian work, it is not Wisdom (*sophia*) but the Word (*logos*) who is responsible for the production of confusion and error in heaven, out of "shadows [and] reflections and semblances (*henhaibes m[ᵉn] heneidōlon mᵉn hᵉntantᵉn*)," terms that indicate faulty, inferior representations of reality, especially in Platonic contexts.[66] From these "shadows and reflections" appear for the first time beings outside the aeonic heaven, who represent negative mental states, degradations of the divine Intellect. Their knowledge of the Father is only shadowy and seeming, and so, like the blind demiurge of Gnostic myth, they believe that there are no powers above them:[67]

> For they thought about themselves that they were self-constituted beings, and (that) they were without source, since they do not see anything else existing prior to them. For this reason did they [live] off of[68] acts of defi-

---

63   On the notion of necessity in *Enn.* 3.2–3, see Adamson, "Making a Virtue," 23–25.

64   Plot. *Enn.* 3.2 [47] 2.23–32, tr. Armstrong in LCL 442:49.

65   Rightly Ilievski, "Stoic Influences," 32.

66   On the terminology of 'image' (*eikōn*) versus 'reflection' (*eidōlon*, etc.) from Plato through Plotinus and the 'Platonizing' Sethian treatises, see Burns, *Apocalypse*, 64–70; for parallels in Valentinian literature, see Thomassen, "Commentaire," 339.

67   On the parallel between the hylic powers' ignorance of the celestial world and the Gnostic demiurge's ignorance of his own origins, see Attridge and Pagels, "*Tripartite Tractate*: Notes," 316; Thomassen, "Commentaire," 345–346; cf. Kenney, "Platonism," 197.

68   For *ōnh ebol hn* with this meaning, see Crum, *Coptic Dictionary*, 252b. Thomassen and

HOW GOD CARES

ance [and] acts of rebellion, without humbling themselves before that one on account of [whom] they came into existence. They wished to order one another around, dominating each other [in] their empty lust for glory, for the glory which they possessed held a cause of the structure[69] that was to come. Therefore, given that they are imitations of the higher things, ⟨they⟩ elevated themselves to tyranny, each one of them according to the stature of the name of which it is but a shadow, making believe that it is actually greater than its brethren ... It happened that many came forth as begotten ones—fighters they are, warriors, destroyers, rebels, defiant ones, tyrants, [and] all the other ones of this kind from them![70]

This is a very different scenario than that we have just seen in *On Providence*, where "Intellect made all things in unperturbed quietness" by sharing its *logos* with matter, with the result being a song of harmony. The *logos* of *Tri. Trac.* has, on the contrary, made a lot of noise.[71] However, it repents its error, and through this repentance then generates another set of sub-intelligible beings who, while not of perfect, spiritual (*pneumatikos*) character, are not malevolent, either; they are of a 'middle,' "animate" (*psychikos*) character.[72] These animate beings proceed to engage in combat with the tyrannical, violent beings that arose from the *logos*'s initial confusion.[73] Both *Tri. Trac.* and Plotinus in *On Providence* agree that the *logos* brought into existence not only beings in harmony, but also beings who are in enmity and strife. For *Tri. Trac.*, the error of the Word is presented in compatibilist terms that assign a providential faculty of will to God: it happened through the Word's "free will (*ouōše ⁿnnautexousios*)," but was also "by the will of the Father ... for the future dispensation (*auoikonomia esnašōpe*)."[74] In *On Providence*, Plotinus will try to show that worldly conflict is consonant with providential care, but that the latter is exercised by Intellect via the *logos*, not by the first principle.

Painchaud prefer "se sont montrés ...," which requires reading a haplography in the manuscript ("Texte," 119)—reasonable, but not necessary.

69   *Sustasis*, i.e., the cosmos.

70   *Tri. Trac.* NHC I 79.12–80.11, text Thomassen in Thomassen and Painchaud, "Texte," 118, 120, 122, tr. mine, with reference to that of P. Nagel, *Tractatus*, 41–42.

71   As Kenney puts it, "a cursory reading of [*Tri. Trac.*'s—DMB] admittedly rather rococo ontology might suggest to an austere student of philosophical theology that there has been a riot in Plato's cave" (Kenney, "Platonism," 204).

72   *Tri. Trac.* NHC I 82.10–24.

73   *Tri. Trac.* NHC I [84].7–8[5].15.

74   *Tri. Trac.* NHC I 75.35–36, 76.36–77.3, text Thomassen in Thomassen and Painchaud, "Texte," 110, 113, 115, tr. mine. On these passages, see above, chapter four.

286   CHAPTER 7

Therefore, he says, "providence ought to reach everything, and its task ought to be just this: to neglect nothing. So, if we say that this universe depends on Intellect, and that the power of intellect has extended to all things, we must try to show in what way each of them is well disposed."[75] In *On Providence*, reason (*logos*) is the binding agent between Intellect and the terrestrial world: "it is not purely Intellect or strictly Intellect; it does not even belong to the kind of pure soul, although it depends on Soul, and it is a sort of shining out from both."[76] In Treatises 47 and 48, then, providence is supplied with 'content' by Intellect, exercised by the World Soul through *logos*, woven together with destiny in the terrestrial realm, and arrives in the sphere of *heimarmenē* when it reaches matter.[77] Plotinus explains this schema by recourse to a variety of metaphors, the most striking of which is a celebrated, extended description of life as a drama in which everything has a role to play.[78]

A second metaphor is of the martial variety, drawn from Aristotle, who describes the order of the cosmos as dependent both on itself and on its source, just as the order in army depends on both the soldiers and their commander.[79] "The universe," Plotinus states,

> is ordered by the generalship of providence which sees the actions and experiences and what must be at hand—food and drink, and all weapons and war-engines as well. Everything which results from their interweaving is foreseen (*proeōratai*), in order that the result following from them may

---

75   Plot. *Enn.* 3.2 [47] 6.21–26, tr. Armstrong in LCL 442:63; see further Kalligas, *'Enneads'*, 457.

76   Plot. *Enn.* 3.2 [47] 16.13–16, text and tr. Armstrong in LCL 442:94–95, slightly modified. See also *Enn.* 3.3 [48] 5. On the *logos* in *On Providence*, see Armstrong, *Architecture*, 102–104; Gurtler, "Providence," 116–117; Kalligas, *'Enneads'*, 458, 468–470.

77   Armstrong, *Architecture*, 84–85, 104; Kalligas, *'Enneads'*, 478.

78   Plot. *Enn.* 3.2 [47] 15–18; see further Magris, *L'idea di destino*, 2:703–706; Sharples, "Introduction: Cicero," 33; Kalligas, *'Enneads'*, 471–472, 479; Ferguson, *Providence of God*, 18; cf. Plut. *Stoic. Rep.* 1065e–1066a, criticizing the notion of the cosmos as a great drama (cit. O'Brien, *Demiurge*, 93). One cannot help but recall Shakespeare's *As You Like It*, act 2, scene 7: "All the world's a stage, And all the men and women merely players; They have their exits and their entrances, And one man in his time plays many parts ..."

79   Arist. *Metaph.* 12.10 1075a11–15, tr. Ross in Barnes, ed., 1699: "We must consider also in which of two ways the nature of the universe contains the good or the highest good, whether as something separate and by itself, or as the order of the parts. Probably in both ways, as an army does. For the good is found both in the order and in the leader, and more in the latter; for he does not depend on the order but it depends on him." See also Arist. [*Mund.*] 6.399a36–b11, 400b8; Cic. *Nat. d.* 2.85; all cit. Kalligas, *'Enneads'*, 474. See additionally Max. Tyr. *Or.* 13.4.

HOW GOD CARES

be easily accommodated, and that everything comes from the general in an ingenious way—although what his enemies planned to do is out of his control.[80]

That is, "the generalship of providence" supervises actions that are rational and therefore in accordance with it—a very Stoic view, and one consonant with his musings on the actions of the 'good soul' in *On Difficulties About the Soul*—but independent actions not in accordance with this rational generalship are not foreseen. Plotinus's use of the generalissimo metaphor is important in several respects: first, he here ascribes forethought to the divine, but only on the level of Intellect, as applied through *logos*; second, in doing so, he re-formulates the Middle Platonic models examined in chapter one, taking the action of the 'enemies' to be necessary conflicts against which incarnate souls make their decisions and receive consequences.

Most interestingly, though, Plotinus then re-frames the question from an unexpected angle: "but if it was possible for him to command the enemy force as well, if he was really 'the great leader' to whom all things are subject, what would be unordered, what would not be in agreement?"[81] His query appears at first sight to be rhetorical, since the following chapter explicates the question of whom to blame for the fact that human beings make bad choices. (The answer: not the providential *logos*, but embodied beings who are not using their own *logos*.) However, Plotinus's suggestion that the *logos* qua "great leader" could also be responsible for 'enemy forces' and thus for the negative aspects of existence which arise from strife may also be read as questioning the portrayal of the *logos* given in *Tri. Trac.* In *Tri. Trac.*, the repentant *logos* is invested with responsibility for the sub-aeonic beings which it has generated, and which are at war with one another. It begins to organize them into two camps of better and worse sub-aeonic beings: those who are "animate (*psychikos*)" on the "right," and those who are "material (*hylikos*)" on the "left," respectively. Over the latter, he sets "the law of judgment" (*pinomos ⁿtekrisis*), and "powers which the roots (*noune*) brought forth [from] tyranny."[82] Each of these beings is given a station, for the Word wishes to put them and their conflict with one another to good use:

The Word understands the balance of the tyranny of the two orders. He granted to these and all the others their desire, giving to each one

---

80   Plot. *Enn.* 3.3 [48] 2.7–13, text and tr. Armstrong in LCL 442:114–117, slightly modified.
81   Plot. *Enn.* 3.3 [48] 2.13–15, text and tr. Armstrong in LCL 442:116–117, slightly modified.
82   *Tri. Trac.* NHC I 99.7–11, text Thomassen in Thomassen and Painchaud, "Texte," 166, tr. mine. See Attridge and Pagels, "*Tripartite Tractate*: Notes," 387.

(the) established order, and it was commanded that each one became an archon over a place and an activity ... Each one of the archons and its kind and its rank—which its lot had established when they appeared—stood at guard, since it had been entrusted with the dispensation (*oikonomia*). None is without command and none without rulership, from the [limit] of the heavens to the end of the [earth], unto the inhabited regions of [the earth and] whatever is below the [earth. There are] kings, there are lords and commanders—some to punish, others to judge, still others to give reprieve and to heal, others to teach, still others to guard. Over all the [archons] did he appoint an archon, with no one to command him. He is Lord of them all.[83]

This archon appointed over the rest of the archons is of course the demiurge himself.[84] What the *logos* does here is install the warring tribes of sub-celestial beings as administrators of the earth, in the manner of the *daimones* who administer cosmic fate in Middle Platonism.[85] Origen describes how even bad angels have their purpose in cosmic administration;[86] *Tri. Trac.* offers a similarly Platonized reading of the 'mitigated dualism' of apocalyptic literature, wherein even demons have a role in God's plan. When Plotinus in *On Providence* turns Aristotle's martial metaphor of the *logos*-general around by entertaining the notion that a truly sovereign *logos* would be commander of both armies in a battle, he describes precisely the situation as given in *Tri. Trac.*[87]

Here, a genuine philosophical difference between *On Providence* and *Tri. Trac.* emerges. The Valentinian treatise describes at length the emanation of the lower world as proceeding in a chaotic fashion, replete with turmoil and full of conflict. All this, we are told, is part of the Father's salvific plan, which the *logos* providentially carries out. Yet the purpose of these descriptions of negative mental states and the nasty sub-aeonic beings that emerge from them can only be to offer an explanation for the human experience of suffering and disorder. Plotinus, on the other hand, insists "we should not attribute blame at all ... to blame anyone for this would be the same as asking, 'Why are people not

---

83   *Tri. Trac.* NHC I 99.19–100.21, text Thomassen in Thomassen and Painchaud, "Texte," 166, 168, tr. mine.

84   Attridge and Pagels, "*Tripartite Tractate*: Notes," 389–390; Thomassen, "Commentaire," 394.

85   Rightly Thomassen, "Commentaire," 393–394.

86   Orig. *Cels.* 8.31, discussed above, chapter three.

87   Cf. Kalligas, who reads Plotinus here as re-tooling the Aristotelian martial metaphor to ward off any doubt about whether the metaphor implies that the world is in a state of cosmic conflict, and thus subject to "dualistic tendencies popular in his time, especially among the Gnostics" (*'Enneads'*, 474).

what gods are?'"[88] As in Stoicism, the only evil is human evil, while all rational action is consummate with providence: actions "follow upon providence if one does what is pleasing to the gods. For the rational principle of providence (*logos ho pronoias*) is dear to the gods."[89] "So the evil deeds are consequences, but follow from necessity. For they come from us, who are not compelled by providence—rather, we attach them, of our own accord, to the works of providence or works derived from providence ..."[90] This distinction between rational action (providential) and irrational action (beyond the scope of providence) is explicitly linked to the standard Middle Platonic division between providence and fate:

> One thing results from all, and there is one providence. But it is 'fate' beginning from the lower part; the higher is providence alone. For in the intelligible world all things are reason and above reason, for all are Intellect and pure Soul; what comes from there, all that comes from Intellect, is providence ...[91]

Here, Plotinus has returned to the more typically Middle Platonic perspective he had defended in *On Fate* and *On the Difficulties About the Soul*: fate does exert control over embodied existence, but to the extent that humans act rationally, they transcend that fate.

Finally, as is well-known, the conclusion to *On Providence* holds a close parallel to *Tri. Trac.* in a discussion of how providence sustains the cosmos.[92] Plotinus snipes at over-literalistic understandings of Stoic-Christian divine omnipresence: "Altogether, those who make the demand to abolish evil in the universe are abolishing providence itself. For what would it be providence of? Certainly not of itself, or of the better; for when we speak of providence above,

---

88   Plot. *Enn.* 3.3 [48] 3.7–9, tr. Armstrong in LCL 442:117.

89   Plot. *Enn.* 3.3 [48] 5.23–24, tr. Armstrong in LCL 442:127, 129.

90   Plot. *Enn.* 3.3 [48] 5.33–37, text and tr. Armstrong in LCL 442:128–129, slightly modified.

91   Plot. *Enn.* 3.3 [48] 5.15–19, text and tr. Armstrong in LCL 442:126–127, slightly modified. For the Middle Platonic valence of the argument, see Magris, *L'idea di destino*, 2:582–583; Eliasson, "Plotinus on Fate," 215–216. See also the description of the two *logoi* in *Enn.* 3.3 [48] 4.6–15. On these two 'nested *logoi*,' see Armstrong, *Architecture*, 105; Kalligas, '*Enneads*', 475–477, who recalls the two *logoi* of Clem. Alex. apud Photius, *Bibliotheca*, 109. However, it is unlikely that Clement held any such view, although we know Valentinian theologies to have done so (Edwards, "Clement").

92   Zandee, *Terminology*, 32–33; Thomassen, "Commentaire," 262; Turner, "Plotinus and the Gnostics," 392–395. Turner, "Plotinus and the Gnostics," 395, re: *Enn.* 4.4. [28] 11.9–11; 3.8 [30] 10.2–14; 6.8 [39] 15.33–36.

290 CHAPTER 7

we are using the term of its relation to what is below."[93] Rather, he argues, particulars proceed from the One "as from a single root which remains static in itself, but they flower out into a divided multiplicity, each one bearing a reflection (*eidōlon*) of that higher reality."[94] These particulars become branches, then branches upon branches with twigs and flowers and leaves produced close to them:

> And what are like empty spaces between the branches are filled with shoots which also grow from the root, these, too, in a different way; and the twigs on the branches are also affected by these, so that they think the effect on them is only produced by what is close to them; but in fact the acting and being acted upon are in the principle, and the principle itself, too, is dependent.[95]

Arthur Hilary Armstrong, a lion amongst translators of Plotinus, states that "the imagery in this sentence is remarkably obscure," but rightly suggests that the point is that while the growth of a plant can seem disorderly from the perspective of tiny shoots far away from the trunk and root, it nonetheless shares the same source as the other shoots.[96] Other, earlier philosophers describe the cosmos as a tree,[97] but the only close parallel I have found to Plotinus's use of the metaphor here—as regards its developed length and application to the problem of providence—is *Tri. Trac.*, which describes God the Father as a "root of the universe," and "like a root and a tree, with branches and fruits."[98] The aeons He produces "are [seeds], and they are thoughts [of] its birth, and eternally living roots which have appeared"; the Father's Son, too, is "the Intellect of the [unintelligible], the spring which has gushed forth from Him, the root of

---

93   Plot. *Enn.* 3.3 [48] 7.5–8, tr. Armstrong in LCL 442:135. Similarly ibid., 3.2 [47] 9.1–4, text and tr. Armstrong in LCL 442:72–73, modified: "providence ought not to exist in such a way as to make us nothing. If everything belonged to providence and only providence, then it would not exist; for of what would it 'pro-vide'? There would only be the divine."

94   Plot. *Enn.* 3.3 [48] 7.11–13, text and tr. Armstrong in LCL 442:134–137.

95   Plot. *Enn.* 3.3 [48] 7.20–24, tr. Armstrong in LCL 442:137.

96   Armstrong in LCL 442:137.

97   Kalligas, '*Enneads*', 480–481, re: Cic. *Nat. d.* 2.82: the Stoa "speak of nature as the sustaining and governing principle of the world ... like a tree or an animal, displaying ... order and a certain semblance of design" (tr. Rackham in LCL 268:203).

98   *Tri. Trac.* NHC I 51.4, 51.17–19, text Thomassen in Thomassen and Painchaud, "Texte," 50; tr. mine. See Attridge and Pagels, "*Tripartite Tractate*: Notes," 217, 221; Thomassen, "Commentaire," 261.

HOW GOD CARES 291

the planted, the god of the established ones ..."[99] In a passage quoted above, when the Word (*logos*) organizes the sub-aeonic beings who are in opposition, he orders the dark ones who belong to the 'left' by giving them "the law of judgment" and setting over them "powers which the roots (*noune*) brought forth [from] tyranny," the greatest of whom is the demiurge.[100] To be sure, *Tri. Trac.* does not describe the plants' and roots' experience of distance from their source from their perspective, as Plotinus does; yet it offers an explanation for precisely that experience, using the same dendronous metaphors. More generally but no less importantly, *Tri. Trac.* employs the metaphors of tree and spring together to describe the first principle's production of intelligible reality; as Corrigan recently observed, Plotinus is the only other thinker to use the metaphors together in the same way.[101]

To summarize, Plotinus in *On Providence* blends two sorts of argumentation in its defense of divine care for the world. On the one hand, he makes wide use of traditional Stoic and Platonic arguments regarding theodicy, particularly the argument that disorder results from necessary causes and the notion that souls are responsible for their own fates, chosen prior to this life. He also mixes Stoic and Platonic themes in his explanation of how the rational principle organizing the cosmos—the *logos*—administers providence, but how fate exerts control over other aspects of embodied life, which can only be transcended through rational (*logismos*) action. On the other hand, Plotinus repeatedly defends an emanationist scheme of creation in the treatise by assigning Intellect's providential activity to *logos*, through whom Intellect manages to extend itself even to the most remote and material of particulars. Three sections of the treatise, meanwhile, closely recall *Tri. Trac.*: the description of emanation as one replete with strife; the notion of *logos* as a 'general' overseeing two armies in conflict with one another; and the shared employment of fountains and trees as metaphors for emanation.

The parallels with *Tri. Trac.* are important for two reasons. First, they serve as additional evidence tying the treatise to Plotinus in some way. While no dependence of one source on another can be firmly demonstrated in this case, it is obvious that if Plotinus does not engage *Tri. Trac.*, the latter treatise engages

---

99   *Tri. Trac.* NHC I [64].1–4, [66].16–19, text Thomassen in Thomassen and Painchaud, "Texte," 82, 88, respectively; tr. mine. See also NHC I 68.8–11 (on the Son's production of aeons as roots), 74.2–13 (on the Father's unity in multiplicity). See Attridge and Pagels, "*Tripartite Tractate*: Notes," 269–270, 275–276; Thomassen, "Commentaire," 309–310.

100 *Tri. Trac.* NHC I 99.7–11, text Thomassen, 166, tr. mine.

101 Corrigan in Turner, "Plotinus and the Gnostics," 395.

292   CHAPTER 7

him, or the two have a source in common.[102] Regardless of how one dates the
Greek *Vorlage* of this Coptic treatise, the strong parallels between it, *On the
Will of the One*, and *On Providence* point to a larger engagement with Judaeo-
Christian Platonists in the Plotinian corpus even after the treatise *Against the
Gnostics*. *On Providence* includes other swipes at what appears to be Jewish and
Christian philosophy in general: the very beginning of the treatise attacks those
who he thinks reject the notion of providence: Epicureans and Gnostics,[103] and
his attack on prayer and divine intervention assumes an interventionist conception of God—absent to the Aristotelian and Platonic sources he knew, but
common to Jewish and Christian ones (discussed above, chapter two).[104] Even
if one does not believe Plotinus to have *Tri. Trac.*'s *logos* in mind, his description
of *logos* as the mediator of providence recalls not only Philo of Alexandria,[105]
but Justin Martyr and Origen. This engagement culminates in Plotinus's concession to the "reckless statement" in Treatise 39 that God knows and wills, and

---

102   With that caveat in mind, the evidence presented in this chapter does lead me to incline
       towards dating the Greek *Vorlage* of *Tri. Trac.* to a time prior to Plotinus's *floruit*, i.e. in the
       first or second quarter of the third century CE. In each of the examples given above, Ploti-
       nus seems to be addressing an unexpected situation which closely resembles what we see
       in *Tri. Trac.* and correcting it, so as to say: "no, the emanation from the Good was peaceful,
       and not replete with strife; no, *logos*'s oversight over both the 'right' and 'left' forces at war
       could not implicate the *logos* in the suffering that emerges from their conflict; no, even the
       most remote shoots of the divine tree enjoy the same root." *Tri. Trac.*, meanwhile, takes up
       each of these questions on its own terms: the strife between the material and animate
       orders who emerge from the spiritual world projects the tripartite anthropology (mate-
       rial, animate, spiritual) of which Valentinians were fond onto an emanative scheme, and
       its use of the metaphors of spring and tree to denote the Father's emanation is not meant
       to extend to the material 'branches,' which it explicitly states will be destroyed (*Tri. Trac.*
       NHC I 119.8–20; see Attridge and Pagels, "*Tripartite Tractate*: Notes," 449–450; Thomassen,
       "Commentaire," 430–431). Finally, as the previous section has shown, there are additional
       parallels between *Enn.* 6.8's description of the "reckless statement" and *Tri. Trac.*'s descrip-
       tion of the Father's will. This may suggest that Plotinus responded to *Tri. Trac.* in two of his
       greatest works—first, his discussion of the *On the Will of the One*, and again in *On Prov-
       idence*. On the other hand, a reason to doubt that Plotinus has *Tri. Trac.* in mind in *On
       Providence* is his statement at the beginning of the treatise that he wishes to refute the
       view "that it [i.e., providence] does not exist at all, and to others that the world has been
       made by an evil maker" (*Enn.* 3.2 [47] 1.1–2, 7–9). *Tri. Trac.* is in agreement with Plotinus
       on both counts, for it repeatedly affirms the existence of providence and describes the
       demiurge as an ambivalent, if not exactly providential, being (see above, chapter four). If
       Plotinus knows a Greek version of our Coptic Valentinian work, he does not represent its
       depiction of the creator accurately.
103   Plot. *Enn.* 3.2 [47] 1.1–2, 7–9.
104   Cf. also Corrigan and Turner, "Introduction," 25 (re: *Enn.* 6.8).
105   Thus Armstrong, *Architecture*, 107–108; O'Brien, *Demiurge*, 296.

HOW GOD CARES 293

that providence may be regarded as God's 'first thought,' the causal mechanism for the emanation of reality. Yet he walks all of this back in his later treatise *On Providence*, where the One once again achieves its transcendence from even providential activity, and the notion of providence as prior to Intellect rather than posterior to Intellect disappears from Plotinus's writings. Yet it did not disappear from philosophical works of the later third–early fourth centuries CE: together with notions of divine omniscience departing from earlier Platonists, it was explored by Plotinus's student Porphyry—and by authors of the 'Platonizing' Sethian apocalypses.

4   The "Unspeakable First Thought" according to Porphyry and the Anonymous Commentary on Plato's 'Parmenides'

Somewhere in the later third century, a shift occurs in Platonic speculations about divine omniscience. As discussed above in chapter five, the character and limits of the gods' knowledge was an important topic for ancient philosophers, particularly those making sense of the relationship between divination and determinism: while Carneades and Cicero argued that the gods do not have knowledge of contingent events, Origen held that God is omniscient and has knowledge even of future contingents. Plotinus, meanwhile, rejected the One's knowledge of temporal matters and particulars, although he preferred to speak of providence ultimately going back to God due to the One's status as First Cause. Yet later commentators on Plato and Aristotle disagreed with Plotinus's position, turning instead to various articulations that the gods possess foreknowledge which extends even to particulars, and to future contingents—versions of the view that Origen held already in the first half of the third century. Ammonius Hermiou (later fifth–early sixth century CE), for instance, agrees with Plotinus that "there is neither past nor future among the gods, if indeed each of these is not-being ... rather, all things among them are established in the one eternal 'now'." It is therefore "necessary to cast conjectural knowledge (*eikastikēn gnōsin*) somewhere far away from the gods ..."[106] However, Ammonius continues, the gods must then have eternal, non-contingent knowledge of particulars: "one must say both that contingent things are arranged by the gods and that they know their outcome in a definite manner."[107] The principle underlying this claim was, he says, developed by Por-

---

106   *Comm. interp.*, text Busse, 133.19–30; tr. Blank, 96, slightly modified.
107   *Comm. interp.* 134.24–26, tr. Blank, 97.

phyry's younger contemporary Iamblichus of Chalcis, who held that "knowledge is intermediate between the knower and the known, since it is the activity of the knower concerning the known."[108] Since the gods are eternal and divine, contingent matters are not contingent to them; running in the waters of eternity home to the gods, they are foreknown.[109]

Ammonius's teacher Proclus 'Diadochus', writing in the fifth century, valorizes Iamblichus's position by way of excoriating Porphyry, who, he claims, argued the opposite: "the knowledge they [i.e., the Gods] have is characterized by the natures of the objects of knowledge ... (and) that what has no reliability is not reliable in the case of the gods."[110] Proclus counters: "let us rather think that the manner of knowing differs according [to] the diversity of the knowers. For the very same object is known by god unitarily, by intellect holistically, by reason universally, by imagination figuratively, by sense-perception passively. And it is not the case that because the object of knowledge is one, the knowledge is also one [and the same]."[111] Because the gods are immaterial and eternal, they "have prior knowledge" (*proeilēphasi*) of the material, temporal realm.[112] Historians of later Platonism thus commonly refer to it as "Iamblichus's principle of knowing."[113]

Yet as Michael Chase argues, in chapter 33 of the *Sententiae*—short essays elaborating on passages of the *Enneads*—Porphyry clearly defends the same principle taken up later by Iamblichus, Proclus, and Ammonius, albeit with reference to the intelligibles, articulated in terms of parts and multiplicity versus the absence thereof:

---

108 *Comm. interp.* 135.15–17, tr. Blank, 98.

109 For critical discussion of Ammonius's argument, see A. Lloyd, *Anatomy*, 155–159; Sorabji, "Introduction," 6; also Theiler, "Tacitus," 63. Iamblichus's extant remarks on providence and ritual in works such as *De mysteriis* do not touch on the subject of divine omniscience, but are not mutually exclusive with the position assigned to him by Ammonius.

110 Procl. *Comm. Tim.* 1.352.11–13, tr. Runia and Share, 210. Proclus's testimony on Porphyry's views here is widely cited, e.g. by Magris, *L'idea di destino*, 2:665 (who goes too far in identifying Porphyry's view with that of Carneades); Sharples, "Introduction: Cicero," 26; Opsomer, "Middle Platonic Doctrine," 165 n. 112.

111 Procl. *Comm. Tim.* 1.352.15–19, tr. Runia and Share, 210, slightly modified.

112 Procl. *Comm. Tim.* 1.352.23–26, tr. Runia and Share, 210. Runia and Share remark op. cit. that "this priority of their knowledge is meant ontologically, not temporally"; rather, Proclus seems to speak here of the gods' eternal knowledge of temporal matters, as his student Ammonius later would.

113 A. Lloyd, *Anatomy*, 155; similarly Benjamins, *Eingeordnete Freiheit*, 93 n. 82; as much seems implied by Boyd, who dubs the principle "Neoplatonic" and cites no authorities for it earlier than Iamblichus ("Two Ancient," 44).

HOW GOD CARES

On the one hand, that which is without parts and non-multiple is, to that which is by nature multiple and endowed with volume, endowed with volume and multiplicity, and it is in this way that it partakes of it—namely, in a manner in accordance with its own nature, not like that other one. Meanwhile, that which has parts and is multiplied is partless and non-multiple for that which is naturally partless and non-multiple, and is present to it in that mode—that is, the latter is present in a partless and non-multiple and non-local manner, in accordance with its own nature, to that which is by nature divisible and multiple and local, while that which is divisible and multiple and local is present to the other, which is free of these specifications, divisibly and multiply and locally.[114]

As Chase writes, "ici le mode d'expression de Porphyre est difficile, mais l'idée fondamentale me semble claire: dans la perspective des êtres sensibles, les choses intelligibles semblent être pourvues des caractéristiques des êtres sensibles, et *vice versa*."[115] Another passage from the same work points in the same direction, when read closely:

On the subject of that which is beyond Intellect, many statements are made on the basis of intellection, but it may be immediately cognized only by means of a non-intellection superior to intellection; even as concerning sleep many statements may be made in a waking state, but only through sleeping can one gain direct knowledge and comprehension; for like is known by like, because all knowledge consists of assimilation to the object of knowledge.[116]

While the final sentence at first echoes Proclus's quotation of the young Porphyry—that knowledge "is characterized by the natures of the objects of knowledge"—it is clear that Porphyry here means that the character of knowledge beyond cognition is determined by (and solely accessible to) one who is not in a cognizant state. "Only through sleeping can one gain direct knowledge and comprehension" of the experience of sleeping. Finally, it is worth mentioning that, in a treatise on free will only preserved in fragments, *Against Nemertius*, Porphyry assumes divine knowledge of future events:

---

114 Porph. *Sent.* 33.21–30, text Brisson, 1:346, tr. J.M. Dillon in ibid., 2:816–817, modified.
115 Chase, "Porphyre sur la providence," 142.
116 Porph. *Sent.* 25, tr. J.M. Dillon in Brisson, 2:804.

God very often knows beforehand (*eidōs ... phthanei pollakis*) what is to be, as when He brings some children out of life early on account of their piety, and others because of the harm that will befall their relatives because to them, and still others He removes out of pity, given the fact of imminent necessary (*sumphorōn*) disasters.[117]

Chase proposes two possible explanations for the discrepancy between the position staked out by Porphyry in the *Sentences* and that assigned to him by Proclus: either Proclus is unkindly reporting a view of the younger Porphyry, perhaps following Iamblichus, or Porphyry simply changed his mind over time.[118] Regardless, Porphyry here departs from Plotinus, who had rejected the gods' knowledge of temporal and contingent matters in the sub-noetic realm. Porphyry appears to have anticipated the later Platonic turn towards divine omniscience. Interestingly, in the same treatise he takes up Plotinus's notion of a 'pre-noetic' cognitive faculty. The passage in question appears to describe how easily meditation on non-being can lead the contemplator to stumble into the metaphysics of utter absence rather than transcendence:

> One kind of non-being we produce when we are apart from being, while another kind we pre-conceive when cleaving close to being (*to de proen-nooumen echomenoi tou ontos*). For if we should by chance be separated from being, we do not pre-conceive the non-being which is beyond being. Rather, we produce a false experience of non-being, as happens to someone who has departed from his proper state. For one and the same person can, truly and on his own initiative, be elevated towards the non-being which is beyond being—and set astray towards that non-being which constitutes the collapse of being.[119]

That "the non-being which is beyond being" is the transcendent state of the One, which one accesses through a kind of "preapprehension" (*proennoein*)— the supra-cognitive faculty alluded to by Plotinus in *Enn.* 6.7–8 [38–39].

---

117   Porph. Frg. 280, text A. Smith, 316, tr. mine, with reference to that of Maisel, "Fragments." Contingents do not seem to be a question here; the disasters in question are *sumforos* ("expedient, suitable"—LSJ 1688a), and probably then of the type that exists for the care of the whole (i.e., the cosmos) rather than the part (i.e., the souls of the young).

118   Chase, "Porphyre sur la providence," 142–143.

119   Porph. *Sent.* 26, text Brisson, 1:324, tr. J.M. Dillon in ibid., 2:804, significantly modified. On this passage see *inter alia* Hadot, *Porphyre et Victorinus*, 1:117; Turner, *Sethian Gnosticism*, 688–691; Mazur, "Platonizing Background," 253.

HOW GOD CARES

The language of preapprehension or 'first thought' of the First Principle also appears in the anonymous *Commentary on Plato's 'Parmenides'*, whose authorship remains the subject of controversy amongst scholars.[120] This anonymous work is significant in itself as perhaps the earliest surviving specimen of the late ancient tradition of long-form commentary on this most difficult of Plato's dialogues.[121] However, it is also implicated in the reception and adaptation of this tradition in late ancient theological writing, for its thought at times resembles that found in material shared between the fourth-century opponent of Arianism Marius Victorinus and the Coptic Gnostic work *Zostrianos* (NHC VIII,1). Significantly, Porphyry tells us that a version of *Zostrianos* circulated in Plotinus's seminar in Rome along with other apocalypses esteemed by the Christian Gnostics, such as *Allogenes*—a version of which survives as part of the Nag Hammadi find as well (NHC XI,3).[122] Scholars have contested the dating and authorship of the anonymous *Commentary*, offering a variety of hypotheses pre-Plotinian and post-Plotinian alike, including Christian and Gnostic authors, although the most widely held position remains that of the work's major twentieth-century editor and interpreter, Pierre Hadot, who regarded it as a text of Porphyry.[123] The issue is complicated further by the lack of consensus in dating the Greek *Vorlagen* of the extant Coptic versions of the Gnostic apocalypses known to Plotinus.

Scholarship remains at a standoff regarding the dating and authorship of the anonymous *Commentary* as well as the Gnostic works to which it is related in some way.[124] These questions may never be settled once and for all, but Anon. *Comm. Parm.* mentions a supra-cognitive faculty used to know the One, and so it is worth examining here:

---

120   On Anon. *Comm. Parm.* in general, see Hadot, *Porphyre et Victorinus*, 1:103–104, 2:61–113; Bechtle, *Anonymous Commentary*, 17–18; Chase, "Porphyre de Tyr," 1358–1361; Turner, "Anonymous *Parmenides* Commentary," 93–99.

121   See e.g. the discussions in the contributions in Turner and Corrigan, eds., *Plato's "Parmenides."*

122   Tardieu, "Recherches"; see also Hadot, "Porphyre et Victorinus." For discussion, see Abramowski, "Nicänismus und Gnosis"; Chase, "Porphyre de Tyr," 1366–1368; Turner, "Anonymous *Parmenides* Commentary," 101–109.

123   For survey, see Chase, "Porphyre de Tyr," 1362–1371; Turner, "Anonymous *Parmenides* Commentary." For Anon. *Comm. Parm.* as a work of Porphyry, see Hadot, *Porphyre et Victorinus*, 1:107–113, and Chase, "Porphyre de Tyr," 1362–1365; for a pre-Plotinian, Platonist author, see Bechtle, *Anonymous Commentary*, 89–90; for Porphyry or Amelius, see Brisson, "Reception," 61; for a fourth-century, Christian author, see Edwards, "Christians and the *Parmenides*," 195–197; for a Gnostic, see Rasimus, see "Porphyry and the Gnostics," esp. 110.

124   Thus Chase, "Porphyre de Tyr," 1369–1371; Turner, "Anonymous *Parmenides* Commentary," 126.

And thus it is possible, without falling into nothingness or daring to attribute something to That One, to wait in a state of incomprehensible comprehension and a state of thinking that is without thought. Thanks to this exercise, at some point it should happen to you—having turned away from thinking about the things that have come into being on account of Him—to bring about the unspeakable first thought (*arrēton pro{s}ennoian*) of Him which represents Him through silence, without even knowing that it is silent or being aware that it represents Him, without even knowing anything at all, but being simply an image of the unspeakable—with the unspeakable being, well, unspeakable—but not as something that knows, if you can follow me as I try to explain it with imagery.[125]

While Hadot emended the term *prosennoia* as it stands in the manuscript to *proennoia* ("preconception") on grounds of Marius Victorinus's use of the terms *praeintellentia* and *praenoscentia*, Zeke Mazur has suggested emending rather to *protennoia*—"first thought," recalling the incarnation of the goddess providence who appears in the Nag Hammadi treatise *Three Forms of First Thought* (see above, chapter four).[126] As in *Enn.* 6.7–6.8 [38–39], "first thought" and "providence/forethought" coincide for God and the mystic, here a meditative reader of the *Parmenides*, alike.

Hadot has further argued that, strictly speaking, this author (who he believes to be Porphyry) only says one may achieve a non-cognitive state of silence, rather than an actual encounter with the One as described by Plotinus.[127] Yet this non-cognitive state is that state which characterizes the One's mode of cognition, as the commentator says in a passage that, significantly, affirms God's knowledge of the future and the past:

And so we are nothing like That One, but He is the sole truly-existing being—if you know what I mean—prior to everything following from Him, having no comparison with or any relation to them, nor turning away from the solitude proper to Him to experience condition and multi-

---

125 Anon. *Comm. Parm.* 2.14–27, text in Hadot, *Porphyre et Victorinus*, 2:68, 70, tr. mine, with reference to those of Hadot and of Bechtle (*Porphyre et Victorinus*, 2:69, 71, and *Anonymous Commentary*, 42, respectively).

126 Hadot in *Porphyre et Victorinus*, 2:71 n. 2; Mazur, "Gnostic Background," 253, n. 183; also idem, "Self-Manifestation," 9 n. 25; cf. the discussion of Bechtle, *Anonymous Commentary*, 42 n. 27.

127 Hadot, *Porphyre et Victorinus*, 1:118.

HOW GOD CARES

plicity—except that He does not ever stay in ignorance of what shall be, and He knows what has been, He who has never been in a state of ignorance.[128]

The commentary continues: "And so does God know everything? And who then knows as He does? And how, [having] knowledge, is He not multiple?"[129] The answer is that God's knowledge is not ignorance; "rather, that He transcends all knowledge."[130]

The anonymous *Commentary* and Porphyry then both identify the non-cognitive forethought of the contemplator of the One with the One's own knowledge that is no knowledge at all. At the same time, they agree that the One possesses knowledge of the future and the past, presumably by virtue of their eternity. Regardless of whether one identifies the author of the anonymous *Commentary* as pre- or post-Plotinian, its description of divine omniscience departs from that of Plotinus and is more similar to that ascribed by the later commentary tradition to Iamblichus—and, if the reading of Porphyry's *Sententiae* offered here is correct, to that of Porphyry, who describes a supra-cognitive faculty for apprehending the One in similar fashion, although not as a 'first thought.' All this speaks for assigning authorship of the anonymous *Commentary* to Porphyry—or to one of his Christian interlocutors, for we find much of this language about providence and first thought in the Coptic, 'Platonizing' Gnostic apocalypses of Nag Hammadi.

5 'First Thought' and Providence in the 'Platonizing' Sethian Treatises of Nag Hammadi

These Platonizing apocalypses are usually classed by scholars as belonging to the 'Sethian' literary tradition, characterized chiefly by its veneration of the patriarch Seth as revealer and savior.[131] To denote the First Principle, they employ the traditional Sethian title "the Great Invisible Spirit."[132] As John

---

128   Anon. *Comm. Parm.* 4.26–35, text in Hadot, *Porphyre et Victorinus*, 2:76, 78, tr. mine, with reference to the translations of Hadot and of Bechtle (*Porphyre et Victorinus*, 2:77, 79, and *Anonymous Commentary*, 49, respectively).

129   Anon. *Comm. Parm.* 5.7–9.

130   Anon. *Comm. Parm.* 5.15.

131   On Sethian Gnosticism, see esp. Schenke, "Phenomenon"; Turner, *Sethian Gnosticism*; Rasimus, *Paradise Reconsidered*; Burns, *Apocalypse*.

132   This is itself interesting in a Platonic context, where use of the term *pneuma* for the First Principle must have conjured the specter of Stoicism. See Hadot, *Porphyre et Victorinus*,

300   CHAPTER 7

D. Turner and Mazur have discussed, two of these texts, *Zostrianos* and *Allogenes*, contain descriptions of the Invisible Spirit's "pre-noetic" capacity, a sort of transcendent 'self-knowing' or 'primary revelation,' whose eternal act of tautology generates the aeon of Barbelo—roughly equivalent to Plotinian *nous*.[133] Such language is also found in the Coptic Gnostic works *Apocryphon of John* as well as *Three Forms of First Thought*.[134]

This doctrine and its attendant terminology parallel discussions of the One's self-knowledge and the generation of Intellect in Plotinus as well as the supra-cognitive faculty described in the anonymous *Commentary* discussed above. What remains to be studied, however, is the position of these treatises on divine knowledge of the sub-divine realm—i.e., the way in which the Invisible Spirit knows the universe, if It knows it at all. While this question is interesting in itself, it may prove to be particularly incisive for the 'Platonizing' Sethian treatises, since we know that there was a marked shift within the Platonic tradition after Plotinus regarding divine omniscience of particular beings and contingent events, as discussed in the previous section.

Zostrianos, the first tractate of Nag Hammadi Codex VIII, describes the existential torment of its eponymous seer and his subsequent ascent into the heavens, where he engages in revelation-dialogues with agents of the Barbelo aeon.[135] A characteristic of these 'Platonizing' treatises is the subdivision of this aeon into the subaeons dubbed Kaluptos ('Hidden'), Prōtophanes ('Primary Manifestation'), and Autogenes ('Self-Generated'), in turn corresponding roughly to the three stages of emanating Intellect (*nous*) in Plotinus: self-contemplating, contemplative, and demiurgical-discursive, respectively.[136] While Plotinus locates providential activity in diverse sectors of the cosmos throughout his corpus (as discussed above), the 'Platonizing' treatises agree with the account in *Enn.* 6.7–8 [38–39] that God exercises foreknowledge in

---

1:295–297; Rasimus, "Porphyry and the Gnostics," 2:94–95, 103. Cf. Abramowski, "Nicänismus und Gnosis," 537–539, 549.

133   See esp. Mazur, "Platonizing Background," 220–266; also idem, "Self-Manifestation"; Turner, *Sethian Gnosticism*, 686–692.

134   Thus, Rasimus suggests a second-century 'Gnostic' origin for this later Platonic nomenclature ("Porphyry and the Gnostics," esp. 2:89, 99 n. 81–82, 101–103; idem, "Johannine Background," 398–403; for survey, see also Burns, "First Thoughts," 38–40). However, they are absent from our sole second-century witness to the text, Ir. *Haer.* 1.29, and so the appearance of this terminology in the later Coptic MSS likely indicates the redacted character of the latter (Burns, op. cit. 40–41).

135   On the frame-narrative of *Zost.*, see Burns, "Apocalypse of Zostrianos"; more recently, van den Kerchove, "Rhétorique."

136   *Nous noētos, nous noeros*, and *nous dianooumenos* or simply *psukhē*. See Turner, *Sethian Gnosticism*, 532–553, 696–697.

HOW GOD CARES 301

Intellect. Thus does *Zostrianos* tell us that Intellect—in its instantiation as the Prōtophanes, 'primary manifestation'—has knowledge of individuals:

> [And] this male (being) is a [model] and [species of the] perfect [Intellect], since it does not have [...] through [unique] knowledge, like that one. [And] it is a [measure] of the individuals; it is [a] unique knowledge of the individuals, [whether] universally [or individually], perfectly. And the [male, perfect] intellect [is knowledge of] the Hidden One.[137]

This aeon—"Hidden One" (Grk., *Kaluptos*)—is the highest grade of Intellect, and it has universal knowledge of individuals and individual actions:

> [It is] he (i.e., the Hidden One) [who] knows every deed of them all, since it is completely perfect. From him derives every power, and everyone, and their entire aeon. To him do they all go, from him do they [all] come—the power of them [all], the source of them [all]. If one were to know him, he would be a [second] aeon, and a [second] unbegottenness.[138]

Yet the Invisible Spirit also has knowledge:

> And the [Invisible] Spirit [is] an [animate] and [intellectual] power, a knower and [a] fore-knower.[139]

Similarly, a passage on the One—extensively restored on the basis of parallels with Marius Victorinus—says:

> [He is prior to them all, for] He is [a first principle of every principle, and He is] a first [thought] of [every] thought.[140]

Yet the text is somewhat less confident in a later discussion, where we are told that

> [Indeed], because That One pre-exists and exists before everything, pre-existing, it is known as thrice-powered. [The] Invisible Spirit absolutely

---

137   *Zost.* NHC VIII 41.12–22, text Barry, Funk, and Poirier, 316, tr. mine.
138   *Zost.* NHC VIII [121].9–22, text Barry, Funk, and Poirier, 458, tr. mine.
139   *Zost.* NHC VIII [58].16–20, text Barry, Funk, and Poirier, 348, tr. mine.
140   *Zost.* NHC VIII [65].4–8, text Barry, Funk, and Poirier, 362, tr. mine.

302   CHAPTER 7

has never been ignorant—[nor was He] cognizant—rather, He [existed] as perfection, [and] Blessedness.[141]

Zostrianos here appears to hew to a position like that of Plotinus: it is Intellect that has knowledge of individuals, but the transcendent God is beyond cognition, and therefore is not itself cognizant. (The latter claim was also made in the anonymous *Commentary*, as noted in the previous section.) At the same time, it would be wrong to deny the Invisible Spirit foreknowledge, since it does have a kind of knowing proper only to itself, a knowledge identical to the emergence of Intellect, as the text explicitly states:

> The Barbelo—the aeon, the [knowledge] of the Invisible, Thrice-Powered, Perfect Spirit ...[142]

The case is less clear with *Allogenes*. The third tractate of Nag Hammadi Codex XI, this work is another apocalypse where the seer—here named 'Foreigner' (*allogenēs*, "other-born, alien," a *sobriquet* for Seth)—enjoys revelation-dialogues about the divine realm of the Platonists. In *Allogenes*, the Invisible Spirit is not just the cause of all beings, but even contains them—a rather strong statement:

> [Now], concerning the Thrice-Powered, Invisible Spirit, listen! [It] exists as one, invisible—[for It] is incomprehensible for them all, since It has all of them inside of itself, for [they] all exist thanks to [It].[143]

More specifically, the Invisible Spirit is explicitly said to care for all things, by virtue of its productivity and bestowal of revelation:

> Since it is impossible for the [individuals] to comprehend the universe that is established in the place that is more than perfect, they receive (revelation) by means of forethought. Not in the manner of Being; [rather] It gives Being with [the] hiddenness [of] existence, in its care (*sahne*) for all things,[144] since it is this that comes into being when It conceives itself.[145]

---

141   *Zost.* NHC VIII [80].14–23, text Barry, Funk, and Poirier, 384, tr. mine. See also Turner, "Commentary," 573–574 (clearly with reference to the passage quoted here, rather than "81.19–23," as stated).

142   *Zost.* NHC VIII 1[1]8.9–11, text Barry, Funk, and Poirier, 452, tr. mine.

143   *Allogenes* NHC XI [47].7–14, text Funk in Funk and Scopello, "Texte," 194, tr. mine.

144   *Sahne* does not translate any Greek terms directly relating to care; it is more concerned with provision or supply (Crum, *Coptic Dictionary*, 385b).

145   *Allogenes* NHC XI [48].9–19, text Funk in Funk and Scopello, "Texte," 196, tr. mine, with

HOW GOD CARES 303

A longer passage states much the same:

> And It is [One], for it is established as a true [cause] and a source—
> and immaterial [matter, and] unnumerable [number, and formless] form,
> and [shapeless shape], and [a powerlessness of] power, [and a substance
> without substance ... and an inactive activity—except insofar as It is a
> provider] of [care, and] a divinity [of] divinity. But if they should receive
> (Being), they receive from the primary Vitality, and an undivided activity,
> a hypostasis of the first (activity) of the One that truly exists.[146]

These passages do not in themselves denote a departure from Plotinus's position—at least as articulated in *Enn.* 6.8 [39], where he comes closest to calling
the One itself providential. But *Allogenes* appears to state something like the
principle that the status of divine knowledge is determined by the knower,
rather than the known:

> [...] the substance [(...)] should it grasp anything, [it is grasped by] that
> one, and [by] that one who is comprehended, which is the same. There-
> fore, the one who comprehends and who knows is greater than that one
> who is comprehended and known.[147]

Here, the degree of comprehension is decided by the subject, not the object.
One might ask if this treatise maintains divine transcendence alongside divine
care because it agrees with Iamblichus—and, as argued in the previous section,
Porphyry—that the quality of transcendence grants the knower more knowledge, not less.

On the other hand, *Allogenes* also states that "The Unknowable One" cannot
desire or will:

> As for That One—[should] someone contemplate [It, It cannot desire]
> anything, for It [exists] prior to those [who have existence. For It is the
> source from which they all have been produced ...][148]

And in a later passage on God's unknowable knowledge, the treatise says that
God does not care:

---

 reference to that of Turner, who also glosses the passages, cleverly, to refer to the three
 subaeons of Barbelo ("Introduction: *Allogenes*," 175).

146 *Allogenes* NHC XI [48].19–37, text Funk in Funk and Scopello, "Texte," 196, tr. mine.
147 *Allogenes* NHC XI [57].6–15, text Funk in Funk and Scopello, "Texte," 214, tr. mine.
148 *Allogenes* NHC XI [47].21–28, text Funk in Funk and Scopello, "Texte," 194, tr. mine.

⟨If one were to see It⟩—how exactly It is unknowable,[149] or if one were to see It in the way that it exists, in some form, or if one would say about It: "It exists as something like knowledge"—that one has sinned against It, being liable to judgment because he has not known God. He will not receive judgment from that one—who does not care for anything, nor does he have any will—rather, it comes from himself, since he has not found the source that truly exists.[150]

The lacunose nature of the manuscript makes it difficult to offer a sure judgment reconciling these views, but my hypothesis is that perhaps we are dealing here with something like Iamblichus's thesis that there are two Ones: a truly transcendent One that is completely removed from everything, and a One that serves as first cause.[151] We find such a schema outlined on page 66 of *Allogenes*, where the text refuses to predicate care (or anything) of what it calls "the Unknowable One," before

[...] and It [does not] care [for] anything. Nor, if one were to take of It, would that one prevail. Nothing acts on It, in accordance with its singularity—which is still in itself—for It is unknowable. Indeed, It is a place without breath,[152] belonging to the boundlessness. Since It is boundless, and without power and being, It does not bestow Being; rather, It holds everything in Itself—being still in Itself, and standing. From that One who stands eternally manifested eternal life, the Invisible Spirit, and the Thrice-Powered One, the One who is in everything that exists and which surrounds them all, for it is superior to them all ...[153]

---

149   Turner proposes the emendation *ē eš⟨če ouen oua efnau erof⟩ če*, adopted by Funk (see the apparatus criticus in Funk and Scopello, "Texte," 228–229) and so followed here.

150   *Allogenes* NHC XI [64].15–30, text Funk in Funk and Scopello, "Texte," 228, tr. mine. The sense is that the one who has not known God condemns oneself.

151   Regarding *Allogenes* and the Thrice-Powered One, cf. Finamore, "Iamblichus," 237–238, 244. On Iamblichus's theory that there are two Ones, see Damascius, *Questions and Solutions on First Principles*, 43, 50, 51; for discussion, see Finamore, op. cit., 227–228, 249–250, 254. It has been suggested that the 'Silent One' of *Mars.* is inspired by the 'second One' of Porphyry and Iamblichus's student, Theodore of Asine (Turner, "Introduction: *Marsanes*," 209–212, 226–230, 234–235; idem, *Sethian Gnosticism*, 707–708; idem, "Introduction: Marsanes"; cf. Finamore, op. cit., 248–249).

152   Or "place without spirit," so as to imply that the First Principle transcends even its traditional Sethian title ("Great Invisible Spirit").

153   *Allogenes* NHC XI [66].17–38, text Funk in Funk and Scopello, "Texte," 232, tr. mine, with reference to that of Funk, "Allogenes," 786.

HOW GOD CARES   305

It is also worth briefly examining an even more poorly-preserved 'Platonizing' Sethian work, *Marsanes*, from Nag Hammadi Codex X. This text mainly
deals with matters of occult philosophy and ritual,[154] but it opens with an
exhortation to persevere in the face of difficulty, and on the first page of the
MS, we are told:

> Those [who have received] you shall be given an excellent reward for
> [their] constancy, and [they shall] persevere [in the face of] evil. [Now],
> let no one [of] us grieve [and] think [in] his heart that the great Father
> is [uninvolved.] For He surveys the universe, [and] is concerned about
> everyone (*f[qō]šᵉt gar ačᵉm ptērᵉf [auō] ᵉffi ᵉmpourauš tē[rou]*).[155]

Among the Platonizing Sethian literature from Nag Hammadi, this is the clear-
est statement that the first principle has knowledge of and cares for worldly
affairs. It is a striking departure from *Zostrianos* and *Allogenes*—and from Plotinus, who even in *Enn.* 6.8 [39] is so hesitant regarding the One's knowledge and
willing of anything. By *On Providence*, he has retreated back to the more conservative position that *pronoia* belongs to Intellect although it may in a sense
be predicated of the One as cause of the universe. Now, *Zostrianos* is on ter-
rain similar to that of Plotinus, since it tries to restrict the prenoetic faculty
to the Prōtophanes and Kaluptos aeons, even though it does not want to say
the Invisible Spirit is non-cognizant. Meanwhile, *Allogenes* explicitly affirms
the principle expressed by Iamblichus and (as argued above) Porphyry that
the status of divine knowledge is determined by the knower—not the object
known. It also states that the Invisible Spirit cares for all, while, later in the
treatise, the One does not—perhaps an indication of a division in the First Principle regarding care and transcendence. Again, this would recall Iamblichus.
Marsanes states unambiguously that God cares for—and, therefore, knows—
the universe. Finally, while none of these three 'Platonizing' apocalypses explicitly ties the character of divine knowledge to the eternity of the divine world
by way of argument, all three emphasize the eternal character of the divine
world and everything in it, insofar as they make ready and free usage of what
is probably the most common term for heaven and its inhabitants in Gnostic
literature: *aiōn* (Grk. "eternity"). It is difficult to imagine that these works see
divine knowledge as possessing a non-eternal character.[156]

---

154   On ritual practices in *Mars.*, see Turner, *Sethian Gnosticism*, 614–633; idem, "Introduction:
       Marsanes," 20, 81, 231–234; Burns, *Apocalypse*, 113–122.
155   *Mars.* NHC X [1].14–25, text Funk in Funk and Poirier, "Texte," 250, tr. mine.
156   Again, *Allogenes* presents itself as most tantalizing in this regard, explicitly identifying

306   CHAPTER 7

From the perspective of the doxography of God's faculties of providence and care in late ancient Platonism, *Allogenes* and *Marsanes* fall on the post-Plotinian side of the spectrum, while *Zostrianos*'s view is more or less like that of Plotinus. This may indicate a later dating for the *Vorlagen* of our extant Coptic versions of *Marsanes* and *Allogenes*. This should not surprise us. Over fifteen years ago, Turner demonstrated that *Marsanes*'s analysis of the configurations of the soul recalls Theodore of Asine, whose *floruit* may be dated to the early fourth century.[157] I have argued elsewhere that the negative theology of *Allogenes*, which uses negations and paradoxes, is more similar to what we find in Proclus and Iamblichus, perhaps then reflecting fourth-century thought rather than the mysticism of Plotinus.[158] The same can be said of the anonymous *Commentary on Plato's 'Parmenides'*, whose position on the mystical supra-cognitive faculty and God's foreknowledge resembles that of Porphyry, if the analysis of the previous section is correct. On the other hand, the same inclination to assign the godhead knowledge and providence which is pronounced in Neoplatonism after Plotinus is simply emblematic of Christian Platonism.

6   Conclusions: A Christianizing Turn in Platonist Conceptions of Divine Foreknowledge

As discussed above in chapters two and five, Jewish and Christian philosophers of the first centuries CE, committed to the positive truth-value of biblical passages regarding the omnipresence and omniscience of the God of Israel, did not hesitate to affirm God's foreknowledge of and involvement in worldly affairs. The general inclination of the Platonizing Sethian texts to affirm the Invisible Spirit's knowledge of particulars, even in the subcelestial realm, would not be unusual in a Christian context of any century. (Once again, *Tri. Trac.* presents itself as a useful comparandum, insofar as it is a work whose understanding of the first principle and the heavenly world is deeply Neoplatonic, but which nonetheless affirms God's providential foreknowledge of the salvific plan.) In other words, the positions of *Allogenes* and *Marsanes* on divine omniscience may not necessarily be later by virtue of their departure from Plotinus, because they are not unusual positions for Jewish and Christian thinkers of the

---

"the knowledge [of] the wholes" (*tignōsis* [ⁿ*te*] *niptērⁿf*—i.e., "knowledge of the universe" < Grk. *gnōsis tōn holōn*) as "the aeon of Barbelo" (NHC XI [59].1–3).

157   Turner, "Introduction: *Marsanes*," 209–230.
158   Burns, "Apophatic Strategies."

HOW GOD CARES 307

first centuries CE.[159] The same might be said of the anonymous *Commentary*, which comfortably asserts God's knowledge of all future and past events even as it maintains divine transcendence. One could then marshal this observation in service of Tuomas Rasimus's thesis that the *Commentary* was authored by Christian Gnostics; yet Porphyry and Iamblichus, no followers of Christ, adopted similar positions, and so one could also plausibly interpret this evidence as indicating Porphyry's authorship of the *Commentary*.

In other words, at the beginning of the third century, it was distinctively characteristic of Jewish and Christian philosophers, as well as the Stoa, to ascribe omniscience and foreknowledge to God; by the end of the century, Platonists had come to do the same, whether one looks at God's eternal knowledge of future and past (as do Porphyry and allegedly Iamblichus), or of God's knowledge of particulars. One need not pursue the (perhaps insoluble) questions of decisively dating the anonymous *Commentary* and the Greek *Vorlagen* of the 'Platonizing' Sethian texts—to say nothing of *Tri. Trac.*—in order to observe this shift in third-century Platonist conceptions of providence and divine omniscience. Yet one can hardly read this shift as a Platonist concession to Stoic contemporaries, for they do not appear to have had any; the Stoa had disappeared by the third century.[160] Moreover, the third-century Platonists who assigned some kind of knowledge to the First Principle also all discuss in some fashion the sort of pre-noetic, mystical 'first thought' mentioned by Plotinus in *Enn.* 6.8, a notion removed from Stoic concerns.

Yet we know the Platonists of the second and third centuries to have had some experience dealing with Christians. The circulation in Plotinus's seminar in Rome of Platonizing works and apocalypses esteemed by Christian Gnostics has already been mentioned; to this we may add Numenius's famous remarks on Moses and the book of Genesis, and the exegesis of the Fourth Gospel by Plotinus's student Amelius.[161] It is striking that historians of philosophy discussing the problem of divine foreknowledge of future conditionals have found only one clear parallel to the views of Iamblichus and Proclus prior to the fourth century: the Christian Origen, in his treatise *On Prayer*.[162] The specter of Pla-

---

159 On Sethian Gnosticism as a phenomenon that appears to have emerged from the boundaries modern scholars have drawn between ancient Judaism and Christianity, see Burns, *Apocalypse*, 143–147.

160 The final Stoic philosopher of note is Marcus Aurelius, although the Neoplatonists remained interested in Stoic sources, particularly Epictetus. On the disappearance of the Stoa around the beginning of the third century CE, see Long, "Stoicism," 366–368.

161 On Numenius's engagement with biblical authorities, see Burns, *Apocalypse*, 23; for Amelius's reading of the Fourth Gospel, see Brisson, "Amélius," 840–843.

162 Orig. *Or.* 6.4–11; thus Sharples, "Introduction: Cicero," 27 and Opsomer, "Middle Platonic Doctrine," 165 n. 112; cf. Gibbons, "Human Autonomy," 678.

tonist dialogue with Christian philosophers has already presented itself in this chapter: Plotinus's response in *Enn.* 6.8 [39] to the "reckless statement" that his philosophy of the One does not permit God to will anything; significant parallels between his description of the logos in *On Providence* and that of *Tri. Trac.*, in addition to other shared metaphors for divine emanation; and the proximity of his ideas about a supra-cognitive 'first thought,' together with those of Porphyry and the anonymous *Commentary*, to parallels in the Coptic Gnostic evidence.

Did Christian notions of divine omniscience lead thinkers after Plotinus to re-think how providence functions, how God cares? Conversely, evidence which has been taken to suggest that the anonymous *Commentary* was authored by an unknown Christian or a Gnostic may rather be evidence suggesting a wider dialogue between Christian and Hellenic thinkers.[163] From this perspective, Porphyry emerges as the pivotal figure: Porphyry engaged Christian sources from his youth, employed them in his early works, wrote a refutation of the *Apocalypse of Zoroaster* at Plotinus's request, and eventually became known as the most dangerous intellectual opponent of Christianity in the ancient world.[164] Despite whatever misgivings he may have had about Christianity, perhaps Porphyry found Christian descriptions of God's omnipresence and omniscience more appealing than Plotinus's relatively austere notion of providence, and wrote accordingly.

Regardless, given Iamblichus's adoption of a position resembling those Origen and other Christians held about divine omniscience, the terms of debate had changed for good. Andrew Louth has explained the increased focus on providence in Neoplatonic philosophy with reference to the "greater appeal of religious considerations" in late antique philosophy rather than "Christian influence on Neoplatonism."[165] 'Influence' may be too brusque a word; yet, given that we know Hellenic and Christian thinkers to have been in intense dis-

---

163 For Christian or Gnostic authorship of Anon. *Comm. Parm.*, see above, n. 122.

164 The present argument does not turn on the controversial questions over whether the young Porphyry actually met the Christian thinker Origen, whether he authored a work *Against the Christians* and the relationship of said work to the fragments of the *Philosophy from Oracles*, and if he is philosopher Lactantius claims helped instigate the Great Persecution. The literature on these issues is vast; see recently *inter alia* Simmons, *Universal Salvation*, esp. 10–13, 30, 64, 90, 279–280; see also Digeser, *Threat*, esp. 167–168, 185–186; Goulet, "Hypothèses récentes"; Johnson, *Religion and Identity*, 25; Addey, *Divination and Theurgy*, 84–88, 90–91; Becker, "Einleitung," 22–27.

165 Louth, "Pagans and Christians," 293. Cf. also Noble and Powers, "Creation and Divine Providence," 69–70, who observe the contrast between Plotinus and Proclus's respective views on divine providence, but do not explain it.

HOW GOD CARES 309

cussion in the mid–late third century CE, it is perhaps even more roughshod to denote this shift of the Platonists' views in the direction of their Christian contemporaries as an isolated development that had nothing to do with Christianity. Perhaps by Iamblichus's day, Christian thinkers had, after nearly two hundred years of writing about providence, 'moved the goalposts' for all philosophers dealing with the question.

Meanwhile, what of the fate of philosophers' language about God's 'first thought,' a kind of supra-cognitive state accessible to human souls? Strangely enough, it seems to disappear from the Platonic tradition after Porphyry.[166] Iamblichus and Proclus prefer a different metaphor for the faculty engaged on the border with the One: the "flower of Intellect" (*anthos nou*) of the *Chaldaean Oracles*.[167] Nor do Christian Neoplatonists of the third–fifth centuries employ the jargon of God's mystical 'first thought' surveyed above. Origen tells of being visited by 'the Bridegroom' when reading Scripture at the highest, anagogic level.[168] Augustine describes the noetic ascent he takes with his mother in Ostia, days before her death, as a voyage beyond intellect and into eternity.[169] Pseudo-Dionysius, a primary conduit for the transfusion of Neoplatonism into medieval Christian thought, does not use any language related to providence or 'first thought' in his *Mystical Theology*. Rather, some kind of terminology of 'first thought' appears in Byzantine ascetic literature: at the end of the fourth century, Evagrius Ponticus writes: "he who brings the practice of prayer to perfection offers to God the fruits of his every first thought (*prōtonoia*)."[170] Evagrius here could be understood here as using Plotinus's terminology to explore the

---

166 *Pace* Mazur, "Platonizing Background," 269–270, who argues that a "connection between *pronoia* and mystical *pronoêsis* ... was made explicit by later Neoplatonists," recalling Iamblichus's reference to "innate knowledge" about the gods (*emphutos gnōsis*; *On the Mysteries*, 5.15–16) and Proclus's description of providence as "activity prior to intellect" (*pro nou*; *Elements of Theology*, 120.10–14). These references are misleading. Iamblichus describes a general human impulse towards religiosity; Proclus, the ineffable character of God's providential activity. In neither passage does the author refer to a supra-cognitive faculty employed by humans. This is not to say Iamblichus and Proclus did not explore such a faculty; rather, they did it without reference to the language of providence. See following note.

167 Iamblichus, *Commentary on Plato's 'Parmenides'* frgs. 2a–b (in J.M. Dillon, ed., *In Platonis*, 208–211), Procl. *Commentary on the Chaldaean Oracles*, in des Places, ed. and tr., *Oracles chaldaïques*, 210.28–211.1; both re: *Chald. Or.* frag. 1. See further Tanaseanu-Döbler, *Theurgy*, 221–222.

168 E.g. Orig. *Homilies on the Song of Songs*, 1.7, discussed in Edwards, *Origen Against Plato*, 111–112, 146–147.

169 Aug. *Conf.* 9.10; on this episode, see Kenney, *Mysticism*, 78–86.

170 Evagrius Ponticus, *De oratione* 126 (PG 79:1193). For this and the following citations, I am indebted to PLG 1200b and a Thesaurus Linguae Graecae full corpus search, s.v. *prōtonoia*.

philosophical approach to Christian prayer developed by Origen. Yet it is more likely that the usage is consonant with that of later authors, such as Marcus Eremita (fifth century) or Johannes Climacus (seventh century), who use the term without any Gnostic-Platonic connotation to describe the first thought of the day that the contemplative offers to God.[171] The supra-cognitive, mystical sense of language about providence does not seem to outlive Plotinus and the Gnostics by much. Although our evidence here is admittedly scanty, this may speak for the Gnostic provenance of such language after all.

---

171 Marcus Eremita, *De baptismo* 11.36–39, 16.22–33, 17.50–55; Johannes Climacus, *Scala Paradisi* 26 (PG 88:1036). I thank Michael Chase for pushing my own thinking on this point (in correspondence).

Conclusions

Scholarship currently enjoys a number of fierce debates over questions regarding the development of philosophy in the third century CE that are at once tantalizing, but also, on the face of the evidence we possess at time of writing, not possible to answer decisively. Chapter seven has already discussed the question of Plotinus's engagement with Christian and especially Gnostic sources, and the degree to which this engagement impacted some of his most important works, such as *On the Will of the One* (*Enn.* 6.8) and *On Providence* (*Enn.* 3.2–3). The same chapter also examined the heated question of the authorship of the anonymous *Commentary on Plato's 'Parmenides'*, whose thought closely resembles that of the material shared between the Coptic Gnostic treatise *Zostrianos* and the fourth-century theologian Marius Victorinus. These debates are recent, sparked in large part by the translation and publication of the Coptic sources from Nag Hammadi in the 1950s–1990s. A third case has been ongoing for centuries: the debate about the identity of Plotinus's own teacher, Ammonius Saccas, and the problem of whether the former's fellow-pupil 'Origen,' known in the Hellenic Platonist tradition, is to be identified with the Christian theologian Origen of Alexandria.

In each of these three cases, the scholarly discussions are vibrant, but inconclusive. While considerable support has been won for the view that Plotinus's debate with the Gnostics was integral to his development as a philosopher, the question of how much this should change our evaluation of the significance of Gnostic literature for the history of philosophy remain controversial. The authorship of the anonymous *Commentary* is still mysterious, with many competing hypotheses, and the analysis given in this book could as easily point to Porphyry as to a Christian or Gnostic author. And of course, the figure of Ammonius is as enigmatic as ever, and scholars continue to disagree about whether 'Origen the Platonist' and 'Origen the Christian' are the same.[1]

Why do these debates continue? As noted in the introduction to this book, historians of philosophy have until very recently maintained early Christian thought to be lacking in innovations or contributions to the history of philosophy on its own terms, rather than those of Christian theology. This is what is at stake in scholarly discussion about Plotinus and the Gnostics, the author-

---

1   The dossier on this question is enormous. For the history of scholarship through the 1970s, see Schroeder, "Ammonius"; further, Digeser, *Threat*, 23–48; For recent *status quaestionis* on the side of identifying the two Origens, see Digeser, op. cit., 49–71; Ramelli, "Origen." For a recent *status quaestionis* doubting this identification, see Edwards, "One Origen or Two?".

© KONINKLIJKE BRILL NV, LEIDEN, 2020 | DOI:10.1163/9789004432994_010

ship of the anonymous *Commentary*, and Ammonius and Origen. If it can be demonstrated that doctrines once thought to first appear in Plotinus actually can be found in Gnostic sources which antedate him, or that the Plotinian corpus or the anonymous *Commentary* are impossible to understand adequately without recourse to Christian or Gnostic literature, then ancient Christian or Gnostic sources must be regarded as significant contributors to the history of philosophy. Meanwhile, as Frederic Schroeder wrote decades ago regarding the hypothesis that Ammonius Saccas taught an Origen who was both the Platonist and Christian known to us from the record, "then Ammonius would increase greatly in stature. He would not only, as teacher of Plotinus, be father of pagan Neoplatonism, but also, as preceptor of Origen, would be the ancestor of a major direction in patristic thought."[2]

I will conclude this book by arguing that regardless of what position one takes on these three fascinating (and likely insoluble) questions, Jewish, Christian, and Gnostic sources of the first three centuries CE contributed in deeply significant and interesting ways to the history of ancient philosophy. Indeed, what this book has shown is that Jewish, Christian, and Gnostic sources constitute major and hitherto largely untapped resources for our understanding of providence in Roman philosophical circles. They are brimming with original and ingenious (if not always compelling) arguments, some of which continue to be debated today in terms not all that distant from those described in this book. These Jewish, Christian, and Gnostic sources should be guaranteed inclusion and close examination in histories of philosophy in the Roman Empire, and merit further revaluation by historians of philosophy on grounds of their philosophical merit and influence.[3]

Which sources, exactly, contributed in an invaluable fashion to ancient philosophy by way of their discussions of providence, and how? Recalling that Hellenic philosophers were not all of like stature and achievement,[4] which Jewish, Christian, and Gnostic thinkers and works stand out as having made particularly strong contributions to Roman thought about providence, and how? At the outset, it is helpful to distinguish two, albeit closely related, forms of 'con-

---

2 Schroeder, "Ammonius," 495.

3 Here, I merely attempt to relate some of the issues discussed in this book to a few, contemporary philosophical discussions of the same problems, in hopes of illustrating the relevance of the ancient materials at hand. A full engagement of modern philosophy of religion with ancient Greek, Jewish, Christian, and Gnostic sources would occupy its own monograph, and an aim of this project has been to set the foundation for further historical and comparative studies.

4 Rightly emphasized for the context of early Christian philosophy by Karamanolis, *Philosophy*, 18–19.

CONCLUSIONS 313

tribution': further development and transformation of a pre-existing tradition, and genuine 'innovation' of notions that simply do not have appeared to exist in pre-existing traditions. As far as innovation goes, the list of standouts is not very surprising: Philo, Marcion, Bardaiṣan, Origen, and the Gnostics. However, the greater trends in the transformation of philosophy in the early Roman Empire by ancient Jewish and Christian writers are less predictable, and indeed constitute a large part of what gives this 'short list' meaning.

A recent article emphasizes that early Christian authors contributed to Platonism by way of developing "the Platonic tradition in new and unexpected ways, asking new questions to the tradition that they engaged with and using it for problem-solving that was unknown to the Platonists themselves. From this point of view, it can meaningfully be said that the Platonic tradition was subject to development from the Christians."[5] The same could be said for Stoicism; indeed, the recognition that ancient Christian ethics are largely grounded in Stoic theory, and thus serve as the vehicle for an afterlife of Stoicism, is so widespread as to have achieved the status of scholarly cliché.[6] This book has shown that Stoic thought about providence forms the bedrock for ancient Jewish and Christian philosophizing on the subject, and thus marks another case (related to but distinct from ethics) where Stoicism was transformed by Jewish and Christian writers.[7] One instance is the problem of the reach of divine care. Chapter two examined how the deep emphasis on divine care for virtuous Jews and Christians in Philo, Josephus, or Justin Martyr is best explained not with reference to their belief in a 'more personal' God, but with reference to the way in which the Stoa and Stoicizing historians emphasized providential care for virtuous individuals and even nations. The indebtedness of second and early third-century apologists to the Stoa regarding divine immanence is evident in the trouble they had distinguishing their views from those of 'the school of the porch.'

A second case of ancient Jewish and Christian adaptations and transformations of Stoic philosophy of providence presents itself with the subject of divine omniscience and prophecy, as discussed in chapter five. A variety of biblically-informed thinkers—Philo, Justin, Clement, the author of the *Teachings of Silvanus*—maintain God's omniscience, including his knowledge of future events, broadly agreeing with the Stoa. Yet a case of innovation also presents itself here, with Origen's argument that God's foreknowledge of future actions is caused by the future action in question, rather than the other way

---

5   Janby, et al., "Introduction," 3.
6   See Long, "Stoicism," 367.
7   Rightly noted by Ferguson, *Providence of God*, 43.

around. Notably, in the *Consolatio philosophiae*, Boethius rejects Origen's solution, on grounds that (*a*) it does not do away with the necessary character of the foreseen answer in question, (*b*) makes eternal foreknowledge dependent on temporal affairs, and (*c*) imputes to God a foreknowledge more akin to opinion than any knowledge worthy of the name.[8] To the best of my knowledge, while it is possible that Boethius knew the argument of 'foreknowledge by future causes' via sources after Origen, the argument does not pre-date Origen, or even seem to have any transmission outside of early Christian sources.[9] In any case, Boethius's treatment of Origen constitutes a 'pre-history' of the emergence of debate about God's 'middle knowledge,' wherein the possibility of divine knowledge of freely-made, human choices (ostensibly) ensures the compatibility of God's omniscience with human free will, a line of argument which remains vital in philosophy of religion today.[10]

The problems of divine care for individuals as well as knowledge of future events—alongside the transformation of Stoic and Platonic traditions alike—come together in the third-century CE debates regarding the status of the transcendent first principle's knowledge, discussed in chapter seven. Middle Platonic writers as well as Plotinus appear to answer this question in a firm negative, but by the end of the century, Platonists have gone the the way of the Stoa and third-century Christian writers, including many Gnostic texts. To be sure, beginning with Porphyry and Iamblichus, Platonists—including ostensibly Christian ones, like Boethius—explained divine foreknowledge with reference to a different philosophical presupposition than did Origen: God's eternal character, not the causality of future events. Yet here, too, there is a biblically-informed antecedent, over two hundred years prior to Iamblichus: Philo of Alexandria.[11] More immediate to the third-century milieu of Plotinus and Porphyry, on the other hand, are the Coptic Gnostic sources *Zostrianos*, *Allogenes*, and *Marsanes*. As argued in chapter seven, *Allogenes* explicitly states the principle that the character of the known is determined by the knower.

---

8   *Cons.* 5.3.9–27; for discussion, see Craig, *Problem*, 80–82, and esp. Sharples, "Commentary: Cicero," 219–220.

9   Klingner had adduced John Chrysostom, *Homilies on Matthew* 60.1 (PG 58:574) and Jerome, *Commentary on Ezekiel* 1.2.5 as possible sources for Boethius; see the discussions of Huber, *Vereinbarkeit*, 30–32; Sharples, "Commentary: Cicero," 219. Huber argues (op. cit., 31–32) that these sources all indicate a lost philosophical doctrine used by Christian authors rather than an innovation by Christians to solve a philosophical problem, a view with which the present discussion is plainly at odds.

10 The subject of Craig, *Problem*. A particularly influential discussion can be found in Plantinga, *Nature*, esp. 174–190; for a critical discussion, see van Inwagen, *Problem*, 79–80.

11 See esp. *Deus* 29–31, discussed above, chapter five.

CONCLUSIONS 315

Another case where transformation of Stoic and Platonic arguments by Jewish, Christian, and Gnostic sources overlap is the problem of free will. As the beginning of chapter six observed, scholarship has hitherto regarded the early Christian innovation of 'free will' as an outgrowth of Stoic thinking in response to the challenge of Gnosticism. Certainly, Stoic models—as well as Aristotelian terminology—play an enormous role in early Christian thinking about human responsibility (as they do for Platonist thinking, too). However, the chapter demonstrated that our most protracted, detailed discussions of human autonomy and free will and in early Christian sources—the *Book of the Laws of the Countries* (Bardaiṣan or his school), Basilides (*apud* Clement), and Origen's *On Free Will*—all articulate the question with respect to the soul's pre-existence, at times with specific reference to *Resp.* 617e. Plotinus, then, was hardly the first to combine the Platonist account of the soul's autonomy with a Stoicizing ethics in the context of the pre-existent soul's embodied state. More innovative is the competing model, already envisaged in Theophilus, Irenaeus, and Tertullian, of free will as God's 'gift' to humanity, beginning with Adam and Even in the Garden of Eden—the standpoint that Augustine and so many subsequent Christian thinkers, including some of the most well-known philosophers of religion today, would take up.[12] Equally innovative, if less successful (at least in Greek and Latin Christendom) is the *Book of the Laws of the Countries*, which stands out as a highly original—and perhaps the oldest—work of Christian Peripateticism.

Finally, the question of reconciling divine care with the experience of evil was discussed in ancient Jewish, Christian, and Gnostic sources with chief reference to the Platonic and Stoic traditions alike—albeit not exclusively, and in innovative and even transgressive ways. Well-known are the various adaptations by Christian authors of Platonic and especially Stoic theodicies: that evil is a necessary byproduct of creation, or a coincidence of it (the concomitance argument), or that suffering serves to make us better (the service of bedbugs).[13] Equally well-known are the transformations of the *Timaeus* in Philo and Gnostic literature, where God has his helpers (angelic 'young gods,'

---

12   For recourse to the 'free-will defence' and the argument that virtue is only possible given the possibility of vice as central planks in contemporary philosophy of religion, see e.g. Swinburne, *Providence and the Problem of Evil*, 39–47, 131–165. 199–222; van Inwagen, *Problem*, 70, 84–112.

13   On these arguments, see above, chapters one and three. They continue to be invoked today, as by Swinburne, *Providence and the Problem of Evil*, 166–198. The arguments that evil is a necessary byproduct of creation, a happy coincidence, good for us in some way, or simply non-existent are rejected, on the other hand, by van Inwagen, *Problem*, 56–70, given the presupposition of God's omnipotence.

whether good or bad) construct the human body, as discussed in chapter four. Particularly interesting is the ambivalence with which Philo and Christian philosophers regarded the Middle Platonist theory of 'conditional fate,' due to their belief that the *daimones* of Graeco-Roman civic cult could only be instigators of human sin. As chapter three showed, Athenagoras welds the Middle Platonic and Enochic models anyway; Clement and Origen are more creative in their adaptations of them, preferring to render divine mediators as human teachers (not *daimones*), or to flatten the ontological hierarchy of angel, demon, and human, respectively. Meanwhile, the allusions of Philo and Origen to the 'great king' of Persia (see chapters two and three, respectively) reflect not the point that pseudo-Aristotle wishes to make in *On the World*, namely, the deep but diminishing presence of divine power into the world. Rather, they use the simile to make a rather Platonic argument: that the divine power extends into the world via a hierarchy populated by semi-divine subordinates.

The dualism of demiurge and matter found in the *Timaeus* exegeses of Plutarch and Numenius was also taken up by Hermogenes, Apelles, and, if Tertullian is to be believed, Marcion. However, the Christian dualisms explored by Marcion and the Gnostics are of deeply innovative characters without any parallel at all in the 'pagan' intellectual tradition. While Plutarch and Numenius negotiate some kind of differentiation between God and demiurge given the latter's involvement with evil matter, they nonetheless identify the demiurge as providential. Marcion, on the other hand, distinguishes the second, creating deity from the first, providential deity. This raises the question of why this higher deity would be providential at all (thus Irenaeus's attempt to pillory Marcion—and Valentinus—as propagating a *deus otiosus*), as discussed in chapter three. Even more distinctive are those sources in chapter four called 'Gnostic,' since they divorce providence from the creator even as they identify human beings as divine and under providential care, and therefore superior to the creator and his creation. Marcionite theology and especially Gnosticism are certainly innovative views from the perspective of the history of philosophy, and even if heresiographers and the Neoplatonists rejected them, they have enjoyed vigorous revivals and adaptations in twentieth-century *Krisis-Theologie*, existentialism, and Jewish philosophy.[14]

Epistemologically, meanwhile, Gnosticism may be regarded as something of an early, optimistic precursor of Descartes's hypothesis of the 'evil demon' and the 'brains-in-a-vat' discussed in contemporary philosophy. Exploring system-

---

14   A useful discussion can be found in Lazier, *God Interrupted*, esp. 27–64.

CONCLUSIONS   317

atic doubt in the first of his *Meditations on First Philosophy*, Descartes entertains various possible setups where everything we know to be true is false. In
one setup, he asks if God is deceiving him, filling his head only with illusions
of the external world and indeed of his very own body, or that an evil demon
may have done the same.[15] In like manner do Gnostic myths such as the *Apocryphon of John* and *On the Origin of the World* suggest that our material and
animate components (*hylikos* and *psychikos*, respectively)—the seats of our
corporeal and sensate selves—are controlled by malevolent, external beings.
These beings have godlike powers but are not actually God, and in fact have
made humanity 'blind,' 'asleep,' or 'in fetters' (i.e., under illusion). The way out
lies in the revelation of humanity's divine (in these two texts, "spiritual," *pneumatikos*) nature, both created and communicated via divine providence, and
its identification with the rational faculty. To be sure, there are also substantial differences between the Gnostic demiurge and the Cartesian demon, chief
among them being that the point of the demon scenario is to raise the specter
of skepticism, not to solve the problem of evil.[16] The Gnostic view is rather more
akin to the 'brain-in-a-vat' scenario, explored in contemporary epistemology.[17]
The 'brain-in-a-vat' hypothesis was popularized in the early 2000s via the hit
film *The Matrix* (1999), and it is probably instructive that this film is a favorite
reference in philosophy of mind and discussions of the reception-history of
Gnosticism alike.[18] The comparison is particularly interesting if we read the
'brain-in-a-vat' hypothesis as does David Chalmers, as presenting us with the
possibility of an alternate metaphysics rather than a prod to confront radical
skepticism.[19] What Chalmers writes about the 'brain-in-a-vat'/*Matrix* scenar-

---

15   For a reading of the argument of the *Meditations* vis-à-vis the demon, see Frankfurt,
     Demons. Descartes's sources for this thought-experiment are unknown. For examination
     of the problem with a suggestion that he draws from medieval meditative traditions, par-
     ticularly as represented by Teresa of Ávila, see Mercer, "Descartes."
16   I set aside here the complicating fact that before he introduces the demon, Descartes
     entertains the scenario of a deceiving but omnipotent God who puts him under illusion.
     The upshot is that just as he cannot be sure that there is or is not a demon who deceives
     him, he cannot be sure that God is or is not benevolent and not deceiving. However, it
     is unclear as to whether the deceiving God scenario is meant to illustrate anything other
     than what is illustrated by that of the demon. For a recent reading that more or less elides
     the two scenarios as far as their import for skepticism goes, see C. Wilson, *Descartes's Med-
     itations*, 40–45.
17   A classic discussion of the problem (and attempted solution) is Putnam, "Brains in a Vat."
18   For the former, see the previous note; for the latter, see the survey of Kwiatkowski, "Cin-
     ema."
19   Chalmers, "Matrix," esp. 466–468; it should be observed here that his reading is not typical,
     although I find it persuasive.

ios is also true of the Gnostic scenario: namely, they both make claims "about the reality underlying physics, about the nature of our minds, and about the creation of the world," specifically, that "first, physical processes are fundamentally computational. Second, our cognitive systems are separate from physical processes but interact with them. Third, physical reality was created by beings outside physical space-time."[20] My (very provisory) sense is that Gnostic literature usually and readily agrees with the second and third statements, while the first is true, in a sense, for those works which (like the *Apocryphon of John*) describe the 'real' heavenly world as emanating in Neo-Pythagorean, i.e. arithmetical, terms.

Finally, the 'innovation' which weaves together all the sources and discussions in chapters two through six is the incorporation of biblical proof-texts and exegetical debate about them into philosophical debate. Recognition that there is no 'fixed' Bible, canon, or orthodoxy in the first three centuries CE should not distract us from the very clear impact that debate about biblical texts had on discussions of providence in Roman philosophy—and the emergence of what we might call a distinctive 'early Christian philosophy.' An index of the scriptural passages invoked by writers about providence lies beyond the scope of the present discussion, but it is worth highlighting a few proof-texts which played particularly important roles in the preceding chapters. Most obvious is God's care for the hairs on the head of the apostles, and for the sparrows (Matt 10:29–30 = Luke 12:6–7), a favorite passage of Origen's but allegedly missing from Marcion's gospel, as discussed in chapter three. The wide influence of the *Book of the Watchers* (1 En. 1–36) on early Christian demonology, with its attendant effects on their approach to Middle Platonists' notions about providence and the 'young gods' of the *Timaeus*, has already been noted above. The problematic portrayal of God and the creation of humanity in Gen 1–3 and the jealous character of the God of Israel in various Septuagintal passages (e.g., Exod 20:5; Is 44:6, 45:5–6) were foundational for Marcionite and Gnostic exegesis. 2 Pet 3:5, Col 1:16, and the Wisdom of Solomon furnished important proof-texts for proto-orthodox thinkers who believed rather that Christ the providential *logos* (at times viz. *sophia*) was responsible for creation, per chapter four. When Origen wishes to defend God's foreknowledge of all future events, he refers to Sus 42–43 LXX and John 2:25, as described in chapter five. As chapter six explained, the vast bulk of his discussion of free will in his treatise *On Free Will* is concerned with combatting Marcionite and, perhaps, Gnostic exegesis of scripture, particularly regarding the possibility of actually fulfill-

---

20   Chalmers, "Matrix," 459.

CONCLUSIONS   319

ing the Ten Commandments, an issue addressed by Basilides, Clement, and the author of the *Book of the Laws of the Countries* as well.

A catalogue of further such passages adduced in an ancient debate about providence would be useful, but even this cursory list suffices to remind us of a larger point: the incorporation of biblical proof-texts into philosophical debate about providence shaped the arguments and the very terms of that debate. Thus, by the time we reach chapter seven, two hundred years of Jewish and Christian philosophers arguing that the first principle must be both providential and omniscient, with the latter connoting knowledge of future events (in some fashion), may explain why we see a drastic turn in Platonist conceptions of divine foreknowledge after Plotinus. Interestingly, and perhaps not coincidentally, it is precisely where this mutual impact and intertwining of 'biblicizing' and 'pagan' philosophical debate becomes most visible—around the persons of Origen, Plotinus, Porphyry, and their Gnostic interlocutors, in the middle third of the third century CE—that something of the 'parting of the ways' between 'Christian theology' and 'Greek philosophy' also begins to become concrete.[21] This emerging separation between Christian and Greek thought, with the Great Persecution and the ascension of the first Christian Emperor of Rome on the horizon, was not solely a question of competing claims to authority among 'schools' with their *dogmata*. It was in the process of becoming a question of competing bodies of texts and interpretations of texts—'biblical' and 'Greek,' canons of 'theology' and 'philosophy'—which ostensibly provide answers to our perennial questions about whether the gods exist, how we should worship, and if they do, in fact, care. When we ask ourselves these questions and investigate their early history today, we already know what we can learn by approaching them through these canons as forged by post-Constantinian philosophers, theologians, and historians.[22] This book has endeavored to offer a hint at what we might learn by setting those canons aside, and reading these pre-Constantinian philosophers not as theologians *avant la lettre*, but as writers of Roman philosophy.

---

21   On the "acute Hellenization of the Platonic tradition" following the Plotinus-Gnostic controversy, see Burns, *Apocalypse*, 147–154; cf. also the discussion of Digeser, *Threat*, 1–22.

22   As discussed in the introduction.

Bibliography

Aalders, G.J.D. *Plutarch's Political Thought*. Amsterdam: North-Holland, 1982.

Abramowski, Luise. "Nicänismus und Gnosis im Rom des Bischofs Liberius: Der Fall des Marius Victorinus." *ZAC* 8 (2005): 513–566.

Adamson, Peter. "Making a Virtue of Necessity: *Anagkē* in Plato and Plotinus." *Études Platoniciennes* 8 (2011): 9–30.

Adamson, Peter. *Philosophy in the Hellenistic and Roman Worlds. A History of Philosophy without any Gaps, volume 2*. Oxford: Oxford University Press, 2015.

Adamson, Peter. "State of Nature: Human and Cosmic Rulership in Ancient Philosophy." Pages 79–94 in *Menschennatur und politische Ordnung*. Edited by Andreas Höfele and Beate Kellner, with Christian Kaiser. Paderborn: Wilhelm Fink, 2016.

Addey, Crystal. *Divination and Theurgy in Neoplatonism: Oracles of the Gods*. Ashgate Studies in Philosophy and theology in Late Antiquity. Aldershot: Ashgate, 2014.

Aitken, James K. "Divine Will and Providence." Pages 282–301 in *Ben Sira's God. Proceedings of the International Ben Sira Conference Durham—Ushaw College 2001*. Edited by Renate Egger-Wenzel. Beihefte zur Zeitschrift für die alttestamentliche Wissenschaft 321. Berlin; New York: De Gruyter, 2002.

Aland (Ehlers), Barbara. "Bardesanes von Edessa—ein syrischer Gnostiker. Bemerkungen aus Anlaß des Buches von H. J. W. Drijvers, *Bardaiṣan von Edessa*." Pages 355–374 in *Was ist Gnosis? Studien zum frühen Christentum, zu Marcion und zur kaiserzeitlichen Philosophie*. Edited by Barbara Aland. *WUNT* 239. Tübingen: Mohr Siebeck, 2015.

Aland (Ehlers), Barbara. "Marcion: Versuch einer neuer Interpretation." Pages 291–317 in *Was ist Gnosis? Studien zum frühen Christentum, zu Marcion und zur kaiserzeitlichen Philosophie*. Edited by Barbara Aland. *WUNT* 239. Tübingen: Mohr Siebeck, 2015.

Aland (Ehlers), Barbara. "Sünde und Erlösung bei Marcion und die Konsequenz für die sog. Beiden Götter Marcions." Pages 147–157 in *Marcion und seine kirchengeschichtliche Wirkung. Vorträge der Internationalen Fachkonferenz zu Marcion, gehalten vom 15.–19. August 2001 in Mainz*. Edited by Gerhard May, Katharina Greschat, and Martin Meiser. *TUGAL* 150. Berlin: De Gruyter, 2002.

Alcinous. *Enseignement des doctrines de Platon*. Edited by John Whittaker. Translated by Pierre Louis. Paris: Belles Lettres, 1990.

Alcinous. *The Handbook of Platonism*. Translated by John M. Dillon. Clarendon Later Ancient Philosophers. Oxford: Clarendon Press, 1993.

Alessandrelli, Michele. "Cleante e Crisippo sul rapport tra provvidenza e fato a proposito di Calc. *In Plat. Tim.* 144." Pages 145–157 in *Fate, Chance, and Fortune in Ancient*

Thought. Edited by Francesca Guadalupe Masi and Stefano Maso. Lexis Ancient Philosophy 9. Amsterdam: Adolf M. Hakkert, 2013.

Alexander of Aphrodisias. *Alexandri Aphrodisiensis praeter commentaria scripta minora*. Edited by Ivo Bruns. Commentaria in Aristotelem Graeca supplementum 2.2. Berlin: Reimer, 1892.

Alexander of Aphrodisias. *Die arabischen Fassungen von zwei Schriften von Alexander von Aphrodisias: über die Vorsehung und über die liberum arbitrium*. Edited and translated by Hans-Jochen Ruland. Ph.D. Diss., Universität des Saarlandes, 1975.

Alexander of Aphrodisias. *On Fate*. Edited and translated by Robert W. Sharples. London: Duckworth, 2003.

Algra, Keimpe. "Plutarch and the Stoic Theory of Providence." Pages 117–135 in *Fate, Providence and Moral Responsibility in Ancient, Medieval and Early Modern Thought: Studies in Honour of Carlos Steel*. Edited by Pieter d'Hoine and Gerd van Riel. AMP 1. Leuven: Leuven University Press, 2014.

Algra, Keimpe. "Stoic Theology." Pages 153–178 in *The Cambridge Companion to the Stoics*. Edited by Brad Inwood. Cambridge: Cambridge University Press, 2003.

Alt, Karin. *Weltflucht und Weltbejahung. Zur Frage des Dualismus bei Plutarch, Numenios, Plotin*. Abhandlungen der Geistes- und Sozialwissenschaftlichen Klasse 8. Mainz; Stuttgart: Akademie der Wissenschaften und der Literatur; Steiner, 1993.

Amand, Dom David. *Fatalisme et liberté dans l'Antiquité grecque. Recherches sur la survivance de l'argumentation morale antifataliste de Carnéade chez les philosophes grecs et les théologiens chrétiens des quatre premiers siècles*. Recueil de Travaux d'Histoire et de Philologie, 3ᵉ série, 19ᵉ fasc. Louvain: Bibliothèque de l'Université, 1945.

Ambrose of Milan. *Hexameron, Paradise, and Cain and Abel*. Translated by John J. Savage. FC 42. Washington: Catholic University of America Press, 1961.

Ammonius Hermiae. *Ammonius in Aristotelis de interpretatione commentaria*. Edited by Adolphus Busse. Commentaria in Aristotelem Graeca 4.5. Berlin: Reimer, 1897.

Ammonius Hermiae. "Ammonius the Son of Hermeias: Commentary on *On Interpretation* 9." Pages 91–117 in *Ammonius: On Aristotle On Interpretation 9 with Boethius On Aristotle On Interpretation 9*. Translated by David Blank and Norman Kretzmann, with essays by Richard Sorabji, Norman Kretzmann, and Mario Mignucci. ACA: London: Duckworth, 1998.

(Pseudo-)Apollodorus. *The Library*. Edited and translated by Sir James George Frazer. 2 vols. LCL 121, 122. London; New York: G.P. Putnam's Sons, 1921.

Apuleius. *Platon und seine Lehre*. Edited by Paolo Siniscalco. Translated by Karl Albert. Texte zur Philosophie 4. Sankt Augustin: Hans Richarz, 1981.

Apuleius. *Rhetorical Works*. Translated by Stephen Harrison, John Hilton, and Vincent Hunink. Edited by Stephen Harrison. Oxford: Oxford University Press, 2002.

Aristotle. *The Complete Works of Aristotle: Revised Oxford Translation*. Edited by Jonathan Barnes. 2 vols. Princeton: Princeton University Press, 1984.

BIBLIOGRAPHY

(Pseudo-)Aristotle. *On the Cosmos*. Edited and translated by Johan Thom. Pages 20–57 in *Cosmic Order and Divine Power*. Edited by Johan Thom. SAPERE 23. Tübingen: Mohr Siebeck, 2014.

Armstrong, Arthur H. *The Architecture of the Intelligible Universe in the Philosophy of Plotinus. An Analytical and Historical Study*. Cambridge Classical Studies. Amsterdam: Adolf M. Hakkert, 1967.

Armstrong, Arthur H. "Dualism: Platonic, Gnostic, and Christian." Pages 33–54 in *Neoplatonism and Gnosticism*. Edited by Richard T. Wallis and Jay Bregman. SNAM 6. Albany: SUNY Press, 1992.

Armstrong, Arthur H. "Two Views of Freedom: A Christian Objection in Plotinus, *Enneads* VI 8. [39] 7, 11–15?" Pages 397–406 in *Studia Patristica* 17. Edited by Elizabeth A. Livingstone. Leuven: Peeters, 1989.

Ashwin-Siejkowski, Piotr. "Clement of Alexandria." Pages 84–97 in *The Wiley Blackwell Companion to Patristics*. Edited by Ken Parry. West Sussex: John Wiley & Sons, 2015.

Athanassiadi, Polymnia. "The Fate of Oracles in Late Antiquity: Didyma and Delphi." Δελτίον 15 (1989–1990): 271–278.

Athenagoras. *Legatio and De Resurrectione*. Edited and translated by William R. Schoedel. OECT. Oxford: Clarendon Press, 1972.

Atticus. *Fragments*. Edited and translated by Édouard des Places. Paris: Belles Lettres, 1977.

Attridge, Harold W. "Divine Sovereignty and Human Responsibility in the Fourth Gospel." Pages 183–199 in *Revealed Wisdom: Studies in Apocalyptic in Honour of Christopher Rowland*. Edited by John Ashton. Ancient Judaism and Early Christianity 88. Leiden; Boston: Brill, 2014.

Attridge, Harold W. *The Interpretation of Biblical History in the Antiquitates Judaicae of Flavius Josephus*. Harvard Dissertations in Religion 7. Missoula: Scholars Press, 1976.

Attridge, Harold W. and George MacRae, eds. and trs. "The *Gospel of Truth*: Introduction, Text, and Translation." Pages 55–122 in *Nag Hammadi Codex I (The Jung Codex). Introductions, Texts, Translations, Indices*. Edited by Harold W. Attridge. NHS 22. Leiden: Brill, 1985.

Attridge, Harold W. and Elaine H. Pagels. "The *Tripartite Tractate*: Notes." Pages 217–497 in *Nag Hammadi Codex I (The Jung Codex). Notes*. Edited by Harold W. Attridge. NHS 23. Leiden: Brill, 1985.

Attridge, Harold W. and Elaine H. Pagels. "The *Tripartite Tractate*: Introduction." Pages 159–191 in *Nag Hammadi Codex I (The Jung Codex). Introductions, Texts, Translations, Indices*. Edited by Harold W. Attridge. NHS 22. Leiden: Brill, 1985.

Aune, David E. "Dualism in the Fourth Gospel and the Dead Sea Scrolls: A Reassessment of the Problem." Pages 281–303 in *Neotestamentica et Philonica: Studies in Honor of Peder Borgen*. Edited by David E. Aune, Torrey Seland, and Jarl Henning Ulrichsen, Jarl Henning. Supplements to Novum Testamentum 106. Leiden; Boston: Brill, 2003.

Babut, Daniel. *Plutarque et le stoïcisme*. Paris: Presses Universitaires de France, 1969.

Bak Halvgaard, Tilde. "Life, Knowledge, and Language in Classic Gnostic Literature: Reconsidering the Role of the Female Spiritual Principle and Epinoia." Pages 237–252 in *Women and Knowledge in Early Christianity: Festschrift Antti Marjanen*. Edited by Ulla Tervahauta, Ivan Miroshnikov, Outi Lehtipuu, and Ismo Dunderberg. VCSup 144. Leiden; Boston: Brill, 2017.

Bak Halvgaard, Tilde. *Linguistic Manifestations in the 'Trimorphic Protennoia' and the 'Thunder: Perfect Mind'. Analysed against the Background of Platonic and Stoic Dialectics*. NHMS 91. Leiden; Boston: Brill, 2014.

Bammel, Caroline P. "Origen's Definitions of Prophecy and Gnosis." *JTS* 40:2 (1989): 489–493.

Barc, Bernard and Louis Painchaud. "La réécriture de l'*Apocryphon de Jean* à la lumière de l'hymne final de la version longue." *Le Muséon* 112 (1999): 317–333.

Barnard, Leslie W. *Athenagoras: A Study in Second Century Christian Apologetic*. Paris: Beauchesne, 1972.

Barnes, Jonathan. "Cicero's *de fato* and a Greek Source." Pages 495–509 in idem, *Mantissa: Essays in Ancient Philosophy IV*. Edited by Maddalena Bonelli. Oxford: Oxford University Press, 2015.

Barry, Catherine, Wolf-Peter Funk and, Paul-Hubert Poirier, eds. and trs. "Texte et traduction." Pages 236–481 in *Zostrien* (*NH VIII,1*). Edited and translated by Catherine Barry, Wolf-Peter Funk, Paul-Hubert Poirier, and John D. Turner. BCNH Section "Textes" 24. Louvain: Peeters, 2000.

Beagon, Mary. *Roman Nature: The Thought of Pliny the Elder*. Oxford Classical Monographs. Oxford: Clarendon Press, 1992.

Beard, Mary. "Cicero and Divination: The Formation of a Latin Discourse." *Journal of Roman Studies* 76 (1986): 33–46.

Bechtle, Gerald. *The Anonymous Commentary on Plato's "Parmenides"*. Bern: Paul Haupt, 1999.

Becker, Matthias. "Einleitung," Pages 3–112 in *Porphyrios, 'Contra Christianos.' Neue Sammlung der Fragmente, Textimonien und Dubia mit Einleitung, Übersetzung, und Anmerkungen*. Edited and translated by Matthias Becker. Texte und Kommentare 52. Berlin: De Gruyter, 2015.

BeDuhn, Jason D. *The First New Testament: Marcion's Scriptural Canon*. Salem: Polebridge, 2013.

Begemann, Elisabeth. "Cicero's Theology and the Concept of Fate." *Archiv für Religionsgeschichte* 15:1 (2014): 225–246.

Behr, John. "Introduction." Pages xv–lxxxviii in *Origen. On First Principles. Volume One*. Edited and translated by John Behr. OECT. Oxford: Oxford University Press, 2017.

Belo, Catarina. *Chance and Determinism in Avicenna and Averroes*. Islamic Philosophy, Theology, and Science. Texts and Studies 69. Leiden; Boston: Brill, 2007.

BIBLIOGRAPHY

Bénatouïl, Thomas. "How Industrious Can Zeus Be? The Extent and Objects of Divine Activity in Stoicism," Pages 23–45 in *God and the Cosmos in Stoicism*. Edited by Ricardo Salles. New York: Oxford University Press, 2009.

Benjamins, Hendrik S. *Eingeordnete Freiheit. Freiheit und Vorsehung bei Origenes*. VCSup 28. Leiden; New York; Köln: Brill, 1994.

Bergjan, Silke-Petra. "Celsus the Epicurean? The Interpretation of an Argument in Origen, contra Celsum." *HTR* 94 (2001): 149–204.

Bergjan, Silke-Petra. "Clement of Alexandria on God's Providence and the Gnostic's Life Choice: The Concept of *Pronoia* in the *Stromateis*, Book VII with Appendix: Fragments from Clement of Alexandria, Περὶ προνοίας." Pages 63–92 in *The Seventh Book of the Stromateis: Proceedings of the Colloquium on Clement of Alexandria (Olomouc, October 21–23, 2010)*. Edited by Matyáš Havrda, Vít Hušek, and Jana Plátová. VCSup 117. Leiden: Brill, 2015.

Bergjan, Silke-Petra. *Der Fürsorgende Gott, Der Begriff der ΠΡΟΝΟΙΑ Gottes in der apologetischen Literatur der Alten Kirche*. Arbeiten zur Kirchengeschichte 81. Berlin: De Gruyter, 2002.

Berkouwer, G.C. *The Providence of God*. Translated by Lewis B. Smedes. Grand Rapids: Wm. B. Eerdmans, 1983.

Berno, Francesco. "Rethinking Valentinianism: Some Remarks on the *Tripartite Tractate*, with Special Reference to Plotinus' *Enneads* II, 9." *Augustinianum* 56 (2016): 331–345.

Betegh, Gàbor and Pavel Gregoric. "Multiple Analogy in Ps.-Aristotle, *De Mundo* 6." *CQ* 64:2 (2014): 574–591.

Bianchi, Ugo. "The Category of Dualism in the Historical Phenomenology of Religion." *Temenos: Nordic Journal of Comparative Religion* 16 (1980): 10–25.

Bianchi, Ugo. "Plutarch und der Dualismus." *ANRW* 2.36.1 (1987): 350–365.

Bitton-Ashkelony, Brouria. "The Limit of the Mind (ΝΟΥΣ): Pure Prayer According to Evagrius Ponticus and Isaac of Nineveh." *ZAC* 15:2 (2011): 291–321.

Blank, David. "Notes to Ammonius' Commentary." Pages 118–128 in Ammonius, *Ammonius: On Aristotle On Interpretation 9 with Boethius On Aristotle On Interpretation 9*. Translated by David Blank and Norman Kretzmann, with essays by Richard Sorabji, Norman Kretzmann, and Mario Mignucci. ACA. London: Duckworth, 1998.

Bobzien, Susanne. *Determinism and Freedom in Stoic Philosophy*. Oxford: Oxford University Press, 1998.

Bobzien, Susanne. "Early Stoic Determinism." *Revue de métaphysique et de morale* 48 (2004–2005): 489–516.

Bobzien, Susanne. "The Inadvertent Conception and Late Birth of the Free Will Problem." *Phronesis* 43 (1998): 133–175.

Boethius. *The Consolation of Philosophy*. Translated by David R. Slavitt. Cambridge; London: Harvard University Press, 2008.

Bonazzi, Mauro. "Middle Platonists on Fate and Human Autonomy: A Confrontation with the Stoics." Pages 283–294 in *What is Up to Us? Studies on Agency and Responsibility in Ancient Philosophy*. Edited by Pierre Destrée, Ricardo Salles, and Marco Zingano. SAMPP 1. Leiden: Sankt Augustin: Academia Verlag, 2014.

Bos, Abraham. *Providentia Divina: The Theme of Divine Pronoia in Plato and Aristotle*. Assen/Amsterdam: Van Gorcum & Comp. B.V., 1976.

Bos, Abraham. "Basilides as an Aristotelianizing Gnostic." *VC* 54:1 (2000): 44–60.

Boyd, Gregory A. "Two Ancient (and Modern) Motivations for Ascribing Exhaustively Definite Foreknowledge to God: a Historic Overview and Critical Assessment." *Religious Studies* 46 (2010): 41–59.

Boys-Stones, George. "Human Autonomy and Divine Revelation in Origen." Pages 489–499 in *Severan Culture*. Edited by Simon Swain, Stephen Harrison, and Jas Elsner. Cambridge: Cambridge University Press, 2007.

Boys-Stones, George. "'Middle' Platonists on Fate and Human Autonomy." Pages 431–447 in *Greek and Roman Philosophy 100 BC–200 AD*. Edited by Robert W. Sharples and Richard Sorabji. BICSSup 94. 2 vols. London: Institute of Classical Studies, University of London, 2007.

Boys-Stones, George. "Providence and Religion in Middle Platonism." Pages 317–338 in *Theologies of Ancient Greek Religion*. Edited by Edith Eidenow, Julia Kindt, and Robin Osborne. Cambridge: Cambridge University Press, 2016.

Brakke, David. *The Gnostics: Myth, Ritual, and Diversity in Early Christianity*. Boston: Harvard University Press, 2010.

Brakke, David. "Valentinians and Their Demons: Fate, Seduction, and Deception in the Quest for Virtue." Pages 13–27 in *From Gnostics to Monastics: Studies in Coptic and Early Christianity*. Edited by David Brakke, Stephen J. Davis, and Stephen Emmel. Orientalia Lovaniensia Analecta 263. Louvain: Peeters, 2017.

Braun, René. *Deus Christianorum. Recherches sur le vocabulaire doctrinal de Tertullian*. Paris: Études Augustiniennes, 1977.

Brenk, Frederick E. "An Imperial Heritage: The Religious Spirit of Plutarch of Chaironeia." *ANRW* 2.36.1 (1987): 248–349.

Brenk, Frederick E. "Plutarch's Middle-Platonic God: About to Enter (or Remake) the Academy." Pages 27–48 in *Gott und die Götter bei Plutarch: Götterbilder—Gottesbilder—Weltbilder*. Edited by Rainer Hirsch-Luipold. Religionsgeschichtliche Versuche und Vorarbeiten 54. Berlin; New York: De Gruyter, 2005.

Brent, Allan. *A Political History of Early Christianity*. Edinburgh: T&T Clark, 2009.

Brisson, Luc. "Amélius: Sa vie, son oeuvre, son style." *ANRW* 2.36.2 (1987): 793–861.

Brisson, Luc. "The Reception of the *Parmenides* before Proclus." Translated by Michael Chase. Pages 2:49–63 in in *Plato's "Parmenides" and Its Heritage, 2. vols*. Edited by Kevin Corrigan and John D. Turner. WGRWSup 2–3. Atlanta: SBL, 2010.

Broadie, Sarah. *Nature and Divinity in Plato's Timaeus*. New York: Cambridge University Press, 2011.

BIBLIOGRAPHY

Brouwer, René. "Polybius and Stoic *Tyche.*" *Greek, Roman, and Byzantine Studies* 51 (2011): 111–132.

Brown, Raymond E., and Thomas Aquinas Collins. "Church Pronouncements." Pages 1167–1174 in *The New Jerome Biblical Commentary*. Edited by Raymond E. Brown, Joseph A. Fitzmyer, and Roland E. Murphy. Englewood Cliffs: Prentice Hall, 1990.

Burkert, Walter. "Signs, Commands, and Knowledge: Ancient Divination between Enigma and Epiphany." Pages 29–49 in *Mantikê: Studies in Ancient Divination*. Edited by Sarah Iles Johnston and Peter Struck. RGRW 155. Leiden; Boston: Brill, 2005.

Burns, Dylan M. *Apocalypse of the Alien God: Platonism and the Exile of Sethian Gnosticism*. Divinations. Philadelphia: University of Pennsylvania Press, 2014.

Burns, Dylan M. "The *Apocalypse of Zostrianos* and Iolaos: A Platonic Reminiscence of the Heracleidae at NHC VIII,1.4," *Le Muséon* 126:1–2 (2013): 29–44.

Burns, Dylan M. "Apocalypses amongst Gnostics and Manichaeans." Pages 358–372 in *The Oxford Handbook of Apocalyptic Literature*. Edited by John J. Collins. New York: Oxford New York, 2014.

Burns, Dylan M. "Apophatic Strategies in *Allogenes* (NHC XI,3)." *HTR* 103:2 (2010): 161–179.

Burns, Dylan M. "Astrological Determinism, Free Will, and Desire According to St. Thecla in the *Symposium* of Methodius of Olympus." Pages 206–220 in *Women and Knowledge in Early Christianity: Festschrift Antti Marjanen*. Edited by Ulla Tervahauta, Ivan Miroshnikov, Outi Lehtipuu, and Ismo Dunderberg. VCSup 144. Leiden; Boston: Brill, 2017.

Burns, Dylan M. "Care or Prayer? Justin Martyr's *Dialogue with Trypho* 1.4 Revisited." *VC* 68:2 (2014): 178–191.

Burns, Dylan M. "First Thoughts on the Structure of the *Apocryphon of John* (NHC II,1 and par.) and Divine Providence in 'Classic Gnostic' Literature." Pages 29–54 in *From Gnostics to Monastics: Studies in Coptic and Early Christianity*. Edited by David Brakke, Stephen J. Davis, and Stephen Emmel. Orientalia Lovaniensia Analecta 263. Louvain: Peeters, 2017.

Burns, Dylan M. "Gnosis Undomesticated: Archon-Seduction, Demon Sex, and Sodomites in the *Paraphrase of Shem* (NHC VII,1)." *Gnosis: Journal of Gnostic Studies* 1–2 (2016): 132–156.

Burns, Dylan M. "Magical, Coptic, Christian: The Great Angel Eleleth and the 'Four Luminaries' in Egyptian Literature of the First Millennium C.E." Pages 141–162 in *The Nag Hammadi Codices in the Context of Fourth- and Fifth-century Christianity in Egypt*. Edited by Hugo Lundhaug and Lance Jenott. STAC 110. Tübingen: Mohr Siebeck, 2018.

Burns, Dylan M. "The Philosophical Contexts of the Providence Doxographies in the *Wisdom of Jesus Christ*, *Eugnostos*, and the *Tripartite Tractate*." In *Texts in Context: Situating Early Christian Writings in the History and Development of Christian The-*

ology. Edited by Joseph Verheyden, Jens Schröter, and Tobias Nicklas. Bibliotheca Ephemeridum Theologicarum Lovaniensium. Leuven: Peeters, forthcoming.

Burns, Dylan M. "Providence, Creation, and Gnosticism According to the Gnostics." *JECS* 24:1 (2016): 55–79.

Burns, Dylan M. "There Is No Soul in a Sect, Only Spirit and Flesh: Soteriological Determinism in the *Tripartite Tractate* (NHC I,5) and the 'Vision of Hagu' (*4QInstruction*)." In *The Dead Sea Scrolls and the Nag Hammadi Codices*. Edited by Dylan M. Burns and Matthew Goff. NHMS. Leiden; Boston: Brill, forthcoming.

Burton, Anne. *Diodorus Siculus. Book I. A Commentary*. EPRO 59. Leiden: Brill, 1972.

Butterworth, George W. "Translator's Introduction." Pages xi–lxxvi in *Origen. On First Principles*. Translated by George W. Butterworth. Christian Classics. Notre Dame: Ave Maria Press, 2013.

Calcidius. *On Plato's 'Timaeus'*. Edited and translated by John Magee. Dumbarton Oaks Medieval Library 41. Cambridge; London: Harvard University Press, 2016.

Cameron, Averil. "Divine Providence in Late Antiquity." Pages 118–142 in *Predicting the Future*. Edited by Leo Howe and Alan Wain. Cambridge; New York: Cambridge University Press, 1993.

Camplani, Alberto. "Bardaisan's Psychology: Known and Unknown Testimonies and Current Scholarly Perspectives." Pages 259–278 in *Syriac Encounters: Papers from the Sixth North American Syriac Symposium, Duke University, 26–29 June 2011*. Edited by Maria E. Doerfler, Emanuel Fiano, and Kyle Richard Smith. Eastern Christian Studies 20. Leuven: Peeters, 2015.

Camplani, Alberto. "Bardesane et les bardesanites." *Annuaires de l'École des hautes études* 112 (2003): 29–50.

Casanova, Angelo. "Plutarch as Apollo's Priest at Delphi." Pages 118–142 in *Predicting the Future*. Edited by Leo Howe and Alan Wain. Cambridge; New York: Cambridge University Press, 1993.

Chadwick, Henry. *Early Christian Thought and the Classical Tradition*. Oxford: Oxford University Press, 1984.

Chadwick, Henry. "Origen, Celsus, and the Stoa." *JTS* 48 (1947): 34–49.

Chadwick, Henry, ed. and tr. *The Sentences of Sextus: A Contribution to the History of Early Christian Ethics*. Cambridge: Cambridge University Press, 1959.

Chadwick, Henry and J.E.L. Oulton, eds. and trs. *Alexandrian Christianity: Selected Translations of Clement and Origen*. Library of Christian Classics. Louisville: Westminster John Knox Press, 2006.

Chalmers, David. J. "The Matrix as Metaphysics." Pages 455–494 in idem, *The Character of Consciousness*. Oxford: Oxford University Press, 2010.

Charlesworth, Martin Percival. "Providentia and Aeternitas." *HTR* 29:2 (1936): 107–132.

Charlesworth, James H., ed. *Old Testament Pseudepigrapha*. 2 vols. Anchor Yale Bible Reference Library. New York: Doubleday, 1983.

BIBLIOGRAPHY

Chase, Michael. "Porphyre de Tyr: Commentaires à Platon et à Aristote." Pages 1349–1376 in *Dictionnaire des Philosophes Antiques. Tome V, de Paccius à Rutilius Rufus. 2e Partie—V b, de Plotina à Rutilius Rufus*. Edited by Richard Goulet. Paris: CNRS Editions, 2012.

Chase, Michael. "Porphyre sur la providence." *Chōra. RÉAM* 13 (2015): 125–147.

Chiapparini, Giulo. "Irenaeus and the Gnostic Valentinus: Orthodoxy and Heresy in the Church of Rome around the Middle of the Second Century." *ZAC* 18 (2014): 95–119.

Chiaradonna, Riccardo. "Plotinus' Account of Demiurgic Causation and Its Philosophical Background." Pages 31–50 in *Causation and Creation in Late Antiquity*. Edited by Anna Marmodoro and Brian D. Prince. Cambridge: Cambridge University Press, 2015.

Cicero. *On the Nature of the Gods. Academics*. Edited and translated by Harris Rackham. LCL 268. Cambridge: Harvard University Press, 1979.

Cicero. *On the Orator: Book 3. On Fate. Stoic Paradoxes. Divisions of Oratory*. Edited and translated by Harris Rackham. LCL 349. Cambridge: Harvard University Press, 1992.

Cicero. *On Fate. & Boethius: The Consolation of Philosophy IV.5–7, V*. Edited and translated by Robert W. Sharples. Aris & Phillips Classical Texts. Oxford; Havertown, 2015.

Cicero. *On Old Age. On Friendship. On Divination*. Edited and translated by W.A. Falconer. LCL 154. Cambridge: Harvard University Press, 1923.

Clark, Elizabeth A. *Clement's Use of Aristotle. The Aristotelian Contribution to Clement of Alexandria's Refutation of Gnosticism*. Texts and Studies of Religion 13. New York; Toronto: Edwin Mellen Press, 1977.

Cleanthes. *Cleanthes' Hymn to Zeus*. Translated by Johan C. Thom. STAC 33. Tübingen: Mohr Siebeck, 2005.

Clement of Alexandria. *Extraits de Theodote*. Edited and translated by Francois Sagnard. SC 23. Paris: Éditions du Cerf, 1948.

Clement of Alexandria. *Le protreptique*. Edited and translated by C. Mondésert. SC 2. Paris: Éditions du Cerf, 1949.

Clement of Alexandria. *Stromata Buch I–VI*. Edited by Otto Stählin. GCS 52. Berlin: Akademie, 1970.

Clement of Alexandria. *Stromata Buch VI–VII—Excerpta ex Theodoto—Eclogae Propheticae—Quis dives salvetur—Fragmente*. Edited by Otto Stählin. GCS 17. Berlin: Akademie, 1960.

Clement of Alexandria. *Stromateis: Books 1–3*. Translated by John Ferguson. FC 85. Washington: Catholic University of America Press, 1991.

Cohen, Shaye J.D. "Josephus, Jeremiah, and Polybius." *History and Theory* 21:3 (1982): 366–381.

Collins, John J. *Apocalypticism in the Dead Sea Scrolls*. London: Routledge, 2002.

Collins, John J. "Introduction: Towards the Morphology of a Genre." *Semeia* 14 (1979): 1–19.

Collins, John J. "The Mythology of Holy War in Daniel and the Qumran War Scroll: A Point of Transition in Jewish Apocalyptic." *Vetus Testamentum* 25:3 (1975): 596–612.

Collins, John J. "What is Apocalyptic Literature?" Pages 1–16 in *The Oxford Handbook of Apocalyptic Literature*. Edited by John J. Collins. New York: Oxford University Press, 2014.

Collins, John J. "Wisdom, Apocalypticism and Generic Compatibility." Pages 385–404 in idem, *Seers, Sybils and Sages in Hellenistic-Roman Judaism*. JSJSup 54. Boston; Leiden: Brill, 1997.

Cook, John Granger. *The Interpretation of the Old Testament in Greco-Roman Paganism*. STAC 23. Tübingen: Mohr Siebeck, 2004.

Cooper, John M. and Douglas S. Hutchinson, eds. *Plato: Complete Works*. Indianapolis: Hackett, 1997.

Copenhaver, Brian P. Hermetica. *The Greek 'Corpus Hermeticum' and the Latin 'Asclepius' in a New English Translation, with Notes and Introduction*. Cambridge: Cambridge University Press, 1998.

Corrigan, Kevin. "Divine and Human Freedom: Plotinus' New Understanding of Creative Agency." Pages 131–148 in *Causation and Creation in Late Antiquity*. Edited by Anna Marmodoro and Brian D. Prince. Cambridge: Cambridge University Press, 2015.

Corrigan, Kevin. "Positive and Negative Matter in Later Platonism: The Uncovering of Plotinus's Dialogue with the Gnostics." Pages 19–56 in *Gnosticism and Later Platonism: Themes, Figures, and Texts*. Edited by John D. Turner and Ruth Majercik. SBL Symposium Series 12. Atlanta: Society of Biblical Literature, 2001.

Corrigan, Kevin and John D. Turner. "Commentary." Pages 123–396 in idem, *Plotinus. Ennead VI.8. On the Voluntary and on the Free Will of the One. Translation with an Introduction and Commentary*. The *Enneads* of Plotinus With Philosophical Commentaries. Las Vegas; Zürich; Athens: Parmenides Publishing, 2017.

Corrigan, Kevin and John D. Turner. "Introduction to the Treatise." Pages 17–59 in idem, *Plotinus. Ennead VI.8. On the Voluntary and on the Free Will of the One. Translation with an Introduction and Commentary*. The *Enneads* of Plotinus With Philosophical Commentaries. Las Vegas; Zürich; Athens: Parmenides Publishing, 2017.

Couliano, Ioan P. *The Tree of Gnosis: Gnostic Mythology from Early Christianity to Modern Nihilism*. Translated by H.S. Wiesner and Ioan P. Couliano. San Francisco: HarperSanFrancisco, 1992.

Craig, William Lane. *The Problem of Divine Foreknowledge and Future Contingents from Aristotle to Suarez*. Brill's Studies in Intellectual History 7. Leiden; New York; København; Köln: Brill, 1988.

Crenshaw, James L. *Old Testament Wisdom: An Introduction*. Atlanta: John Knox Press, 1981.

Crouzel, Henri. "Theological Construction and Research: Origen on Free Will." Pages

BIBLIOGRAPHY

239–265 in *Scripture, Tradition, and Reason: A Study in the Criteria of Christian Doctrine. Essays in Honour of Richard P. C. Hanson.* Edited by Richard J. Bauckham and Benjamin Drewery. Edinburgh: T&T Clark, 1988.

Crum, Walter Ewing. *A Coptic Dictionary.* Oxford: Clarendon Press, 1962.

Davidson, Arnold I. "Introduction." Pages 1–45 in *Philosophy as a Way of Life: Spiritual Exercises from Socrates to Foucault,* by Pierre Hadot. Edited by Arnold I. Davidson. Translated by Michael Chase. Malden; Oxford; Victoria: Blackwell, 1995.

de Blois, Lukas. "The Perception of Politics in Plutarch's Roman 'Lives.'" *ANRW* 2.33.6 (1992): 4568–4615.

de Vogel, Cornelia J. "Problems concerning Justin Martyr: Did Justin Find a Certain Continuity between Greek Philosophy and Christian Faith?" *Mnemosyne* 31:4 (1978): 360–388.

de Vogel, Cornelia J. *Pythagoras and Early Pythagoreanism. An Interpretation of Neglected Evidence on the Philosopher Pythagoras.* Assen: Van Gorcum & Co., 1966.

DeConick, April. "Crafting Gnosis: Gnostic Spirituality in the Ancient New Age." Pages 285–307 in *Gnosticism, Platonism, and the Late Ancient World. Essays in Honour of John D. Turner.* Edited by Kevin Corrigan and Tuomas Rasimus, with Dylan M. Burns, Lance Jenott, and Zeke Mazur. NHMS 82. Leiden; Boston: Brill, 2013.

den Boeft, Jan. *Calcidius on Fate: His Doctrine and Sources.* PA 18. Leiden: Brill, 1970.

den Dulk, Matthijs. *Between Jews and Heretics: Refiguring Justin Martyr's Dialogue with Trypho.* London; New York: Routledge, 2018.

des Places, Édouard, ed. and tr. *Oracles chaldaïques. Avec un choix de commentaires anciens.* Paris: Les belles lettres, 1971.

Dell, Katherine J. "Wisdom." Pages 409–419 in *The Oxford Handbook to Biblical Studies.* Edited by J.W. Rogerson and Judith M. Lieu. Oxford: Oxford University Press, 2008.

Denzey (Lewis), Nicola. "Bardaisan." Pages 159–184 in *A Companion to Second-Century Christian "Heretics."* Edited by Antti Marjanen and Petri Luomanen. VCSup 76. Leiden: Brill, 2005.

Denzey (Lewis), Nicola. *Cosmology and Fate in Gnosticism and Graeco-Roman Antiquity: Under Pitiless Skies.* NHMS 81. Leiden: Brill, 2013.

Denzey (Lewis), Nicola. "Facing the Beast: Justin, Christian Martyrdom, and Freedom of the Will." Pages 176–198 in *Stoicism in Early Christianity.* Edited by Tuomas Rasimus, Troels Engberg-Pedersen, and Ismo Dunderberg. Grand Rapids: Baker Academic, 2010.

Denzey (Lewis), Nicola. "Genesis Traditions in Conflict?: the Use of Some Exegetical Traditions in the *Trimorphic Protennoia* and the Johannine Prologue." *VC* 55:1 (2001): 20–44.

Denzey (Lewis), Nicola. "A New Star on the Horizon: Astral Christologies and Stellar Debates in Early Christian Discourse." Pages 207–221 in *Prayer, Magic, and the*

Stars in the Ancient and Late Antique World. Edited by Scott Noegel, Joel Walker, and Brannon Wheeler. Magic in History. Philadelphia: Penn State University Press, 2003.

Diels, Hermann, and Walther Kranz, eds. *Die Fragmente der Vorsokratiker*. Berlin: Weidmann, 1951.

Digeser, Elizabeth DePalma. *A Threat to Public Piety: Christians, Platonists, and the Great Persecution*. Ithaca: Cornell University Press, 2012.

Dihle, Albrecht. "Astrology in the Doctrine of Bardesanes." Pages 160–168 in *Studia Patristica* 20. Edited by Elizabeth A. Livingstone. Leuven: Peeters, 1989.

Dihle, Albrecht. "Philosophische Lehren von Schicksal und Freiheit." *JAC* 30 (1987): 14–28.

Dihle, Albrecht. *The Theory of Will in Classical Antiquity*. Sather Classical Lectures 48. Berkeley: University of California Press, 1982.

Dihle, Albrecht. "Zur Schicksalslehre des Bardesanes." Pages 123–135 in *Kerygma und Logos. Beiträge zu den geistesgeschichtlichen Beziehungen zwischen Antike und Christentum; Festschrift für Carl Andresen zum 70. Geburtstag*. Edited by Adolf Martin Ritter. Göttingen: Vandenhoeck & Ruprecht, 1979.

Dillon, John M. "Commentary." Pages 51–211 in Alcinous, *The Handbook of Platonism*. Translated by John M. Dillon. Clarendon Later Ancient Philosophers. Oxford: Clarendon Press, 1993.

Dillon, John M. "The Descent of the Soul in Middle Platonic and Gnostic Theory." Pages 1:357–364 in *The Rediscovery of Gnosticism: Proceedings of the International Conference on Gnosticism*. Edited by Bentley Layton. 2 vols. Leiden: Brill, 1980.

Dillon, John M. *The Heirs of Plato. A Study of the Old Academy (347–274 BC)*. Oxford: Clarendon Press, 2003.

Dillon, John M. "Introduction." Pages ix–xliii in Alcinous, *The Handbook of Platonism*. Translated by John M. Dillon. Clarendon Later Ancient Philosophers. Oxford: Clarendon Press, 1993.

Dillon, John M. *The Middle Platonists*. London: Duckworth, 1977.

Dillon, John M. "Signs and Tokens: Do the Gods of Neoplatonism Really Care?" Pages 227–238 in *Fate, Providence and Moral Responsibility in Ancient, Medieval and Early Modern Thought: Studies in Honour of Carlos Steel*. Edited by Pieter d'Hoine and Gerd van Riel. AMP 1. Leuven: Leuven University Press, 2014.

Diodorus Siculus. *Library of History, Volume I: Books 1–2.34*. Edited and translated by C.H. Oldfather. LCL 279. Cambridge: Harvard University Press, 1933.

Diogenes Laertius. *Lives of Eminent Philosophers*. Edited and translated by Robert D. Hicks. 2 vols. LCL 184, 185. Cambridge: Harvard University Press, 1925.

Dorandi, Tiziano. "Chronology." Pages 31–54 in *The Cambridge History of Hellenistic Philosophy*. Edited by Keimpe Algra, Jonathan Barnes, Jaap Mansfeld, and Malcolm Schofield. Cambridge: Cambridge University Press, 1999.

Dorival, Gilles. "Modes of Prayer in the Hellenic Tradition." Pages 27–45 in *Platonic Theories of Prayer*. Edited by John M. Dillon and Andrei Timotin. SPNPT 19. Leiden: Brill, 2015.

Dörrie, Heinrich. "Der Begriff Pronoia in Stoa und Platonismus." *Freiburger Zeitschrift für Philosophie und Theologie* 24 (1977): 60–87.

Dörrie, Heinrich. "Dualismus." *Reallexikon für Antike und Christentum* 4 (1959): 334–350.

Dörrie, Heinrich, and Matthias Baltes, eds. and trs. *Der Platonismus in der Antike*. 6 vols. Stuttgart: Frommann-Holzboog, 1987–2002.

Dragona-Monachou, Myrto. "Divine Providence in the Philosophy of the Empire." *ANRW* 2.36.7 (1994): 4417–4490.

Drecoll, Volker Henning. "Martin Hengel and the Origins of Gnosticism." Pages 139–165 in *Gnosticism, Platonism, and the Late Ancient World: Essays in Honour of John D. Turner*. Edited by Kevin Corrigan and Tuomas Rasimus, with Dylan M. Burns, Lance Jenott, and Zeke Mazur. NHMS 82. Leiden: Brill, 2013.

Drews, Friedemann. "Asinus Philosophans: Allegory's *Fate* and Isis' *Providence* in the *Metamorphoses*." Pages 107–131 in *Aspects of Apuleius' 'Golden Ass,' volume III: the Isis-Book. A Collection of Original Papers*. Edited by W.H. Keulen and Ulrike Egelhaaf-Gaiser. Leiden; Boston: Brill, 2012.

Drijvers, Han J.W. *Bardaiṣan of Edessa*. Assen: van Gorcum & Co., 1966.

Drijvers, Han J.W. "Bardaisan's Doctrine of Free Will, the Pseudo-Clementines, and Marcionism in Syria." Pages 13–30 in *Liberté chrétienne et libre arbitre*. Edited by Guy Bedouelle. Fribourg: O. Fatio, 1994.

Drijvers, Han J.W., ed. and tr. *The Book of the Laws of the Countries. Dialogue on Fate of Bardaiṣan of Edessa*. Assen: van Gorcum & Co., 1965.

Dubois, Jean-Daniel. "Le *Traité Tripartite* (Nag Hammadi I, 5). Est-il antérieur à Origéne?" Pages 303–316 in *Origeniana Octava. Origen and the Alexandrian Tradition. Origene e la tradizione alessandrina: Papers on the 8th International Origen Congress. Pisa, 27–31 August 2001*. Edited by Lorenzo Perrone, in collaboration with P. Bernardino and D. Marchini. Leuven: Leuven University Press; Peeters, 2003.

Dubois, Jean-Daniel. "Once Again, the Valentinian Expression 'Saved by Nature'." Pages 193–204 in *Valentinianism: New Studies*. Edited by Einar Thomassen and Christoph Markschies. NHMS 96. Leiden; Boston: Brill, 2019.

Dudley, John. "The Fate of Providence and Plato's World-Soul in Aristotle." Pages 159–173 in *Fate, Providence and Moral Responsibility in Ancient, Medieval and Early Modern Thought: Studies in Honour of Carlos Steel*. Edited by Pieter d'Hoine and Gerd van Riel. AMP 1. Leuven: Leuven University Press, 2014.

Dunderberg, Ismo. *Beyond Gnosticism: Myth, Lifestyle, and Society in the School of Valentinus*. New York: Columbia University Press, 2008.

Dunderberg, Ismo. "Valentinian Theories on Classes of Humankind." Pages 113–128 in *Zugänge zur Gnosis: Akten zur Tagung der Patristischen Arbeitsgemeinschaft vom*

02.–05.01.2011 in Berlin-Spandau. Edited by Christoph Markschies and Johannes van Oort. Patristic Studies 12. Leuven: Peeters, 2013.

Dunning, Benjamin H. *Aliens and Sojourners: Self as Other in Early Christianity*. Divinations. Philadelphia: University of Pennsylvania Press, 2009.

Dunning, Benjamin H. "What Sort of Thing Is This Luminous Woman? Thinking Sexual Difference in On the Origin of the World." *JECS* 17:1 (2009): 55–84.

Edwards, Mark J. "Christians and the *Parmenides*." Pages 2:189–198 in in *Plato's "Parmenides" and Its Heritage, 2. vols*. Edited by Kevin Corrigan and John D. Turner. WGRWSup 2–3. Atlanta: SBL, 2010.

Edwards, Mark J. "Clement of Alexandria and His Doctrine of the Logos." *VC* 54 (2000): 159–177.

Edwards, Mark J. "Numenius of Apamea." Pages 115–125 in *The Cambridge History of Philosophy in Late Antiquity*. Edited by Lloyd P. Gerson. 2 vols. Cambridge: Cambridge University Press, 2010.

Edwards, Mark J. "One Origen or Two? The *Status Quaestionis*." *Symbolae Osloenses* 89:1 (2015): 81–103.

Edwards, Mark J. *Origen Against Plato*. Aldershot: Ashgate, 2002.

Eidinow, Esther. *Oracles, Curses, and Risk Among the Ancient Greeks*. Oxford: Oxford University Press, 2013.

Eliasson, Erik. "Plotinus on Fate (EIMARMENH)." Pages 199–220 in *Fate, Chance, and Fortune in Ancient Thought*. Edited by Francesca Guadalupe Masi and Stefano Maso. Lexis Ancient Philosophy 9. Amsterdam: Adolf M. Hakkert, 2013.

Elliott, Mark W. *Providence Perceived. Divine Action from a Human Point of View*. Arbeiten zur Kirchengeschichte 124. Berlin; München: De Gruyter, 2015.

Emmel, Stephen, ed. and tr. "Text and Translation." Pages 37–95 in *Nag Hammadi Codex III,5. The Dialogue of the Savior*. Edited by Stephen Emmel. NHS 26. Leiden: Brill, 1984.

Engberg-Pedersen, Troels. "Introduction: A Historiographical Essay." Pages 1–26 in *From Stoicism to Platonism: The Development of Philosophy, 100 BCE–100 CE*. Edited by Troels Engberg-Pedersen. Cambridge: Cambridge University Press, 2017.

Engberg-Pedersen, Troels. "Setting the Scene: Stoicism and Platonism in the Transitional Period in Ancient Philosophy." Pages 1–14 in *Stoicism in Early Christianity*. Edited by Tuomas Rasimus, Troels Engberg-Pedersen, and Ismo Dunderberg. Grand Rapids: Baker Academic, 2010.

Ephraem Syrus. *S. Ephraim's Prose Refutations of Mani, Marcion, and Bardaisan. Of Which the Greater Part has been Transcribed from the Palimpsest B.M. Add. 14623 and is Now First Published*. Edited and translated by Charles W.S. Mitchell. 2 vols. London; Oxford: Williams and Norgate, 1912.

Epictetus. *The Discourses: Books 1–2*. Edited and translated by William A. Oldfather. LCL 131. Cambridge: Harvard University Press, 1925.

BIBLIOGRAPHY

Epictetus. *The Discourses: Books 3–4. Fragments. The Encheiridion.* Edited and translated by William A. Oldfather. LCL 218. Cambridge: Harvard University Press, 1928.

Epiphanius of Salamis. *Panarion.* Translated by Frank Williams. 2 vols. NHMS 63, 79. Leiden: Brill, 2009.

Eshel, Hanan. "The Bar Kochba Revolt, 132–135 CE." Pages 105–127 in *The Cambridge History of Judaism, Vol. 4: The Late Roman-Rabbinic Period.* Edited by Steven T. Katz. Cambridge: Cambridge University Press, 2006.

Euripides. *Suppliant Women. Electra. Heracles.* Edited and translated by David Kovacs. LCL 9. Cambridge: Harvard University Press, 1998.

Eusebius. *Ecclesiastical History: Books 1–4.* Edited and translated by Kirsopp Lake. LCL 153. Cambridge: Harvard University Press, 2001.

Ewing, Jon. *Clement of Alexandria's Reinterpretation of Divine Providence: The Christianization of the Hellenistic Idea of 'Pronoia'.* Lewiston: Edwin Mellen Press, 2008.

Feldmeier, Reinhard. "Wenn die Vorsehung ein Gesicht erhält: Theologische Transformation einer problematischen Kategorie." Pages 147–170 in *Vorsehung, Schicksal, und göttliche Macht. Antike Stimmen zu einem aktuellen Thema.* Edited by Reinhard G. Kratz and Hermann Spieckermann. Tübingen: Mohr Siebeck, 2008.

Ferguson, David. *The Providence of God: A Polyphonic Approach.* Cambridge: Cambridge University Press, 2018.

Finamore, John F. "Iamblichus, the Sethians, and Marsanes." Pages 221–257 in *Gnosticism and Later Platonism: Themes, Figures, and Texts.* Edited by John D. Turner and Ruth Majercik. SBL Symposium Series 12. Atlanta: Society of Biblical Literature, 2001.

Fishwick, Duncan. *The Imperial Cult in thr Latin West. Studies on the Ruler Cult of the Western Providences of the Roman Empire.* Volume I,1. EPRO 108/1. Leiden; New York; Köln: Brill, 1993.

Förster, Hans. *Wörterbuch der griechischen Wörter in den koptischen dokumentarischen Texten.* TUGAL 148. Berlin; New York: De Gruyter, 2002.

Frede, Dorothea. "Could Paris (Son of Priam) Have Chosen Otherwise? A Discussion of R. W. Sharples, *Alexander of Aphrodisias: de Fato.*" *Oxford Studies in Ancient Philosophy* 2 (1984): 279–292.

Frede, Dorothea. "The Dramatization of Determinism: Alexander of Aphrodisias' *De Fato.*" *Phronesis* 27:3 (1982): 276–298.

Frede, Dorothea. "Free Will in Aristotle?" Pages 39–58 in *What is Up to Us? Studies on Agency and Responsibility in Ancient Philosophy.* Edited by Pierre Destrée, Ricardo Salles, and Marco Zingano. SAMPP 1. Leiden: Sankt Augustin: Academia Verlag, 2014.

Frede, Dorothea. "Theodicy and Providential Care in Stoicism." Pages 85–117 in *Traditions of Theology: Studies in Hellenistic Theology, its Background and Aftermath.* Edited by Dorothea Frede and André Laks. PA 89. Leiden: Brill, 2002.

Frede, Michael. *A Free Will: Origins of the Notion in Ancient Thought.* Sather Classical Lectures 68. Berkeley; Los Angeles; Oxford: University of California Press, 2011.

Frede, Michael. "Galen's Theology." Pages 73–126 in *Galien et la philosophie: huit exposés suivis de discussions*. Edited by Jonathan Barnes. Genève: Foundation Hardt, 2003.

Frede, Michael. "Numenius." *ANRW* 2.32.2 (1987): 1034–1075.

Fredriksen, Paula. *Sin: The Early History of an Idea*. Princeton; Oxford: Princeton University Press, 2012.

Frey, Jörg. "Apocalyptic Dualism." Pages 271–294 in *The Oxford Handbook of Apocalyptic Literature*. Edited by John J. Collins. New York: Oxford University Press, 2014.

Frick, Peter. *Divine Providence in Philo of Alexandria*. TSAJ 77. Tübingen: Mohr Siebeck, 1999.

Funk, Wolf-Peter. "Allogenes (NHC XI,3)." Pages 2:763–787 in *Nag Hammadi Deutsch*. Edited by Hans-Martin Schenke, Hans-Gebhard Bethge, and Ursula Ulrike Kaiser. GCS 8. 2 vols. Berlin; New York: De Gruyter, 2001, 2003.

Funk, Wolf-Peter, and Paul-Hubert Poirier, eds. and trs. "Texte et traduction." Pages 249–357 in *Marsanès (NH X)*. Edited and translated by Wolf-Peter Funk, Paul-Hubert Poirier, and John D. Turner. BCNH Section "Textes" 27. Québec: Presses de l'université Laval; Leuven: Peeters, 2000.

Funk, Wolf-Peter, and Madeleine Scopello, eds. and trs. "Texte et traduction." Pages 189–239 in *L'Allogène (NH XI,3)*. Edited and translated by Wolf-Peter Funk, Madeleine Scopello, and John D. Turner. BCNH Section "Textes" 30. Québec: Presses de l'université Laval; Leuven: Peeters, 2004.

Gabba, Emilio. "The Social, Economic and Political History of Palestine 63 BCE–70 CE." Pages 94–168 in *The Cambridge History of Judaism, Vol. 3: The Early Roman Period*. Edited by William Horbury, W.D. Davies, and John Sturdy. Cambridge: Cambridge University Press, 1999.

Gabor, Gary. "When Should a Philosopher Consult Divination? Epictetus and Simplicius on Fate and What is Up to Us." Pages 325–340 in *Fate, Providence and Moral Responsibility in Ancient, Medieval and Early Modern Thought: Studies in Honour of Carlos Steel*. Edited by Pieter d'Hoine and Gerd van Riel. AMP 1. Leuven: Leuven University Press, 2014.

Gager, John. "Marcion and Philosophy." *VC* 26 (1972): 53–59.

Galen. *On the Usefulness of the Parts of the Human Body*. Translated by Margaret Tallmadge May. 2 vols. Ithaca: Cornell University Press, 1968.

Gardner, Iain. "Dualism." In *Vocabulary for the Study of Religion*. Edited by Robert A. Segal and Kocku von Stuckrad. Brill Online, 2016. Available from: http://reference works.brillonline.com/entries/vocabulary-for-the-study-of-religion/dualism-COM _00000283.

Gaskin, Richard. *The Sea Battle and the Master Argument: Aristotle and Diodorus Cronus on the Metaphysics of the Future*. Quellen und Studien zur Philosophie 40. Berlin: De Gruyter, 1995.

Gasparro, Giulia Sfameni. *"Daimôn and Tuchê* in the Hellenistic Religious Experience."

BIBLIOGRAPHY

Pages 67–109 in *Conventional Values of the Hellenistic Greeks*. Edited by Per Bilde, Troels Engberg-Pedersen, Lise Hannestad, and Jan Zahle. Studies in Hellenistic Civilization 8. Aarhus: Aarhus University Press, 1997.

Geach, Peter T. *Providence and Evil*. Cambridge: Cambridge University Press, 1977.

Gercke, Alfred. "Eine platonische Quelle des Neuplatonismus." *Rheinisches Museum* 41 (1886): 266–291.

Gerson, Lloyd P. "General Introduction." Pages 1–10 in *The Cambridge History of Philosophy in Late Antiquity*. Edited by Lloyd P. Gerson. 2 vols. Cambridge: Cambridge University Press, 2010.

Gibbons, Kathleen. "Human Autonomy and its Limits in the Thought of Origen of Alexandria." *CQ* 66:2 (2017): 673–690.

Giulea, Dragoş-Andrei. "The Watchers' Whispers: Athenagoras's *Legatio* 25,1–3 and the *Book of the Watchers*." *VC* 61 (2007): 266–273.

Givens, Terryl L. *When Souls Had Wings: Pre-Mortal Existence in Western Thought*. Oxford: Oxford University Press, 2009.

Good, Deirdre. *Reconstructing the Tradition of Sophia in Gnostic Literature*. Atlanta, GA: Society of Biblical Literature, 1987.

Goulet, Richard. "Hypothèses récentes sur le traité de Porphyre Contre les Chrétiens." Pages 61–109 in *Hellénisme et christianisme*. Edited by Michel Narcy and Éric Rebillard. Paris: Presses Universitaires du Septentrion, 2004.

Graf, Fritz. "Rolling the Dice for an Answer." Pages 51–97 in *Mantikê: Studies in Ancient Divination*. Edited by Sarah Iles Johnston and Peter Struck. RGRW 155. Leiden; Boston: Brill, 2005.

Graverini, Luca. "*Prudentia* and *Providentia*: Book XI in Context." Pages 86–106 in *Aspects of Apuleius' 'Golden Ass,' volume III: the Isis-Book. A Collection of Original Papers*. Edited by W.H. Keulen and Ulrike Egelhaaf-Gaiser. Leiden; Boston: Brill, 2012.

Greschat, Katharina. *Apelles und Hermogenes. Zwei theologische Lehrer des zweiten Jahrhunderts*. VCSup 10. Leiden; Boston; Köln: Brill, 2000.

Grypeou, Emmanouela and Helen Spurling. *The Book of Genesis in Late Antiquity: Encounters between Jewish and Christian Exegesis*. Jewish and Christian Perspectives 24. Leiden; Boston: Brill, 2013.

Gundel, W. "Heimarmene." *Paulys Real-Encyclopädie der classischen Altertumswissenschaft* 7 (1912): 2622–2645.

Gurtler, Gary M. "Providence: The Platonic Demiurge and Hellenistic Causality." Pages 99–124 in *Neoplatonism and Nature*. Edited by Michael F. Wagner. SNAM 8. Albany: State University of New York Press, 2001.

Hadot, Pierre. "Philosophy, Exegesis, and Creative Mistakes." Pages 71–78 in idem, *Philosophy as a Way of Life: Spiritual Exercises from Socrates to Foucault*. Edited by Arnold I. Davidson. Translated by Michael Chase. Malden; Oxford; Victoria: Blackwell, 1995.

Hadot, Pierre. *Porphyre et Victorinus*. 2 vols. Paris: Études Augustiniennes, 1968.

Hadot, Pierre. "Porphyre et Victorinus: Questions et hypothèses." *Res Orientales* 9 (1996): 117–125.

Hammerstaedt, Jürgen. *Die Orakelkritik des Kynikers Oenomaus*. Beiträge zur Klassischen Philologie 188. Frankfurt am Main: Athenaeum, 1988.

Hanegraaff, Wouter J. "Gnosticism." Pages 790–798 in *The Brill Dictionary of Religion*. Edited by Kocku von Stuckrad. Leiden; Boston: Brill, 2006.

Hanson, Paul D. *The Dawn of Apocalyptic. The Historical and Sociological Roots of Jewish Apocalyptic Eschatology*. Philadelphia: Fortress Press. 1979.

Harrison, Stephen. *Apuleius: A Latin Sophist*. Oxford: Oxford University Press, 2000.

Harper, Kyle. *From Shame to Sin. The Christian Transformation of Sexual Morality in Late Antiquity*. Revealing Antiquity 20. Cambridge: Harvard University Press, 2013.

Hägg, Tomas. "A Professor and His Slave: Conventions and Values in the *Life of Aesop*." Pages 177–203 in *Conventional Values of the Hellenistic Greeks*. Edited by Per Bilde, Troels Engberg-Pedersen, Lise Hannestad, and Jan Zahle. Studies in Hellenistic Civilization 8. Aarhus: Aarhus University Press, 1997.

Harl, Marguerite. "La préexistence des âmes dans l'œuvre d'Origène." Pages 238–258 in *Origeniana Quarta. Die Referate des 4. Internationalen Origeneskongresses (Innsbruck, 2.-6. September 1985)*. Edited by Lothar Lies. Innsbrucker theologische Studien 19. Innsbruck-Wien: Tyrloia Verlag, 1987.

Havrda, Matyáš. "Grace and Free Will According to Clement of Alexandria." *JECS* 19:1 (2011): 21–48.

Healey, John F. "The Edessan Milieu and the Birth of Syriac†." *Hugoye: Journal of Syriac Studies* 10:2 (2007). Accessed 28 January 2020. https://hugoye.bethmardutho.org/article/hv10n2healey

Hegedus, Tim. *Early Christianity and Ancient Astrology*. Patristic Studies 6. New York: Peter Lang, 2007.

Hegedus, Tim. "Necessity and Free Will in the Thought of Bardaisan of Edessa." *Laval théologique et philosophique* 59:2 (2003): 333–344.

Herodotus. *The Persian Wars, Volume II: Books 3–4*. Edited and translated by A.D. Godley. LCL 118. Cambridge: Harvard University Press, 1921.

Hoheisel, Karl. "Das frühe Christentum und die Seelenwanderung." *JAC* 27/28 (1984/85): 24–46.

Homer. *Iliad*. Edited and translated by Augustus T. Murray. 2 vols. LCL 170–171. Cambridge: Harvard University Press, 1979.

Homer. *Odyssey*. Edited and translated by Augustus T. Murray. 2 vols. LCL 104–105. Cambridge: Harvard University Press, 1979.

Horner, Timothy J. *Listening to Trypho: Justin's 'Dialogue with Trypho' Reconsidered*. Contributions to Biblical Exegesis & Theology 28. Leuven: Peeters, 2001.

BIBLIOGRAPHY

Horsley, Greg H.R. *New Documents Illustrating Early Christianity. A Review of the Greek Inscriptions and Papyri Published in 1978*. North Ryde: The Ancient History Documentary Research Centre, Macquarie University, 1983.

Huber, Peter (Thomas Morus). *Die Vereinbarkeit von göttlicher Vorsehung und menschlicher Freiheit in der Consolatio Philosophiae des Boethius*. Zürich: Juris, 1976.

Hyldahl, Niels. *Philosophie und Christentum. Eine Interpretation der Einleitung zum Dialog Justins*. Acta Theologica Danica 9. Kopenhagen: Prostant apud Munksgaard, 1966.

Iamblichus. *In Platonis Dialogos Commentariorum Fragmenta*. Edited and translated by John M. Dillon. Leiden: Brill, 1973.

Iamblichus. *On the Mysteries*. Edited and translated by Emma C. Clarke, John M. Dillon, and Jackson P. Hershbell. WGRW 4. Atlanta: SBL, 2003.

Ilievski, Viktor. "Stoic Influences on Plotinus' Theodicy?" *ELPIS* 2 (2018): 23–36.

Irenaeus of Lyons. *Against the Heresies Book 1*. Translated by Dominic J. Unger. Revised by John J. Dillon. ACW 55. New York; Mahwah: Newman, 1992.

Irenaeus of Lyons. *Against the Heresies Book 2*. Translated by Dominic J. Unger and Matthew Craig Steenberg. Revised by John J. Dillon. ACW 65. New York; Mahwah: Newman, 2012.

Irenaeus of Lyons. *Against the Heresies Book 3*. Translated by Dominic J. Unger. ACW 64. New York; Mahwah: Newman, 2012.

Irenaeus of Lyons. *Contre les hérésies: denonciation et réfutation de la gnose au nom menteur*. Edited and translated by Louis Doutreleau and Adelin Rousseau, et al. 10 vols. SC 100, 152–153, 210–211, 263–264, 293–294. Paris: Éditions du Cerf, 1974–2006.

Jackson, B. Darrell. "Sources of Origen's Doctrine of Freedom." *Church History* 35 (1966): 13–23.

Jacobsen, Anders Christian Lund. "Freedom and Providence in Origen's Theology." *Church Studies* 3 (2006): 65–77.

Janby, Lars Fredrik, Eyjólfur Kjalar Emilsson, Torstein Theodor Tollefsen, and Panagiotis G. Pavlos. "Introduction." Pages 1–13 in *Platonism and Christian Thought in Late Antiquity*. Edited by Panagiotis G. Pavlos, Lars Fredrik Janby, Eyjólfur Kjalar Emilsson, and Torstein Theodor Tollefsen. Studies in Philosophy and Theology in Late Antiquity. London; New York: Routledge, 2019.

Jenott, Lance. "Emissaries of Truth and Justice: The Seed of Seth as Agents of Divine Providence." Pages 43–62 in *Gnosticism, Platonism, and the Late Ancient World*. Edited by Kevin Corrigan and Tuomas Rasimus, with Dylan M. Burns, Lance Jenott, and Zeke Mazur. NHMS 82. Leiden: Brill, 2013.

Johnson, Aaron P. *Religion and Identity in Porphyry of Tyre. The Limits of Hellenism in Late Antiquity*. Cambridge: Cambridge University Press, 2013.

Joly, Robert. *Christianisme et philosophie: Etudes sur Justin et les apologists grecs du deux-*

ième siècle. Éditions de l'université de Bruxelles 52. Bruxelles: Université libre de Bruxelles, 1973.

Joly, Robert. "Notes pour le moyen platonisme." Pages 311–321 in *Kerygma und Logos: Beiträge zu den geistesgeschichtlichen Beziehungen zwischen Antike und Christentum. Festschrift für Carl Andresen zum 70. Geburtstag*. Edited by Adolf Martin Ritter. Göttingen: Vandenhoeck & Ruprecht, 1979.

Jonas, Hans. "The Concept of God After Auschwitz: A Jewish Voice." *Journal of Religion* 67:1 (1987): 1–13.

Josephus. *Jewish Antiquities: Books 5–8*. Edited and translated by H.St.J. Thackeray and Ralph Marcus. LCL 281. Cambridge: Harvard University Press; London: William Heinemann, 1934.

Josephus. *Jewish Antiquities: Books 9–11*. Edited and translated by Ralph Marcus. LCL 326. Cambridge: Harvard University Press; 1937.

Josephus. *Jewish Antiquities: Books 16–17*. Edited and translated by Ralph Marcus and Allen Wikgren. LCL 410. Cambridge: Harvard University Press, 1969.

Josephus. *Jewish War: Books 5–7*. Edited and translated by Henry St. John Thackeray. LCL 210. Cambridge: Harvard University Press, 1928.

Jourdan, Fabienne. "Introduction." *Chōra*. RÉAM 13:Sup (2015): 7–17.

Justin Martyr. *Iustini Martyris Apologiae pro Christianis. Iustini Martyris Dialogus cum Tryphone*. Edited by Miroslav Marcovich. Berlin; Boston: De Gruyter, 2011.

Justin Martyr. *St. Justin Martyr. Dialogue with Trypho*, Translated by Thomas B. Falls. Revised by Thomas P. Halton. Edited by Michael Slusser. Selections from the Fathers of the Church 3. Washington: Catholic University of America Press, 2003.

Justin Martyr. *St. Justin Martyr. The First Apology, the Second Apology, Dialogue with Trypho, Exhortation to the Greeks, Discourse to the Greeks, The Monarchy of the Rule of God*. Translated by Thomas B. Falls. FC 6. Washington: Catholic University of America Press, 1948.

Kahn, Charles H. "Discovering Will from Aristotle to Augustine." Pages 234–259 in *The Question of "Eclecticism": Studies in Later Greek Philosophy*. Edited by John M. Dillon and Anthony A. Long. Berkeley: University of California Press, 1988.

Kalligas, Anthony. *The 'Enneads' of Plotinus: A Commentary. Volume 1*. Translated by Elizabeth Key Fowden and Nicolas Pilavachi. Princeton: Princeton University Press, 2014.

Karamanolis, George E. *The Philosophy of Early Christianity*. Ancient Philosophies. London: Routledge, 2014.

Karanika, Andromache. "Homer the Prophet: Homeric Verses and Divination in the *Homeromanteion*." Pages 255–277 in *Sacred Words: Orality, Literacy, and Religion*. Edited by André Lardinois, Josine Blok, and M.G.M. van der Poel. Mnemosyne Supplements 332. Leiden; Boston: Brill, 2011.

Karavites, Peter. *Evil, Freedom, & the Road to Perfection in Clement of Alexandria*. VCSup 43. Leiden; Boston; Köln: Brill, 1999.

BIBLIOGRAPHY

Kenney, John Peter. *The Mysticism of Saint Augustine: Rereading the* Confessions. New York; London: Routledge, 2005.

Kenney, John Peter. "The Platonism of the *Tripartite Tractate* (NH I, 5)." Pages 187–206 in *Neoplatonism and Gnosticism*. Edited by Richard T. Wallis and Jay Bregman. SNAM 6. Albany: SUNY Press, 1992.

Kerkeslager, Allen. "The Jews in Egypt and Cyrenaica, 66–c. 235 CE." Pages 53–68 in *The Cambridge History of Judaism, Vol. 4: The Late Roman-Rabbinic Period*. Edited by Steven T. Katz. Cambridge: Cambridge University Press, 2006.

King, Karen L. "A Distinctive Intertextuality: Genesis and Platonizing Philosophy in the 'Secret Revelation of John'." Pages 3–22 in *Gnosticism, Platonism, and the Late Ancient World: Essays in Honour of John D. Turner*. Edited by Kevin Corrigan and Tuomas Rasimus, with Dylan M. Burns, Lance Jenott, and Zeke Mazur. NHMS 82. Leiden: Brill, 2013.

King, Karen L. *The Secret Revelation of John*. Cambridge: Harvard University Press, 2006.

King, Karen L. *What is Gnosticism?* Cambridge: Harvard University Press, 2003.

Kippenberg, Hans G. "Versuch einer soziologischen Verortung des antiken Gnostizismus." *Numen* 17 (1970): 211–232.

Klawans, Jonathan. *Josephus and the Theologies of Ancient Judaism*. Oxford: Oxford University Press, 2012.

Kocar, Alexander. "'Humanity Came to Be According to Three Essential Types': Anthropogony and Ethical Responsibility in the *Tripartite Tractate*." Pages 193–211 in *Jewish and Christian Cosmogony in Late Antiquity*. Edited by Lance Jenott and Sarit Kattan Gribetz. Texts and Studies in Ancient Judaism 155. Tübingen: Mohr Siebeck, 2013.

Koch, Hal. *Pronoia und Paideusis. Studien über Origenes und sein Verhältnis zum Platonismus*. Berlin; Leipzig: Walter de Gruyter & Co., 1932.

Kraabel, A. Thomas. "Pronoia at Sardis." *Te'uda* 12 (1996): 75–96.

Krayer, Jill. "Disputes over the Authorship of *De mundo* between Humanism and *Altertumswissenschaft*." Pages 181–197 in *Cosmic Order and Divine Power*. Edited by Johan Thom. SAPERE 23. Tübingen: Mohr Siebeck, 2014.

Kwiatkowski, Fryderyk. "Cinema: Evil Demiurges in Hollywood Films at the Threshold of the Twenty-First Century." Pages 679–687 in *The Gnostic World*. Edited by Garry W. Trompf, with Gunner B. Mikkelsen and Jay Johnston. Routledge Worlds. London; New York: Routledge, 2019.

Labarriére, Pierre-Jean. "Providence." *Dictionnaire de spiritualité ascétique et mystique* 12 (1986):2464–2476.

Larson, Jennifer. *Understanding Greek Religion: A Cognitive Approach*. Understanding the Ancient World. London; New York: Routledge, Taylor & Francis Group, 2016.

Lashier, Jackson. *Irenaeus on the Trinity*. VCSup. 127. Leiden; Boston: Brill, 2014.

Layton, Bentley. *The Gnostic Scriptures*. New York: Doubleday, 1987.

Layton, Bentley. "The *Hypostasis of the Archons*. Critical Edition and Translation." Pages

234–259 in *Nag Hammadi Codex II, 2–7. Vol. 1*. Edited by Bentley Layton. NHS 20. Leiden: Brill, 1989.

Layton, Bentley. "Prolegomena to the Study of Ancient Gnosticism." Pages 334–350 in *The Social World of the First Christians: Essays in Honor of Wayne Meeks*. Edited by L. Michael White and Larry O. Yarbrough. Minneapolis: Fortress Press, 1995.

Layton, Bentley. "The Significance of Basilides in Ancient Christian Thought."*Representations* 28 (1989): 135–151.

Lazier, Benjamin. *God Interrupted: Heresy and the European Imagination between the World Wars*. Princeton: Princeton University Press, 2008.

Leo XIII. "Providentissimus Deus." Accessed 21 August 2019. http://w2.vatican.va/content/leo-xiii/en/encyclicals/documents/hf_l-xiii_enc_18111893_providentissimus-deus.html

Leonhardt-Balzer, Jutta. "Evil at Qumran." Pages 17–33 in *Evil in Second Temple Judaism and Early Christianity*. Edited by Chris Keith and Loren T. Tuckenbruck. WUNT 417. Tübingen: Mohr Siebeck, 2016.

Létourneau, Pierre. "Creation in Gnostic Christian Texts, or: What Happens to the Cosmos when its Maker is not the Highest God?" Pages 415–434 in *Theologies of Creation in Early Judaism and Ancient Christianity. In Honour of Hans Klein*. Edited by Tobias Nicklas, Korinna Zamfir, and Heike Braun. Deuterocanonical and Cognate Literature Studies 6. Berlin; New York: De Gruyter, 2010.

Liddell, Henry George and Robert Scott, eds. *A Greek-English lexicon: With a revised supplement. Compiled by Henry George Liddell and Robert Scott. Revised and augmented throughout by Henry Stuart Jones with the assistance of Roderick McKenzie and with the cooperation of many scholars*, 9th edition. Oxford: Clarendon Press, 1940.

Lienhard, Joseph T. "Introduction." Pages xv–xxxix in *Origen. Homilies on Luke. Fragments on Luke*. FC 94. Washington: Catholic University of America Press, 2009.

Lieu, Judith. *Marcion and the Making of a Heretic: God and Scripture in the Second Century*. New York: Cambridge University Press, 2015.

Lilla, Salvatore R.C. *Clement of Alexandria. A Study in Christian Platonism and Gnosticism*. Oxford: Oxford University Press, 1971.

Lincoln, Abraham. "Second Inaugural Address." Accessed 20 August 2019. https://www.bartleby.com/124/pres32.html

Linjamaa, Paul. *The Ethics of 'The Tripartite Tractate' (NHC I,5). A Study of Determinism and Early Christian Philosophy of Ethics*. NHMS 95. Leiden; Boston: Brill, 2019.

Litwa, M. David. "The God 'Human' and Human Gods: Modes of Deification in Irenaeus and the *Apocryphon of John*," ZAC 18:1 (2013): 70–94.

Litwa, M. David, ed. and tr. *Refutation of All Heresies*. WGRW 40. Atlanta: SBL Press, 2016.

Lloyd, Antony C. *The Anatomy of Neoplatonism*. Oxford: Clarendon Press, 1990.

Lloyd, Genevieve. *Providence Lost*. Cambridge: Harvard University Press, 2008.

BIBLIOGRAPHY

Long, Anthony A. *Epictetus: A Stoic and Socratic Guide to Life*. Oxford: Oxford University Press, 2002.

Long, Anthony A. *Hellenistic Philosophy: Stoics, Epicureans, Skeptics*. Berkeley; Los Angeles: University of California Press, 1986.

Long, Anthony A. "Stoicism in the Philosophical Tradition: Spinoza, Lipsius, Butler." Pages 365–392 in *The Cambridge Companion to the Stoics*. Edited by Brad Inwood. Cambridge: Cambridge University Press, 2003.

Long, Anthony A., and David Sedley, eds. and trs. *The Hellenistic Philosophers*. 2 vols. Cambridge: Cambridge University Press, 1987.

Losekam, Claudia. *Die Sünde der Engel. Die Engelfalltradition in frühjüdischen und gnostischen Texten*. Texte und Arbeiten zum Neutestamentlichen Zeitalter 41. Tübingen: Franke, 2012.

Louth, Andrew. "Pagans and Christians on Providence." Pages 279–297 in *Texts and Culture in Late Antiquity: Inheritance, Authority, and Change*. Edited by J.H.D. Scourfield. Swansea: The Classical Press of Wales, 2007.

Löhr, Winrich. *Basilides und seine Schule: Eine Studie zur Theologie- und Kirchengeschichte des zweiten Jahrhunderts*. WUNT 83. Tübingen: Mohr, 1996.

Löhr, Winrich. "Did Marcion Distinguish Between a Just God and a Good God?" Pages 131–146 in *Marcion und seine kirchengeschichtliche Wirkung. Vorträge der Internationalen Fachkonferenz zu Marcion, gehalten vom 15.–19. August 2001 in Mainz*. Edited by Gerhard May, Katharina Greschat, and Martin Meiser. TUGAL 150. Berlin: De Gruyter, 2002.

Löhr, Winrich. "Gnostic Determinism Reconsidered." *VC* 46 (1992): 381–390.

Macaskill, Grant. "History, Providence, and the Apocalyptic Paul." *Scottish Journal of Theology* 70:4 (2017): 409–426.

Macaskill, Grant. *Revealed Wisdom and Inaugurated Eschatology in Ancient Judaism and Early Christianity*. JSJSup 115. Leiden: Brill, 2007.

MacRae, George, ed. and tr. "*Authoritative Teaching*." Pages 257–289 in *Nag Hammadi Codices V,2–5 and VI, with Papyrus Berolinensis 8502, "1" and "4*." Edited by Douglas M. Parrott. NHS 11. Leiden: Brill, 1979.

MacRae, George. "The Jewish Background of the Gnostic Sophia Myth." *Novum Testamentum* 12 (1970): 86–101.

Machinist, Peter. "Fate, *miqreh*, and Reason: Some Reflections on Qohelet and Biblical Thought." Pages 159–175 in *Solving Riddles and Untying Knots: Biblical Epigraphic and Semitic Studies in Honor of Jonas C. Greenfield*. Edited by Ziony Zevit, Seymour Gitin, and Michael Sokoloff. Winona Lake: Eisenbrauns, 1995.

Magee, John. "Introduction." Pages vii–xxvi in Calcidius. *On Plato's 'Timaeus'*. Edited and translated by John Magee. Dumbarton Oaks Medieval Library 41. Cambridge; London: Harvard University Press, 2016.

Mahé, Jean-Pierre, ed. and tr. *Le Témoignage Véritable (NH IX,3): Gnose et martyre*. BCNH

Section "Textes," 23. Québec; Louvain; Paris: Les presses de l'université Laval; Peeters, 1996.

Majercik, Ruth, ed. and tr. *The Chaldean Oracles: Text, Translation, and Commentary.* Studies in Greek and Roman Religion 5. Leiden: Brill, 1989.

Magris, Aldo. *L'idea di destino nel pensiero antico.* 2 vols. Università degli Studi di Trieste, Facoltà di Magistero IIIe serie, 15. Udine: Del Bianco editore, 1984–1985.

Manilius. *Astronomica.* Edited and translated by George P. Gould. LCL 469. Cambridge; London: Harvard University Press, 1997.

Mansfeld, Jaap. "Bad World and Demiurge: A Gnostic Motif from Parmenides and Empedocles to Lucretius and Philo." Pages 261–314 in *Studies in Gnosticism and Hellenistic Religions: Studies Presented to Gilles Quispel on the Occasion of his 65th Birthday.* Edited by Roelof van den Broek and Maarten J. Vermaseren. EPRO 91. Leiden: Brill, 1981.

Mansfeld, Jaap. "*Diaphonia*: the Argument of Alexander *De fato* chs. 1–2." *Phronesis* 33:2 (1988): 181–207.

Mansfeld, Jaap. "Providence and the Destruction of the Universe in Early Stoicism." Pages 129–188 in *Studies in Hellenistic Religions.* Edited by Maarten J. Vermaseren. EPRO 68. Leiden: Brill, 1979.

Mansfeld, Jaap. "Theology." Pages 462–478 in *The Cambridge History of Hellenistic Philosophy.* Edited by Keimpe Algra, Jonathan Barnes, Jaap Mansfeld, and Malcolm Schofield. Cambridge: Cambridge University Press, 1999.

Marchetti, Sandra Citroni. *Plinio il Vecchio e la traditzione del moralismo romano.* Biblioteca di Materiali e discussion per l'analisi dei testi classici 9. Pisa: Giardini, 1991.

Marcovich, Miroslav. "Introduction." Pages 3–22 in *Pseudo-Iustinus. Cohoratio ad Graecos, De monarchia, Oratio ad Graecos.* Edited by Miroslav Marcovich. Patristische Texte und Studien 32. Berlin; New York; De Gruyter, 1990.

Marcus Aurelius. *Marcus Aurelius.* Edited and translated by C.R. Haines. LCL 58. Cambridge; London: Harvard University Press, 1999.

Marcus Eremita. *Traités I.* Edited and translated by Georges-Matthieu de Durand. SC 445. Paris: Éditions du Cerf, 1999.

Marjanen, Antti. "Gnosticism." Pages 203–217 in *The Oxford Handbook of Early Christian Studies.* Edited by Susan Ashbrook Harvey and David G. Hunter. Oxford: Oxford University Press, 2008.

Markschies, Christoph. "Die valentinianische Gnosis und Marcion—einige neue Perspektiven." Pages 159–175 in *Marcion und seine kirchengeschichtliche Wirkung. Vorträge der Internationalen Fachkonferenz zu Marcion, gehalten vom 15.–19. August 2001 in Mainz.* Edited by Gerhard May, Katharina Greschat, and Martin Meiser. TUGAL 150. Berlin: De Gruyter, 2002.

Markschies, Christoph. *Gnosis.* Translated by John Bowden. London: T&T Clark, 2003.

Markschies, Christoph. "New Research on Ptolemaeus Gnosticus." *ZAC* 4:2 (2000): 225–254.

Markschies, Christoph. *Valentinus Gnosticus? Untersuchungen zur valentinianischen Gnosis; mit einem Kommentar zu den Fragmenten Valentins.* WUNT 65. Tübingen: Mohr Siebeck, 1992.

Martens, Peter W. "Embodiment, Heresy, and the Hellenization of Christianity: The Descent of the Soul in Plato and Origen." *HTR* 108:4 (2015): 594–620.

Martens, Peter W. "Origen's Doctrine of Pre-Existence and the Opening Chapters of Genesis." *ZAC* 16 (2013): 516–549.

Martin, Dale. "When Did Angels Become Demons?" *JBL* 129:4 (2010): 657–677.

Martin, Jean-Pierre. *Providentia deorum: recherches sur certains aspects religieux du pouvoir impérial romain.* Roma: École française de Rome, 1982.

Martin, Luther. "Josephus' Use of Heimarmene in the Jewish Antiquities XIII,171–3." *Numen* 28 (1981): 127–131.

Martínez, Florentino García, and Eibert J.C. Tigchelaar, eds. and trs. *The Dead Sea Scrolls: Study Edition.* 2 vols. Leiden: Brill, 1997.

Mason, Steve. "Text and Commentary." Pages 1–420 in idem, *Flavius Josephus. Translation and Commentary. Volume 1 B. Judean War 2.* Leiden; Boston: Brill, 2008.

Mason, Steve. "Jews, Judaeans, Judaizing, Judaism: Problems of Categorization in Ancient History." *Journal for the Study of Judaism* 38:4 (2005): 457–512

Mattila, Sharon Lea. "Ben Sira and the Stoics: A Reexamination of the Evidence." *JBL* 119:3 (2000): 473–501.

Maximus of Tyre. *Dissertationes.* Edited by Michael B. Trapp. Bibliotheca scriptorium Graecorum et Romanorum Teubneriana. Leipzig: B.G. Teubner, 2011.

Maximus of Tyre. *The Philosophical Orations.* Translated by Michael B. Trapp. Oxford: Clarendon Press, 1997.

May, Gerhard. "Eschatologie v. Alte Kirche." *TRE* 10:299–305.

Mazur, Zeke. "The Platonizing Sethian Gnostic Background of Plotinus' Mysticism." Ph.D. diss., University of Chicago, 2010.

Mazur, Zeke. "Self-Manifestation and 'Primary Revelation' in the Platonizing Sethian Ascent Treatises and Plotinian Mysticism." Paper presented at the Nag Hammadi and Gnosticism section at the annual meeting of the Society of Biblical Literature in Boston, November 2008.

Melton, Brittany. *Where is God in the 'Megilloth'? A Dialogue on the Ambiguity of Divine Presence and Absence.* Oudtestamentische Studiën 73. Leiden; Boston: Brill, 2018.

Meyer, Marvin. "Thought, Forethought, and Afterthought in the *Secret Book of John.*" Pages 217–231 in *Beyond the Gnostic Gospels: Studies Building on the Work of Elaine Pagels.* Edited by Eduard Iricinschi, Lance Jenott, Nicola Denzey Lewis, and Philippa Townsend. STAC 82. Tübingen: Mohr Siebeck, 2013.

Meyer, Susan Sauvé. "Chain of Causes: What is Stoic Fate?" Pages 71–89 in *God and the Cosmos in Stoicism.* Edited by Ricardo Salles. Oxford: Oxford University Press, 2010.

Michalewski, Alexandra. "Faut-il préférer Épicure à Aristote? Quelques réflexions sur la providence." Pages 123–142 in *Réceptions de la théologie aristotélicienne. D'Aristote à*

Michel d'Éphèse. Edited by Fabienne Baghdassarian and Gweltaz Guyomarc'h. Aristote. Traductions et Études. Louvain-la-neuve: Peeters, 2017.

Mignucci, Mario. "Logic and Omniscience: Alexander of Aphrodisias and Proclus." *Oxford Studies in Ancient Philosophy* 3 (1985): 219–246.

Mincius Felix. *Octavius*. Edited and translated by Gerald H. Rendall. LCL 250. Cambridge: Harvard University Press, 1977.

Mitralexis, Sotiris, and Georgios Steiris and Sebastian Lilla. "Introduction." Pages xxi–xxiv in *Maximus Confessor as a European Philosopher*. Veritas 25. Eugene: Cascade, 2017.

Moore, George Foot. "Fate and Free Will in the Jewish Philosophies According to Josephus." *HTR* 22:4 (1929): 371–389.

Moreschini, Claudio. "Tertullian's *Adversus Marcionem* and Middleplatonism." *ZAC* 21:1 (2017): 140–163.

Mayhew, Robert. "Aristotle on Prayer." *Rhizai* 4:2 (2007): 295–309.

Meijering, Eginhard P. *Tertullian Contra Marcion. Gotteslehre in der Polemik. Adversus Marcionen I–II*. Philosophia Patrum 3. Leiden: Brill, 1977.

Michalka, Wolfgang (ed.). *Das Dritte Reich: Dokumente zur Innen- und Außenpolitik. Band 2. Weltmachtanspruch und nationaler Zusammenbruch, 1939–1945*. München: Deutscher Taschenbuch, 1985.

Morrow, Glenn. "Necessity and Persuasion in Plato's *Timaeus*." *Philosophical Review* 59:2 (1950): 147–163.

Murphy, Francesca Aran and Philip G. Ziegler, eds. *The Providence of God*. London; New York: T&T Clark, 2009.

Musurillo, Herbert, ed. and tr. *The Acts of the Christian Martyrs*. Oxford: Clarendon Press, 1972.

Müller, Jörn, and Roberto Hofmeister Pich. "Auf dem Weg zum Willen? Eine problemgeschichtliche Hinführung zur Genese des philosophischen Willensbegriffs in Kaiserzeit und Spätantike." Pages 1–22 in *Wille und Handlung in der Philosophie der Kaiserzeit und Spätantike*. Edited by Jörn Müller and Roberto Hofmeister Pich. BzA 287. Berlin; Boston: De Gruyter, 2010.

Nagel, Peter. "Über das Verhältnis von Gnosis und Manichäismus, oder: Wie gnostisch ist die Gnosis des Mani?" Pages 121–139 in *Vom "Troglodytenland" ins Reich der Scheherazade. Archäologie, Kunst und Religion zwischen Okzident und Orient. Festschrift für Piotr O. Scholz zum 70. Geburtstag*. Edited by Magdalena Drugosz. Berlin: Frank & Timme 2014.

Nagel, Peter, tr. *Der Tractatus Tripartitus aus Nag Hammadi Codex I (Codex Jung)*. STAC 1. Tübingen: Mohr Siebeck, 1998.

Nagel, Svenja. "Mittelplatonische Konzepte der Göttin Isis bei Plutarch und Apuleius im Vergleich mit ägyptischen Quellen der griechischrömischen Zeit." Pages 79–126 in *Platonismus und spätägyptische Rebligion. Plutarch und die Ägyptenrezeption in der römischen Kaiserzeit*. Edited by Michael Erler and Martin A. Stadler. BzA 364. Berlin; Boston: De Gruyter, 2017.

Narbonne, Jean-Marc. *Plotinus in Dialogue with the Gnostics*. SPNPT 11. Leiden: Brill, 2011.

Nasrallah, Laura Salah. "'I Do Not Wish to Be Rich': the 'Barbarian' Christian Tatian Responds to *Sortes*." Pages 290–308 in *My Lots are in Thy Hands: Sortilege and its Practitioners in Late Antiquity*. Edited by AnneMarie Luijendijk and William E. Klingshirn, with Lance Jenott. RGRW 188. Leiden; Boston: Brill, 2019.

Nasrallah, Laura Salah. "Lot Oracles and Fate: On Early Christianity among Others in the Second Century." Pages 214–232 in *Christianity in the Second Century: Themes and Developments*. Edited by James Carleton Paget and Judith Lieu. Cambridge: Cambridge University Press, 2017.

Nautin, Pierre. "Les fragments de Basilide sur la souffrance et leur interpretations par Clément d'Alexandrie et Origène." Pages 393–404 in *Mélanges d'histoire des religions offert à Henri-Charles Puech*. Paris: Presses Universitaires de France, 1974.

Nautin, Pierre. *Origène. Sa vie et son oeuvre*. Christianisme antique 1. Paris: Beauchesne, 1977.

Nemesius of Emesa. *On the Nature of Man*. Translated by Robert W. Sharples and Philip J. van der Eijk. TTH 49. Liverspool: Liverpool University Press, 2008.

Niehoff, Maren R. *Philo of Alexandria: An Intellectual Biography*. New Haven; London: Yale University Press, 2018.

Noble, Christopher Isaac and Nathan M. Powers. "Creation and Divine Providence in Plotinus." Pages 51–70 in *Causation and Creation in Late Antiquity*. Edited by Anna Marmodoro and Brian D. Prince. Cambridge: Cambridge University Press, 2015.

Nock, Arthur Darby, and Andre-Jean Festugière, eds. and trs. *Corpus Hermeticum*. 4 vols. Paris: Belles Lettres, 1946–1954.

Nongbri, Brent. *Before Religion: A History of a Modern Concept*. New Haven: Yale University Press, 2013.

Norelli, Enrico. "Marcion: ein christlicher Philosoph oder ein Christ gegen die Philosophie?" Pages 113–130 in *Marcion und seine kirchengeschichtliche Wirkung. Vorträge der Internationalen Fachkonferenz zu Marcion, gehalten vom 15.–19. August 2001 in Mainz*. Edited by Gerhard May, Katharina Greschat, and Martin Meiser. TUGAL 150. Berlin: De Gruyter, 2002.

Numenius. *Numénius. Fragments*. Edited and translated by Édouard des Places. Collection des universités de France Série grecque 226. Paris: Les Belles Lettres, 1973.

O'Brien, Carl Séan. *The Demiurge in Ancient Thought: Secondary Gods and Divine Mediators*. Cambridge: Cambridge University Press, 2015.

O'Brien, Carl Séan. "Prayer in Maximus of Tyre." Pages 58–71 in *Platonic Theories of Prayer*. Edited by John M. Dillon and Andrei Timotin. SPNPT 19. Leiden: Brill, 2015.

O'Meara, Dominic J. "Introduction." Pages ix–xviii in *Neoplatonism and Christian*

Thought. Edited by Dominic J. O'Meara. SNAM 3. Norfolk: International Society for Neoplatonic Studies, 1982.

Onuki, Takashi. *Gnosis und Stoa. Eine Untersuchung zum apokryphon des Johannes.* Novum Testamentum et Orbis Antiquus 9. Freiburg; Göttingen: Van den Hoeck & Ruprecht, 1989.

Onuki, Takashi. "Die dreifache Pronoia. Zur Beziehung zwischen Gnosis, Stoa und Mittelplatonismus." Pages 240–270 in idem, *Heil und Erlösung*. WUNT 165. Tübingen: Mohr Siebeck, 2004.

Opsomer, Jan. "The Middle Platonic Doctrine of Conditional Fate." Pages 137–167 in *Fate, Providence and Moral Responsibility in Ancient, Medieval and Early Modern Thought: Studies in Honour of Carlos Steel*. Edited by Pieter d'Hoine and Gerd van Riel. AMP 1. Leuven: Leuven University Press, 2014.

Opsomer, Jan and Carlos Steel. "Evil Without a Cause: Proclus' Doctrine on the Origin of Evil, and its Antecedents in Hellenistic Philosophy." Pages 229–260 in *Zur Rezeption der hellenistischen Philosophie in der Spätantike. Akten der 1. Tagung der Karl-und-Gertrud-Abel-Stiftung vom 22.–25. September 1997 in Trier*. Edited by Therese Fuhrer and Michael Erler, with Karin Schlapbach. Philosophie der Antike 9. Stuttgart: Steiner, 1999.

Origen. *Commentary on the Epistle to the Romans*. Translated by Thomas P. Scheck. 2 vols. FC 103–104. Washington: Catholic University of America Press, 2001–2002.

Origen. *Commentary on the Gospel According to John: Books 1–10*. Translated by Ronald E. Heine. FC 80. Washington: Catholic University of America Press, 1989.

Origen. *Contra Celsus*. Translated by Henry Chadwick. Cambridge: Cambridge University Press, 1980.

Origen. *Contre Celse*. Edited and translated by Marcel Borret. 5 vols. SC 132, 136, 147, 150, 227. Paris: Éditions du Cerf, 1967–1976.

Origen. *Homilies on Luke. Fragments on Luke*. Translated by Joseph Lienhard. FC 94. Washington: Catholic University of America Press, 2009.

Origen. *Homélies sur S. Luc. Texte latin et fragments grecs*. Edited and translated by Henri Crouzel, François Fournier, and Pierre Périchon. SC 87. Paris: Éditions du Cerf, 1962.

Origen. *Homilies on Jeremiah, Homily on 1 Kings 28*. Translated by John Clark Smith. FC 97. Washington: Catholic University of America Press, 1998.

Origen. *On First Principles*. Edited and translated by John Behr. 2 vols. OECT. Oxford: Oxford University Press, 2017–2018.

Origen. *Philocalia*. Edited and translated by Eric Junod. SC 226. Paris: Éditions du Cerf, 2006.

Osborn, Eric. *Clement of Alexandria*. Cambridge: Cambridge University Press, 2005.

Osborn, Eric. *Irenaeus of Lyons*. Cambridge: Cambridge University Press, 2001.

O'Sullivan, Timothy M. *Walking in Roman Culture*. Cambridge: Cambridge University Press, 2011.

BIBLIOGRAPHY

Pagels, Elaine. "'The Demiurge and His Archons': A Gnostic View of the Bishop and Presbyters?" *HTR* 69:3/4 (1976): 301–324.

Pagels, Elaine. *The Johannine Gospel in Gnostic Exegesis. Heracleon's Commentary on John*. Nashville: Abingdon Press, 1973.

Pagels, Elaine. "The Social History of Satan, the 'Intimate Enemy': A Preliminary Sketch." *HTR* 84:2 (1991): 105–128.

Painchaud, Louis. "Commentaire: *L'écrit sans titre*." Pages 219–526 in *L'écrit sans titre. Traité sur l'origine du monde (NH II, 5 et XIII, 2 et Brit. Lob. Or. 4926[1])*. Edited and translated by Louis Painchaud. BCNH Section "Textes," 21. Québec; Louvain: Les presses de l'université Laval; Peeters, 1995.

Painchaud, Louis, ed. and tr. "Texte et traduction: *L'écrit sans titre*," Pages 145–218 in *L'écrit sans titre. Traité sur l'origine du monde (NH II, 5 et XIII, 2 et Brit. Lob. Or. 4926[1])*. Edited and translated by Louis Painchaud. BCNH "Textes," 21. Québec; Louvain: Les presses de l'université Laval; Peeters, 1995.

Parker, Robert. "The Origins of Pronoia: A Mystery." Pages 84–94 in *Apodosis. Essays presented to Dr W. W. Cruickshank to mark his eightieth birthday*. London: St. Paul's School, 1992.

Parma, Christian. *Pronoia und Providentia. Der Vorsehungsbegriff Plotins und Augustins. Studien zur Problemgeschichte der antiken und mittelalterlichen Philosophie* 6. Leiden: Brill, 1971.

Parthenius. *The Love Romances*. Translated by S. Gaselee. LCL 69. London; New York; William Heinemann; G.P. Putnam's Sons, 1916.

Payne Smith, J. *A Compendious Syriac Dictionary. Founded Upon the 'Thesaurus Syriacus' of R. Payne Smith, D.D.* Oxford: Oxford University Press, 1957.

Pearson, Birger. "Basilides the Gnostic." Pages 1–31 in *A Companion to Second-Century Christian "Heretics"*. Edited by Antti Marjanen and Petri Luomanen. VCSup. 76. Leiden; Boston: Brill, 2008.

Pearson, Birger. "Philo and Gnosticism." *ANRW* 2.22.1 (1984): 295–342.

Pedersen, Nils Arne. *Demonstrative Proof in Defence of God: A Study of Titus of Bostra's 'Contra Manichaeos'—The Work's Sources, Aims and Relation to its Contemporary Theology*. NHMS 56. Leiden; Boston: Brill, 2004.

Peel, Malcolm, ed. and tr. "The *Teachings of Silvanus*: Text, Translation, and Notes." Pages 278–369 in *Nag Hammadi Codex VII*. Edited by Birger Pearson. NHMS 30. Leiden: Brill, 1996.

Pépin, Jean. "Cosmic Piety." Pages 408–435 in *Classical Mediterranean Spirituality: Egyptian, Greek, Roman*. Edited by Arthur Hillary Armstrong. World Spirituality: an Encyclopedic History of the Religious Quest 15. London: Routledge & Kegan Paul, 1986.

Pépin, Jean. "Prière et providence au 2e siècle." Pages 111–125 in *Images of Man. Studia G. Verbeke Dicata*. Edited by Fernand Bossier. Leuven: Leuven University Press, 1976.

Perkams, Matthias. "Einheit und Vielfalt der Philosophie von der Kaiserzeit zur ausgehenden Antike." Pages 3–32 in *PHILOSOPHIA in der Konkurrenz von Schulen, Wissenschaften Und Religionen: Zur Pluralisierung des Philosophiebegriffs in Kaiserzeit Und Spätantike*. Edited by Christoph Riedweg. Philosophie der Antike 34. Berlin; Boston: De Gruyter, 2017.

Perkams, Matthias. "Ethischer Intellektualismus und Willensbegriff. Handlungstheorie beim griechischen und lateinischen Origenes." Pages 239–258 in *Wille und Handlung in der Philosophie der Kaiserzeit und Spätantike*. Edited by Jörn Müller and Roberto Hofmeister Pich. BzA 287. Berlin; Boston: De Gruyter, 2010.

Perkins, Pheme. *The Gnostic Dialogue: The Early Church and the Crisis of Gnosticism*. New York: Paulist Press, 1980.

Perkins, Pheme. "*On the Origin of the World* (CG II,5): A Gnostic Physics." *VC* 34:1 (1980): 36–46.

Perkins, Pheme. "Ordering the Cosmos: Irenaeus and the Gnostics." Pages 221–238 in *Nag Hammadi, Gnosticism, & Early Christianity*. Edited by Charles W. Hedrick and Robert Hodgson. Peabody: Hendrickson Publishers, 1986.

Perkins, Pheme. "Logos Christologies in the Nag Hammadi Codices." *VC* 35:4 (1981): 379–396.

Perrin, Andrew B. "An Almanac of Tobit Studies: 2000–2014." *Currents in Biblical Research* 13:1 (2014): 107–142.

Perrone, Lorenzo. "For the Sake of a 'Rational Worship': The Issue of Prayer and Cult in Early Christian Apologetics." Pages 231–264 in *Critique and Apologetics*. Edited by Anders-Christian Jacobsen, Jörg Ulrich, and David Brakke. Early Christianity in the Context of Antiquity 4. Frankfurt am Main: Peter Lang, 2009.

Perrone, Lorenzo. "Ἴχνος ἐνθουσιασμοῦ. Origen, Plato, and the Inspired Scriptures." *Phasis* 2–3 (2000): 319–326.

Perry, Ben Edwin. *Studies in the Text History of the Life and Fables of Aesop*. Philological Monographs Published by the American Philological Association 7. American Philological Association: Haverford, 1936.

Perry, Ben Edwin, ed. *Aesopica. A Series of Texts Relating to Aesop or Ascribed to Him or Closely Connected with the Literary Tradition that Bears His Name. Volume One: Greek and Latin Texts*. Urbana: University of Illinois Press, 1952.

Petersen, William L. "Tatian the Assyrian." Pages 125–158 in *A Companion to Second-Century Christian "Heretics."* Edited by Antti Marjanen and Petri Luomanen. VCSup 76. Leiden: Brill, 2005.

Philippson, Robert. "Die Quelle der epikureischen Götterlehre in Ciceros erstem Buche *De natura deorum*." *Symbolae Osloenses* 19:1 (1939): 15–40.

Philo of Alexandria. *Every Good Man is Free. On the Contemplative Life. On the Eternity of the World. Against Flaccus. Apology for the Jews. On Providence*. Edited and translated by Francis H. Colson. LCL 363. Cambridge: Harvard University Press, 1941.

BIBLIOGRAPHY   351

Philo of Alexandria. *On Abraham. On Joseph. On Moses.* Edited and translated by Francis H. Colson. LCL 289. Cambridge: Harvard University Press, 1935.

Philo of Alexandria. *On the Cherubim. The Sacrifices of Abel and Cain. The Worse Attacks the Better. On the Posterity and Exile of Cain. On the Giants.* Edited and translated by Francis H. Colson and George H. Whitaker, LCL 227. Cambridge: Harvard University Press, 1929.

Philo of Alexandria. *On the Creation. Allegorical Interpretation of Genesis 2 and 3.* Edited and translated by Francis H. Colson and George H. Whitaker, LCL 226. Cambridge: Harvard University Press, 1929.

Philo of Alexandria. *On the Decalogue. On Special Laws.* Edited and translated by Francis H. Colson. LCL 320. Cambridge: Harvard University Press, 1929.

Philo of Alexandria. *On Flight and Finding. On the Change of Names. On Dreams.* Edited and translated by Francis H. Colson and George H. Whitaker. LCL 275. Cambridge: Harvard University Press, 1934.

Philo of Alexandria. *On the Unchangeableness of God. On Husbandry. Concerning Noah's Work As a Planter. On Drunkenness. On Sobriety.* Edited and translated by Francis H. Colson and George H. Whitaker. LCL 247. Cambridge: Harvard University Press, 1930.

Philo of Alexandria. *Questions on Genesis.* Edited and translated by Ralph Marcus. LCL 380. Cambridge: Harvard University Press, 1953.

Pich, Roberto Hofmeister. "Προαίρεσις und Freiheit bei Epiktet: Ein Beitrag zur philosophischen Geschichte des Willensbegriffs." Pages 95–127 in *Wille und Handlung in der Philosophie der Kaiserzeit und Spätantike.* Edited by Jörn Müller and Roberto Hofmeister Pich. BzA 287. Berlin; Boston: De Gruyter, 2010.

Pietersma, Albert and Benjamin G. Wright, eds. *A New English Trnaslation of the Septuagint and the Other Greek Translations Traditionally Included under That Title.* New York; Oxford: Oxford University Press, 2007.

Plantinga, Alvin. *The Nature of Necessity.* Oxford: Clarendon Press, 1982.

Pleše, Zlatko. "Evil and its Sources in Gnostic Traditions." Pages 101–132 in *Die Wurzel allen Übels. Vorstellungen über die Herkunft des Bösen und schlechten in der Philosophie und Religion des 1.–4. Jahrhunderts.* Edited by Fabienne Jourdan and Rainer Hirsch-Luipold. Ratio Religionis Studien 3. Tübingen: Mohr Siebeck, 2014.

Pleše, Zlatko. "Fate, Providence, and Astrology in Gnosticism (1): The *Apocryphon of John.*" *MHNH: International Journal of Research on Ancient Magic and Astrology* 7 (2007): 237–268

Pleše, Zlatko. "Gnostic Literature." Pages 163–198 in *Religiöse Philosophie und philosophische Religion der frühen Kaiserzeit. Literaturgeschichtliche Perspektiven.* Edited by Rainer Hirsch-Luipold, Herwig Görgemanns, and Michael von Albrecht, with Tobias Thum. Ratio Religionis Studien 1/STAC 51. Tübingen: Mohr Siebeck, 2009.

Pliny the Elder. *Natural History: Books 1–2.* Edited and translated by Harris Rackham. LCL 330. Cambridge: Harvard University Press, 1938.

Pliny the Elder. *Natural History: Books 3–7*. Edited and translated by Harris Rackham. LCL 352. Cambridge: Harvard University Press, 1942.

Plotinus. *Enneads*. Edited and translated by Arthur Hilary Armstrong. 7 vol. LCL 440–445, 468. Cambridge: Harvard University Press, 1966–1988.

Plutarch. *Moralia, Volume V: Isis and Osiris. The E at Delphi. The Oracles at Delphi No Longer Given in Verse. The Obsolescence of Oracles*. Edited and translated by Frank Cole Babbitt. LCL 306. Cambridge; London: Harvard University Press, 1993.

Plutarch. *Moralia, Volume VII: On Love of Wealth. On Compliancy. On Envy and Hate. On Praising Oneself Inoffensively. On the Delays of Divine Vengeance. On the Sign of Socrates. On Exile. Consolation to His Wife*. Edited and translated by Phillip H. de Lacy and Benedict Einarson. LCL 405. Cambridge; London: Harvard University Press, 1953.

Poirier, Paul-Hubert. "Deux doxographies sur le destin et le gouvernement du monde." Pages 761–786 in *Coptica—Gnostica—Manichaica: Mélanges offerts à Wolf-Peter Funk*. Edited by Louis Painchaud and Paul-Hubert Poirier. BCNH Section "Études" 7. Québec: Presses de l'université Laval; Leuven: Peeters, 2006.

Poirier, Paul-Hubert. "The *Three Forms of First Thought* and the *Secret Book of John*." Pages 23–39 in *Gnosticism, Platonism, and the Late Ancient World. Essays in Honour of John D. Turner*. Edited by Kevin Corrigan and Tuomas Rasimus, with Dylan M. Burns, Lance Jenott, and Zeke Mazur. NHMS 82. Leiden: Brill, 2013.

Poirier, Paul-Hubert, ed. and tr. *La pensée première à la triple forme*. BCNH Section "Textes" 32. Québec: Presses de l'université Laval; Leuven: Peeters, 2006.

Polybius. *The Histories: Books 1–2*. Translated by William R. Paton. LCL 128. Cambridge: Harvard University Press, 1922.

Popović, Mladen. "Apocalyptic Determinism." Pages 255–270 in *The Oxford Handbook of Apocalyptic Literature*. Edited by John J. Collins. New York: Oxford University Press, 2014.

Porphyry. *Fragmenta*. Edited by Andrew Smith. Leipzig: Teubner, 1999.

Porphyry. "The Fragments of Porphyry's *Against Nemertius* in Translation, With an Appendix." Translated by Ludwig Maisel. Unpublished.

Porphyry. *Sentences*. Edited by Luc Brisson. 2 vols. Histoire des doctrines de l'antiquité classique 33. Paris: J. Vrin, 2005.

Possekel, Ute. "Bardaisan of Edessa: Philosopher or Theologian?" *ZAC* 10:3 (2007): 442–461.

Possekel, Ute. "Bardaisan and Origen on Fate and the Power of Stars." *JECS* 20:4 (2012): 515–541.

Possekel, Ute. "Bardaisan's Influence on Late Antique Christianity." *Hugoye: Journal of Syriac Studies* 21:1 (2018): 81–125.

Pouderon, Bernard. *Athénagore d'Athènes: Philosophe chrétien*. Théologie historique 82. Paris: Beauchesne, 1989.

Preisigke, Friedrich. *Wörterbuch der griechischen Papyrusurkunden mit Einschluß der*

BIBLIOGRAPHY

griechischen Inschriften, Aufschriften, Ostraka, Mumienschilder usw. aus Ägypten. Edited by Emil Kießling. Berlin: privately printed, 1925–1931.

Price, Simon. "Latin Christian Apologetics: Minucius Felix, Tertullian, and Cyprian." Pages 105–129 in in *Apologetics in the Roman Empire: Pagans, Jews, and Christians.* Edited by Mark Edwards, Martin Goodman, and Simon Price, with Christopher Rowland. Oxford: Oxford University Press, 1999.

Proclus. *Commentary on Plato's "Timaeus." Vol. 1, book 1: Proclus on the Socratic State and Atlantis.* Translated by Harold Tarrant. Cambridge: Cambridge University Press, 2007.

Proclus. *Commentary on Plato's "Timaeus." Vol. 2, book 2: Proclus on the Causes of the Cosmos and its Creation.* Translated by David Runia and Michael Share. Cambridge: Cambridge University Press, 2008.

Proclus. *Elements of Theology.* Edited and translated by Eric R. Dodds. Oxford: Oxford University Press, 1963.

Proclus. *In Platonis Timaeum Commentarii.* Edited by Ernst Diehl. 3 vols. Leipzig: Teubner, 1903–1906.

Proclus. *Théologie Platonicienne.* Edited and translated by Henri-Dominique Saffrey and Leendert Gerrit Westerink. 6 vols. Paris: Les belles lettres, 1968–1997.

Procter, Everett. *Christian Controversy in Alexandria: Clement's Polemic against the Basilideans and Valentinians.* American University Studies 172. New York: Peter Lang, 1995.

Putnam, Hilary. "Brains in a Vat." Pages 1–21 in idem, *Reason, Truth, and History.* Cambridge: Cambridge University Press, 1981.

Radice, Roberto. "Philo's Theology and Theory of Creation." Translated by Adam Kamesar. Pages 124–154 in the *Cambridge Companion to Philo.* Edited by Adam Kamesar. Cambridge: Cambridge University Press, 2009.

Rajak, Tessa. "The Gifts of God at Sardis." Pages 229–240 in *Jews in a Greco-Roman World.* Edited by Martin Goodman. Oxford: Clarendon Press, 1998.

Rajak, Tessa. "Talking at Trypho: Christian Apologetic as Anti-Judaism in Justin's *Dialogue with Trypho the Jew.*" Pages 59–80 in *Apologetics in the Roman Empire: Pagans, Jews, and Christians.* Edited by Mark Edwards, Martin Goodman, and Simon Price, with Christopher Rowland. Oxford: Oxford University Press, 1999.

Rapp, Christof. "Tackling Aristotle's Notion of the Will." *International Philosophical Inquiry* 41:2–3 (2017): 67–79.

Ramelli, Ilaria L.E. *Bardaiṣan of Edessa: A Reassessment of the Evidence and a New Interpretation.* Piscataway: Gorgias Press, 2009.

Ramelli, Ilaria L.E. "Origen and the Platonic Tradition." *Religions* 8(2):21 (2017).

Rankin, David. *Athenagoras: Philosopher and Theologian.* Farnham; Burlington: Ashgate, 2009.

Rasimus, Tuomas. "The Johannine Background of the Being-Life-Mind Triad." Pages

369–409 in *Gnosticism, Platonism, and the Late Ancient World. Essays in Honour of John D. Turner*. Edited by Kevin Corrigan and Tuomas Rasimus, with Dylan M. Burns, Lance Jenott, and Zeke Mazur. NHMS 82. Leiden; Boston: Brill, 2013.

Rasimus, Tuomas. *Paradise Reconsidered in Gnostic Mythmaking: Rethinking Sethianism in Light of the Ophite Evidence*. NHMS 68. Leiden: Brill, 2009.

Rasimus, Tuomas. "Porphyry and the Gnostics: Reassessing Pierre Hadot's Thesis in Light of the Second- and Third-Century Sethian Treatises." Pages 2:81–110 in *Plato's "Parmenides" and Its Heritage*. Edited by Kevin Corrigan and John D. Turner. 2. vols. WGRWSup 2–3. Atlanta: SBL, 2010.

Rasimus, Tuomas. "The Three Descents of Barbelo and Sethian Initiation in the *Trimorphic Protennoia*." Pages 241–252 in *Christianisme des origines: Mélanges en l'honneur du Professeur Paul-Hubert Poirier*. Edited by Eric Crégheur, Julio Cesar Dias Chaves, and Steve Johnston. Judaïsme antique et origines du christianisme 11. Turnhout: Brepols, 2018.

Räisänen, Heikki. "Marcion." Pages 100–124 *in A Companion to Second-Century "Heretics."* Edited by Antti Marjanen and Petri Luomanen. VCSup 76. Leiden: Brill, 2005.

Reed, Annette Yoshiko. *Fallen Angels and the History of Judaism and Christianity: The Reception of Enochic Literature*. Cambridge: Cambridge University Press, 2005.

Regev, Eyal. "Early Christianity in Light of New Religious Movements." *Numen* 63:5–6 (2016): 483–510.

Reydams-Schils, Gretchen J. *Demiurge and Providence: Stoic and Platonist Readings of Plato's 'Timaeus.'* Turnhout: Brépols, 1999.

Reydams-Schils, Gretchen J. "Maximus of Tyre on God and Providence." Pages 125–139 in *Selfhood and the Soul: Essays on Ancient Thought and Literature in Honour of Christopher Gill*. Edited by Richard Seaford, John Wilkins, and Matthew Wright. Oxford: Oxford University Press, 2017.

Reydams-Schils, Gretchen J. "Seneca's Platonism: The Soul and its Divine Origin." Pages 196–215 in *Ancient Models of Mind: Studies in Human and Divine Rationality*. Edited by Andrea Nightingale and David Sedley. Cambridge: Cambridge University Press, 2010.

Riley, Gregory, ed. and tr. "The *Second Treatise of the Great Seth*: Text, Translation, and Notes." Pages 146–199 in *Nag Hammadi Codex VII*. Edited by Birger Pearson. NHMS 30. Leiden: Brill, 1996.

Rist, John M. "The Greek and Latin Texts of the Discussion on Free Will in *De Principiis*, Book III." Pages 97–111 in *Origeniana. Premier colloque international des études origéniennes (Montserrat, 18–21 septembre 1973)*. Edited by Henri Crouzel, Gennaro Lomiento, and Josep Rius-Camps. Quaderni di "Vetera Christianorum" 12. Bari: Istitutio di letteratura christiana antica; Università di Bari, 1975.

Roberge, Michel, ed. and tr. *La Paraphrase de Sem (NH VII, 1)*. BCNH Section "Textes" 25. Québec; Leuven: Les presses de l'Université Laval; Éditions Peeters, 2000.

Robertson, Paul. "Greco-Roman Ethical-Philosophical Influences in Bardaisan's 'Book of the Laws of the Countries'." *VC* 71 (2017): 511–540.

Robinson, James M. *The Nag Hammadi Story*. 2 vols. NHMS 86. Leiden: Brill, 2014.

Rollston, Christopher A. "An Ur-History of the New Testament Devil." Pages 1–16 in *Evil in Second Temple Judaism and Early Christianity*. Edited by Chris Keith and Loren T. Tuckenbruck. WUNT 417. Tübingen: Mohr Siebeck, 2016.

Rosen-Zvi, Ishay. *Demonic Desires: "Yetzer Hara" and the Problem of Evil in Late Antiquity*. Divinations. Philadelphia: University of Pennsylvania Press, 2011.

Roth, Dieter T. "Evil in Marcion's Conception of the Old Testament God." Pages 340–356 in *Evil in Second Temple Judaism and Early Christianity*. Edited by Chris Keith and Loren T. Stuckenbruck. WUNT 417. Tübingen: Mohr Siebeck, 2016.

Roth, Dieter T. *The Text of Marcion's Gospel*. New Testament Tools, Studies and Documents 49. Leiden; Brill, 2015.

Runia, David. *Philo of Alexandria and the 'Timaeus' of Plato*. PA 44. Leiden: Brill, 1986.

Runia, David. "Philo and the Early Christian Fathers." Pages 210–230 in *The Cambridge Companion to Philo*. Edited by Adam Kamesar. Cambridge: Cambridge University Press, 2009.

Runia, David. "Philo and Hellenistic Doxography." Pages 271–312 in *Aëtiana: The Method and Intellectual Context of a Doxographer. Volume Three: Studies in the Doxographical Traditions of Ancient Philosophy*. Edited by Jaap Mansfeld and David Runia. PA 118. Leiden: Brill, 2009.

Russell, Jeffrey Burton. *The Devil: Perceptions of Evil from Antiquity to Primitive Christianity*. Ithaca; London: Cornell University Press, 1977.

Russell, Jeffrey Burton. *Satan: The Early Christian Tradition*. Ithaca; London: Cornell University Press, 1987.

Rüpke, Jörg. "Göttliche Macht ohne Gesicht. Eine religionswissenschaftliche Sondierung." Pages 1–22 in *Vorsehung, Schicksal, und göttliche Macht. Antike Stimmen zu einem aktuellen Thema*. Edited by Reinhard G. Kratz and Hermann Spieckermann. Tübingen: Mohr Siebeck, 2008.

Sacks, Kenneth S. *Diodorus Siculus and the First Century*. Princeton: Princeton University Press, 1990.

Santangelo, Frederico. "Prediction and Divination in Diodorus." *Dialogues d'histoire ancienne* 33:2 (2007): 115–126.

Schallenberg, Magnus. *Freiheit und Determinismus. Ein philosophischer Kommentar zu Ciceros Schrift 'De fato'*. Quellen und Studien zur Philosophie 75. De Gruyter: Berlin; New York, 2008.

Schäfer, Peter. *The Mirror of His Beauty: Feminine Images of God from the Bible to the Early Kabbalah*. Princeton; Oxford: Princeton University Press, 2002.

Scheffczyk, Leo. *Schöpfung und Vorsehung*. Handbuch der Dogmengeschichte 2.2a. Freiburg; Basel; Wien: Herder, 1963.

Schellenberg, Ryan S. "Suspense, Simultaneity, and Divine Providence in the Book of Tobit." *JBL* 130:2 (2011): 313–327.

Schenke, Hans-Martin. "The Phenomenon and Significance of Gnostic Sethianism." Translated by Bentley Layton. Pages 2:588–616 in *The Rediscovery of Gnosticism: Proceedings of the International Conference on Gnosticism*. Edited by Bentley Layton. 2 vols. Leiden: Brill, 1980.

Schmitz, Barbara. "Gott als Figur in deuterokanonischer Literatur." Pages 217–237 in *Gott als Figur. Narratologische Analysen biblischer Texte und ihrer Adaptionen*. Edited by Ute Eisen and Ilse Müllner. Herders Bibilische Studien 82. Freiburg: Herder, 2016.

Schmitz, Barbara. "... Using Different Names, as Zeus and Dis (Arist 16). Concepts of 'God' in the Letter of Aristeas." Pages 703–716 in *Die Septuaginta—Orte und Intentionen. 5. Internationale Fachtagung veranstaltet von Septuaginta Deutsch (LXX.D), Wuppertal 24.–26. Juli 2014*. Edited by Siegfried Kreuzer, Martin Meiser, and Marcus Sigismund. WUNT 361. Tübingen: Mohr Siebeck, 2016.

Schoedel, William R. "Theophilus of Antioch: Jewish Christian?" *Illinois Classical Studies* 18 (1993): 270–297.

Schofield, Malcolm. "Cicero For and Against Divination." *Journal of Roman Studies* 76 (1986): 47–65.

Schottroff, Luise. "*Animae naturaliter salvandae*: Zum Problem der himmlischen Herkunft des Gnostikers." Pages 65–97 in *Christentum und Gnosis*. Edited by Walther Eltester. Beiheft zur Zeitschrift für die neutestamentliche Wissenschaft 37. Berlin: Alfred Töpelmann, 1969.

Schrage, Wolfgang. *Vorsehung Gottes? Zur Rede von der providentia Dei in der Antike und im Neuen Testament*. Neukirchen-Vluyn: Neukirchener Verlag, 2005.

Schroeder, Frederic M. "Ammonius Saccas," *ANRW* 2.36.1 (1987): 493–526.

Schroeder, Frederic M. "Aseity and Connectedness in the Plotinian Philosophy of Providence." Pages 303–317 in *Gnosticism and Later Platonism: Themes, Figures, and Texts*. Edited by John D. Turner and Ruth Majercik. SBL Symposium Series 12. Atlanta: Society of Biblical Literature, 2001.

Schüngel, Paul. "Gnostische Gotteslehren: Zum 7. Und 8. Fragment des Basilides, zu Valentins 5. Fragment und zwei antiken Kommentaren zu diesem Fragment." *VC* 53 (1999): 361–394.

Scott, Alan. *Origen and the Life of the Stars: A History of an Idea*. Oxford: Oxford University Press, 1994.

Scott, Mark S.M. *Journey Back to God: Origen on the Problem of Evil*. Oxford: Oxford, University Press, 2015.

Swartz, Michael D. *The Mechanics of Providence*. Texts and Studies in Ancient Judaism 182. Tübingen: Mohr Siebeck, 2018.

Sebti, Meryem and Daniel De Smet, eds. *The Reception of Avicenna's Theory of Provi-*

dence in Post-Avicennism. Special issue of *Intellectual History of the Islamicate World* 7:1 (2019).

Sedley, David. "The Origins of Stoic God." Pages 41–83 in *Traditions of Theology: Studies in Hellenistic Theology, its Background and Aftermath.* Edited by Dorothea Frede and André Laks. PA 89. Leiden: Brill, 2002.

Sedley, David. *Creationism and its Critics in Antiquity.* Sather Classical Lectures 66. Berkeley: University of California Perss, 2007.

Seneca. *Epistles.* Edited and translated by Richard M. Gummere. 3 vols. LCL 75–77. Cambridge: Harvard University Press, 1918–1920.

Seneca. *Natural Questions.* Edited and translated by T.H. Corcoran. 2 vols. LCL 450, 457. Cambridge: Harvard University Press, 1971–1972.

Sextus Empiricus. *I. Outlines of Pyrrhonism.* Edited and translated by R.G. Bury. LCL 273. Cambridge: Harvard University Press, 1933.

Sextus Empiricus. *Against the Physicists. Against the Ethicists.* Edited and translated by R.G. Bury. LCL 311. Cambridge; London: Harvard University Press; William Heinemann Ltd, 1968.

Sharples, Robert W. "Alexander of Aphrodisias, *De Fato*: Some Parallels." *CQ* 28:2 (1978): 243–266.

Sharples, Robert W. "Alexander of Aphrodisias on Divine Providence: Two Problems." *CQ* 32:1 (1982): 198–211.

Sharples, Robert W. "Aristotelian Theology after Aristotle." Pages 1–40 in *Traditions of Theology.* Edited by Dorothea Frede and André Laks. PA 89. Leiden: Brill, 2002.

Sharples, Robert W. "Commentary: Alexander." Pages 126–178 in Alexander of Aphrodisias. *Alexander of Aphrodisias: On Fate.* Edited and translated by Robert W. Sharples. London: Duckworth, 2003.

Sharples, Robert W. "Commentary: Cicero *On fate*; Appendix: Parallel texts; Excursus: Terminology for Causes; Boethius *Consolation of Philosophy* IV.5–7 and V." Pages 159–231 in Cicero, *On Fate. & Boethius: The Consolation of Philosophy IV.5–7, V.* Edited and translated by Robert W. Sharples. Aris & Phillips Classical Texts. Oxford; Havertown, 2015.

Sharples, Robert W. "Introduction: Alexander." Pages 3–37 in Alexander of Aphrodisias. *Alexander of Aphrodisias: On Fate.* Edited and translated by Robert W. Sharples. London: Duckworth, 2003.

Sharples, Robert W. "Introduction: Cicero." Pages 1–50 in Cicero. *On Fate. & Boethius: The Consolation of Philosophy IV.5–7, V.* Edited and translated by Robert W. Sharples. Aris & Phillips Classical Texts. Oxford; Havertown, 2015.

Sharples, Robert W. "The Stoic Background to the Middle Platonist Discussion of Fate." Pages 169–187 in *Platonic Stoicism—Stoic Platonism. The Dialogue between Platonism and Stoicism in Antiquity.* Edited by Mauro Bonazzi and Christoph Helmig. Leuven: Leuven University Press, 2007.

Sharples, Robert W. "Threefold Providence: the History and Background of a Doctrine." Pages 107–127 in *Ancient Approaches to Plato's 'Timaeus'*. Edited by Robert W. Sharples and Anne D.R. Sheppard. *BICSSup* 78. London: University of London, 2003.

Sharples, Robert W. and Philip J. van der Eijk. "Introduction." Pages 1–32 in Nemesius of Emesa. *On the Nature of Man*. Translated by Robert W. Sharples and Philip J. van der Eijk. TTH 49. Liverpool: Liverpool University Press, 2008.

Sharples, Robert W. and Philip J. van der Eijk. "Notes." Pages 35–221 in Nemesius of Emesa. *On the Nature of Man*. Translated by Robert W. Sharples and Philip J. van der Eijk. TTH 49. Liverpool: Liverpool University Press, 2008.

Sherk, Robert K., ed. *Rome and the Greek East to the Death of Augustus*. Translated Documents of Greece and Rome 4. Cambridge: Cambridge University Press, 1984.

Shoemaker, Stephen. "Early Christian Apocryphal Literature." Pages 521–548 in *The Oxford Handbook of Early Christian Studies*. Edited by Susan Ashbrook Harvey and David G. Hunter. Oxford: Oxford University Press, 2008.

Simmons, Michael Bland. *Universal Salvation in Late Antiquity: Porphyry of Tyre and the Pagan-Christian Debate*. Oxford Studies in Late Antiquity. Oxford; New York: Oxford University Press, 2015.

Simonetti, Elsa Giovanna. *A Perfect Medium? Oracular Divination in the Thought of Plutarch*. Plutarchea Hypomnemata. Leuven: Leuven University Press, 2017.

Simplicius. *Simplicii in Aristotelis physicorum libros octo commentaria*. Edited by Hermann Diels. Commentaria in Aristotelem Graeca 9 & 10. Berlin: Reimer, 1882–1895.

Smith, Geoffrey S. *Guilt by Association: Heresy Catalogues in Early Christianity*. Oxford: Oxford University Press, 2015.

Smith, Geoffrey S. "Irenaeus, the Will of God, and Anti-Valentinian Polemics: A Closer Look at *Against the Heresies* 1.12.1." Pages 93–123 in *Beyond the Gnostic Gospels: Studies Building on the Work of Elaine Pagels*. Edited by Eduard Iricinschi, Lance Jenott, Nicola Denzey Lewis and Philippa Townsend. STAC 82. Tübingen: Mohr Siebeck, 2013.

Sokoloff, Michael. *A Syriac Lexicon: A Translation from the Latin, Correction, Expansion, and Update of C. Brockelmann's 'Lexicon Syriacum'*. Winona Lake; Piscataway: Eisenbrauns; Gorgias Press, 2009.

Solmsen, Friedrich. "Providence and the Souls: A Platonic Chapter in Clement of Alexandria." Pages 352–374 in *Kleine Schriften*, 3 vols. Edited by Friedrich Solmsen. Hildesheim: Georg Olms Verlag, 1982.

Sorabji, Richard. "Introduction: The Three Deterministic Arguments Opposed by Ammonius." Pages 3–15 in Ammonius, *Ammonius: On Aristotle On Interpretation 9 with Boethius On Aristotle On Interpretation 9*. Translated by David Blank and Norman Kretzmann, with essays by Richard Sorabji, Norman Kretzmann, and Mario Mignucci. ACA: London: Duckworth, 1998.

BIBLIOGRAPHY

Spanneut, Michel. *Le stoicisme des pères de l'église. De Clément de Rome à Clément d'Alexandrie*. Paris: Faculté des lettres, 1957.

Spanu, Nicola. *Plotinus, 'Ennead' II 9 [33] 'Against the Gnostics': A Commentary*. Studia Patristica Supplement Series 1. Leuven: Peeters, 2012.

Spiteri, Donat. "The Specific Contribution of Divino afflante Spiritu." *Melita Theologica* 26:1–2 (1974): 7–15.

Stead, Christopher. *Philosophy in Christian Antiquity*. Cambridge: Cambridge University Press, 1994.

Steenberg, Matthew Craig. "Children in Paradise: Adam and Eve as 'Infants' in Irenaeus of Lyons." *JECS* 12:1 (2004):1–22.

Steenberg, Matthew Craig. *Irenaeus on Creation: The Cosmic Christ and the Saga of Redemption*. VCSup 91. Leiden: Brill, 2008.

Stettner, Walter. *Die Seelenwanderung bei Griechen und Römern*. Tübinger Beiträge zur Altertumswissenschaft 22. Stuttgart: W. Kohlhammer, 1934.

Stoyanov, Yuri. *The Other God: Dualist Religions from Antiquity to the Cathar Heresy*. London; New Haven: Yale University Press, 2000.

Stroumsa, Gedaliahu G. *Another Seed: Studies in Gnostic Mythology*. NHS 24. Leiden: Brill, 1984

Stroumsa, Gedaliahu G. *The Making of the Abrahamic Religions in Late Antiquity*. Oxford Studies in the Abrahamic Religions 1. Oxford: Oxford University Press, 2015.

Stuckenbruck, Loren T. "The Origins of Evil in Jewish Apocalyptic Tradition: The Interpretation of Genesis 6:1–4 in the Second and Third Centuries B.C.E." Pages 87–118 in *The Fall of the Angels*. Edited by Christoph Auffarth and Loren T. Stuckenbruck. Themes in Biblical Narrative 6. Leiden; Boston: Brill; 2004.

Stuckenbruck, Loren T. "Satan and Demons." Pages 173–197 in *Jesus Among Friends and Enemies: A Historical and Literary Introduction to Jesus in the Gospels*. Edited by Chris Keith and Larry W. Hurtado. Grand Rapids: Baker Academic, 2011.

Suda On Line. "Diodorus." Translated by Kenneth Mayer. Edited by David Whitehead, et al. 2016. Accessed 9 July, 2019. http://www.stoa.org/sol-entries/delta/1151.

Suda On Line. "Pronoia." Translated by David Whitehead. Edited by Catharine Roth, et al. 2011. Accessed 30 July, 2019. http://www.stoa.org/sol-entries/pi/2534.

Suda On Line. "Pronoia Athena." Translated by Catharine Roth. Edited by David Whitehead, et al. 2016. Accessed 30 July, 2019. http://www.stoa.org/sol-entries/pi/2535.

Sutcliffe, Edmund F. *Providence and Suffering in the Old and New Testaments*. London: Thomas Nelson and Sons Ltd., 1953.

Swain, Simon. *Hellenism and Empire: Language, Classicism, and Power in the Greek World, AD 50–250*. Oxford: Oxford University Press, 1996.

Swain, Simon. "Plutarch: Chance, Providence, and History." *AJP* 110 (1989): 272–302.

Swinburne, Richard. *Providence and the Problem of Evil*. Oxford: Oxford University Press, 1998.

Tanaseanu-Döbler, Ilinca. *Theurgy in Late Antiquity: The Invention of a Ritual Tradition*. Beiträge zur Europäischen Religionsgeschichte 1. Göttingen: Vandenhoeck & Ruprecht, 2013.

Tardieu, Michel. "Recherches sur la formation de l'Apocalypse de Zostrien et les sources de Marius Victorinus." *Res Orientales* 9 (1996): 7–114.

Tarrant, Harold. "Platonism before Plotinus." Pages 63–99 in *The Cambridge History of Philosophy in Late Antiquity*. Edited by Lloyd P. Gerson. 2 vols. Cambridge: Cambridge University Press, 2010.

Tatian. *'Oratio ad Graecos' and Fragments*. Edited and translated by Molly Whittaker. OECT. Oxford: Clarendon Press, 1982.

Tertullian. *Adversus Marcionem*. Edited and translated by Ernest Evans. 2 vols. Oxford: Clarendon Press, 1972.

Tertullian. *Apology. De Spectaculis*. Edited and translated by Terrot R. Glover. LCL 250. Cambridge: Harvard University Press, 1977.

Tertullian. *Opera I. Opera catholica. Adversus Marcionem*. Edited by E. Dekkers, et al. Corpus Christianorum Series Latina 1. Turnhout; Brepols, 1954.

Tertullian. *Quinti Septimi Florentis Tertulliani. 'De anima.'* Edited by Jan H. Waszink. VCSup 100. Leiden; Boston: Brill, 2010.

Tertullian. *Traité de la prescription contre les hérétiques*. Edited and translated by Francois Refoulé. SC 46. Paris: Cerf, 1957.

Tertullian. *Tertullian's Treatise on the Resurrection*. Edited and translated by Ernest Evans. London: SPCK, 1960.

Tertullian. *The Treatise against Hermogenes*. Translated by Jan H. Waszink. Ancient Christian Writers. Westminster; London: Newman Press; Longmans, Green and Co, 1956.

Theiler, Willy. "Tacitus und die antike Schicksalslehre." Pages 46–103 in *Forschungen zum Neuplatonismus*. Edited by Willy Theiler. Berlin: De Gruyter, 1966.

Theophilus of Antioch. *Ad Autolycum*. Edited and translated by Robert M. Grant. OECT. Oxford: Clarendon Press, 1970.

Thévenaz, Pierre. *L'ame du monde, le devenir et la matiere chez Plutarque*. Paris: 1938.

Thom, Johan. "Introduction." Pages 3–17 in *Cosmic Order and Divine Power*. Edited by Johan Thom. SAPERE 23. Tübingen: Mohr Siebeck, 2014.

Thomassen, Einar. "Commentaire: Le Traité Tripartite." Pages 260–453 in *Le Traité Tripartite (NH I, 5)*. BCNH Section "Textes" 19. Québec: Les presses de l'Université Laval, 1989.

Thomassen, Einar. "Introduction: Le Traité Tripartite." Pages 1–48 in *Le Traité Tripartite (NH I, 5)*. BCNH Section "Textes" 19. Québec: Les presses de l'Université Laval, 1989.

Thomassen, Einar. "Saved by Nature? The Question of Human Races and Soteriological Determinism in Valentinianism." Pages 129–150 in *Zugänge zur Gnosis: Akten zur Tagung der Patristischen Arbeitsgemeinschaft vom 02.–05.01.2011 in Berlin-Spandau*.

BIBLIOGRAPHY

Edited by Christoph Markschies and Johannes van Oort. Patristic Studies 12. Leuven: Peeters, 2013.

Thomassen, Einar. *The Spiritual Seed: The Church of the 'Valentinians.'* Leiden; Boston: Brill, 2008.

Thomassen, Einar. "The Structure of the Transcendent World in the Tripartite Tractate (NHC I, 5)." *VC* 34 (1980): 358–375.

Thomassen, Einar and Louis Painchaud, eds. and trs. "Texte et Traduction." Pages 49–259 in *Le Traité Tripartite (NH I, 5)*. BCNH Section "Textes" 19. Québec: Les presses de l'Université Laval, 1989.

Thorsteinsson, Runar M. "Justin and Stoic Cosmo-Theology." *JTS* 63:2 (2012): 533–571.

Timotin, Andrei. *La démonologie platonicienne. Histoire de la notion de daimōn de Platon aux derniers néoplatoniciens*. PA 128. Leiden; Boston: Brill, 2012.

Timotin, Andrei. *La prière dans la tradition platonicienne, de Platon à Proclus*. Recherches sur les rhétoriques religieuses 22. Turnhout: Brepols, 2017.

Tite, Philip L. "Voluntary Martyrdom and Gnosticism." *JECS* 23:1 (2015): 27–54.

Trigg, Joseph W. *Origen*. Early Church Fathers. New York: Routledge, 2012.

Turner, John D. "The Anonymous *Parmenides* Commentary, Marius Victorinus, and the Sethian Platonizing Apocalypses: State of the Question." Pages 93–126 in *Gnose et Manichéisme. Entre les oasis d'Égypte et la route de la soie. Hommage à Jean-Daniel Dubois*. Edited by Anna van den Kerchove and Luciana Gabriela Soares Santoprete. Bibliothèque de l'École des Hautes Études Sciences Religieuses 176. Turnhout: Brepols, 2017.

Turner, John D. "Commentary." Pages 483–662 in *Zostrien (NH VIII,1)*. Edited and translated by Catherine Barry, Wolf-Peter Funk, Paul-Hubert Poirier, and John D. Turner. BCNH Section "Textes" 24. Louvain: Peeters, 2000.

Turner, John D. "Introduction: *Allogenes*." Pages 1–188 in *L'Allogène (NH XI,3)*. Edited and translated by Wolf-Peter Funk, Madeleine Scopello, and John D. Turner. BCNH Section "Textes" 30. Québec: Presses de l'université Laval; Leuven: Peeters, 2004.

Turner, John D. "Introduction: *Marsanes*." Pages 1–248 in *Marsanès (NH X)*. Edited and translated by Wolf-Peter Funk, Paul-Hubert Poirier, and John D. Turner. BCNH Section "Textes" 27. Québec: Presses de l'université Laval; Leuven: Peeters, 2000.

Turner, John D. "Plotinus and the Gnostics: The *Tripartite Tractate*?" Pages 373–411 in *Valentinianism: New Studies*. Edited by Einar Thomassen and Christoph Markschies. NHMS 96. Leiden; Boston: Brill, 2019.

Turner, John D. *Sethian Gnosticism and the Platonic Tradition*. BCNH Section "Études" 6. Québec: Université Laval. Leuven: Peeters, 2001.

Turner, John D., and Kevin Corrigan, eds. *Plato's "Parmenides" and Its Heritage*. 2 vols. WGRWSup 2–3. Atlanta: Society of Biblical Literature, 2010.

van den Broek, Roelof. *Gnostic Religion in Antiquity*. Cambridge: Cambridge University Press, 2013.

van den Broek, Roelof. "The Theology of the Teachings of Silvanus." *VC* 40 (1986): 1–23.

van den Hoek, Annewies. "Clement of Alexandria on Martyrdom." Pages 324–331 in *Studia Patristica* 26. Edited by Elizabeth A. Livingstone. Leuven: Peeters, 1993.

van den Kerchove, Anna. "Rhétorique de la véracité: la prologue 'autobiographique' du *Zostrien* (NH VIII,1)." Pages 275–396 in *Nag Hammadi à 70 ans. Qu'avons-nous appris? Nag Hammadi at 70: What Have We Learned? (Colloque international, Québec, Université Laval, 29–31 mai 2015)*. Edited by Eric Crégheur, Louis Painchaud, and Tuomas Rasimus. BCNH Section "Études" 10. Leuven: Peeters, 2019.

van der Horst, Pieter Willem. "Commentary." Pages 88–245 in *Philo of Alexandria. Philo's 'Flaccus': The First Pogrom*. Translated by Pieter Willem van der Horst. Philo of Alexandria Commentary Series 2. Leiden; Boston: Brill, 2003.

van der Horst, Pieter Willem. "Introduction." Pages 1–53 in *Philo of Alexandria. Philo's 'Flaccus': The First Pogrom*. Translated by Pieter Willem van der Horst. Philo of Alexandria Commentary Series 2. Leiden; Boston: Brill, 2003.

van Inwagen, Peter. *The Problem of Evil: The Gifford Lectures Delivered in the University of St Andrews in 2003*. Oxford: Clarendon Press, 2006.

van Kooten, George. "The Anthropological Trichotomy of Spirit, Soul and Body in Philo of Alexandria and Paul of Tarsus." Pages 87–119 in *Anthropology in the New Testament and Its Ancient Context: Papers from the EABS-Meeting in Piliscsaba/Budapest*. Edited by Michael Labahn and Outi Lehtipuu. Contributions to Biblical Exegesis and Theology 54. Leuven: Peeters, 2010.

van Nuffelen, Peter. *Rethinking the Gods: Philosophical Readings of Religion in the Post-Hellenistic Period*. Cambridge: Cambridge University Press, 2011.

van Oort, Johannes. "Alexander of Lycopolis, Manichaeism and Neoplatonism." Pages 275–283 in *Gnosticism, Platonism, and the Late Ancient World. Essays in Honour of John D. Turner*. Edited by Kevin Corrigan and Tuomas Rasimus, with Dylan M. Burns, Lance Jenott, and Zeke Mazur. NHMS 82. Leiden: Brill, 2013.

van Unnik, Willem C. "An Attack on the Epicureans by Flavius Josephus." Pages 341–355 in *Romanitas et Christianitas. Studia Ianoa Henrico Waszink. A.D. VI Kal. Nov. A. MCMLXXIII XIII lustra complenti oblata*. Edited by Jan H. Waszink, Willem den Boer, Pieter Gijsbertus van der Nat, and C.M.J. Sicking. Amsterdam; London: North-Holland Publishing Company, 1973.

van Winden, J.C.M. *Calcidius on Matter: His Doctrine and Sources. A Chapter in the History of Platonism*. PA 9. Leiden: Brill, 1965.

van Winden, J.C.M. *An Early Christian Philosopher: Justin Martyr's Dialogue with Trypho, chapters one to nine*. Philosophia Patrum 1. Leiden: Brill, 1971.

VanderKam, James C. "1 Enoch, Enochic Motifs, and Enoch in Early Christian Literature." Pages 33–101 in *The Jewish Apocalyptic Heritage in Early Christianity*. Edited by James C. vanderKam and William Adler. Compendia Rerum Iudaicarum ad Novum Testamentum 3.4. Minneapolis: Fortress Press, 1996.

BIBLIOGRAPHY

Vielhauer, Philipp and Georg Strecker. "Apocalypses and Related Subjects: Introduction." Pages 2:559–602 in *New Testament Apocrypha*. Edited by Edgar Hennecke and Wilhelm Schneemelcher. Translated by Robert McLachlan Wilson. 2 vols. Louisville: Westminster John Knox Press, 2003.

von Arnim, Johannes, ed. *Stoicorum Veterum Fragmenta*, 4 vols. Stuttgart: Teubner, 1924.

Walbank, Frank W. *A Historical Commentary on Polybius. Volume I. Commentary on Books I–VI*. Oxford: Clarendon Press, 1957.

Waldstein, Michael. "Das Apocryphon des Johannes (NHC II,1; III,1; IV,1; und BG 2)." Pages 1:95–150 in *Nag Hammadi Deutsch*. Edited by Hans-Martin Schenke, Hans-Gebhard Bethge, and Ursula Ulrike Kaiser. GCS 8. 2 vols. Berlin; New York: De Gruyter, 2001, 2003.

Waldstein, Michael. "The Providence Monologue in the *Apocryphon of John* and the Johannine Prologue." *JECS* 3:4 (1995): 369–402.

Waldstein, Michael and Frederik Wisse. "Introduction." Pages 1–8 in *The Apocryphon of John: Synopsis of Nag Hammadi Codices II,1; III,1; and IV,1 with BG 8502,2*. Edited by Michael Waldstein and Frederik Wisse. NHS 33. Leiden: Brill, 1995.

Waldstein, Michael and Frederik Wisse, eds. and trs. "Synopsis." Pages 11–195. *The Apocryphon of John: Synopsis of Nag Hammadi Codices II,1; III,1; and IV,1 with BG 8502,2*. Edited by Michael Waldstein and Frederik Wisse. NHS 33. Leiden: Brill, 1995.

Wallis, Richard T. "Soul and Nous in Plotinus, Numenius, and Gnosticism." Pages 461–482 in *Neoplatonism and Gnosticism*. Edited by Richard T. Wallis and Jay Bregman. SNAM 6. Albany: SUNY Press, 1992.

Walsh, James. "Introduction." Pages 11–17 in James Walsh and P.G. Walsh. *Divine Providence & Human Suffering*. Message of the Fathers of the Church 17. Wilmington: Michael Glazier, 1985.

Walsh, James and P.G. Walsh. *Divine Providence & Human Suffering*. Message of the Fathers of the Church 17. Wilmington: Michael Glazier, 1985.

Wasserman, Emma. "Beyond Apocalyptic Dualism: Ranks of Divinities in 1 Enoch and Daniel." Pages 189–199 in *"The One Who Sows Bountifully": Essays in Honor of Stanley K. Stowers*. Edited by Caroline Johnson Hodge, Saul M. Olyan, Daniel Ullucci, and Emma Wasserman. Brown Judaic Studies 356. Providence: Brown University Press, 2013.

Waszink, Jan H. "Observations on Tertullian's Treatise *Against Hermogenes*." *VC* 9:2 (1955): 129–147.

Webb, Stephen H. "From Prudentius to President Bush: Providence, Empire, and Paranoia." Pages 231–254 in *The Providence of God*. Edited by Francesca Aran Murphy and Philip G. Ziegler. London; New York: T&T Clark, 2009.

White, Benjamin L. "Justin Between Paul and the Heretics: The Salvation of Christian Judaizers in the Dialogue with Trypho." *JECS* 26:2 (2018): 163–189.

Whittaker, John. "Notes complémentaires." Pages 73–154 in Alcinous. *Enseignement des doctrines de Platon*. Edited by John Whittaker. Translated by Pierre Louis. Paris: Belles Lettres, 1990.

Whittaker, John. "Valentinus Fr. 2." Pages 455–460 in *Kerygma und Logos: Beiträge zu den geistesgeschichtlichen Beziehungen zwischen Antike und Christentum. Festschrift für Carl Andresen zum 70. Geburtstag*. Edited by Adolf Martin Ritter. Göttingen: Vandenhoeck & Ruprecht, 1979.

Wicke-Reuter, Ursel. "Ben Sira und die Frühe Stoa: Zum Zusammenhang von Ethik und dem Glauben an eine göttliche Providenz." Pages 268–281 in *Ben Sira's God. Proceedings of the International Ben Sira Conference Durham—Ushaw College 2001*. Edited by Renate Egger-Wenzel. Beihefte zur Zeitschrift für die alttestamentliche Wissenschaft 321. Berlin; New York: De Gruyter, 2002.

Wilberding, James. "The Myth of Er and the Problem of Constitutive Luck." Pages 87–105 in *Ancient Approaches to Plato's 'Republic'*. Edited by Anne Sheppard. BICSSup 117. London: Institute of Classical Studies School of Advanced Study, University of London, 2013..

Wildberg, Christian. "The Will and its Freedom: Epictetus and Simplicius on What is Up to Us." Pages 329–350 in *What is Up to Us? Studies on Agency and Responsibility in Ancient Philosophy*. Edited by Pierre Destrée, Ricardo Salles, and Marco Zingano. SAMPP 1. Leiden: Sankt Augustin: Academia Verlag, 2014.

Williams, Michael Allen. "Higher Providence, Lower Providences and Fate in Gnosticism and Middle Platonism." Pages 483–507 in *Neoplatonism and Gnosticism*. Edited by Richard T. Wallis and Jay Bregman. SNAM 6. Albany: SUNY Press, 1992.

Williams, Michael Allen. *Rethinking "Gnosticism": Arguments for Dismantling a Dubious Category*. Princeton: Princeton University Press, 1995.

Williams, Michael Allen. "'Wisdom, Our Innocent Sister': Reflections on a Mytheme." Pages 253–290 in *Women and Knowledge in Early Christianity: Festschrift Antti Marjanen*. Edited by Ulla Tervahauta, Ivan Miroshnikov, Outi Lehtipuu, and Ismo Dunderberg. VCSup 144. Leiden; Boston: Brill, 2017.

Willing, Meike. "Die neue Frage des Marcionschülers Apelles—zur Rezeption marcionitischen Gedankenguts." Pages 221–231 in *Marcion und seine kirchengeschichtliche Wirkung. Vorträge der Internationalen Fachkonferenz zu Marcion, gehalten vom 15.–19. August 2001 in Mainz*. Edited by Gerhard May and Katharina Greschat. TUGAL 150. Berlin: De Gruyter, 2013.

Wilson, Barrie A. "Bardaisan: On Nature, Fate, and Freedom." *International Philosophical Quarterly* 24 (1984): 165–178.

Wilson, Catherine. *Descartes's Meditations: An Introduction*. Cambridge; New York: Cambridge University Press, 2003.

Winston, David. "Philo and the Wisdom of Solomon on Creation, Revelation, and Providence: The High-Water Mark of Jewish Hellenistic Fusion." Pages 109–130 in *Shem in the Tents of Japhet: Essays on the Encounter of Judaism and Hellenism*. JSJSup 74. Edited by James L. Kugel. Leiden; Boston; Köln: Brill, 2002.

Winston, David. "Theodicy and the Creation of Man in Philo of Alexandria." Pages 105–111 in *Hellenica et Judaica: Hommage à Valentin Nikiprowetzky*. Edited by André Caquot, Mireille Hadas-Lebel, and Jean Riaud. Leuven; Paris: Peeters, 1986.

Winston, David. *The Wisdom of Solomon: A New Translation with Introduction and Commentary*. Anchor Bible 43. Garden City; New York: Doubleday, 1979.

Wiśniewski, Robert. "Pagans, Jews, Christians, and a Type of Book Divination in Late Antiquity." *JECS* 24:4 (2016): 553–568.

Wisse, Frederik, ed. and tr. "The *Letter of Peter to Philip*: Text, Translation and Notes." Pages 234–251 in *Nag Hammadi Codex VIII*. Edited by John H. Sieber. NHS 31. Leiden: Brill, 1991.

Wisse, Frederik, ed. and tr. "The *Paraphrase of Shem*: Text, Translation, and Notes." Pages 24–127 in *Nag Hammadi Codex VII*. Edited by Birger Pearson. NHMS 30. Leiden: Brill, 1996.

Wright, Benjamin G. III. *The Letter of Aristeas. 'Aristeas to Philocrates' or 'On the Translation of the Law of the Jews'*. Commentaries on Early Jewish Literature. Berlin; Boston: De Gruyter, 2015.

Wyse Rhodes, Jackie. "The Natural World as a Model for Human Righteousness in Jewish Apocalyptic Literature." Conference paper delivered at the Annual Meeting of the Society of Biblical Literature. November 19, 2011.

Xenophon. *Memorabilia. Oeconomicus. Symposium. Apology*. Translated by E.C. Marchant and O.J. Todd. LCL 168. Cambridge; London: Harvard University Press, 1997.

Xeravits, Géza G., ed. *Dualism at Qumran*. London: T&T Clark, 2010.

Zachhuber, Johannes. "Review of Karamanolis, *The Philosophy of Early Christianity*." *Notre Dame Philosophical Reviews* 2015.07.32.

Zagzebski, Linda Trinkaus. "Recent Work on Divine Foreknowledge and Free Will." Pages 45–64 in *The Oxford Handbook of Free Will*. Edited by Robert Kane. Oxford: Oxford University Press, 2002.

Zandee, Jan. *The Terminology of Plotinus and of Some Gnostic Writings, Mainly the Fourth Treatise of the Jung Codex*. Istanbul: Nederlands historisch-archaeologisch instituut in het nabije oosten, 1961.

Ziegler, Konrad. "Plutarchos." *Paulys Real-Encyclopädie der classischen Altertumswissenschaft* 21 (1951): 636–952.

Index

Abraham
  children born out of providence   77, 123
  God of   96, 97, 138, 159
  God's providence sought by   80
  Josephus on   86
Academicae quaestiones (Cicero)   18, 31, 45n138
accountability. *See* personal accountability (responsibility)
action
  Aristotle's account of   43, 227–228, 240, 277
  voluntary   227, 237, 245, 249, 275, 277
Acts
  2:23   216n97
  7:53   116n67
  divine intervention in   56n7
Adam and Eve
  Adam receives divine *pneuma*   172
  cast into matter   176n100
  created as children   160
  divine foreknowledge and   213n88
  expulsion from the Garden   266
  fall of   117, 213, 249, 267n234
  freedom of   266
  God offers choice to   264, 315
  God's ignorance of Adam's whereabouts   214
  God's test of obedience of   266, 267
  Nature of the Rulers on creation of Adam   177
  On the Origin of the World on creation of   164, 167
  poor choices made by   112
  sinning of   144, 146
  Tatian the Assyrian on   265
  Theophilus of Antioch on   266
Adamson, Paul   8, 9
aeons
  in *Apocryphon of John*   165, 175
  in *On the Origin of the World*   177
  in 'Sethian' treatises   305
  in *Tripartite Tractate*   179, 179n114, 181, 275, 290
  in *Zostrianos*   300
Aesop   51–52

Aëtius   32–33
Against Celsus (Origen)
  on care for individuals   130n130, 130–131
  on determinism and personal responsibility   193
  on divine foreknowledge   192, 193, 210–211, 212, 215–216, 256
  excerpt inserted in *On Fate*   192, 210
  on 'Oracle to Laius'   12, 193, 210, 211, 212, 216
  on personal accountability   193, 211, 222
  on prophecy   210–211
  on providence and evil   132–133
  on providence as demiurgic   156
  on 'what is up to us' (*to eph'hēmin*)   193
Against Heresies (Irenaeus of Lyons)   139–141, 160, 267
Against Hermogenes (Tertullian)   137, 137n153
Against Marcion (Tertullian)   141–143, 144–146, 267
Against Nemertius (Porphyry of Tyre)   295–296
Against the Gnostics (Plotinus)   153, 172, 183, 271, 282, 291
Aland (Ehlers), Barbara   142n174, 186, 186n147, 232n49
Alcinous
  conditional fate doctrine of   46, 48
  Handbook of Platonism   207–209, 218
  on matter as creative principle   106
  on 'Oracle to Laius'   193, 198
  on prophecy   12
  on will   270n2
Alexander, Tiberius   84, 85
Alexander of Aphrodisias
  Book of the Laws of the Countries compared with   238
  on conditional fate   226
  on divination   12, 204–207
  on 'freedom to do otherwise'   224
  on free will   229
  household argument appropriated by   62n35, 207
  as interpreter of Aristotle   204n52
  On Providence   206–207

INDEX

on regret 264
on Stoic pantheism 62
on *tuchē* 238n80
on virtuous character 230
See also On Fate (Alexander of Aphrodisias)
Algra, Keimpe 31, 39n111
Allegorical Interpretation (Philo of Alexandria) 82
Allogenes
circulated in Plotinus's seminar 297
on first thought 13, 272
on Invisible Spirit 300, 302–304
Marsanes contrasted with 305
negative theology of 306
as post-Plotinian 306
Ambrose of Milan 149, 213
ameleia 5
Amelius 307
Ammonius Hermiou 293
Ammonius Saccus 219n103, 311, 312
Anaxagoras 20, 20n16
Angel of Darkness 113, 114
angels
Athenagoras of Athens on 120–121, 124, 135, 136, 138
Book of the Laws of the Countries on 235
Byzantine view of 136–137
Clement of Alexandria on 122, 123, 124, 126, 138
early Christian writers on 100
evil 114–115, 116, 132, 136, 138, 146, 149, 185, 265, 288
fallen 104, 112, 113, 118, 120, 121, 124, 126–127, 131, 137
Greek gods as sinning 119, 124
Justin Martyr on 119, 124, 136, 264
Origen on 131–132, 133–134, 138, 222, 288
personal accountability in 264, 265
Satan as 116
Tertullian on 148
Tripartite Tractate on 171, 181
Annals (Tacitus) 46, 46n144
anthropocentrism
in early Christianity 174
in Gnosticism 183
in Stoicism 36, 58, 60, 61–62, 174
Apelles
on divine foreknowledge 213

dualism of 11, 104, 137, 151, 152, 316
on evil 148, 152
on fiery angel 148–149
on God 155
on imperfection 104
Marcion and 146–147, 148–149
on one principle 147, 149
on pre-existing souls 147, 268n237
on providential and inferior gods 137
on sin 138
Apocalypse of Zoroaster 308, 318
apocalyptic literature 104, 112–118, 136, 175
Apocryphon of John 165–169
aeons in 165, 175
archons in 166, 167, 172, 173, 174
as compilation of pre-existing sources 165
creation and providence separated in 175
on the demiurge 166, 172, 177, 182
Descartes's evil demon compared with 317
Irenaeus of Lyons and Porphyry know 184
language of divine care in 154, 183
on matter 167, 176
On the Origin of the World compared with 167
on providence 161–165, 174–176, 177
on rational divine character of humans 174
'Sethian' treatises compared with 300
Three Forms of First Thought as dependent on 169n71
two kinds of providence in 174–176
Wisdom in 165–166, 168, 175n93, 176
Yaldabaoth in 166, 167, 171, 174
Apuleius
Athenagoras of Athens compared with 121
conditional fate doctrine of 46
on *daimones* 100, 151
on divine intervention 63n45
Archaic poets 19
archons
in *Apocryphon of John* 166, 167, 172, 173, 174
Basilides on 179n112
evil associated with 175

Gnostics on   215
in *On the Origin of the World*   161, 162–163, 164, 173, 174, 185
in *Second Treatise on the Great Seth*   173
in *Sentences of Sextus*   184
in *Three Forms of First Thought*   170, 177
in *Tripartite Tractate*   181–182, 288
argument from design   20–21, 26, 36, 80, 156, 273
Aristotle
on actions made by choice   43, 227–228, 240, 277
Alexander of Aphrodisias as interpreter of   204n52
Athenagoras of Athens on   121
Clement of Alexandria on free will and   241
Epicurus compared with   26–27
on failure to consistently choose virtue   236
on God as not involved in sublunary realm   206, 207
Metaphysics   27–28, 29, 30
Nicomachaean Ethics   43, 227–228, 236
On Philosophy   28–29
on order of the cosmos   286, 286n79, 288
on Prime Mover   28n52, 33n78
public support for teaching of   204
on Pythagorean Table of Opposites   105
on questions deserving punishment   128
theology of   27–29, 33
on two causes in Plato   106
on virtuous character   230, 230n38
on walking   48n151
on 'what is up to us'   43, 227, 236, 245, 249
Armstrong, Arthur Hilary   112, 113, 290, 290n93
astrological determinism
Book of the Laws of the Countries on   233, 239, 240
in emergence of concept of free will   224–225
Origen and   12, 193, 195, 215, 259
astrology
Astrological Book on   116
Book of the Watchers on   115
nomima barbarika argument in polemics against   239

Origen's *Commentary on Genesis* on   193–195, 213, 215, 219–222
Origen's *On Fate* on   192, 193, 219–222
Tatian the Assyrian on   265
See also astrological determinism
Astronomical Book   115, 116
Athenagoras of Athens   118–122
on angels   120–121, 124, 135, 136, 138
on conditional fate   262n
on *daimones*   100, 124, 129, 135–136, 152, 237, 316
Embassy for the Christians   120
on evil   10, 104, 120, 136, 152
on general and specific providence   90n202
on God   120, 121
on responsibility for creation   156
on Satan   121, 135, 136
Stoic influence on   97
Atticus   26–27, 27n45, 27n46, 29, 107n17, 270n2
Attridge, Harold   85, 87–88
augury   203, 220
Augustine, St.   13, 217n97, 218, 224, 225, 309, 315
Augustus, Emperor   67–68
Authoritative Teaching   178
Autogenes   300
autonomy
Book of the Laws of the Countries on   235, 236, 237–238, 239, 240, 262
Chrysippus on   229
demonology in development of concept of   136
moral   235
Origen's *On First Principles* on   255, 257, 261, 262
Paul on   258
Platonism on   231n48
shift in notion of human accountability to freedom from   268
See also free will, *ḥiʾrutāʾ*

Bak Halvgaard, Tilde   170n75
baptism   264, 265–266, 267
Barbelo   165, 167–168, 169, 300, 302
Barc, Bernard   165, 169
Bardaiṣan
on Adam's disobedience   267, 267n234

INDEX

Book of the Laws of the Countries and
232, 232n49, 233
dualism attributed to 236
on fate as controlling the body 240,
240n90
Barnes, Jonathan 211n79
Basilides
Clement of Alexandria on 240–251
determinism attributed to 252
as earliest known Christian philosopher
55n4, 90n203
earliest known remarks on providence
and accountability by Christian
philosopher 242
Exegetica 244
on free will 12, 268, 315
on Great Archon 179n112
Justin Martyr on 94, 138
on martyrdom 226, 245n122, 249n147,
250, 251
monism of 245, 251
Origen on 260
on personal accountability 245, 246, 250
on pre-existence of souls 246, 251–252,
261, 262, 315
on punishment 226, 244, 245–246, 247,
251
reincarnation attributed to 246
salvation by nature doctrine and 252,
258n189
on sin 244, 250, 251
on Ten Commandments 244–245, 319
Basil of Caesarea 192
Beagon, Mary 70n81
Beard, Mary 203
Beliar 113–114, 117
Benjamins, Hendrik S. 195n10, 217n97
Bergjan, Silke-Petra
on Christians and Stoic doctrine of fate
57n12
on Clement on providence 125
on God's care as interaction with humanity 269, 268n240
on Origen on punishment 256, 256n182
on prophecy and providence 193n
on providence for distinguishing between
philosophical schools 91
on question of God's providence 18n8
as source for this study 2n5

Berkouwer, G.C. 2n7
Bianchi, Ugo 107, 150n213
Bible. *See* New Testament; Old Testament
biblical proof-texts 56, 57, 96, 113, 117, 129,
146, 156, 225, 253n159, 255, 318–319
bibliomancy 219, 219n102
binitarianism 149, 149n210
Bobzien, Susanne
on Chrysippus and Laius oracle 198n24
on Chrysippus on 'freedom to do otherwise' 41n123
on cylinder metaphor in Chrysippus
42n125
on divination 202n40
on faculty of choosing and the soul
225–226
on 'freedom to do otherwise' 224, 225
on General Causal Principle 38
on Origen 211n79, 212n82
on Philopator on freedom and fate
228n30
on providence in later writings about fate
18n9
on Pseudo-Plutarch on Aristotle 48n152
on Stoics on fate 31, 199n30
body, human. *See* human body
Boethius 4, 13, 191, 314
Book of the Laws of the Countries 232–240
on autonomy 235, 236, 237–238, 239,
240, 262
Bardaiṣan and authorship of 232,
232n49
catalogue of customs in 232, 239
on choice 233, 234, 235, 240
Dihle and 226n19
on free will 232, 233, 234–235, 240, 268,
315
on human accountability 226, 233, 234–
235, 236, 238, 240
on keeping the commandments 235–
236, 238, 239, 240, 259
nomima barbarika argument in 220,
239
Peripatetic influence on 233n51
on pre-existing souls 237–238, 240, 246,
261, 262, 315
on Ten Commandments 235–236, 238,
239, 240, 262, 319
on 'what is up to us' 234, 245

Book of the Watchers
   on angels   114–115
   Apelles and   149
   Book of the Laws of the Countries and
     235
   Christian philosophers and   135, 318
   on idolatry   114
   on introduction of forbidden arts   248
   Marcion and   146
   Middle Platonism and   155
   Origen and   129
   Tertullian on   119, 148
Book of Zoroaster   176n100
Bos, Abraham   29
Boyd, Gregory A.   294n113
Boys-Stones, George
   on Aristotle on Prime Mover   28n52
   on Atticus and Aristotle   27n46
   on divine foreknowledge   218n109
   on 'Middle Platonism'   45n140
   on multi-tiered providence in Middle Platonism   64, 64n54
   on Origen   217n97, 261n210
   on Pseudo-Plutarch   49n158, 230, 231n48
'brain-in-a-vat' scenario   317–318
Brakke, David   153, 154, 154n4, 184n135
Braun, René   143n182
Broadie, Sarah   22–23
Brouwer, René   66n61

Calcidius
   conditional fate doctrine of   46, 47
   on evil   109–110
   on fate and providence   39n111
   fragment of Numenius of Apamea in 109
   on grades of providence   47n145
   on will   270n2
Cameron, Averil   4
Camplani, Alberto   232n49, 236n69
Carneades   39n111, 45, 61, 202, 216, 293
carum esse   5
causality
   Alexander of Aphrodisias's *On Fate* on 206
   Aristotle on final cause   28
   Book of the Laws of the Countries on   233, 238, 239, 240

causal dualism   231, 232
   as central to problem of providence   103
   Christian philosophical contributions on 9
   compatibilism and   41
   in debate about evil   52–53
   of demons   114, 122, 151, 222
   divine foreknowledge and   104, 195–196, 199, 200, 210, 212
   dualism and   103
   of evil   10, 46, 134, 149, 151
   fate and   38
   General Causal Principle   38, 42, 43, 199, 228–229
   Middle Platonists on   46–47
   number of causal principles   10, 104, 121–122, 149, 150, 152
   Origen on   260, 261
   of personifications of evil   114
   Platonists on   47, 230–231
   Plotinus on   273, 274, 293
   prophecy and   211, 213
   Pseudo-Plutarch on   49–50
   Stoics on   38, 47, 59, 199
   Stoics on god's causal efficacy   31
   third century shift in notion of   269
Celsus
   eternal return and   49n158
   Origen's *Against Celsus*   130n130, 130–131, 132–133, 210–211, 215–216
Chadwick, Henry   216n93
Chaldaean Oracles   309
Chalmers, David   317–318
chance
   Alexander of Aphrodisias on   238n80
   character and   230
   Cicero on   39n111
   Josephus on   87
   Numenius of Apamea on   110
   personal responsibility and   231
   Platonists on   230–231
   Plotinus on   278
   Polybius on   65–66, 66n60, 70
   Pseudo-Plutarch on   48–49, 231, 231n46
   tertiary providence and   63n45
   See also contingency; *tuchē*
character   37, 43, 229, 230
Chase, Michael   294, 295, 296
Chiaradonna, Riccardo   280n47

INDEX   371

choice
  Adam and Eve's   112, 264
  Alexander of Aphrodisias's *On Fate*   229,
     264
  Aristotle on   43, 227–228, 240, 277
  Athenagoras of Athens on angels'   121
  Book of the Laws of the Countries on   233,
     234, 235, 240
  Clement of Alexandria on   241, 249
  in conditional fate doctrine   48
  by demons   151
  Epictetus on   43n131
  Josephus on   88
  Justin Martyr on   264
  Middle Platonists on   53, 151
  natural cosmos seen as capable of   115
  Origen on   222, 254, 257, 261
  Platonists on   47
  Plato on   25–26, 208, 225, 249, 252, 261,
     264, 268
  in Plato's *Republic*   25, 105, 208, 209
  Plotinus on   279, 287
  pre-natal   231n48, 240, 246, 261, 262, 264,
     283
  Pseudo-Plutarch on   48, 231
  responsibility and   26
  sin and   136
  Stoics on   41n122
  Tatian the Assyrian on   265
  Tertullian on   267
  Theophilus of Antioch on   266
  what we choose now   223–269
Christ. *See* Jesus Christ
Christianity. *See* early Christianity
Chrysippus
  on autonomy   229
  on co-fated events   12, 198, 201, 203,
     205n55, 261
  compatibilism of   41, 41n123, 202
  cylinder metaphor of   41–42
  on *daimones*   60, 60n25
  on divination   199–200
  on divine foreknowledge   214, 258
  on dog tied to moving cart   41n123
  on evil   35, 282
  on fate   38–39
  on flaws in creation   35n88
  on foot delighting in getting muddy
     41n123

  on General Causal Principle   38, 199
  on god as united with matter   33n78
  household argument of   60–61
  on 'lazy argument' (*agros logos*)   39, 193,
     198n24, 201, 212
  on Middle Platonists' semi-divine beings
     60
  On Destiny   38–39
  On Fate   34
  On the World   38
  on 'Oracle to Laius'   193, 198, 201–202,
     203, 206, 208, 216
  on prophecy   200, 216
  on providence as present in parts   60
  on successive world-cycles   34, 34n85
  on vice as punishment   62
  on what is up to us   40, 43
Cicero
  Academicae quaestiones   18, 31, 45n138
  Aristotle's *On Philosophy* quoted by   28,
     29
  Carneades as source for   202
  on chance   39n111
  on Epicureans   18, 31
  evidence on providence in   7
  on free will   39n116
  on General Causal Principle   38
  on the gods knowing everything   33–34,
     34n83, 293
  On Divination   199, 203
  Philo of Alexandria compared with   78
  providentia in writings of   5
  See also On Fate (Cicero); *On the Nature of
     the Gods* (Cicero)
civic piety
  Alcinous's *Handbook of Platonism* on
     209, 218
  Alexander of Aphrodisias's *On Fate* on
     206, 207, 218
  care of the gods and the civic cult   267
  Cicero's *On the Nature of the Gods* on
     203–204, 207, 218
Clark, Elizabeth A.   250n151
Cleanthes   32, 33, 34, 39, 39n111, 72, 97
Clement of Alexandria
  on Adam's disobedience   267
  on angels   122, 123, 124, 126, 138
  argument from design in   156
  on Basilides   240–251

on choice   241, 249

on demons   122, 136, 152, 242n106

on divine care   1, 122–125

on divine foreknowledge   216, 313

on evil   10, 104, 136, 150, 152, 247–248, 316

on free will   240–241, 251, 257

on God   57n12, 123, 247–248

on human accountability   226, 241, 243, 246–247, 249, 249n147, 250–252

on martyrdom   226, 242–244, 245–246

on punishment   127, 226, 249n147, 250, 251

'resident alien' motif in   251

on salvation by nature   253

on sin   124, 250

on the soul   251

and Stoic conception of Zeus's omni-science   33n78

Stromateis (*Miscellanies*)   122–128, 241–251

on subordinating philosophy to Christian instruction   127–128

on Ten Commandments   241n96, 249, 259, 262

on true Gnostics   124–125, 126–127, 135, 241, 242, 251

on 'what is up to us'   241, 241n96, 246, 249–250

Collins, John J.   112n40, 113n42

Colossians 1:16   156, 318

Commentary on Genesis (Origen)   210–216

on astrology   193–195, 213, 215, 219–222

on determinism   210, 213

on divine foreknowledge   11–12, 195–196, 212, 216, 218–219, 256

extracts of inserted in *On Fate*   192, 210, 222

nomima barbarika argument in   220, 239

on prophecy   193, 210, 211, 213, 215, 218–219, 221

whom it was written against   212

Commentary on Plato's 'Parmenides'

attributed to Porphyry   297, 298, 299, 306, 308, 311

authorship of   297, 308, 311–312

on divine foreknowledge   298, 306, 307

on first thought   13, 272, 297–299, 308

on God as not self-cognizant   298, 302

on supra-cognitive faculty   272, 300, 306

Community Rule   113–114, 136

compatibilism

of Chrysippus   41, 41n123, 202

of Josephus   86n178

Middle Platonists and   209, 232

of Sirach   73, 74

of Stoicism   41, 41n123, 47, 230, 253

in *Tripartite Tractate*   284

concomitance argument

Aesop and   52

of Chrysippus   35n88, 35–36, 44

Clement of Alexandria and   249

in early Christian philosophers   175, 315

Origen and   131, 136

conditional fate

Alcinous on   46, 48

Alexander of Aphrodisias on   226

Apuleius on   46

Athenagoras of Athens on   262n

Calcidius on   46, 47

choice in   48

Justin Martyr on   263–264

in Middle Platonism   12, 45–51, 207, 208, 209, 225, 226, 230–232, 261, 263–264, 316

Pseudo-Plutarch on   46, 47, 207, 230

contingency

in early Christian ontology   267

fate governs the contingent   271

God's knowledge of contingent events   293–294

Philo of Alexandria on   217–218

Pseudo-Plutarch on   48

Stoicism on   199

See also chance

1 Corinthians

2:14–15   253

10:19–22   116–117

15:20–22   117

Corrigan, Kevin   275, 277n30, 279n41, 291

Couliano, Ioan   174

Craig, William Lane   212n82

creation

Apocryphon of John on providence and   175

creator-god   10, 11, 37, 104, 112, 120, 156, 164, 172, 173, 178, 179

INDEX

373

flaws in 35, 35n88, 53
Irenaeus of Lyons's creation-theology
155–160
Plato on 21–24, 32
Crouzel, Henri 261n208

daimones
Alcinous's *Handbook of Platonism* on
209
Apuleius on 100, 151
Athenagoras of Athens on 100, 124, 129,
135–136, 152, 237
Chrysippus on 60, 60n25
in discussions about providence 112
Epictetus on 62–63
evil associated with 10–11
Graeco-Roman deities as 113, 124, 129,
135, 155, 265, 316
Middle Platonism on 12, 45, 47, 53, 58,
59–60, 63–64, 65, 100, 104, 108, 118,
121, 122, 126, 132, 152, 155, 165, 242, 288,
316
Philo of Alexandria on 80, 99, 100
Platonic source of 51
in Plato's *Republic* 25
Plutarch on 64, 70, 100, 108, 151
Pseudo-Plutarch on 50–51, 209
as translation of Hebrew words 116n63
See also demons
David the Psalmist 211, 266
Dead Sea Scrolls 113–114
death
Adam acquires 266
fate and 238
free will and 262
Graeco-Roman gods and 104
as limitation of embodiment 237
Satan and 74, 242
sin associated with 117
souls after 24, 64, 252, 252n155, 253, 281
Tatian the Assyrian on 265
De fato treatises
stock arguments in 6n23
See also On Fate
demiurge (*dēmiourgos*)
in *Apocryphon of John* 166, 172, 177, 182
Christian teachers compared with 127
in discussions about providence 112
evil associated with 174

Gnosticism seen as biblical demiurgicalism 185–187
Gnostics and 153, 174, 215, 282, 284, 317
Irenaeus of Lyons and 140, 160–161
Marcion and 138, 139, 142, 145
Middle Platonists on 10
in Numenius of Apamea 109, 316
Origen and 156
Philo of Alexandria on 80, 81
in Plato's *Timaeus* 21, 22–23, 32, 50, 84,
105, 106n7, 122, 152, 155, 164, 174, 316
Plutarch on 107, 109, 316
repenting 179
Valentinians on 171–172, 178–179, 182,
186, 215n92, 288
Democritus 20, 107
demons
apocalyptic perspective and 150
arch-demon 116
associated with sacrificial cults and idols
116–117, 119–120
causality of 114, 122, 151, 222
Clement of Alexandria on 122, 136, 152,
242n106
in Dead Sea Scrolls 113
Descartes's evil demon 316–317
as divine administrators 121–122
in dualism 104
early Christian writers on 100, 103, 118
evil 113, 115, 124n106, 175, 316, 317
Gnostics on superiority of human beings
to 173
in the Gospels 116
Graeco-Roman gods identified with 113,
124
as imposters 116
in New Testament 118
Origen on 131, 132–136, 152, 222
sin introduced into world by 117
in *Three Forms of First Thought* 170,
170n72
Valentinus on sin and 119
in worldview of first centuries CE 112–
113
See also daimones; Satan (the Devil)
De natura deorum (Cicero). *See On the Nature
of the Gods* (Cicero)
den Boeft, Jan 47n145
den Dulk, Matthijs 91n205

Denzey (Lewis), Nicola   2n5, 6n23, 173, 265n227, 267
Descartes, René   316–317, 317n16
determinism
    Alexander of Aphrodisias's *On Fate* on   204, 205, 206
    Basilides associated with   252
    Book of the Laws of the Countries on   233, 236, 237, 238
    epistemic versus logical   202
    Gnostic   226, 252
    God's knowledge and divination and   293
    hard determinism (incompatibilism)   43–44
    Irenaeus of Lyons on   268
    Middle Platonists on   47
    Origen's *Against Celsus* on   193
    Origen's *Commentary on Genesis* on   210, 213
    Origen's *On First Principles* on   253–262
    Platonists on   231
    in Plato's *Republic*   25
    Pseudo-Plutarch on   50, 230
    in Stoicism   6, 37–44, 57, 103, 206, 218, 226, 256
    Tatian the Assyrian on   265
    Tertullian on   268
    See also astrological determinism; compatibilism
Devil, the. *See* Satan (the Devil)
Dialogue with Trypho (Justin Martyr)   10, 58, 89–96, 138
Dihle, Albrecht   224, 225, 225n13, 226n19, 235n67, 238n80, 252n156, 254n167
Dillon, John M.   45n138, 47, 277n30
Diodore of Tarsus   240n91
Diodorus Cronus   199n30
Diodorus Siculus   58, 65, 66–68, 70
Diogenes Laertius   20, 31, 40
Diogenes of Apollonia   20
divination
    Alcinous's *Handbook of Platonism* on   209, 218
    Alexander of Aphrodisias's *On Fate* on   204–207, 218
    Bible-centered   219
    Chrysippus on   199–200, 218
    Cicero's *On Fate* on   199–200, 203

    civic   218
    daimones in   51
    God's knowledge and determinism and   293
    Origen on   193, 218–219, 220
    philosophical debates over   197
    Stoics on   199, 199n29, 200
    Tatian the Assyrian on   265
    See also prophecy
divine foreknowledge   191–222
    Alcinous's *Handbook of Platonism* on   207–209, 214
    Alexander of Aphrodisias's *On Fate* on   204–207, 214, 215
    Carneades on   216
    causality and   104, 195–196, 199, 200, 210, 212
    Christianizing turn in Platonic conceptions of   306–310
    Chrysippus on   214, 258
    Cicero's *On Fate* on   203, 214
    Clement of Alexandria on   216, 313
    Commentary on Plato's 'Parmenides' on   298, 306, 307
    of future conditionals   193, 209, 216, 293–294, 295–296, 307–308, 313–314, 318
    Gnostics on   213–214
    Justin Martyr on   216, 263, 313
    Marcion on   12, 143, 213, 215
    'Oracle to Laius' and   12
    Origen's *Against Celsus* on   192, 193, 210–211, 212, 215–216, 256
    Origen's *Commentary on Genesis* on   11–12, 195–196, 212, 216, 218–219, 256
    Origen's *On Fate* on   12, 192
    Origen's *On First Principles* on   258
    personal accountability (responsibility) and   196, 212
    Philo of Alexandria on   217–218, 313
    Plotinus on   11, 13, 300–301
    Sirach on   73–74
    Stoicism on   216, 307
    Teachings of Silvanus on   216, 217n97, 313
    Tripartite Tractate on   276, 306
    Zostrianos on   302
Dörrie, Heinrich   57n12
Drijvers, Han J.W.   233n54
dualism   101–188
    of Apelles   11, 104, 137, 151, 152, 316

INDEX   375

Book of the Laws of the Countries on   233,
    234, 236, 240
causal   231, 232
Christianity as moderately dualist   150, 151
eschatology associated with   117
evil and   103
of Gnostics   11, 152, 153, 185, 316
Irenaeus of Lyons's opposition to   157
iterations of   150n213
in Jewish apocalyptic literature   104, 112–
    118, 136, 149, 175
of light and darkness   169
of Marcion   11, 104, 151, 152, 186, 213, 222,
    234, 316
mitigated   112, 117, 118, 149, 183, 288
in Nag Hammadi manuscripts   187
of Numenius of Apamea   11, 104, 106,
    108–109, 111, 152, 316
of Platonism   103, 104, 105, 106
in Plato's *Timaeus*   316
of Plutarch   11, 104, 106, 111, 150n213, 152,
    316
of Pythagoreanism   105
religious   11, 149–152
Dudley, John   28
Dunderberg, Ismo   163n40

early Christianity
anthropocentrism in   174
biblical proof-texts in writings of   318–
    319
Book of the Watchers' influence on   135,
    318
Christianizing turn in Platonic con-
    ceptions of divine foreknowledge
    306–310
Clement of Alexandria and Christian phi-
    losophy   125, 126–128
and creation   156
and demons   100, 103, 118
Enochic literature and   119, 135
Epicurean arguments used against   99
and evil   103, 151, 175
and free will   9, 12, 103, 223, 226, 252–253,
    262, 267, 315
Gnostics and   154
God of   97
Greek philosophy and Christian philoso-
    phy part ways   319

and liberation from enslavement to fate
    173, 195
and metempsychosis   246
Middle Platonism's influence on   100,
    104, 135
mitigated dualism in   118, 183
as moderately dualist   150, 151
Nag Hammadi manuscripts' perspective
    distinguished from   187
and pagan contemporaries on providence
    57–58
and personal accountability   9, 225, 253
personal God of   54–58
philosophy practiced in   55, 318
Platonism's relationship to   13–14, 307–
    308
Plato's influence on   12–13
Plotinus's engagement with   14, 307–
    308, 311, 312
and providence and mitigated dualism
    118
reassessing philosophical contributions of
    311–312
'resident alien' motif in   251
Stoic influence on   10, 97, 152, 168, 225,
    313
Stoicism distinguished from   99, 100
Stoicism adopted and transformed by
    313–314
two ontological strata in   267
Edwards, Mark J.   109n24
election   58, 253
eleutheria   39
Eliasson, Erik   280, 281
Elliott, Mark W.   31n67, 39n116, 56n9,
    86n178, 90n202, 254n171
emanation
Apelles and   147n260
Apocryphon of John on   318
Hermogenes on   137n153
Plotinus on   271, 273, 282, 283, 291,
    292n102, 293, 308
Tripartite Tractate on   288, 291, 292n102
Embassy for the Christians (Athenagoras of
    Athens)   120
Empedocles   20
Enneads (Plotinus)   271
    Against the Gnostics   153, 172, 183, 271,
        282, 291

How the Multitude of Forms Came into Being, and on the Good 273–274

on the knowledge and will of the Good 273–281, 284

On Destiny 219n103, 271

On Difficulties About the Soul 280–281, 287, 289

On Fate 289

On the Good, or the One 272

On the Will of the One 13, 274–275

Porphyry of Tyre's *Sententiae* on 294

See also On Providence (Plotinus)

1 Enoch

as anthology 114

Astronomical Book 115, 116

on demons 117

on idolatry 115

Tertullian on 119

See also Book of the Watchers

Enochic literature

on angels 126, 136–137

apocalyptic perspective of 113, 150, 151

Christian philosophers and 119, 135

mitigated dualism of 149

Origen's familiarity with 129

Philo of Alexandria and 118

See also 1 Enoch

Ephraem Syrus 213, 267, 267n234

Epictetus

on character 43

on choice 241

on *daimones* 62–63

on God having no need of a spectator 184

on god knowing everything 33

Origen draws from 254, 254n169

on personal responsibility 223

on providential care of the virtuous 62, 96

taxonomy of providence and fate 6n23

on what is up to us 42–43

"you are an offshoot of God" 62, 187

Epicureans

on chance 39n116

Cicero on 18, 31

on God not causing what we experience 151

Josephus on 88–89

Marcion associated with 141, 143, 144, 145, 146, 157

Marcus Aurelius on 60

providence rejected by 17–18, 26, 79, 282, 291

on Stoicism 18, 59, 99

Stoics' response to 35

Valentinus associated with 157

Epicurus

atomism of 107

providence rejected by 17–18, 26–27, 30, 97, 98

Tertullian on 98

See also Epicureans

epimeleia 5, 55, 65, 65n55

epimeleisthai 77, 84n163

Epiphanius of Salamis 146

Epistle (Letter) of Aristeas 71–72, 75, 83, 96, 98

Esther 76

eternal return 34, 49, 200, 216

Eudorus of Alexandria 105

Euhemerus 97

Euripides 20, 121, 208n64

Eusebius of Caesarea 84, 89n198, 146–147, 219, 232n49

Evagrius Ponticus 309–310

evil

accounts of 315–316

angels 114–115, 116, 132, 136, 138, 146, 149, 185, 265, 288

Apelles on 148, 152

apocalyptic perspective and 150

Astronomical Book on origins of 115, 116

Athenagoras of Athens on 10, 104, 120, 136, 152, 316

Basilides on 247

Book of the Laws of the Countries on 233, 235, 236, 238

causality of 10, 46, 134, 149, 151

Chrysippus on 35, 282

Clement of Alexandria on 10, 104, 136, 150, 152, 247–248, 316

as concern of biblical texts 96

cosmic 114, 150, 151

daimones associated with 10–11

demiurge associated with 174

INDEX

demons   113, 115, 124n106, 175, 316, 317
Descartes's evil demon   316–317
dualism and   103
early Christian philosophers on   103, 151, 175
free will associated with   175
Gnosticism on   185
Greek philosophy on the gods' care and   18
Irenaeus of Lyons on   159–160
Jewish apocalyptic literature on   117–118
Josephus on   87
Justin Martyr on   118, 151
Marcion on   139, 152
matter associated with   10, 22, 53, 106, 109–110, 136, 137, 151
Maximus of Tyre on   111
Middle Platonists on   10, 46, 53, 106, 122, 151
monotheism and problem of   151
natural   35, 36, 44, 111, 124n106
Numenius of Apamea on   10, 111–112, 134, 136, 137
Origen on   10, 104, 128–137, 150, 151, 152, 260, 316
personifications of   107, 113, 114
Philo of Alexandria on   83–84, 118, 315
Plato on   22, 23, 34–35, 105, 109
Plotinus on   136, 282, 283, 288–290
Plutarch on   10, 107, 107n17, 111–112, 134, 136, 137
proto-orthodox view of   10
providence despite apparent existence of   52–53
Pythagoreanism on   105
Stoics on   34–36, 37, 53, 83, 103, 105, 108, 111, 118, 136, 151, 289
Tatian the Assyrian on   265
Tertullian on   119, 267
vice identified with   36
in worldview of first centuries CE   112
See also sin; theodicy; vice
Exegetica (Basilides)   244

fatalism
Book of the Laws of the Countries on   232
in Homeric epics   19
Josephus on Sadducees on   86n178

Philo of Alexandria's On Providence on   31n67
Pliny the Elder on   68n71
fate
Alcinous's Handbook of Platonism on   207–208
the body governed by   175
Book of the Laws of the Countries on   237, 238, 239, 240
co-fated events   12, 198, 201, 203, 205n55, 261
cosmic   195, 241n96, 264, 266, 267, 288
in essence and in action   46
Greek philosophy on the gods' care and   18
Josephus on   87, 88
Justin Martyr on   263–264
liberation from enslavement to   173, 195
in Oedipus story   198
Origen's Philocalia on   192
Platonists on   231
Plato on   207, 271
Plato's language in discussions of   24
Presocratics on   20
providence and   6n23, 18, 31, 37, 38, 39, 46, 50, 65, 191, 261n207, 289
Stoics on   6, 6n23, 31, 37–44, 57, 216, 230
See also conditional fate; fatalism
Feldmeier, Reinhard   6–7, 6n24, 56n9, 58
Ferguson, David   84n164
Final Judgment   225, 252n155, 259, 266, 268
First Apology (Justin Martyr)   89n196, 94, 119, 138–139, 234n60, 263
First Principle
Alcinous on   209
Barbelo as image of   167
as both providential and omniscient   319
Commentary on Plato's 'Parmenides' on   297
as Great Invisible Spirit   299–300
as knowing   269, 314
Marsanes on   305
matter and   106
Refutation of All Heresies on   214
Tripartite Tractate on   180, 275, 276, 291, 306
See also God; One, The
first thought (prōtē noēsis)
in Apocryphon of John   165

Christian and Hellenistic philosophers' engagement regarding 191

Commentary on Plato's 'Parmenides' on 13, 272, 297–299, 308

disappears from Platonic tradition 309–310

in 'Platonizing' Sethian treatises 299–306

Plotinus on 13, 270–271, 272, 274, 280, 293, 308

Porphyry of Tyre and forethought 272, 293–296, 299, 308, 309

Three Forms of First Thought on 169, 170, 177, 272, 298

Flaccus (Philo of Alexandria) 78–79, 85, 99

Flavius Josephus. *See* Josephus

Frede, Dorothea 37, 61–62, 206n57, 230n38

Frede, Michael 63n44, 224, 225, 227–228, 259, 277n27, 277n30

free will
Alexander of Aphrodisias on 229
Athenagoras of Athens on angels' 121
Basilides on 12, 268, 315
Book of the Laws of the Countries on 232, 233, 234–235, 240, 268, 315
in Christian theology and philosophy 9, 12, 103, 223, 226, 262, 267, 315
Clement of Alexandria on 240–241, 251, 257
divine omniscience as compatible with 314
emergence of concept of 191, 223–226, 252–253, 262, 315
evil associated with 175
'freedom to do otherwise' 41n123, 224, 226, 228, 234, 236
Justin Martyr on 263
Maximus of Tyre on 111
Origen on 134, 191, 192, 252–262, 268, 315
Plotinus on 275
in second and third century Roman philosophy 12
shift in notion of human accountability from autonomy to freedom 268
Stoicism on 39, 223, 261, 315
Tatian the Assyrian on 265
Theophilus of Antioch on 266, 267, 315

Tripartite Tractate on 180n116, 285
See also compatibilism; ḥi'rutā'; 'what is up to us' (*to eph'hēmin*)

Frick, Peter 81, 81n151, 82, 82n153

Gager, John 143, 144
Gaius, school of 46n144
Galen 63n44, 228n30
Genesis
1–3 318
1:26 144, 148, 159
1:27 156
2:3 12, 112, 193
2:7 253
2:8–13 144
3 143
6:1–4 112, 114, 136, 137
23:4 251
25:21–26 258
See also Adam and Eve

Gibbons, Kathleen 212n82, 217n97

Gnosticism
alternative terms for 185–188
anthropocentrism of 183
as anticosmic dualism 185, 185n139
biblical proof-texts of 318
'brain-in-a-vat' scenario compared with 317–318
on the demiurge 153, 174, 215, 282, 284, 317
Descartes's evil demon compared with 316–317
determinism attributed to 226, 252
on divine foreknowledge 213–214
dualism of 11, 152, 153, 185, 316
emergence of concept of will and 223, 224
on evil 185, 315
as genuine innovation 313
as 'Gnosis' 187
versus 'Gnostics' 153–155
on God's care for particulars 272
on humans as good and the world as bad 174
Irenaeus of Lyons on 11, 160, 187
language of providence in 188
Marcionism distinguished from 186n144, 186–187
martyrdom and 242n107

INDEX

379

mutual impact of biblicizing and pagan
philosophy on   319
and the One   277
Origen on   226
Plotinus's criticism of   153, 172, 282, 292,
311
Plotinus's engagement with   14, 307–
308, 311, 312
Porphyry of Tyre on   11, 153, 187
Stoicism contrasted with   175, 187, 315
term criticized   153–154
See also Nag Hammadi Codices
God
of Abraham   96, 97, 138, 159
Apelles on   155
in Aristotle's theology   27–29, 33
Athenagoras of Athens on   120, 121
Book of the Laws of the Countries on   233,
234, 235, 239
as cause of everything   38
Clement of Alexandria on   57n12, 123,
247–248
creator-god   10, 11, 37, 104, 112, 114, 120,
156, 164, 172, 173, 178, 179
demons as divine administrators   121–
122
eventual triumph over evil   112–113
in Hellenistic Jewish writings   58, 71–
76
ignorance of Adam's whereabouts in the
Garden   214
immanent   10, 28, 37, 82, 97, 98, 100, 130,
313
impersonal   57, 57n12, 58, 268
Irenaeus of Lyons on   11, 158–159, 160
of Israel   10, 72–76, 83, 88, 95–96, 140,
147n200, 155, 306, 318
Jewish apocalyptic literature on   117–118
Justin Martyr's *Dialogue with Trypho* on
88–96
knowledge of contingent events   293–
294, 305
knowledge of particulars   293–294, 306,
307
"let *us* make"   144, 159
Marcion on   137–149, 155, 260
memory of   271–272
middle knowledge of   314
monotheism   151, 266

Nature of the Rulers on   177
Numenius of Apamea on   108
of Old Testament   11, 141, 143, 144,
186n144, 260
as omnipotent   32, 56n7, 61, 75, 88, 97,
100, 159, 270, 315n13, 317n16
as omnipresent   31, 32, 53, 58, 61, 75, 88,
97, 100, 108, 124–125, 130, 133, 152, 272,
274, 275, 289, 306, 308
as omniscient   13, 31, 33, 53, 61, 75, 88,
104, 159, 193, 194, 201, 216–217, 221, 256,
271, 272, 289, 293, 296, 299, 300, 306,
307, 308, 313–314, 319
Origen on evil and   260
personal   54–64, 76, 83, 90, 96–100, 152,
214n91, 268, 313
Philo of Alexandria on   11, 76, 77, 80–81,
99, 155, 157
of Platonism   57, 96, 105
Plato on creation of the world by   21–24
Plotinus on   271–272, 292
Pseudo-Aristotle on   29–30
shift in identity of   10, 90, 92n206, 93, 95,
96–97, 268
of Stoics   31–37, 53, 57, 58, 59–60, 61,
72, 96, 97, 98, 100, 130, 155, 208, 218,
268
Tertullian on   149
transcendent   28, 60n21, 74n103, 79, 81,
82n153, 99, 108, 125, 158, 182n128, 209,
218n100, 272, 275, 277, 299, 302, 303,
304, 307
Tripartite Tractate on   181, 182, 290–291,
292n102
will of   17, 87, 132–133, 177, 178, 183, 194,
255n172, 270n2, 272, 279n41
See also divine foreknowledge; providence; theodicy
gods
in Archaic poets   19
behavior proper to   141
Cicero on their knowing everything   33–
34, 34n83, 293
Graeco-Roman as angels   119, 124
Graeco-Roman identified with demons
113, 124, 129, 135, 155, 265, 316
in Homeric epics   19
pantheism   32n71, 61, 62
Presocratics on   20

young gods of Plato's *Timaeus*   22, 23, 26, 30, 37, 53, 136, 152, 155, 174, 315, 318
See also God
Good, the
does not care   279, 281–282
the One and   273, 277
Plotinus on the knowledge and will of   273–281, 284
Tripartite Tractate on the knowledge and will of   275–277
Gospels
Adam's fall absent in   117
apocalyptic heritage in   113, 122, 150, 151
Satan in   114, 116, 121
See also John; Luke; Mark; Matthew
grace   241, 241n97, 257
Gregory of Nazianzus   192
Greschat, Katharina   147

Hadot, Pierre   8n27, 274, 297, 298
Hägg, Tomas   52n167, 52n170
Handbook of Platonism (Alcinous)   207–209, 218
Harper, Kyle   225, 225n13, 226n19, 239n80, 262, 263
Havrda, Matyáš   63n44, 241, 241n96, 242n106
heimarmenē   5
Alexander of Aphrodisias's *Peri heimar-menēs*   204
Bardaiṣan's *Peri heimarmenēs*   232n49
in Gnostic literature   175
Josephus's use of   87
Justin Martyr on   263
Origen's *Commentary on Genesis* on   194
Plotinus on   281, 286
versus *pronoia*   5, 39, 44
in Stoicism   38–39, 44
See also fate, *On Fate*
Heraclitus   20, 242
Hermogenes
on co-existence of matter and God   137
dualism of   11, 316
on imperfection   104
on matter as source of chaos   151
Numenius's influence on   108n23
Tertullian's polemic against   137, 137n153
Herodotus   20, 20n20, 26, 65, 197
Hesiod   19, 33

Hitler, Adolf   3, 3n11, 6
holos   23, 24n34
Homer   19, 111
Homilies on Jeremiah (Origen)   257n184
Homilies on Luke (Origen)   129, 129n125, 131
household argument   60–61, 62n35, 125, 207
How the Multitude of Forms Came into Being, and on the Good (Plotinus)   273–274
Huber, Peter   314n9
human body
Apelles on creator of   138, 148, 149
Apocryphon of John on creator of   167, 171
Book of the Laws of the Countries on   240
Clement of Alexandria on   251
fate as controlling   240, 240n90, 289
Gnostics on   173, 175
On the Origin of the World on creator of   165
Plato on caring for   243
Plotinus on souls' descent into   280
resurrection of   265, 266, 268
Socratic argument from design regarding   36
Tertullian on creator of   148
young gods of *Timaeus* as creators of   22, 152, 315
Hyde, Thomas   150n213
Hymn to Zeus (Cleanthes)   32, 72, 97
Hypothetica (Philo of Alexandria)   80

ḥi'rutā'   233–236, 238, 240

Iamblichus
Allogenes compared with   303, 304, 305, 306
on flower of the One   309
on God's foreknowledge of future conditionals   218, 299, 307, 308, 314
on impulse toward religiosity   309n166
on knowledge as intermediate   294, 294n109
on Plotinus on soul's descent into matter   106n9
providence in writings of   7
on two Ones   304
idolatry   115, 116, 126, 131, 135
If God Makes Good, Whence Comes Evil? (Maximus of Tyre)   111
Iliad (Homer)   19, 33

INDEX

Ilievski, Viktor 282n59
individual responsibility. *See* personal accountability (responsibility)
Irenaeus of Lyons
  Against Heresies 139–141, 160, 267
  creation-theology of 155–160
  demiurge and 140, 160–161
  emphasis on thinkers whose views resemble those of 13
  on evil 159–160
  on free will 267, 268, 315
  on Gnostics 11, 160, 187
  Gnostic texts known by 184, 185
  on God as providential creator 11, 158–159, 160
  on humanity coming to possess intellect 171
  on Marcion 138, 139–141, 143, 157, 316
  on matter 158, 161
  on Plato 140n161, 157, 157n18
  on the Son 159, 186
  on the soul as seat of accountability 268
  Valentinians and 160, 178, 182, 316
  on Wisdom 160, 161
Isocrates 65n55

Janssens, Yvonne 169n71
Jerome, St. 143, 213, 314n9
Jesus Christ
  Apelles on 148
  Basilides and suffering of 244–245
  Clement of Alexandria on 125, 127
  'consider how the wild flowers grow' 56
  on God's care for sparrows 96, 132
  Judas's betrayal of 195, 196, 210, 211, 212, 215, 256
  Justin Martyr on 89, 93–94, 95, 97, 156
  in *Letter of Peter to Philip* 172–173
  as *logos* 156, 170, 211
  Marcion on 138, 139, 141, 142, 144
  Origen on 129, 130
  in *Second Treatise on the Great Seth* 173
  on sin 117
  Tripartite Tractate on 276
  See also early Christianity
Jewish Antiquities (Josephus) 85, 86–88, 89n195
Jewish War (Josephus) 85, 86, 87

Jews
  apocalyptic literature of 112–118, 136
  departure to Sinai 75
  God in writings of Hellenistic 58
  God of Israel 10, 72–76, 83, 88, 95–96, 140, 147n200, 155, 306, 318
  Jewish writings as untapped resource 312
  Josephus on providential history as Jewish history 85–89
  Justin Martyr's *Dialogue with Trypho* on 89, 94–96
  language of providence used by philosophically-inclined 55
  on life based on *anagkē* 241n96
  Philo of Alexandria on God's providential care of 77, 78–80, 83, 99
  providence in Hellenistic Jewish literature 71–76
  under Roman domination 54, 72
  Stoicism influenced by 313
  Tertullian on 98
  wisdom literature of 58, 72, 73n92
  See also Abraham; Enochic literature; Moses; Old Testament
Job
  1–2 114, 117
  2:10 131
  14:4 245
Johannes Climacus 310
John
  2:25 212, 318
  4:24 130
  12:27 56n7
  14:6 170
  16:8 266
  Amelius's exegesis of 307
Joly, Robert 91n205, 92
Joseph 77
Josephus 85–89
  on interventionist providence 85–89, 96
  Jewish Antiquities 85, 86–88, 89n195
  Jewish War 85, 86, 87
  on omnipresence of the divine 100
  on Stoic model of providential care 58, 98
Judas 195, 196, 210, 211, 212, 215, 256
Judith 76
Junod, Eric 195n10

Justin (Gnostic)   213–214

Justin Martyr
  on angels   119, 124, 136, 264
  on baptism   264, 267
  on *daimones*   100
  Dialogue with Trypho   10, 58, 89–96, 138
  on divine foreknowledge   216, 263, 313
  on evil   118, 151
  on fate   263–264
  First Apology   89n196, 94, 118, 138–139, 234n60, 263
  on free will   263
  God of   96–97, 234n60
  on Greek gods as sinning angels   119
  on Jesus Christ   89, 93–94, 95, 97, 156
  on *logos*   264, 292
  on Marcion   94, 138–139
  on personal accountability   262, 263
  on punishment   263, 264
  Second Apology   118
  Stoicism and   118
  on will   223

Kalligas, Anthony   20n20, 288n87, 289n91, 290n97
Kaluptos   300, 301, 305
Karamanolis, George E.   2n5, 103, 151n216, 186, 186n144, 220n106, 265n227
Kenney, John Peter   284n71
King, Karen L.   167n57
Kippenberg, Hans G.   163n40
Klawans, Jonathan   6n23, 88
Klingner, Friedrich   314n9
knowledge
  Allogenes on divine   303–304
  God as omniscient   13, 31, 33, 53, 61, 75, 88, 104, 159, 193, 194, 201, 216–217, 221, 256, 271, 272, 289, 293, 296, 299, 300, 306, 307, 308, 313–314, 319
  God's knowledge of contingent events   293–294
  God's knowledge of particulars   293–294, 306, 307
  God's middle knowledge   314
  Marsanes on divine   305
  Zostrianos on Intellect as having   300–303
  See also divine foreknowledge
Kraabel, A. Thomas   4n14, 96n223

Labarriére, Pierre-Jean   9n33
Lachesis   25, 242n106
Laws (Plato)
  Myth of Er contrasted with   25
  Philo of Alexandria influenced by   79
  Stoic God contrasted with   37
  on whole-part in God's relationship to the world   23–24, 50, 53, 60, 61, 271, 282, 283
  on World Soul   105, 107
Layton, Bentley   153, 154, 154n4, 176n99
'lazy argument' (*argos logos*)
  Alexander of Aphrodisias's *On Fate* on   205
  Chrysippus on   39, 193, 198n24, 201, 212
  Cicero's *On Fate* on   201, 211
  Clement of Alexandria and   247, 253
  Origen on   211, 216
Leo XIII, Pope   2–3, 3n10
Létourneau, Pierre   172
Letter (Epistle) of Aristeas   71–72, 75, 83, 96, 98
Letter of Peter to Philip   172–173
Library of History (Diodorus Siculus)   66–68
Lieu, Judith   213
Life of Aesop   51–52
Life of Moses (Philo of Alexandria)   77–78, 79–80
Lincoln, Abraham   2
Litwa, M. David   167n57
logos
  Christ as   156, 170, 211
  Chrysippus on   40
  Clement of Alexandria on   241
  in John   170
  Justin Martyr on   264, 292
  Origen on   156, 292
  Philo of Alexandria on   81–82, 82n156, 83, 156, 292
  Plotinus on   279, 282, 284, 285, 286, 287, 289, 291, 292, 308
  Tripartite Tractate on   179, 186, 276, 284–285, 287, 288, 291, 292, 308
  See also reason (rationality)
Löhr, Winrich   249n144, 249n147, 250n150
Louth, Andrew   57, 308
Lucian   51n157, 93n210
Lucretius   17

INDEX   383

Luke
    4:5–7   116
    4:16–18   129
    12:6–7   57, 96, 129, 318
    12:27–30   56, 144–145
    22:22   145–146

Macaskill, Grant   73n92
Maccabees   76
Magris, Aldo   1n5, 86n178, 135n150, 154n6, 206n57, 294n110
Manichaeism   153, 187
Mansfeld, Jaap   20n16, 33n78, 174, 185n141
Marcion   137–149
    Apelles contrasted with   148–149
    astrology and   195
    biblical proof-texts of   318
    Clement of Alexandria and   248
    on divine foreknowledge   12, 143, 213, 215
    dualism of   11, 104, 151, 152, 186, 213, 222, 234, 316
    Epicureanism attributed to   141, 143, 144, 145, 146, 157
    on evil   139, 152
    exegesis of Genesis 2:3   12, 193
    as genuine innovator   313
    Gnosticism and Marcionism distinguished   186n144, 186–187
    on God   137–149, 155, 260
    Irenaeus of Lyons on   138, 139–141, 143, 157
    Justin Martyr on   94, 138–139
    Luke 12:6–7 absent from Gospel of   318
    Origen's attack on   12, 194–195, 210, 213, 215, 218, 222, 260
    providence in writings of   7, 137–149
    salvation by nature doctrine and   252
    on sin   142
    Tertullian on   138, 141–143, 144–146, 157, 213, 316
    Tripartite Tractate and   181, 182
Marcovich, Miroslav   127n118
Marcus Aurelius   39, 43n134, 59, 60, 204, 307n160
Marcus Eremita   310
Marcus Sergius   69–70
Marius Victorinus   297, 298, 301, 311
Marjanen, Antti   184n135

Mark
    4:12   255n172
    14:36   56n7
Marsanes   13, 304n151, 305–306, 314
martyrdom
    Basilides on   226, 245n122, 249n147, 250, 251
    Clement of Alexandria on   226, 242–244, 245–246
    by Gnostics   242n107
    providence and   243–247
Mastema   113
matter
    Adam cast into   176n100
    in *Apocryphon of John*   167, 176
    Aristotle on   28
    Athenagoras of Athens on   120
    Authoritative Teaching on   178
    as chaotic   22, 82, 104, 110, 111, 151, 158
    Chrysippus on God and   33n78
    in discussions about providence   112
    evil associated with   10, 22, 53, 106, 109–110, 136, 137, 151
    Hermogenes on   137
    Irenaeus of Lyons on   158, 161
    Maximus of Tyre on   111
    Middle Platonists on   53, 106
    Numenius of Apamea on   106, 108–109, 111–112, 137
    On the Origin of the World on   177
    Origen on   106, 134, 136
    Philo of Alexandria on   82, 82n156, 99
    Plato on form and   106, 109
    in Plato's *Timaeus*   84, 105, 106, 110, 316
    Plotinus on   106, 106n9
    Plutarch on   106–108, 111, 137
    as resistant to ordering   112
    Stoicism on   105, 155
    Tertullian on creation from   142
    Three Forms of First Thought on   176, 177
    Tripartite Tractate on   182
    Zeno on Fate and   38
    See also human body
Matthew
    4:8   116
    10:29–30   56, 96, 128–129, 318
    26:39   56n7
Maximus of Tyre
    on *daimones*   64

on divine intervention 63n45
on evil 111
If God Makes Good, Whence Comes Evil? 111
medical metaphor of 94
Plutarch compared with 51
on prayer 93, 93n210, 94
Mazur, Zeke 281n52, 298, 300, 309n166
Melki-Resa 113
Memorabilia (Xenophon) 20–21, 26
Menander 147, 176
Menedemus 72, 98
Metaphysics (Aristotle) 27–28, 29, 30
metempsychosis 147, 231n48, 246
Meyer, Marvin 170
Meyer, Susan Sauvé 229
Michalewski, Alexandra 27n45, 280n49
Middle Platonism
    Alcinous's *Handbook of Platonism* and 207
    Athenagoras of Athens compared with 121
    compatibilism and 209, 232
    on conditional fate 12, 45–51, 207, 208, 209, 225, 226, 230–232, 261, 263–264, 316
    on *daimones* 12, 45, 47, 53, 58, 59–60, 63–64, 65, 100, 104, 108, 118, 121, 122, 126, 132, 152, 155, 165, 242, 288, 315
    on divine foreknowledge 212
    early Christians contrasted with 55
    early Christians influenced by 100, 104, 135
    on evil 10, 46, 53, 106, 122, 151
    on First Principle as knowing 314
    grades of providence in 46, 47, 50–51, 155, 175
    location between Academic Skepticism and Plotinus 45
    on matter 106
    Origen and 212
    Plotinus and 45, 278, 280, 287, 289
    on providence and fate 46, 65, 289
    on second creative principle 106
    Stoicism contrasted with 59
    weakness of the term 45n140
    on will 270n2
    Yaldabaoth compared with 164
Mignucci, Mario 206n59

Minucius Felix 99, 100, 123, 130
miracles 56n7, 77–78, 79
Miscellanies (*Stromateis*) (Clement of Alexandria) 122–128, 241–251
Moderatus of Gades 106, 109
monism 103, 147, 150, 150n212, 151n216, 245, 251
monotheism 151, 266
Moore, George F. 42n124
Moreschini, Claudio 141n168
Moses 77–78, 79–80, 86, 98, 264
Mystical Theology (Pseudo-Dionysius) 309

Nag Hammadi Codices
    biblical demiurgicalism and 186
    debates sparked by 311
    dualism in 187
    on first thought 272
    general perspective on divine providence in 187
    'Gnostic' literature in 153, 154
    Jesus in 172
    language of providence in 11, 171, 172–173
    Platonizing Sethian literature in 13, 191
    Plotinus and 191
    on providence and the present world 175–176
    on repenting demiurges 179
    Teachings of Silvanus 216, 217n97, 313
    See also Allogenes; Apocryphon of John; Authoritative Teaching; Letter of Peter to Philip; Marsanes; On the Origin of the World; Paraphrase of Shem; 'Sethian' treatises; *Three Forms of First Thought* (*Trimorphic Protennoia*); *Tripartite Tractate*; *Zostrianos*
Narbonne, Jean-Marc 277n30
Nasrallah, Laura Salah 6, 91n205, 265n227
Natural History (Pliny the Elder) 68n70, 68–70
nature
    Book of the Laws of the Countries on 237, 238, 239
    salvation by 252, 253, 258, 258n189, 260, 261
Nature of the Rulers 177, 183
Nautin, Pierre 249n147
Nemesis 25

INDEX

385

Nemesius of Emesa   34, 46, 47n145, 200–
    201, 216, 228n30, 230
Neoplatonism
    on God's foreknowledge of future condi-
        tionals   218
    increased focus on providence in   308–
        309
    on matter as creative principle   106
    Middle Platonists and   45
    Tripartite Tractate and   306
    See also Iamblichus; Plotinus; Porphyry of
        Tyre
Nephilim   114, 115
New Testament
    on demons   118
    divine interventions in   55–56
    personal sense of the divine in   10
    pronoia qua 'providence' absent in   7, 55,
        96
    See also Acts; 1 Corinthians; Gospels;
        2 Peter; Romans
Nicomachaean Ethics (Aristotle)   43, 227–
    228, 236
Niehoff, Maren   85
Noble, Christopher Isaac   308n165
nomima barbarika argument   220, 239
non-being   296
Norelli, Enrico   141n167
nous
    Alcinous on   209
    Aristotle on   27
    Plato on   106
    Plotinus on   273, 277, 278, 279, 300
numen   5, 69
Numenius of Apamea
    Apelles contrasted with   148
    on the demiurge   109, 316
    dualism of   11, 104, 106, 108–109, 111, 152,
        316
    on evil   10, 111–112, 134, 136, 137
    on matter   106, 108–109, 111, 112, 137
    Philo of Alexandria compared with   99
    providence in writings of   7
    remarks on Moses and Genesis   307
    sees himself as Pythagorean   109
    on World Soul   108, 111–112, 152

O'Brien, Carl   107, 112, 178n110
Octavius (Minucius Felix)   99

Odyssey (Homer)   19, 111
Oedipus Rex (Sophocles)   209–210
Old Academy   45, 45n138, 51
Old Testament
    God of   11, 141, 143, 144, 186n144, 260
    Septuagint   76, 83, 113, 114, 116, 117, 318
    Tanakh   96
    See also Genesis; Job; Psalms
On Difficulties About the Soul (Plotinus)
    280–281, 287, 289
On Divination (Cicero)   199, 203
One, the
    activity and providence ascribed to
        274–275
    Allogenes on   303–304
    Gnostic use of the term   277
    the Good and   273, 277
    Iamblichus on two   304
    knowledge of particulars   293, 301, 305
    Marsanes on   305
    particulars proceed from   290
    Plotinus on   13, 271, 293, 300, 301, 305, 314
    self-knowledge of   300
    supra-cognitive faculty for knowing
        297–299
    transcendence of   293
    Zostrianos on   301–302
On Fate (Alexander of Aphrodisias, *Peri
    heimarmenēs*)   204–207
    on Anaxagoras on fate   20n16
    on choice   229, 264
    civic piety and   206, 207, 218
    dedication of   204, 207
    on divine foreknowledge   204–207, 214,
        215
    on 'Oracle to Laius'   193, 198, 204, 205,
        210, 213, 218–219
    on 'what is up to us'   228–229
On Fate (Chrysippus, *Peri heimarmenēs*)   34,
    38–39
On Fate (Cicero, *De fato*)
    civic values animate   203
    on divination   199–200, 203
    on divine foreknowledge   203, 214
    doctrine of co-fated events preserved in
        12, 201
    on 'lazy argument'   201, 211
    on Milo wrestling at the Olympics
        201n39

on 'Oracle to Laius' 193, 198, 201, 202–203

On Fate (Origen, *Peri heimarmenēs*) 192, 210–216
  on astrology 192, 193, 219–222
  on divine foreknowledge 12, 192
  as extract from *Commentary on Genesis* 192, 210, 222
  insertion from *Against Celsus* in 192
  subject matter of 11–12, 219

On Fate (Plotinus, *Peri heimarmenēs*) 219n103, 271, 289

On Fate (Pseudo-Plutarch, *Peri heimarmenēs*) 9–10, 46, 46n141, 207, 230

On First Principles (Origen)
  on individual autonomy 255, 257, 261, 262
  on determinism 253–262
  Enoch cited by 131
  on keeping the commandments 254, 259
  on nothing happening without God 128–129
  on personal accountability 253, 261, 262
  on pre-existent intellects 133–134
  on punishment 253, 256n182, 256–257
  subject matter of 191
  on Wisdom, *logos*, and *pronoia* 156
  See also On Free Will (Origen), *On the Opposing Powers* (Origen)

On Flight (Philo of Alexandria) 82–83

On Free Will (Origen) 12, 226, 253, 315, 318–319

On Isis and Osiris (Plutarch) 106–108, 111–112

On Philosophy (Aristotle) 28–29

On Prayer (Origen) 307

On Providence (Alexander of Aphrodisias, *Peri pronoias*) 206–207

On Providence (Philo of Alexandria, *Peri pronoias*) 31n67, 84–85

On Providence (Plotinus, *Peri pronoias*) 281–293
  Christian and Gnostic influence on 311
  on divine plan 272n7
  generalissimo metaphor in 286–287
  on life as a drama 286
  on *logos* 284, 285, 286, 287, 289, 291, 292, 308

retreats to more conservative position 272, 305

Tripartite Tractate and 13, 272, 282, 284–285, 288–292, 292n102

On the Cherubim (Philo of Alexandria) 81

On the Creation of the World (Philo of Alexandria) 77

On the Decline of Oracles (Plutarch) 64

On the Fortune of the Romans (Plutarch) 70–71

On the Good, or the One (Plotinus) 272

On the Nature of the Gods (Cicero)
  civic values animate 203–204, 207, 218
  on divine causality entailing divine providence 34, 36–37
  on God leaving the small stuff aside 60, 61, 61n29, 100
  on human reason as gift of providence 62
  on Plato's *Timaeus* 18
  on *pronoia* 18
  on Stoic God 32, 59, 61

On the Opposing Powers (Origen) 259n194

On the Origin of the World 161–165
  Apocryphon of John compared with 167
  archons in 161, 162–163, 164, 173, 174, 185
  creation and providence separated in 175
  on the demiurge 172
  Descartes's evil demon compared with 317
  Irenaeus of Lyons and Porphyry know 184
  on matter 177
  on providence 154, 161–165, 174–176, 177
  on rational divine character of humans 174
  tensions in 183
  two kinds of providence in 174–176
  Wisdom in 161, 162, 163, 164, 165
  Yaldabaoth in 160–162, 163, 164–165, 171, 174

On the Soul (Tertullian) 137n153, 267–268

On the Special Laws (Philo of Alexandria) 77, 81, 82

On the Unchangeableness of God (Philo of Alexandria) 217–218

On the Will of the One (Plotinus) 13, 274–275, 292, 292n102, 311

INDEX

387

On the World (Chrysippus) 38

On the World (*De mundo*) (Pseudo-Aristotle)
 29–30
  dating and authorship of 29n57
  Epicurean views on providence distinguished from 27
  Epicurus mocked by 30, 30n66
  'Great King' reference in 29, 30, 51, 125–126, 316
  Middle Platonists influenced by 53
  Philo of Alexandria and 80

Opsomer, Jan 34n83, 41n122, 49n158,
  49n159, 63n45, 231, 231n48

'Oracle to Laius' 197–213
  Alcinous on 193, 198, 208–209
  Alexander of Aphrodisias on 193, 198,
   204, 205, 210, 213
  Chrysippus on 193, 198, 201–202, 203,
   206, 208, 216
  Cicero on 193, 198, 201, 202–203
  Origen on 12, 193, 210, 211, 212, 216, 218–219
  Plotinus and 277
  Sophocles's *Oedipus Rex* and 209–210

Origen
  on angels 131–132, 133–134, 138, 222,
   288
  astrological determinism and 12, 193,
   195, 215, 259
  on the Bridegroom 309
  on choice 222, 254, 257, 261
  as Christian theologian and Platonist
   philosopher 311, 312
  Chrysippus and 39, 193, 198n24, 201, 212
  on demons 131, 132–136, 152, 222
  on the Devil 132, 134–135, 135n148
  on divination 193, 218–219, 220
  eternal return and 49n158
  on evil 10, 104, 128–137, 150, 151, 152, 259,
   316
  on free will 134, 191, 192, 252–262, 268,
   315
  as genuine innovator 313
  on Gnosticism 226
  on God's foreknowledge of future conditionals 193, 216, 218, 293, 307, 313–314,
   318
  'Great King' analogy used by 30, 132, 133,
   316

Homilies on Jeremiah 257n184
Homilies on Luke 129, 129n125, 131
  on 'lazy argument' 211, 216
  on *logos* 156, 292
  on Luke 12:6–7 57, 129, 318
  on Marcion 12, 194–195, 210, 213, 215, 218,
   222, 260
  on matter 106, 134, 136
  mutual impact of biblicizing and pagan
   philosophy on 157
On Free Will 12, 226, 253, 315, 318–319
On Prayer 307
On the Opposing Powers 259n194
  on 'Oracle to Laius' 12, 193, 210, 211, 212,
   216, 218–219
  Plotinus and 219, 219n103
  on prayer 310
  on pre-existing souls 133–134, 246,
   253n164, 257–258, 260, 261, 262, 315
  on providence 7, 128–137, 156–157, 191–196
  on sin 133, 135, 135n148
  Valentinians and 179, 260
  on will 223
  on Wisdom 134n146, 156
  See also Against Celsus (Origen); *Commentary on Genesis* (Origen); *On Fate*
   (Origen); *On First Principles* (Origen);
   Philocalia (Origen)

Osborn, Eric 57n12

Pagels, Elaine 170
paideia 228, 248, 256n182, 267
Painchaud, Louis 165, 169
pantheism 32n71, 61, 62
Paraphrase of Shem 177–178, 183
Parker, Robert 20n20
Parma, Christian 1n5
Parmenides (Plato) 297
Parthenius 197
Paul, St. 55n4, 113, 116, 117, 258, 270n2
Pearson, Birger 246
Pedersen, Nils Arne 213, 213n88, 214, 214n91
Pépin, Jean 92n207, 93, 93n210, 185n142
Perkins, Pheme 172
Perry, Ben Edwin 51n167
personal accountability (responsibility)
  Alexander of Aphrodisias on 205, 206,
   229–230

Aristotle's account of action in debate on 227

Basilides on 245, 246, 250

in biblical sources 96, 223

Book of the Laws of the Countries on 226, 233, 234–235, 236, 238, 240, 262

in Christian theology and philosophy 9, 225, 253

Clement of Alexandria on 226, 241, 243, 246–247, 249, 249n147, 250–252, 262

divine foreknowledge and 196, 212

early Christian writers on dualism and 103

Greek philosophy on the gods' care and 18

Irenaeus of Lyons on 159

Justin Martyr on 262, 263

Middle Platonists on 45, 46, 53

nominalistic versus voluntaristic notions of 224

Origen's *Against Celsus* on 193, 211, 222

Origen's *On First Principles* on 253, 261, 262

Plato on 25–26, 208, 225, 249, 252, 261, 264, 268

Plotinus on 278

pre-natal 225, 240, 246, 249, 262, 268

providence and 191, 223, 227

shift in notion of 268

Sirach on 73

Socrates on 25–26

the soul seen as seat of 12, 263, 266, 268

Stoics on 37, 39–44, 151, 152, 223, 223n4, 224, 225, 254, 264

Tatian the Assyrian on 265

Tertullian on 267–268

tripartion of providence and 50

See also 'what is up to us' (*to eph'hēmin*)

2 Peter 3:5 156, 318

Phaedo (Plato) 20n16

Phaedrus (Plato) 24–25, 105, 283

Philocalia (Origen)
  as compilation 191–192
  on fate 192
  on free will 191, 192, 253
  On Free Will excerpted in 226, 253
  as point of departure on divine fore-knowledge 191

See also On Fate (Origen); *On Free Will* (Origen)

Philo of Alexandria 76–85
  on Abraham 77, 123
  Allegorical Interpretation 82
  on *daimones* 80, 99, 100
  on divine foreknowledge 217–218, 313
  embassy to Rome 85
  evidence on providence in 7
  on evil 83–84, 118, 315
  Flaccus 78–79, 85, 99
  as genuine innovator 313
  on God 11, 76, 77, 80–81, 99, 155, 157
  on God's powers 81, 83, 185
  on God's will 270n2
  'Great King' analogy used by 30, 80, 316
  Hypothetica 80
  Josephus and 85, 86
  Life of Moses 77–78, 79–80
  on *logos* 81–82, 82n156, 83, 156, 292
  On Flight 82–83
  On Providence 31n67, 84–85
  On the Cherubim 81
  On the Creation of the World 77
  On the Special Laws 77, 81, 82
  On the Unchangeableness of God 217–218
  parental metaphor in 77, 81, 83
  personalization of providence of 58, 96
  in shift in identity of the divine 10
  Stoicism and 58, 76, 79, 80, 85, 98, 118

Philopator 228n30

philosophy
  Academic Skepticism 32, 45, 61, 204n52, 212
  biblical proof texts in 318–319
  boundary between theology and 9
  Clement of Alexandria on 123–124, 127–128
  debates regarding third century development of 311–312
  in early Christianity 55, 318
  Nag Hammadi manuscripts' perspective distinguished from 187
  Parting of the ways between Christian philosophy and 319
  Presocratics 20
  providence in Greek 17–53, 59–64, 104–112, 196–210, 271–298

INDEX

Pythagoreanism 105, 109, 318

religious dualism in Roman 149–152

See also Aristotle; Plato; Platonism; Stoicism

Pich, Roberto Hofmeister 43n132

Plato

Alcinous's *Handbook of Platonism* on 207

on caring for the body 243

eschatological myths of 24–25

on evil 22, 23, 34–35, 105, 109

on fate 207, 271

on flaws in creation 35, 35n88, 53

Irenaeus of Lyons and 140n161, 157, 157n18

on matter 106, 109, 158

on metempsychosis 147, 231n48

Numenius of Apamea compared with 109

Parmenides 297

Phaedo 20n16

Phaedrus 24–25, 105, 283

Politicus 23

on pre-existence of souls 246, 249, 283

pronoia in 5, 20, 18n9, 57

providential crucifixion predicted by 127

Theaetetus 105

"the responsibility lies with the one who chooses" 25–26, 208, 225, 249, 252, 261, 264, 268

on two causes 105–106

Tripartite Tractate compared with 182

Zeno and 32

See also Laws (Plato); *Republic* (Plato); *Timaeus* (Plato); Platonism

Platonism

causal dualism of 231, 232

Christianizing turn in Platonic conceptions of divine foreknowledge 306–310

compatibilism attributed to 230

dualism in 103, 104, 105, 106

early Christian philosophy's relationship to 13–14, 307–308

fusion of Pythagoreanism and 105

on God 57, 96, 105

in Nag Hammadi manuscripts 13, 191

Old Academy 45, 45n138, 51

'Platonizing' Sethian treatises 299–306

shift in speculation about divine omniscience in 293, 296, 319

Stoicism opposed by 45

Tertullian on 98

on will 270

See also Middle Platonism; Neoplatonism

Pleše, Zlatko 182n128

Pliny the Elder 58, 65, 68n71, 68–70, 96

Plotinus

on causality 273, 274, 293

on divine foreknowledge 11, 13, 300–301

on emanation 271, 273, 282, 283, 291, 292n102, 293, 308

engagement with Christian and Gnostic sources 14, 307–308, 311, 312

on evil 136, 282, 283, 288–290

on first thought 13, 270–271, 272, 274, 280, 293, 308

on Gnostics 153, 172, 282, 292, 311

on God 271–272, 292

on the knowledge and will of the Good 273–281

on *logos* 279, 282, 284, 285, 286, 287, 289, 291, 292, 308

Marsanes contrasted with 305

on matter as creative principle 106, 106n9

Middle Platonists and 45, 278, 280, 287, 289

mutual impact of biblicizing and pagan philosophy on 157

on *nous* 273, 277, 278, 279, 300

on the One 13, 271, 293, 300, 301, 305, 314

Origen and 219, 219n103

on personal accountability 278

Platonizing works circulate in seminar of 297, 307, 314

on pre-existence of souls 283, 315

on pre-noetic cognitive faculty 296

on providence 279–283, 303, 308

on "reckless statement" 275, 277, 292n102, 292–293, 308

Stoicism compared with 282, 287, 291

on theodicy 272, 282, 283

Tripartite Tractate and 179, 182, 183, 271, 277

on will 13, 271, 272, 277, 278, 283
on World Soul 279, 286
Zostrianos and *Allogenes* and 297, 305
See also Enneads (Plotinus)
Plutarch
on causality and personal responsibility 230
on *daimones* 64, 70, 100, 108, 151
on demiurge 107, 109, 316
on divination 197
on divine intervention 63n45, 64
dualism of 11, 104, 106, 111, 150n213, 152, 316
on evil 10, 107, 107n17, 111–112, 134, 136, 137
Josephus and 87
on matter 106–108, 111, 137
On Isis and Osiris 106–108, 111–112
On the Decline of Oracles 64
On the Fortune of the Romans 70–71
personalization of providence of 58
Philo of Alexandria compared with 78, 99
on *tuchē* 71, 71n84
on World Soul 107, 109, 109n24, 111, 152
Poirer, Paul-Hubert 169n71
Polemo 45n138
Politicus (Plato) 23
Polybius 65–66
on chance 3n11 (*tuchē*), 65–66, 66n60, 70, 87
Josephus and 87
Philo of Alexandria and 78
philosophical context of 58
on providence in history 65–66, 96
Porphyry of Tyre
Against Nemertius 295–296
Allogenes compared with 303, 305, 314
Calcidius and 47n145
Christian sources engaged by 308, 308n164
Commentary on Plato's 'Parmenides' attributed to 297, 298, 299, 306, 308, 311
as editor of Plotinus's *Enneads* 271, 273
on forethought, first thought 272, 293–296, 299, 308, 309
on Gnosticism 11, 153, 187
Gnostic texts known by 184, 185

on God's foreknowledge of future conditionals 218, 295–296, 314
on gods' knowing 294–296, 305, 307
mutual impact of biblicizing and pagan philosophy on 157
on pre-noetic cognitive faculty 296
Sententiae 294, 296, 299
Zostrianos and 297, 314
Posidonius 67, 200
Powers, Nathan M. 308n165
prayer 90, 91, 92–95, 97, 292, 310
pre-existence of souls
Apelles on 147, 268n237
Basilides on 246, 251–252, 261, 262, 315
Book of the Laws of the Countries on 237–238, 240, 246, 261, 262, 315
Irenaeus of Lyons on 268
Origen on 133–134, 246, 253n164, 257–258, 260, 261, 262, 315
Plato on 246, 249, 283
Plotinus and 283, 315
pre-natal choice 231n48, 240, 246, 261, 262, 264, 283
Tatian the Assyrian on 264–265
Tertullian on 268
Presocratics 20
Prince of Lights 114
Proclus 'Diadochus' 109n24, 294, 295, 296, 306, 309, 309n166
pronoia 17–53, 78n126, 88, 97, 108, 121n19, 125, 127, 130n129, 139, 157, 172, 178, 197, 205, 206, 218, 242, 243, 248, 256, 279, 289
Athene Pronoia 196–197
Clement of Alexandria and questions about 1
Diodorus Siculus on 67
earliest reference in Jewish literature 72
in Gnostics 154–155
in Herodotus 20
imperial tone taken on by 65–66
Josephus's use of 86
in Justin Martyr's *Dialogue with Trypho* 58, 94
in Plato 5, 18n9, 57
sovereigns appropriate language of 55, 67–68
See also On Providence, providence

INDEX

prophecy
Alcinous on 12
Alcinous's *Handbook of Platonism* on 209
Alexander of Aphrodisias's *On Fate* on 205
causality and 211, 213
Chrysippus on 200, 216
Origen's *Against Celsus* on 210–211
Origen's *Commentary on Genesis* on 193, 210, 211, 213, 215, 218–219, 221
providence and 193
Theophilus of Antioch on 266
See also divination
Prōtophanes 300, 301, 305
providence 15–100
Allogenes on Invisible Spirit as caring 302–304
Apocryphon of John on 165–169, 174–176, 177
Athenagoras of Athens on 118–122
balkanization of scholarship on 5–7
Book of the Laws of the Countries on 233, 233n51
causality as central to problem of 103, 150
challenges in study of 2–9
character and 230
Clement of Alexandria on 1, 122–128
and creation 153–188
determinism and 191
dualism and 105
earliest known remarks on by Christian philosopher 242
in early Roman historians 65–71
Epicureans reject 17–18, 26, 79, 282, 291
Epicurus rejects 17–18, 26–27, 30, 97, 98
fate and 6n23, 18, 31, 37, 38, 39, 46, 50, 65, 191, 261n207, 289
and first thought of The One 13
Gnosticism on 154–155, 184–188
grades of 46, 47, 50–51, 118, 155, 175
in Greek philosophy 17–53
in Hellenistic Jewish literature 71–76
how God cares 270–319
for human beings 11, 19, 20–21, 27, 98, 144, 146, 161, 171, 174, 175–176, 183, 184
implicit 56, 57
Irenaeus of Lyons on 155–160

Josephus on providential history 85–89
Justin Martyr's *Dialogue with Trypho* on 89–96
language of 2–3
Marcion on 7, 137–149
Marsanes on 305–306
in Nag Hammadi manuscripts 11, 160–184
Neoplatonism's increasing focus on 308–309
Numenius of Apamea on 110
On the Origin of the World on 154, 161–165, 174–176, 177
Origen on 7, 128–137, 156–157, 191–196
for particulars 28, 31, 49, 55–56, 59, 70, 85–86, 90, 91–92, 94, 96–97, 99, 122, 129, 130, 131, 132, 146, 155, 207, 272, 275, 281–282, 314
persecution of martyrs and 243–247
personal 10, 55, 58, 62, 65, 67, 71, 80, 88, 96, 100, 144, 152, 155
personal accountability and 191, 223, 227
Philo of Alexandria on 76–85
philosophy as locus of talk of 54
in 'Platonizing' Sethian treatises 299–306
Plato's language in discussions of 24
Plotinus on 279–283, 303, 308
Plutarch on 58, 108
providential punishment 226, 248n143, 248–249, 250
rational action and 289
significance in ancient philosophy 1–2
sovereigns appropriate language of 55
Stoicism on 7, 18–19, 55, 155, 313
term absent in New Testament 7, 55, 96
Theophilus of Antioch on 266
third-century shift in notion of 268–269
in *Three Forms of First Thought* 169–171
Tripartite Tractate on 179–183
unevenness in surviving ancient sources 7–8
See also On Providence; pronoia
providentia 2, 5, 36, 39, 55, 70n82, 109, 137n153, 143n182
in Cicero 5
Epicureans on 18
civic or imperial tone taken on by 65, 210

sovereigns appropriate language of 67–68

See also providence

Psalms

50:10 266

84:3 56

108 211

Pseudo-Apollodorus 197–198

Pseudo-Aristotle. *See On the World (De mundo)* (pseudo-Aristotle)

Pseudo-Clement 192, 222

Pseudo-Dionysius 309

Pseudo-Justin Martyr 127n118

Pseudo-Plutarch

Athenagoras of Athens compared with 121

on causality 49–50

on chance 48–49, 231, 231n46

on choice 48, 231

conditional fate doctrine of 46, 47, 207, 230

on *daimones* 50–51, 209

eternal return and 49n159

on grades of providence 47n145

'Great King' analogy used by 30, 51

on 'what is up to us' 48, 49–50, 231n47, 231n48

will and 270n2

See also On Fate (Pseudo-Plutarch)

Ptolemy 138n154, 178, 178n111, 182

punishment

Basilides on 226, 244, 245–246, 247, 251

Book of the Laws of the Countries on 240

Clement of Alexandria on 127, 226, 249n147, 250, 251

divine 70n81, 74n98, 86, 88, 142, 217n97

in Greek philosophy 127

Josephus on 86, 88

Justin Martyr on 263, 264

in 'Oracle to Laius' 208

Origen's *On First Principles* on 253, 256n182, 256–257

Philo of Alexandria on 79

Pliny the Elder on 69, 70n81

providential 226, 248n143, 248–249, 250

Sirach on 74n98

Stoicism on 62, 74n98

Tertullian on 142

Theophilus of Antioch on 266–267

Tripartite Tractate on 181

wickedness as its own 62, 74n98

Pythagoras 97, 109–110

Pythagoreanism 105, 109, 318

Radice, Roberto 82n156

Rajak, Tessa 4n14

Ramelli, Ilaria L.E. 235n67, 236n69

Rasimus, Tuomas 154n4, 300n134, 307

reason (rationality)

in *Apocryphon of John* 167–168

Chrysippus on 40

Cicero on 62

Clement of Alexandria on 241

Gnostics on human 172, 174

Irenaeus of Lyons on humanity coming to possess intellect 171

Justin Martyr on 264

Origen on 156–157

Philo of Alexandria on 76–77, 83

Polybius on 66

providence and rational action 289

Stoicism on 58, 62, 63, 88, 96, 100, 152, 168

Tertullian on 100

Theophilus of Antioch on 100

Three Forms of First Thought on 170

See also logos

Recognitions (Pseudo-Clement) 192, 222

Refutation of All Heresies 214

reincarnation 25, 26, 231n48, 246

Republic (Plato)

central to dogmatic interpretation of Plato 45

early Christian thought influenced by 12–13

Myth of Er 24, 25, 208, 209, 225, 242n106, 249, 262

'resident alien' motif 251

responsibility. *See* personal accountability (responsibility)

resurrection 265, 266, 268

Reydams-Schils, Gretchen J. 111n37

Rhodon 147, 149

Rist, John M. 256n182

Romans

5:12 117

8:22 117

INDEX

9:10–13   258
9:18–21   258, 258n189
Rudolph, Kurt   176n95, 185n139
Rufinus   134n147, 255n175, 256n178, 256n182, 257n186
Runia, David   294n112
Russell, Jeffrey Burton   150, 151

Sacks, Kenneth   67
Satan (the Devil)
 apocalyptic perspective and   150
 Athenagoras of Athens on   121, 135, 136
 Book of the Laws of the Countries on   236, 237, 240
 Clement of Alexandria on   246
 as cosmic force   117
 as counter-God   114
 in Dead Sea Scrolls   113
 in Deuteronomistic and Prophetic literature   114
 evil attributed to   175
 as first-born   119
 in the Gospels   114, 116, 121
 in Jewish apocalyptic literature   104
 Origen on   132, 134–135, 135n148
 'the' Satan   114
Schallenberg, Magnus   206n59
Scheffczyk, Leo   97, 174, 186
Schenke, Hans-Martin   154n4
Schmitz, Barbara   71n86, 72, 76n113
Schrage, Wolfgang   57n12
Schroeder, Frederic   312
Schüngel, Paul   243n112, 249n144
Second Apology (Justin Martyr)   118
Second Treatise on the Great Seth   173, 176
Sedley, David   45n138
Seneca
 on divine spirit   60n21
 on Gods' care of individuals   61, 62, 100
 hard determinism (incompatibilism) of   43–44
 on natural evils   35
 on the Stoic's God as Jupiter   32
 on suffering by good people   36
Sentences of Sextus   184
Sententiae (Porphyry of Tyre)   294, 296, 299
Septuagint   76, 83, 113, 114, 116, 117, 318
'Sethian' treatises   299–306
 Gnostic myths compared with   154n4

 on Invisible Spirit's knowledge of particulars   306
 on providence as prior to Intellect   293
 subdivision of the aeons in   300
 See also Allogenes; Zostrianos
Sextus Empiricus   17, 52
Share, Michael   294n112
Sharples, Robert W.
 on Alexander of Aphrodisias   205n55, 206, 206n57
 on Aristotle's generalissimo metaphor   28
 on Chrysippus   198n24, 201
 on Laius oracle   202n40, 208, 209
 as source for this study   2n5
sin
 of Adam and Eve   117, 144, 146
 Apelles on   138
 Basilides on   244, 250, 251
 Book of the Laws of the Countries on   236–237, 238, 239
 choice in   136, 151
 Clement of Alexandria on   124, 250
 death associated with   117
 introduction into the world   112, 117, 119, 129, 136
 Irenaeus of Lyons on   159
 Marcion on   142
 Origen on   133, 135, 135n148
 Paul on   117
 Satan as cause of   114
 Second Treatise on the Great Seth on Jesus and   173
Sirach   58, 72, 73–74, 74n98, 75, 83
Skepticism, Academic   32, 45, 61, 204n52, 212
Smith, Geoffrey S.   270n2
Socrates
 argument from design in   20–21, 26, 36, 273
 Epictetus on   33
 on responsibility for virtue   25
 'voice' of   63
'sons of God' (b'nai Elohim)   112, 114–115
Sophia (Wisdom)
 in *Apocryphon of John*   165–166, 168, 175n93, 176
 innocence of   176
 Irenaeus of Lyons on   160, 161

in *On the Origin of the World* 161, 162, 163, 164, 165
Origen on 134n146, 156
Philo of Alexandria on *logos* and 81
Tripartite Tractate on 172, 179
in Wisdom of Solomon 74
Sophocles 209–210
souls
after death 24, 64, 252, 252n155, 253, 281
Clement of Alexandria on 251, 252n155
as faculty of decision-making 264
immaterial 226, 263, 265, 283
immortality of 92n206, 177, 257
Plato on their choosing their incarnate existence 25, 231n48, 261n207
Plotinus on 280–281
reincarnation of 25, 26, 231n48, 246
as seat of accountability 12, 263, 266, 268
Tatian the Assyrian on 265
See also pre-existence of souls; World Soul
Stead, George Christopher 8–9, 256n180
Steel, Carlos 34n83
Stobaeus, Johannes 270n2
Stoicism
anthropocentrism of 36, 58, 60, 61–62, 174
Basilides compared with 247
on causality 38, 47, 59, 199
on character development 37
Clement of Alexandria and 123, 241
compatibilism of 41, 41n123, 47, 230, 253
cosmic eschatology of 34
and determinism 6, 37–44, 57, 103, 206, 218, 226, 256
Diodorus Cronus and 199n30
disappearance of 307
on divination 199, 199n29, 200
on divine foreknowledge 216, 307
early Christian adoption and transformation of 313
early Christian philosophy influenced by 10, 97, 152, 168, 225, 313
early Christians distinguish themselves from 99, 100
Epicureans on 18, 59, 99
on eternal return 34, 49, 200, 216
on evil 34–36, 37, 53, 83, 103, 105, 108, 111, 118, 136, 151, 289

on fate 6, 6n23, 37–44, 57, 216, 230
first thought and 274
free will and 39, 223, 261, 315
Gnosticism contrasted with 175, 187, 315
God of 31–37, 53, 57, 58, 59–60, 61, 72, 96, 97, 98, 100, 130, 155, 208, 218, 268
on God's involvement in the world 10, 59–63
household argument of 125
Josephus and 58, 98
Justin Martyr and 118
on matter 105, 155
Middle Platonism contrasted with 59
monism of 103, 104–105
On the Origin of the World and 177
pantheism of 61, 62
on personal accountability (responsibility) 37, 39–44, 151, 152, 223, 223n4, 224, 225, 254, 264
Philo of Alexandria and 58, 76, 79, 80, 85, 98, 118
Pliny the Elder associated with 68
Plotinus compared with 282, 287, 291
Plutarch on 107, 108
on providence 7, 18–19, 55, 155, 313
on reason 58, 62, 63, 88, 96, 100, 152, 168
Roman historians influenced by 70
Sirach and 73–74
Tertullian on 98–99
on theodicy 35, 291, 315
Stoyanov, Yuri 151, 152
Stromateis (*Miscellanies*) (Clement of Alexandria) 122–128, 241–251
Stuckenbruck, Loren 112
Suda (lexicon) 197
Susanna 42–43 195, 318
Swartz, Michael D. 57n10

Tacitus 46, 46n144
Tatian the Assyrian 119, 262, 264–266, 267
Teachings of Silvanus 216, 217n97, 313
Tertullian
Against Hermogenes 137, 137n153
Against Marcion 141–143, 144–146, 267
on angels 148
on Apelles 147
binitarianism of 149n210
Christians and philosophers distinguished by 98

INDEX

Clement of Alexandria compared with 123

divine mediators absent in 100

emphasis on thinkers whose views resemble those of 13

on *1 Enoch* 119

on evil 119, 267

on free will 268, 315

on God 149

on Hermogenes 137, 137n153

on Marcion 138, 141–143, 144–146, 157, 213, 316

On the Soul 137n153, 267–268

on personal accountability 267–268

on responsibility for creation 156

on Stoicism 98–99, 100

To the Gentiles (*Ad Nationes*) 98–99

unde bonum? (reply to *unde malum?*) 186–187

Testimony of Truth 214, 215

Theaetetus (Plato) 105

Theiler, Willy 33n81, 228n30, 230n42, 231n48

theodicy

Basilides and 245

dualism and 117

God's ignorance and 214

Philo of Alexandria and 84

Plato's language in discussions of 24

Plotinus and 272, 282, 283, 291

Stoic 35, 291, 315

Theodore of Asine 306

Theophilus of Antioch

divine mediators absent in 100

on free will 266, 267, 315

on personal accountability 262, 266

on providence 97–98, 266

on punishment 266–267

on responsibility for creation 156

Stoic influence on 97, 100

To Autolycus 266

Thorsteinsson, Runar M. 43n134

Three Forms of First Thought (*Trimorphic Protennoia*) 169–171

on archons 170, 177

creation and providence separated in 175

on demons 170, 170n72

as dependent on *Apocryphon of John* 169n71

on first thought 169, 170, 177, 272, 298

on matter 176, 177

on rationality 170

'Sethian' treatises compared with 300

Wisdom in 176

Timaeus (Plato)

Cicero's agreement with 36

consistent philosophy attributed to 45

demiurge (*dēmiourgos*) in 21, 22–23, 32, 50, 84, 105, 106n7, 122, 152, 155, 164, 174, 316

dualism of 316

early Christian philosophers and 10

Epicureans on 18

on error in the world 34–35, 44, 284, 315

on God's creation of the universe 21–24, 32

'Great Year' doctrine in 49

on matter 84, 105, 106, 110, 316

Numenius of Apamea and 110

Philo of Alexandria influenced by 82, 84

on receptacle 105, 106

tripartion of providence and 50

young gods in 22, 23, 26, 30, 37, 53, 136, 152, 155, 174, 315, 318

Titus of Bostra 213

To Autolycus (Theophilus of Antioch) 266

Tobit 75–76

To the Gentiles (*Ad Nationes*) (Tertullian) 98 99

Trimorphic Protennoia. See Three Forms of First Thought (*Trimorphic Protennoia*)

Trinity 120

Tripartite Tractate 179–183

on aeons 179, 179n114, 181, 275, 290

on angels 171, 181

on archons 181–182, 288

dating of 179n115, 292n102

on the demiurge 182, 186, 215n92, 284

on emanation 288, 291, 292n102

on First Principle 180, 275, 276, 291, 306

on free will 180n116, 285

on God 181, 182, 290–291, 292n102

on the knowledge and will of the Good 275–277

on *logos* 179, 186, 276, 284–285, 287, 288, 291, 292, 308

on matter 182

as Neoplatonic 306

Plotinus compared with   179, 182, 183, 271, 277
Plotinus's *On Providence* compared with   13, 272, 282, 284–285, 288–292, 292n102
on sub-aeonic beings   284–285, 287–288, 291
on will   179–180, 271, 275–277
tuchē
Diodorus Siculus on   67
Josephus on   87
Platonists on   230–231
Plotinus on   278
Plutarch on   71, 71n84
Polybius on   65–66, 66n60
Pseudo-Plutarch on   48
See also chance
Turner, John D.   299–300, 305

Valentinus
associated with Epicureanism   157
on demons and sin   119
divine mediators absent in   100
Irenaeus of Lyons and   160, 178, 182, 316
Origen and   260
salvation by nature doctrine and   252, 258n189
Stoic influence on   97
van den Broek, Roelof   217n97
van Nuffelen, Peter   71n85
van Winden, J.C.M.   91n205, 92n209
Vespasian, Emperor   68
vice
in concomitance argument   36
Josephus on   88
Philo of Alexandria on   84
Plato on   35, 44
as punishment   62
voluntary action   227, 237, 245, 277

Wasserman, Emma   117–118
'what is up to us' (*to eph'hēmin*)
Alexander of Aphrodisias's *On Fate* on   228–229
Aristotle on   43, 227, 236, 245, 249
Book of the Laws of the Countries on   234, 245
character and   229

Chrysippus on   42
Clement of Alexandria on   241, 241n96, 246, 249–250
divine foreknowledge and   196n13
Epictetus on   42–43
human responsibility framed in terms of   9, 39–40
Origen's *Against Celsus* on   193
Platonists on   271
Plotinus on   275, 278
Pseudo-Plutarch on   48, 49–50, 231n47, 231n48
tertiary providence and   63n45
Wicke-Reuter, Ursel   56n10
will   189–310
Aristotle's account of action in debate on   227–228
divine   17, 87, 132–133, 177, 178, 183, 194, 255n172, 270n2, 272, 279n41
of the Father   11, 177, 180, 181n122, 183, 184, 276, 285
natural cosmos seen as having a   115
Origen's *On First Principles* on   257
Platonism and   270
Plotinus on   13, 271, 272, 277, 278, 283
Plotinus on the knowledge and will of the Good   273–281
Tripartite Tractate on   179–180, 271, 275–277
See also free will
Williams, Michael Allen   153n1, 153–154, 175n92, 175n93, 176, 185
Willing, Meike   147–148
Winston, David   60n21, 83n157
Wisdom. *See* Sophia (Wisdom)
Wisdom of Solomon   58, 72, 74–75, 83, 96, 318
World Soul
Calcidius on   47n145
Middle Platonism on   64n54, 106
Numenius of Apamea on   108, 111–112, 152
Plato on   105, 107
Plotinus on   279, 286
Plutarch on   107, 109, 109n24, 111, 152

Xenocrates   51, 64
Xenophon   20–21, 26, 36

INDEX

Yaldabaoth
in *Apocryphon of John* 166, 167, 171, 174
as not accidental 176
in *On the Origin of the World* 160–162, 163, 164–165, 171, 174

Zachhuber, Johannes 8n29
Zeno of Citium 31–32, 34, 38, 41n123
Zostrianos
circulated in Plotinus's seminar 297

Commentary on Plato's 'Parmenides' compared with 297, 311
on first thought 13, 272
on Intellect as having knowledge 300–303
on Invisible Spirit's pre-noetic capacity 300, 305
Marsanes contrasted with 305
Plotinus compared with 297, 305

Printed in the United States
By Bookmasters